The Postal Service
Guide to U.S. Stamps

The Postal Service
Guide to U.S. Stamps

28th Edition
Updated Stamp Values

UNITED STATES
POSTAL SERVICE®

HarperResource
An Imprint of HarperCollinsPublishers

HarperCollins books may be purchased for educational, business, or sales
promotional use. For information please write: Special Markets Department,
HarperCollins Publishers Inc., 10 East 53rd Street, New York, NY 10022.

Printed in the United States of America.

Library of Congress Cataloging-in-Publication Data has been applied for.

ISBN 0-06-095855-3

01 02 03 04 RRD 10 9 8 7 6 5 4 3 2 1

Table of Contents

Drawn to Perfection

Stamp Collecting Offers a Unique Perspective on the Artist's Craft

AL PARKER

This year's focus on the work of American illustrators shows just how fascinating stamp collecting can be. Did you know that an illustration by Al Parker appeared on a 1961 stamp honoring nursing? Or that this year marks the fourth time Frederic Remington has been honored with a stamp? Stamp collectors do—because they know that American stamps have long recognized great artists and their work. Stamps have shown the tender nostalgia of Norman Rockwell, the flappers of John Held, Jr., and famous poster art by N. C. Wyeth and James Montgomery Flagg. You never know what—or who—will turn up on a stamp, and that's all part of the fun.

N. C. WYETH

Stamp collecting can be a lifelong hobby. It's fun and educational for all ages, and it's easy to start without a big investment. Read on to find out how to start or build your very own collection.

What is philately?

The word philately (fi-latt'-eh-lee) means the study of stamps and other postal materials. Stamp collectors are sometimes called philatelists.

How do I start collecting stamps?

It's easy. You can start by simply saving stamps from letters, packages, and postcards. Ask your friends and family to save stamps from their mail.

Neighborhood businesses that get a lot of mail—banks, stores, travel agencies, and others—might save their envelopes for you, too.

Or, start your collection by choosing one or two favorite subjects. Then, collect stamps that fit your theme—art, history, sports, transportation, science, animals, and others—whatever you choose! This is called topical or thematic stamp collecting. See the stamps pictured in these feature articles for ideas to get you started on a space theme!

Will it cost me a lot to start a collection?

No! Start with used stamps and a few inexpensive accessories (such as a small album and a package of stamp hinges), and you can have a great time on a limited budget. Remember to put stamps, albums, and hinges on your birthday and holiday wish lists, too!

What kinds of stamps are there?

There are a number of different types of stamps. Their purposes can be described as commemorative, definitive, or special; their formats can be in sheets, booklets, or coils. And all of these now exist with conventional adhesive (the "lick-and-stick" gum) or self-adhesive (the "no-lick, peel-and-stick" type).

Definitive stamps (also called "regular issues") are the most common type of postage stamp. They feature everything from statesmen to animals and from the American flag to historic vehicles. They tend to be fairly small (generally less than an inch square), with denominations

(the face value printed on the stamp) from one cent to many dollars. They are printed in large quantities, often more than once, and tend to be available for several years.

Commemorative stamps are usually larger and more colorful than definitives. They are printed in smaller quantities and typically are printed only once. They remain on sale for a limited period of time, generally about a year; many post offices carry them for only a few months. They are issued for specific rates, most often the prime letter rate. They honor, or commemorate, important people, events, or subjects, all of which reflect some aspect of American culture.

Special stamps supplement the regular issues and tend to be more commemorative in appearance (larger and more colorful), while meeting specific needs. They may be reprinted, but tend to remain on sale for only the life of the specific rate for which they are issued. These include Christmas and Love stamps, Holiday Celebration stamps, international rate stamps (previously known as airmail stamps), Priority Mail, and Express Mail stamps.

Sheet stamps are printed as large press sheets, then trimmed into smaller units called panes, most of which measure less than eight by ten inches. Panes generally contain twenty stamps, but may contain up to a hundred or as few as one stamp; smaller commemorative panes, with fewer than ten stamps, are often called souvenir sheets, depending on their purpose. Individual stamps tend to have perfs (perforations) or die-cut edges (generally with a wavy pattern) on all sides.

Booklet stamps are designed to be folded into a convenient unit. Booklets generally contain twenty stamps and may contain separate panes of stamps in a small folder or may be issued in a flat unit designed to be folded into a booklet by the customer. Most individual booklet stamps have at least one straight edge (no perfs or die-cuts) and sometimes two adjacent straight edges.

Coil stamps are issued in rolls. Customers often buy them in rolls of a hundred stamps; business mailers can buy them in rolls of up to ten thousand stamps. Individual coil stamps usually have two straight edges on opposite sides.

How do I remove stamps from envelopes?

If you wish, you can save whole envelopes with stamps on them and store them anywhere—from shoe boxes to special albums. These are called "covers." Collecting entire envelopes reflects a specialty called "postal history." It's a good idea to save the whole envelope if there's something special about the address or return address (famous places or people for example), or the postmark (a date or location of some historic significance). See also the information below on collectible "first day covers" later in this article.

If you want to remove stamps from envelopes, it pays to be careful. The best way to remove stamps from envelopes is to soak them. Here's how:

1. Tear or cut off the upper right-hand corner of the envelope, leaving enough margin around the stamps to ensure they aren't damaged.
2. Place it, stamp side down, in a small pan of warm (not hot) water. If the stamp is affixed to a piece of colored envelope, use colder water; it may take longer, but any dyes from the paper are less likely to run and discolor the stamp. After a few minutes, the stamp should sink to the bottom. Remove the envelope piece from the water as soon as the stamp is off.
3. Wait a few more minutes for any remaining gum to dislodge from the stamp. The newer self-adhesive gums tend to take a bit longer.
4. Lift the stamp out. If you use your fingers, be sure your hands are clean, since oil from your skin can hasten discoloration of the stamps over time. Tongs—a good stamp- collecting tool like tweezers—can be used to minimize contact. Wet stamps are delicate and should be handled carefully.
5. Place the stamp between two paper towels and put a heavy object, such as a book, on top. This will keep the stamp from curling as it dries. Leave the stamp there overnight.
6. If the stamp shows signs of remaining adhesive, even after lengthy soaking, dry it face down on a single paper towel with nothing touching the back. If necessary, it can be flattened after it's dried; otherwise, it may stick to surfaces when drying.

How do I collect
First Day Covers?

The fastest way to get a First Day Cover is to buy the stamp yourself (it will usually go on sale the day after the first day of issue), attach it to your own envelope (or cover), and send it to the first day post office for cancellation. You can submit up to fifty envelopes, up to thirty days after the stamp's issue date. Here's how:

1. Write your address in the lower right-hand corner of each first day envelope, at least 5/8 inch from the bottom. Leave plenty of room for the stamp(s) and cancellation. Use a peel-off label if you prefer.
2. Insert a piece of cardboard (about as thick as a postcard) into each envelope. You can tuck the flap in or seal the envelope.
3. Affix your stamp(s) to your first day envelope(s).
4. Put your first day envelope(s) inside another, larger envelope and mail it to "Customer-Affixed Envelopes" in care of the postmaster of the first day city. Your envelopes will be canceled and returned.

Or, you can purchase a plain envelope with the stamp(s) already affixed and canceled. These are now sold directly by mail order through the U.S. Postal Service.

How should I organize my stamps?

However you want to, of course—it's your collection. But be sure to protect them so they don't get damaged or lost. You can attach your stamps to loose-leaf paper and put them in a three-ring binder. Or, arrange them in a more formal album, which you can buy in stores or by mail order.

What kinds of stamp albums can I buy?

Some stamp albums feature specific categories with pictures of the stamps that should appear on each page. You may want to select one with loose-leaf pages so you can add pages as your collection grows. Personal computers can help you design your own pages, featuring your collection in a totally personalized manner. Software programs can help you with stamp-album pages, and common page-design programs can help you customize any design.

A *stock book* is an album with plastic or paper pockets on each page. There are no pictures of stamps, so you can organize the stock book in any way. These books are especially useful for holding duplicate stamps, stamps for trading, and stamps that you've saved but haven't yet had time to put in the album containing your permanent collection.

How do I put a stamp in the album?

It's best to use a stamp hinge—a small strip of thin material (often glassine) with gum on one side. Unlike tape or glue (which should *never* be used), hinges let you peel the stamp off the page without damaging it. Hinges come either folded or unfolded. Here's how to use a folded hinge:

1. Lightly moisten about three fourths of the short end of the hinge, leaving the area nearest the fold unmoistened. Press the hinge to the back of the stamp, placing the fold about 1/8 inch from the top of the stamp; that way, it can't be seen once the stamp is mounted in the album.

2. Lightly moisten most of the long end of the hinge (again, leaving the area closest to the fold unmoistened), position the stamp where you want it in the album, and press down to secure it.
3. Using tongs, gently lift the stamp from the bottom to make sure it's not stuck to the page.

If you have an unfolded hinge, simply fold it about one third the length (gummed side out), giving you short and long ends, and proceed as above.

Instead of a hinge, you can insert the entire stamp into a mount—a small, clear plastic sleeve. Mounts are more expensive than hinges, but they protect stamps from air, dirt, and moisture. Hinges are fine for used stamps (stamps without adhesive that you've removed from mail), but mounts offer better protection for mint stamps (new stamps with adhesive, such as those you buy from the post office).

Is there anything else I need?
Here's a list of other materials and accessories you may find helpful:

Glassine envelopes are made of a special thin, see-through paper that protects stamps from grease and air. You can use them to keep stamps until you put them in your album.

A *stamp catalog* is a reference book with illustrations to help you identify stamps (like this book). It also lists the values of used and unused (mint) stamps.

A *magnifying glass* (or *loupe*) helps you examine stamps by making them appear larger. Sometimes it's important to examine certain details of stamps more closely.

A *perforation gauge* measures perforations along the edges of stamps. Sometimes the size and number of perfs are needed to identify stamps. The same principle can be used to measure the distance between peaks or ridges on newer die-cut self-adhesive stamps, with wavy die cuts that simulate perforations.

A *watermark tray* (and *watermark fluid*) help make watermarks on stamps more visible. A watermark is a design or pattern that is pressed into some stamp paper during manufacturing. This equipment is necessary only with stamps—mostly older stamps—with watermarks that help to identify them.

| Superb | Very Fine | Fine | Good |

How can I tell what a stamp is worth?

Ask yourself two questions: "How rare is it?" and "What condition is it in?" The price listed in a stamp catalog gives you some idea of how rare it is. However, the stamp may sell at more or less than the catalog price, depending on its condition. Catalog prices and condition are discussed further below.

Always try to find stamps in the best possible condition.

How should I judge the condition of a stamp?

Stamp dealers put stamps into categories according to their condition. Look at the pictured examples to see the differences among categories. A stamp in mint condition is the same as when purchased from the post office. An unused stamp has no cancellation but may not have any gum on the back. Mint stamps are usually worth more than unused stamps. Hinge marks on mint stamps can reduce value, which is why the use of stamp mounts is recommended for mint stamps.

You can begin to judge the condition of a stamp by examining the front of it. Are the colors bright or faded? Is the stamp clean, dirty, or stained? Is the stamp torn or creased? Torn stamps are not considered "collectible," but you may want to keep an example as a space filler until you get a better copy.

Are all the perforations intact? Has the stamp been canceled? A stamp with a light cancellation is in better condition than one with heavy marks across it.

Is the stamp design centered on the paper, crooked, or off to one side? In the examples pictured, this centering can range from "superb" (perfectly centered on the stamp) to "good" (the design on at least one side is marred somewhat by the perfs). Anything

Light Cancel–Very Fine

Medium Cancel–Fine

Heavy Cancel

FRIDA KAHLO USA34
2001

less would be graded "fair" or "poor" and, like torn copies, should be saved only as space fillers. Centering varies widely on older stamps; modern production techniques make it unlikely that copies with less than "fine" centering could be found.

Now look at the back of the stamp. Is there a thin spot in the paper? If so, it may have been caused by careless removal from a hinge or envelope.

The values listed in this book are for used and unused stamps in "very fine" condition that may have been hinged.

Where else can I find stamps?

Check the classified ads in philatelic newspapers and magazines at your local library. Some are listed under "periodicals" in this book (see page 562), and most will send you a free sample copy on request. There also are a number of stamp-related sites on the Internet, which can be accessed through most search programs and services.

What other stamp materials can I collect?

Postal stationery products are popular among some collectors. These have the stamp design printed and/or embossed (with an impressed or raised image) directly on them.

Stamped envelopes were first issued in the United States in 1853. More than five hundred million of them are printed each year.

Stamped cards (also called *postal cards*) were first issued in 1873. The first U.S. multicolored commemorative stamped cards were released in 1956. Several different stamped card designs are issued each year.

Aerogrammes (also called *air letters*) are designed to be letters and envelopes all in one. They are specially stamped, marked for folding, and gummed for sealing.

Other philatelic collectibles include:

Plate numbers (including *plate blocks*) appear on or adjacent to stamps. These are most common on sheet stamps. Plate blocks are the group of stamps (usually four) which have the printing plate numbers in the adjoining selvage—or margin (usually in the corner of the pane). On coils, these numbers appear in the margins of the stamps themselves, and collectors may save a *plate number strip* of three or five stamps with the number on the center stamp. On booklets, the plate numbers usually appear on the booklet "tab" by which the panes are affixed to the booklet cover.

Booklet panes are panes of stamps affixed in, or as part of, a thin folder to form a booklet. With self-adhesive stamps, a newer convertible booklet format has been created, so that the stamps, liner, and booklet are all one unit. Usually, collectors of booklet panes save the entire pane or the entire booklet.

Marginal blocks (including **copyright blocks**) feature marginal inscriptions other than the plate numbers. The most common is the copyright block, which features the copyright symbol ©, copyright date, and U.S. Postal Service information. All U.S. stamp designs since 1978 are copyrighted.

First Day Covers (FDCs) are envelopes bearing new stamps that are postmarked on the first day of sale. For each new postal issue, the U.S. Postal Service generally selects one location, usually related to the stamp subject, as the place for the first day dedication ceremony and the first day postmark. See page 10 for information on how to collect these covers.

First day ceremony programs are given to persons who attend first day ceremonies. They contain a list of participants, information on the stamp subject, and the actual stamp attached and postmarked.

Are there any stamp groups I can join?

Yes! Stamp clubs can be a great source for new stamps and stamp collecting advice. These clubs often meet at schools, libraries, and community centers. Ask your local postmaster or librarian for the locations of stamp clubs in your area and other contact information (including Internet sites, in some cases).

The Art of Illustration

Advances in printing and publishing made possible by changes in technology ushered in a new era for American illustrators during the last quarter of the 19th century, allowing their work to be reproduced with increasing fidelity and attracting some of the country's finest talents to the field. The public could now view famous works of fine art as engravings or chromolithographs in the pages of newspapers and general-interest magazines. By the early decades of the 20th century, many illustrators had built reputations on the artwork they created for books and magazine covers. Whether focused on fashions and fads or pivotal moments in history, they documented what they saw around them, preserving visual memories of these important times for future generations.

While some artists were interested in revealing the contemporary American experience, others, such as Frederic Remington, were inclined to interpret modern life more romantically. His paintings and magazine illustrations captured the waning years of the Old West and romanticized the American cowboy. But Remington was also a keen observer of the important events of his day, serving as an artist and correspondent in Cuba during the Spanish-American War and reproducing what he saw with vivid proficiency.

Other illustrators are remembered today for their impressive book illustrations. N. C. Wyeth gained renown for his illustrations to accompany an edition of Robert Louis Stevenson's *Treasure Island*. Wyeth brought a strong sense of drama to his work, and his paintings evoke adventure in exotic and faraway places populated by heroes and villains.

EDWIN AUSTIN ABBEY

ROCKWELL KENT

JAMES MONTGOMERY FLAGG

His artistic legacy continues with the work of his son Andrew and grandson James.

N.C.WYETH

The career of artist Rockwell Kent defies easy classification. As a painter, lithographer, illustrator, muralist, and writer, he was both versatile and prolific. Like N. C. Wyeth, Kent is also remembered for his illustrations for books, including *The Bridge of San Luis Rey*, *Leaves of Grass*, and *Paul Bunyan*. Editions of each of these already impressive works were further enhanced by the bold, precise lines of his illustrations. Many of his works are considered masterpieces of design; the wood engravings he made for a 1930 edition of *Moby Dick* brought a striking new dimension to an American literary classic.

Sometimes the work of illustrators has the power to take us back to a scene from days long gone. Norman Rockwell painted more than 300 covers for *The Saturday Evening Post* that chronicled the lives of everyday people—images that have become icons of idealized American life. While Rockwell embraced small-town ideals, J. C. Leyendecker and John Held, Jr., focused on the sophistication and allure of the Jazz Age. Leyendecker's Arrow Collar Man embodied confidence, elegance, and poise—a model of gentlemanly behavior and an object of romance. Meanwhile, Held's flappers appeared to glide from one raucous party to the next, celebrating life, love, and merriment along the way.

FREDERIC REMINGTON—

While Leyendecker's elegantly dressed figures and Held's convivial flappers defined an era for some Americans, Jessie Willcox Smith explored a more serene and domestic world in her work. Her best known subjects were mothers and children, often depicted together in quiet and reflective moments. Suffused with dignity, her work illustrated the unwavering commitment of maternal love, and was perhaps close to the everyday experience

JOHN HELD, JR.

MAXFIELD PARRISH

ROSE O'NEILL

of many American women at the time.

Illustrating her own verse, self-trained artist Rose O'Neill created a universe populated by cherubic, cupid-like Kewpies. Whimsical and sweet, the Kewpies' popularity led to the creation of dolls that are still prized collector's items. O'Neill's cartoonish creations conveyed a sense of optimism and innocence—but her illustrations could also venture into haunting and mystical subjects as well. A versatile artist, O'Neill was also a talented sculptor, novelist, and poet.

Neysa McMein's covers for popular magazines, such as *The Saturday Evening Post*, *Collier's*, and *McCall's*, reflected her own sophistication. Surrounded by fashionable society, McMein often drew on her immediate experience for inspiration, and one recurring subject JESSIE WILLCOX SMITH was the well-bred, attractive, and fashionably dressed girl. "I just take a pretty girl and draw her as she is," she once said. However, McMein did not limit her palette only to lovely socialites: President Warren G. Harding, Chief Justice Charles Evans Hughes, and Charlie Chaplin all sat for portraits.

On its own, an illustration can evoke adventure, suspense, romance, or whimsy. Combined with text, an image takes on even greater power, adding depth and authenticity to a story and bringing its scenes and characters to life. Illustrators have always known how to harness their artistic powers in the service of effective storytelling. Clarity of expression and distinctive stylistic approaches have allowed them to create unique records of human experience— whether in books and magazines or on exquisitely designed postage stamps.

COLES PHILLIPS

Masterpieces in Miniature

The Power of Postage Stamp Illustration

The U.S. Postal Service has regularly used illustration to create lasting testimonials to the achievements of Americans in all walks of life. Postage stamps have honored writers, musicians, composers, architects, artists, nature, holidays, educational and public institutions, athletes, and actors, with stamp illustrators interpreting each subject in unique and memorable ways. This year, the Postal Service recognizes the art of illustration with a Classic Collection of 20 stamp designs that honors the role of illustrators in American culture.

The U.S. stamp program includes examples of the best in modern illustration. Nationally recognized artists such as Steve Buchanan, John D. Dawson, and Drew Struzan all contribute regularly to the stamp program, distilling complex subjects into works of art that retain their effectiveness even at the size of a postage stamp.

Probably the most common subjects for stamps are portraits of important Americans. Drew Struzan brings a wholly modern approach to this popular tradition. Recognized internationally for his dramatic poster art, Struzan has masterfully captured the essence of individuals such as Broadway legends Alfred Lunt and Lynn Fontanne and film star Edward G. Robinson, rendering

them immediately recognizable even at stamp size.

John D. Dawson's detailed natural history illustrations are equally as stunning. For the award-winning Nature of America series, Dawson brings mammals, birds, reptiles, amphibians, insects, and native plant species together into a single scene representing an entire biological community. Dawson began his work on the series in 1999 with the Sonoran Desert issuance, followed by Pacific Coast Rain Forest in 2000; he is already hard at work on new designs for future years.

Steve Buchanan shares Dawson's passion for precise nature illustrations. His attention to detail is evident in the intricate poses and subtle coloration of the 1999 Insects and Spiders stamps. Buchanan also captured the vibrant forms and vivid colors of plant life in the popular Tropical Flowers stamps in 1999.

This year, new works by each of these artists have been included in the U.S. stamp program. Lucille Ball by Drew Struzan, Nature of America: Great Plains Prairie by John D. Dawson, and Carnivorous Plants by Steve Buchanan join with American Illustrators to make 2001 an especially fine year for stamp illustration.

Biographies and photographs of many of the illustrators and designers who have contributed to stamp art over the years are interspersed throughout the pages of this guide. A number of their original canvases can be seen in the traveling exhibition "Pushing the Envelope: The Art of the Postage Stamp." Organized by the Norman Rockwell Museum in Stockbridge, Massachusetts, in collaboration with the U.S. Postal Service, the exhibit recognizes the significance and allure of postage stamps as "objects of unexpected beauty that convey a sense of history and national identity through image and word."

**Federal Eagle
Stamped Envelope**

Statue of Liberty

Lunar New Year (Year of the Snake)

Federal Eagle Stamped Envelope   #U646

Eagles—such as the one featured on this First-Class stamped envelope—were popular decorative elements on letter boxes in the past. Michael Doret used graphics software to create the art for this First-Class stamped envelope.

Date of Issue: January 7, 2001   Printing: Flexo
Place of Issue: Washington, DC
Designer: Michael Doret

Statue of Liberty   #3466

The Statue of Liberty—one of the world's most recognized symbols of freedom and democracy—is the subject chosen by the U.S. Postal Service for these First-Class stamp, self-adhesive coils of 3,000 and 10,000. Dedicated on October 28, 1886, the colossal statue stands on Liberty Island in New York Harbor.

Date of Issue: January 7, 2001   Photographer: Paul Hardy
Place of Issue: Washington, DC   Printing: Gravure
Designer: Derry Noyes

Love Letters   #3496
(Not Shown)

The U.S. Postal Service pays tribute to the art of letter writing and the centuries-old tradition of expressing love in letters, with the issuance of a new love stamp. The non-denominated, First-Class, one-ounce stamp design features a red rose superimposed on the elegant script of a handwritten letter. The letter—written by John Adams to Abigail Smith on April 20, 1763, during their courtship—underscores the enduring nature of profound sentiment expressed in writing. John Adams—who was President of the United States from 1797 to 1801—and Abigail Smith were married in 1764.

Date of Issue: January 19, 2001   Photographer: Renée Comet
Place of Issue: Tucson, AZ   Printing: Offset
Designer: Lisa Catalone

Lunar New Year (Year of the Snake)   #3500

In the Chinese lunar calendar, the Year of the Snake begins January 24, 2001 and ends February 11, 2002. The U.S. Postal Service will mark the occasion with the issuance of the ninth stamp in the award-winning Lunar New Year series. The first stamp in the series of twelve was the Year of the Rooster, followed by the Year of the Dog, Boar, Rat, Ox, Tiger, Hare, and Dragon. The snake—the sixth of twelve animals associated with the Chinese lunar calendar—is a symbol of wisdom and charm. People born in the Year of the Snake are said to be intelligent and philosophical. Known for elegance and style, they often enjoy active social lives. The Chinese characters—drawn in grass-style calligraphy by Lau Bun—translate into English as "Year of the Snake."

Date of Issue: January 20, 2001   Illustrator: Clarence Lee
Place of Issue: Oakland, CA   Printing: Offset/ Microprint
Designer: Clarence Lee   ("USPS")

Roy Wilkins   #3501

With this 24th stamp in the Black Heritage series, the U.S. Postal Service honors civil rights leader Roy Wilkins. Born August 30, 1901, in St. Louis, Missouri, Wilkins graduated from the University of Minnesota in 1923. He led the National Association for the Advancement of Colored People (NAACP) from 1955 to 1977 as executive secretary and executive director. Wilkins advocated nonviolent means and the use of the legal system to achieve racial equality and to advance the rights of African Americans. Under his leadership, the NAACP campaigned for the Civil Rights Act of 1964, the Voting Rights Act of 1965, and the Fair Housing Act of 1968. In 1964, he was awarded the NAACP's Spingarn Medal, an annual award honoring outstanding achievement by an African American. Wilkins died on September 8, 1981, at the age of 80.

Date of Issue: January 24, 2001
Place of Issue: Minneapolis, MN
Designer: Richard Sheaff

Photographers: Morgan and Marvin Smith
Printing: Offset/Microprint ("USPS")

$3.50 U.S. Capitol   #3472

An architectural landmark in the nation's capital, the U.S. Capitol is the subject chosen by the U.S. Postal Service for this Priority Mail stamp. The stamp art is a color photograph of the dome of the U.S. Capitol.

Date of Issue: January 29, 2001
Place of Issue: Washington, DC
Designer: Derry Noyes

Photographer: Robert Llewellyn
Printing: Offset, with Scrambled Indicia ®

$12.25 Washington Monument   #3473

A prominent landmark in the nation's capital, the Washington Monument is the subject chosen by the U.S. Postal Service for this Express Mail stamp. The stamp art is a color photograph of the Washington Monument at sunrise.

Date of Issue: January 29, 2001
Place of Issue: Washington, DC
Designer: Derry Noyes

Photographer: Patricia Fisher
Printing: Offset, with Scrambled Indicia ®

Roy Wilkins

U.S. Capitol

Washington Monument

American Illustrators

CLASSIC COLLECTION

.34
x 20
$6.80

AMERICAN ILLUSTRATORS

JAMES MONTGOMERY FLAGG	MAXFIELD PARRISH	J.C. LEYENDECKER	ROBERT FAWCETT	COLES PHILLIPS
AL PARKER	A.B. FROST	HOWARD PYLE	ROSE O'NEILL	DEAN CORNWELL
EDWIN AUSTIN ABBEY	JESSIE WILLCOX SMITH	NEYSA McMEIN	JON WHITCOMB	HARVEY DUNN
FREDERIC REMINGTON	ROCKWELL KENT	N.C. WYETH	NORMAN ROCKWELL	JOHN HELD, JR.

© 2000
USPS

PLATE POSITION

X1111

American Illustrators

Farm Flag

American Illustrators   #3502a-t

In 2001, the U.S. Postal Service pays tribute to the unique history of illustration in America. The American Illustrators stamp pane, part of the Classic Collection, features details of works by selected illustrators that were recommended by a panel of experts convened by the Society of Illustrators. The Society celebrated its centennial on February 1, 2001. The stamp designs depict illustrations originally used for several purposes, including books, advertisements, magazine covers, murals, and posters. Honored on the stamp pane are Edwin Austin Abbey, Dan Cornwell, Harvey Dunn, Robert Fawcett, James Montgomery Flagg, Arthur Burdett Frost, John Held, Jr., Rockwell Kent, Joseph Christian Leyendecker, Neysa McMein, Rose O'Neill, Al Parker, Maxfield Parrish, Coles Phillips, Howard Pyle, Frederic Remington, Norman Rockwell, Jessie Willcox Smith, Jon Whitcomb, and Newell Convers Wyeth. Artwork by Franklin Booth appears on the selvage. All of the illustrators featured on the stamp pane are members of the Society of Illustrators' Hall of Fame.

Date of Issue: February 1, 2001   Printing: Gravure
Place of Issue: New York, NY
Designer: Carl Herrman

Statue of Liberty   #3476-3477, 3485a-b, BK283
(not shown)

This definitive stamp was previously issued in self-adhesive coils of 3,000 and 10,000.

> Water-activated coil of 3,000 and 10,000 – #3476
> Self-adhesive coil of 100 – #3477
> Convertible booklet of 10 – #3485a
> Convertible booklet of 20 – #3485b
> Vending booklet of 20 – #BK283

Date of Issue: February 7, 2001   Photographer: Paul Hardy
Place of Issue: New York, NY   Printing: Gravure
Designer: Derry Noyes

Farm Flag   #3469

An agricultural motif is depicted on this pane of 100 First-Class stamps featuring the U.S. flag. The stamp art—a painting by Hiro Kimura—depicts his vision of the classic American farm. Barns, silos, and other outbuildings are clustered on the horizon behind a neatly furrowed field. The stars and stripes of the U.S. flag appear in the foreground. Kimura also illustrated the City Flag and Classroom Flag stamps that were issued in 1999.

Date of Issue: February 7, 2001   Illustrator: Hiro Kimura
Place of Issue: New York, NY   Printing: Offset/Microprint
Designer: Richard Sheaff   ("USPS")

Flowers
#3458-3461, 3478-3481,
3487-3490

Four cut flowers—a freesia, a cymbidium orchid, and two lilies—
are featured on these First-Class stamps. Photographs by Robert
Peak capture their color and delicacy. The stamps were issued in coils
of 100 (#3458-3461), self-adhesive vending booklets of 20 (#3478-
3481), and convertible booklets of 20 (#3487-3490).

Date of Issue: February 7, 2001   Photographer: Robert Peak
Place of Issue: New York, NY   Printing: Gravure
Designer: Derry Noyes

Love Letters
#3497-3498

This First-Class, one-ounce stamp design features a red rose superimposed on the elegant script of a handwritten letter. The design reflects
in self-adhesive convertible (#3497) and vending (#3498) booklets what
was previously issued in non-denominated form.

Date of Issue: February 14, 2001   Photographer: Renée Comet
Place of Issue: Lovejoy, GA   Printing: Offset/Microprint
Designer: Lisa Catalone   ("USPS")

Love Letters
#3499

This First-Class, two-ounce stamp design features a pink rose superimposed on the elegant script of a handwritten letter. The letter—
written by Abigail Smith to John Adams on August 11, 1763, during
their courtship—underscores the enduring nature of profound
sentiment expressed in writing.

Date of Issue: February 14, 2001   Photographer: Renée Comet
Place of Issue: Lovejoy, GA   Printing: Offset/Microprint
Designer: Lisa Catalone   ("USPS")

Lovebirds Stamped Envelope
#U647

With its depiction of two birds as mirror images within a single heart,
the Lovebirds First-Class stamped envelope embodies the intimacy of
true love.

Date of Issue: February 14, 2001   Artist: Robert Brangwynne
Place of Issue: Lovejoy, GA   Printing: Flexo
Designer: Robert Brangwynne

Flowers

Love Letters

Love Letters

Lovebirds Stamped Envelope

Community Colleges Stamped Envelope

Hattie Caraway

Badlands Stamped Card

Community Colleges Stamped Envelope   #U648

Using as a benchmark the 1901 founding of Joliet Junior College—considered the first publicly funded and continuously operating two-year college in the United States—the U.S. Postal Service issued a First-Class stamped envelope in commemoration of community college education. In an effort to sustain their commitment to the public, community colleges emphasize cultural diversity, broad and ongoing community interaction, affordable tuition, and quality education. According to the American Association of Community Colleges (AACC), more than five million students—nearly half of all undergraduates in the United States—attend a community college each fall.

Date of Issue: February 20, 2001   Illustrator: Steve McCracken
Place of Issue: Joliet, IL   Printing: Offset
Designer: Howard Paine

Hattie Caraway   #3431

The U.S. Postal Service honors Hattie Wyatt Caraway (1878-1950), the first woman elected the U.S. Senate. Mrs. Caraway was appointed to the Senate on November 13, 1931, a few days after the death of her husband, Senator Thaddeus Caraway. On January 12, 1932, she won a special election to fill the remaining months of her late husband's term. She was subsequently elected to two six-year terms. In 1933, Mrs. Caraway became the first woman to chair a Senate committee. On October 19, 1943, she was appointed president pro tempore of the Senate and became the first woman to preside over that chamber. A Democrat from Arkansas, Mrs. Caraway served in the Senate until 1945. On her last day in office, the Senate tendered her the high honor of standing ovation.

Date of Issue: February 21, 2001   Illustrator: Mark Summers
Place of Issue: Little Rock, AR   Printing: Offset/Intaglio
Designer: Richard Sheaff

Badlands Stamped Card   #UXC28

Located in southwestern South Dakota, 242,756-acre Badlands National Park preserves a portion of the White River Badlands as well as the largest remnant of mixed-grass prairie in the U.S. Established as a national monument in 1939, the area was redesignated as a national park in 1978. The buttes, spires, and gulches that comprise the park's spectacular and formidable landforms (called badlands) are carved by erosion, which also continuously uncovers rich Oligocene epoch fossil beds. This international-rate stamped card features a color photograph of the Badlands at sunrise.

Date of Issue: February 22, 2001   Photographer: David Muench
Place of Issue: Wall, SD   Printing: Offset
Designer: Ethel Kessler

Art Deco Eagle   #3471

Eagles—such as the one featured on this First-Class, two-ounce stamp—were popular decorative elements on art deco letter boxes in the 1920s and 1930s. These letter boxes were made of a variety of metals—bronze, brass, cast aluminum, and alloys. The stamp art by Nancy Stahl is a composite rendering based on photographs of several eagles that decorate art deco letter boxes dating from the 1920s and 1930s.

Date of Issue: February 22, 2001   Illustrator: Nancy Stahl
Place of Issue: Wall, SD   Printing: Gravure
Designer: Carl Herrman

George Washington   #3482-3483, BK281A, BK282A

George Washington—first President of the United States—is the subject chosen by the U.S. Postal Service for this postcard-rate stamp. The stamp art is based on a black-and-white photograph of a bust of George Washington by Jean-Antoine Houdon. The bust—which is signed and dated 1785—is on display at George Washington's Mount Vernon estate in Virginia. This stamp was issued in a convertible booklet of 10 (#3483) and a criss-cross vending booklet of 10 (BK281A).

Date of Issue: February 22, 2001   Printing: Offset/Microprint
Place of Issue: Wall, SD   ("USPS")
Designer: Richard Sheaff

Bison   #3468, 3475

The bison, a symbol of the American West, appears on this First-Class, second-ounce stamp. The stamp art by Tom Nikosey is based on a color photograph of a bison. It was issued in a self-adhesive pane of 20 (#3468) and a coil of 100 (#3475).

Date of Issue: February 22, 2001   Illustrator: Tom Nikosey
Place of Issue: Wall, SD   Printing: Gravure
Designer: Carl Herrman

Official Mail   #O158

Date of Issue: February 27, 2001   Printing: Offset
Place of Issue: Washington, DC
Designer: Bradbury Thompson

Official Mail Stamped Envelope   #UO90

Date of Issue: February 27, 2001   Printing: Flexo/Deboss
Place of Issue: Washington, DC
Designer: Bradbury Thompson

Art Deco Eagle

George Washington

Bison

Official Mail (coil)

Official Mail Stamped Envelope

Nine-Mile Prairie

Apple and Orange

Diabetes Awareness

Nine-Mile Prairie   #C136

Nine-Mile Prairie is the subject chosen by the U.S. Postal Service for this international postcard-rate stamp. Located five miles west and four miles north of Lincoln, Nebraska, these 230 acres of tall grass prairie—210 of which have never been plowed—are preserved for teaching, research, and nature study. The stamp art is a color photo by Nebraska photographer Michael Forsberg of "six-foot-high big bluestem...laid out over the rolling countryside" of Nine-Mile Prairie.

Date of Issue: March 6, 2001
Place of Issue: Lincoln, NE
Designer: Ethel Kessler
Photographer: Michael Forsberg
Printing: Offset/Microprint ("USPS")

Farm Flag   #3470
(not shown)

This definitive stamp, issued as a self-adhesive pane of 20, was issued earlier as a pane of 100.

Date of Issue: March 6, 2001
Place of Issue: Lincoln, NE
Designer: Richard Sheaff
Illustrator: Hiro Kimura
Printing: Offset/Microprint ("USPS")

Apple and Orange   #3491-3492

The U.S. Postal Service selected familiar fruits—an apple (#3491) and an orange (#3492)—for these First-Class stamps, which were issued for general mail use in self-adhesive booklets. The stamp art by Ned Seidler continues the theme of his earlier illustrations for the Peaches and Pears (1995) and the Fruit Berries (1999) stamps.

Date of Issue: March 6, 2001
Place of Issue: Lincoln, NE
Designer: Ned Seidler
Illustrator: Ned Seidler
Printing: Offset/Microprint ("USPS")

Diabetes Awareness   #3503

With the issuance of the Diabetes stamp, the U.S. Postal Service continues a tradition of raising public awareness of health and social issues. Diabetes is a chronic disease that prevents the body from making enough insulin or using insulin effectively. Insulin is a hormone that helps cells take in glucose, or sugar. By interfering with the production or use of insulin, diabetes deprives cells of energy and causes a buildup of glucose in the blood. Some 16 million people in the United States have diabetes and about one-third of them are unaware that they have the disease. Diabetes was the seventh leading cause of death in the U.S. in 1996-1997. Current research focuses on discovering the causes of diabetes, finding ways to prevent and cure the disease, and finding ways to prevent and treat its complications.

Date of Issue: March 16, 2001
Place of Issue: Boston, MA
Designer: Richard Sheaff
Illustrator: James Steinberg
Printing: Offset/Microprint ("USPS")

The Nobel Prize   #3504

In partnership with Sweden Post, the U.S. Postal Service honors the centennial of the distinguished Nobel Prize. Since 1901 the Nobel Foundation has awarded five annual prizes for outstanding achievement in Physics, Chemistry, Physiology or Medicine, Literature, and Peace. In 1968 the Bank of Sweden Prize in Economic Sciences in Memory of Alfred Nobel was established. The prizes—established in the will of Swedish-born inventor and industrialist Alfred Bernhard Nobel (1833-1896)—are presented each year on December 10, the anniversary of Nobel's death. A Nobel Prize winner receives a gold medal, a diploma, and a check for the amount of the prize. The Peace Prize is awarded in Oslo, Norway, and the remaining prizes are awarded in Stockholm, Sweden. Erik Lindberg, a Swedish sculptor and engraver, designed these four medals.

Date of Issue: March 22, 2001   Engraver: Czeslaw Slania
Place of Issue: Washington, DC   Printing: Offset/Intaglio
Designer: Olöf Baldursdottir

The Pan-American Inverts   #3505

The Pan-American Exposition was held in Buffalo, New York, from May 1 to November 1, 1901. The exhibits highlighted advancements in industry, transportation, manufacturing, and the arts. On the opening day of the Pan-American Exposition, the U.S. Post Office Department issued a series of six bicolored stamps commemorating the exposition. The stamps celebrated the theme of transportation and were on sale from May 1 through October 31, 1901. On three of the six, a limited number of the panes were printed with inverted centers: the one-cent stamp that depicted the steamship *City of Alpena*, the two-cent stamp that depicted the train *Empire State Express*; and the four-cent stamp that depicted an early electric automobile.

Date of Issue: March 29, 2001   Printing: Offset/Intaglio
Place of Issue: New York, NY
Designer: Richard Sheaff

Yale University Stamped Card   #UX361

The U.S. Postal Service commemorates the 300th anniversary of the founding of Yale University, with a stamped card issued as part of the Historic Preservation series. Chartered as the Collegiate School on October 9, 1701, the third oldest university in the United States was renamed Yale College in 1718 (after benefactor Elihu Yale). A contemporary photograph of Connecticut Hall—a symbol of Yale's long-standing commitment to tradition—appears on the stamped card. The first of Yale's brick buildings and the oldest remaining academic structures on the campus, Connecticut Hall is a national historic landmark. It was listed on the National Register of Historic Places on October 15, 1966.

Date of Issue: March 30, 2001   Printing: Offset
Place of Issue: New Haven, CT
Designer: Derry Noyes

The Nobel Prize

The Pan-American Inverts

Yale University Stamped Card

Mt. McKinley

Great Plains Prairie

**University of South Carolina
Stamped Card**

Mt. McKinley   #C137

Mount McKinley—located in Alaska's Denali National Park and Preserve—is featured on this international letter-rate stamp. At 20,320 feet, Mount McKinley is the highest mountain in North America.

Date of Issue: April 17, 2001
Place of Issue: Fairbanks, AK
Designer: Ethel Kessler

Photographers: John Eastcott and Yva Momatiuk
Printing: Gravure

Great Plains Prairie   #3506a-j

The Great Plains Prairie pane is the third in an educational series designed to promote appreciation of North America's major plant and animal communities. The prior issuances in the Nature of America series were Sonoran Desert (1999) and Pacific Coast Rain Forest (2000). The prairie stretches from the edge of the eastern woodlands and oak savannas to the foothills of the Rocky Mountains. An important part of the American landscape, many people often underestimate the prairie's complexity and significance as an ecosystem. It is one of the largest grasslands in the world.

Date of Issue: April 19, 2001
Place of Issue: Lincoln, NE
Designer: Ethel Kessler

Illustrator: John D. Dawson
Printing: Offset

University of South Carolina   #UX362
Stamped Card

Chartered as the South Carolina College on December 19, 1801, the University of South Carolina celebrates its bicentennial in 2001. Classes began at the South Carolina College in 1805. Reestablished as the University of South Carolina in 1906, the school prides itself on being the first institution of higher learning funded entirely by a state. The stamped card features a detail of a circa 1820 painting that depicts the historic Horseshoe district on the main campus in Columbia. Listed on the National Register of Historic Places as the "Old Campus District," this site is the original campus of the university.

Date of Issue: April 26, 2001
Place of Issue: Columbia, SC
Designer: Ethel Kessler

Printing: Offset

Northwestern University #UX363
Stamped Card

The U.S. Postal Service commemorates the 150th anniversary of the founding of Northwestern University with a stamped card. The university's act of incorporation was approved by the Illinois State Legislature and signed into law by Governor Augustus C. French on January 28, 1851. University Hall, Northwestern's oldest building, is on the Evanston campus, which borders Lake Michigan. This Gothic-style structure originally contained a chapel, a library, a museum, dormitories, and classrooms. Today it houses the English department of the Judd A. and Marjorie Weinberg College of Arts and Sciences.

Date of Issue: April 28, 2001   Illustrator: Arnold C. Holeywell
Place of Issue: Evanston, IL   Printing: Offset
Designer: Howard Paine

University of Portland #UX364
Stamped Card

The U.S. Postal Service commemorates the 100th anniversary of the founding of the University of Portland with the issuance of a stamped card as part of the Historic Preservation series. Founded by Archbishop Alexander Christie, Columbia University—as it was known then—held its first classes on September 5, 1901. The University was renamed University of Portland in 1935. Waldschmidt Hall—the oldest building on campus—was constructed in the early 1890s, before the university's inception. Considered the university's signature building, Waldschmidt Hall was listed on the National Register of Historic Places on September 22, 1977.

Date of Issue: May 1, 2001   Illustrator: John Pirman
Place of Issue: Portland, OR   Printing: Offset
Designer: Richard Sheaff

Peanuts #3507

This stamp commemorates the comic strip "Peanuts," which celebrated its 50th anniversary in 2000. Drawn by Charles M. Schulz (1922-2000), "Peanuts" began in syndication on October 2, 1950. The installment published on Sunday, February 13, 2000, was the last original comic strip by Schultz, who died the previous day. "Peanuts" appears in some 2,600 newspapers in 75 countries and is translated into 21 languages. "Peanuts" inspired numerous Emmy Award-winning animated television specials, including *A Charlie Brown Christmas* (1965), and *You're a Good Sport, Charlie Brown* (1975). The pane of 20 stamps consists of a single stamp design featuring Snoopy on top of his doghouse, imagining himself as a World War I flying ace.

Date of Issue: May 17, 2001   Printing: Offset/Microprint
Place of Issue: Santa Rosa, CA   ("USPS")
Designer: Paige Braddock,
  Charles M. Schulz Creative Associates

**Northwestern University
Stamped Card**

**University of Portland
Stamped Card**

Peanuts

Honoring Veterans

Acadia National Park

Frida Kahlo

Honoring Veterans   #3508

With the issuance of this stamp, the U.S. Postal Service honors the patriotic dedication of all the men and women who have served in the U.S. armed forces. The present population of U.S. veterans is estimated to be nearly 25 million. Many veterans continue to serve their country, their fellow veterans, and their communities by becoming members of veteran service organizations. These organizations provide aid to veterans and their families, including assistance with benefit applications, transportation to VA medical facilities, and burial and memorial services. Local communities also benefit from the work of veterans service organizations, through scholarship programs, youth sports activities and other programs designed to promote civic pride.

Date of Issue: May 23, 2001   Printing: Offset
Place of Issue: Washington, DC
Designer: Carl Herrman

Acadia National Park   #C138

Acadia National Park is the subject chosen by the U.S. Postal Service for this international postcard-rate stamp. Located in Bar Harbor, Maine, Acadia encompasses over 35,000 acres of mountains, wood-lands, forests, lakes, ponds, and ocean shoreline. On January 19, 1929, Acadia became the first national park established east of the Mississippi River. Acadia National Park was established to protect the area's vast resources, beautiful scenic views, and natural native plant and animal life. Visitors can experience spectacular sunrises atop Cadillac Mountain.

Date of Issue: May 30, 2001   Photographer: Carr Clifton
Place of Issue: Bar Harbor, ME   Printing: Offset
Designer: Ethel Kessler

Frida Kahlo

The U.S. Postal Service continues its celebration of the fine arts with this stamp honoring Mexican painter Frida Kahlo. Frida Kahlo, best know for her striking self-portraits, was born in Coyoacán, Mexico, on July 6, 1907. Stricken by polio in early childhood and seriously injured in an accident at the age of 18, Kahlo endured severe pain throughout her life. Her physical suffering, inability to bear children, and tumul-tuous marriage to Mexican muralist Diego Rivera are reflected in much of her work. After her death on July 13, 1954, Frida Kahlo's audience grew. Her work has influenced Chicana artists in the United States, and since the mid-1970s she has been a role model for women in the Mexican-American and feminist communities. The stamp art features a Frida Kahlo self-portrait painted in 1933.

Date of Issue: June 21, 2001   Printing: Offset
Place of Issue: Phoenix, AZ
Designer: Richard Sheaff

Baseball's Legendary Playing Fields

In partnership with Major League Baseball, the U.S. Postal Service commemorates eleven legendary playing fields. Appearing on the ten stamps are: Cominskey Park in Chicago, Crosley Field in Cincinnati, Ebbets Field in Brooklyn, Fenway Park in Boston, Forbes Field in Pittsburgh, Polo Grounds in New York City, Shibe Park in Philadelphia, Tiger Stadium in Detroit, Wrigley Field in Chicago, and Yankee Stadium in New York City. Sportsman's Park in St. Louis is featured on the header. Only four of these eleven legendary playing fields still stand. Fenway Park, Wrigley Field, and Yankee Stadium are still used as home fields by their respective teams. The fate of Tiger Stadium—no longer used by the Detroit Tigers—is uncertain.

Date of Issue: June 27, 2001   Printing: Offset
Place of Issue: Boston, MA;
  Chicago, IL; Detroit, MI; New York, NY
Designer: Phil Jordan

Atlas

This presorted standard stamp features the bronze sculpture *Atlas* that stands in front of the International Building at Rockefeller Center in New York City. American sculptor Lee Oskar Lawrie (1877-1963) created this striking example of art deco in 1937. The sculpture portrays the giant Atlas who, according to Greek mythology, bore the heavens on his shoulders. Lawrie's *Atlas* holds an armillary sphere, an old astronomical instrument composed of interlocking rings. The sphere contains the twelve signs of the zodiac and its axis points to the North Star.

Date of Issue: June 29, 2001   Illustrator: Kevin Newman
Place of Issue: New York, NY   Printing: Gravure
Designer: Carl Herrman

Leonard Bernstein

Leonard Bernstein (1918-1990)—conductor, composer, pianist, teacher, and author—brought worldwide recognition to American composers and musicians. He was noted for his passion for—and achievements in—multiple genres of music, from symphonies to Broadway shows. He composed symphonies, chamber music, and vocal music, as well as works for ballet, opera, film, and the Broadway musical stage. His many contributions to the musical theater include the score for *West Side Story*, which was made into an Academy Award-winning film. He received an Academy Award nomination for his score for the film *On the Waterfront*.

Date of Issue: July 10, 2001   Photographer: Don Hunstein
Place of Issue: New York, NY   Printing: Offset
Designer: Howard Payne

Baseball's Legendary Playing Fields

Atlas

Leonard Bernstein

Woody Wagon

Lucille Ball

Amish Quilts

Woody Wagon

This presorted nondenominated stamp at the First-Class card rate features a woody station wagon. Wood-paneled vehicles, or woodies, captured the imagination of the American public from the 1930s through the 1950s. Woodies came in several models, including sedans, convertibles, station wagons, and trucks. Originally designed as stylish cars for wealthy buyers, woodies were later marketed as practical transportation for families, who found woody wagons ideal for shopping trips and vacations. Woodies enjoyed a revival in the 1950s and 1960s among surfers, who bought used woody wagons to carry their boards to the beach.

Date of Issue: August 3, 2001
Place of Issue: Denver, CO
Designer: Carl Herrman

Illustrator: Kevin Newman
Printing: Gravure

Lucille Ball

This is the seventh stamp issued in the Legends of Hollywood series. Lucille Ball (1911-1989) was a prominent star of stage, screen, radio, and especially television. For nearly three decades, Lucille Ball regularly appeared on television programs including the enormously popular show *I Love Lucy* (1951-1957). She also appeared in more than 70 movies. She won four Emmy Awards®, was one of the first inductees into the Academy of Television Arts & Sciences Hall of Fame in 1984, and received the Kennedy Center Honors in 1986. She was posthumously awarded the Presidential Medal of Freedom in 1989. The selvage photograph depicting Lucille Ball as Lucy Ricardo in a state of openmouthed surprise is from Episode 175 of *I Love Lucy*. This episode, entitled "Housewarming," first aired April 1, 1957.

Date of Issue: August 6, 2001
Place of Issue: Los Angeles, CA
Designer: Derry Noyes

Illustrator: Drew Stuzan
Printing: Offset

Amish Quilts

The U.S. Postal Service pays tribute to one of the most colorful traditions in American design—the Amish quilt. Distinctive in its simplicity, symmetry, deft needlework, and broad fields of deep color, the Amish quilt is a uniquely American folk art form. Amish quilting traditions vary from region to region, yet all are influenced by the religious and social values of Amish daily life: humility, simplicity, modesty, and serviceability. The four quilts repeated on this pane of 20 stamps display the vibrant colors, bold graphic patterns, and central design motifs characteristic of quilts made in Lancaster County, Pennsylvania, during the first half of the 20th century.

Date of Issue: August 9, 2001
Place of Issue: Nappanee, IN
Designer: Derry Noyes

Printing: Offset

Carnivorous Plants

Four carnivorous plant species and their prey are portrayed on this striking pane of twenty commemorative stamps. The Carnivorous Plants stamps are the featured issuance during National Stamp Collecting Month. All plants on the pane are native to—but not necessarily restricted to—North America. The Venus flytrap (*Dionaea muscipula*) is shown with a little metalmark—a kind of butterfly—caught in one of its leaves. A fly perches on the lip of the yellow trumpet (*Sarracenia flava*), also known as the trumpet or yellow pitcherplant. An unwary wasp is drawn towards the mouth of the cobra lily (*Darlingtonia californica*), a plant native to the West Coast. The English sundew (*Drosera anglica)* is a small plant that uses its sticky leaves to trap insects. Here an unlucky syrphid fly has been caught by the plant.

Date of Issue: August 23, 2001   Illustrator: Steve Buchanan
Place of Issue: Des Plaines, IL   Printing: Gravure
Designer: Phil Jordan

Holiday Celebration: Eid

Issued as part of the Holiday Celebrations series, this stamp commemorates the two most important festivals—or eids—in the Islamic calendar: Eid al-Fitr and Eid al-Adha. On these days, Muslims wish each other *Eid mubarak*, the phrase featured in Islamic calligraphy on the stamp. *Eid mubarak* translates literally as "blessed festival," and can be paraphrased "May your religious holiday be blessed." The first day of the Muslim lunar month of Shawwal, Eid al-Fitr signifies "The Feast of Breaking the Fast." This festival marks the end of Ramadan, the month of fasting. Signifying "The Feast of the Sacrifice," Eid al-Adha occurs approximately two months and ten days after Eid al-Fitr. Eid al-Adha comes at the end of the hajj—the annual period of pilgrimage to the holy city of Mecca—and commemorates Ibrahim's willingness to sacrifice his son Ismail.

Date of Issue: September 1, 2001   Printing: Gravure
Place of Issue: Des Plaines, IL
Designer and Calligrapher: Mohamed Zakariya

Enrico Fermi

This stamp commemorates the centenary of Enrico Fermi's birth on September 29, 1901, in Rome, Italy. Enrico Fermi received a Ph.D. in physics from the University of Pisa in 1922, and went on to become one of the preeminent physicists of the atomic age. In 1934, while experimenting with neutron bombardment of uranium, Fermi—without realizing it at the time—became the first physicist to split the atom. Fermi was awarded the Nobel Prize in Physics in 1938. In January 1942 he supervised the design and assembly of the first nuclear reactor as part of the secret Manhattan Project. He was present when the first atomic bomb was tested. In 1955, the Institute for Nuclear Studies was renamed the Enrico Fermi Institute for Nuclear Studies in his memory.

Date of Issue: September 29, 2001   Printing: Offset
Place of Issue: Chicago, IL
Designer: Richard Sheaff

Carnivorous Plants

Holiday Celebrations: Eid

Enrico Fermi

Porky Pig

Holiday Traditional

Holiday Contemporary

Porky Pig

The U.S. Postal Service, in partnership with Warner Bros., is pleased to feature Porky Pig on this fifth and last stamp in the Looney Tunes series. The first true star of the Looney Tunes cast, Porky Pig is popular with audiences of all ages. He has appeared in more than 160 cartoons, often playing straight man to Daffy Duck. Previous stamps in the Looney Tunes series featured Bugs Bunny (1997), Sylvester and Tweety (1998), Daffy Duck (1999), and Wile E. Coyote and Road Runner (2000). Porky Pig ends the series with his classic line "That's all Folks!"

Date of Issue: October 1, 2001 Character Art: Frank Espinosa,
Place of Issue: Burbank, CA Warner Bros.
Designer: Ed Wleczyk, Warner Bros. Printing: Gravure

Holiday Traditional

Coinciding with the 125th anniversary of the Philadelphia Museum of Art in 2001, this latest offering in the Holiday Traditional series features a detail of Italian Renaissance painter Lorenzo Costa's oil-on-panel *Virgin and Child*, circa 1490. The painting is a part of the John G. Hohnson Collection at the Philadelphia Museum of Art. Lorenzo Costa's work is well represented in major European galleries; this painting a rare example of Costa's work in an American museum.

Date of Issue: October 10, 2001 Illustrator: Lorenzo Costa
Place of Issue: Philadelphia, PA Printing: Gravure
Designer: Richard Sheaff

Holiday Contemporary

These stamps feature four images that represent part of the rich folklore of Santa Claus. Over the centuries, numerous cultures have contributed to the legend, and these images are part of that tradition.

Date of Issue: October 10, 2001 Printing: Gravure
Place of Issue: Santa Claus, IN
Designer: Richard Sheaff

Holiday Celebrations: Thanksgiving

The U.S. Thanksgiving holiday, observed the fourth Thursday of every November, stems from a rich history of celebration. The best known of these if the first harvest festival at Plymouth, where in autumn 1621, some 50 colonists and 90 Native Americans gathered for a three-day feast to offer thanks for a bountiful harvest. In 1863, President Abraham Lincoln issued a Proclamation of Thanksgiving, marking the beginning of national recognition of an annual Thanksgiving holiday in the U.S.

Date of Issue: October, 2001   Illustrator: Margaret Cusack
Place of Issue: Dallas, TX   Printing: Offset
Designer: Richard Sheaff

James Madison

The U.S. Postal Service marks the 250th anniversary of James Madison's birth with the issuance of this commemorative stamp in 2001. Madison, the fourth President of the United States, is also remembered as the "father of the U.S. Constitution." Born March 16, 1751, in Port Conway, Virginia, Madison graduated from the College of New Jersey (later Princeton University) in 1771. He was elected to the Virginia Constitutional Convention in 1776 and to the Continental Congress in December 1779. Madison was instrumental in organizing the body of delegates that wrote the U.S. Constitution in 1787, and his extensive study of ancient republics led to his many contributions to that document. He was also an important figure in the ratification of the Constitution. Later, while a member of the U.S. House of Representatives, Madison played a leading role in the creation and passage of the first ten amendments to the Constitution. These amendments, known as the Bill of Rights, were proposed in 1789 and adopted in 1791. Madison was elected President in 1808 and reelected in 1812 after asking Congress to declare war on Britain. Upon leaving office, Madison retired to Montpelier, his Virginia estate. He died there on June 28, 1836.

Date of Issue: October 18, 2001   Illustrator: John Thompson
Place of Issue: New York, NY   Printing: Offset/Intaglio
Designer: Carl Herrman

**Holiday Celebrations:
Thanksgiving**

James Madison

Explanation of Catalog Prices

The United States Postal Service sells only the commemoratives and special issues released during the past few years. Current postal stationery and regular issues remain on sale for longer periods of time. Prices in this book are called "catalog prices" by stamp collectors. Collectors use catalog prices as guidelines when buying or trading stamps. **It is important to remember the prices are simply guidelines to the stamp values. Stamp condition is very important in determining the actual value of a stamp.**

Prices are Estimated

Listed prices are estimates of how much you can expect to pay for a stamp from a dealer. **A 20-cent minimum valuation has been established that represents a fair-market price to have a dealer locate and provide a single stamp to a customer. Dealers may charge less per stamp to provide a group of such stamps, and may charge less for such a single stamp. Similarly, a $1.00 minimum has been established for First Day Covers (FDCs).** If you sell a stamp to a dealer, he or she may offer you much less than the catalog price. Dealers pay based on their interest in owning a particular stamp. If they already have a full supply, they may only buy additional stamps at a low price.

Condition Affects Value

The catalog prices are given for unused (mint) stamps and used (canceled) stamps that have been hinged and are in "very fine" condition. Stamps in "superb" condition that have never been hinged may cost more than the listed price. Stamps in less than "fine" condition may cost less.

The prices for used stamps are based on a light cancellation; a heavy cancellation lessens a stamp's value. Canceled stamps may be worth more than uncanceled stamps. This happens if the cancellation is of a special type or for a significant date. Therefore, it is important to study an envelope before removing a stamp and discarding its "cover." Additional information about and examples of stamp conditions can be found in the Introduction to this book.

Sample Listing

				Un	U	PB/LP/PNC	#	FDC	Q(M)
3069	32¢	Georgia O'Keefe	05/23/96	.65	.20	2.75	(4)	1.25	156

Scott Catalog Number (bold type indicates stamp is pictured)

Description Denomination

Date of Issue

Unused Catalog Price

Used Catalog Price

Plate Block Price, Line Pair Price or Plate Number Coil Price

Number of stamps in Plate Block, Line Pair or Plate Number Coil

First Day Cover Price

Quantity Issued in Millions (where known)

3069

Understanding the Listings

■ Prices in **regular type** for single unused and used stamps are taken from the *Scott 2001 Specialized Catalogue of U.S. Stamps & Covers,* whose editors have based these prices on **actual retail values** as they found them in the marketplace. The Scott numbering system for stamps is used in this book. Prices quoted for unused and used stamps are for "very fine" condition, except where "very fine" is not available.

■ Stamp values in *italic* generally refer to items difficult to value accurately.

■ A dash (—) in a value column means the item is known to exist but information is insufficient for establishing a value.

■ The stamp listings contain a number of additions designated "*a,*" "*b,*" "*c,*" etc. These represent recognized variations of stamps as well as errors. These listings are as complete as space permits.

Occasionally, a new stamp or major variation may be inserted by the catalog editors into a series or sequence where it was not originally anticipated. These additions are identified by capital letters "*A,*" "*B*" and so forth. For example, a new stamp which logically belonged between 1044 and 1045 is designated 1044A, even though it is entirely different from 1044. The insertion was preferable to a complete renumbering of the series.

■ Prices for Plate Blocks, First Day Covers, American Commemorative Panels and Souvenir Pages are taken from *Scott 2001 Specialized Catalogue of U.S. Stamps & Covers.*

Sample Variation Listing

			Un	U	PB/LP/PNC	#	FDC	Q(M)
2281	25¢ Honeybee	09/02/88	.45	.20	3.25	(3)	1.25	
a	Imperf. pair		*45.00*					
b	Black omitted		*65.00*					
d	Pair, imperf. between		*1,000.00*					

■ Scott Catalog Number (bold type indicates stamp is pictured)

■ Description Denomination

■ Date of Issue

2281

■ Unused Catalog Price

■ Used Catalog Price

■ Plate Block Price, Line Pair Price or **Plate Number** Coil Price

■ First Day Cover Price

Quantity Issued in **Millions** (where known)

Number of stamps in Plate Block, Line Pair or Plate Number Coil

Commemorative and Definitive Stamps

1847-1875

1

2

3

4

5

11

12

14

17

Issues of 1847	Un	U
Thin, Bluish Wove Paper,		
July 1, Imperf., Unwmkd.		
1 5¢ Benjamin Franklin	5,750.00	600.00
b 5¢ orange brown	7,000.00	850.00
c 5¢ red orange	12,500.00	5,000.00
Pen cancel		300.00
Double transfer of top or top and		
bottom frame lines		725.00
Double transfer of top, bottom and		
left frame lines and numerals		3,000.00
2 10¢ George		
Washington	27,500.00	1,400.00
Pen cancel		750.00
Vertical line through second "F"		
of "OFFICE"	—	1,900.00
With "stick pin" in tie, or		
with "harelip"	—	1,900.00
Double transfer in lower		
right "X," or of left and		
bottom frame lines	—	2,000.00
Double transfer in		
"POST OFFICE"	—	2,500.00
Issues of 1875, Reproductions		
of 1 and 2, Bluish Paper, Without Gum		
3 5¢ Franklin	850.00	—
4 10¢ Washington	1,100.00	—

5¢. On the originals, the left side of the white shirt frill touches the oval on a level with the top of the "F" of "Five." On the reproductions, it touches the oval about on a level with the top of the figure "5."

10¢. On the originals, line of coat points to "T" of TEN and right line of coat points between "T" and "S" of CENTS.

On the reproductions left, line of coat points to right tip of "X" and right line of coat points to center of "S" of CENTS.

On the reproductions, the eyes have a sleepy look, the line of the mouth is straighter, and in the curl of hair near the left cheek is a strong black dot, while the originals have only a faint one.

Issues of 1851-57, Imperf.		
5 1¢ Franklin, type I	175,000.00	40,000.00
5A 1¢ blue, type Ib	14,000.00	5,500.00
#6-9: Franklin (5), 1851		
6 1¢ dark blue, type Ia	35,000.00	9,500.00
7 1¢ blue, type II	1,100.00	160.00
Cracked plate	1,350.00	375.00
8 1¢ blue, type III	11,500.00	2,750.00
8A 1¢ blue, type IIIa	4,250.00	975.00
9 1¢ blue, type IV	750.00	125.00
Triple transfer,		
one inverted	900.00	175.00

Issues of 1851-57	Un	U
#10-11, 25-26a all had plates on which at		
least four outer frame lines (and usually much		
more) were recut, adding to their value.		
10 3¢ orange brown		
Washington, type I (11)	3,000.00	100.00
3¢ copper brown	3,500.00	170.00
On part-India paper	—	500.00
11 3¢ Washington, type I	240.00	10.00
3¢ deep claret	325.00	18.00
Double transfer,		
"GENTS" for "CENTS"	375.00	35.00
12 5¢ Jefferson, type I	17,500.00	1,100.00
13 10¢ green Washington,		
type I (14)	14,000.00	800.00
14 10¢ green, type II	3,500.00	225.00
15 10¢ Washington, type III	3,500.00	225.00
16 10¢ green, type IV (14)	25,000.00	1,600.00
17 12¢ Washington	4,500.00	325.00
Issues of 1857-61, Perf. 15.5 (Issued in		
1857 except #18, 27, 28A, 29, 30, 30A, 35,		
36b, 37, 38, 39)		
#18-24: Franklin (5)		
18 1¢ blue, type I	1,750.00	550.00
19 1¢ blue, type Ia	19,000.00	5,500.00
20 1¢ blue, type II	1,000.00	250.00
21 1¢ blue, type III	12,000.00	2,000.00
22 1¢ blue, type IIIa	1,800.00	450.00
23 1¢ blue, type IV	7,250.00	650.00
24 1¢ blue, type V	175.00	40.00
"Curl" on shoulder	240.00	67.50
"Earring" below ear	350.00	95.00
Long double		
"curl" in hair	300.00	80.00
b Laid paper	—	
#25-26a: Washington (11)		
25 3¢ rose, type I	2,100.00	80.00
Major cracked plate	3,500.00	525.00
26 3¢ dull red, type II	75.00	5.00
3¢ brownish carmine	140.00	16.00
3¢ claret	170.00	21.00
Left or right frame		
line double	110.00	15.00
Cracked plate	750.00	250.00
26a 3¢ dull red, type IIa	200.00	45.00
Double transfer	300.00	100.00
Left frame line double	—	140.00

5
Bust of Benjamin
Franklin.

Detail of **#7, 20** Type II

Lower scrollwork
incomplete (lacks little
balls and lower plume
ornaments). Side orna-
ments are complete.

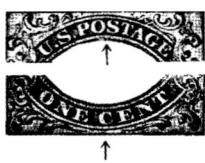

Detail of **#9, 23** Type IV

Similar to Type II, but
outer lines recut top,
bottom or both.

Detail of **#5, 18, 40**
Type I

Has curved, unbroken
lines outside labels.
Scrollwork is substan-
tially complete at top,
forms little balls at
bottom.

Detail of **#8, 21** Type III

Outer lines broken in
the middle. Side orna-
ments are substantially
complete.

Detail of **#8A, 22**
Type IIIa

Outer lines broken top
or bottom but not
both.

Detail of **#24** Type V

Similar to Type III of
1851-57 but with side
ornaments partly cut
away.

Detail of **#6, 19** Type Ia

Same as Type I at bot-
tom but top ornaments
and outer line partly
cut away. Lower scroll-
work is complete.

Detail of **#5a** Type Ib

Lower scrollwork is
incomplete, the little
balls are not so clear.

3¢ Washington Types I-IIa, Series 1851-1857, 1857-1861, 1875

10
Bust of George Washington

Detail of **#10, 11, 25, 41**
Type I

There is an outer frame line at top and bottom.

Detail of **#26**
Type II

The outer frame line has been removed at top and bottom. The side frame lines were recut so as to be continuous from the top to the bottom of the plate.

Detail of **#26a**
Type IIa

The side frame lines extended only to the bottom of the stamp design.

5¢ Jefferson Types I-II, Series 1851-1857, 1857-1861

12
Portrait of
Thomas Jefferson

Detail of **#12, 27-29**
Type I

There are projections on all four sides.

Detail of **#30-30a**
Type II

The projections at top and bottom are partly cut away.

10¢ Washington Types I-IV, Series 1851-1857, 1857-1861, 1875

15
Portrait of
George Washington

Detail of **#13, 31, 43**
Type I

The "shells" at the lower corners are practically complete. The outer line below the label is very nearly complete. The outer lines are broken above the middle of the top label and the "X" in each upper corner.

Detail of **#14, 32**
Type II

The design is complete at the top. The outer line at the bottom is broken in the middle. The shells are partly cut away.

Detail of **#15, 33**
Type III

The outer lines are broken above the top label and the "X" numerals. The outer line at the bottom and the shells are partly cut away, as in Type II.

Detail of **#16, 34** Type IV

The outer lines have been recut at top or bottom or both. Types I, II, III and IV have complete ornaments at the sides of the stamps and three pearls at each outer edge of the bottom panel.

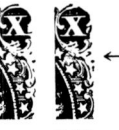
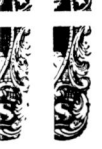

Detail of **#35**
Type V

(Two typical examples.) Side ornaments slightly cut away. Outer lines complete at top except over right "X." Outer lines complete at bottom and shells nearly so.

Issues of 1857-61	Un	U
Perf. 15.5		
#27-29: Jefferson (12)		
27 5¢ brick red, type I	22,500.00	1,300.00
28 5¢ red brown, type I	4,000.00	650.00
b 5¢ brt. red brn., type I	4,250.00	850.00
28A 5¢ Indian red, type I	30,000.00	3,000.00
29 5¢ brown, type I	2,200.00	350.00
Defective transfer	—	—
30 5¢ orange brown, type II	1,150.00	1,100.00
30A 5¢ brown, type II (30)	1,800.00	260.00
b Printed on both sides	4,250.00	4,500.00
#31-35: Washington (15)		
31 10¢ green, type I	16,000.00	850.00
32 10¢ green, type II	4,750.00	275.00
33 10¢ green, type III	4,750.00	275.00
"Curl" on forehead		
or in left "X"		350.00
34 10¢ green, type IV	32,500.00	2,250.00
35 10¢ green, type V	275.00	65.00
Small "curl" on forehead	325.00	77.50
"Curl" in "e" or		
"t" of "Cents"	350.00	90.00
Plate I Outer frame lines complete		
36 12¢ blk. Washington		
(17), plate I	1,200.00	210.00
Triple transfer	1,500.00	
36b 12¢ black, plate III	725.00	175.00
Vertical line		
through rosette	900.00	250.00
37 24¢ gray lilac	1,500.00	350.00
a 24¢ gray	1,500.00	350.00
38 30¢ orange Franklin	1,800.00	450.00
Recut at bottom	2,100.00	575.00
39 90¢ blue Washington	2,600.00	6,000.00
Double transfer		
at top or bottom	2,750.00	—
Pen cancel		1,750.00

Note: Beware of forged cancellations of #39. Genuine cancellations are rare

Issues of 1875	Un	U
Government Reprints, White Paper		
Without Gum, Perf. 12		
40 1¢ bright blue Franklin (5)	650.00	
41 3¢ scarlet Wash. (11)	2,750.00	
42 5¢ orange brown		
Jefferson (30)	1,100.00	
43 10¢ blue green		
Washington (14)	2,250.00	
44 12¢ greenish black		
Washington (17)	3,000.00	
45 24¢ blackish violet		
Washington (37)	3,000.00	
46 30¢ yellow orange		
Franklin (38)	3,000.00	
47 90¢ deep blue		
Washington (39)	4,500.00	
48-54 Not assigned		
Issue of 1861, Thin,		
Semi-Transparent Paper		
#55-62 are no longer considered postage stamps. Many experts consider them to be essays and/or trial color proofs.		
62B 10¢ dark green		
Washington (58)	6,500.00	900.00

30

37

38

39

40

62B

63

64

65

67

68

69

70

71

72

73

77

Details

Issues of 1861-62, 1861-66, 1867 and 1875

Detail of **#63, 86, 92**

There is a dash in 63, 86 and 92 added under the tip of the ornament at the right of the numeral in upper left corner.

Detail of **#67, 75, 80, 95**

There is a leaf in 67, 75, 80 and 95 added to the foliated ornaments at each corner.

Detail of **#69, 85E, 90, 97**

In 69, 85E, 90 and 97, ovals and scrolls have been added at the corners.

Detail of **#64-66, 74, 79, 82-83, 85, 85C, 88, 94**

In 64-66, 74, 79, 82-83, 85, 85C, 88 and 94, ornaments at corners have been enlarged and end in a small ball.

Detail of **#68, 85D, 89, 96**

There is an outer line in 68, 85D, 89 and 96 cut below the stars and an outer line added to the ornaments above them.

Detail of **#72, 101**

In 72 and 101, parallel lines form an angle above the ribbon containing "U.S. Postage"; between these lines a row of dashes has been added, along with a point of color to the apex of the lower line.

Issues of 1861-62		Un	U
Perf. 12			
63	1¢ blue Franklin	325.00	32.50
	Double transfer	—	45.00
	Dot in "U"	350.00	37.50
a	1¢ ultramarine	700.00	250.00
b	1¢ dark blue	525.00	80.00
c	Laid paper	—	—
d	Vert. pair, imperf. horiz.		—
e	Printed on both sides		2,500.00
64	3¢ pink Washington	7,000.00	700.00
a	3¢ pigeon blood pink	16,000.00	3,500.00
b	3¢ rose pink	500.00	140.00
65	3¢ rose Washington	130.00	2.50
	Cracked plate	—	—
	Double transfer	150.00	5.50
b	Laid paper	—	—
d	Vertical pair,		
	imperf. horizontally	3,500.00	750.00
e	Printed on both sides	3,250.00	2,750.00
f	Double impression		6,000.00
66	3¢ lake Washington is considered		
	a Trial Color Proof		
67	5¢ buff Jefferson	16,500.00	750.00
68	10¢ yellow green		
	Washington	700.00	50.00
	10¢ deep yellow green		
	on thin paper	850.00	60.00
	Double transfer	775.00	55.00
a	10¢ dark green	750.00	52.50
b	Vert. pair, imperf. horiz.		3,500.00
69	12¢ blk. Washington	1,100.00	90.00
	12¢ intense black	1,150.00	95.00
	Double transfer of top		
	or bottom frame line	1,200.00	110.00
	Double transfer of top		
	and bottom frame lines	1,250.00	115.00
70	24¢ red lilac		
	Washington	1,700.00	150.00
	Scratch under "A"		
	of "POSTAGE"		—
a	24¢ brown lilac	1,500.00	130.00
b	24¢ steel blue	7,500.00	600.00
c	24¢ violet	9,500.00	1,100.00
d	24¢ grayish lilac	3,000.00	900.00
71	30¢ orange Franklin	1,500.00	150.00
a	Printed on both sides		—
72	90¢ bl. Washington	2,500.00	400.00
a	90¢ pale blue	2,500.00	400.00
b	90¢ dark blue	2,750.00	475.00
Issues of 1861-66			
73	2¢ blk. Andrew Jackson	350.00	50.00
	Double transfer	400.00	55.00
	Major double transfer of top		
	left corner and "POSTAGE"		12,500.00
	Cracked plate	—	—

Issues of 1861-66		Un	U
Perf. 12			
	#74 3¢ scarlet Washington was not regularly		
	issued and is considered a Trial Color Proof.		
75	5¢ red brown		
	Jefferson (67)	4,270.00	450.00
76	5¢ brown Jefferson (67)	1,100.00	110.00
a	5¢ dark brown	1,250.00	160.00
	Double transfer of top		
	or bottom frame line	1,200.00	125.00
77	15¢ blk. Lincoln	1,500.00	150.00
	Double transfer	1,600.00	160.00
78	24¢ lilac Washington (70)	1,000.00	95.00
a	24¢ grayish lilac	1,000.00	95.00
b	24¢ gray	1,000.00	95.00
c	24¢ blackish violet	30,000.00	1,750.00
d	Printed on both sides		3,500.00
Grills on U.S. Stamps			
	Between 1867 and 1870, postage stamps		
	were embossed with pyramid-shaped grills		
	that absorbed cancellation ink to prevent		
	reuse of canceled stamps.		
Issues of 1867, With Grills			
	Grills A, B and with C: Points Up		
A. Grill Covers Entire Stamp			
79	3¢ rose Washington (56)	4,500.00	1,000.00
b	Printed on both sides		—
80	5¢ brown Jefferson (57)	—	80,000.00
a	5¢ dark brown		80,000.00
81	30¢ orange Franklin (61)		50,000.00
B. Grill about 18 x 15mm			
82	3¢ rose Washington (56)		160,000.00
C. Grill about 13 x 16mm			
83	3¢ rose Washington (56)	4,750.00	900.00
	Double grill	6,250.00	2,250.00
Grills, D, Z, E, F with Points Down			
D. Grill about 12 x 14mm			
84	2¢ black Jackson (73)	13,000.00	2,250.00
85	3¢ rose Washington (56)	5,750.00	900.00
	Split grill		1,000.00
Z. Grill about 11 x 14mm			
85A	1¢ blue Franklin (55)		935,000.00
85B	2¢ black Jackson (73)	7,000.00	1,000.00
	Double transfer	7,500.00	1,050.00
85C	3¢ rose Washington (56)	10,000.00	2,750.00
	Double grill	11,500.0	
85D	10¢ grn. Washington (58)		90,000.00
85E	12¢ blk. Washington (59)	9,000.00	1,250.00
	Double transfer		
	of top frame line		1,350.00
85F	15¢ black Lincoln (77)		220,000.00
E. Grill about 11 x 13mm			
86	1¢ blue Franklin (55)	2,750.00	450.00
a	1¢ dull blue	2,750.00	425.00
	Double grill	—	575.00
	Split grill	2,850.00	500.00

Issues of 1867	Un	U
With Grills, Perf. 12		
87 2¢ black Jackson (73)	1,350.00	125.00
2¢ intense black	1,450.00	150.00
Double grill	—	—
Double transfer	1,450.00	135.00
88 3¢ rose Washington (65)	750.00	20.00
a 3¢ lake red	800.00	25.00
Double grill	—	—
Very thin paper	775.00	22.50
89 10¢ grn. Washington (68)	4,500.00	300.00
Double grill	5,750.00	500.00
90 12¢ blk. Washington (69)	4,250.00	325.00
Double transfer of top or bottom frame line	4,500.00	350.00
91 15¢ black Lincoln (77)	8,250.00	625.00
Double grill	—	950.00
F. Grill about 9 x 13mm		
92 1¢ blue Franklin (63)	1,000.00	190.00
Double transfer	1,050.00	225.00
Double grill	—	350.00
93 2¢ black Jackson (73)	450.00	45.00
Double grill	—	175.00
Very thin paper	500.00	52.50
94 3¢ red Washington (65)	350.00	6.00
a 3¢ rose	350.00	6.00
Double grill	—	
End roller grill		325.00
Quadruple split grill	625.00	125.00
c Vertical pair, imperf. horizontally	1,100.00	
d Printed on both sides	2,250.00	
95 5¢ brown Jefferson (67)	3,000.00	700.00
a 5¢ black brown	3,250.00	825.00
96 10¢ yellow green Washington (68)	2,400.00	200.00
a 10¢ dark green	2,400.00	200.00
Double transfer	—	—
Quadruple split grill		625.00
97 12¢ blk. Washington (69)	2,750.00	225.00
Double transfer of top or bottom frame line	3,000.00	240.00
Triple grill		—
98 15¢ black Lincoln (77)	3,000.00	300.00
Double transfer of upper right corner	—	—
Double grill	—	450.00
Quadruple split grill	3,750.00	625.00
99 24¢ gray lilac Washington (70)	5,250.00	750.00
100 30¢ orange Franklin (71)	5,250.00	700.00
Double grill	7,000.00	1,500.00
101 90¢ bl. Washington (72)	9,500.00	1,400.00
Double grill	13,500.00	

Issues of 1875	Un	U
Reissue of 1861-66 Issues, Without Grill, Perf. 12		
102 1¢ blue Franklin (63)	750.00	1,000.00
103 2¢ black Jackson (73)	3,000.00	4,500.00
104 3¢ brown red Washington (65)	3,250.00	5,000.00
105 5¢ brown Jefferson (67)	2,500.00	2,750.00
106 10¢ grn. Washington (68)	2,650.00	4,500.00
107 12¢ blk. Washington (69)	3,500.00	5,250.00
108 15¢ black Lincoln (77)	3,500.00	5,500.00
109 24¢ deep violet Washington (70)	4,500.00	7,000.00
110 30¢ brownish orange Franklin (71)	4,750.00	8,000.00
111 90¢ bl. Washington (72)	5,750.00	40,000.00
Issues of 1869, With Grill, Hardware Paper		
G. Grill about 9.5 x 9mm		
112 1¢ buff Franklin	700.00	150.00
Double grill	1,100.00	325.00
b Without grill	4,250.00	
113 2¢ br. Post Horse and Rider	650.00	60.00
Split grill	800.00	85.00
Double transfer		80.00
114 3¢ Locomotive	300.00	20.00
Triple grill	—	—
Sextuple grill	—	3,250.00
Gray paper	—	95.00
a Without grill	1,100.00	
d Double impression		3,500.00
115 6¢ Washington	2,500.00	210.00
Quadruple split grill	—	825.00
116 10¢ Shield and Eagle	1,850.00	140.00
End roller grill	—	—
117 12¢ S.S. Adriatic	2,000.00	150.00
Split grill	2,400.00	165.00
118 15¢ Columbus Landing, type I	7,000.00	600.00
119 15¢ type II (118)	3,000.00	250.00
b Center inverted	275,000.00	18,500.00
c Center double, one inverted		35,000.00
120 24¢ Declaration of Independence	6,500.00	750.00
b Center inverted	275,000.00	20,000.00
121 30¢ Shield, Eagle and Flags	6,500.00	550.00
Double grill	—	1,100.00
b Flags inverted	210,000.00	65,000.00
122 90¢ Lincoln	8,750.00	2,200.00
Split grill	—	—
Issues of 1875, Reissue of 1869 Issue, Without Grill, Hard White Paper, Perf. 12		
123 1¢ buff (112)	500.00	325.00
124 2¢ brown (113)	650.00	450.00
125 3¢ blue (114)	5,000.00	14,000.00
126 6¢ blue (115)	1,500.00	1,500.00

112

113

114

115

116

117

118

120

121

122

Details

15¢ Landing of Columbus, Types I-III, Series 1869-1875

Detail of **#118** Type I
Picture unframed.

Detail of **#119** Type II
Picture framed.

#129 Type III

Same as Type I but
without fringe of
brown shading lines
around central

134

135

136

137

138

139

140

141

142

143

144

156

157

158

Details

Detail of **#134, 145**

Detail of **#135, 146**

Detail of **#136, 147**

Detail of **#156, 167, 182, 192**

1¢. In the pearl at the left of the numeral "1" there is a small crescent.

Detail of **#157, 168, 178, 180, 183, 193**

2¢. Under the scroll at the left of "U.S." there is a small diagonal line. This mark seldom shows clearly.

Detail of **#158, 169, 184, 194**

3¢. The under part of the upper tail of the left ribbon is heavily shaded.

Issues of 1875		Un	U
127	10¢ yellow (116)	2,000.00	1,600.00
128	12¢ green (117)	2,500.00	2,500.00
129	15¢ brown and blue,		
	type III (118)	1,900.00	1,000.00
a	Imperf. horizontally	3,500.00	—
130	24¢ grn. & violet (120)	2,000.00	1,300.00
131	30¢ bl. & carmine (121)	2,750.00	2,500.00
132	90¢ car. & black (122)	5,000.00	5,500.00
	Issue of 1880, Reissue of 1869,		
	Soft Porous Paper		
133	1¢ buff (112)	325.00	200.00
a	1¢ brown orange,		
	issued without gum	240.00	175.00
	Issues of 1870-71		
	With Grill, White Wove Paper,		
	No Secret Marks		
	H. Grill about 10 x 12mm		
134	1¢ Franklin	1,900.00	125.00
	End roller grill		575.00
135	2¢ Jackson	1,100.00	65.00
136	3¢ Washington	725.00	19.00
	Cracked plate	—	90.00
137	6¢ Lincoln	4,000.00	500.00
	Double grill	—	850.00
138	7¢ Edwin M. Stanton	2,750.00	400.00
139	10¢ Jefferson	4,500.00	650.00
140	12¢ Henry Clay	21,000.00	2,750.00
141	15¢ Daniel Webster	5,250.00	1,200.00
142	24¢ Gen. Winfield Scott	—	6,500.00
143	30¢ Alexander Hamilton	12,000.00	2,250.00
144	90¢ Commodore Perry	13,500.00	1,500.00
	Split grill	—	1,550.00

Issues of 1870-71		Un	U
	Without Grill, White Wove Paper,		
	No Secret Marks		
145	1¢ ultra. Franklin (134)	450.00	15.00
146	2¢ red brn. Jackson (135)	325.00	9.00
147	3¢ grn. Washington (136)	300.00	1.50
148	6¢ carmine Lincoln (137)	625.00	25.00
	6¢ violet carmine	650.00	30.00
149	7¢ verm. Stanton (138)	800.00	90.00
150	10¢ brown Jefferson (139)	700.00	20.00
151	12¢ dull violet Clay (140)	1,650.00	150.00
152	15¢ brt. or. Webster (141)	1,800.00	150.00
153	24¢ purple Scott (142)	1,500.00	140.00
154	30¢ black Hamilton (143)	4,500.00	175.00
155	90¢ carmine Perry (144)	4,000.00	300.00
	Issues of 1873, Without Grill,		
	White Wove Paper, Thin to Thick,		
	Secret Marks		
156	1¢ ultra. Franklin	225.00	3.25
	Paper with silk fibers	—	22.50
f	Imperf. pair	—	550.00
157	2¢ br. Jackson	375.00	17.50
	Double paper	500.00	35.00
c	With grill	1,850.00	750.00
158	3¢ gr. Washington	130.00	.40
	olive green	375.00	15.00
	Cracked plate	—	32.50

Richard Sheaff

Since 1983 Richard Sheaff has served as a design consultant to the Citizens' Stamp Advisory Committee for the U.S. Postal Service. In that capacity he has been responsible for the design and art direction of more than 200 U.S. postage stamps. In addition to designing the

© 1998 CRAIG WELLS

Pan-American Inverts stamp pane issued in 2001, he also designed this year's Black Heritage stamp honoring Roy Wilkins and provided art direction for the Diabetes Awareness stamp. Educated at Dartmouth College and Syracuse University, where he earned a master of fine arts degree in visual communication and design, he has had a distinguished design career for more than 30 years. He is the president and creative consultant of R. Dana Sheaff & Company in Scottsdale, Arizona. Working with corporations and institutions, he provides marketing strategy development, creative direction, project management, and publication and graphic design. ■

1873-1879

Issues of 1873	Un	U
Without Grill, White Wove Paper, Thin to Thick, Secret Marks		
159 6¢ dull pk. Lincoln	425.00	17.50
b With grill	1,800.00	
160 7¢ or. verm. Stanton	1,000.00	80.00
Ribbed paper	—	95.00
161 10¢ br. Jefferson	700.00	18.00
162 12¢ bl. vio. Clay	1,700.00	95.00
163 15¢ yel. or. Webster	1,900.00	100.00
a With grill	5,000.00	
164 24¢ pur. Scott	—	
165 30¢ gray blk. Hamilton	2,100.00	100.00
166 90¢ rose carm. Perry	2,750.00	250.00
Issues of 1875, Special Printing, Hard, White Wove Paper, Without Gum, Secret Marks		
Although perforated, these stamps were usually cut apart with scissors. As a result, the perforations are often much mutilated and the design is frequently damaged.		
167 1¢ ultra. Franklin (156)	10,500.00	
168 2¢ dk. br. Jackson (157)	4,750.00	
169 3¢ blue green Washington (158)	12,500.00	—
170 6¢ dull rose Lincoln (159)	11,500.00	
171 7¢ reddish vermilion Stanton (160)	2,850.00	
172 10¢ pale brown Jefferson (161)	11,500.00	
173 12¢ dark vio. Clay (162)	4,250.00	

Issues of 1875	Un	U
174 15¢ bright orange Webster (163)	11,500.00	
175 24¢ dull pur. Scott (142)	2,750.00	5,000.00
176 30¢ greenish black Hamilton (143)	8,500.00	
177 90¢ vio. car. Perry (144)	10,500.00	
Regular Issue, Yellowish Wove Paper		
178 2¢ verm. Jackson (157)	400.00	10.00
c With grill	750.00	
179 5¢ Zachary Taylor, June	525.00	20.00
Cracked plate	—	170.00
Double paper	600.00	
Paper with silk fibers	—	32.50
c With grill	1,600.00	
Special Printing, Hard, White Wove Paper, Without Gum		
180 2¢ carmine vermilion Jackson (157)	29,000.00	
181 5¢ br. bl. Taylor (179)	48,000.00	
Issues of 1879, Soft, Porous Paper, Thin to Thick, Perf. 12		
182 1¢ dark ultramarine Franklin (156)	300.00	2.75
183 2¢ verm. Jackson (157)	130.00	2.75
a Double impression	—	500.00

Derry Noyes

For more than a decade, Derry Noyes has designed and provided art direction for dozens of United States postage stamps and stamp products. She holds a bachelor of arts degree from Hampshire College and a master of fine arts degree from Yale University. She worked as a graphics designer at Beveridge and Associates, a Washington, D.C., firm, until 1979 when she established her own design firm, Derry Noyes Graphics. Her clients have included museums, corporations, foundations, and architectural and educational institutions. Her work has been honored by the Art Directors Club of Metropolitan Washington, *Communication Arts*, *Critique* magazine, and *Graphis*. Before becoming an art director for the United States Postal Service, she served as a member of the Citizens' Stamp Advisory Committee from 1981-1983. Noyes currently lives in Washington, D.C., is married, and has five children. ∎

159

160

161

162

163

179

Details

Detail of **#137, 148**

Detail of **#138, 149**

Detail of **#139, 150, 187**

Detail of **#159, 170, 186, 195**

Detail of **#160, 171, 196**

Detail of **#161, 172, 188, 197**

6¢. The first four vertical lines of the shading in the lower part of the left ribbon have been strengthened.

7¢. Two small semi-circles are drawn around the ends of the lines that outline the ball in the lower righthand corner.

10¢. There is a small semi-circle in the scroll at the right end of the upper label.

Detail of **#140, 151**

Detail of **#141, 152**

Detail of **#143, 154, 165, 176**

Detail of **#162, 173, 198**

Detail of **#163, 174, 189, 199**

Detail of **#190**

12¢. The balls of the figure "2" are crescent-shaped.

15¢. In the lower part of the triangle in the upper left corner two lines have been made heavier, forming a "V." This mark can be found on some of the Continental and American (1879) printings, but not all stamps show it.

30¢. In the "S" of "CENTS," the vertical spike across the middle section of the letter has been broadened.

205   **206**   **207**   **208**

209   **210**   **211**   **212**

219   **220**   **221**   **222**   **223**   **224**

225   **226**   **227**   **228**   **229**

Details

Issues of 1881-82, Re-engravings of 1873 Designs

Detail of **#206**

1¢. Upper vertical lines have been deepened, creating a solid effect in parts of background. Upper arabesques shaded.

Detail of **#207**

3¢. Shading at sides of central oval is half its previous width A short horizontal dash has been cut below the "TS" of "CENTS."

Detail of **#208**

6¢. Has three vertical lines instead of four between the edge of the panel and the outside of the stamp.

Detail of **#209**

10¢. Has four vertical lines instead of five between left side of oval and edge of the shield. Horizontal lines in lower part of background strengthened.

Issues of 1879		Un	U
184	3¢ grn. Washington (158)	100.00	.40
	Double transfer	—	—
	Short transfer	—	6.00
185	5¢ blue Taylor (179)	500.00	12.00
186	6¢ pink Lincoln (159)	950.00	20.00
187	10¢ brown Jefferson		
	(139) (no secret mark)	2,000.00	25.00
188	10¢ brown Jefferson		
	(161) (with secret mark)	1,500.00	25.00
	black brown	1,600.00	37.50
	Double transfer		45.00
189	15¢ red or. Webster (163)	340.00	22.50
190	30¢ full blk. Hamilton (143)	1,100.00	55.00
191	90¢ carmine Perry (144)	2,250.00	250.00
Issues of 1880, Special Printing,			
Soft Porous Paper, Without Gum, Perf. 12			
192	1¢ dark ultramarine		
	Franklin (156)	22,500.00	
193	2¢ blk. br. Jackson (157)	9,000.00	
194	3¢ blue green		
	Washington (158)	32,500.00	
195	6¢ dull rose		
	Lincoln (159)	17,000.00	
196	7¢ scarlet vermilion		
	Stanton (160)	3,500.00	
197	10¢ deep brown		
	Jefferson (161)	17,000.00	
198	12¢ blk. pur. Clay (162)	5,000.00	
199	15¢ or. Webster (163)	17,000.00	
200	24¢ dk. vio. Scott (142)	5,000.00	
201	30¢ greenish black		
	Hamilton (143)	12,500.00	
202	90¢ dull carmine		
	Perry (144)	12,500.00	
203	2¢ scarlet vermilion		
	Jackson (157)	26,000.00	
204	5¢ dp. bl. Taylor (179)	45,000.00	
Issues of 1882, Perf. 12			
205	5¢ Garfield, Apr. 10	250.00	8.00
Special Printing, Soft Porous			
Paper, Without Gum, Perf. 12			
205C	5¢ gray brown		
	Garfield (205)	28,500.00	
Issues of 1881-82, Designs			
of 1873 Re-engraved			
206	1¢ Franklin, Aug. 1881	80.00	.90
	Double transfer	105.00	6.00
207	3¢ Washington,		
	July 16, 1881	80.00	.55
	Double transfer	—	12.00
	Cracked plate	—	
208	6¢ Lincoln, June 1882	525.00	80.00
a	6¢ deep brown red	475.00	110.00
209	10¢ Jefferson, Apr. 1882	160.00	4.75
	10¢ pur. or. olive brown	175.00	5.00
b	10¢ black brown	700.00	45.00

Issues of 1883		Un	U
210	2¢ Washington, Oct. 1	50.00	.40
	Double transfer	55.00	2.00
211	4¢ Jackson, Oct. 1	250.00	14.00
	Cracked plate	—	
Special Printing, Soft Porous Paper, Perf. 12			
211B	2¢ pale red brown		
	Washington (210)	525.00	—
c	Horizontal pair,		
	imperf. between	2,000.00	
211D	4¢ deep blue green		
	Jackson (211) no gum	26,000.00	
Issues of 1887, Perf. 12			
212	1¢ Franklin, June	110.00	1.40
	Double transfer		—
213	2¢ green Washington		
	(210), Sept. 10	50.00	.35
	Double transfer	—	3.25
b	Printed on both sides		—
214	3¢ vermilion Washington		
	(207), Oct. 3	80.00	55.00
Issues of 1888, Perf. 12			
215	4¢ carmine		
	Jackson (211), Nov.	225.00	17.50
216	5¢ indigo		
	Garfield (205), Feb.	240.00	12.00
217	30¢ orange brown		
	Hamilton (165), Jan.	450.00	100.00
218	90¢ pur. Perry (166),		
	Feb.	1,300.00	240.00
Issues of 1890-93, Perf. 12			
219	1¢ Franklin, Feb. 22, 1890	27.50	.35
	Double transfer	—	
219D	2¢ lake Washington		
	(220), Feb. 22, 1890	210.00	.90
	Double transfer	—	—
220	2¢ Washington, 1890	22.50	.30
	Double transfer	—	3.25
a	Cap on left "2"	80.00	2.50
c	Cap on both "2s"	400.00	20.00
221	3¢ Jackson, Feb. 22, 1890	72.50	7.50
222	4¢ Lincoln, June 2, 1890	75.00	2.75
	Double transfer	90.00	—
223	5¢ Grant, June 2, 1890	72.50	2.75
	Double transfer	90.00	3.25
224	6¢ Garfield, Feb. 22, 1890	75.00	20.00
225	8¢ Sherman, Mar. 21, 1893	57.50	13.00
226	10¢ Webster,		
	Feb. 22, 1890	155.00	3.50
	Double transfer	—	—
227	15¢ Clay, Feb. 22, 1890	200.00	20.00
	Double transfer	—	—
	Triple transfer	—	
228	30¢ Jefferson,		
	Feb. 22, 1890	325.00	30.00
	Double transfer	—	—
229	90¢ Perry, Feb. 22, 1890	500.00	125.00
	Short transfer at bottom	—	—

1893

	Issues of 1893		Un	U	PB	#	FDC	Q(M)
	Columbian Exposition Issue, Printed by The American Bank Note Co., Perf. 12							
230	1¢ Columbus in Sight of Land	01/02/93	25.00	40	350.00	(6)	4,000.00	449
	Double transfer		30.00	.75				
	Cracked plate		95.00					
231	2¢ Landing of Columbus	01/02/93	22.50	.20	275.00	(6)	3,500.00	1,464
	Double transfer		27.50	.30				
	Triple transfer		67.50	—				
	Quadruple transfer		100.00					
	Broken hat on third							
	figure left of Columbus		70.00	.30				
	Broken frame line		24.00	.25				
	Recut frame lines		24.00	—				
	Cracked plate		95.00	—				
232	3¢ *Santa Maria*, Flagship	01/02/93	62.50	15.00	750.00	(6)	6,000.00	12
	Double transfer		82.50	—				
233	4¢ ultramarine, Fleet	01/02/93	87.50	7.50	1,050.00	(6)	9,500.00	19
a	4¢ blue (error)		19,000.00	15,000.00	87,500.00	(4)		
	Double transfer		125.00	—				
234	5¢ Columbus Soliciting							
	Aid from Isabella	01/02/93	95.00	8.00	1,400.00	(6)	16,000	35
	Double transfer		145.00	—				
235	6¢ Columbus Welcomed							
	at Barcelona	01/02/93	90.00	22.50			20,000.00	5
a	6¢ red violet		90.00	22.50	1,250.00	(6)		
	Double transfer		115.00	30.00				
236	8¢ Columbus Restored to Favor	03/93	80.00	11.00	875.00	(6)		11
	Double transfer		92.50	—				
237	10¢ Columbus							
	Presenting Natives	01/02/93	135.00	8.00	3,250.00	(6)	7,500.00	17
	Double transfer		175.00	12.50				
	Triple transfer		—					
238	15¢ Columbus							
	Announcing His Discovery	01/02/93	240.00	65.00	3,750.00	(6)		2
	Double transfer		—	—				
239	30¢ Columbus at La Rábida	01/02/93	300.00	85.00	8,500.00	(6)		0.6
240	50¢ Recall of Columbus	01/02/93	600.00	160.00	13,000.00	(6)		0.2
	Double transfer		—	—				
	Triple transfer		—	—				
241	$1 Isabella							
	Pledging Her Jewels	01/02/93	1,500.00	650.00	47,500.00	(6)		0.05
	Double transfer		—	—				
242	$2 Columbus in Chains	01/02/93	1,550.00	600.00	70,000.00	(6)	52,500.00	0.05
243	$3 Columbus Describing							
	His Third Voyage	01/02/93	2,400.00	1,000.00				0.03
a	$3 olive green		2,400.00	1,000.00	90,000.00	(6)		
244	$4 Isabella and Columbus	01/02/93	3,250.00	1,350.00				0.03
a	$4 rose carmine		3,250.00	1,350.00	250,000.00	(6)		
245	$5 Portrait of Columbus	01/02/93	3,750.00	1,600.00	190,000.00	(6)		0.03

230

231

232

233

234

235

236

237

238

239

240

241

242

243

244

245

1894

246

248

253

254

255

256

257

258

259

Details

2¢ Washington Types I-III, Series 1894-98

Triangle of **#248-50, 265** Type I

Horizontal lines of uniform thickness run across the triangle.

Triangle of **#251, 266** Type II

Horizontal lines cross the triangle, but are thinner within than without.

Triangle of **#252, 267, 279B-279Be** Type III

The horizontal lines do not cross the double frame lines of the triangle.

Issues of 1894		Un	U	PB	#
Unwmkd., Perf. 12					

Bureau Issues Starting in 1894 and continuing until 1979, the Bureau of Engraving and Printing in Washington produced all U.S. postage stamps except #909-21, 1335, 1355, 1410-18 and 1789. Beginning in 1979, security printers in addition to the Bureau of Engraving and Printing started producing postage stamps under contract with the U.S. Postal Service.

			Un	U	PB	#
246	1¢ Franklin	10/94	32.50	4.00	360.00	(6)
	Double transfer		40.00	5.00		
247	1¢ blue Franklin (246)	11/94	67.50	2.00	650.00	(6)
	Double transfer		—	3.50		
248	2¢ pink Washington, type I	10/94	27.50	3.00	250.00	(6)
	Double transfer		—	—		
249	2¢ carmine lake, type I (248)	10/94	145.00	2.75	1,400.00	(6)
	Double transfer		—	3.25		
250	2¢ carmine, type I (248)		30.00	1.10		
a	2¢ rose		30.00	.40		
b	2¢ scarlet		30.00	.40	300.00	(6)
	Double transfer		—	3.00		
c	Vertical pair, imperf. horizontally		1,500.00			
d	Horizontal pair, imperf. between		1,500.00			
251	2¢ carmine, type II (248)		250.00	5.50	2,250.00	(6)
252	2¢ carmine, type III (248)		110.00	3.75		
a	2¢ scarlet		120.00	5.50	1,350	(6)
b	Horizontal pair, imperf. vertically		1,500.00		—	
c	Horizontal pair, imperf. between		1,750.00			
253	3¢ Jackson	09/94	105.00	8.00	1,100.00	(6)
254	4¢ Lincoln	09/94	135.00	3.75	1,500.00	(6)
255	5¢ Grant	09/94	100.00	5.50	975.00	(6)
	Worn plate, diagonal lines missing in oval background		100.00	4.50		
	Double transfer		125.00	6.50		
c	Vertical pair, imperf. horiz.		1,750.00			
256	6¢ Garfield	07/94	150.00	21.00	2,250.00	(6)
a	Vertical pair, imperf. horizontally		900.00		13,000.00	(6)
257	8¢ Sherman	03/94	140.00	14.00	1,300.00	(6)
258	10¢ Webster	09/94	250.00	10.00	2,750.00	(6)
	Double transfer		290.00	11.50		
259	15¢ Clay	10/94	300.00	50.00	4,500.00	(6)

	Issues of 1894		Un	U	PB	#	
260	50¢ Jefferson	11/94	475.00	110.00	*9,000.00*	(6)	
261	$1 Perry, type I	11/94	1,000.00	325.00	*17,000.00*	(6)	
261A	$1 black Perry, type II (261)	11/94	2,300.00	650.00	*22,500.00*	(6)	
262	$2 James Madison	12/94	3,100.00	1,000.00	*40,000.00*	(6)	
263	$5 John Marshall	12/94	4,500.00	2,100.00	*21,000.00*	(3)	
	Issues of 1895, Wmkd. (191), Perf. 12						
264	1¢ blue Franklin (246)	04/95	6.50	.25	210.00	(6)	
265	2¢ carmine Washington,						
	type I (248)	05/95	30.00	.80	375.00	(6)	
	Double transfer		45.00	3.25			
266	2¢ carmine, type II (248)		30.00	3.00	410.00	(6)	
267	2¢ carmine, type III (248)		5.50	.25	175.00	(6)	
268	3¢ purple Jackson (253)	10/95	37.50	1.10	650.00	(6)	
	Double transfer		45.00	2.75			
269	4¢ dark brown Lincoln (254)	06/95	40.00	1.60	700.00	(6)	
	Double transfer		45.00	3.00			
270	5¢ chocolate Grant (255)	06/11/95	37.50	1.90	600.00	(6)	
	Double transfer		45.00	3.25			
	Worn plate, diagonal lines						
	missing in oval background		40.00	2.50			
271	6¢ dull brown Garfield (256)	08/95	95.00	4.25	2,250.00	(6)	
	Very thin paper		105.00	4.50			
a	Wmkd. USIR		*2,750.00*	*1,000.00*			
272	8¢ violet brown Sherman (257)	07/95	65.00	1.25	750.00	(6)	
	Double transfer		80.00	2.75			
a	Wmkd. USIR		*2,250.00*	250.00	*9,000.00*	(3)	
273	10¢ dark green Webster (258)	06/95	95.00	1.50	1,600.00	(6)	
	Double transfer		120.00	3.50			
274	15¢ dark blue Clay (259)	09/95	225.00	9.00	3,250.00	(6)	
275	50¢ orange Jefferson (260)	11/95	300.00	20.00	5,750.00	(6)	
a	50¢ red orange		325.00	24.00	5,750.00	(6)	
276	$1 black Perry, type I (261)	08/95	650.00	70.00	*12,000.00*	(6)	
276A	$1 black Perry, type II (261)	08/95	1,300.00	160.00	*24,000.00*	(6)	
277	$2 bright blue Madison (262)	08/95	1,100.00	325.00			
a	$2 dark blue		1,100.00	325.00	*20,000.00*	(6)	
278	$5 dark green Marshall (263)	08/95	2,500.00	450.00	*72,500.00*	(6)	

260   261

262   263

277

Watermark 191
Double-line
"USPS" in
capital letters;
detail at right.

Details

$1 Perry, Types I-II, Series 1894

Detail of **#261, 276**
Type I

The circles enclosing
$1 are broken.

Detail of **#261A, 276A**
Type I

The circles enclosing
$1 are complete.

Issues of 1898-1900		Un	U	PB	#	FDC	Q(M)
Wmkd. (191), Perf. 12							
279	1¢ deep grn. Franklin (246) 01/98	9.00	.25	175.00	(6)		
	Double transfer	12.00	.85				
279B	2¢ red Washington, type III (248) 01/98	9.00	.25	200.00	(6)		
c	2¢ rose carmine, type III	240.00	65.00	2,650.00	(6)		
d	2¢ orange red, type III	10.00	.30	210.00	(6)		
e	Booklet pane of 6 04/16/00	425.00	425.00				
f	2¢ carmine, type IV	10.00	.25	210.00	(6)		
g	2¢ pink, type IV	11.00	.40	230.00	(6)		
h	2¢ vermillion, type IV	10.00	.25	210.00	(6)		
i	2¢ brown orange, type IV	100.00	5.00	400.00	(3)		
280	4¢ rose brn. Lincoln (254) 10/98	30.00	.90				
a	4¢ lilac brown	30.00	.90				
b	4¢ orange brown	30.00	.90	600.00	(6)		
	Extra frame line at top	50.00	4.00				
281	5¢ dark blue Grant (255) 03/98	35.00	.75	600.00	(6)		
	Double transfer	45.00	2.00				
	Worn plate, diagonal lines missing in oval background	40.00	.90				
282	6¢ lake Garfield (256) 12/98	45.00	2.50	800.00	(6)		
	Double transfer	57.50	3.50				
a	6¢ purple lake	60.00	3.50	1,000.00	(6)		
282C	10¢ brown Webster (258), type I 11/98	180.00	2.50	2,250.00	(6)		
	Double transfer	200.00	4.25				
283	10¢ orange brown Webster (258), type II	110.00	2.00	1,600.00	(6)		
284	15¢ olive grn. Clay (259) 11/98	150.00	7.50	2,000.00	(6)		
Issues of 1898, Trans-Mississippi Exposition Issue							
285	1¢ Marquette on the Mississippi 06/17/98	30.00	6.00	300.00	(6)	12,500.00	71
	Double transfer	40.00	7.25				
286	2¢ Farming in the West 06/17/98	27.50	1.50	275.00	(6)	9,500.00	160
	Double transfer	42.50	2.25				
	Worn plate	30.00	1.75				
287	4¢ Indian Hunting Buffalo 06/17/98	150.00	22.50	1,400.00	(6)	27,500.00	5
288	5¢ Frémont on the Rocky Mountains 06/17/98	140.00	20.00	1,300.00	(6)	17,500.00	8
289	8¢ Troops Guarding Wagon Train 06/17/98	180.00	40.00	2,750.00	(6)	20,000	3
a	Vertical pair, imperf. horizontally	19,000.00		75,000.00	(4)		
290	10¢ Hardships of Emigration 06/17/98	180.00	25.00	3,000.00	(6)	27,500.00	5
291	50¢ Western Mining Prospector 06/17/98	650.00	180.00	25,000	(6)	30,000.00	0.5
292	$1 Western Cattle in Storm 06/17/98	1,250.00	525.00	50,000.00	(6)	—	0.06
293	$2 Mississippi River Bridge 06/17/98	2,100.00	950.00	150,000.00	(6)		0.06

282C

285

286

287

288

289

290

291

292

293

Details

10¢ Webster Types I-II, Series 1898

Detail of **#282C**
Type I

The tips of the foliate ornaments do not impinge on the white curved line below "TEN CENTS."

Detail of **#283**
Type II

The tips of the ornaments break the curved line below the "E" of "TEN" and the "T" of "CENTS."

The **Subscription Program**

An affordable way to acquire beautiful collectibles!

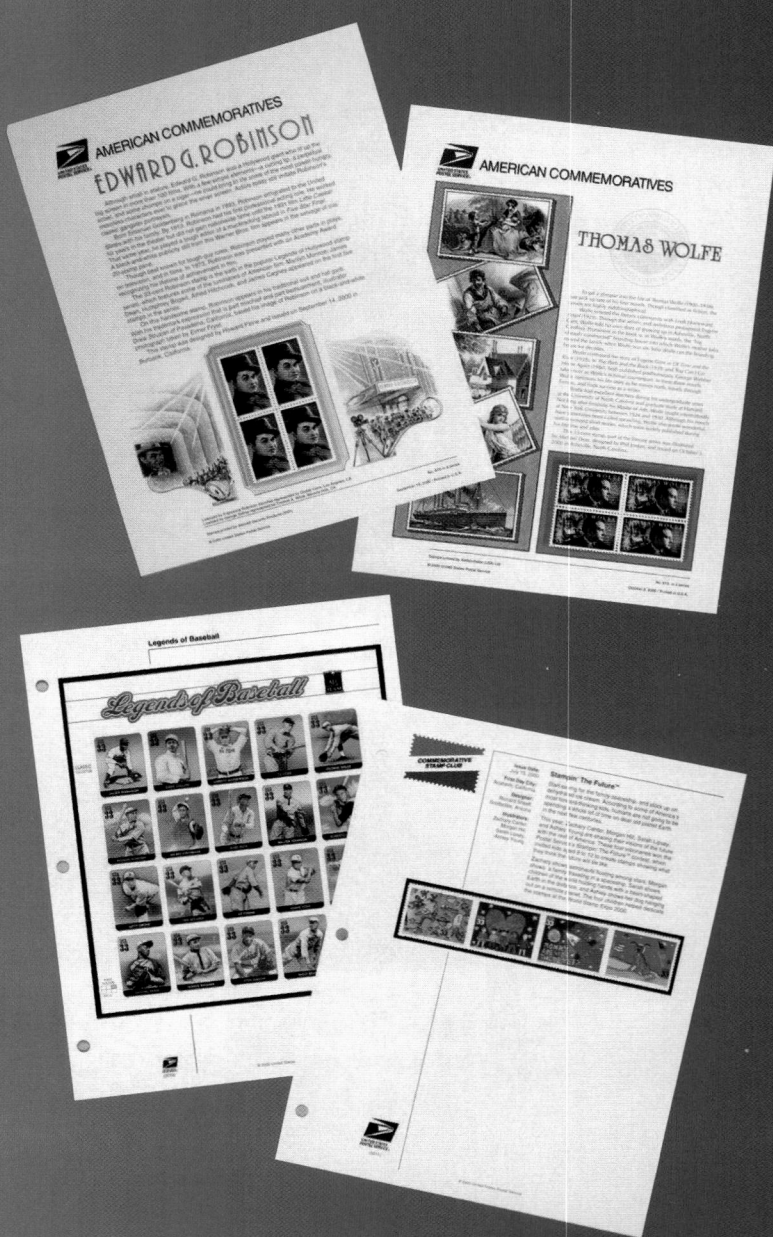

Choose any or all of the following
Subscription Program items to
uniquely display your stamps.

Commemorative Panels

Prized for engravings of stamp-related subjects— you will also receive mint condition stamps and background information presented on beautifully designed pages. About $6.00* each, depending on the value of the stamps.

Commemorative Stamp Club

An easy and uniform way to collect and learn about the stamps being issued. Simply mount the stamps on the sheet and place them in a three ring binder. Just $48.95* for the yearly membership.

Souvenir Pages

The most colorful way to present your collection— for your pleasure and convenience, we've mounted stamp(s) against a colorful background specially tinted to coordinate with the stamps. About $2.00* each, depending on the value of the stamps.

Order Now. Establish your Subscription Program account(s).

To order or for more information call **1 800 STAMP-24**. Customers may order online by visiting the Postal Service's Web site at **www.usps.com** and clicking on the Postal Store.

Source Code: #39001

*Prices subject to change without notice.

294

295

296

297

298

299

300

301

302

303

304

305

306

307

308

309

310

311

312

313

Issues of 1901-03			Un	U	PB	#	FDC	Q(M)
Issues of 1901, Pan-American Exposition Issue, Perf. 12								
294	1¢ Great Lakes Steamer	05/01/01	18.00	3.00	230.00	(6)	4,500.00	91
a	Center inverted		10,000.00	7,000.00	75,000.00	(4)		
295	2¢ An Early Locomotive	05/01/01	17.50	1.00	225.00	(6)	2,750.00	210
a	Center inverted		42,500.00	17,500.00	275,000.00	(4)		
296	4¢ Automobile	05/01/01	82.50	15.00	2,250.00	(6)		6
a	Center inverted		22,500.00		140,000.00	(4)		
297	5¢ Bridge at Niagara Falls	05/01/01	95.00	14.00	2,500.00	(6)	15,000.00	7
298	8¢ Canal Locks at							
	Sault Ste. Marie	05/01/01	120.00	50.00	4,250.00	(6)		5
299	10¢ American Line Steamship	05/01/01	170.00	25.00	7,000.00	(6)		5
Wmkd. (191), Perf. 12 (All issued in 1903 except #300b, 306, 308)								
300	1¢ Franklin	02/03	12.00	.20	200.00	(6)		
	Double transfer		17.50	1.00				
	Worn plate		13.00	.30				
	Cracked plate		14.00	.30				
b	Booklet pane of 6	03/06/07	550.00	—				
301	2¢ Washington	01/17/03	16.00	.20	240.00	(6)	2,750.00	
	Double transfer		27.50	1.00				
	Cracked plate		—	1.00				
c	Booklet pane of 6	01/24/03	475.00	—				
302	3¢ Jackson	02/03	55.00	2.75	725.00	(6)		
	Double transfer		77.50	3.75				
	Cracked plate		—	—				
303	4¢ Grant	02/03	60.00	1.25	725.00	(6)		
	Double transfer		77.50	2.75				
304	5¢ Lincoln	01/03	60.00	1.50	725.00	(6)		
305	6¢ Garfield	02/03	72.50	2.50	850.00	(6)		
	6¢ brownish lake		72.50	2.50				
	Double transfer		77.50	3.50				
306	8¢ M. Washington	12/02	45.00	2.00	675.00	(6)		
	8¢ lavender		55.00	2.75				
307	10¢ Webster	02/03	67.50	1.40	1,000.00	(6)		
308	13¢ B. Harrison	11/18/02	50.00	7.50	625.00	(6)		
309	15¢ Clay	05/27/03	170.00	4.75	3,000.00	(6)		
	Double transfer		210.00	9.00				
310	50¢ Jefferson	03/23/03	475.00	22.50	7,000.00	(6)		
311	$1 David G. Farragut	06/05/03	775.00	55.00	18,000.00	(6)		
312	$2 Madison	06/05/03	1,250.00	190.00	32,500.00	(6)		
313	$5 Marshall	06/05/03	3,000.00	750.00	82,500.00	(6)		

For listings of #312 and 313 with perf. 10, see #479 and 480.

	Issues of 1906-08		Un	U	PB/LP	#	FDC	Q(M)
	Imperf. (All issued in 1908 except #314)							
314	1¢ bl. grn. Franklin (300)	10/02/06	19.00	15.00	170.00	(6)		
314A	4¢ brown Grant (303)	04/08	30,000.00	25,000.00				
	#314A was issued imperforated, but all copies were privately perforated at the sides.							
315	5¢ blue Lincoln (304)	05/12/08	260.00	*600.00*	2,500.00	(6)		
	Coil Stamps, Perf. 12 Horizontally							
316	1¢ bl. grn. pair Franklin (300)	02/18/08	*105,000*	—	175,000.00	(2)		
317	5¢ blue pair Lincoln (304)	02/24/08	*12,500.00*	—	28,000.00	(2)		
	Coil Stamp, Perf. 12 Vertically							
318	1¢ bl. grn. pair Franklin (300)	07/31/08	11,000.00	—	*17,000.00*	(2)		
	Issues of 1903, Perf. 12							
319	2¢ Washington	11/12/03	6.00	.20	105.00	(6)		
a	2¢ lake, type I		—	—				
b	2¢ carmine rose, type I		8.00	.35	150.00	(6)		
c	2¢ scarlet, type I		6.00	.25	100.00	(6)		
d	Vertical pair, imperf.							
	horizontally		*5,000.00*					
e	Vertical pair, imperf.							
	between		*1,250.00*					
f	2¢ lake, type II		8.00	.25	250.00	(6)		
g	Booklet pane of 6,							
	carmine, type I	12/03/03	120.00	*175.00*				
h	Booklet pane of 6,							
	carmine, type II		260.00					
i	2¢ carmine, type II		27.50	*50.00*				
j	2¢ carmine rose, type II		20.00	.75	500.00	(6)		
k	2¢ scarlet, type II		18.00	.45	500.00	(6)		
m	Booklet pane of 6, lake		*2,500.00*					
n	Booklet pane of 6, carmine rose		180.00	*250.00*				
p	Booklet pane of 6, scarlet		160.00	*200.00*				
q	Booklet pane of 6, lake		200.00	*375.00*				
	Issues of 1906, Washington (319), Imperf.							
320	2¢ carmine	10/02/06	18.00	12.00	210.00	(6)		
	Double transfer		25.00	16.00				
a	2¢ lake, die II		50.00	40.00	750.00	(6)		
b	2¢ scarlet		18.00	12.50	210.00	(6)		
c	2¢ carmine rose, type I		55.00	40.00				
d	2¢ carmine, type II		—					
	Issues of 1908, Coil Stamp (319), Perf. 12 Horizontally							
321	2¢ carmine pair, type I	02/18/08	*125,000.00*		—	(2)		
	Coil Stamp, Perf. 12 Vertically							
322	2¢ carmine pair, type II	07/31/08	10,000.00	—	*12,500.00*	(2)		
	Issues of 1904, Louisiana Purchase Exposition Issue, Perf. 12							
323	1¢ Robert R. Livingston	04/30/04	30.00	4.00	275.00	(6)	*6,000.00*	80
	Diagonal line through left "1"		50.00	11.00				
324	2¢ Thomas Jefferson	04/30/04	27.50	1.50	275.00	(6)	*4,750.00*	193
325	3¢ James Monroe	04/30/04	90.00	30.00	950.00	(6)	*5,000.00*	5
326	5¢ William McKinley	04/30/04	95.00	25.00	1,000.00	(6)	*22,500.00*	7
327	10¢ Map of Louisiana							
	Purchase	04/30/04	180.00	27.50	2,250.00	(6)	*24,000.00*	4
	Issues of 1907, Jamestown Exposition Issue, Wmkd. (191), Perf. 12							
328	1¢ Captain John Smith	04/26/07	30.00	4.00	275.00	(6)	*6,000.00*	78
	Double transfer		35.00	5.00				
329	2¢ Founding of							
	Jamestown, 1607	04/26/07	35.00	3.50	375.00	(6)	*9,000.00*	149
330	5¢ Pocahontas	04/26/07	135.00	27.50	2,600.00	(6)		

319

323

324

325

326

327

328

329

330

Details

2¢ Washington Die I-II, Series 1903

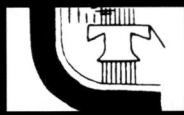

-Detail of #319a, 319b, 319g Die I

Detail of #319c, 319f, 319h, 319i Die II

331

332

333

334

335

336

337

338

339

340

341

342

Details

3¢ Washington Types I-IV, Series 1908-19

Detail of **#333, 345, 359, 376, 389, 394, 426, 445, 456, 464, 483, 493, 501-01b**
Type I

Top line of toga rope is weak and rope shading lines are thin. Fifth line from left is missing. Line between lips is thin.

Detail of **#484, 494, 502, 541** Type II

Top line of toga rope is strong and rope shading lines are heavy and complete. Line between lips is heavy.

Detail of **#529**
Type I

Top row of toga rope is strong but fifth shading line is missing as in Type I. Toga button center shading line consists of two dashes, central dot. "P," "O" of "POSTAGE" are separated by line of color.

Detail of **#530, 535**
Type IV

Top rope shading lines are complete. Second, fourth toga button shading lines are broken in middle, third line is continuous with dot in center. "P," "O" of "POSTAGE" are joined.

	Issues of 1908-09		Un	U	PB/LP	#
	Wmkd. (191) Perf. 12 (All issued in 1908 except #336, 338-42, 345-47)					
331	1¢ Franklin	12/08	7.25	.20	75.00	(6)
	Double transfer		9.50	.60		
a	Booklet pane of 6	12/02/08	160.00	*140.00*		
332	2¢ Washington	11/08	6.75	.20	67.50	(6)
	Double transfer		12.50	—		
	Cracked plate		—	—		
a	Booklet pane of 6	11/16/08	135.00	*125.00*		
333	3¢ Washington, type I	12/08	35.00	2.50	375.00	(6)
a	"China Clay" paper		*1,000.00*		*9,000.00*	(6)
334	4¢ Washington	12/08	42.50	1.00	425.00	(6)
	Double transfer		55.00	—		
a	"China Clay" paper		*1,300.00*			
335	5¢ Washington	12/08	52.50	2.00	550.00	(6)
a	"China Clay" paper		*1,000.00*			
336	6¢ Washington	01/09	65.00	5.00	750.00	(6)
a	"China Clay" paper		*750.00*			
337	8¢ Washington	12/08	50.00	2.50	500.00	(6)
	Double transfer		57.50	—		
a	"China Clay" paper		*1,000.00*			
338	10¢ Washington	01/09	70.00	1.40	825.00	(6)
a	"China Clay" paper		*1,000.00*			
339	13¢ Washington	01/09	42.50	19.00	500.00	(6)
	Line through "TAG" of "POSTAGE"		70.00	—		
a	"China Clay" paper		*1,000.00*			
340	15¢ Washington	01/09	70.00	5.50	650.00	(6)
a	"China Clay" paper		*1,000.00*			
341	50¢ Washington	01/13/09	350.00	20.00	*7,000.00*	(6)
342	$1 Washington	01/29/09	525.00	75.00	*13,500.00*	(6)
	Imperf.					
343	1¢ green Franklin (331)	12/08	5.25	4.50	50.00	(6)
	Double transfer		11.00	7.00		
344	2¢ carmine Washington (332)	12/10/08	6.50	3.00	80.00	(6)
	Double transfer		12.50	4.00		
	Foreign entry, design of 1¢		*1,250.00*	—		
	#345-47: Washington (333-35)					
345	3¢ deep violet, type I	1809	12.00	20.00	160.00	(6)
	Double transfer		22.50	—		
346	4¢ orange brown	02/25/09	20.00	22.50	180.00	(6)
	Double transfer		37.50	—		
347	5¢ blue	02/25/09	37.50	35.00	300.00	(6)
	Cracked plate		—			
	Issues of 1908-10, Coil Stamps, Perf. 12 Horizontally					
	#350-51, 354-56: Washington (Designs of 334-35, 338)					
348	1¢ green Franklin (331)	12/29/08	37.50	19.00	290.00	(2)
349	2¢ carmine Washington (332)	01/09	70.00	11.00	500.00	(2)
	Foreign entry, design of 1¢		—	*1,750.00*		
350	4¢ orange brown	08/15/10	160.00	100.00	1,150.00	(2)
351	5¢ blue	01/09	175.00	140.00	1,150.00	(2)
	Issues of 1909, Coil Stamps, Perf. 12 Vertically					
352	1¢ green Franklin (331)	01/09	80.00	40.00	600.00	(2)
	Double transfer		—	—		

	Issues of 1909		Un	U	PB/LP	#	FDC	Q(M)
	Coil Stamps, Perf. 12 Vertically							
353	2¢ carmine Washington (332)	01/12/09	87.50	11.00	575.00	(2)		
354	4¢ orange brown	02/23/09	200.00	75.00	1,450.00	(2)		
355	5¢ blue	02/23/09	210.00	100.00	1,450.00	(2)		
356	10¢ yellow	01/07/09	2,500.00	1,100.00	10,000.00	(2)		
	Bluish Paper, Perf. 12, #359-66: Washington (Designs of 333-40)							
357	1¢ green Franklin (331)	02/16/09	95.00	100.00	1,000.00	(6)		
358	2¢ carmine Washington (332)	02/16/09	90.00	100.00	975.00	(6)		
	Double transfer		—					
359	3¢ deep violet, type I	1909	2,000.00	2,500.00	22,500.00	(6)		
360	4¢ orange brown	1909	24,000.00		110,000.00	(3)		
361	5¢ blue	1909	5,000.00	9,000.00	60,000.00	(6)		
362	6¢ red orange	1909	1,500.00	2,250.00	16,500.00	(6)		
363	8¢ olive green	1909	26,000.00		115,000.00	(3)		
364	10¢ yellow	1909	1,800.00	2,750.00	32,500.00	(6)		
365	13¢ blue green	1909	3,000.00	2,400.00	30,000.00	(6)		
366	15¢ pale ultramarine	1909	1,450.00	8,000.00	11,000.00	(6)		
	Lincoln Memorial Issue, Wmkd. (191)							
367	2¢ Bust of Abraham Lincoln	02/12/09	5.50	1.75	150.00	(6)	500.00	148
	Double transfer		7.50	2.50				
	Imperf.							
368	2¢ carmine (367)	02/12/09	21.50	20.00	190.00	(6)	12,500.00	1
	Double transfer		42.50	27.50				
	Bluish Paper							
369	2¢ carmine (367)	02/09	225.00	260.00	2,900.00	(6)		0.6
	Alaska-Yukon Pacific Exposition Issue							
370	2¢ Willam H. Seward	06/01/09	9.00	2.00	225.00	(6)	3,000.00	153
	Double transfer		11.00	4.50				
	Imperf.							
371	2¢ carmine (370)	06/09	26.00	25.00	230.00	(6)		0.5
	Double transfer		40.00	30.00				
	Hudson-Fulton Celebration Issue, Wmkd. (191)							
372	2¢ Half Moon & Clermont	09/25/09	12.50	4.50	290.00	(6)	750.00	73
	Double transfer		15.00	4.75				
	Imperf.							
373	2¢ carmine (372)	09/25/09	29.00	25.00	250.00	(6)	7,000.00	0.2
	Double transfer		42.50	30.00				
	Issues of 1910-11, Wmkd. (190) #376-82: Washington (Designs of 333-38, 340)							
374	1¢ green Franklin (331)	11/23/10	6.75	.20	77.50	(6)		
	Double transfer		13.50	—				
	Cracked plate		—	—				
a	Booklet pane of 6	10/07/10	150.00	125.00				
375	2¢ carmine Washington (332)	11/23/10	6.75	.20	85.00	(6)		
	Cracked plate		—	—				
	Double transfer		11.50	—				
	Foreign entry, design of 1¢		—	1,000.00				
a	Booklet pane of 6	11/30/10	95.00	95.00				
b	2¢ lake		250.00					
376	3¢ deep violet, type I	01/16/11	20.00	1.40	200.00	(6)		

367

370

372

USPS

Watermark 190
Single-line
"USPS"
in capital letters;
detail at right.

397

398

399

400

	Issues of 1911		Un	U	PB/LP	#	FDC	Q(M)
	Wmkd. (190), Perf. 12							
377	4¢ brown	01/20/11	32.50	.50	290.00	(6)		
	Double transfer		—	—				
378	5¢ blue	01/25/11	32.50	.50	340.00	(6)		
	Double transfer		—	—				
379	6¢ red orange	01/25/11	37.50	.70	500.00	(6)		
380	8¢ olive green	02/08/11	115.00	12.50	1,100.00	(6)		
381	10¢ yellow	01/24/11	105.00	3.75	1,150.00	(6)		
382	15¢ pale ultramarine	03/01/11	275.00	15.00	2,400.00	(6)		
	Issues of 1910, Imperf.							
383	1¢ green Franklin (331)	12/10	2.50	2.00	45.00	(6)		
	Double transfer		6.50	—				
384	2¢ carmine Washington (332)	12/10	4.00	2.50	130.00	(6)		
	Foreign entry, design of 1¢		1,500.00					
	Double transfer		7.50	—				
	Rosette plate, crack on head		100.00	—				
	Issues of 1910, Coil Stamps, Perf. 12 Horizontally							
385	1¢ green Franklin (331)	11/01/10	32.50	15.00	400.00	(2)		
386	2¢ carmine Washington (332)	11/01/10	62.50	20.00	775.00	(2)		
	Issues of 1910-11, Coil Stamps, Wmkd. (190), Perf. 12 Vertically							
387	1¢ green Franklin (331)	11/01/10	140.00	50.00	600.00	(2)		
388	2¢ carmine Washington							
	(332)	11/01/10	875.00	350.00	5,750.00	(2)		
389	3¢ deep violet Washington,							
	type I (333)	01/24/11	57,500.00	11,500.00	125,000.00	(2)		
	Issues of 1910-13, Coil Stamps, Perf. 8.5 Horizontally							
390	1¢ green Franklin (331)	12/12/10	4.75	6.00	35.00	(2)		
	Double transfer		—	—				
391	2¢ carmine Washington							
	(332)	12/23/10	37.50	12.50	240.00	(2)		
	Coil Stamps, Perf. 8.5 Vertically #394-96: Washington (Designs of 333-35)							
392	1¢ green Franklin (331)	12/12/10	22.00	19.00	165.00	(2)		
	Double transfer		—	—				
393	2¢ carmine Washington							
	(332)	12/16/10	42.50	7.75	275.00	(2)		
394	3¢ deep violet, type I	09/18/11	52.50	47.50	380.00	(2)		
395	4¢ brown	04/15/12	52.50	42.50	380.00	(2)		
396	5¢ blue	03/13	52.50	42.50	380.00	(2)		
	Issues of 1913, Panama Pacific Exposition Issue, Wmkd. (190), Perf. 12							
397	1¢ Vasco Nunez de Balboa	01/01/13	17.50	1.50	175.00	(6)	5,000.00	167*
	Double transfer		22.50	2.50				
398	2¢ Pedro Miguel Locks,							
	Panama Canal	01/13	21.00	.50	275.00	(6)		251*
	Double transfer		40.00	2.00				
a	2¢ carmine lake		575.00					
399	5¢ Golden Gate	01/01/13	75.00	9.50	1,900.00	(6)	21,000.00	14*
400	10¢ yellow Discovery of							
	San Francisco Bay	01/01/13	130.00	20.00	2,400.00	(6)	10,000.00	8*
400A	10¢ orange (400)	08/13	210.00	16.00	11,500.00	(6)		

*Includes perf. 10 printing quantities.

	Issues of 1914-15		Un	U	PB/LP	#
	Perf. 10					
401	1¢ green (397)	12/14	25.00	5.50	340.00	(6)
402	2¢ carmine (398)	01/15	75.00	1.50	2,000.00	(6)
403	5¢ blue (399)	02/15	175.00	15.00	4,000.00	(6)
404	10¢ irabge (400)	07/15	925.00	62.50	12,500.00	(6)
	Issues of 1912-14, Wmkd. (190), Perf. 12					
405	1¢ green	02/12	6.00	.20	87.50	(6)
	Cracked plate		14.00	—		
	Double transfer		7.00	—		
a	Vertical pair, imperf. horizontally		650.00	—		
b	Booklet pane of 6	02/08/12	60.00	50.00		
406	2¢ carmine, type I	02/12	6.00	.20	110.00	(6)
	Double transfer		8.25	—		
a	Booklet pane of 6	02/08/12	60.00	60.00		
b	Double impression		—			
c	2¢ lake		350.00	—		
407	7¢ black	04/14	80.00	11.00	1,200.00	(6)
	Imperf. #408-13: Washington (Designs of 405-6)					
408	1¢ green	03/12	1.10	.55	19.00	(6)
	Double transfer		2.40	1.00		
	Cracked plate		—	—		
409	2¢ carmine, type I	02/12	1.30	.60	37.50	(6)
	Cracked plate		14.00	—		
	Coil Stamps, Perf. 8.5 Horizontally					
410	1¢ green	03/12	6.00	4.00	30.00	(2)
	Double transfer		—	—		
411	2¢ carmine, type I	03/12	10.00	3.75	55.00	(2)
	Double transfer		12.50	—		
	Coil Stamps, Perf. 8.5 Vertically					
412	1¢ green	03/18/12	25.00	5.50	120.00	(2)
413	2¢ carmine, type I	03/12	42.50	1.10	240.00	(2)
	Double transfer		45.00	—		
	Perf. 12					
414	8¢ Franklin	02/12	45.00	1.25	475.00	(6)
415	9¢ Franklin	04/14	55.00	12.50	650.00	(6)
416	10¢ Franklin	01/12	45.00	.40	500.00	(6)

 **405**  **406**  **407**  **414**  **415** 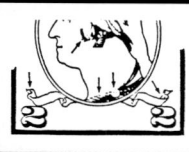 **416**

Details

2¢ Washington, Types I-VII, Series 1912-21

Detail of **#406-06a, 411, 413, 425-25e, 442, 444, 449, 453, 461, 463-63a, 482, 499-99f** Type I

One shading line in first curve of ribbon above left "2" and one in second curve of ribbon above right "2." Toga button has only a faint outline. Top line of toga rope, from button to front of the throat, is very faint. Shading lines of face end in the front of the ear, with little or no joining, to form lock of hair.

Detail of **#482a, 500** Type Ia

Similar to Type I but all lines are shorter.

Detail of **#454, 487, 491, 539** Type II

Shading lines in ribbons as in Type I. Toga button, rope and rope shading lines are heavy. Shading lines of face at lock of hair end in strong vertical curved line.

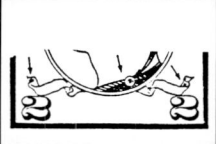

Detail of **#450, 455, 488, 492, 540, 546** Type III

Two lines of shading in curves of ribbons.

Detail of **#526, 532** Type IV

Top line of toga rope is broken. Toga button shading lines form "DID." Line of color in left "2" is very thin and usually broken.

Detail of **#527, 533** Type V

Top line of toga rope is complete. Toga button has five verticle shading lines. Line of color in left "2" is very thin and usually broken. Nose shading dots are as shown.

Detail of **#528, 534** Type Va

Same as Type V except third row from bottom of nose shading dots has four dots instead of six. Overall height of design is 1/3mm shorter than Type V.

Detail of **#528A, 534A** Type VI

Generally same as Type V except line of color in left "2" is very heavy.

Detail of **#528B, 534B** Type VII

Line of color in left "2" is continuous, clearly defined and heavier than in Type V or Va but not as heavy as Type VI. An additional vertical row of dots has been added to upper lip. Numerous additional dots appear in hair at top of head.

417

418

419

420

421

423

434

After 1915 (from 1916 to date),
all postage stamps, except #519 and 832b,
are on unwatermarked paper.

Issues of 1912-14		Un	U	PB	#
417	12¢ Franklin 04/14	50.00	4.25	625.00	(6)
	Double transfer	55.00	—		
	Triple transfer	72.50	—		
418	15¢ Franklin 02/12	85.00	3.50	850.00	(6)
	Double transfer	—			
419	20¢ Franklin 04/14	200.00	15.00	2,000.00	(6)
420	30¢ Franklin 04/14	125.00	15.00	1,500.00	(6)
421	50¢ Franklin 08/14	425.00	17.50	10,00.00	(6)
	Wmkd. (191)				
422	50¢ Franklin (421) 02/12/12	250.00	15.00	4,750.00	(6)
423	$1 Franklin 02/12/12	525.00	60.00	12,000.00	(6)
	Double transfer	550.00			
	Issues of 1914-15, Wmkd. (190), Perf. 10 #424-30: Wash. (Designs of 405-06, 333-36, 407)				
424	1¢ green 09/05/14	2.30	.20	40.00	(6)
	Cracked plate	—	—		
	Double transfer	4.50	—		
	Experimental precancel, New Orleans		—		
a	Perf. 12 x 10	2750.00	2,500.00		
b	Perf. 10 x 12		2,250.00		
c	Vertical pair, imperf. horizontally	1,500.00	750.00		
d	Booklet pane of 6	4.75	3.25		
e	As "d", imperf.	1,600.00			
425	2¢ rose red, type I 09/05/14	2.20	.20	27.50	(6)
	Cracked plate	9.50	—		
	Double transfer	—	—		
c	Perf. 10 x 12		—		
d	Perf. 12 x 10	6,500.00	3,500.00		
e	Booklet pane of 6 01/06/14	16.00	15.00		
426	3¢ deep violet, type I 09/18/14	14.00	1.25	180.00	(6)
427	4¢ brown 09/07/14	35.00	.50	500.00	(6)
	Double transfer	45.00	—		
428	5¢ blue 09/14/14	32.50	.50	400.00	(6)
a	Perf. 12 x 10		6,500.00		
429	6¢ red orange 09/28/14	47.50	1.40	550.00	(6)
430	7¢ black 09/10/14	85.00	4.00	975.00	(6)
	#431-33, 435, 437-40: Franklin (414-21, 423)				
431	8¢ pale olive green 09/26/14	35.00	1.50	475.00	(6)
	Double impression	—			
432	9¢ salmon red 10/06/14	50.00	7.50	725.00	(6)
433	10¢ orange yellow 09/09/14	47.50	.40	850.00	(6)
434	11¢ Franklin 08/11/15	22.50	7.50	250.00	(6)
435	12¢ claret brown 09/10/14	26.00	4.00	300.00	(6)
	Double transfer	32.50	—		
	Triple transfer	37.50	—		
a	12¢ copper red	29.00	4.00	330.00	(6)
436	Not assigned				
437	15¢ gray 09/16/14	125.00	7.25	1,150.00	(6)
438	20¢ ultramarine 09/19/14	210.00	4.00	3,400.00	(6)
439	30¢ orange red 09/19/14	250.00	16.00	4,250.00	(6)
440	50¢ violet 12/10/15	550.00	16.00	15,000.00	(6)

	Issues of 1914		Un	U	PB/LP	#
	Coil Stamps, Perf. 10 Horizontally #441-59: Wash.					
	(Designs of 405-06, 333-35; Flat Press, 18.5-19 x 22mm)					
441	1¢ green	11/14/14	1.00	1.00	7.75	(2)
442	2¢ carmine, type I	07/22/14	8.00	6.00	47.50	(2)
	Coil Stamps, Perf. 10 Vertically					
443	1¢ green	05/29/14	22.50	5.00	140.00	(2)
444	2¢ carmine, type I	04/25/14	35.00	1.50	250.00	(2)
445	3¢ violet, type I	12/18/14	220.00	125.00	1,250.00	(2)
446	4¢ brown	10/02/14	120.00	42.50	700.00	(2)
447	5¢ blue	07/30/14	42.50	27.50	250.00	(2)
	Issues of 1915-16, Coil Stamps, Perf. 10 Horizontally					
	(Rotary Press, Designs 18.5-19 x 22.5mm)					
448	1¢ green	12/12/15	6.00	3.25	40.00	(2)
449	2¢ red, type I	12/05/15	2,600.00	500.00	*15,000*	(2)
450	2¢ carmine, type III	02/16	9.50	3.00	75.00	(2)
451	Not assigned					
	Issues of 1914-16, Coil Stamps, Perf. 10 Vertically (Rotary Press, Designs 19.5 20 x 22mm)					
452	1¢ green	11/11/14	10.00	2.00	75.00	(2)
453	2¢ carmine rose, type I	07/03/14	140.00	4.25	725.00	(2)
	Cracked plate		—			
454	2¢ red, type II	06/15	82.50	10.00	425.00	(2)
455	2¢ carmine, type III	12/15	8.50	1.00	50.00	(2)
456	3¢ violet, type I	02/02/16	240.00	90.00	1,200.00	(2)
457	4¢ brown	02/18/16	25.00	17.50	150.00	(2)
	Cracked plate		35.00	—		
458	5¢ blue	03/09/16	30.00	17.50	180.00	(2)
	Issue of 1914, Horizontal Coil Stamp, Imperf.					
459	2¢ carmine, type I	06/30/14	250.00	*950.00*	1,050.00	(2)
	Issues of 1915, Wmkd. (191), Perf. 10					
460	$1 violet black Franklin (423)	02/08/15	850.00	85.00	*12,000.00*	(6)
	Double transfer		900.00	—		
	Perf. 11					
461	2¢ pale carmine red Washington					
	(406), type I	06/17/15	140.00	*275.00*	*1,450.00*	(6)
	Privately perforated copies of #409 have been made to resemble 461.					
	Issues of 1916-17, Unwmkd., Perf. 10 #462-69: Wash. (Designs of 405-06, 333-36, 407)					
462	1¢ green	09/27/16	7.00	.35	160.00	(6)
	Experimental precancel, Springfield, MA,					
	or New Orleans, LA			10.00		
a	Booklet pane of 6	10/15/16	9.50	*5.00*		
463	2¢ carmine, type I	09/25/16	4.50	.25	135.00	(6)
	Experimental precancel, Springfield, MA			22.50		
	Double transfer		6.50	—		
a	Booklet pane of 6	10/08/16	95.00	*65.00*		
464	3¢ violet, type I	11/11/16	75.00	12.50	1,400.00	(6)
	Double transfer in "CENTS"		*90.00*	—		
465	4¢ orange brown	10/07/16	45.00	1.70	675.00	(6)
466	5¢ blue	10/17/16	75.00	1.70	950.00	(6)
	Experimental precancel, Springfield, MA			175.00		
467	5¢ carmine (error in plate of 2¢)		575.00	*700.00*		
468	6¢ red orange	10/10/16	95.00	7.00	1,400.00	(6)
	Experimental precancel, Springfield, MA			175.00		
469	7¢ black	10/10/16	120.00	11.00	1,400.00	(6)
	Experimental precancel, Springfield, MA			175.00		

	Issues of 1916-17		Un	U	PB/LP	#	FDC
	#470-78: Franklin (Designs of 414-16, 434, 417-21, 423)						
470	8¢ olive green	11/13/16	57.50	5.50	575.00	(6)	
	Experimental precancel, Springfield, MA			165.00			
471	9¢ salmon red	11/16/16	57.50	14.00	775.00	(6)	
472	10¢ orange yellow	10/17/16	105.00	1.25	1,400.00	(6)	
473	11¢ dark green	11/16/16	37.50	16.00	375.00	(6)	
	Experimental precancel, Springfield, MA			575.00			
474	12¢ claret brown	10/10/16	50.00	5.00	650.00	(6)	
	Double transfer		60.00	6.00			
	Triple transfer		72.50	9.00			
475	15¢ gray	11/16/16	190.00	10.50	3,250.00	(6)	
476	20¢ light ultramarine	12/05/16	240.00	12.00	3,700.00	(6)	
476A	30¢ orange red		4,000.00	—		(6)	
477	50¢ light violet	03/02/17	1,050.00	60.00	57,500.00	(6)	
478	$1 violet black	12/22/16	775.00	17.50	13,500.00	(6)	
	Double transfer		825.00	22.50			
479	$2 dark blue Madison (312)	03/22/17	300.00	40.00	4,150.00	(6)	
480	$5 light green Marshall (313)	03/22/17	240.00	42.50	3,000.00	(6)	
	Issues of 1916-17, Imperf.						
	#481-96: Washington (Designs of 405-06, 333-35)						
481	1¢ green	11/16	1.00	.55	14.00	(6)	
	Double transfer		2.50	1.25			
482	2¢ carmine, type I	12/08/16	1.40	1.25	24.00	(6)	
482A	2¢ deep rose, type Ia			15,000.00			
483	3¢ violet, type I	10/13/17	13.50	7.50	120.00	(6)	
	Double transfer		18.00	—			
484	3¢ violet, type II		10.50	5.00	95.00	(6)	
	Double transfer		13.00	—			
485	5¢ carmine (error in plate of 2¢)	03/17	10,500.00		140.00	(6)	
	Issues of 1916-22, Coil Stamps, Perf. 10 Horizontally						
486	1¢ green	01/18	.90	.25	4.75	(2)	
	Double transfer		2.25	—			
487	2¢ carmine, type II	11/15/16	14.00	3.00	110.00	(2)	
488	2¢ carmine, type III	1919	2.50	1.75	15.00	(2)	
	Cracked plate		12.00	7.50			
489	3¢ violet, type I	10/10/17	5.00	1.50	32.50	(2)	
	Coil Stamps, Perf. 10 Vertically						
490	1¢ green	11/17/16	.55	.25	3.50	(2)	
	Cracked plate (horizontal)		7.50	—			
	Cracked plate (vertical) retouched		9.00	—			
	Rosette crack		50.00	—			
491	2¢ carmine, type II	11/17/16	2,250.00	600.00	11,500.00	(2)	
492	2¢ carmine, type III		9.50	.25	55.00	(2)	
493	3¢ violet, type I	07/23/17	16.00	3.00	110.00	(2)	
494	3¢ violet, type II	02/04/18	10.00	1.00	75.00	(2)	
495	4¢ orange brown	04/15/17	10.00	4.00	75.00	(2)	
	Cracked plate		25.00	—			
496	5¢ blue	01/15/19	3.50	1.00	30.00	(2)	
497	10¢ orange yellow						
	Franklin (416)	01/31/22	20.00	10.50	140.00	(2)	4,500.00

	Issues of 1917-19		Un	U	PB	#
	Perf. 11, #498-507: Washington (Designs of 405-06, 333-36, 407)					
498	1¢ green	03/17	.35	.25	17.50	(6)
	Cracked plate		7.50	—		
a	Vertical pair, imperf. horizontally		175.00			
b	Horizontal pair, imperf. between		100.00			
c	Vertical pair, imperf. between		*450.00*			
d	Double impression		175.00			
e	Booklet pane of 6	04/06/17	2.50	*1.00*		
f	Booklet pane of 30	09/17	*1,000.00*			
g	Perf. 10 top or bottom		—	—		
499	2¢ rose, type I	03/17	.35	.25	17.50	(6)
	Double transfer		6.00	—		
a	Vertical pair, imperf. horizontally		150.00			
b	Horizontal pair, imperf. vertically		*450.00*	*225.00*		
c	Vertical pair, imperf. between		*650.00*	*225.00*		
e	Booklet pane of 6	03/31/17	4.00	*1.25*		
f	Booklet pane of 30	09/17	*28,000.00*			
g	Double impression		160.00	—		
500	2¢ deep rose, type Ia		275.00	225.00	2,200.00	(6)
	Pair, types I and Ia		*1,275.00*			
501	3¢ light violet, type I	03/17	11.00	.25	125.00	(6)
b	Booklet pane of 6	10/17/17	70.00	*45.00*		
c	Vertical pair, imperf. horizontally, type I		350.00			
d	Double impression		275.00			
502	3¢ dark violet, type II		14.00	.40	150.00	(6)
b	Booklet pane of 6	02/28/18	60.00	*45.00*		
c	Vertical pair, imperf. horizontally		250.00	*125.00*		
d	Double impression		200.00			
e	Perf. 10, top or bottom		—	3,500		
503	4¢ brown	03/17	10.00	.25	140.00	(6)
504	5¢ blue	03/17	9.00	.25	130.00	(6)
	Double transfer		11.00	—		
505	5¢ rose (error in plate of 2¢)		360.00	500.00		
506	6¢ red orange	03/17	12.50	.25	175.00	(6
507	7¢ black	03/17	27.50	1.10	260.00	(6)
	#508-12, 514-18: Franklin (Designs of 414-16, 434, 417-21, 423)					
508	8¢ olive bister	03/17	12.00	.50	175.00	(6)
b	Vertical pair, imperf. between		—	—		
c	Perf. 10 top or bottom			*3,250.00*		
509	9¢ salmon red	03/17	14.00	1.75	150.00	(6)
510	10¢ orange yellow	03/17	17.00	.20	190.00	(6)
511	11¢ light green	05/17	9.00	2.50	130.00	(6)
	Double transfer		12.50	3.25		
512	12¢ claret brown	05/17	9.00	.35	130.00	(6)
a	12¢ brown carmine		9.50	.40		
b	Perf. 10, top or bottom		—	*3,000.00*		
513	13¢ apple green	01/10/19	11.00	6.00	130.00	(6)
	13¢ deep apple green		12.50	6.50		
514	15¢ gray	05/17	37.50	1.00	575.00	(6)
515	20¢ light ultramarine	05/17	47.50	.25	625.00	(6)
	20¢ deep ultramarine		50.00	.25		
b	Vertical pair, imperf. between		*1,000.00*			
c	Double impression		*1,250.00*			
d	Perf. 10 at top or bottom		—	*4,500.00*		
516	30¢ orange red	05/17	37.50	1.00	600.00	(6)
a	Perf. 10 top or bottom		*5,000.00*	—		

498 499 500 501 502

503 504 505

506 507 508 509 510

511 512 512a 513 514

515 516

Read about the newest issues in the "2001 Issues—New U.S. Postage Stamps" section.

517

523

524

Issues of 1917		Un	U	PB	#	FDC	Q(M)
Wmkd. (191), Perf. 11							
517 50¢ red violet	05/17	67.50	.50	1,650.00	(6)		
b Vertical pair, imperf. between							
and at bottom		—	7,000.00				
c Perf. 10, top or bottom			4,500.00				
518 $1 violet brown	05/17	52.50	1.50	1,350.00	(6)		
b $1 deep brown		1,900.00	1,050.00				
519 2¢ carm. Washington (332)	10/10/17	400.00	1,100.00	2,700.00	(6)		
Privately perforated copies of #344 have been made to resemble #519.							
520-22 Not assigned							
Issues of 1918, Unwmkd.							
523 $2 Franklin	08/19/18	625.00	230.00	12,000.00	(8)		
524 $5 Franklin	08/19/18	220.00	35.00	4,250.00	(8)		
Issues of 1918-20 #525-35: Washington (Designs of 405-06, 333)							
525 1¢ gray green	12/18	2.50	.50	25.00	(6)		
1¢ Emerald		3.50	1.00				
a 1¢ dark green		2.75	.95				
c Horizontal pair, imperf. between		100.00					
d Double impression		27.50	25.00				
526 2¢ carmine, type IV	03/06/20	27.50	3.50	250.00	(6)	800.00	
Gash on forehead		40.00	—				
Malformed "2" at left		37.50	6.00				
527 2¢ carmine, type V	03/20/20	20.00	1.00	175.00	(6)		
Line through "2" and "EN"		30.00	—				
a Double impression		60.00	10.00				
b Vertical pair, imperf. horizontally		600.00					
c Horizontal pair, imperf. vertically		1,000.00					
528 2¢ carmine, type Va	05/04/20	9.25	.25	85.00	(6)		
c Double impression		27.50					
g Vertical pair, imperf. between		2,000.00					
528A 2¢ carmine, type VI	06/24/20	52.50	1.50	450.00	(6)		
d Double impression		160.00					
f Vertical pair, imperf. horizontally		—					
h Vertical pair, imperf. between		1,000.00					
528B 2¢ carmine, type VII	11/03/20	22.50	.35	185.00	(6)		
Retouched on cheek		400.00	—				
e Double impression		70.00					
529 3¢ violet, type III	03/18	3.25	.25	60.00	(6)		
a Double impression		32.50	—				
b Printed on both sides		450.00					
530 3¢ purple, type IV		1.60	.20	18.50	(6)		
"Blister" under "U.S."		4.50	—				
Recut under "U.S."		4.50	—				
a Double impression		20.00	6.00	—			
b Printed on both sides		250.00					
Imperf.							
531 1¢ green	01/19	9.50	8.00	90.00	(6)		
532 2¢ carmine rose, type IV	03/20	40.00	27.50	350.00	(6)		
533 2¢ carmine, type V	05/04/20	130.00	80.00	1,150.00	(6)		
534 2¢ carmine, type Va	05/25/20	11.00	6.50	110.00	(6)		
534A 2¢ carmine, type VI	07/26/20	45.00	22.50	400.00	(6)		
534B 2¢ carmine, type VII	12/02/20	2,150.00	1,000.00	17,000.00	(6)		
535 3¢ violet, type IV	1918	9.00	5.00	77.50	(6)		
a Double impression		100.00	—				
Issues of 1919, Perf. 12.5							
536 1¢ gray green							
Washington (405)	08/15/19	22.50	20.00	210.00	(6)		
a Horizontal pair, imperf. vertically		700.00					

	Issues of 1919		Un	U	PB	#	FDC	Q(M)
	Perf. 11							
537	3¢ Allied Victory	03/03/19	10.00	3.25	110.00	(6)	*750.00*	100
	Double transfer		—	—				
a	deep red violet		*1,150.00*	*1,500.00*	4,250.00	(6)		
b	light reddish violet		10.00	3.00	110.00	(6)		
c	red violet		40.00	12.00				
	Issues of 1919, George Washington, Unwmkd., Perf. 11 x 10							
538	1¢ green	06/19	12.00	8.50	115.00	(4)		
	Double transfer		17.50	—				
a	Vertical pair, imperf. horizontally		50.00	*100.00*	900.00	(4)		
539	2¢ carmine rose, type II		2,750.00	*4,750.00*	15,000.00	(4)		
540	2¢ carmine rose, type III	06/14/19	14.00	8.50	110.00	(4)		
	Double transfer		22.50	—				
a	Vertical pair, imperf. horizontally		50.00	*100.00*	750.00	(4)		
b	Horizontal pair, imperf. vertically		*750.00*					
541	3¢ violet, type II	06/19	45.00	30.00	375.00	(4)		
	Issue of 1920, Perf. 10 x 11							
542	1¢ green	05/26/20	14.00	1.10	175.00	(6)	*1,750.00*	
	Issues of 1921, Perf. 10							
543	1¢ green	05/21	.50	.25	15.00	(4)		
	Double transfer			—				
	Triple transfer		—	—				
a	Horizontal pair, imperf. between		*1,100.00*					
	Issue of 1922, Perf. 11							
544	1¢ green		*15,000.00*	*3,250.00*				
	Issues of 1921							
545	1¢ green	05/21	190.00	175.00	1,150.00	(4)		
546	2¢ carmine rose, type III	05/21	125.00	*160.00*	825.00	(4)		
	Recut in hair		140.00	185.00				
a	Perf. 10 at left		—					
	Issue of 1920							
547	$2 Franklin	11/01/20	200.00	40.00	4,350.00	(8)		
	Pilgrim Tercentenary Issue							
548	1¢ The *Mayflower*	12/21/20	4.50	2.25	45.00	(6)	*900.00*	138
	Double transfer		—	—				
549	2¢ Landing of the Pilgrims	12/21/20	6.50	1.60	65.00	(6)	*700.00*	196
550	5¢ Signing of the Compact	12/21/20	42.50	12.50	450.00	(6)	—	11
	Issues of 1922-25 (See also #581-91, 594-606, 622-23, 631-42, 658-79, 684-87, 692-701, 723)							
551	½¢ Nathan Hale	04/04/25	.20	.20	5.75	(6)	17.50	(4)
	"Cap" on fraction bar		.75	.20				
552	1¢ Franklin	01/17/23	1.50	.20	22.50	(6)	25.00	(2)
	Double transfer		3.50	—				
a	Booklet pane of 6	08/11/23	6.00	*2.00*				
553	1½¢ Harding	03/19/25	2.60	.20	27.50	(6)	30.00	(2)
554	2¢ Washington	01/15/23	1.40	.20	20.00	(6)	37.50	
	Double transfer		2.50	.80				
a	Horizontal pair, imperf. vertically		200.00					
b	Vertical pair, imperf. horizontally		*750.00*					
c	Booklet pane of 6	02/10/23	6.75	*2.00*				
d	Perf. 10 at top or bottom		—	3,500.00				
555	3¢ Lincoln	02/12/23	18.00	1.00	160.00	(6)	35.00	
556	4¢ M. Washington	01/15/23	19.00	.25	160.00	(6)	60.00	
a	Vertical pair, imperf. horizontally		—					
b	Perf. 10, top or bottom		*2,250.00*	—				
557	5¢ T. Roosevelt	10/27/22	19.00	.20	190.00	(6)	*125.00*	
a	Imperf., pair		*1,500.00*					
b	Horizontal pair, imperf. vertically		—					
c	Perf. 10, top or bottom		—	*3,250.00*				

537

547

548

549

550

551

552

553

554

555

556

557

558

559

560

561

562

563

564

565

566

567

568

569

570

571

572

573

	Issues of 1922-23		Un	U	PB	#	FDC
	Perf. 11						
558	6¢ Garfield	11/20/22	35.00	.85	400.00	(6)	225.00
	Double transfer		55.00	2.00			
	Same, recut		55.00	2.00			
559	7¢ McKinley	05/01/23	9.25	.55	70.00	(6)	175.00
	Double transfer		—	—			
560	8¢ Grant	05/01/23	50.00	.60	575.00	(6)	175.00
	Double transfer		—	—			
561	9¢ Jefferson	01/15/23	14.00	1.10	160.00	(6)	175.00
	Double transfer		—	—			
562	10¢ Monroe	01/15/23	18.00	.20	200.00	(6)	175.00
a	Vertical pair, imperf. horizontally		*1,500.00*				
b	Imperf., pair		*1,250.00*				
c	Perf. 10 at top or bottom			2,250.00			
563	11¢ Hayes	10/04/22	1.40	.40	27.50	(6)	600.00
d	Imperf., pair			17,500.00			
564	12¢ Cleveland	03/20/23	6.00	.20	72.50	(6)	175.00
a	Horizontal pair, imperf. vertically		*1,000.00*				
565	14¢ American Indian	05/01/23	4.00	.75	47.50	(6)	400.00
	Double transfer		—	—			
566	15¢ Statue of Liberty	11/11/22	23.00	.20	250.00	(6)	550.00
567	20¢ Golden Gate	05/01/23	22.00	.20	230.00	(6)	*500.00*
a	Horizontal pair, imperf. vertically		*1,500.00*				
568	25¢ Niagara Falls	11/11/22	18.00	.45	240.00	(6)	*650.00*
b	Vertical pair, imperf. horizontally		*1,750.00*				
c	Perf. 10 at one side		*3,000.00*				
569	30¢ Buffalo	03/20/23	32.50	.35	230.00	(6)	*850.00*
	Double transfer		55.00	—			
570	50¢ Arlington Amphitheater	11/11/22	55.00	.20	600.00	(6)	*1,250.00*
571	$1 Lincoln Memorial	02/12/23	45.00	.45	300.00	(6)	*7,000.00*
	Double transfer		90.00	1.50			
572	$2 U.S. Capitol	03/20/23	90.00	9.00	675.00	(6)	*15,000.00*
573	$5 Head of Freedom, Capitol Dome	03/20/23	150.00	15.00	1,900.00	(8)	*25,000.00*
a	Carmine lake and dark blue		175.00	16.00	2,100.00	(8)	
574	Not assigned						
	Issues of 1923-25, Imperf.						
575	1¢ green Franklin (552)	03/20/23	7.25	5.00	70.00	(6)	
576	1½¢ yel. brn. Harding (553)	04/04/25	1.50	1.50	20.00	(6)	45.00
577	2¢ carmine Washington (554)		1.60	1.25	25.00	(6)	
	Issues of 1923, Perf. 11 x 10						
578	1¢ green Franklin (552)	1923	100.00	*140.00*	800.00	(4)	
579	2¢ carmine Washington (554)	1923	90.00	*125.00*	600.00	(4)	
	Recut in eye		*110.00*	*150.00*			
	Issues of 1923-26, Perf. 10 (See also #551-73, 622-23, 631-42, 658-79, 684-87, 692-701, 723)						
580	Not assigned						
581	1¢ green Franklin (552)	04/21/23	11.00	.65	120.00	(4)	*6,000.00*
582	1½¢ brn. Harding (553)	03/19/25	5.50	.60	45.00	(4)	40.00
	Pair with full horiz. gutter between		*160.00*				
583	2¢ carm. Wash. (554)	04/14/24	3.00	.25	32.50	(4)	
a	Booklet pane of 6		08/27/26	90.00	*50.00*			*1,500.00*
584	3¢ violet Lincoln (555)	08/01/25	32.50	2.25	260.00	(4)	55.00
585	4¢ yellow brown Martha Washington (556)	03/25	19.00	.45	230.00	(4)	55.00
586	5¢ blue T. Roosevelt (557)	12/24	19.00	.25	225.00	(4)	57.50
587	6¢ red orange Garfield (558)	03/25	9.25	.35	95.00	(4)	60.00
588	7¢ black McKinley (559)	05/29/26	13.50	5.50	115.00	(4)	70.00

	Issues of 1925-26		Un	U	PB/LP	#	FDC	Q(M)
	Perf. 11 x 10							
589	8¢ olive grn. Grant (560)	05/29/26	30.00	3.50	240.00	(4)	72.50	
590	9¢ rose Jefferson (561)	05/29/26	6.00	2.25	50.00	(4)	72.50	
591	10¢ orange Monroe (562)	06/08/25	72.50	.25	475.00	(4)	95.00	
592-93	Not assigned							
	Issues of 1923, Perf. 11							
594	1¢ green Franklin (552),							
	design 19.75 x 22.25mm	1923	18,000.00	6,000.00				
595	2¢ carmine Washington (554),							
	design 19.75 x 22.25mm	1923	300.00	325.00	2,100.00	(4)		
596	1¢ green Franklin (552),							
	design 19.25 x 22.5mm	1923		70,000.00				
	Issues of 1923-29, Coil Stamps, Perf. 10 Vertically							
597	1¢ green Franklin (552)	07/18/23	.30	.20	2.25	(2)	600.00	
	Gripper cracks or double transfer		2.60	1.00				
598	1½¢ brown Harding (553)	03/19/25	1.00	.20	4.75	(2)	60.00	
599	2¢ carmine Washington							
	(554), type I	01/23	.40	.20	2.30	(2)	1,500.00	
	Double transfer		1.90	1.00				
	Gripper cracks		2.30	2.00				
599A	2¢ carmine Washington							
	(554), type II	03/29	125.00	11.00	675.00	(2)		
600	3¢ violet Lincoln (555)	05/10/24	7.25	.20	25.00	(2)	80.00	
601	4¢ yellow brown							
	M. Washington (556)	08/05/23	4.50	.35	30.00	(2)		
602	5¢ dark blue T. Roosevelt (557)	03/05/24	1.75	.20	10.00	(2)	85.00	
603	10¢ orange Monroe (562)	12/01/24	4.00	.20	26.50	(2)	100.00	
	Coil Stamps, Perf. 10 Horizontally							
604	1¢ yel. grn. Franklin (552)	07/19/24	.35	.20	3.75	(2)	90.00	
605	1½¢ yel. brn. Harding (553)	05/09/25	.35	.20	3.50	(2)	70.00	
606	2¢ carmine Washington (554)	12/31/23	.35	.20	2.60	(2)	125.00	
607-09	Not assigned							
	Issues of 1923, Harding Memorial Issue, Perf. 11							
610	2¢ blk. Harding	09/01/23	.65	.20	20.00	(6)	30.00	1,459
	Double transfer		1.75	.50				
a	Horizontal pair, imperf. vertically		1,750.00					
	Imperf.							
611	2¢ blk. Harding (610)	11/15/23	6.25	4.00	75.00	(6)	90.00	0.8
	Perf. 10							
612	2¢ blk. Harding (610)	09/12/23	17.50	1.75	300.00	(4)	100.00	100
	Perf. 11							
613	2¢ black Harding (610)	1923		27,500.00				
	Issues of 1924, Huguenot-Walloon Tercentary Issue, May 1							
614	1¢ Ship *Nieu Nederland*	01/05/24	2.75	3.25	35.00	(6)	40.00	51
615	2¢ Walloons' Landing							
	at Fort Orange (Albany)	01/05/24	5.50	2.10	60.00	(6)	55.00	78
	Double transfer		12.00	3.50				
616	5¢ Huguenot Monument to							
	Jan Ribault at Mayport, Florida	01/05/24	22.50	12.50	225.00	(6)	80.00	6

599   **610**

614   **615**   **616**

Details

2¢ Washington, Types I-II, Series 1923-29

Detail of **#599, 634**
Type I

No heavy hair lines at top
center of head.

Detail of **#599A, 634A**
Type II

Three heavy hair lines at
top center of head.

617

618

619

620

621

622

623

627

628

629

630

	Issues of 1925		Un	U	PB	#	FDC	Q(M)
	Lexington-Concord Issue, Perf. 11							
617	1¢ Washington at Cambridge	04/04/25	2.50	2.40	35.00	(6)	35.00	16
618	2¢ "The Birth of Liberty,"							
	by Henry Sandham	04/04/25	5.00	3.90	60.00	(6)	37.50	27
619	5¢ "The Minute Man,"							
	by Daniel Chester French	04/04/25	20.00	12.50	210.00	(6)	85.00	5
	Line over head		42.50	18.50				
	Norse-American Issue							
620	2¢ Sloop *Restaurationen*	05/18/25	4.00	3.00	180.00	(8)	25.00	9
621	5¢ Viking Ship	05/18/25	15.00	10.50	525.00	(8)	40.00	2
	Issues of 1925-26 (See also #551-79, 581-91, 594-606, 631-42, 658-79, 684-87, 692-701, 723)							
622	13¢ B. Harrison	01/11/26	13.50	.45	145.00	(6)	22.50	
623	17¢ Wilson	12/28/25	15.00	.25	160.00	(6)	27.50	
624-26	Not assigned							
	Issues of 1926							
627	2¢ Independence							
	Sesquicentennial Exposition	05/10/26	3.25	.50	37.50	(6)	10.00	308
628	5¢ John Ericsson Memorial	05/29/26	6.50	3.25	80.00	(6)	30.00	20
629	2¢ Battle of White Plains	10/18/26	2.25	1.70	35.00	(6)	6.25	41
a	Vertical pair, imperf. between		—					
	International Philatelic Exhibition Souvenir Sheet							
630	2¢ Battle of White Plains,							
	sheet of 25 with selvage							
	inscription (629)	10/18/26	375.00	450.00			1,500.00	0.1
	Dot over first "S" of "States"		400.00	475.00				
	Imperf. (See also #551-79, 581-91, 594-606, 622-23, 658-79, 684-87, 692-701, 723)							
631	1½¢ yellow brown							
	Harding (553)	08/27/26	1.90	1.70	62.50	(4)	35.00	
	Issues of 1926-34, Perf. 11 x 10.5 (See also #551-73, 575-79, 581-91, 594-606, 622-23, 631-42, 684-87, 692-701, 723)							
632	1¢ green Franklin (552)	06/10/27	.20	.20	2.00	(4)	45.00	
	Pair with full vertical gutter between		150.00	—				
	Cracked plate		—	—				
a	Booklet pane of 6	11/02/27	5.50	2.25			3,250.00	
b	Vertical pair, imperf. between		*1,600.00*	125.00				
c	Horizontal pair, imperf. between		—					
633	1½¢ yellow brown							
	Harding (553)	05/17/27	1.90	.20	62.50	(4)	45.00	
634	2¢ carmine Washington							
	(554), type I	12/10/26	.20	.20	1.75	(4)	47.50	
	Pair with full vertical gutter between		200.00					
b	2¢ carmine lake, type I		—	—	—	(4)		
c	Horizontal pair, imperf. between		2,000.00					
d	Booklet pane of 6	02/25/27	1.75	*1.10*				
634A	2¢ carmine Washington							
	(554), type II	12/28/27	350.00	13.50	2,000.00	(4)		
	Pair with full vertical or							
	horizontal gutter between		1,000.00	—				
635	3¢ violet Lincoln (555)	02/03/27	.40	.20	12.00	(4)	47.50	
a	3¢ bright violet Lincoln	02/07/34	.20	.20	5.50	(4)	25.00	
	Gripper cracks		3.25	2.00				
636	4¢ yellow brown Martha							
	Washington (556)	05/17/27	2.10	.20	72.50	(4)	50.00	
	Pair with full vertical gutter between		*200.00*					
637	5¢ dark blue Theodore							
	Roosevelt (557)	03/24/27	2.10	.20	14.00	(4)	50.00	
	Pair with full vertical gutter between		*275.00*					

	Issues of 1927-31		Un	U	PB/LB	#	FDC	Q(M)
	Perf. 11 x 10.5							
638	6¢ red orange Garfield (558)	07/27/27	2.10	.20	14.00	(4)	57.50	
	Pair with full vert. gutter between		*200.00*					
639	7¢ black McKinley (559)	03/24/27	2.10	.20	14.00	(4)	57.50	
a	Vertical pair, imperf.							
	between		*275.00*	85.00				
640	8¢ olive green Grant (560)	06/10/27	2.10	.20	15.00	(4)	62.50	
641	9¢ orange red Jefferson (561)	1931	2.10	.20	15.00	(4)	72.50	
642	10¢ orange Monroe (562)	02/03/27	3.50	.20	21.00	(4)	90.00	
	Double transfer		—	—				
	Perf. 11							
643	2¢ Vermont Sesquicentennial	08/03/27	1.40	.80	37.50	(6)	6.00	40
644	2¢ Burgoyne Campaign	08/03/27	3.50	2.10	32.50	(6)	12.50	26
	Issues of 1928							
645	2¢ Valley Forge	05/26/28	1.05	.40	25.00	(6)	4.00	101
	Perf. 11 x 10.5							
646	2¢ Battle of Monmouth/							
	Molly Pitcher	10/20/28	1.10	1.10	32.50	(4)	15.00	10
	Wide spacing, vertical pair		50.00	—				
	Hawaii Sesquicentennial Issue							
647	2¢ Washington (554)	08/13/28	5.00	4.50	135.00	(4)	15.00	6
	Wide spacing, vertical pair		100.00					
648	5¢ Theodore Roosevelt (557)	08/13/28	14.50	13.50	260.00	(4)	22.50	1
	Aeronautics Conference Issue, Perf. 11							
649	2¢ Wright Airplane	12/12/28	1.25	.80	10.00	(6)	7.00	51
650	5¢ Globe and Airplane	12/12/28	5.25	3.25	50.00	(6)	10.00	10
	Plate flaw "prairie dog"		27.50	12.50				
	Issues of 1929							
651	2¢ George Rogers Clark	02/25/29	.65	.50	10.00	(6)	6.00	17
	Double transfer		4.25	2.25				
652	Not assigned							
	Perf. 11 x 10.5							
653	½¢ olive brown Nathan							
	Hale (551)	5/25/29	.20	.20	1.50	(4)	27.50	
	Electric Light's Golden Jubilee Issue, Perf. 11							
654	2¢ Thomas Edison's First Lamp	06/05/29	.70	.70	25.00	(6)	10.00	32
	Perf. 11 x 10.5							
655	2¢ carmine rose (654)	06/11/29	.65	.20	35.00	(4)	80.00	210
	Coil Stamp, Perf. 10 Vertically							
656	2¢ carmine rose (654)	06/11/29	14.00	1.75	75.00	(2)	90.00	133
	Perf. 11							
657	2¢ Sullivan Expedition	06/17/29	.70	.60	25.00	(6)	4.00	51
a	2¢ lake		500.00	—				

643   **644**   **645**

646   **647**   **648**

649   **650**

651

654   **657**

658 **669**

680 **681**

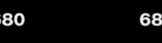

682 **683**

Issues of 1929		Un	U	PB/LP	#	FDC	Q(M)
#658-68 overprinted "Kans.," Perf. 11 x 10.5							
(See also #551-73, 575-79, 581-91, 594-606, 622-23, 631-42, 684-87, 692-701, 723)							
658 1¢ Franklin	05/01/29	2.50	2.00	35.00	(4)	50.00	13
a Vertical pair, one without overprint		325.00					
659 1½¢ brown Harding (553)	05/01/29	4.00	2.90	50.00	(4)	52.50	8
Wide spacing, pair		70.00					
660 2¢ carmine Washington (554)	05/01/29	4.50	1.10	47.50	(4)	52.50	87
661 3¢ violet Lincoln (555)	05/01/29	22.50	15.00	210.00	(4)	60.00	3
662 4¢ yellow brown Martha Washington (556)	05/01/29	22.50	9.00	210.00	(4)	62.50	2
663 5¢ deep blue T. Roosevelt (557)	05/01/29	14.00	9.75	150.00	(4)	80.00	3
664 6¢ red orange Garfield (558)	05/01/29	32.50	18.00	450.00	(4)	90.00	1
665 7¢ black McKinley (559)	05/01/29	30.00	27.50	500.00	(4)	100.00	1
666 8¢ olive green Grant (560)	05/01/29	110.00	75.00	825.00	(4)	125.00	2
667 9¢ light rose Jefferson (561)	05/01/29	16.00	11.25	225.00	(4)	140.00	1
668 10¢ orange yel. Monroe (562)	05/01/29	25.00	12.00	350.00	(4)	175.00	3
#669-79 overprinted "Nebr."							
669 1¢ Franklin	05/01/29	4.00	2.25	50.00	(4)	50.00	8
a Vertical pair, one without overprint		—					
670 1½¢ brown Harding (553)	05/01/29	3.75	2.50	52.50	(4)	50.00	9
671 2¢ carmine Washington (554)	05/01/29	3.75	1.30	42.50	(4)	55.00	73
672 3¢ violet Lincoln (555)	05/01/29	15.00	12.00	165.00	(4)	65.00	2
673 4¢ yellow brown Martha Washington (556)	05/01/29	22.50	15.00	250.00	(4)	75.00	2
Wide spacing, pair		120.00					
674 5¢ deep blue T. Roosevelt (557)	05/01/29	20.00	15.00	275.00	(4)	75.00	2
675 6¢ red orange Garfield (558)	05/01/29	47.50	24.00	525.00	(4)	100.00	1
676 7¢ black McKinley (559)	05/01/29	27.50	18.00	300.00	(4)	100.00	0.8
677 8¢ olive green Grant (560)	05/01/29	37.50	25.00	400.00	(4)	125.00	1
678 9¢ light rose Jefferson (561)	05/01/29	42.50	27.50	525.00	(4)	140.00	0.5
679 10¢ orange yel. Monroe (562)	05/01/29	135.00	22.50	950.00	(4)	175.00	2
Warning: Excellent forgeries of the Kansas and Nebraska overprints exist.							
Perf. 11							
680 2¢ Battle of Fallen Timbers	09/14/29	.80	.80	22.50	(6)	3.50	29
681 2¢ Ohio River Canalization	10/19/29	.70	.65	15.00	(6)	3.50	33
Issues of 1930							
682 2¢ Mass. Bay Colony	04/08/30	.60	.50	22.50	(6)	3.50	74
683 2¢ Carolina-Charleston	04/10/30	1.20	1.20	42.50	(6)	3.50	25
Perf. 11 x 10.5							
684 1½¢ Warren G. Harding	12/01/30	.35	.20	1.75	(4)	4.50	
Pair with full horizontal gutter between		175.00					
Pair with full vertical gutter between		—					
685 4¢ William H. Taft	06/04/30	.90	.20	11.00	(4)	6.00	
Gouge on right "4"		2.10	.60				
Recut right "4"		2.10	.65				
Pair with full horizontal gutter between		—					
Coil Stamps, Perf. 10 Vertically							
686 1½¢ brn. Harding (684)	12/01/30	1.80	.20	6.50	(2)	5.00	
687 4¢ brown Taft (685)	09/18/30	3.25	.45	13.00	(2)	20.00	

1930-1932

	Issues of 1930		Un	U	PB	#	FDC	Q(M)
	Perf. 11							
688	2¢ Battle of Braddock's Field	07/09/30	1.00	.85	30.00	(6)	4.00	26
689	2¢ Gen. von Steuben	09/17/30	.55	.55	20.00	(6)	4.00	66
a	Imperf., pair		2,500.00		12,000.00	(6)		
	Issues of 1931							
690	2¢ General Pulaski	01/16/31	.30	.20	10.00	(6)	4.00	97
691	Not assigned							
	Perf. 11 x 10.5 (See also #551-73, 575-79, 581-91, 594-606, 622-23, 631-42, 658-79, 684-87, 723)							
692	11¢ light bl. Hayes (563)	09/04/31	2.60	.20	13.50	(4)	100.00	
	Retouched forehead		20.00	1.00				
693	12¢ brown violet Cleveland (564)	08/25/31	5.50	.20	27.50	(4)	100.00	
694	13¢ yellow green Harrison (622)	09/04/31	2.00	.20	12.50	(4)	100.00	
695	14¢ dark blue American Indian (565)	09/08/31	3.75	.25	22.50	(4)	100.00	
696	15¢ gray Statue of Liberty (566)	08/27/31	8.00	.20	40.00	(4)	125.00	
	Perf. 10.5 x 11							
697	17¢ black Wilson (623)	07/25/31	4.50	.20	27.50	(4)	2,750.00	
698	20¢ carmine rose Golden Gate (567)	09/08/31	8.75	.20	40.00	(4)	325.00	
	Double transfer		20.00	—				
699	25¢ blue green Niagara Falls (568)	07/25/31	9.00	.20	47.50	(4)	2,000.00	
700	30¢ brown Buffalo (569)	09/08/31	17.50	.20	72.50	(4)	300.00	
	Cracked plate		27.50	.85				
701	50¢ lilac Arlington Amphitheater (570)	09/04/31	40.00	.20	200.00	(4)	425.00	
	Perf. 11							
702	2¢ Red Cross	05/21/31	.25	.20	1.90	(4)	3.00	99
a	Red cross omitted		40,000.00					
703	2¢ Yorktown	10/19/31	.40	.25	2.25	(4)	3.50	25
a	2¢ lake and black		4.50	.75				
b	2¢ dark lake and black		375.00		2,000.00	(4)		
c	Pair, imperf. vertically		5,000.00		—	(6)		
	Issues of 1932, Washington Bicentennial Issue, Perf. 11 x 10.5							
704	½¢ Portrait by Charles W. Peale	01/01/32	.20	.20	5.75	(4)	5.00 (4)	88
	Broken circle		.75	.20				
705	1¢ Bust by Jean Antoine Houdon	01/01/32	.20	.20	4.25	(4)	4.00 (2)	1,266
706	1½¢ Portrait by Charles W. Peale	01/01/32	.40	.20	14.50	(4)	4.00 (2)	305
707	2¢ Portrait by Gilbert Stuart	01/01/32	.20	.20	1.50	(4)	4.00	4,222
	Gripper cracks		1.75	.65				
708	3¢ Portrait by Charles W. Peale	01/01/32	.55	.20	16.50	(4)	4.00	456
709	4¢ Portrait by Charles P. Polk	01/01/32	.25	.20	5.50	(4)	4.00	151
	Broken bottom frame line		1.50	.50				
710	5¢ Portrait by Charles W. Peale	01/01/32	1.60	.20	16.50	(4)	4.00	171
	Cracked plate		5.25	1.10				
711	6¢ Portrait by John Trumbull	01/01/32	3.25	.20	50.00	(4)	4.00	112
712	7¢ Portrait by John Trumbull	01/01/32	.25	.20	9.00	(4)	4.00	83
713	8¢ Portrait by Charles B.J.F. Saint Memin	01/01/32	2.75	.50	50.00	(4)	4.50	97
	Pair, full vert. gutter between		—					
714	9¢ Portrait by W. Williams	01/01/32	2.40	.20	32.50	(4)	4.50	76
715	10¢ Portrait by Gilbert Stuart	01/01/32	10.00	.20	85.00	(4)	4.50	147

688 689 690

702 703

704 705 706

707 708 709

710 711 712

1932-1933

 **716**

 **717**

 **718**

 **719**

 **720**

 **724**

 **725**

 **726**

 **727**

 **728**

 **729**

 **730**

 **731**

 732

 **733**

	Issues of 1932		Un	U	PB/LP	#	FDC	Q(M)
	Olympic Winter Games Issue, Perf. 11							
716	2¢ Ski Jumper	01/25/32	.40	.20	10.00	(6)	6.00	51
	Recut		3.50	1.50				
	Colored "snowball"		25.00	5.00				
	Perf. 11 x 10.5							
717	2¢ Arbor Day	04/22/32	.20	.20	6.50	(4)	4.00	100
	Olympic Summer Games Issue, Perf. 11 x 10.5							
718	3¢ Runner at Starting Mark	06/15/32	1.40	.20	11.50	(4)	6.00	168
	Gripper cracks		4.25	.75				
719	5¢ Myron's Discobolus	06/15/32	2.20	.20	20.00	(4)	8.00	53
	Gripper cracks		4.25	1.00				
720	3¢ Washington	06/16/32	.20	.20	1.30	(4)	7.50	
	Pair with full vertical or							
	horizontal gutter between		200.00					
	Recut lines on nose		2.00	.75				
b	Booklet pane of 6	07/25/32	37.50	7.50			100.00	
c	Vertical pair, imperf. between		1,250.00	1,000.00				
	Coil Stamp, Perf. 10 Vertically							
721	3¢ deep violet (720)	06/24/32	2.75	.20	10.00	(2)	15.00	
	Recut lines around eyes		—	—				
	Coil Stamp, Perf. 10 Horizontally							
722	3¢ deep violet (720)	10/12/32	1.50	.35	6.25	(2)	15.00	
	Coil Stamp, Perf. 10 Vertically (See also #551-73, 575-79, 581-91, 594-606, 622-23, 631-42, 684-87, 692-701)							
723	6¢ deep orange Garfield (558)	08/18/32	11.00	.30	60.00	(2)	15.00	
	Perf. 11							
724	3¢ William Penn	10/24/32	.30	.20	8.00	(6)	3.25	49
a	Vertical pair, imperf. horizontally		—					
725	3¢ Daniel Webster	10/24/32	.30	.25	16.50	(6)	3.25	49
	Issues of 1933							
726	3¢ Georgia Settlement	02/12/33	.30	.20	10.00	(6)	3.25	61
	Perf. 10.5 x 11							
727	3¢ Peace of 1783	04/19/33	.20	.20	4.00	(4)	3.50	73
	Century of Progress Issue							
728	1¢ Restoration of Fort Dearborn	05/25/33	.20	.20	1.90	(4)	3.00 (3)	348
	Gripper cracks		2.00	—				
729	3¢ Federal Building at Chicago	05/25/33	.20	.20	2.25	(4)	3.00	480
	American Philatelic Society Issue Souvenir Sheets, Without Gum, Imperf.							
730	1¢ sheet of 25 (728)	08/25/33	27.50	27.50			100.00	0.4
a	Single stamp from sheet		.75	.45			3.25 (3)	11
731	3¢ sheet of 25 (729)	08/25/33	25.00	25.00			100.00	0.4
a	Single stamp from sheet		.65	.45			3.25	11
	Perf. 10.5 x 11							
732	3¢ NRA	08/15/33	.20	.20	1.50	(4)	3.25	1,978
	Gripper cracks		1.50	—				
	Recut at right		2.00					
	Perf. 11							
733	3¢ Byrd Antarctic Expedition II	10/09/33	.50	.50	14.00	(6)	10.00	5
	Double transfer		2.75	1.00				
734	5¢ Kosciuszko	10/13/33	.55	.25	27.50	(6)	4.50	45
a	Horizontal pair, imperf. vertically		2,250.00		25,000.00	(8)		

	Issues of 1934		Un	U	PB	#	FDC	Q(M)
	National Stamp Exhibition Issue Souvenir Sheet, Without Gum, Imperf.							
735	3¢ sheet of 6 (733)	02/10/34	12.50	10.00			40.00	0.8
a	Single stamp from sheet		2.00	1.65			5.00	4
	Perf. 11							
736	3¢ Maryland Tercentenary	03/23/34	.20	.20	6.00	(6)	1.60	46
	Double transfer		—	—				
	Mothers of America Issue, Perf. 11 x 10.5							
737	3¢ Portrait of his Mother,							
	by James A. McNeill Whistler	05/02/34	.20	.20	1.00	(4)	1.60	193
	Perf. 11							
738	3¢ deep violet (737)	05/02/34	.20	.20	4.25	(6)	1.60	15
739	3¢ Wisconsin Tercentenary	07/07/34	.20	.20	3.00	(6)	1.10	64
a	Vert. pair, imperf. horizontally		350.00					
b	Horiz. pair, imperf. vertically		500.00					
	National Parks Issue, Unwmkd.							
740	1¢ El Capitan, Yosemite							
	(California)	07/16/34	.20	.20	1.00	(6)	2.25	84
	Recut		1.50	.50				
a	Vertical pair, imperf.							
	horizontally, with gum		450.00					
741	2¢ Grand Canyon (Ariz.)	07/24/34	.20	.20	1.25	(6)	2.25	74v
	Double transfer		1.25	—				
a	Vertical pair, imperf.							
	horizontally, with gum		450.00					
b	Horizontal pair, imperf.							
	vertically, with gum		500.00					
742	3¢ Mirror Lake, Mt. Rainier							
	(Washington)	08/03/34	.20	.20	1.75	(6)	2.50	95
a	Vertical pair, imperf.							
	horizontally, with gum		425.00					
743	4¢ Cliff Palace, Mesa Verde							
	(Colorado)	09/25/34	.35	.40	7.00	(6)	2.25	19
a	Vertical pair, imperf.							
	horizontally, with gum		700.00					
744	5¢ Old Faithful, Yellowstone							
	(Wyoming)	07/30/34	.70	.65	8.75	(6)	2.25	30
a	Horizontal pair, imperf.							
	vertically, with gum		500.00					
745	6¢ Crater Lake (Oregon)	09/05/34	1.10	.85	15.00	(6)	3.00	16
746	7¢ Great Head, Acadia							
	Park (Maine)	10/02/34	.60	.75	10.00	(6)	3.00	15
a	Horizontal pair, imperf.							
	vertically, with gum		700.00					
747	8¢ Great White Throne,							
	Zion Park (Utah)	09/18/34	1.60	1.50	15.00	(6)	3.25	15
748	9¢ Glacier National Park							
	(Montana)	08/27/34	1.50	.65	15.00	(6)	3.50	17
749	10¢ Great Smoky Mountains							
	(North Carolina)	10/08/34	3.00	1.25	22.50	(6)	6.00	18
	American Philatelic Society Issue Souvenir Sheet, Imperf.							
750	3¢ sheet of 6 (742)	08/28/34	30.00	27.50			40.00	0.5
a	Single stamp from sheet		3.50	3.25			3.25	3
	Trans-Mississippi Philatelic Exposition Issue Souvenir Sheet							
751	1¢ sheet of 6 (740)	10/10/34	12.50	12.50			35.00	0.7
a	Single stamp from sheet		1.40	1.60			3.25 (3)	4

735

736

737

739

740

741

742

744

743

745

746

747

748

749

750

751

Examples of Special Printing Position Blocks

Gutter Block 752

Centerline Block 754

Line Block 756

Arrow Block 763

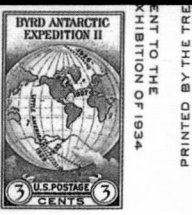

Cross-Gutter Block 768

	Issues of 1935		Un	U	PB	#	FDC	Q(M)
	Special Printing (#752-71), Without Gum, Perf. 10.5 x 11							
752	3¢ violet Peace of 1783 (727)	03/15/35	.20	.20	20.00	(4)	5.00	3
	Perf. 11							
753	3¢ blue Byrd Expedition II (733)	03/15/35	.50	.45	17.50	(6)	6.00	2
	Imperf.							
754	3¢ dp. vio. Whistler's Mother (737)	03/15/35	.60	.60	16.00	(6)	6.00	2
755	3¢ deep violet Wisconsin (739)	03/15/35	.60	.60	16.00	(6)	6.00	2
756	1¢ green Yosemite (740)	03/15/35	.20	.20	5.25	(6)	6.00	3
757	2¢ red Grand Canyon (741)	03/15/35	.25	.25	6.00	(6)	6.00	3
	Double transfer		—					
758	3¢ deep violet Mt. Rainier (742)	03/15/35	.50	.45	15.00	(6)	6.00	2
759	4¢ brown Mesa Verde (743)	03/15/35	.95	.95	20.00	(6)	6.50	2
760	5¢ blue Yellowstone (744)	03/15/35	1.50	1.30	25.00	(6)	6.50	2
	Double transfer		—					
761	6¢ dark blue Crater Lake (745)	03/15/35	2.40	2.10	35.00	(6)	6.50	2
762	7¢ black Acadia (746)	03/15/35	1.50	1.40	30.00	(6)	6.50	2
	Double transfer		—					
763	8¢ sage green Zion (747)	03/15/35	1.60	1.50	37.50	(6)	7.50	2
764	9¢ red orange Glacier (748)	03/15/35	1.90	1.65	42.50	(6)	7.50	2
765	10¢ gray black Smoky Mts. (749)	03/15/35	3.75	3.25	50.00	(6)	7.50	2
766	1¢ yellow grn. (728), pane of 25	03/15/35	25.00	25.00			250.00	0.1
a	Single stamp from pane		.70	.40			5.50 (3)	2
767	3¢ violet (729), pane of 25	03/15/35	23.50	23.50			250.00	0.09
a	Single stamp from pane		.60	.40			5.50	2
768	3¢ dark blue (733), pane of 6	03/15/35	20.00	15.00			250.00	0.3
a	Single stamp from pane		2.80	2.40			6.50	2
769	1¢ green (740), pane of 6	03/15/35	12.50	11.00			250.00	0.3
a	Single stamp from pane		1.85	1.80			4.00	2
770	3¢ deep violet (742), pane of 6	03/15/35	30.00	24.00			250.00	0.2
a	Single stamp from pane		3.25	3.10			5.00	1
771	16¢ dark blue Great Seal of U.S.	03/15/35	2.40	2.25	52.50	(6)	12.50	1
	For perforate variety, see #CE2.							

A number of position pieces can be collected from the panes or sheets of the 1935 Special Printing issues, including horizontal and vertical gutter (#752, 766-70) or line (#753-65, 771) blocks of four (HG/L and VG/L), arrow-and-guideline blocks of four (AGL) and crossed-gutter or centerline blocks of four (CG/L). Pairs sell for half the price of blocks of four. Arrow-and-guideline blocks are top or bottom only.

	HG/L	VG/L	AGL	CG/L		HG/L	VG/L	AGL	CG/L
752	11.50	19.00		50.00	762	8.50	7.50	8.25	14.00
753	4.50	50.00	52.50	57.50	763	7.50	9.50	11.00	17.50
754	3.50	2.80	3.00	7.25	764	10.00	9.00	10.50	22.50
755	3.50	2.80	3.00	7.25	765	18.00	21.00	24.00	30.00
756	.90	1.10	1.25	3.00	766	11.00	14.00		15.00
757	1.40	1.10	1.25	3.50	767	10.50	13.50		15.00
758	2.80	2.50	2.75	5.25	768	15.00	18.00		20.00
759	5.50	4.50	4.75	8.50	769	12.00	18.00		15.00
760	7.00	8.50	9.00	15.00	770	25.00	22.00		30.00
761	13.00	11.00	12.50	20.00	771	13.00	11.00	12.50	60.00

Issues of 1935		Un	U	PB	#	FD	Q(M)
Perf. 11 x 10.5							
Beginning with #772, unused values are for never-hinged stamps.							
772	3¢ Connecticut 04/26/35	.20	.20	1.40	(4)	10.00	71
	Defect in cent design	1.00	.25				
773	3¢ California Pacific						
	International Expo 05/29/35	.20	.20	1.25	(4)	10.00	101
	Pair with full vertical gutter between	—					
	Perf. 11						
774	3¢ Boulder Dam 09/30/35	.20	.20	1.65	(6)	10.00	74
	Perf. 11 x 10.5						
775	3¢ Michigan Statehood 11/01/35	.20	.20	1.25	(4)	10.00	76
	Issues of 1936						
776	3¢ Republic of Texas 03/02/36	.20	.20	1.10	(4)	17.50	124
	Perf. 10.5 x 11						
777	3¢ Rhode Island 05/04/36	.20	.20	1.10	(4)	9.00	67
	Pair with full gutter between	200.00					
	Third International Philatelic Exhibition Issue Souvenir Sheet, Imperf.						
778	Sheet of 4 different stamps						
	(#772, 773, 775 and 776) 05/09/36	1.75	1.75			13.00	3
a-d	Single stamp from sheet	.40	.30				3
779-81	Not assigned						
	Perf. 11 x 10.5						
782	3¢ Arkansas Statehood 06/15/36	.20	.20	1.10	(4)	9.00	73
783	3¢ Oregon Territory 07/14/36	.20	.20	1.10	(4)	8.50	74
	Double transfer	1.00	.50				
784	3¢ Susan B. Anthony 8/26/36	.20	.20	.75	(4)	9.00	270
	Period missing after "B"	.75	.25				

Howard Paine

A member of the Citizens' Stamp Advisory Committee before being named art director in 1981, Howard Paine has supervised the design of more than 400 U.S. postage stamps. As art director for the National Geographic Society for more than 30 years, he redesigned its magazine, developed the children's  magazine, *National Geographic World*, and designed Explorers Hall. A popular lecturer, he has spoken at Yale and New York University, among others, and presented programs for the National Park Service and the Smithsonian Institution. He judges art shows and design competitions and has taught magazine design at the George Washington University. A resident of Delaplane, Virginia, he has been a stamp collector since childhood. He designed the catalog, *Pushing The Envelope: The Art of the Postage Stamp*, for The Norman Rockwell Museum exhibit which opened in November 2000. ■

772

773

774

775

776

777

UNDER AUTHORITY OF
JAMES A. FARLEY, POSTMASTER GENERAL

NEW YORK, N.Y., MAY 9-17, 1936
PLATE NUMBER 21558

778

785

786

787

788

789

790

791

792

793

794

795

796

798

799

800

801

802

	Issues of 1936-37		Un	U	PB	#	FDC	Q(M)
	Army Issue, Perf. 11 x 10.5							
785	1¢ George Washington, Nathaniel Green and Mount Vernon	12/15/36	.20	.20	.85	(4)	6.00	105
	Pair with full vertical gutter between		—					
786	2¢ Andrew Jackson, Winfield Scott and The Hermitage	01/15/37	.20	.20	.85	(4)	6.00	94
787	3¢ Generals Sherman, Grant and Sheridan	02/18/37	.20	.20	1.10	(4)	6.00	88
788	4¢ Generals Robert E. Lee and "Stonewall" Jackson and Stratford Hall	03/23/37	.30	.20	8.00	(4)	6.00	36
789	5¢ U.S. Military Academy at West Point	05/26/37	.60	.20	8.50	(4)	6.00	37
	Navy Issue							
790	1¢ John Paul Jones, John Barry, *Bon Homme Richard* and *Lexington*	12/15/36	.20	.20	.85	(4)	6.00	105
791	2¢ Stephen Decatur, Thomas Macdonough and *Saratoga*	01/15/37	.20	.20	.75	(4)	6.00	92
792	3¢ David G. Farragut and David D. Porter, *Hartford* and *Powhatan*	02/18/37	.20	.20	1.00	(4)	6.00	93
793	4¢ Admirals William T. Sampson, George Dewey and Winfield S. Schley	03/23/37	.30	.20	8.50	(4)	6.00	35
794	5¢ Seal of U.S. Naval Academy and Naval Cadets	05/26/37	.60	.20	8.50	(4)	6.00	37
	Issues of 1937							
795	3¢ Northwest Territory Ordinance	07/13/37	.20	.20	1.10	(4)	7.00	85
	Perf. 11							
796	5¢ Virginia Dare	08/18/37	.20	.20	6.50	(6)	9.00	25
	Society of Philatelic Americans Issue Souvenir Sheet, Imperf.							
797	10¢ blue green (749)	08/26/37	.60	.40			8.00	5
	Perf. 11 x 10.5							
798	3¢ Constitution Sesquicentennial	09/17/37	.20	.20	1.00	(4)	8.00	100
	Territorial Issues, Perf. 10.5 x 11							
799	3¢ Hawaii	10/18/37	.20	.20	1.25	(4)	8.00	78
	Perf. 11 x 10.5							
800	3¢ Alaska	11/12/37	.20	.20	1.25	(4)	8.00	77
	Pair with full gutter between		—					
801	3¢ Puerto Rico	11/25/37	.20	.20	1.25	(4)	8.00	81
802	3¢ Virgin Islands	12/15/37	.20	.20	1.25	(4)	8.00	76
	Pair with full vertical gutter between	275.00						

Issues of 1938-39		Un	U	PB	#	FDC
Presidential Issue, Perf. 11 x 10.5 (#804b, 806b, 807a issued in 1939, 832b in 1951, 832c in 1954, rest in 1938; see also 839-51)						
803	½¢ Benjamin Franklin 05/19/38	.20	.20	.35	(4)	2.25
804	1¢ George Washington 04/25/38	.20	.20	.25	(4)	2.50
	Pair with full vertical gutter between	160.00	—			
b	Booklet pane of 6 01/27/39	2.00	.35			
805	1½¢ Martha Washington 05/05/38	.20	.20	.20	(4)	2.50
	Pair with full horizontal gutter between	175.00				
b	Horizontal pair, imperf. between	160.00	30.00			
806	2¢ John Adams 06/03/38	.20	.20	.30	(4)	2.50
	Recut at top of head	3.00	1.50			
b	Booklet pane of 6 01/27/39	4.75	.85			15.00
807	3¢ Thomas Jefferson 06/16/38	.20	.20	.25	(4)	2.50
a	Booklet pane of 6 01/27/39	8.50	1.25			17.50
b	Horizontal pair, imperf. between	900.00	—			
c	Imperf., pair	2,500.00				
808	4¢ James Madison 07/01/38	.75	.20	3.75	(4)	2.50
809	4½¢ The White House 07/11/38	.20	.20	1.50	(4)	2.50
810	5¢ James Monroe 07/21/38	.20	.20	1.00	(4)	2.50
811	6¢ John Quincy Adams 07/28/38	.20	.20	1.00	(4)	2.50
812	7¢ Andrew Jackson 08/04/38	.25	.20	1.25	(4)	2.50
813	8¢ Martin Van Buren 08/11/38	.30	.20	1.40	(4)	2.50
814	9¢ William H. Harrison 08/18/38	.30	.20	1.40	(4)	3.00
	Pair with full vertical gutter between	—				
815	10¢ John Tyler 09/02/38	.25	.20	1.25	(4)	3.00
816	11¢ James K. Polk 09/08/38	.65	.20	3.00	(4)	3.50
817	12¢ Zachary Taylor 09/14/38	.90	.20	4.25	(4)	3.50
818	13¢ Millard Fillmore 09/22/38	1.25	.20	6.50	(4)	3.50
819	14¢ Franklin Pierce 10/06/38	.90	.20	4.50	(4)	3.50
820	15¢ James Buchanan 10/13/38	.40	.20	1.90	(4)	3.50
821	16¢ Abraham Lincoln 10/20/38	.90	.25	4.50	(4)	5.00
822	17¢ Andrew Johnson 10/27/38	.85	.20	4.50	(4)	5.00
823	18¢ Ulysses S. Grant 11/03/38	1.75	.20	8.75	(4)	5.00
824	19¢ Rutherford B. Hayes 11/10/38	1.25	.35	6.25	(4)	5.00
825	20¢ James A. Garfield 11/10/38	.70	.20	3.50	(4)	5.00
826	21¢ Chester A. Arthur 11/22/38	1.25	.20	7.00	(4)	5.50
827	22¢ Grover Cleveland 11/22/38	1.00	.40	9.50	(4)	5.50
828	24¢ Benjamin Harrison 12/02/38	3.50	.20	17.00	(4)	5.50
829	25¢ William McKinley 12/02/38	.60	.20	3.00	(4)	6.25
830	30¢ Theodore Roosevelt 12/08/38	3.50	.20	16.00	(4)	7.75
831	50¢ William Howard Taft 12/08/38	5.50	.20	24.00	(4)	10.00

832

833

834

835

836

837

838

852

853

854

855

856

857

858

Issues of 1938-54			Un	U	PB/LP	#	FDC	Q(M)
Perf. 11								
832	$1 Woodrow Wilson	08/29/38	7.00	.20	35.00	(4)	50.00	
a	Vertical pair, imperf. horizontally		*1,600.00*					
b	Watermarked "USIR" (1951)			250.00	65.00	1,550.00	(4)	
c	$1 red violet and black	08/31/54	6.00	.20	30.00	(4)	25.00	
d	As "c," vert. pair, imperf. horiz.		*1,250.00*					
e	Vertical pair, imperf. between		*2,750.00*					
f	As "c," vert. pair, imperf. between		*7,000.00*					
833	$2 Warren G. Harding	09/29/38	20.00	3.75	95.00	(4)	100.00	
834	$5 Calvin Coolidge	11/17/38	95.00	3.00	440.00	(4)	150.00	
a	$5 red, brown and black		3,250.00	4,000.00				
Issues of 1938, Perf. 11 x 10.5								
835	3¢ Constitution Ratification	06/21/38	.25	.20	3.50	(4)	9.00	73
Perf. 11								
836	3¢ Swedish-Finnish Tercentenary	06/27/38	.20	.20	2.50	(6)	9.00	59
Perf. 11 x 10.5								
837	3¢ Northwest Territory	07/15/38	.20	.20	7.50	(4)	9.00	66
838	3¢ Iowa Territorial Centennial	08/24/38	.20	.20	5.00	(4)	9.00	47
	Pair with full vertical gutter between		—					
Issues of 1939, Coil Stamps, Perf. 10 Vertically								
839	1¢ green Washington (804)	01/20/39	.30	.20	1.40	(2)	4.75	
840	1½¢ bister brn.							
	Martha Washington (805)	01/20/39	.30	.20	1.50	(2)	4.75	
841	2¢ rose carmine							
	John Adams (806)	01/20/39	.40	.20	1.75	(2)	4.75	
842	3¢ deep violet Jefferson (807)	01/20/39	.50	.20	2.00	(2)	4.75	
	Gripper cracks		—					
	Thin, translucent paper		2.50	—				
843	4¢ red violet Madison (808)	01/20/39	8.00	.40	27.50	(2)	5.00	
844	4½¢ dark gray							
	White House (809)	01/20/38	.70	.40	5.00	(2)	5.00	
845	5¢ bright blue Monroe (810)	01/20/39	5.00	.35	27.50	(2)	5.00	
846	6¢ red orange							
	John Quincy Adams (811)	01/20/39	1.10	.20	7.50	(2)	6.50	
847	10¢ brown red Tyler (815)	01/20/39	11.00	.50	42.50	(2)	9.00	
Coil Stamps, Perf. 10 Horizontally								
848	1¢ green Washington (804)	01/27/39	.85	.20	2.75	(2)	5.00	
849	1½¢ bister brn.							
	Martha Washington (805)	01/27/39	1.25	.30	4.50	(2)	5.00	
850	2¢ rose carmine							
	John Adams (806)	01/27/39	2.50	.40	6.50	(2)	5.00	
851	3¢ deep violet Jefferson (807)	01/27/39	2.25	.35	6.25	(2)	5.50	
Perf. 10.5 x 11								
852	3¢ Golden Gate Exposition	02/18/39	.20	.20	1.25	(4)	6.00	114
853	3¢ New York World's Fair	04/01/39	.20	.20	1.75	(4)	12.50	102
Perf. 11								
854	3¢ Washington's Inauguration	04/30/39	.40	.20	3.50	(6)	6.00	73
Perf. 11 x 10.5								
855	3¢ Baseball	06/12/39	1.75	.20	7.50	(4)	35.00	81
Perf. 11								
856	3¢ Panama Canal	08/15/39	.25	.20	3.00	(6)	6.50	68
Perf. 10.5 x 11								
857	3¢ Printing	09/25/39	.20	.20	1.00	(4)	5.00	71
Perf. 11 x 10.5								
858	3¢ 50th Anniversary of Statehood (Montana, North Dakota, South Dakota, Washington)	11/02/39	.20	.20	1.10	(4)	5.00	67

1940

Issues of 1940			Un	U	PB	#	FDC	Q(M)
Famous Americans Issue, Perf. 10.5 x 11								
Authors								
859	1¢ Washington Irving	01/29/40	.20	.20	.95	(4)	2.00	56
860	2¢ James Fenimore Cooper	01/29/40	.20	.20	.95	(4)	2.00	53
861	3¢ Ralph Waldo Emerson	02/05/40	.20	.20	1.25	(4)	2.00	53
862	5¢ Louisa May Alcott	02/05/40	.30	.20	8.25	(4)	3.00	22
863	10¢ Samuel L. Clemens							
	(Mark Twain)	02/13/40	1.65	1.20	32.50	(4)	4.50	13
Poets								
864	1¢ Henry W. Longfellow	02/16/40	.20	.20	1.75	(4)	2.00	52
865	2¢ John Greenleaf Whittier	02/16/40	.20	.20	1.75	(4)	2.00	52
866	3¢ James Russell Lowell	02/20/40	.20	.20	2.25	(4)	2.00	52
867	5¢ Walt Whitman	02/20/40	.35	.20	9.00	(4)	4.00	22
868	10¢ James Whitcomb Riley	02/24/40	1.75	1.25	30.00	(4)	6.00	12
Educators								
869	1¢ Horace Mann	03/14/40	.20	.20	1.90	(4)	2.00	52
870	2¢ Mark Hopkins	03/14/40	.20	.20	1.25	(4)	2.00	52
871	3¢ Charles W. Eliot	03/28/40	.20	.20	2.25	(4)	2.00	52
872	5¢ Frances E. Willard	03/28/40	.40	.20	9.00	(4)	4.00	21
873	10¢ Booker T. Washington	04/07/40	1.25	1.10	25.00	(4)	6.50	14
Scientists								
874	1¢ John James Audubon	04/08/40	.20	.20	.95	(4)	2.00	59
875	2¢ Dr. Crawford W. Long	04/08/40	.20	.20	.95	(4)	2.00	58
876	3¢ Luther Burbank	04/17/40	.20	.20	1.10	(4)	2.00	58
877	5¢ Dr. Walter Reed	04/17/40	.25	.20	5.00	(4)	3.00	24
878	10¢ Jane Addams	04/26/40	1.10	.85	16.00	(4)	5.00	15
Composers								
879	1¢ Stephen Collins Foster	05/03/40	.20	.20	1.00	(4)	2.00	57
880	2¢ John Philip Sousa	05/03/40	.20	.20	1.00	(4)	2.00	58
881	3¢ Victor Herbert	05/13/40	.20	.20	1.10	(4)	2.00	56
882	5¢ Edward A. MacDowell	05/13/40	.40	.20	9.25	(4)	3.00	21
883	10¢ Ethelbert Nevin	06/10/40	3.75	1.35	32.50	(4)	5.00	13
Artists								
884	1¢ Gilbert Charles Stuart	09/05/40	.20	.20	1.00	(4)	2.00	54
885	2¢ James A. McNeill Whistler	09/05/40	.20	.20	.95	(4)	2.00	54
886	3¢ Augustus Saint-Gaudens	09/16/40	.20	.20	1.00	(4)	2.00	55
887	5¢ Daniel Chester French	09/16/40	.50	.20	8.00	(4)	3.00	22
888	10¢ Frederic Remington	09/30/40	1.75	1.25	20.00	(4)	5.00	14
Inventors								
889	1¢ Eli Whitney	10/07/40	.20	.20	1.90	(4)	2.00	48
890	2¢ Samuel F.B. Morse	10/07/40	.20	.20	1.10	(4)	2.00	53
891	3¢ Cyrus Hall McCormick	10/14/40	.25	.20	1.75	(4)	2.00	54
892	5¢ Elias Howe	10/14/40	1.10	.30	12.50	(4)	3.00	20
893	10¢ Alexander Graham Bell	10/28/40	11.00	2.00	65.00	(4)	7.50	14

859 860 861 862 863

864 865 866 867 868

869 870 871 872 873

874 875 876 877 878

879 880 881 882 883

884 885 886 887 888

889 890 891 892 893

894

895

896

897

898

899

900

901

902

903

904

905

906

907

908

	Issues of 1940		Un	U	PB	#	FDC	Q(M)
894	3¢ Pony Express	04/03/40	.25	.20	2.75	(4)	6.00	46
	Perf. 10.5 x 11							
895	3¢ Pan American Union	04/14/40	.20	.20	2.75	(4)	4.50	48
	Perf. 11 x 10.5							
896	3¢ Idaho Statehood	07/03/40	.20	.20	1.75	(4)	4.50	51
	Perf. 10.5 x 11							
897	3¢ Wyoming Statehood	07/10/40	.20	.20	1.50	(4)	4.50	50
	Perf. 11 x 10.5							
898	3¢ Coronado Expedition	09/07/40	.20	.20	1.50	(4)	4.50	61
	National Defense Issue							
899	1¢ Statue of Liberty	10/16/40	.20	.20	.45	(4)	4.25	
	Cracked plate		3.00					
	Gripper cracks		3.00					
a	Vertical pair, imperf. between		650.00	—				
b	Horizontal pair, imperf. between		35.00	—				
	Pair with full vertical gutter between		200.00					
900	2¢ 90mm Antiaircraft Gun	10/16/40	.20	.20	.45	(4)	4.25	
a	Horizontal pair, imperf. between		40.00	—				
	Pair with full vertical gutter between		275.00					
901	3¢ Torch of Enlightenment	10/16/40	.20	.20	.60	(4)	4.25	
a	Horizontal pair, imperf. between		27.50	—				
	Pair with full vertical gutter between		—					
	Perf. 10.5 x 11							
902	3¢ Thirteenth Amendment	10/20/40	.20	.20	3.00	(4)	7.50	44
	Issue of 1941, Perf. 11 x 10.5							
903	3¢ Vermont Statehood	03/04/41	.20	.20	1.75	(4)	7.00	55
	Issues of 1942							
904	3¢ Kentucky Statehood	06/01/42	.20	.20	1.10	(4)	4.00	64
905	3¢ Win the War	07/04/42	.20	.20	.40	(4)	3.75	
	Pair with full vertical or horizontal gutter between		175.00					
b	3¢ purple		—	—				
906	5¢ Chinese Resistance	07/07/42	.85	.20	10.00	(4)	6.00	21
	Issues of 1943							
907	2¢ Allied Nations	01/14/43	.20	.20	.30	(4)	3.50	1,700
	Pair with full vertical or horizontal gutter between		225.00					
908	1¢ Four Freedoms	02/12/43	.20	.20	.60	(4)	3.50	1,200

Ethel Kessler

Ethel Kessler has been an art director for the U.S. Postal Service since 1996. The Breast Cancer semipostal, first of her more than 50 released stamp designs, was issued in July 1998. Sales of this stamp have raised more than $19 million for breast cancer research. After graduating from the Maryland Institute, College of Art with a degree in visual communications, she worked as a graphic designer and exhibits project manager at the United States Information Agency. In 1981, she established Kessler Design Group. A designer, art director, and design consultant, her clients include corporations, museums, and public and private institutions. Honored by numerous design organizations including *Graphis*, *Communications Arts*, the Art Directors Club in New York and Washington, D.C., and the Society of Illustrators, she is enthusiastic about interpreting America's story in such a challenging medium. ■

Issues of 1943-44		Un	U	PB	#	FDC	Q(M)
Overrun Countries Issue, Perf. 12							
909	5¢ Poland	06/22/43	.20	.20	4.50*	(4)	7.50	20
910	5¢ Czechoslovakia	07/12/43	.20	.20	2.75*	(4)	4.00	20
911	5¢ Norway	07/27/43	.20	.20	1.40*	(4)	4.00	20
912	5¢ Luxembourg	08/10/43	.20	.20	1.30*	(4)	4.00	20
913	5¢ Netherlands	08/24/43	.20	.20	1.30*	(4)	4.00	20
914	5¢ Belgium	09/14/43	.20	.20	1.15*	(4)	4.00	20
915	5¢ France	09/28/43	.20	.20	1.25*	(4)	4.00	20
916	5¢ Greece	10/12/43	.35	.25	11.00*	(4)	4.00	15
917	5¢ Yugoslavia	10/26/43	.25	.20	4.50*	(4)	4.00	15
918	5¢ Albania	11/09/43	.20	.20	4.25*	(4)	4.00	15
919	5¢ Austria	11/23/43	.20	.20	3.75*	(4)	4.00	15
920	5¢ Denmark	12/07/43	.20	.20	5.75*	(4)	4.00	15
921	5¢ Korea	11/02/44	.20	.20	4.75*	(4)	5.00	15
	"KORPA" plate flaw		17.50	12.50				
*Instead of plate numbers, the selvage is inscribed with the name of the country.							
Issues of 1944, Perf. 11 x 10.5							
922	3¢ Transcontinental Railroad	05/10/44	.20	.20	1.40	(4)	6.00	61
923	3¢ Steamship	05/22/44	.20	.20	1.25	(4)	4.00	61
924	3¢ Telegraph	05/24/44	.20	.20	.90	(4)	3.50	61
925	3¢ Philippines	09/27/44	.20	.20	1.10	(4)	3.50	50
926	3¢ Motion Pictures	10/31/44	.20	.20	.90	(4)	4.00	53

Phil Jordan

Phil Jordan grew up in New Bern, North Carolina, and attended East Carolina University. After Army service in Alaska, he graduated from Virginia Commonwealth University with a degree in visual communications. He worked in advertising and in design at a trade association before joining Beveridge and Associates, Inc., where he provided art direction for corporate, institutional, and government design projects. A partner in the firm, he left after 18 years to establish his own design firm where he has managed projects for USAir, NASA, McGraw-Hill, IBM, and Smithsonian Books, among others. He was Design Director of *Air & Space/Smithsonian* magazine for 15 years. His work has appeared in numerous exhibitions and publications such as *Graphis* and *Communications Arts*. A past president of the Art Directors Club of Metropolitan Washington, he has been an art director for the U.S. Postal Service since 1991. A resident of Falls Church, Virginia, he is an avid glider pilot and a member of the Skyline Soaring Club. ■

UNITED STATES POSTAGE
5 POLAND 5 CENTS
909

UNITED STATES POSTAGE
5 CZECHOSLOVAKIA 5 CENTS
910

UNITED STATES POSTAGE
5 NORWAY 5 CENTS
911

UNITED STATES POSTAGE
5 LUXEMBURG 5 CENTS
912

UNITED STATES POSTAGE
5 NETHERLANDS 5 CENTS
913

UNITED STATES POSTAGE
5 BELGIUM 5 CENTS
914

UNITED STATES POSTAGE
5 FRANCE 5 CENTS
915

UNITED STATES POSTAGE
5 GREECE 5 CENTS
916

UNITED STATES POSTAGE
5 YUGOSLAVIA 5 CENTS
917

UNITED STATES POSTAGE
5 ALBANIA 5 CENTS
918

UNITED STATES POSTAGE
5 AUSTRIA 5 CENTS
919

UNITED STATES POSTAGE
5 DENMARK 5 CENTS
920

UNITED STATES POSTAGE
5 KOREA 5 CENTS
921

1869 1944
COMPLETION OF FIRST TRANSCONTINENTAL RAILROAD
UNITED STATES OF AMERICA
3¢
922

FIRST STEAMSHIP TO CROSS THE ATLANTIC
1819 1944
3¢
UNITED STATES POSTAGE
923

CENTENARY OF THE TELEGRAPH
WHAT HATH GOD BROUGHT
1844 1944
3¢
UNITED STATES POSTAGE
924

UNITED STATES OF AMERICA
CORREGIDOR
5¢

UNITED STATES OF AMERICA
3¢ 50TH ANNIVERSARY OF MOTION PICTURES
POSTAGE

927

928

929

930

931

932

933

934

935

936

937

938

939

940

941

942

943

944

945

946

947

	Issues of 1945, Perf. 11 x 10.5		Un	U	PB	#	FDC	Q(M)
927	3¢ Florida Statehood	03/03/45	.20	.20	.50	(4)	4.50	62
928	5¢ United Nations Conference	04/25/45	.20	.20	.45	(4)	5.00	76
	Perf. 10.5 x 11							
929	3¢ Iwo Jima (Marines)	07/11/45	.20	.20	.40	(4)	10.00	137
	Issues of 1945-46, Franklin D. Roosevelt Issue, Perf. 11 x 10.5							
930	1¢ Roosevelt and Hyde Park							
	Residence	07/26/45	.20	.20	.20	(4)	3.50	128
931	2¢ Roosevelt and "The Little White House"							
	at Warm Springs, Ga.	08/24/45	.20	.20	.25	(4)	3.50	67
932	3¢ Roosevelt and White House	06/27/45	.20	.20	.30	(4)	3.50	134
933	5¢ Roosevelt, Map of Western							
	Hemisphere and Four Freedoms	01/30/46	.20	.20	.45	(4)	3.50	76
934	3¢ Army, Sept. 28	09/28/45	.20	.20	.40	(4)	6.00	128
935	3¢ Navy	10/27/45	.20	.20	.40	(4)	6.00	136
936	3¢ Coast Guard	11/10/45	.20	.20	.40	(4)	6.00	112
937	3¢ Alfred E. Smith	11/26/45	.20	.20	.40	(4)	2.50	309
	Pair with full vertical gutter between	—						
938	3¢ Texas Statehood	12/29/45	.20	.20	.30	(4)	4.00	171
	Issues of 1946							
939	3¢ Merchant Marine	02/26/46	.20	.20	.40	(4)	5.00	136
940	3¢ Veterans of World War II	05/09/46	.20	.20	.35	(4)	4.00	260
941	3¢ Tennessee Statehood	06/01/46	.20	.20	.30	(4)	1.50	132
942	3¢ Iowa Statehood	08/03/46	.20	.20	.30	(4)	1.50	132
943	3¢ Smithsonian Institution	08/10/46	.20	.20	.30	(4)	1.50	139
944	3¢ Kearny Expedition	10/16/46	.20	.20	.30	(4)	1.50	115
	Issues of 1947, Perf. 10.5 x 11							
945	3¢ Thomas A. Edison	02/11/47	.20	.20	.35	(4)	3.00	157
	Perf. 11 x 10.5							
946	3¢ Joseph Pulitzer	04/10/47	.20	.20	.35	(4)	1.50	120
947	3¢ Postage Stamps Centenary	05/17/47	.20	.20	.30	(4)	1.50	127

Carl Herrman

An art director for the U.S. Postal Service since 1992, Carl Herrman has designed more than 250 commemorative stamps including those honoring Marilyn Monroe, James Dean, Legendary Football Coaches, Comic Strip Classics, and American Illustrators. Educated at the New York College of Technology, Syracuse University, and American University, he has held public relations and marketing positions at universities in Florida and California. A teacher and lecturer, he has provided consulting services for clients such as BMW of North America, USAir, the President's Council on Physical Fitness and Sports, and the Smithsonian Institution. He has won more than 260 awards from design groups including the Art Directors Club in both New York and Washington, D.C., the Society of Illustrators, and *Communication Arts*. This former editor of *Surfing East* continues to search for the perfect wave and often can be seen driving to the beaches near his Carlsbad, California, home in his restored red Citroën. ∎

Want **More Stamps**?

Buy **Press Sheets**

*Here's a great
way to make
your collection
even more
valuable!*

Press Sheets
are unique collectibles
featuring six or more
panes of the new
stamp issues. They
vary in cost from
$28.00–$62.00.

*Prices subject to
change without notice.

Buy Stamped Cards

Indian Peace Flag
1803

Easton Flag
1814

Star-Spangled Banner
1814

Bennington Flag
c.1820

Legends of Baseball

Produced for select issues only. Press Sheets and Stamp Cards are a great way to augment your collection!

Stamped Cards depict related stamp designs and are issued in sets of 10 or 20, varying in cost from $6.95–$8.95 a set.

To order or for more information call **1 800 STAMP-24**. Customers may order online by visiting the Postal Service's Web site at **www.usps.com** and clicking on the Postal Store. Source Code: #39002.

Issues of 1947		Un	U	PB	#	FDC	Q(M)
Centenary International Philatelic Exhibition Issue Souvenir Sheet, Imperf.							
948 Souvenir sheet of 2							
stamps (#1-2)	05/19/47	.55	.45			2.00	10
a 5¢ single stamp from sheet		.20	.20				
b 10¢ single stamp from sheet		.25	.25				
Perf. 11 x 10.5							
949 3¢ Doctors	06/09/47	.20	.20	.30	(4)	2.50	133
950 3¢ Utah Settlement	07/24/47	.20	.20	.30	(4)	1.00	132
951 3¢ U.S. Frigate *Constitution*	10/21/47	.20	.20	.30	(4)	6.00	131
Perf. 10.5 x 11							
952 3¢ Everglades National Park	12/05/47	.20	.20	.30	(4)	1.00	122
Issues of 1948							
953 3¢ Dr. G.W. Carver	01/05/48	.20	.20	.35	(4)	1.00	122
Perf. 11 x 10.5							
954 3¢ California Gold	01/24/48	.20	.20	.30	(4)	1.00	131
955 3¢ Mississippi Territory	04/07/48	.20	.20	.30	(4)	1.00	123
956 3¢ Four Chaplains	05/28/48	.20	.20	.40	(4)	3.00	122
957 3¢ Wisconsin Statehood	05/29/48	.20	.20	.30	(4)	1.00	115
958 5¢ Swedish Pioneer	06/04/48	.20	.20	.45	(4)	1.00	64
959 3¢ Progress of Women	07/19/48	.20	.20	.30	(4)	1.00	118
Perf. 10.5 x 11							
960 3¢ William Allen White	07/31/48	.20	.20	.40	(4)	1.00	78
Perf. 11 x 10.5							
961 3¢ U.S.-Canada Friendship	08/02/48	.20	.20	.30	(4)	1.00	113
962 3¢ Francis Scott Key	08/09/48	.20	.20	.30	(4)	1.00	121
963 3¢ Salute to Youth	08/11/48	.20	.20	.30	(4)	1.00	78
964 3¢ Oregon Territory	08/14/48	.20	.20	.35	(4)	1.00	52
Perf. 10.5 x 11							
965 3¢ Harlan F. Stone	08/25/48	.20	.20	.60	(4)	1.00	54
966 3¢ Palomar Observatory	08/30/48	.20	.20	.95	(4)	2.00	61
a Vertical pair, imperf. between		550.00					
Perf. 11 x 10.5							
967 3¢ Clara Barton	09/07/48	.20	.20	.30	(4)	3.00	58

James Barkley

An avid stamp collector and award-winning illustrator, James Barkley has created images for America's most prestigious corporations and publications including General Foods, IBM, NBC, PepsiCo, Sony, Columbia Pictures, *Esquire*, *National Geographic,* and *McCall's*. He has taught aspiring illustrators as a professor of art at Bridgeport University and Parsons School of Design and served as a trustee of the Society of Illustrators in New York. Passionate about the environment, he has created nature paintings for the U. S. Department of the Interior, the National Park Service, and the United States Postal Service. ∎

"I have been an avid stamp collector all my life. I felt honored to be a part of United States Postal History."

— James Barkley

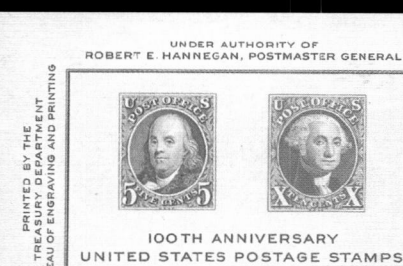

948

949

950

951

952

953

954

955

956

957

958

959

960

961

962

963

964

965

966

967

968

969

970

971

972

973

974

975

976

977

978

979

980

981

982

983

984

985

986

987

988

	Issues of 1948		Un	U	PB	#	FDC	Q(M)
968	3¢ Poultry Industry	09/09/48	.20	.20	.40	(4)	1.25	53
	Perf. 10.5 x 11							
969	3¢ Gold Star Mothers	09/21/48	.20	.20	.35	(4)	1.00	77
	Perf. 11 x 10.5							
970	3¢ Fort Kearny	09/22/48	.20	.20	.35	(4)	1.00	58
971	3¢ Volunteer Firemen	10/04/48	.20	.20	.40	(4)	7.00	56
972	3¢ Indian Centennial	10/15/48	.20	.20	.35	(4)	1.00	58
973	3¢ Rough Riders	10/27/48	.20	.20	.40	(4)	1.00	54
974	3¢ Juliette Gordon Low	10/29/48	.20	.20	.30	(4)	2.25	64
	Perf. 10.5 x 11							
975	3¢ Will Rogers	11/04/48	.20	.20	.40	(4)	1.50	67
976	3¢ Fort Bliss	11/05/48	.20	.20	1.10	(4)	2.00	65
	Perf. 11 x 10.5							
977	3¢ Moina Michael	11/09/48	.20	.20	.35	(4)	1.00	64
978	3¢ Gettysburg Address	11/19/48	.20	.20	.40	(4)	1.00	63
	Perf. 10.5 x 11							
979	3¢ American Turners	11/20/48	.20	.20	.30	(4)	1.00	62
980	3¢ Joel Chandler Harris	12/09/48	.20	.20	.55	(4)	1.25	57
	Issues of 1949, Perf. 11 x 10.5							
981	3¢ Minnesota Territory	03/03/49	.20	.20	.30	(4)	1.00	99
982	3¢ Washington and Lee University	04/12/49	.20	.20	.30	(4)	1.00	105
983	3¢ Puerto Rico Election	04/27/49	.20	.20	.30	(4)	1.00	109
984	3¢ Annapolis Tercentenary	05/23/49	.20	.20	.30	(4)	1.00	107
985	3¢ Grand Army of the Republic	08/29/49	.20	.20	.30	(4)	1.00	117
	Perf. 10.5 x 11							
986	3¢ Edgar Allan Poe	10/07/49	.20	.20	.45	(4)	1.50	123
	Thin outer frame line at top, inner frame line missing		6.00					
	Issues of 1950, Perf. 11 x 10.5							
987	3¢ American Bankers	01/03/50	.20	.20	.35	(4)	2.00	131
	Perf. 10.5 x 11							
988	3¢ Samuel Gompers	01/27/50	.20	.20	.30	(4)	1.00	128

© 1995 OWEN STAYNER

Sabra Field

Born in Oklahoma, Sabra Field grew up in the metropolitan New York area. She earned a bachelor's degree in the arts from Middlebury College which awarded her its Alumni Achievement Award in 1984 and an honorary doctor of arts degree in 1991. She holds a master's degree from Wesleyan University where she studied printmaking. In 1969 she moved to Vermont and established Tontine Press to publish her hand-pulled wood-block prints. She was named an Extraordinary Vermonter in 1991 and received the Governor's Award for Excellence in the Arts in 1999. Well known for her woodcuts, she also uses IRIS ink jet prints as well as stained glass and collage to create commissioned works. She has had more than 50 solo exhibitions of her prints since 1960. Her first U.S. Postal Service stamp design celebrated Vermont's bicentennial in 1991. ■

	Issues of 1950		Un	U	PB	#	FDC	Q(M)
	National Capital Sesquicentennial Issue, Perf. 10.5 x 11, 11 x 10.5							
989	3¢ Statue of Freedom on							
	Capitol Dome	04/20/50	.20	.20	.30	(4)	1.00	132
990	3¢ Executive Mansion	06/12/50	.20	.20	.40	(4)	1.00	130
991	3¢ Supreme Court	08/02/50	.20	.20	.30	(4)	1.00	131
992	3¢ U.S. Capitol	11/22/50	.20	.20	.40	(4)	1.00	130
	Gripper cracks		1.00	.50				
	Perf. 11 x 10.5							
993	3¢ Railroad Engineers	04/29/50	.20	.20	.35	(4)	1.50	122
994	3¢ Kansas City, MO	06/03/50	.20	.20	.30	(4)	1.00	122
995	3¢ Boy Scouts	06/30/50	.20	.20	.35	(4)	5.00	132
996	3¢ Indiana Territory	07/04/50	.20	.20	.30	(4)	1.00	122
997	3¢ California Statehood	09/09/50	.20	.20	.30	(4)	1.00	121
	Issues of 1951							
998	3¢ United Confederate							
	Veterans	05/30/51	.20	.20	.30	(4)	1.00	119
999	3¢ Nevada Settlement	07/14/51	.20	.20	.30	(4)	1.00	112
1000	3¢ Landing of Cadillac	07/24/51	.20	.20	.30	(4)	1.00	114
1001	3¢ Colorado Statehood	08/01/51	.20	.20	.30	(4)	1.00	114
1002	3¢ American Chemical Society	09/04/51	.20	.20	.35	(4)	2.00	117
1003	3¢ Battle of Brooklyn	12/10/51	.20	.20	.30	(4)	1.00	116
	Issues of 1952							
1004	3¢ Betsy Ross	01/02/52	.20	.20	.35	(4)	1.00	116
1005	3¢ 4-H Club	01/15/52	.20	.20	.30	(4)	1.00	116
1006	3¢ B&O Railroad	02/28/52	.20	.20	.40	(4)	1.75	113
1007	3¢ American Automobile							
	Association	03/04/52	.20	.20	.30	(4)	1.00	117

C.F. Payne

Chris Payne's insightful and impudent portraits of the famous and the infamous are often found on the covers and pages of America's leading publications. Praised for his chameleon flexibility and meticulous craftsmanship, he lives and works in his hometown, Cincinnati, Ohio, where he creates distinctive editorial images for *Esquire*, *Time*, *The New York Times*, *Sports Illustrated*, *Entertainment Weekly, Rolling Stone,* and an impressive roster of advertising clients. The recipient of many professional awards and honors, he chairs the Society of Illustrators' museum committee and teaches at the Columbus College of Art. His artwork appears on five United States postage stamps. ■

"Stamps represent the best of our nation. I can only hope that I was up to the challenge."

— C.F. Payne

989

990

991

992

993

994

995

996

997

998

999

1000

1001

1002

1003

1004

1005

1006

1007

1008

1009

1010

1011

1012

1013

1014

1015

1016

1017

1018

1019

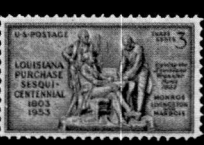

1020

1021

1022

1023

1024

1025

1026

1027

1028

1029

	Issues of 1952		Un	U	PB	#	FDC	Q(M)
1008	3¢ NATO	04/04/52	.20	.20	.30	(4)	1.00	2,900
1009	3¢ Grand Coulee Dam	05/15/52	.20	.20	.30	(4)	1.00	115
1010	3¢ Arrival of Lafayette	06/13/52	.20	.20	.30	(4)	1.00	113
	Perf. 10.5 x 11							
1011	3¢ Mt. Rushmore Memorial	08/11/52	.20	.20	.35	(4)	1.00	116
	Perf. 11 x 10.5							
1012	3¢ Engineering	09/06/52	.20	.20	.30	(4)	1.00	114
1013	3¢ Service Women	09/11/52	.20	.20	.30	(4)	1.00	124
1014	3¢ Gutenberg Bible	09/30/52	.20	.20	.30	(4)	1.00	116
1015	3¢ Newspaper Boys	10/04/52	.20	.20	.30	(4)	1.00	115
1016	3¢ International Red Cross	11/21/52	.20	.20	.30	(4)	1.50	136
	Issues of 1953							
1017	3¢ National Guard	02/23/53	.20	.20	.30	(4)	1.00	115
1018	3¢ Ohio Statehood	03/02/53	.20	.20	.35	(4)	1.00	119
1019	3¢ Washington Territory	03/02/53	.20	.20	.30	(4)	1.00	114
1020	3¢ Louisiana Purchase	04/30/53	.20	.20	.30	(4)	1.00	114
1021	5¢ Opening of Japan	07/14/53	.20	.20	.65	(4)	1.00	89
1022	3¢ American Bar Association	08/24/53	.20	.20	.30	(4)	5.00	115
1023	3¢ Sagamore Hill	09/14/53	.20	.20	.30	(4)	1.00	116
1024	3¢ Future Farmers	10/13/53	.20	.20	.30	(4)	1.00	115
1025	3¢ Trucking Industry	10/27/53	.20	.20	.30	(4)	1.00	124
1026	3¢ General George S. Patton	11/11/53	.20	.20	.40	(4)	4.00	115
1027	3¢ New York City	11/20/53	.20	.20	.35	(4)	1.00	116
1028	3¢ Gadsden Purchase	12/30/53	.20	.20	.30	(4)	1.00	116
	Issue of 1954							
1029	3¢ Columbia University	01/04/54	.20	.20	.30	(4)	1.00	119

Paul Salmon

Award-winning illustrator Paul Salmon has worked with distinguished clients such as the Smithsonian Institution, NBC, the National Geographic Society, Time-Life Books, NASA, and the National Air and Space Museum. His art ranges from pen and ink drawings to full-color paintings which he has created for museums, corporations, and national publications. A graduate of the Richmond Professional Institute, College of William and Mary, he has taught at the Corcoran School of Art in Washington D.C. His work has been honored by the Art Director's Club of Washington, the Society of Illustrators, and Printing Industries of America. Three of his paintings toured with the Smithsonian exhibit "The Artist and the Space Shuttle." The designer of two stamps issued by the U.S. Postal Service, this resident of Burke, Virginia, currently devotes himself to landscape and still-life painting and commissioned work for books and magazines. ■

	Issues of 1954-67		Un	U	PB	#	FDC
	Liberty Issue, Perf. 11 x 10.5						
1030	½¢ Franklin	10/20/55	.20	.20	.25	(4)	1.00
1031	1¢ Washington	03/56	.20	.20	.20	(4)	
	Pair with full vertical or						
	horizontal gutter between		150.00				
b	Wet printing		.20	.20	.20	(4)	1.00
	Perf. 10.5 x 11						
1031A	1¼¢ Palace of the Governors	06/17/60	.20	.20	.45	(4)	1.00
1032	1½¢ Mt. Vernon	02/22/56	.20	.20	1.75	(4)	1.00
	Perf. 11 x 10.5						
1033	2¢ Jefferson	09/15/54	.20	.20	.25	(4)	1.00
	Pair with full vertical or						
	horizontal gutter between		—				
1034	2½¢ Bunker Hill	06/17/59	.20	.20	.50	(4)	1.00
1035	3¢ Statue of Liberty	06/24/54	.20	.20	.25	(4)	
a	Booklet pane of 6	06/30/54	4.00	.90			5.00
b	Tagged	07/06/66	.25	.25	5.00	(4)	15.00
c	Imperf., pair		2,000.00				
d	Horizontal pair, imperf. between		—				
e	Wet printing	06/24/54	.20	.20	.30	(4)	1.00
f	As "a," untagged		5.00	1.10			
g	As "a," vertical imperf. between		5,000.00				
1036	4¢ Lincoln	11/19/54	.20	.20	.35	(4)	
a	Booklet pane of 6	07/31/58	2.75	.80			4.00
b	Tagged	11/02/63	.60	.40	7.50	(4)	50.00
	Perf. 10.5 x 11						
1037	4½¢ The Hermitage	03/16/59	.20	.20	.65	(4)	1.00
	Perf. 11 x 10.5						
1038	5¢ James Monroe	12/02/54	.20	.20	.45	(4)	1.00
	Pair with full vertical gutter between		200.00				
1039	6¢ T. Roosevelt	11/18/55	.25	.20	1.25	(4)	
a	Wet printing	11/18/55	.40	.20	1.80	(4)	1.00
1040	7¢ Wilson	01/10/56	.20	.20	1.00	(4)	1.00
	Perf. 11						
1041	8¢ Statue of Liberty	04/09/54	.25	.20	2.25	(4)	1.00
a	Carmine double impression		650.00				
1042	8¢ Statue of Liberty, redrawn	03/22/58	.20	.20	.90	(4)	1.00
	Perf. 11 x 10.5						
1042A	8¢ Gen. John J. Pershing	11/17/61	.20	.20	.90	(4)	1.00
	Perf. 10.5 x 11						
1043	9¢ The Alamo	06/14/56	.30	.20	1.30	(4)	1.50
1044	10¢ Independence Hall	07/04/56	.30	.20	1.30	(4)	1.00
d	Tagged	07/06/66	2.00	1.00	35.00	(4)	15.00
	Perf. 11						
1044A	11¢ Statue of Liberty	06/15/61	.30	.20	1.25	(4)	1.00
c	Tagged	01/11/67	2.00	1.60	35.00	(4)	22.50

1030

1031

1031A

1032

1033

1034

1035

1036

1037

1038

1039

1040

1041

1042

1042A

1043

1044

1044A

1045

1046

1047

1048

1049

1050

1051

1052

1053

Issues of 1954-67		Un	U	PB/LP	#	FDC
Perf. 11 x 10.5						
1045 12¢ Benjamin Harrison	06/06/59	.35	.20	1.50	(4)	1.00
a Tagged	1968	.35	.20	4.00	(4)	25.00
1046 15¢ John Jay	12/12/58	.60	.20	3.00	(4)	1.00
a Tagged	07/06/66	1.10	.35	12.50	(4)	20.00
Perf. 10.5 x 11						
1047 20¢ Monticello	04/13/56	.40	.20	1.75	(4)	1.25
Perf. 11 x 10.5						
1048 25¢ Paul Revere	04/18/58	1.10	.20	4.75	(4)	1.25
1049 30¢ Robert E. Lee	09/21/55	.70	.20	3.50	(4)	
a Wet printing	09/21/55	1.10	.20	5.00	(4)	2.00
1050 40¢ John Marshall	04/58	1.50	.20	7.50	(4)	
a Wet printing	09/24/55	2.25	.25	12.50	(4)	2.00
1051 50¢ Susan B. Anthony	04/58	1.50	.20	6.75	(4)	
a Wet printing	08/25/55	1.75	.20	10.00	(4)	6.00
1052 $1 Patrick Henry	10/58	4.75	.20	19.00	(4)	
a Wet printing	10/07/55	5.25	.20	22.50	(4)	10.00
Perf. 11						
1053 $5 Alexander Hamilton	03/19/56	75.00	6.75	325.00	(4)	65.00
Issues of 1954-80, Coil Stamps, Perf. 10 Vertically						
1054 1¢ dark green Washington (1031)	08/57	.20	.20	1.00	(2)	
b Imperf., pair		2,500.00	—			
c Wet printing	10/08/54	.35	.20	1.75	(2)	1.00
Coil Stamp, Perf. 10 Horizontally						
1054A 1¼¢ turquoise Palace of the Governors (1031A)	06/17/60	.20	.20	2.25	(2)	1.00
Coil Stamps, Perf. 10 Vertically						
1055 2¢ rose carmine Jefferson (1033)	05/57	.20	.20	.75	(2)	
a Tagged	05/06/68	.20	.20	.75	(2)	11.00
b Imperf., pair (Bureau precanceled)			550.00			
c As "a," imperf., pair		575.00				
d Wet printing	10/22/54	.40	.20	3.50	(2)	1.00
1056 2½¢ gray blue Bunker Hill (1034)	09/09/59	.25	.25	3.50	(2)	2.00
1057 3¢ deep violet Statue of Liberty (1035)	10/56	.20	.20	.55	(2)	
a Imperf., pair		1,750.00	—	2,750.00	(2)	
b Tagged	06/26/67	1.00	.50	25.00	(2)	
c Wet printing	07/20/54	.30	.20	2.00	(2)	1.00
1058 4¢ red violet Lincoln (1036)	07/31/58	.20	.20	2.00	(2)	1.00
a Imperf., pair		120.00	70.00	200.00	(2)	
b Wet printing (Bureau precanceled)		27.50	.50	375.00	(2)	
Coil Stamp, Perf. 10 Horizontally						
1059 4½¢ blue green The Hermitage (1037)	05/01/59	1.50	1.20	14.00	(2)	1.75
Coil Stamp, Perf. 10 Vertically						
1059A 25¢ green Revere (1048)	02/25/65	.50	.30	2.00	(2)	1.25
b Tagged	04/03/73	.65	.20	3.00	(2)	14.00
Dull finish gum	1980	.65		3.00	(2)	
c Imperf., pair		55.00		100.00	(2)	

	Issues of 1954		Un	U	PB	#	FDC	Q(M)
	Perf. 11 x 10.5							
1060	3¢ Nebraska Territory	05/07/54	.20	.20	.30	(4)	1.00	116
1061	3¢ Kansas Territory	05/31/54	.20	.20	.30	(4)	1.00	114
	Perf. 10.5 x 11							
1062	3¢ George Eastman	07/12/54	.20	.20	.30	(4)	1.00	128
	Perf. 11 x 10.5							
1063	3¢ Lewis and Clark Expedition	07/28/54	.20	.20	.30	(4)	1.00	116
	Issues of 1955, Perf. 10.5 x 11							
1064	3¢ Pennsylvania Academy of the Fine Arts	01/15/55	.20	.20	.30	(4)	1.00	116
	Perf. 11 x 10.5							
1065	3¢ Land-Grant Colleges	02/12/55	.20	.20	.30	4)	1.00	120
1066	8¢ Rotary International	02/23/55	.20	.20	.95	(4)	3.00	54
1067	3¢ Armed Forces Reserve	05/21/55	.20	.20	.30	(4)	1.00	176
	Perf. 10.5 x 11							
1068	3¢ New Hampshire	06/21/55	.20	.20	.40	(4)	1.00	126
	Perf. 11 x 10.5							
1069	3¢ Soo Locks	06/28/55	.20	.20	.30	(4)	1.00	122
1070	3¢ Atoms for Peace	07/28/55	.20	.20	.35	(4)	1.00	134
1071	3¢ Fort Ticonderoga	09/18/55	.20	.20	.30	(4)	1.00	119
	Perf. 10.5 x 11							
1072	3¢ Andrew W. Mellon	12/20/55	.20	.20	.30	(4)	1.00	112

Dolli Tingle

Born in Chicago, Dolli Tingle attended the Chicago Academy of Fine Arts, the American Academy of Art, and continued her art studies with Reuben Tam at the Brooklyn Museum Art School in New York. Her paintings won many awards, including first prize for her 1973 Christmas Seal design, and were exhibited widely in shows such as the National Audubon Show and the New England Annual. The United States Postal Service commissioned her to design and execute the 1973 Christmas stamp, the first to be created in needlepoint. In 1974, the American Needlepoint Guild honored that design by naming her Woman of the Year.

In addition to solo exhibits at New York's Kay-Mar Gallery, she also participated in exhibits with her husband, painter and author Ward Brackett, in New York, Connecticut, and Florida. She devoted the last decade of her life almost entirely to painting. She died in 1993. ■

1060

1061

1062

1063

1064

1065

1066

1067

1068

1069

1070

1071

1072

1956

1073

1074

1075

1076

1077

1078

1079

1080

1081

1082

1083

1085

Issues of 1956		Un	U	PB	#	FDC	Q(M)
1073 3¢ Benjamin Franklin	01/17/56	.20	.20	.35	(4)	1.00	129
Perf. 11 x 10.5							
1074 3¢ Booker T. Washington	04/05/56	.20	.20	.30	(4)	1.25	121
Fifth International Philatelic Exhibition Issues Souvenir Sheet, Imperf.							
1075 Sheet of 2 stamps							
(1035, 1041)	04/28/56	2.00	2.00			5.00	3
a 3¢ (1035), single stamp from sheet		.80	.80				
b 8¢ (1041), single stamp from sheet		1.00	1.00				
Perf. 11 x 10.5							
1076 3¢ New York Coliseum and							
Columbus Monument	04/30/56	.20	.20	.30	(4)	1.00	120
Wildlife Conservation Issue							
1077 3¢ Wild Turkey	05/05/56	.20	.20	.35	(4)	1.50	123
1078 3¢ Pronghorn Antelope	06/22/56	.20	.20	.35	(4)	1.50	123
1079 3¢ King Salmon	11/09/56	.20	.20	.35	(4)	1.50	109
Perf. 10.5 x 11							
1080 3¢ Pure Food and Drug Laws	06/27/56	.20	.20	.30	(4)	1.00	113
Perf. 11 x 10.5							
1081 3¢ Wheatland	08/05/56	.20	.20	.30	(4)	1.00	125
Perf. 10.5 x 11							
1082 3¢ Labor Day	09/03/56	.20	.20	.30	(4)	1.00	118
Perf. 11 x 10.5							
1083 3¢ Nassau Hall	09/22/56	.20	.20	.30	(4)	1.00	122
Perf. 10.5 x 11							
1084 3¢ Devils Tower	09/24/56	.20	.20	.30	(4)	1.00	118
Pair with full horizontal gutter between		—					
Perf. 11 x 10.5							
1085 3¢ Children's Stamp	12/15/56	.20	.20	.30	(4)	1.00	101

Bradbury Thompson

(1911-1995)

J. Bradbury Thompson, graphic designer, art director, and professor of fine arts at Yale University, left his mark in many areas of graphic design including limited edition books, art and fashion magazines, museum exhibition catalogues, and postage stamps. The designer of more than 120 U.S. postage stamps, he served as Design Coordinator of the Citizens Stamp Advisory Committee from 1969-1978. He designed or redesigned more than 35 magazines including *Smithsonian, Business Week*, *Harvard Business Review*, and *Progressive Architecture*. In 1969 he was commissioned to create a great lectern Bible. *The Washburn College Bible,* a three-volume folio Bible, was published in 1979. Elected to the Art Directors Club Hall of Fame, he was also honored by the American Institute of Graphic Arts and the National Society of Art Directors. His award-winning artistic autobiography, *The Art of Graphic Design*, was published in 1988. ∎

Issues of 1957		Un	U	PB	#	FDC	Q(M)
1086	3¢ Alexander Hamilton 01/11/57	.20	.20	.30	(4)	1.00	115
	Perf. 10.5 x 11						
1087	3¢ Polio 01/15/57	.20	.20	.30	(4)	1.00	187
	Perf. 11 x 10.5						
1088	3¢ Coast and Geodetic Survey 02/11/57	.20	.20	.30	(4)	1.00	115
1089	3¢ American Institute						
	of Architects 02/23/57	.20	.20	.30	(4)	1.00	107
	Perf. 10.5 x 11						
1090	3¢ Steel Industry 05/22/57	.20	.20	.30	(4)	1.00	112
	Perf. 11 x 10.5						
1091	3¢ International Naval Review-						
	Jamestown Festival 06/10/57	.20	.20	.30	(4)	1.00	118
1092	3¢ Oklahoma Statehood 06/14/57	.20	.20	.35	(4)	1.00	102
1093	3¢ School Teachers 07/01/57	.20	.20	.30	(4)	2.00	102
	Perf. 11						
1094	4¢ Flag 07/04/57	.20	.20	.35	(4)	1.00	84
	Perf. 10.5 x 11						
1095	3¢ Shipbuilding 08/15/57	.20	.20	.30	(4)	1.00	126
	Champion of Liberty Issue, Perf. 11						
1096	8¢ Bust of Ramon Magsaysay on						
	Medal 08/31/57	.20	.20	.85	(4)	1.00	39
	Plate block of 4, ultramarine # omitted	—					
	Perf. 10.5 x 11						
1097	3¢ Lafayette 09/06/57	.20	.20	.30	(4)	1.00	123
	Perf. 11						
1098	3¢ Wildlife Conservation 11/22/57	.20	.20	.35	(4)	1.00	174
	Perf. 10.5 x 11						
1099	3¢ Religious Freedom 12/27/57	.20	.20	.30	(4)	1.00	114
	Issues of 1958						
1100	3¢ Gardening-Horticulture 03/15/58	.20	.20	.30	(4)	1.00	123
1101-03	Not assigned						
	Perf. 11 x 10.5						
1104	3¢ Brussels Universal and						
	International Exhibition 04/17/58	.20	.20	.30	(4)	1.00	114
1105	3¢ James Monroe 04/28/58	.20	.20	.30	(4)	1.00	120
1106	3¢ Minnesota Statehood 05/11/58	.20	.20	.30	(4)	1.00	121
	Perf. 11						
1107	3¢ International Geophysical Year 05/31/58	.20	.20	.35	(4)	1.00	126
	Perf. 11 x 10.5						
1108	3¢ Gunston Hall 06/12/58	.20	.20	.30	(4)	1.00	108

George Giusti (1908-1990)

An influential and internationally recognized innovator in the field of graphic design, George Giusti had the ability to reduce forms and images to their simplified, minimal essence. He was trained at the Reale Accademia di Belle Arti in Milan and owned a design studio in Zurich before emigrating to the United States in 1938. As a freelance artist in New York City, he created award-winning artwork for government agencies and such clients as Geigy Pharmaceuticals, Westinghouse, Random House, *Time, Fortune,* and *TV Guide.* In 1979, he was inducted into the Art Directors Hall of Fame for his extraordinary lifetime achievements. His designs appear on three United States postage stamps. ■

1086

1087

1088

1089

1090

1091

1092

1093

1094

1095

1096

1097

1098

1099

1100

1104

1105

1106

1107

1108

1109

1110

1111

1112

1113

1114

1115

1116

1117

1118

1119

1120

1121

1122

1123

1124

1125

1126

1127

1128

1129

1130

1131

Issues of 1958		Un	U	PB	#	FDC	Q(M)
Perf. 10.5 x 11							
1109 3¢ Mackinac Bridge	06/25/58	.20	.20	.30	(4)	1.00	107
Champion of Liberty Issue							
1110 4¢ Bust of Simon Bolivar on							
Medal	07/24/58	.20	.20	.35	(4)	1.00	115
Perf. 11							
1111 8¢ Bust of Bolivar on Medal	07/24/58	.20	.20	1.25	(4)	1.00	39
Plate block of four, ocher # only		—					
Perf. 11 x 10.5							
1112 4¢ Atlantic Cable	08/15/58	.20	.20	.35	(4)	1.00	114
Issues of 1958-59, Lincoln Sesquicentennial Issue, Perf. 10.5 x 11							
1113 1¢ Portrait by George Healy	02/12/59	.20	.20	.20	(4)	1.25	120
1114 3¢ Sculptured Head by							
Gutzon Borglum	02/27/59	.20	.20	.30	(4)	1.25	91
Perf. 11 x 10.5							
1115 4¢ Lincoln and Stephen Douglas							
Debating, by Joseph							
Boggs Beale	08/27/58	.20	.20	.35	(4)	1.25	114
1116 4¢ Statue in Lincoln Memorial							
by Daniel Chester French	05/30/59	.20	.20	.40	(4)	1.25	126
Champion of Liberty Issue, Perf. 10.5 x 11							
1117 4¢ Bust of Lajos Kossuth on							
Medal	09/19/58	.20	.20	.30	(4)	1.00	120
Perf. 11							
1118 8¢ Bust of Kossuth on Medal	09/19/58	.20	.20	1.10	(4)	1.00	44
Perf. 10.5 x 11							
1119 4¢ Freedom of the Press	09/22/58	.20	.20	.30	(4)	1.00	118
Perf. 11 x 10.5							
1120 4¢ Overland Mail	10/10/58	.20	.20	.30	(4)	1.00	125
Perf. 10.5 x 11							
1121 4¢ Noah Webster	10/16/58	.20	.20	.35	(4)	1.00	114
Perf. 11							
1122 4¢ Forest Conservation	10/27/58	.20	.20	.30	(4)	1.00	156
Perf. 11 x 10.5							
1123 4¢ Fort Duquesne	11/25/58	.20	.20	.35	(4)	1.00	124
Issues of 1959							
1124 4¢ Oregon Statehood	02/14/59	.20	.20	.30	(4)	1.00	120
Champion of Liberty Issue, Perf. 10.5 x 11							
1125 4¢ Bust of José de San Martin							
on Medal	02/25/59	.20	.20	.30	(4)	1.00	133
a　　Horizontal pair, imperf. between		1,500.00					
Perf. 11							
1126 8¢ Bust of San Martin							
on Medal	02/25/59	.20	.20	.85	(4)	1.00	45
Perf. 10.5 x 11							
1127 4¢ NATO	04/01/59	.20	.20	.30	(4)	1.00	122
Perf. 11 x 10.5							
1128 4¢ Arctic Explorations	04/06/59	.20	.20	.40	(4)	1.00	131
1129 8¢ World Peace Through							
World Trade	04/20/59	.20	.20	.85	(4)	1.00	47
1130 4¢ Silver Centennial	06/08/59	.20	.20	.30	(4)	1.00	123
Perf. 11							
1131 4¢ St. Lawrence Seaway	06/26/59	.20	.20	.35	(4)	1.25	126
Pair with full horizontal gutter between		—					

	Issues of 1959		Un	U	PB	#	FDC	Q(M)
1132	4¢ 49-Star Flag	07/04/59	.20	.20	.40	(4)	1.00	209
1133	4¢ Soil Conservation	08/26/59	.20	.20	.35	(4)	1.00	121
	Perf. 10.5 x 11							
1134	4¢ Petroleum Industry	08/27/59	.20	.20	.40	(4)	1.25	116
	Perf. 11 x 10.5							
1135	4¢ Dental Health	09/14/59	.20	.20	.40	(4)	3.00	118
	Champion of Liberty Issue, Perf. 10.5 x 11							
1136	4¢ Bust of Ernst Reuter on Medal	09/29/59	.20	.20	.30	(4)	1.00	112
	Perf. 11							
1137	8¢ Bust of Reuter on Medal	09/29/59	.20	.20	.85	(4)	1.00	43
	Perf. 10.5 x 11							
1138	4¢ Dr. Ephraim McDowell	12/03/59	.20	.20	.40	(4)	1.50	115
a	Vertical pair, imperf. between		450.00					
b	Vertical pair, imperf. horizontally		350.00					
	Issues of 1960-61, American Credo Issue, Perf. 11							
1139	4¢ Quotation from Washington's Farewell Address	01/20/60	.20	.20	.40	(4)	1.25	126
1140	4¢ Benjamin Franklin Quotation	03/31/60	.20	.20	.40	(4)	1.25	125
1141	4¢ Thomas Jefferson Quotation	05/18/60	.20	.20	.45	(4)	1.25	115
1142	4¢ Francis Scott Key Quotation	09/14/60	.20	.20	.45	(4)	1.25	122
1143	4¢ Abraham Lincoln Quotation	11/19/60	.20	.20	.50	(4)	1.25	121
	Pair with full horizontal gutter between		—					
1144	4¢ Patrick Henry Quotation	01/11/61	.20	.20	.50	(4)	1.25	113
	Issues of 1960							
1145	4¢ Boy Scouts	02/08/60	.20	.20	.40	(4)	3.50	139
	Olympic Winter Games Issue, Perf. 10.5 x 11							
1146	4¢ Olympic Rings and Snowflake	02/18/60	.20	.20	.40	(4)	1.00	124
	Champion of Liberty Issue							
1147	4¢ Bust of Thomas Masaryk on Medal	03/07/60	.20	.20	.30	(4)	1.00	114
a	Vertical pair, imperf. between		3,250.00					
	Perf. 11							
1148	8¢ Bust of Masaryk on Medal	03/07/60	.20	.20	.95	(4)	1.00	44
a	Horizontal pair, imperf. between		—					
	Perf. 11 x 10.5							
1149	4¢ World Refugee Year	04/07/60	.20	.20	.30	(4)	1.00	113
	Perf. 11							
1150	4¢ Water Conservation	04/18/60	.20	.20	.35	(4)	1.00	122
	Perf. 10.5 x 11							
1151	4¢ SEATO	05/31/60	.20	.20	.35	(4)	1.00	115
a	Vertical pair, imperf. between		160.00					

1132

1133

1134

1135

1136

1137

1138

1139

1140

1141

1142

1143

1144

1145

1146

1147

1148

1149

1150

1151

1152

1153

1154

1155

1156

1157

1158

1159

1160

1161

1162

1164

1163

1165

1166

1167

1168

1169

1170

1171

1172

1173

Issues of 1960			Un	U	PB	#	FDC	Q(M)
	Perf. 11 x 10.5							
1152	4¢ American Woman	06/02/60	.20	.20	.30	(4)	1.25	111
	Perf. 11							
1153	4¢ 50-Star Flag	07/04/60	.20	.20	.30	(4)	1.00	153
	Perf. 11 x 10.5							
1154	4¢ Pony Express	07/19/60	.20	.20	.40	(4)	1.25	120
	Perf. 10.5 x 11							
1155	4¢ Employ the Handicapped	08/28/60	.20	.20	.30	(4)	1.00	118
1156	4¢ 5th World Forestry Congress	08/29/60	.20	.20	.30	(4)	1.00	118
	Perf. 11							
1157	4¢ Mexican Independence	09/16/60	.20	.20	.30	(4)	1.00	112
1158	4¢ U.S.-Japan Treaty	09/28/60	.20	.20	.30	(4)	1.00	125
	Champion of Liberty Issue, Paderewski, Perf. 10.5 x 11							
1159	4¢ Bust of Ignacy Jan Paderewski on Medal	10/08/60	.20	.20	.30	(4)	1.00	120
	Perf. 11							
1160	8¢ Bust of Paderewski on Medal	10/08/60	.20	.20	.90	(4)	1.00	43
	Perf. 10.5 x 11							
1161	4¢ Sen. Robert A. Taft Memorial	10/10/60	.20	.20	.35	(4)	1.00	107
	Perf. 11 x 10.5							
1162	4¢ Wheels of Freedom	10/15/60	.20	.20	.30	(4)	1.00	110
	Perf. 11							
1163	4¢ Boys' Clubs of America	10/18/60	.20	.20	.30	(4)	1.00	124
1164	4¢ First Automated Post Office	10/20/60	.20	.20	.30	(4)	1.00	124
	Champion of Liberty Issue, Perf. 10.5 x 11							
1165	4¢ Bust of Gustaf Mannerheim on Medal	10/26/60	.20	.20	.30	(4)	1.00	125
	Perf. 11							
1166	8¢ Bust of Mannerheim on Medal	10/26/60	.20	.20	.80	(4)	1.00	42
1167	4¢ Camp Fire Girls	11/01/60	.20	.20	.35	(4)	1.00	116
	Champion of Liberty Issue, Perf. 10.5 x 11							
1168	4¢ Bust of Giusseppe Garibaldi on Medal	11/02/60	.20	.20	.30	(4)	1.00	126
	Perf. 11							
1169	8¢ Bust of Garibaldi on Medal	11/02/60	.20	.20	.85	(4)	1.00	43
	Perf. 10.5 x 11							
1170	4¢ Sen. Walter F. George Memorial	11/05/60	.20	.20	.35	(4)	1.00	124
1171	4¢ Andrew Carnegie	11/25/60	.20	.20	.35	(4)	1.00	120
1172	4¢ John Foster Dulles Memorial	12/06/60	.20	.20	.35	(4)	1.00	117
	Perf. 11 x 10.5							
1173	4¢ Echo I-Communications for Peace	12/15/60	.20	.20	.65	(4)	2.50	124

	Issues of 1961		Un	U	PB	#	FDC	Q(M)
	Champion of Liberty Issue, Perf. 10.5 x 11							
1174	4¢ Bust of Gandhi on Medal	01/26/61	.20	.20	.30	(4)	1.00	113
	Perf. 11							
1175	8¢ Bust of Gandhi on Medal	01/26/61	.20	.20	1.00	(4)	1.00	42
1176	4¢ Range Conservation	02/02/61	.20	.20	.40	(4)	1.00	111
	Perf. 10.5 x 11							
1177	4¢ Horace Greeley	02/03/61	.20	.20	.30	(4)	1.00	99
	Issues of 1961-65, Civil War Centennial Issue, Perf. 11 x 10.5							
1178	4¢ Fort Sumter	04/12/61	.20	.20	.85	(4)	3.00	101
1179	4¢ Shiloh	04/07/62	.20	.20	.75	(4)	3.00	125
	Perf. 11							
1180	5¢ Gettysburg	07/01/63	.20	.20	.85	(4)	3.00	80
1181	5¢ The Wilderness	05/05/64	.20	.20	.60	(4)	3.00	125
1182	5¢ Appomattox	04/09/65	.25	.25	1.20	(4)	3.00	113
a	Horizontal pair, imperf. vertically	4,500.00						
1183	4¢ Kansas Statehood	05/10/61	.20	.20	.35	(4)	1.00	106
	Perf. 11 x 10.5							
1184	4¢ Sen. George W. Norris	07/11/61	.20	.20	.35	(4)	1.00	111
1185	4¢ Naval Aviation	08/20/61	.20	.20	.35	(4)	1.00	117
	Pair with full vertical gutter between	150.00						
	Perf. 10.5 x 11							
1186	4¢ Workmen's Compensation	09/04/61	.20	.20	.35	(4)	1.00	121
	With plate # inverted				.60	(4)		
	Perf. 11							
1187	4¢ Frederic Remington	10/04/61	.20	.20	.40	(4)	1.25	112
	Perf. 10.5 x 11							
1188	4¢ Republic of China	10/10/61	.20	.20	.45	(4)	3.00	111
1189	4¢ Naismith-Basketball	11/06/61	.20	.20	.50	(4)	6.00	109
	Perf. 11							
1190	4¢ Nursing	12/28/61	.20	.20	.50	(4)	7.50	145
	Issues of 1962							
1191	4¢ New Mexico Statehood	01/06/62	.20	.20	.30	(4)	1.25	113
1192	4¢ Arizona Statehood	02/14/62	.20	.20	.30	(4)	1.25	122
1193	4¢ Project Mercury	02/20/62	.20	.20	.35	(4)	3.00	289
1194	4¢ Malaria Eradication	03/30/62	.20	.20	.30	(4)	1.00	120
	Perf. 10.5 x 11							
1195	4¢ Charles Evans Hughes	04/11/62	.20	.20	.30	(4)	1.00	125

Stevan Dohanos (1907-1994)

A celebrated illustrator of the American scene, Stevan Dohanos is renowned for the memorable *Saturday Evening Post* covers that he created during the 1940s and 1950s. He helped to define the look of United States postage stamps during the second half of the twentieth century through his involvement with the stamp design program from 1959 to 1989. As a United States Postal Service art director and as chairman of the Citizens' Stamp Advisory Committee, he advised the Postmaster General in the selection of stamp subjects and designs. His artwork appears on 40 United States postage stamps and he commissioned designs for more than 300 others. A founding member of the Famous Artists School, he was elected to the Society of Illustrators' Hall of Fame. ■

1174 **1175** **1176** **1177**

1178 **1179** **1180**

1181 **1183**

1182

1184 **1185** **1186** **1187**

1188 **1189** **1190** **1191**

1193 **1194**

1196

1197

1198

1199

1200

1201

1202

1203

1204

1205

1206

1207

1208

1209

1213

1230

1231

1232

1233

1234

	Issues of 1962		Un	U	PB/LP	#	FDC	Q(M)
	Perf. 11							
1196	4¢ Seattle World's Fair	04/25/62	.20	.20	.30	(4)	1.00	147
1197	4¢ Louisiana Statehood	04/30/62	.20	.20	.30	(4)	1.00	119
	Perf. 11 x 10.5							
1198	4¢ Homestead Act	05/20/62	.20	.20	.30	(4)	1.00	123
1199	4¢ Girl Scout Jubilee	07/24/62	.20	.20	.30	(4)	4.00	127
	Pair with full vertical gutter between		250.00					
1200	4¢ Sen. Brien McMahon	07/28/62	.20	.20	.35	(4)	1.00	131
1201	4¢ Apprenticeship	08/31/62	.20	.20	.30	(4)	1.00	120
	Perf. 11							
1202	4¢ Sam Rayburn	09/16/62	.20	.20	.30	(4)	1.00	121
1203	4¢ Dag Hammarskjold	10/23/62	.20	.20	.30	(4)	1.00	121
1204	4¢ black, brown and yellow (yellow inverted), Dag Hammarskjold, special printing	11/16/62	.20	.20	1.10	(4)	5.00	40
	Christmas Issue							
1205	4¢ Wreath and Candles	11/01/62	.20	.20	.30	(4)	1.10	862
1206	4¢ Higher Education	11/14/62	.20	.20	.35	(4)	1.50	120
1207	4¢ Winslow Homer	12/15/62	.20	.20	.45	(4)	1.25	118
a	Horizontal pair, imperf. between		6,750.00					
	Issue of 1963-66							
1208	5¢ Flag over White House	01/09/63	.20	.20	.40	(4)	1.00	
	Pair with full horizontal gutter between		—					
a	Tagged	08/25/66	.20	.20	2.00	(4)	25.00	
b	Horizontal pair, imperf. between		1,500.00					
	Issues of 1962-66, Perf. 11 x 10.5							
1209	1¢ Andrew Jackson	03/22/63	.20	.20	.20	(4)	1.00	
	Pair with full vertical gutter between		—					
a	Tagged	07/06/66	.20	.20	.40	(4)	25.00	
1210-12	Not assigned							
1213	5¢ George Washington	11/23/62	.20	.20	.40	(4)	1.00	
a	Booklet pane of 5 + label		3.00	1.75			4.00	
b	Tagged	10/28/63	.50	.20	4.50	(4)	25.00	
c	As "a," tagged	10/28/63	2.00	1.50			100.00	
1214-24	Not assigned							
	Coil Stamps, Perf. 10 Vertically							
1225	1¢ green Jackson (1209)	05/31/63	.20	.20	2.25	(2)	1.00	
a	Tagged	07/06/66	.20	.20	.75	(2)	15.00	
1226-28	Not assigned							
1229	5¢ dark blue gray Washington (1213)	11/23/62	1.25	.20	4.00	(2)	1.00	
a	Tagged	10/28/63	1.40	.20	6.50	(2)	25.00	
b	Imperf., pair		450.00		1,250.00	(2)		
	Issues of 1963, Perf. 11							
1230	5¢ Carolina Charter	04/06/63	.20	.20	.40	(4)	1.00	130
1231	5¢ Food for Peace-Freedom from Hunger	06/04/63	.20	.20	.40	(4)	1.00	136
1232	5¢ West Virginia Statehood	06/20/63	.20	.20	.40	(4)	1.00	138
1233	5¢ Emancipation Proclamation	08/16/63	.20	.20	.40	(4)	1.50	132
1234	5¢ Alliance for Progress	08/17/63	.20	.20	.40	(4)	1.00	136

Issues of 1963		Un	U	PB	#	FDC	Q(M)
1235 5¢ Cordell Hull	10/05/63	.20	.20	.45	(4)	1.00	131
Perf. 11 x 10.5							
1236 5¢ Eleanor Roosevelt	10/11/63	.20	.20	.45	(4)	1.00	133
Perf. 11							
1237 5¢ The Sciences	10/14/63	.20	.20	.40	(4)	1.00	130
1238 5¢ City Mail Delivery	10/26/63	.20	.20	.50	(4)	1.00	128
a Tagged omitted		7.50					
1239 5¢ International Red Cross	10/29/63	.20	.20	.40	(4)	1.25	119
Christmas Issue							
1240 5¢ National Christmas Tree and White House	11/01/63	.20	.20	.40	(4)	1.25	1,300
Pair with full horizontal gutter between		—					
a Tagged	11/02/63	.65	.40	5.00	(4)	60.00	
1241 5¢ John James Audubon, (See also #C71)	12/07/63	.20	.20	.45	(4)	1.00	175
Issues of 1964, Perf. 10.5 x 11							
1242 5¢ Sam Houston	01/10/64	.20	.20	.45	(4)	1.00	126
Perf. 11							
1243 5¢ Charles M. Russell	03/19/64	.20	.20	.40	(4)	1.25	128
Perf. 11 x 10.5							
1244 5¢ New York World's Fair	04/22/64	.20	.20	.45	(4)	1.50	146
Perf. 11							
1245 5¢ John Muir	04/29/64	.20	.20	.45	(4)	1.00	120
Perf. 11 x 10.5							
1246 5¢ President John Fitzgerald Kennedy Memorial	05/29/64	.20	.20	.60	(4)	2.50	512
Perf. 10.5 x 11							
1247 5¢ New Jersey Settlement	06/15/64	.20	.20	.45	(4)	1.00	124
Perf. 11							
1248 5¢ Nevada Statehood	07/22/64	.20	.20	.40	(4)	1.00	123
1249 5¢ Register and Vote	08/01/64	.20	.20	.45	(4)	1.00	453
Perf. 10.5 x 11							
1250 5¢ Shakespeare	08/14/64	.20	.20	.40	(4)	1.50	123
1251 5¢ Doctors William and Charles Mayo	09/11/64	.20	.20	.60	(4)	3.50	123
Perf. 11							
1252 5¢ American Music	10/15/64	.20	.20	.40	(4)	1.50	127
a Blue omitted		1,000.00					
1253 5¢ Homemakers	10/26/64	.20	.20	.40	(4)	1.00	121

Antonio Frasconi

A renowned printmaker and graphic artist, Antonio Frasconi was born in Buenos Aires and emigrated to the United States in 1945 to study art at the Art Students League in New York. Since then, he has enjoyed a long and active career as a visual artist. He has designed and illustrated almost 100 books, illuminating the words of Pablo Neruda, Isaac Bashevis Singer, and Langston Hughes among others. As a professor of visual arts at the State University of New York at Purchase, he has taught design and printmaking to aspiring artists since 1980. His 1963 United States postage stamp image honoring the National Academy of Sciences was chosen from 15 designs in the first competition of its kind. ■

1235

1236

1237

1238

1239

1240

1241

1242

1243

1244

1245

1246

1247

1248

1249

1250

1251

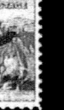

1252

1253

1254   **1255**

1259

1256   **1257 1257b**

1258

1260

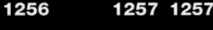

1261

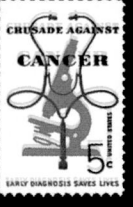

1262   **1263**   **1264**

1265   **1266**

1267   **1268**

1269

1270

1271

1272

1274

1276

Issues of 1964			Un	U	PB	#	FDC	Q(M)
Christmas Issue, Perf. 11								
1254	5¢ Holly	11/09/64	.25	.20			1.00	352
a	Tagged		.60	.50				
1255	5¢ Mistletoe	11/09/64	.25	.20			1.00	352
a	Tagged		.60	.50				
1256	5¢ Poinsettia	11/09/64	.25	.20			1.00	352
a	Tagged		.60	.50				
1257	5¢ Sprig of Conifer	11/09/64	.25	.20			1.00	352
a	Tagged		.60	.50				
b	Block of four, #1254-57		1.10	1.10	1.10	(4)	3.00	
c	As "b," tagged		2.50	2.25			57.50	
Perf. 10.5 x 11								
1258	5¢ Verrazano-Narrows Bridge	11/21/64	.20	.20	.45	(4)	1.00	120
Perf. 11								
1259	5¢ Fine Arts	12/02/64	.20	.20	.40	(4)	1.00	126
Perf. 10.5 x 11								
1260	5¢ Amateur Radio	12/15/64	.20	.20	.50	(4)	1.25	122
Issues of 1965, Perf. 11								
1261	5¢ Battle of New Orleans	01/08/65	.20	.20	.40	(4)	1.00	116
1262	5¢ Physical Fitness-Sokol	02/15/65	.20	.20	.50	(4)	1.25	115
1263	5¢ Crusade Against Cancer	04/01/65	.20	.20	.40	(4)	2.00	120
Perf. 10.5 x 11								
1264	5¢ Winston Churchill Memorial	05/13/65	.20	.20	.40	(4)	1.50	125
Perf. 11								
1265	5¢ Magna Carta	06/15/65	.20	.20	.40	(4)	1.00	120
	Corner block of four, black PB# omitted		—					
1266	5¢ International Cooperation							
	Year-United Nations	06/26/65	.20	.20	.40	(4)	1.00	115
1267	5¢ Salvation Army	07/02/65	.20	.20	.40	(4)	1.50	116
Perf. 10.5 x 11								
1268	5¢ Dante Alighieri	07/17/65	.20	.20	.40	(4)	1.00	115
1269	5¢ President Herbert Hoover							
	Memorial	08/10/65	.20	.20	.45	(4)	1.00	115
Perf. 11								
1270	5¢ Robert Fulton	08/19/65	.20	.20	.40	(4)	1.00	116
1271	5¢ Florida Settlement	08/28/65	.20	.20	.45	(4)	1.00	117
a	Yellow omitted		350.00					
1272	5¢ Traffic Safety	09/03/65	.20	.20	.45	(4)	1.00	114
1273	5¢ John Singleton Copley	09/17/65	.20	.20	.50	(4)	1.00	115
1274	11¢ International							
	Telecommunication Union	10/06/65	.35	.20	3.00	(4)	1.00	27
1275	5¢ Adlai E. Stevenson Memorial	10/23/65	.20	.20	.40	(4)	1.10	128
Christmas Issue								
1276	5¢ Angel with Trumpet							
	(1840 Weather Vane)	11/02/65	.20	.20	.40	(4)	1.00	1,140
a	Tagged	11/15/65	.75	.25	5.50	(4)	42.50	
1277	Not assigned							

Issues of 1965-78		Un	U	PB	#	FDC
Prominent Americans Issue, Perf. 11 x 10.5, 10.5 x 11 (See also #1299, 1303-05C)						
1278 1¢ Jefferson	01/12/68	.20	.20	.20	(4)	1.00
a Booklet pane of 8	01/12/68	1.00	.50			2.50
b Bklt. pane of 4 + 2 labels	05/10/71	.80	.30			12.50
c Untagged (Bureau precanceled)			.20			
d Tagging omitted		3.50	—			
1279 1¼¢ Albert Gallatin	01/30/67	.20	.20	6.25	(4)	1.00
1280 2¢ Frank Lloyd Wright	06/08/66	.20	.20	.25	(4)	1.00
Pair with full vertical gutter between		—				
a Booklet pane of 5 + label	01/08/68	1.25	.60			3.50
b Untagged (Bureau precanceled)			.20			
c Booklet pane of 6	05/07/71	1.00	.50			15.00
d Tagging omitted		3.50	—			
1281 3¢ Francis Parkman	09/16/67	.20	.20	.25	(4)	1.00
a Untagged (Bureau precanceled)			.20			
b Tagging omitted		4.50	—			
1282 4¢ Lincoln	11/19/65	.20	.20	.40	(4)	1.25
a Tagged	12/01/65	.20	.20	.55	(4)	25.00
Pair with full horizontal gutter between		—				
1283 5¢ Washington	02/22/66	.20	.20	.50	(4)	1.00
a Tagged	02/23/66	.20	.20	.60	(4)	75.00
1283B 5¢ redrawn	11/17/67	.20	.20	.50	(4)	1.00
Dull finish gum		.20		1.40	(4)	
d Untagged (Bureau precanceled)			.20			
1284 6¢ Roosevelt	01/29/66	.20	.20	.60	(4)	1.00
a Tagged	12/29/66	.20	.20	.80	(4)	30.00
b Booklet pane of 8	12/28/67	1.50	.75			2.75
c Booklet pane of 5 + label	01/09/68	1.50	.75			100.00
1285 8¢ Albert Einstein	03/14/66	.20	.20	.85	(4)	1.50
a Tagged	07/06/66	.20	.20	.85	(4)	25.00
1286 10¢ Jackson	03/15/67	.20	.20	1.00	(4)	1.00
b Untagged (Bureau precanceled)			.20			
1286A 12¢ Henry Ford	07/30/68	.25	.20	1.00	(4)	1.50
c Untagged (Bureau precanceled)			.25			
1287 13¢ John F. Kennedy	05/29/67	.30	.20	1.50	(4)	2.00
a Untagged (Bureau precanceled)			.35			
b Tagging omitted		20.00	—			
1288 15¢ Oliver Wendell Holmes	03/08/68	.30	.20	1.25	(4)	1.00
a Untagged (Bureau precanceled)			.30			
d Type II		.55	.20	8.00	(4)	
f As "d", tagging omitted		5.00	—			
Booklet Stamp, Perf. 10						
1288B 15¢ magenta, tagged						
(1288), Single from booklet		.35	.20			1.00
c Booklet pane of 8	06/14/78	2.80	1.75			3.00
e As "c," vert. imperf. between		—				
Perf. 11 x 10.5, 10.5 x 11						
1289 20¢ George C. Marshall	10/24/67	.40	.20	1.75	(4)	1.10
a Tagged	04/03/73	.40	.20	1.75	(4)	25.00
1290 25¢ Frederick Douglass	02/14/67	.55	.20	2.00	(4)	1.75
a Tagged	04/03/73	.45	.20	2.00	(4)	27.50
b Magenta		25.00	—	150.00		
1291 30¢ John Dewey	10/21/68	.65	.20	2.90	(4)	1.75
a Tagged	04/03/73	.50	.20	2.25	(4)	27.50
1292 40¢ Thomas Paine	01/29/68	.80	.20	3.25	(4)	1.75
a Tagged	04/03/73	.65	.20	2.75	(4)	27.50
1293 50¢ Lucy Stone	08/13/68	1.00	.20	4.25	(4)	2.00
a Tagged	04/03/73	.80	.20	3.50	(4)	30.00

1278

1279

1280

1281

1282

1283

1283B

1284

1285

1286

1286A

1287

1288

1289

1290

1291

1292

1293

1294

1295

1305

1306

1307

1308

1309

1310

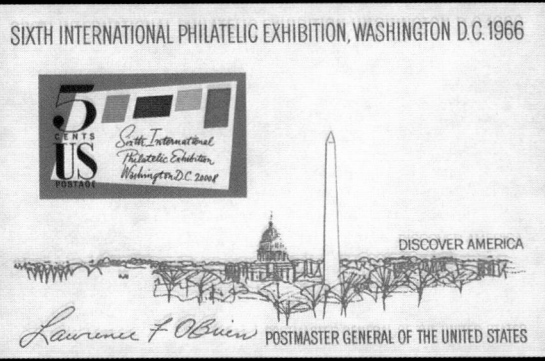

1311

1312

1313

1314

	Issues of 1966-73		Un	U	PB/LP	#	FDC	Q(M)
	Perf. 11 x 10.5, 10.5 x 11							
1294	$1 Eugene O'Neill	10/16/67	2.25	.20	10.00	(4)	7.50	
a	Tagged	04/03/73	1.65	.20	6.75	(4)	35.00	
1295	$5 John Bassett Moore	12/03/66	9.50	2.25	40.00	(4)	40.00	
a	Tagged	04/03/73	8.00	2.00	32.50	(4)	80.00	
1296	Not assigned							
	Issues of 1967-75, Coil Stamps, Perf. 10 Horizontally							
1297	3¢ violet Parkman (1281)	11/04/75	.20	.20	.45	(2)	1.00	
a	Imperf., pair		30.00		55.00	(2)		
b	Untagged (Bureau precanceled)			.20				
c	As "b," imperf., pair			6.00	25.00	(2)		
1298	6¢ Roosevelt (1284)	12/28/67	.20	.20	1.25	(2)	1.00	
a	Imperf., pair		2,250.00					
b	Tagging omitted		3.00					
	Issues of 1966-81, Coil Stamps, Perf. 10 Vertically (See also #1279-96)							
1299	1¢ green Jefferson (1278)	01/12/68	.20	.20	.25	(2)	1.00	
a	Untagged (Bureau precanceled)			.20				
b	Imperf., pair		30.00	—	60.00	(2)		
1300-02	Not assigned							
1303	4¢ blk. Lincoln (1282)	05/28/66	.20	.20	.75	(2)	1.00	
a	Untagged (Bureau precanceled)			.20				
b	Imperf., pair		900.00		2,000.00	(2)		
1304	5¢ bl. Washington (1283)	09/08/66	.20	.20	.40	(2)	1.00	
a	Untagged (Bureau precanceled)			.20				
b	Imperf., pair		175.00		400.00	(2)		
e	As "a," imperf. pair			400.00	900.00	(2)		
1304C	5¢ redrawn (1283B)	1981	.20	.20	1.25	(2)		
d	Imperf., pair		800.00					
1305	6¢ gray brown Roosevelt	02/28/68	.20	.20	.55	(2)	1.00	
a	Imperf., pair		75.00		130.00	(2)		
b	Untagged (Bureau precanceled)			.20				
1305E	15¢ magenta, Type I (1288)	06/14/78	.25	.20	1.25	(2)	1.00	
	Dull finish gum		.60		2.00	(2)		
f	Untagged (Bureau precanceled)			.30				
g	Imperf., pair		30.00		75.00	(2)		
h	Pair, imperf. between		200.00		550.00	(2)		
i	Type II, dull gum		.35	.20	2.50	(2)		
j	Type II, dull gum, imperf., pair		90.00		300.00	(2)		
1305C	$1 dull purple Eugene O'Neill (1294)	01/12/73	2.00	.40	5.75	(2)	4.00	
d	Imperf., pair		2,250.00		4,000.00	(2)		
	Issues of 1966, Perf. 11							
1306	5¢ Migratory Bird Treaty	03/16/66	.20	.20	.40	(4)	1.50	117
1307	5¢ Humane Treatment of Animals	04/09/66	.20	.20	.40	(4)	1.25	117
1308	5¢ Indiana Statehood	04/16/66	.20	.20	.40	(4)	1.00	124
1309	5¢ American Circus	05/02/66	.20	.20	.50	(4)	2.50	131
	Sixth International Philatelic Exhibition Issue							
1310	5¢ Stamped Cover	05/21/66	.20	.20	.40	(4)	1.00	122
	Souvenir Sheet, Imperf.							
1311	5¢ Stamped Cover (1310) and Washington, D.C., Scene	05/23/66	.20	.20			1.10	15
	Perf. 11							
1312	5¢ The Bill of Rights	07/01/66	.20	.20	.45	(4)	1.00	114
	Perf. 10.5 x 11							
1313	5¢ Poland's Millennium	07/30/66	.20	.20	.45	(4)	1.00	128
	Perf. 11							
1314	5¢ National Park Service	08/25/66	.20	.20	.45	(4)	1.00	120
a	Tagged	08/26/66	.30	.25	2.00	(4)	30.00	

1966-1967

	Issues of 1966		Un	U	PB	#	FDC	Q(M)
1315	5¢ Marine Corps Reserve	08/29/66	.20	.20	.45	(4)	1.50	125
a	Tagged		.30	.20	2.00	(4)	30.00	
b	Black and bister omitted		16,000.00					
1316	5¢ Women's Clubs	09/12/66	.20	.20	.45	(4)	1.00	115
a	Tagged	09/13/66	.30	.20	2.00	(4)	30.00	
	American Folklore Issue							
1317	5¢ Johnny Appleseed and							
	Apple	09/24/66	.20	.20	.45	(4)	1.50	124
a	Tagged	09/26/66	.30	.20	2.00	(4)	30.00	
1318	5¢ Beautification of America	10/05/66	.20	.20	.45	(4)	1.00	128
a	Tagged		.30	.20	2.00	(4)	30.00	
1319	5¢ Great River Road	10/21/66	.20	.20	.45	(4)	1.00	128
a	Tagged	10/22/66	.30	.20	2.00	(4)	30.00	
1320	5¢ Savings Bond-Servicemen	10/26/66	.20	.20	.45	(4)	1.00	116
a	Tagged	10/27/66	.30	.20	1.75	(4)	30.00	
b	Red, dark bl. and blk. omitted		5,000.00					
c	Dark blue omitted		9,000.00					
	Christmas Issue							
1321	5¢ Madonna and Child,							
	by Hans Memling	11/01/66	.20	.20	.40	(4)	1.00	1,174
a	Tagged	11/02/66	.30	.20	1.50	(4)	30.00	
1322	5¢ Mary Cassatt	11/17/66	.20	.20	.60	(4)	1.00	114
a	Tagged		.30	.25	1.75	(4)	30.00	
	Issues of 1967							
1323	5¢ National Grange	04/17/67	.20	.20	.40	(4)	1.00	121
a	Tagging omitted		5.00	—				
1324	5¢ Canada	05/25/67	.20	.20	.40	(4)	1.00	132
a	Tagging omitted		5.00	—				
1325	5¢ Erie Canal	07/04/67	.20	.20	.40	(4)	1.00	119
a	Tagging omitted		10.00	—				
1326	5¢ Search for Peace	07/05/67	.20	.20	.40	(4)	1.00	122
a	Tagging omitted		5.00	—				
1327	5¢ Henry David Thoreau	07/12/67	.20	.20	.45	(4)	1.00	112
1328	5¢ Nebraska Statehood	07/29/67	.20	.20	.40	(4)	1.00	117
a	Tagging omitted		6.00	—				
1329	5¢ Voice of America	08/01/67	.20	.20	.40	(4)	1.00	112
a	Tagging omitted		10.00	—				
	American Folklore Issue							
1330	5¢ Davy Crockett	08/17/67	.20	.20	.40	(4)	1.10	114
a	Vertical pair, imperf. between		6,000.00					
b	Green omitted		—					
c	Black and green omitted		—					
e	Tagging omitted		5.00					
	Accomplishments in Space Issue							
1331	5¢ Space-Walking Astronaut	09/29/67	.50	.20			3.00	60
b	Tagging omitted		10.00	—				
1332	5¢ Gemini 4 Capsule							
	and Earth	09/29/67	.50	.20	2.75	(4)	3.00	60
a	Tagging omitted		10.00	—				
b	Pair, #1331-1332		1.10	1.25			7.50	
c	As "b", Tagging omitted		40.00	—				
1333	5¢ Urban Planning	10/02/67	.20	.20	.50	(4)	1.00	111
1334	5¢ Finland Independence	10/06/67	.20	.20	.50	(4)	1.00	111

1315

1316

1317

1318

1319

1320

1321

1322

1323

1324

1325

1326

1327

1328

1329

1330

1331   1332   1332b

1333

1334

1335

1336

1337

1338

1339

1340

1341

1342

1343

1344

1345

1346

1347

1348

1349

1350

1351

1352

1353

1354

1354a

Issues of 1967		Un	U	PB	#	FDC	Q(M)
Perf. 12							
1335 5¢ Thomas Eakins	11/02/67	.20	.20	.50	(4)	1.00	114
Christmas Issue, Perf. 11							
1336 5¢ Madonna and Child,							
by Hans Memling	11/06/67	.20	.20	.40	(4)	1.00	1,209
a Tagging omitted		4.00	—				
1337 5¢ Mississippi Statehood	12/11/67	.20	.20	.50	(4)	1.00	113
a Tagging omitted		6.00	—				
Issues of 1968-1971							
1338 6¢ Flag over White House							
(design 19 x 22mm)	01/24/68	.20	.20	.45	(4)	1.00	
k Vertical pair, imperf. between		550.00					
m Tagging omitted		4.00	—				
Coil Stamp, Perf. 10 Vertically							
1338A 6¢ dk bl, rd and grn (1338)	05/30/69	.20	.20	.30	(2)	1.00	
b Imperf., pair		500.00					
q Tagging omitted		8.50	—				
Perf. 11 x 10.5							
1338D 6¢ dark blue, red and green							
(1338, design 18.25 x 21mm)	08/07/70	.20	.20	2.60	(20)	1.00	
e Horizontal pair, imperf. between		175.00					
n Tagging omitted		5.00	—				
1338F 8¢ dk bl, rd and slt grn (1338)	05/10/71	.20	.20	3.00	(20)	1.00	
i Imperf., vertical pair		45.00					
j Horizontal pair, imperf. between		55.00					
o Tagging omitted		5.00	—				
Coil Stamp, Perf. 10 Vertically							
1338G 8¢ dk bl, rd and slt grn (1338)	05/10/71	.20	.20	.40	(2)	1.00	
h Imperf., pair		55.00					
r Tagging omitted		4.00	—				
Issues of 1968, Perf. 11							
1339 6¢ Illinois Statehood	02/12/68	.20	.20	.50	(4)	1.00	141
1340 6¢ HemisFair '68	03/30/68	.20	.20	.50	(4)	1.00	144
a White omitted		1,300.00					
1341 $1 Airlift	04/04/68	2.25	1.25	10.00	(4)	7.00	
Pair with full horizontal gutter between			—				
1342 6¢ Support Our Youth-Elks	05/01/68	.20	.20	.50	(4)	1.00	147
a Tagging omitted		7.00	—				
1343 6¢ Law and Order	05/17/68	.20	.20	.50	(4)	1.50	130
1344 6¢ Register and Vote	06/27/68	.20	.20	.50	(4)	1.00	159
Historic Flag Issue							
1345 6¢ Ft. Moultrie Flag, 1776	07/04/68	.40	.25			3.00	23
1346 6¢ Ft. McHenry (U.S.)							
Flag, 1795-1818	07/04/68	.30	.25			3.00	23
1347 6¢ Washington's							
Cruisers Flag, 1775	07/04/68	.25	.25			3.00	23
1348 6¢ Bennington Flag, 1777	07/04/68	.25	.25			3.00	23
1349 6¢ Rhode Island Flag, 1775	07/04/68	.25	.25			3.00	23
1350 6¢ First Stars and							
Stripes, 1777	07/04/68	.25	.25			3.00	23
1351 6¢ Bunker Hill Flag, 1775	07/04/68	.25	.25			3.00	23
1352 6¢ Grand Union Flag, 1776	07/04/68	.25	.25			3.00	23
1353 6¢ Philadelphia Light Horse							
Flag, 1775	07/04/68	.25	.25			3.00	23
1354 6¢ First Navy Jack, 1775	07/04/68	.25	.25			3.00	23
a Strip of 10, #1345-54		2.75	2.75	6.50	(20)	17.50	

	Issues of 1968		Un	U	PB	#	FDC	Q(M)
	Perf. 12							
1355	6¢ Walt Disney	09/11/68	.20	.20	.90	(4)	15.00	153
a	Ocher omitted		600.00	—				
b	Vertical pair, imperf. horizontally		700.00					
c	Imperf., pair		675.00					
d	Black omitted		2,000.00					
e	Horizontal pair, imperf. between		4,750.00					
f	Blue omitted		2,250.00					
g	Tagging omitted		10.00	—				
	Perf. 11							
1356	6¢ Father Marquette	09/20/68	.20	.20	.50	(4)	1.00	133
	American Folklore Issue							
1357	6¢ Pennsylvania Rifle, Powder Horn,							
	Tomahawk, Pipe and Knife	09/26/68	.20	.20	.50	(4)	1.10	130
1358	6¢ Arkansas River Navigation	10/01/68	.20	.20	.50	(4)	1.00	132
1359	6¢ Leif Erikson	10/09/68	.20	.20	.50	(4)	1.00	129
	Perf. 11 x 10.5							
1360	6¢ Cherokee Strip	10/15/68	.20	.20	.60	(4)	1.00	125
a	Tagging omitted		5.00	—				
	Perf. 11							
1361	6¢ John Trumbull	10/18/68	.20	.20	.60	(4)	1.00	128
1362	6¢ Waterfowl Conservation	10/24/68	.20	.20	.65	(4)	1.50	142
a	Vertical pair, imperf. between		550.00					
b	Red and dark blue omitted		900.00					
	Christmas Issue							
1363	6¢ Angel Gabriel, from							
	"The Annunciation," by							
	Jan Van Eyck	11/01/68	.20	.20	2.00	(10)	1.00	1,411
a	Untagged	11/02/68	.20	.20	2.00	(10)	10.00	
b	Imperf., pair (tagged)		225.00					
c	Light yellow omitted		65.00					
d	Imperf., pair (untagged)		300.00					
1364	6¢ American Indian	11/04/68	.20	.20	.70	(4)	1.50	125
	Issues of 1969, Beautification of America Issue							
1365	6¢ Capitol, Azaleas and Tulips	01/16/69	.30	.20			1.00	48
1366	6¢ Washington Monument,							
	Potomac River and Daffodils	01/16/69	.30	.20			1.00	48
1367	6¢ Poppies and Lupines							
	along Highway	01/16/69	.30	.20			1.00	48
1368	6¢ Blooming Crabapple Trees							
	Lining Avenue	01/16/69	.30	.20			1.00	48
a	Block of 4, #1365-68		1.25	1.75	1.50	(4)	4.00	
1369	6¢ American Legion	03/15/69	.20	.20	.45	(4)	1.00	149
	American Folklore Issue							
1370	6¢ "July Fourth" by							
	Grandma Moses	05/01/69	.20	.20	.50	(4)	1.00	139
a	Horizontal pair, imperf. between		225.00					
b	Black and Prussian blue omitted		850.00					
c	Tagging omitted		6.00	—				
1371	6¢ Apollo 8	05/05/69	.20	.20	.65	(4)	3.00	187
1372	6¢ W.C. Handy	05/17/69	.20	.20	.45	(4)	1.25	126
a	Tagging omitted		6.00	—				
1373	6¢ California Settlement	07/16/69	.20	.20	.45	(4)	1.00	144
1374	6¢ John Wesley Powell	08/01/69	.20	.20	.45	(4)	1.00	136
a	Tagging omitted		7.50	—				
1375	6¢ Alabama Statehood	08/02/69	.20	.20	.45	(4)	1.00	151

1355

1356

1357

1358

1359

1360

1361

1362

1365   1366

1363

1364

1367   1368   1368a

1369

1370

1371

1372

1969-1970

1376 **1377**

1378 **1379** **1379a**

1380

1381

1382

1383

1384

1384 Precancel

1385

1386

1387 **1388**

1391

1389 **1390** **1390a**

1392

Issues of 1969		Un	U	PB	#	FDC	Q(M)
Botanical Congress Issue, Perf. 11							
1376	6¢ Douglas Fir (Northwest) 08/23/69	.40	.20			1.50	40
1377	6¢ Lady's Slipper (Northeast) 08/23/69	.40	.20			1.50	40
1378	6¢ Ocotillo (Southwest) 08/23/69	.40	.20			1.50	40
1379	6¢ Franklinia (Southeast) 08/23/69	.40	.20			1.50	40
a	Block of 4, #1376-79	1.75	2.25	2.00	(4)	5.00	
Perf. 10.5 x 11							
1380	6¢ Dartmouth College Case 09/22/69	.20	.20	.50	(4)	1.00	130
Perf. 11							
1381	6¢ Professional Baseball 09/24/69	.65	.20	3.00	(4)	12.00	131
a	Black omitted	*1,100.00*					
1382	6¢ College Football 09/26/69	.20	.20	.85	(4)	6.50	139
1383	6¢ Dwight D. Eisenhower 10/14/69	.20	.20	.50	(4)	1.00	151
Christmas Issue, Perf. 11 x 10.5							
1384	6¢ Winter Sunday in Norway, Maine 11/03/69	.20	.20	1.40	(10)	1.00	1,710
	Precanceled	.50	.20				
b	Imperf., pair	*1,000.00*					
c	Light green omitted	*22.50*					
d	Light green and yellow omitted	*1,000.00*	—				
e	Yellow omitted	*2,250.00*					
f	Tagging omitted	*5.00*	—				
Precanceled versions issued on an experimental basis in four cities whose names appear on the stamps: Atlanta, GA; Baltimore, MD; Memphis, TN; and New Haven, CT.							
Perf. 11							
1385	6¢ Hope for the Crippled 11/20/69	.20	.20	.50	(4)	1.25	128
1386	6¢ William M. Harnett 12/03/69	.20	.20	.55	(4)	1.00	146
Issues of 1970, Natural History Issue							
1387	6¢ American Bald Eagle 05/06/70	.20	.20			1.50	50
1388	6¢ African Elephant Herd 05/06/70	.20	.20			1.50	50
1389	6¢ Tlingit Chief in Haida Ceremonial Canoe 05/06/70	.20	.20			1.50	50
1390	6¢ Brontosaurus, Stegosaurus and Allosaurus from Jurassic Period 05/06/70	.20	.20			1.50	50
a	Block of 4, #1387-90	.55	.60	.70	(4)	4.00	
1391	6¢ Maine Statehood 07/09/70	.20	.20	.50	(4)	1.50	172
Perf. 11 x 10.5							
1392	6¢ Wildlife Conservation 07/20/70	.20	.20	.50	(4)	1.00	142

Paul Wenzel

During his forty-two year career as a graphic artist with the Walt Disney Company, Paul Wenzel created thousands of fine illustrations for motion picture advertising and retail merchandising. One of his many film-advertising illustrations was for the Academy Award® winner, *Mary Poppins*, first released in 1964. Recently retired, he continues to accept commercial assignments on a freelance basis and paint more personal images for exhibition and enjoyment. His vibrant portrait of Walt Disney appears on a 1968 United States postage stamp. ■

	Issues of 1970-74		Un	U	PB/LP	#	FDC	Q(M)
1393	6¢ Eisenhower	08/06/70	.20	.20	.50	(4)	1.00	
a	Booklet pane of 8		1.50	.65			3.00	
b	Booklet pane of 5 + label		1.50	.65			1.50	
c	Untagged (Bureau precanceled)			.20				
	Perf. 10.5 x 11							
1393D	7¢ Franklin	10/20/72	.20	.20	.60	(4)	1.00	
e	Untagged (Bureau precanceled)			.20				
f	Tagging omitted		4.00	—				
	Perf. 11							
1394	8¢ Eisenhower	05/10/71	.20	.20	.60	(4)	1.00	
	Pair with full vertical gutter between		—					
a	Tagging omitted		4.00	—				
	Perf. 11 x 10.5							
1395	8¢ deep claret Eisenhower							
	(1394), Single from booklet		.20	.20			1.00	
a	Booklet pane of 8	05/10/71	1.80	*1.25*			2.50	
b	Booklet pane of 6	05/10/71	1.25	.90			2.50	
c	Booklet pane of 4 + 2							
	labels	01/28/72	1.65	.80			2.00	
d	Booklet pane of 7 +							
	label	01/28/72	1.90	*1.00*			1.75	
1396	8¢ U.S. Postal Service	07/01/71	.20	.20	2.00	(12)	1.00	
1397	14¢ Fiorello H. LaGuardia	04/24/72	.25	.20	1.20	(4)	1.00	
a	Untagged (Bureau precanceled)			.25				
1398	16¢ Ernie Pyle	05/07/71	.30	.20	1.25	(4)	1.25	
a	Untagged (Bureau precanceled)			.35				
1399	18¢ Dr. Elizabeth Blackwell	01/23/74	.35	.20	1.50	(4)	1.25	
1400	21¢ Amadeo P. Giannini	06/27/73	.40	.20	1.65	(4)	1.25	
	Coil Stamps, Perf. 10 Vertically							
1401	6¢ dark blue gray Eisenhower							
	(1393)	08/06/70	.20	.20	.50	(2)	1.00	
a	Untagged (Bureau precanceled)			.20				
b	Imperf., pair		*2,000.00*		—	(2)		
1402	8¢ deep claret Eisenhower							
	(1394)	05/10/71	.20	.20	.55	(2)	1.00	
a	Imperf., pair		45.00		70.00	(2)		
b	Untagged (Bureau precanceled)			.20				
c	Pair, imperf. between		*6,250.00*					
1403-04	Not assigned							
	Issues of 1970, Perf. 11							
1405	6¢ Edgar Lee Masters	08/22/70	.20	.20	.50	(4)	1.00	138
a	Tagging omitted		30.00	—				
1406	6¢ Woman Suffrage	08/26/70	.20	.20	.50	(4)	1.00	135
1407	6¢ South Carolina Settlement	09/12/70	.20	.20	.50	(4)	1.00	136
1408	6¢ Stone Mountain Memorial	09/19/70	.20	.20	.50	(4)	1.00	133
1409	6¢ Ft. Snelling	10/17/70	.20	.20	.50	(4)	1.00	135
	Anti-Pollution Issue, Perf. 11 x 10.5							
1410	6¢ Save Our Soil							
	Globe and Wheat Field	10/28/70	.25	.20			1.25	40
1411	6¢ Save Our Cities							
	Globe and City Playground	10/28/70	.25	.20			1.25	40
1412	6¢ Save Our Water							
	Globe and Bluegill Fish	10/28/70	.25	.20			1.25	40
1413	6¢ Save Our Air							
	Globe and Seagull	10/28/70	.25	.20			1.25	40
a	Block of 4, #1410-13		1.10	1.25	2.25	(10)	4.00	

1393

1393D

1394

1396

1397

1398

1399

1400

1405

1406

1407

1408

1409

1410   **1411**

1412   **1413**   **1413a**

1414   1414a

1415   1416

1417   1418   1418b

1419

1420

1421   1422   1422a

1423

1424

1425

1426

1427   1428

1429   1430   1430a

	Issues of 1970		Un	U	PB	#	FDC	Q(M)
	Christmas Issue, Perf. 10.5 x 11							
1414	6¢ Nativity, by Lorenzo Lotto	11/05/70	.20	.20	1.10	(8)	1.25	639*
a	Precanceled		.20	.20	1.90	(8)	7.50	358
b	Black omitted		550.00					
c	As "a," blue omitted		1,500.00					
d	Type II		.20	.20	2.75	(8)		
e	Type II, precanceled		.25	.20	4.00	(8)		

#1414a-18a were furnished to 68 cities. Unused prices are for copies with gum and used prices are for copies with or without gum but with an additional cancellation. *Includes #1414a.

	Perf. 11 x 10.5							
1415	6¢ Tin and Cast-iron							
	Locomotive	11/05/70	.30	.20			1.40	122
a	Precanceled		.75	.20				110
b	Black omitted		2,500.00					
1416	6¢ Toy Horse on Wheels	11/05/70	.30	.20			1.40	122
a	Precanceled		.75	.20				110
b	Black omitted		2,500.00					
c	Imperf., pair			4,000.00				
1417	6¢ Mechanical Tricycle	11/05/70	.30	.20			1.40	122
a	Precanceled		.75	.20				110
b	Black omitted		2,500.00					
1418	6¢ Doll Carriage	11/05/70	.30	.20			1.40	122
a	Precanceled		.75	.20				110
b	Block of 4, #1415-18		1.25	1.50	3.25	(8)	5.00	
c	Block of 4, #1415a-18a		3.25	3.25	6.50	(8)	15.00	
d	Black omitted		2,500.00					
	Perf. 11							
1419	6¢ United Nations	11/20/70	.20	.20	.50	(4)	1.25	128
	Pair with full horizontal gutter between		—					
1420	6¢ Landing of the Pilgrims	11/21/70	.20	.20	.50	(4)	1.00	130
a	Orange and yellow omitted		900.00					
	Disabled American Veterans and Servicemen Issue							
1421	6¢ Disabled American							
	Veterans Emblem	11/24/70	.20	.20			2.00	67
1422	6¢ U.S. Servicemen	11/24/70	.20	.20			2.00	67
a	Attached pair, #1421-22		.30	.30	1.00	(4)	3.00	
	Issues of 1971							
1423	6¢ American Wool Industry	01/19/71	.20	.20	.50	(4)	1.00	136
a	Tagging omitted		9.00	—				
1424	6¢ Gen. Douglas MacArthur	01/26/71	.20	.20	.50	(4)	1.10	135
1425	6¢ Blood Donor	03/12/71	.20	.20	.50	(4)	1.10	131
a	Tagging omitted		11.00					
	Perf. 11 x 10.5							
1426	8¢ Missouri Statehood	05/08/71	.20	.20	2.00	(12)	1.00	161
	Wildlife Conservation Issue, Perf. 11							
1427	8¢ Trout	06/12/71	.20	.20			1.25	44
1428	8¢ Alligator	06/12/71	.20	.20			1.25	44
1429	8¢ Polar Bear	06/12/71	.20	.20			1.25	44
1430	8¢ California Condor	06/12/71	.20	.20			1.25	44
a	Block of 4, #1427-30		.80	.90	.90	(4)	3.00	
b	As "a," light green and dark green omitted from #1427-28		4,500.00					
c	As "a," red omitted from #1427, 1429-30		9,000.00					

	Issues of 1971		Un	U	PB	#	FDC	Q(M)
1431	8¢ Antarctic Treaty	06/23/71	.20	.20	.65	(4)	1.00	139
a	Tagging omitted		7.00					
	American Revolution Bicentennial Issue							
1432	8¢ Bicentennial Commission							
	Emblem	07/04/71	.20	.20	.85	(4)	1.00	138
a	Gray and black omitted		650.00					
b	Gray omitted		1,150.00					
1433	8¢ John Sloan	08/02/71	.20	.20	.70	(4)	1.00	152
a	Tagging omitted		—					
	Space Achievement Decade Issue							
1434	8¢ Earth, Sun and Landing							
	Craft on Moon	08/02/71	.20	.20				88
a	Tagging omitted		25.00					
1435	8¢ Lunar Rover and							
	Astronauts	08/02/71	.20	.20	.65	(4)		88
a	Tagging omitted		25.00					
b	Pair #1434-1435		.40	.45				
c	As "b", tagging omitted		—					
d	As "b", blue & red omitted		1,500.00					
1436	8¢ Emily Dickinson	08/28/71	.20	.20	.65	(4)	1.00	143
a	Black and olive omitted		800.00					
b	Pale rose omitted		7,500.00					
1437	8¢ San Juan, Puerto Rico	09/12/71	.20	.20	.65	(4)	1.00	149
a	Tagging omitted		7.50					
	Perf. 10.5 x 11							
1438	8¢ Prevent Drug Abuse	10/04/71	.20	.20	1.00	(6)	1.00	139
1439	8¢ CARE	10/27/71	.20	.20	1.25	(8)	1.00	131
a	Black omitted		4,750.00					
b	Tagging omitted		5.00					
	Historic Preservation Issue, Perf. 11							
1440	8¢ Decatur House,							
	Washington, D.C.	10/29/71	.20	.20			1.25	43
1441	8¢ Whaling Ship Charles W. Morgan,							
	Mystic, Connecticut	10/29/71	.20	.20			1.25	43
1442	8¢ Cable Car, San Francisco	10/29/71	.20	.20			1.25	43
1443	8¢ San Xavier del Bac Mission,							
	Tucson, Arizona	10/29/71	.20	.20			1.25	43
a	Block of 4, #1440-43		.75	.85	.90	(4)	3.00	
b	As "a," black brown omitted		2,250.00					
c	As "a," ocher omitted		—					
d	As "a," tagging omitted		60.00					
	Christmas Issue, Perf. 10.5 x 11							
1444	8¢ Adoration of the Shepherds,							
	by Giorgione	11/10/71	.20	.20	1.80	(12)	1.10	1,074
a	Gold omitted		550.00					
1445	8¢ Partridge in a Pear Tree	11/10/71	.20	.20	1.80	(12)	1.10	980

1431

1432

1433

1434   **1435**   **1435b**

1436

1437

1438

1439

1440   **1441**

1442   **1443**   **1443a**

1972

1446

1447

1448   1449

1450   1451   1451a

1452

1454

1453

1455

1456   1457

1458   1459   1459a

1460

1461

1462

	Issues of 1972		Un	U	PB	#	FDC	Q(M)
1446	8¢ Sidney Lanier	02/03/72	.20	.20	.65	(4)	1.00	137
a	Tagging omitted		15.00					
	Perf. 10.5 x 11							
1447	8¢ Peace Corps	02/11/72	.20	.20	1.00	(6)	1.00	150
a	Tagging omitted		5.00					
	National Parks Centennial Issue (See also #C84)							
1448	2¢ Ship at Sea	04/05/72	.20	.20				43
1449	2¢ Cape Hatteras Lighthouse	04/05/72	.20	.20				43
1450	2¢ Laughing Gulls on Driftwood	04/05/72	.20	.20				43
1451	2¢ Laughing Gulls and Dune	04/05/72	.20	.20				43
a	Block of 4, #1448-51		.25	.25	.50	(4)	2.50	
b	As "a," black omitted		2,750.00					
1452	6¢ Performance at Wolf Trap Farm, Shouse Pavilion	06/26/72	.20	.20	.55	(4)	1.00	104
a	Tagging omitted		9.00					
1453	8¢ Old Faithful, Yellowstone	03/01/72	.20	.20	.70	(4)	1.00	164
a	Tagging omitted		15.00					
1454	15¢ View of Mount McKinley in Alaska	07/28/72	.30	.20	1.30	(4)	1.00	54

Note: Beginning with this National Parks Centennial issue, the USPS began to offer stamp collectors first day cancellations affixed to 8" x 101/2" souvenir pages. The pages are similar to the stamp announcements that have appeared on Post Office bulletin boards beginning with Scott #1132. See "Souvenir Pages" listed in the back of this book (see Table of Contents)

	Issues of 1972		Un	U	PB	#	FDC	Q(M)
1455	8¢ Family Planning	03/18/72	.20	.20	.65	(4)	1.00	153
a	Yellow omitted		1,250.00					
b	Dark brown and olive omitted		—					
c	Dark brown omitted		9,500.00					
	American Bicentennial Issue, Perf. 11 x 10.5							
1456	8¢ Glassblower	07/04/72	.20	.20			1.00	50
1457	8¢ Silversmith	07/04/72	.20	.20			1.00	50
1458	8¢ Wigmaker	07/04/72	.20	.20			1.00	50
1459	8¢ Hatter	07/04/72	.20	.20			1.00	50
a	Block of 4, #1456-59		.65	.75	.80	(4)	2.50	
	Olympic Games Issue, (See also #C85)							
1460	6¢ Bicycling and Olympic Rings	08/17/72	.20	.20	1.25	(10)	1.00	67
	Cylinder flaw (broken red ring)		10.00					
1461	8¢ Bobsledding and Olympic Rings	08/17/72	.20	.20	1.60	(10)	1.00	180
a	Tagging omitted		5.00					
1462	15¢ Running and Olympic Rings	08/17/72	.30	.20	3.00	(10)	1.00	46
1463	8¢ Parent Teachers Association	09/15/72	.20	.20	.65	(4)	1.00	180

	Issues of 1972		Un	U	PB	#	FDC	Q(M)
	Wildlife Conservation Issue, Perf. 11							
1464	8¢ Fur Seals	09/20/72	.20	.20			1.50	50
1465	8¢ Cardinal	09/20/72	.20	.20			1.50	50
1466	8¢ Brown Pelican	09/20/72	.20	.20			1.50	50
1467	8¢ Bighorn Sheep	09/20/72	.20	.20			1.50	50
a	Block of 4, #1464-67		.65	.75	.75	(4)	3.00	
b	As "a," brown omitted		4,000.00					
c	As "a," green and blue omitted		4,750.00					
d	As "a," red & brown omitted		4,000.00					

Note: With this Wildlife Conservation issue the USPS introduced the "American Commemorative Series" Stamp Panels. Each panel contains a block of four or more mint stamps with text and background illustrations. See pages 493-497 for a complete listing.

			Un	U	PB	#	FDC	Q(M)
1468	8¢ Mail Order Business	09/27/72	.20	.20	1.75	(12)	1.00	185
	Perf. 10.5 x 11							
1469	8¢ Osteopathic Medicine	10/09/72	.20	.20	1.00	(6)	1.00	162
	American Folklore Issue, Perf. 11							
1470	8¢ Tom Sawyer Whitewashing							
	a Fence, by Norman Rockwell	10/13/72	.20	.20	.65	(4)	1.00	163
a	Horizontal pair, imperf. between		4,500.00					
b	Red and black omitted		1,900.00					
c	Yellow and tan omitted		2,400.00					
	Christmas Issue, Perf. 10.5 x 11							
1471	8¢ Angels from "Mary, Queen of Heaven"							
	by the Master of the							
	St. Lucy Legend	11/09/72	.20	.20	1.75	(12)	1.00	1,003
a	Pink omitted		150.00					
b	Black omitted		4,000.00					
1472	8¢ Santa Claus	11/09/72	.20	.20	1.75	(12)	1.00	1,017
	Perf. 11							
1473	8¢ Pharmacy	11/10/72	.20	.20	.65	(4)	6.00	166
a	Blue and orange omitted		825.00					
b	Blue omitted		2,250.00					
c	Orange omitted		2,250.00					
1474	8¢ Stamp Collecting	11/17/72	.20	.20	.65	(4)	1.00	167
a	Black omitted		700.00					
	Issues of 1973, Perf. 11 x 10.5							
1475	8¢ Love	01/26/73	.20	.20	1.00	(6)	2.50	320
	American Bicentennial Issue, Perf. 11							
1476	8¢ Printer and Patriots Examining							
	Pamphlet	02/16/73	.20	.20	.65	(4)	1.00	166
1477	8¢ Posting a Broadside	04/13/73	.20	.20	.65	(4)	1.00	163
	Pair with full horizontal gutter between		—					
1478	8¢ Postrider	06/22/73	.20	.20	.65	(4)	1.00	159
1479	8¢ Drummer	09/28/73	.20	.20	.65	(4)	1.00	147
	Boston Tea Party							
1480	8¢ British Merchantman	07/04/73	.20	.20			1.00	49
1481	8¢ British Three-Master	07/04/73	.20	.20			1.00	49
1482	8¢ Boats and Ship's Hull	07/04/73	.20	.20			1.00	49
1483	8¢ Boat and Dock	07/04/73	.20	.20			1.00	49
a	Block of 4, #1480-83		.65	.75	.75	(4)	3.00	
b	As "a," blk. (engraved) omitted		1,500.00					
c	As "a," blk. (lithographed) omitted		1,400.00					

1464 **1465**

1466 **1467** **1467a**

1468

1469 **1470**

1473

1474

1471 **1472**

1475

1476

1477

1478

1479

1480 **1481**

1482 **1483**

1483a

1484

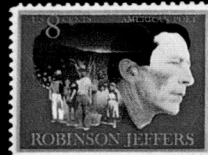

1485

1486

1487

1488

1489

1490

1491

1492

1493

Nearly 27 billion U.S. stamps are sold yearly to carry your letters to every corner of the world.

People Serving You

Mail is picked up from nearly a third of a million local collection boxes, as well as your mailbox.

People Serving You

More than 87 billion letters and packages are handled yearly—almost 300 million every delivery day.

People Serving You

The People in your Postal Service handle and deliver more than 500 million packages yearly.

People Serving You

Thousands of machines, buildings, and vehicles must be operated and maintained to keep your mail moving.

People Serving You

1494

1495

1496

1497

1498

The skill of sorting mail manually is still vital to delivery of your mail.

People Serving You

Employees use modern, high-speed equipment to sort and process huge volumes of mail in central locations.

People Serving You

Thirteen billion pounds of mail are handled yearly by postal employees as they speed your letters and packages.

People Serving You

Our customers include 54 million urban and 12 million rural families, plus 9 million businesses.

People Serving You

Employees cover 4 million miles each delivery day to bring mail to your home or business.

People Serving You

Issues of 1973		Un	U	PB	#	FDC	Q(M)
American Arts Issue, Perf 11							
1484 8¢ George Gershwin and Scene							
from "Porgy and Bess"	02/28/73	.20	.20	1.75	(12)	1.00	139
a Vertical pair, imperf. horizontally		*240.00*					
1485 8¢ Robinson Jeffers, Man and Children							
of Carmel with Burro	08/13/73	.20	.20	1.75	(12)	1.00	128
a Vertical pair, imperf. horizontally		*250.00*					
1486 8¢ Henry Ossawa Tanner,							
Palette and Rainbow	09/10/73	.20	.20	1.75	(12)	1.00	146
1487 8¢ Willa Cather, Pioneer Family							
and Covered Wagon	09/20/73	.20	.20	1.75	(12)	1.00	140
a Vertical pair, imperf. horizontally		*275.00*					
1488 8¢ Nicolaus Copernicus	04/23/73	.20	.20	.65	(4)	1.75	159
a Orange omitted		*1,000.00*					
b Black omitted		*1,000.00*					
Postal Service Employees Issue, Perf. 10.5 x 11							
1489 8¢ Stamp Counter	04/30/73	.20	.20			1.00	49
1490 8¢ Mail Collection	04/30/73	.20	.20			1.00	49
1491 8¢ Letter Facing on Conveyor	04/30/73	.20	.20			1.00	49
1492 8¢ Parcel Post Sorting	04/30/73	.20	.20			1.00	49
1493 8¢ Mail Canceling	04/30/73	.20	.20			1.00	49
1494 8¢ Manual Letter Routing	04/30/73	.20	.20			1.00	49
1495 8¢ Electronic Letter Routing	04/30/73	.20	.20			1.00	49
1496 8¢ Loading Mail on Truck	04/30/73	.20	.20			1.00	49
1497 8¢ Carrier Delivering Mail	04/30/73	.20	.20			1.00	49
1498 8¢ Rural Mail Delivery	04/30/73	.20	.20			1.00	49
a Strip of 10, #1489-98		1.75	1.75	3.25	(20)	5.00	

#1489-98 were the first United States postage stamps to have printing on the back.
(See also 1559-62.)

Robert Indiana

Born Robert E. Clark, renowned American Pop artist Robert Indiana adopted the name of his native state early in his career. A painter of the American environment, he creates images from words and numbers that are inspired by the world of signs— in particular, signs of the highway that refer allegorically to life's journey. His paintings, sculpture, and graphics are exhibited internationally and are included in the permanent collections of the Museum of Modern Art and the Smithsonian Institution among many others. In 1978, he left New York City for the solitude of Vinalhaven, Maine, the small fishing community and summer vacation spot where he lives and works today. His 1973 Love was the first love stamp ever issued by the United States Postal Service and the artist's only stamp design. ■

	Issues of 1973		Un	U	PB	#	FDC	Q(M)
	Perf. 11							
1499	8¢ Harry S. Truman	05/08/73	.20	.20	.65	(4)	1.00	157
	Progress in Electronics Issue, (See also #C86)							
1500	6¢ Marconi's Spark							
	Coil and Gap	07/10/73	.20	.20	.55	(4)	1.00	53
1501	8¢ Transistors and Printed							
	Circuit Board	07/10/73	.20	.20	.70	(4)	1.00	160
a	Black omitted		500.00					
b	Tan and lilac omitted		1,250.00					
1502	15¢ Microphone, Speaker, Vacuum							
	Tube, TV Camera Tube	07/10/73	.30	.20	1.30	(4)	1.00	39
a	Black omitted		1,500.00					
1503	8¢ Lyndon B. Johnson	08/27/73	.20	.20	1.90	(12)	1.00	153
a	Horizontal pair, imperf. vertically		350.00					
	Issues of 1973-74, Rural America Issue							
1504	8¢ Angus and Longhorn Cattle,							
	by F.C. Murphy	10/05/73	.20	.20	.65	(4)	1.00	146
a	Green and red brown omitted		950.00					
b	Vertical pair, imperf. between			—				
1505	10¢ Chautauqua Tent and							
	Buggies	08/06/74	.20	.20	.85	(4)	1.00	151
1506	10¢ Wheat Fields and Train	08/16/74	.20	.20	.85	(4)	1.00	141
a	Black and blue omitted		750.00					
	Issues of 1973, Christmas Issue, Perf. 10.5 x 11							
1507	8¢ Small Cowper Madonna,							
	by Raphael	11/07/73	.20	.20	1.75	(12)	1.00	885
	Pair with full vertical gutter between		—					
1508	8¢ Christmas Tree in							
	Needlepoint	11/07/73	.20	.20	1.75	(12)	1.00	940
	Pair with full horizontal gutter between		—					
a	Vertical pair, imperf. between		300.00					
	Issues of 1973-74, Perf. 11 x 10.5							
1509	10¢ 50-Star and							
	13-Star Flags	12/08/73	.20	.20	4.25	(20)	1.00	
a	Horizontal pair, imperf. between		50.00	—				
b	Blue omitted		175.00					
c	Imperf., pair		950.00					
d	Horizontal pair, imperf. vertically		1,000.00					
e	Tagging omitted		7.50					
1510	10¢ Jefferson Memorial	12/14/73	.20	.20	.85	(4)	1.00	
a	Untagged (Bureau precanceled)			.20				
b	Booklet pane of 5 + label		1.65	.55			2.25	
c	Booklet pane of 8		1.65	.70			2.50	
d	Booklet pane of 6	08/05/74	5.25	1.00			3.00	
e	Vertical pair, imperf. horizontally		525.00					
f	Vertical pair, imperf. between		—					
g	Tagging omitted		5.00					

1499

1500

1501

1502

1503

1504

1505

1506

1507

1508

1509

1510

1974

1511

1518

1525

1526

1527

1528

1529

1530   1531   1532   1533

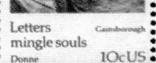
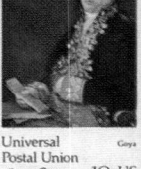

1537a

1534   1535   1536   1537

Issues of 1973-74		Un	U	PB/LP	#	FDC	Q(M)
1511 10¢ ZIP Code	01/04/74	.20	.20	1.75	(8)	1.00	
Pair with full horizontal gutter between		—					
a Yellow omitted		65.00					
1512-17 Not assigned							
Coil Stamps, Perf. 10 Vertically							
1518 6.3¢ Liberty Bell	10/01/74	.20	.20	.80	(2)	1.00	
a Untagged (Bureau precanceled)			.20	.80	(2)		
b Imperf., pair		200.00		550.00	(2)		
c As "a," imperf., pair			100.00	250.00	(2)		
1519 10¢ red and blue Flags (1509)	12/08/73	.20	.20			1.00	
a Imperf., pair		37.50					
1520 10¢ blue Jefferson Memorial (1510)	12/14/73	.25	.20	.75	(2)	1.00	
a Untagged (Bureau precanceled)			.25				
b Imperf., pair		40.00		70.00	(2)		
1521-24 Not assigned							
Issues of 1974, Perf. 11							
1525 10¢ Veterans of Foreign Wars	03/11/74	.20	.20	.85	(4)	2.00	149
Perf. 10.5 x 11							
1526 10¢ Robert Frost	03/26/74	.20	.20	.85	(4)	1.00	145
Perf. 11							
1527 10¢ Expo '74 World's Fair	04/18/74	.20	.20	2.50	(12)	1.00	135
Perf. 11 x 10.5							
1528 10¢ Horse Racing	05/04/74	.20	.20	2.50	(12)	2.00	156
a Blue omitted		900.00					
b Red omitted		—					
Perf. 11							
1529 10¢ Skylab	05/14/74	.20	.20	.85	(4)	1.50	164
a Vertical pair, imperf. between		—					
Universal Postal Union Issue							
1530 10¢ Michelangelo, from "School of Athens," by Raphael	06/06/74	.20	.20			1.00	24
1531 10¢ "Five Feminine Virtues," by Hokusai	06/06/74	.20	.20			1.00	24
1532 10¢ "Old Scraps," by John Fredrick Peto	06/06/74	.20	.20			1.00	24
1533 10¢ "The Lovely Reader," by Jean Etienne Liotard	06/06/74	.20	.20			1.00	24
1534 10¢ "Lady Writing Letter," by Gerard Terborch	06/06/74	.20	.20			1.00	24
1535 10¢ Inkwell and Quill, from "Boy with a Top," by Jean-Baptiste Simeon Chardin	06/06/74	.20	.20			1.00	24
1536 10¢ Mrs. John Douglas, by Thomas Gainsborough	06/06/74	.20	.20			1.00	24
1537 10¢ Don Antonio Noriega, by Francisco de Goya	06/06/74	.20	.20			1.00	24
a Block of 8, #1530-37		1.75	1.60	3.50	(16)	4.00	
b As "a," imperf. vertically		7,500.00					

	Issues of 1974		Un	U	PB	#	FDC	Q(M)
	Mineral Heritage Issue, Perf. 11							
1538	10¢ Petrified Wood	06/13/74	.20	.20			1.00	42
a	Light blue and yellow omitted		—					
1539	10¢ Tourmaline	06/13/74	.20	.20			1.00	42
a	Light blue omitted		—					
b	Black and purple omitted		—					
1540	10¢ Amethyst	06/13/74	.20	.20			1.00	42
a	Light blue and yellow omitted		—					
1541	10¢ Rhodochrosite	06/13/74	.20	.20			1.00	42
a	Block of 4, #1538-41		.80	.90	.90	(4)	2.50	
b	As "a," light blue and							
	yellow omitted		1,900.00					
c	Light blue omitted		—					
d	Black and red omitted		—					
1542	10¢ First Kentucky Settlement-							
	Ft. Harrod	06/15/74	.20	.20	.85	(4)	1.00	156
a	Dull black omitted		850.00					
b	Green, black and blue omitted		3,750.00					
c	Green omitted		—					
d	Green and black omitted		—					
e	Tagging omitted			—				
	American Bicentennial Issue, First Continental Congress							
1543	10¢ Carpenters' Hall	07/04/74	.20	.20			1.00	49
1544	10¢ "We Ask but for Peace,							
	Liberty and Safety"	07/04/74	.20	.20			1.00	49
1545	10¢ "Deriving Their Just Powers							
	from the Consent of							
	the Governed"	07/04/74	.20	.20			1.00	49
1546	10¢ Independence Hall	07/04/74	.20	.20			1.00	49
a	Block of 4, #1543-46		.80	.90	.90	(4)	2.75	
1547	10¢ Energy Conservation	09/23/74	.20	.20	.85	(4)	1.00	149
a	Blue and orange omitted		900.00					
b	Orange and green omitted		650.00					
c	Green omitted		825.00					
	American Folklore Issue							
1548	10¢ Headless Horseman							
	and Ichabod Crane	10/10/74	.20	.20	.85	(4)	2.00	157
1549	10¢ Retarded Children	10/12/74	.20	.20	.85	(4)	1.00	150
a	Tagging omitted		7.50					
	Christmas Issue, Perf. 10.5 x 11							
1550	10¢ Angel from Perussis							
	Altarpiece	10/23/74	.20	.20	2.10	(10)	1.00	835
	Perf. 11 x 10.5							
1551	10¢ "The Road-Winter," by							
	Currier and Ives	10/23/74	.20	.20	2.50	(12)	1.00	883
a	Buff omitted		35.00					
	Precanceled Self-Adhesive, Imperf.							
1552	10¢ Dove Weather Vane atop							
	Mount Vernon	11/15/74	.20	.20	4.25	(20)	1.00	213
	Issues of 1975, American Arts Issue, Perf. 10.5 x 11							
1553	10¢ Benjamin West,							
	Self-Portrait	02/10/75	.20	.20	2.10	(10)	1.00	157
	Perf. 11							
1554	10¢ Paul Laurence Dunbar							
	and Lamp	05/01/75	.20	.20	2.10	(10)	1.00	146
a	Imperf., pair		1,300.00					
1555	10¢ D.W. Griffith and							
	Motion-Picture Camera	05/27/75	.20	.20	.85	(4)	1.00	149
a	Brown omitted		625.00					

1538

1539

1540

1541 1541a

1542

1543 1544

1545 1546 1546a 1547

1548

1549

1550 1551

1552

1553

1554

1555

1556

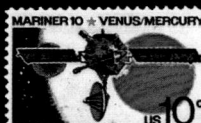

1557

1558

1559

1560

1561

YOUTHFUL HEROINE
On the dark night of April 26, 1777, 16-year-old Sybil Ludington rode her horse "Star" alone through the Connecticut countryside rallying her father's militia to repel a raid by the British on Danbury.

GALLANT SOLDIER
The conspicuously courageous actions of black foot soldier Salem Poor at the Battle of Bunker Hill on June 17, 1775, earned him citations for his bravery and leadership ability.

FINANCIAL HERO
Businessman and broker Haym Salomon was responsible for raising most of the money needed to finance the American Revolution and later to save the new nation from collapse.

1562

1563

1564

FINANCIAL HERO
Businessman and broker Haym Salomon was responsible for raising most of the money needed to finance the American Revolution and later to save the new nation from collapse.

1565 **1566** **1569**

1567 **1568** **1568a**

1570 **1570a**

Issues of 1975		Un	U	PB	#	FDC	Q(M)
Space Issues, Perf. 11							
1556	10¢ Pioneer 10 Passing						
	Jupiter	02/28/75	.20	.20	.85	(4)	2.00	174
a	Red and yellow omitted		1,400.00					
b	Blue omitted		950.00					
c	Tagging omitted		7.50					
1557	10¢ Mariner 10, Venus						
	and Mercury	04/04/75	.20	.20	.85	(4)	2.00	159
a	Red omitted		500.00					
b	Ultramarine and bister omitted		2,000.00					
c	Tagging omitted		7.50					
1558	10¢ Collective Bargaining	03/13/75	.20	.20	1.75	(8)	1.00	153
	Imperfs. of #1558 exist from printer's waste							
American Bicentennial Issue Perf. 11 x 10.5							
1559	8¢ Sybil Ludington						
	Riding Horse	03/25/75	.20	.20	1.50	(10)	1.00	63
a	Back inscription omitted		225.00					
1560	10¢ Salem Poor Carrying						
	Musket	03/25/75	.20	.20	2.10	(10)	1.00	158
a	Back inscription omitted		225.00					
1561	10¢ Haym Salomon						
	Figuring Accounts	03/25/75	.20	.20	2.10	(10)	1.00	167
a	Back inscription omitted		225.00					
b	Red omitted		250.00					
1562	18¢ Peter Francisco						
	Shouldering Cannon	03/25/75	.35	.20	3.60	(10)	1.00	45
Battle of Lexington & Concord, Perf. 11							
1563	10¢ "Birth of Liberty,"						
	by Henry Sandham	04/19/75	.20	.20	2.50	(12)	1.00	144
a	Vertical pair, imperf. horizontally		425.00					
Battle of Bunker Hill							
1564	10¢ "Battle of Bunker						
	Hill," by John Trumbull	06/17/75	.20	.20	2.50	(12)	1.00	140
Military Uniforms							
1565	10¢ Soldier with Flintlock						
	Musket, Uniform Button	07/04/75	.20	.20			1.00	45
1566	10¢ Sailor with Grappling						
	Hook, First Navy Jack, 1775	07/04/75	.20	.20			1.00	45
1567	10¢ Marine with Musket,						
	Full-Rigged Ship	07/04/75	.20	.20			1.00	45
1568	10¢ Militiaman with						
	Musket, Powder Horn	07/04/75	.20	.20			1.00	45
a	Block of 4, #1565-68		.85	.90	2.50	(12)	2.50	
Apollo Soyuz Space Issue							
1569	10¢ Apollo and Soyuz						
	after Docking and Earth	07/15/75	.20	.20			3.00	81
	Pair with full horizontal gutter between		—					
1570	10¢ Spacecraft before Docking,						
	Earth and Project Emblem	07/15/75	.20	.20			3.00	81
a	Attached pair, #1569-70		.45	.40	2.50	(12)	5.00	
b	As "a", tagging omitted		30.00					
c	As "a," vertical pair,						
	imperf. horizontally		2,000.00					

	Issues of 1975		Un	U	PB	#	FDC	Q(M)
	Perf. 11 x 10.5							
1571	10¢ International							
	Women's Year	08/26/75	.20	.20	1.30	(6)	1.00	146
	Postal Service Bicentennial Issue							
1572	10¢ Stagecoach and							
	Trailer Truck	09/03/75	.20	.20			1.00	42
1573	10¢ Old and New							
	Locomotives	09/03/75	.20	.20			1.00	42
1574	10¢ Early Mail Plane and Jet	09/03/75	.20	.20			1.00	42
1575	10¢ Satellite for Mailgrams	09/03/75	.20	.20			1.00	42
a	Block of 4, #1572-75		.85	.90	2.50	(12)	1.25	
b	As "a," red "10¢" omitted		9,500.00					
	Perf. 11							
1576	10¢ World Peace Through Law	09/29/75	.20	.20	.85	(4)	1.25	147
a	Tagging omitted		6.00					
	Banking and Commerce Issue							
1577	10¢ Engine Turning, Indian Head							
	Penny and Morgan Silver Dollar	10/06/75	.25	.20			1.00	73
1578	10¢ Seated Liberty Quarter, $20							
	Gold Piece and Engine Turning	10/06/75	.25	.20			1.00	73
a	Attached pair, #1577-78		.50	.40	1.20	(4)	1.25	
b	Brown and blue omitted		2,250.00					
c	As "a," brn., blue and yel. omitted		2,750.00					
	Christmas Issue							
1579	(10¢) Madonna and Child,							
	by Domenico Ghirlandaio	10/14/75	.20	.20	2.50	(12)	1.00	739
a	Imperf., pair		90.00					
	Plate flaw ("d" damaged)		5.00	—				
	Perf. 11.2							
1580	(10¢) Christmas Card,							
	by Louis Prang, 1878	10/14/75	.20	.20	2.50	(12)	1.00	879
a	Imperf., pair		90.00					
c	Perf. 10.9		.25	.20	3.50	(12)		
	Perf. 10.5 x 11.3							
1580B	(10¢) Christmas Card,							
	by Louis Prang, 1878		.60	.20	15.00	(12)		
	Issues of 1977-1981, Americana Issue, Perf. 11 x 10.5 (Designs 18.5 x 22.5mm; #1590-90a, 17.5 x 20mm; see also 1606, 1608, 1610-19, 1622-23, 1625, 1811, 1813, 1816)							
1581	1¢ Inkwell & Quill	12/08/77	.20	.20	.25	(4)	1.00	
a	Untagged (Bureau precanceled)			.20				
d	Tagging omitted		4.50					
1582	2¢ Speaker's Stand	12/08/77	.20	.20	.25	(4)	1.00	
a	Untagged (Bureau precanceled)			.20				
b	Cream paper, dull gum, 1981		.20	.20	.25	(4)		
c	Tagging omitted		4.50					
1583	Not assigned							
1584	3¢ Early Ballot Box	12/08/77	.20	.20	.30	(4)	1.00	
a	Untagged (Bureau precanceled)			.20				
b	Tagging omitted		6.00					
1585	4¢ Books, Eyeglasses	12/08/77	.20	.20	.40	(4)	1.00	
a	Untagged (Bureau precanceled)			1.25				
1586-89	Not assigned							
	Booklet Stamp							
1590	9¢ Capitol Dome, single (1591)							
	from booklet (1623a)	03/11/77	.45	.20			1.00	
	Booklet Stamp, Perf. 10							
1590A	Single (1591) from booklet (1623c)		22.50	15.00				
	#1590 is on white paper; #1591 is on gray paper.							

1571

1572

1573

1574

1575

1575a

1576

1577

1578

1578a

1579

1580

1581

1582

1591

1592

1593

1594

1595

1596

1597

1599

1603

1604

1605

1606

	Issues of 1975-81		Un	U	PB/LP	#	FDC
	Americana Issue (continued), Perf. 11 x 10.5						
1591	9¢ Capitol Dome	11/24/75	.20	.20	.85	(4)	1.00
a	Untagged (Bureau precanceled)			.20			
b	Tagging omitted		5.00				
1592	10¢ Contemplation of Justice	11/17/77	.20	.20	.90	(4)	1.00
a	Untagged (Bureau precanceled)			.25			
b	Tagging omitted		7.00				
1593	11¢ Printing Press	11/13/75	.20	.20	.90	(4)	1.00
a	Tagging omitted		4.00				
1594	12¢ Torch	04/08/81	.25	.20	1.60	(4)	1.00
a	Tagging omitted		5.00				
1595	13¢ Liberty Bell, single from booklet		.30	.20			1.00
a	Booklet pane of 6	10/31/75	2.25	.75			2.00
b	Booklet pane of 7 + label		2.25	.75			2.75
c	Booklet pane of 8		2.25	1.00			2.50
d	Booklet pane of 5 + label	04/02/76	1.75	.75			2.25
e	Vertical pair, imperf. between		1,200.00				
	Perf. 11						
1596	13¢ Eagle and Shield	12/01/75	.25	.20	3.25	(12)	1.00
a	Imperf., pair		50.00	—			
b	Yellow omitted		160.00				
d	Line perforated		27.50	—	375.00	(12)	
1597	15¢ Ft. McHenry Flag	06/30/78	.30	.20	1.90	(6)	1.00
a	Imperf., pair		20.00				
b	Gray omitted		600.00				
d	Tagging omitted		4.00				
	Booklet Stamp, Perf. 11 x 10.5						
1598	15¢ Ft. McHenry Flag (1597),						
	single from booklet		.40	.20			1.00
a	Booklet pane of 8	06/30/78	4.25	.80			2.50
1599	16¢ Head of Liberty	03/31/78	.35	.20	1.90	(4)	1.00
1600-02	Not assigned						
1603	24¢ Old North Church	11/14/75	.50	.20	2.25	(4)	1.00
a	Tagging omitted		7.50				
1604	28¢ Ft. Nisqually	08/11/78	.55	.20	2.40	(4)	1.25
	Dull finish gum		1.10		10.00	(4)	
1605	29¢ Sandy Hook Lighthouse	04/14/78	.60	.20	3.00	(4)	2.00
	Dull finish gum		2.00		15.00	(4)	
1606	30¢ One-Rm. Schoolhouse	08/27/79	.55	.20	2.40	(4)	1.25
a	Tagging omitted		15.00				
1607	Not assigned						
	Perf. 11						
1608	50¢ Whale Oil Lamp	09/11/79	.85	.20	3.75	(4)	1.50
a	Black omitted		300.00				
b	Vertical pair, imperf. horizontally		1,750.00				
c	Tagging omitted		10.00				
1609	Not assigned						
1610	$1 Candle and Rushlight						
	Holder	07/02/79	2.00	.20	8.50	(4)	3.00
a	Brown omitted		275.00				
b	Tan, orange and yellow omitted		350.00				
c	Brown inverted		14,500.00				
d	Tagging omitted		15.00				
1611	$2 Kerosene Table Lamp	11/16/78	3.75	.75	16.00	(4)	5.00
1612	$5 Railroad Lantern	08/23/79	8.25	1.75	35.00	(4)	12.50

	Issues of 1975-81		Un	U	PB/LP	#	FDC
	Coil Stamps, Perf. 10 Vertically						
1613	3.1¢ Guitar	10/25/79	.20	.20	1.50	(2)	1.00
a	Untagged (Bureau precanceled)			.50			
b	Imperf., pair		1,400.00		3,600.00	(2)	
1614	7.7¢ Saxhorns	11/20/76	.20	.20	1.00	(2)	1.00
a	Untagged (Bureau precanceled)			.35			
b	As "a," imperf., pair			1,600.00	4,400.00	(2)	
1615	7.9¢ Drum	04/23/76	.20	.20	.75	(2)	1.00
a	Untagged (Bureau precanceled)			.20			
b	Imperf., pair		600.00				
1615C	8.4¢ Piano	07/13/78	.20	.20	3.25	(2)	1.00
d	Untagged (Bureau precanceled)			.30			
e	As "d," pair, imperf. between			60.00	125.00	(2)	
f	As "d," imperf., pair			17.50	35.00	(2)	
	Americana Issue, Perf. 10 Vertically (See also #1581-82, 1584-85, 1590-99, 1603-05, 1811, 1813, 1816)						
1616	9¢ slate green Capitol Dome (1591)	03/05/76	.20	.20	1.00	(2)	1.00
a	Imperf., pair		160.00		375.00	(2)	
b	Untagged (Bureau precanceled)			.35			
c	As "b," imperf., pair			700.00	—	(2)	
1617	10¢ purple Contemplation of Justice (1592)	11/04/77	.20	.20	1.10	(2)	1.00
	Dull finish gum		.30		2.75	(2)	
a	Untagged (Bureau precanceled)			.25			
b	Imperf., pair		60.00		125.00	(2)	
1618	13¢ brown Liberty Bell (1595)	11/25/75	.25	.20	.70	(2)	1.00
a	Untagged (Bureau precanceled)			.45			
b	Imperf., pair		25.00		65.00	(2)	
g	Pair, imperf. between		—				
1618C	15¢ Ft. McHenry Flag (1597)	06/30/78	.40	.20			1.00
d	Imperf., pair		25.00				
e	Pair, imperf. between		150.00				
f	Gray omitted		40.00				
i	Tagging omitted		20.00				
1619	16¢ blue Head of Liberty (1599)	03/31/78	.35	.20	1.50	(2)	1.00
a	Huck Press printing (white background with a bluish tinge, fraction of a millimeter smaller)		.50	.20			
1620-21	Not assigned						
	Perf. 11 x 10.75						
1622	13¢ Flag over Independence Hall	11/15/75	.25	.20	5.75	(20)	1.00
a	Horizontal pair, imperf. between		50.00				
b	Imperf., pair		1,100.00				
c	Perf. 11	1981	.65	.20	60.00	(20)	
d	As "c," vertical pair, imperf.		150.00				
e	Horizontal pair, imperf. vertically		—				
f	Tagging omitted		4.00				
	Perf. 11.25						
1622C	13¢ Flag over Independence Hall		1.00	.25	20.00	(6)	
d	Vertical pair, imperf.		150.00				
	Booklet Stamps, Perf. 11						
1623	13¢ Flag over Capitol, single from booklet (1623a)		.25	.20			1.00
a	Booklet pane of 8, (1 #1590 and 7 #1623)	03/11/77	2.25	1.10			25.00
d	Attached pair, #1590 and 1623		.70	.70			

1613

1614

1615

1615C

1622

1623a

1632

1629   1630   1631   1631a

1633   1634   1635

1636   1637

1638   1639   1640

1641   1642

1643   1644   1645

1646   1647

Issues of 1975-1977		Un	U	PB	#	FDC	Q(M)
Booklet Stamps, Perf. 10 x 9.75							
1623B 13¢ Single from booklet		.80	.80				
c Booklet pane of 8,							
(1 #1590a and 7 #1623b)		29.00	—			12.50	
e Attached pair, #1590a and 1623b		24.00	22.50				
#1623, 1623b issued only in booklets. All stamps are imperf. at one side or imperf. at one side and bottom.							
1624 Not assigned							
Coil Stamp, Perf. 10 Vertically							
1625 13¢ Flag over Independence Hall (1622)	11/15/75	.25	.20			1.00	
a Imperf. pair		25.00					
American Bicentennial Issue, Perf. 11							
1629 13¢ Drummer Boy	01/01/76	.25	.20			1.25	73
1630 13¢ Old Drummer	01/01/76	.25	.20			1.25	73
1631 13¢ Fife Player	01/01/76	.25	.20			1.25	73
a Strip of 3, #1629-31		.75	.65	3.50	(12)	2.00	
b As "a," imperf.		1,050.00					
c Imperf., pair, #1631		800.00					
1632 13¢ Interphil 76	01/17/76	.20	.20	1.00	(4)	1.00	158
State Flags							
1633 13¢ Delaware	02/23/76	.25	.20			1.50	9
1634 13¢ Pennsylvania	02/23/76	.25	.20			1.50	9
1635 13¢ New Jersey	02/23/76	.25	.20			1.50	9
1636 13¢ Georgia	02/23/76	.25	.20			1.50	9
1637 13¢ Connecticut	02/23/76	.25	.20			1.50	9
1638 13¢ Massachusetts	02/23/76	.25	.20			1.50	9
1639 13¢ Maryland	02/23/76	.25	.20			1.50	9
1640 13¢ South Carolina	02/23/76	.25	.20			1.50	9
1641 13¢ New Hampshire	02/23/76	.25	.20			1.50	9
1642 13¢ Virginia	02/23/76	.25	.20			1.50	9
1643 13¢ New York	02/23/76	.25	.20			1.50	9
1644 13¢ North Carolina	02/23/76	.25	.20			1.50	9
1645 13¢ Rhode Island	02/23/76	.25	.20			1.50	9
1646 13¢ Vermont	02/23/76	.25	.20			1.50	9
1647 13¢ Kentucky	02/23/76	.25	.20			1.50	9

Melbourne Brindle (1904-1995) Australian-born Melbourne Brindle began his career as a letterer in a San Francisco department store. An accomplished artist and illustrator, he was renowned and highly sought-after for his automotive paintings, which were commissioned by Ford Motor Company, Packard, General Motors, and Chrysler. Created with astonishing accuracy, his art was informed by his interest in collecting and restoring classic cars. He also created images for such prominent clients as Douglas Aircraft, United Airlines, *The Saturday Evening Post,* and the United States Postal Service. His paintings have been exhibited at the National Air and Space Museum and in Buckingham Palace, among others. ∎

1976

	American Bicentennial Issue (continued), State Flags					
1648	13¢ Tennessee	02/23/76	.25	.20	1.50	9
1649	13¢ Ohio	02/23/76	.25	.20	1.50	9
1650	13¢ Louisiana	02/23/76	.25	.20	1.50	9
1651	13¢ Indiana	02/23/76	.25	.20	1.50	9
1652	13¢ Mississippi	02/23/76	.25	.20	1.50	9
1653	13¢ Illinois	02/23/76	.25	.20	1.50	9
1654	13¢ Alabama	02/23/76	.25	.20	1.50	9
1655	13¢ Maine	02/23/76	.25	.20	1.50	9
1656	13¢ Missouri	02/23/76	.25	.20	1.50	9
1657	13¢ Arkansas	02/23/76	.25	.20	1.50	9
1658	13¢ Michigan	02/23/76	.25	.20	1.50	9
1659	13¢ Florida	02/23/76	.25	.20	1.50	9
1660	13¢ Texas	02/23/76	.25	.20	1.50	9
1661	13¢ Iowa	02/23/76	.25	.20	1.50	9
1662	13¢ Wisconsin	02/23/76	.25	.20	1.50	9
1663	13¢ California	02/23/76	.25	.20	1.50	9
1664	13¢ Minnesota	02/23/76	.25	.20	1.50	9
1665	13¢ Oregon	02/23/76	.25	.20	1.50	9
1666	13¢ Kansas	02/23/76	.25	.20	1.50	9
1667	13¢ West Virginia	02/23/76	.25	.20	1.50	9

Mark English

Born in Hubbard, Texas, Mark English picked cotton, chased rodeos, painted billboards, and served in the Army before studying art at the Art Center College in Los Angeles. He began his career as an art director in advertising, but quickly became known as one of America's leading magazine illustrators. A Hall of Fame illustrator, he is admired for his innovative artistic experiments and has created images for most national publications including *The Saturday Evening Post*, *Good Housekeeping*, *Redbook*, *McCall's*, and *Time*. He has counseled aspiring and professional illustrators as an artist-in-residence at Hallmark Cards in Kansas City and at The Illustration Academy, a school that he founded. His striking designs appear on 12 United States postage stamps. ■

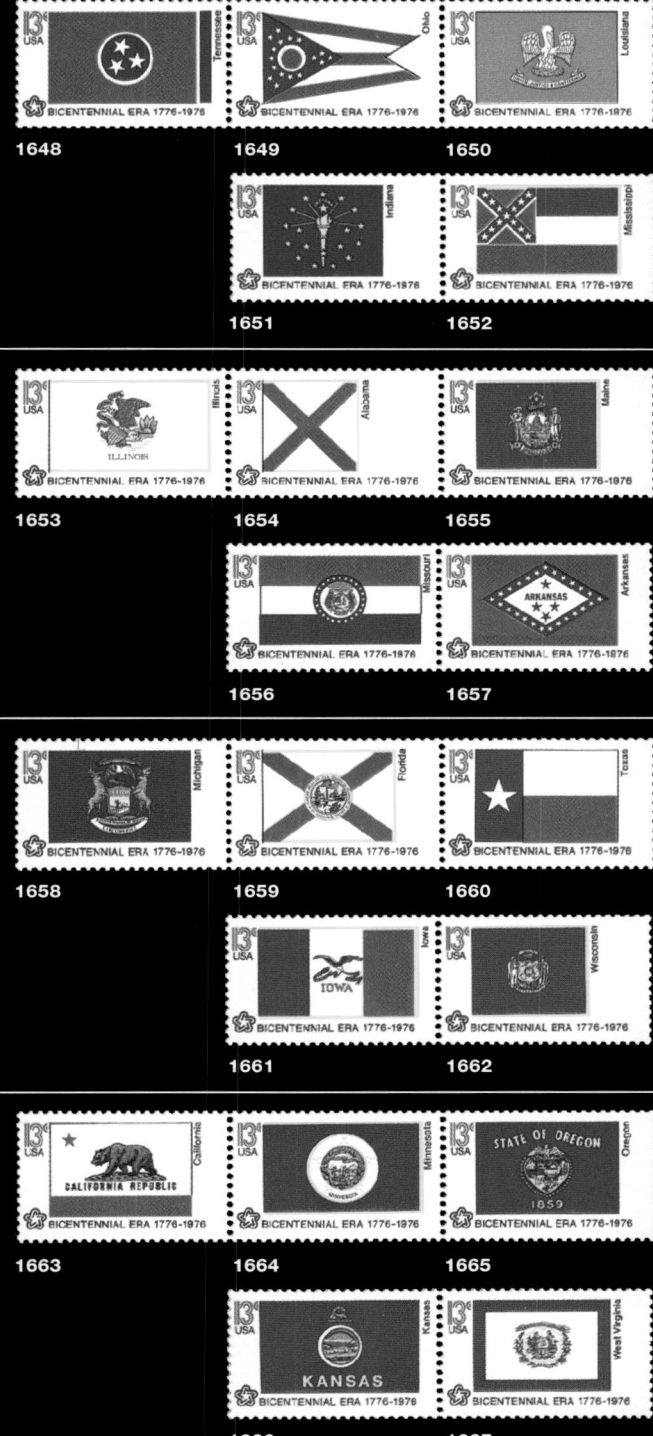

1648

1649

1650

1651

1652

1653

1654

1655

1656

1657

1658

1659

1660

1661

1662

1663

1664

1665

1666

1667

1976

1668   1669   1670

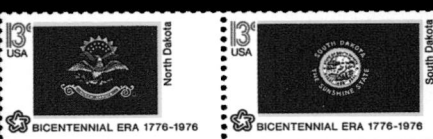

1671   1672

1673   1674   1675

1676   1677

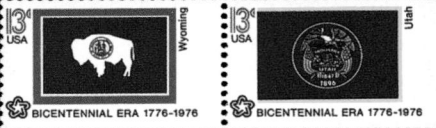

1678   1679   1680

	Issues of 1976		Un	U	FDC	Q(M)
	American Bicentennial Issue (continued), State Flags					
1668	13¢ Nevada	02/23/76	.25	.20	1.50	9
1669	13¢ Nebraska	02/23/76	.25	.20	1.50	9
1670	13¢ Colorado	02/23/76	.25	.20	1.50	9
1671	13¢ North Dakota	02/23/76	.25	.20	1.50	9
1672	13¢ South Dakota	02/23/76	.25	.20	1.50	9
1673	13¢ Montana	02/23/76	.25	.20	1.50	9
1674	13¢ Washington	02/23/76	.25	.20	1.50	9
1675	13¢ Idaho	02/23/76	.25	.20	1.50	9
1676	13¢ Wyoming	02/23/76	.25	.20	1.50	9
1677	13¢ Utah	02/23/76	.25	.20	1.50	9
1678	13¢ Oklahoma	02/23/76	.25	.20	1.50	9
1679	13¢ New Mexico	02/23/76	.25	.20	1.50	9
1680	13¢ Arizona	02/23/76	.25	.20	1.50	9
1681	13¢ Alaska	02/23/76	.25	.20	1.50	9
1682	13¢ Hawaii	02/23/76	.25	.20	1.50	9
a	Pane of 50, #1633-82		15.00	—	27.50	

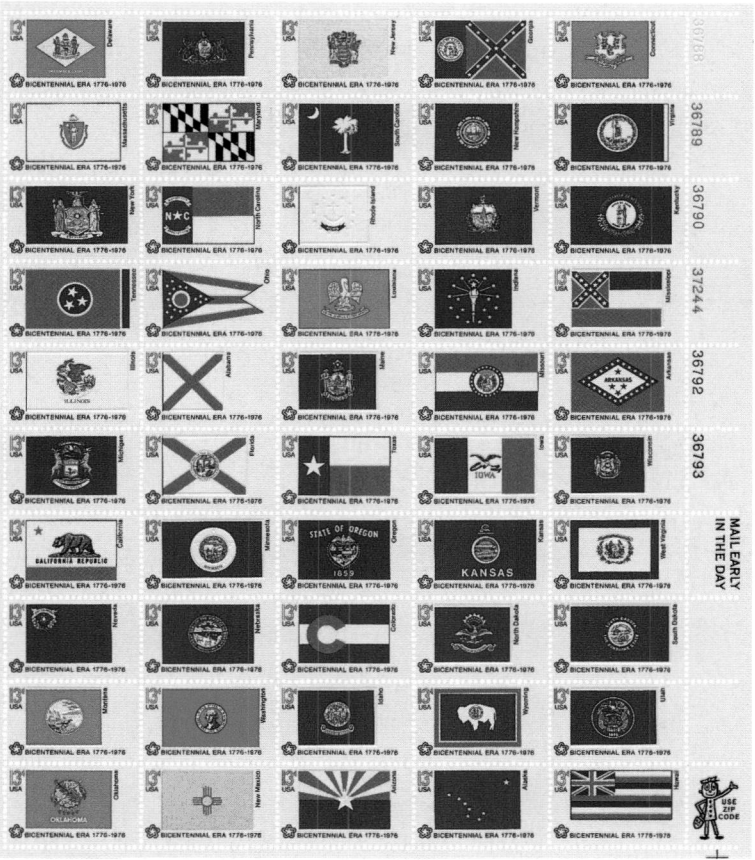

Example of 1682a

1976

	Issues of 1976		Un	U	PB	#	FDC	Q(M)
1683	13¢ Telephone Centennial	03/10/76	.25	.20	1.10	(4)	1.00	158
1684	13¢ Commercial Aviation	03/19/76	.25	.20	2.75	(10)	1.00	156
1685	13¢ Chemistry	04/06/76	.25	.20	3.25	(12)	2.00	158
	Pair with full vertical gutter between		—					
American Bicentennial Issue Souvenir Sheets, 5 stamps each, Perf. 11								
1686	13¢ The Surrender of Lord							
	Cornwallis at Yorktown, by							
	John Trumbull	05/29/76	3.25	—			6.00	2
a	13¢ Two American Officers		.45	.40				2
b	13¢ Gen. Benjamin Lincoln		.45	.40				2
c	13¢ George Washington		.45	.40				2
d	13¢ John Trumbull, Col. David Cobb,							
	General Friedrich von Steuben,							
	Marquis de Lafayette and							
	Thomas Nelson		.45	.40				2
e	13¢ Alexander Hamilton,							
	John Laurens and Walter Stewart		.45	.40				2
f	"USA/13¢" omitted on "b,"							
	"c" and "d," imperf.		—	2,250.00				
g	"USA/13¢" omitted on "a" and "e"		450.00	—				
h	Imperf. (untagged)			2,250.00				
i	"USA/13¢" omitted on "b," "c" and "d"		450.00					
j	"USA/13¢" double on "b"		—					
k	"USA/13¢" omitted on "c" and "d"		750.00					
l	"USA/13¢" omitted on "e"		500.00					
m	"USA/13¢" omitted, imperf.							
	(untagged)		—					
n	As "g", imperf., untagged		—					
1687	18¢ The Declaration of Independence,							
	4 July 1776 at Philadelphia,							
	by John Trumbull	05/29/76	4.25	—			7.50	2
a	18¢ John Adams, Roger Sherman							
	and Robert R. Livingston		.55	.55				2
b	18¢ Thomas Jefferson							
	and Benjamin Franklin		.55	.55				2
c	18¢ Thomas Nelson, Jr., Francis							
	Lewis, John Witherspoon and							
	Samuel Huntington		.55	.55				2
d	18¢ John Hancock and							
	Charles Thomson		.55	.55				2
e	18¢ George Read, John Dickinson							
	and Edward Rutledge		.55	.55				2
f	Design and marginal							
	inscriptions omitted		3,000.00					
g	"USA/18¢" omitted on "a" and "c"		750.00					
h	"USA/18¢" omitted							
	on "b," "d" and "e"		450.00					
i	"USA/18¢" omitted on "d"		500.00	500.00				
j	Black omitted in design		2,000.00					
k	"USA/18¢" omitted,							
	imperf. (untagged)		3,000.00					
m	"USA/18¢" omitted on "b" and "e"		500.00					

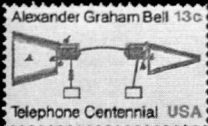

1683

1684

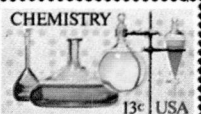

1685

The Surrender of Lord Cornwallis at Yorktown
From a Painting by John Trumbull

1686

The Declaration of Independence, 4 July 1776 at Philadelphia
From a Painting by John Trumbull

1687

Washington Crossing the Delaware
From a Painting by Emanuel Leutze / Eastman Johnson

1688

Washington Reviewing His Ragged Army at Valley Forge
From a Painting by William T. Trego

1689

Issues of 1976		Un	U	FDC	Q(M)
American Bicentennial Issue Souvenir Sheets, 5 stamps each (continued)					
1688	24¢ Washington Crossing the Delaware, by Emanuel Leutze/ Eastman Johnson 05/29/76	5.25	—	8.50	2
a	24¢ Boatmen	.70	.70		2
b	24¢ George Washington	.70	.70		2
c	24¢ Flagbearer	.70	.70		2
d	24¢ Men in Boat	.70	.70		2
e	24¢ Steersman and Men on Shore	.70	.70		2
f	"USA/24¢" omitted, imperf.	3,500.00			
g	"USA/24¢" omitted on "d" and "e"	450.00	450.00		
h	Design and marginal inscriptions omitted	3,500.00			
i	"USA/24¢" omitted on "a," "b" and "c"	500.00	—		
j	Imperf. (untagged)	3,000.00			
k	"USA/24¢" inverted on "d" and "e"	—			
1689	31¢ Washington Reviewing His Ragged Army at Valley Forge, by William T. Trego 05/29/76	6.25	—	9.50	2
a	31¢ Two Officers	.85	.85		2
b	31¢ George Washington	.85	.85		2
c	31¢ Officer and Brown Horse	.85	.85		2
d	31¢ White Horse and Officer	.85	.85		2
e	31¢ Three Soldiers	.85	.85		2
f	"USA/31¢" omitted, imperf.	2,750.00			
g	"USA/31¢" omitted on "a" and "c"	400.00			
h	"USA/31¢" omitted on "b," "d" and "e"	450.00	—		
i	"USA/31¢" omitted on "e"	450.00			
j	Black omitted in design	2,000.00			
k	Imperf. (untagged)		2,250.00		
l	"USA/31¢" omitted on "b" and "d"	—			
m	"USA/31¢" omitted on "a," "c" and "e"	—			
n	As "m," imperf. (untagged)	—			
p	As "h," imperf. (untagged)		2,500.00		
q	As "g," imperf. (untagged)	2,750.00			
r	"USA/31¢" omitted on "d" & "e"	—			
s	As "f", untagged	2,250.00			

	Issues of 1976		Un	U	PB	#	FDC	Q(M)
	American Bicentennial Issue, Perf. 11							
1690	13¢ Bust of Benjamin Franklin,							
	Map of North America, 1776	06/01/76	.25	.20	1.10	(4)	1.00	165
a	Light blue omitted		300.00					
b	Tagging omitted		5.00					
	Declaration of Independence, by John Trumbull							
1691	13¢ Delegates	07/04/76	.30	.20			1.00	41
1692	13¢ Delegates and John Adams	07/04/76	.30	.20			1.00	41
1693	13¢ Roger Sherman, Robert R.							
	Livingston, Thomas Jefferson							
	and Benjamin Franklin	07/04/76	.30	.20			1.00	41
1694	13¢ John Hancock, Charles							
	Thomson, George Read,							
	John Dickinson and							
	Edward Rutledge	07/04/76	.30	.20			1.00	41
a	Strip of 4, #1691-94		1.20	1.10	5.75	(20)	2.00	
	Olympic Games Issue							
1695	13¢ Diver and Olympic Rings	07/16/76	.25	.20			1.00	46
1696	13¢ Skier and Olympic Rings	07/16/76	.25	.20			1.00	46
1697	13¢ Runner and Olympic							
	Rings	07/16/76	.25	.20			1.00	46
1698	13¢ Skater and Olympic							
	Rings	07/16/76	.25	.20			1.00	46
a	Block of 4, #1695-98		1.10	1.10	3.25	(12)	2.00	
b	As "a," imperf.		700.00					
1699	13¢ Clara Maass	08/18/76	.25	.20	3.25	(12)	2.00	131
a	Horizontal pair, imperf. vertically		450.00					
1700	13¢ Adolph S. Ochs	09/18/76	.25	.20	1.10	(4)	1.00	158
	Christmas Issue							
1701	13¢ Nativity, by							
	John Singleton Copley	10/27/76	.25	.20	3.25	(12)	1.00	810
a	Imperf., pair		100.00					
1702	13¢ "Winter Pastime,"							
	by Nathaniel Currier	10/27/76	.25	.20	2.75	(10)	1.00	482*
a	Imperf., pair		100.00					
	*Includes #1703 printing							
1703	13¢ as #1702	10/27/76	.25	.20	6.00	(20)	1.00	
a	Imperf., pair		110.00					
b	Vertical pair, imperf. between		—					
c	Tagging omitted		12.50					

#1702 has overall tagging. Lettering at base is black and usually ½mm below design. As a rule, no "snowflaking" in sky or pond. Pane of 50 has margins on 4 sides with slogans. #1703 has block tagging the size of the printed area. Lettering at base is gray-black and usually ¾mm below design. "Snowflaking" generally in sky and pond. Pane of 50 has margin only at right or left and no slogans.

	Issues of 1977, American Bicentennial Issue							
1704	13¢ Washington, Nassau Hall,							
	Cannon and 13-star Flag, by							
	Charles Willson Peale	01/03/77	.25	.20	2.75	(10)	1.00	150
a	Horizontal pair, imperf. vertically		550.00					
1705	13¢ Sound Recording	03/23/77	.25	.20	1.10	(4)	1.00	177

1690

1691   **1692**   **1693**   **1694**   **1694a**

1695   **1696**

1699   **1700**

1697   **1698**   **1698a**

1701

1702

1703

1704

1705

1706   **1707**

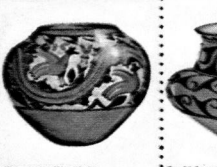

1710

1711

1708   **1709**   **1709a**

1712   **1713**

1716

1714   **1715**   **1715a**

1717   **1718**

1721

1719   **1720**   **1720a**

Issues of 1977			Un	U	PB	#	FDC	Q(M)
American Folk Art Issue, Pueblo Pottery, Perf. 11								
1706	13¢ Zia Pot	04/13/77	.25	.20			1.00	49
1707	13¢ San Ildefonso Pot	04/13/77	.25	.20			1.00	49
1708	13¢ Hopi Pot	04/13/77	.25	.20			1.00	49
1709	13¢ Acoma Pot	04/13/77	.25	.20			1.00	49
a	Block of 4, #1706-09		1.00	1.00	2.75	(10)	2.00	
b	As "a," imperf. vertically		2,500.00					
1710	13¢ Solo Transatlantic Flight	05/20/77	.25	.20	3.25	(12)	3.00	209
a	Imperf. pair		1,050.00					
1711	13¢ Colorado Statehood	05/21/77	.25	.20	3.25	(12)	1.00	192
a	Horizontal pair, imperf. between		600.00					
b	Horizontal pair, imperf. vertically		900.00					
c	Perf. 11.2		.35	.25	20.00	(12)		
	Butterfly Issue							
1712	13¢ Swallowtail	06/06/77	.25	.20			1.00	55
1713	13¢ Checkerspot	06/06/77	.25	.20			1.00	55
1714	13¢ Dogface	06/06/77	.25	.20			1.00	55
1715	13¢ Orange-Tip	06/06/77	.25	.20			1.00	55
a	Block of 4, #1712-15		1.00	1.00	3.25	(12)	2.00	
b	As "a," imperf. horizontally		15,000.00					
	American Bicentennial Issue							
1716	13¢ Marquis de Lafayette	06/13/77	.25	.20	1.10	(4)	1.00	160
	Skilled Hands for Independence							
1717	13¢ Seamstress	07/04/77	.25	.20			1.00	47
1718	13¢ Blacksmith	07/04/77	.25	.20			1.00	47
1719	13¢ Wheelwright	07/04/77	.25	.20			1.00	47
1720	13¢ Leatherworker	07/04/77	.25	.20			1.00	47
a	Block of 4, #1717-20		1.00	1.00	3.25	(12)	1.75	
	Perf. 11 x 10.5							
1721	13¢ Peace Bridge	08/04/77	.25	.20	1.10	(4)	1.00	164

Walter (1926–1998)
and Naiad Einsel

Respected illustrators and graphic designers with compatible artistic sensibilities, Walter and Naiad Einsel have worked collaboratively on many projects including book and magazine illustrations, posters, advertisements, television commercials, package designs, collage boxes, and kinetic sculptures. They met and married when each was an art director at NBC and CBS, respectively, and were the first husband-and-wife team to create stamp designs for the United States Postal Service. Among their credits is an AT&T exhibition at Walt Disney World EPCOT Center in Florida that features 55 intricately mechanized figures of their design. ■

The **2001 Stamp Yearbook**

A Great Way to Collect All of the 2001 Commemorative Stamp Issues!

What a line-up!!!

Featuring beautiful stamp related designs, illustrations and photographs — the 2001 STAMP YEARBOOK has 64 pages featuring more than 70 commemorative stamps.

The 2001 STAMP YEARBOOK is a terrific gift for you and others.

Featuring Dozens of Commemorative Stamps

The Pan-American Inverts

A souvenir sheet with reproductions of three stamps and a cinderella issued to commemorate the opening of the Pan-American Exposition in 1901.

Holiday Celebrations: Thanksgiving

A new addition to the Holiday Celebrations series that recognizes a uniquely American observance.

Holiday Celebration: Eid

Commemorates the two most important festivals—or eids—in the Islamic calendar.

Baseball's Legendary Playing Fields

Depicts ten of America's most notable ballparks.

"That's all Folks!"

The fifth and final stamp in the Looney Tunes series features Porky Pig.

Lucille Ball

The "Queen of Comedy"—everybody loves this star of stage, screen, radio, and television.

American Illustrators

Commemorating twenty renowned illustrators.

Peanuts

Featuring Snoopy as the Red Baron in honor of the unforgettable strip created by Charles Schulz.

Buy the book at local post offices or retail stores nationwide.

Order online by visiting the Postal Service's Web site at **www.usps.com** and clicking on the Postal Store.

Call **1 800 STAMP–24** for purchases or more information.

Source Code: #39003

Issues of 1977		Un	U	PB	#	FDC	Q(M)
American Bicentennial Issue, Perf. 11							
1722	13¢ Herkimer at Oriskany,						
	by Frederick Yohn	08/06/77	.25	.20	2.75	(10)	1.00	156
Energy Issue							
1723	13¢ Energy Conservation	10/20/77	.25	.20			1.25	79
1724	13¢ Energy Development	10/20/77	.25	.20			1.25	79
a	Attached pair, #1723-24		.50	.50	3.25	(12)	1.25	
1725	13¢ First Civil Settlement						
	Alta, California	09/09/77	.25	.20	1.10	(4)	1.00	154
American Bicentennial Issue							
1726	13¢ Members of Continental						
	Congress in Conference	09/30/77	.25	.20	1.10	(4)	1.00	168
1727	13¢ Talking Pictures	10/06/77	.25	.20	1.10	(4)	1.50	157
American Bicentennial Issue							
1728	13¢ Surrender of Burgoyne,						
	by John Trumbull	10/07/77	.25	.20	2.75	(10)	1.00	154
Christmas Issue							
1729	13¢ Washington at Valley						
	Forge, by J.C. Leyendecker	10/21/77	.25	.20	5.75	(20)	1.00	882
a	Imperf., pair		75.00					
1730	13¢ Rural Mailbox	10/21/77	.25	.20	2.75	(10)	1.00	922
a	Imperf., pair		300.00					
Issues of 1978							
1731	13¢ Carl Sandburg	01/06/78	.25	.20	1.10	(4)	1.00	157
Captain Cook Issue							
1732	13¢ Capt. James Cook						
	Alaska, by Nathaniel Dance	01/20/78	.25	.20			2.00	101
1733	13¢ *Resolution* and *Discovery*						
	Hawaii, by John Webber	01/20/78	.25	.20			2.00	101
a	Vertical pair, imperf. horizontally		—					
b	Attached pair, #1732-33		.50	.50	1.10	(4)	3.00	
c	As " b," imperf. between		4,500.00					
1734	13¢ Indian Head Penny	01/11/78	.25	.20	1.25	(4)	1.00	
	Pair with full horizontal gutter between		—					
a	Horizontal pair, imperf. vertically		300.00					
1735	(15¢) "A" Stamp	05/22/78	.25	.20	1.25	(4)	1.00	
a	Imperf., pair		90.00					
b	Vertical pair, imperf. horizontally		700.00					
c	Perf. 11.2		.25	.20	1.75	(2)		
Booklet Stamp, Perf. 11 x 10.5							
1736	(15¢) "A" orange Eagle (1735),						
	single from booklet	05/22/78	.25	.20			1.00	
a	Booklet pane of 8	05/22/78	2.25	.90			2.50	
Roses Booklet Issue, Perf. 10							
1737	15¢ Roses, single from						
	booklet	07/11/78	.25	.20			1.00	
a	Booklet pane of 8	07/11/78	2.25	.90			2.50	
b	As "a," imperf.		—					
c	As "a," tagging omitted		40.00					

#1736-37 issued only in booklets. All stamps are imperf. on one side or on one side and bottom.

1722

1723

1724 **1724a**

1725

1726

1727

1728

1729

1730

1731

1732

1733 **1733b**

1734

1735

1737

1738   1739   1740   1741   1742   1742a

1744

1745   1746
1747   1748   1748a

1750   1752
1749   1751   1752a

1753

1754

1755   1756

	Issues of 1980		Un	U	PB/LP	#	FDC	Q(M)
	Windmills Booklet Issue, Perf. 11							
1738	15¢ Virginia, 1720	02/07/80	.30	.20			1.00	
1739	15¢ Rhode Island, 1790	02/07/80	.30	.20			1.00	
1740	15¢ Massachusetts, 1793	02/07/80	.30	.20			1.00	
1741	15¢ Illinois, 1860	02/07/80	.30	.20			1.00	
1742	15¢ Texas, 1890	02/07/80	.30	.20			1.00	
a	Booklet pane of 10, #1738-42		3.50	3.00			3.50	
b	Strip of 5, #1730-1742		1.50	1.40				
	#1737-42 issued only in booklets. All stamps are imperf. top or bottom, or top or bottom and right side.							
	Issues of 1978 (continued), Coil Stamp, Perf. 10 Vertically							
1743	(15¢) "A" orange Eagle (1735)	05/22/78	.25	.20	.65	(2)	1.00	
a	Imperf., pair		90.00		—	(2)		
	Black Heritage Issue, Perf. 10.5 x 11							
1744	13¢ Harriet Tubman and Cart Carrying Slaves	02/01/78	.25	.20	3.25	(12)	1.00	157
	American Folk Art Issue, Quilts, Perf. 11							
1745	13¢ Basket design, red and orange	03/08/78	.25	.20			1.00	41
1746	13¢ Basket design, red	03/08/78	.25	.20			1.00	41
1747	13¢ Basket design, orange	03/08/78	.25	.20			1.00	41
1748	13¢ Basket design, brown	03/08/78	.25	.20			1.00	41
a	Block of 4, #1745-48		1.00	1.00	3.25	(12)	2.00	
	American Dance Issue							
1749	13¢ Ballet	04/26/78	.25	.20			1.00	39
1750	13¢ Theater	04/26/78	.25	.20			1.00	39
1751	13¢ Folk	04/26/78	.25	.20			1.00	39
1752	13¢ Modern	04/26/78	.25	.20			1.00	39
a	Block of 4, #1749-52		1.00	1.00	3.25	(12)	1.75	
	American Bicentennial Issue, French Alliance							
1753	13¢ King Louis XVI and Benjamin Franklin, by Charles Gabriel Sauvage	05/04/78	.25	.20	1.10	(4)	1.00	103
	Perf. 10.5 x 11							
1754	13¢ Early Cancer Detection	05/18/78	.25	.20	1.10	(4)	1.00	152
	Performing Arts Issue, Perf. 11							
1755	13¢ Jimmie Rodgers with Locomotive, Guitar and Brakeman's Cap	05/24/78	.25	.20	3.25	(12)	1.50	95
1756	15¢ George M. Cohan, "Yankee Doodle Dandy" and Stars	07/03/78	.25	.20	4.00	(12)	1.50	152

	Issues of 1978		Un	U	PB	#	FDC	Q(M)
	CAPEX '78 Souvenir Sheet, Perf. 11							
1757	13¢ Souvenir sheet of 8	06/10/78	2.00	2.00	2.25	(8)	2.75	15
a	13¢ Cardinal		.25	.20				15
b	13¢ Mallard		.25	.20				15
c	13¢ Canada Goose		.25	.20				15
d	13¢ Blue Jay		.25	.20				15
e	13¢ Moose		.25	.20				15
f	13¢ Chipmunk		.25	.20				15
g	13¢ Red Fox		.25	.20				15
h	13¢ Raccoon		.25	.20				15
i	Yellow, green, red, brown and black (litho.) omitted		7,000.00					
1758	15¢ Photography	06/26/78	.30	.20	4.00	(12)	1.50	163
1759	15¢ Viking Missions to Mars	07/20/78	.30	.20	1.35	(4)	2.00	159
	Wildlife Conservation Issue							
1760	15¢ Great Gray Owl	08/26/78	.30	.20			1.00	47
1761	15¢ Saw-Whet Owl	08/26/78	.30	.20			1.00	47
1762	15¢ Barred Owl	08/26/78	.30	.20			1.00	47
1763	15¢ Great Horned Owl	08/26/78	.30	.20			1.00	47
a	Block of 4, #1760-63		1.25	1.25	1.40	(4)	2.00	
	American Trees Issue							
1764	15¢ Giant Sequoia	10/09/78	.30	.20			1.00	42
1765	15¢ White Pine	10/09/78	.30	.20			1.00	42
1766	15¢ White Oak	10/09/78	.30	.20			1.00	42
1767	15¢ Gray Birch	10/09/78	.30	.20			1.00	42
a	Block of 4, #1764-67		1.25	1.25	4.00	(12)	2.00	
b	As "a," imperf. horizontally		15,000.00					

Robert M. Cunningham

Robert M. Cunningham's unique sense of light, color, and design has made an indelible mark on the field of illustration during the past 40 years. Raised in America's heartland, he served as an air cadet in the Navy before attending the Kansas City Art Institute and the Art Students League in New York in pursuit of his artistic dream. His award-winning images have been sought after by America's leading magazines and such companies as General Electric, Mobil, Chevrolet, and American Express. The designer of ten United States postage stamps celebrating the 1980 Olympic Games, he was inducted into the Illustrators Hall of Fame in 1998 for his lifelong achievements. ∎

"I've always enjoyed doing sports. Sports offer unique opportunities to paint bright colors and unusual shapes."

— Robert M. Cunningham

a b c d

1757

e f g h

1758

1759

1760 1761

1762 1763 1763a

1764 1765

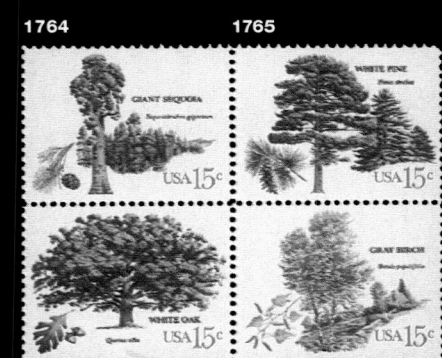

1766 1767 1767a

1768

1769

1770

1771

1772

1773

1774

1775   **1776**

1777   **1778**   **1778a**

1779   **1780**

1781   **1782**   **1782a**

1783   **1784**

1785   **1786**   **1786a**

	Issues of 1978		Un	U	PB	#	FDC	Q(M)
	Christmas Issues, Perf. 11							
1768	15¢ Madonna and Child with Cherubim, by Andrea della Robbia	10/18/78	.30	.20	4.00	(12)	1.00	963
a	Imperf., pair		90.00					
1769	15¢ Child on Hobby Horse and Christmas Trees	10/18/78	.30	.20	4.00	(12)	1.00	917
	Pair with full horizontal gutter between		—					
a	Imperf., pair		100.00					
b	Vertical pair, imperf. horizontally		2,000.00					
	Issues of 1979, Perf. 11							
1770	15¢ Robert F. Kennedy	01/12/79	.35	.20	1.75	(4)	3.00	159
	Black Heritage Issue							
1771	15¢ Martin Luther King, Jr., and Civil Rights Marchers	01/13/79	.30	.20	4.00	(12)	2.50	166
a	Imperf., pair		—					
1772	15¢ International Year of the Child	02/15/79	.30	.20	1.40	(4)	1.00	163
	Literary Arts Issue, Perf. 10.5 x 11							
1773	15¢ John Steinbeck, by Philippe Halsman	02/27/79	.30	.20	1.40	(4)	1.25	155
1774	15¢ Albert Einstein	03/04/79	.35	.20	1.75	(4)	4.00	157
	Pair with full horizontal gutter between		—					
	American Folk Art Issue, Perf. 11							
1775	15¢ Straight-Spout Coffeepot	04/19/79	.30	.20			1.00	44
1776	15¢ Tea Caddy	04/19/79	.30	.20			1.00	44
1777	15¢ Sugar Bowl	04/19/79	.30	.20			1.00	44
1778	15¢ Curved-Spout Coffeepot	04/19/79	.30	.20			1.00	44
a	Block of 4, #1775-78		1.25	1.25	3.25	(10)	2.00	
b	As "a," imperf. horizontally		4,250.00					
	American Architecture Issue							
1779	15¢ Virginia Rotunda, by Thomas Jefferson	06/04/79	.30	.20			1.00	41
1780	15¢ Baltimore Cathedral, by Benjamin Latrobe	06/04/79	.30	.20			1.00	41
1781	15¢ Boston State House, by Charles Bulfinch	06/04/79	.30	.20			1.00	41
1782	15¢ Philadelphia Exchange, by William Strickland	06/04/79	.30	.20			1.00	41
a	Block of 4, #1779-82		1.25	1.25	1.40	(4)	2.00	
	Endangered Flora Issue							
1783	15¢ Persistent Trillium	06/07/79	.30	.20			1.00	41
1784	15¢ Hawaiian Wild Broadbean	06/07/79	.30	.20			1.00	41
1785	15¢ Contra Costa Wallflower	06/07/79	.30	.20			1.00	41
1786	15¢ Antioch Dunes Evening Primrose	06/07/79	.30	.20			1.00	41
a	Block of 4, #1783-86		1.25	1.25	4.00	(12)	2.00	
	As "a," full vertical gutter between		—					
b	As "a," imperf.		600.00					

	Issues of 1979		Un	UPB	PB	#	FDC	Q(M)
1787	15¢ Seeing Eye Dogs	06/15/79	.30	.20	6.50	(20)	1.00	162
a	Imperf., pair		425.00					
b	Tagging omitted		10.00					
1788	15¢ Special Olympics	08/09/79	.30	.20	3.25	(10)	1.00	166
	American Bicentennial Issue, Perf. 11 x 12							
1789	15¢ John Paul Jones,							
	by Charles Willson Peale	09/23/79	.30	.20	3.25	(10)	1.25	160
c	Vertical pair, imperf. horizontally		175.00					
1789A	Perf. 11		.50	.20	4.00	(10)		
d	Vertical pair,							
	imperf. horizontally		150.00					
1789B	Perf. 12		1,750.00	1,000.00	25,000.00	(10)		
	Numerous varieties of printer's waste of #1789 exist							
	Olympic Summer Games Issue, Perf. 11 (See also #C97)							
1790	10¢ Javelin Thrower	09/05/79	.20	.20	3.00	(12)	1.00	67
1791	15¢ Runner	09/28/79	.30	.20			1.00	47
1792	15¢ Swimmer	09/28/79	.30	.20			1.00	47
1793	15¢ Rowers	09/28/79	.30	.20			1.00	47
1794	15¢ Equestrian Contestant	09/28/79	.30	.20			1.00	47
a	Block of 4, #1791-94		1.25	1.25	4.00	(12)	2.00	
b	As "a," imperf.		1,500.00					
	Issues of 1980, Olympic Winter Games Issue, Perf. 11 x 10.5							
1795	15¢ Speed Skater	02/01/80	.35	.20			1.00	52
1796	15¢ Downhill Skier	02/01/80	.35	.20			1.00	52
1797	15¢ Ski Jumper	02/01/80	.35	.20			1.00	52
1798	15¢ Hockey Goaltender	02/01/80	.35	.20			1.00	52
a	Perf. 11, #1795-98		1.05	.60				
b	Block of 4, #1795-98		1.50	1.40	4.50	(12)	2.00	
c	Block of 4, #1795a-98a		4.25	3.50	14.00	(12)		
	Issues of 1979 (continued), Christmas Issue, Perf. 11							
1799	15¢ Virgin and Child with							
	Cherubim, by Gerard David	10/18/79	.30	.20	4.00	(12)	1.00	874
a	Imperf., pair		90.00					
b	Vertical pair, imperf. horizontally		700.00					
c	pair, imperf. between		2,250.00					
1800	15¢ Santa Claus, Christmas							
	Tree Ornament	10/18/79	.30	.20	4.00	(12)	1.00	932
a	Green and yellow omitted		625.00					
b	Green, yellow and tan omitted		700.00					
	Performing Arts Issue							
1801	15¢ Will Rogers and Rogers as a							
	Cowboy Humorist	11/04/79	.30	.20	4.00	(12)	1.50	161
a	Imperf., pair		225.00					
1802	15¢ Vietnam Veterans	11/11/79	.30	.20	3.25	(10)	4.00	173
	Issues of 1980 (continued), Performing Arts Issue							
1803	15¢ W.C. Fields and							
	Fields as a Juggler	01/29/80	.30	.20	4.00	(12)	1.75	169
	Black Heritage Issue							
1804	15¢ Benjamin Banneker							
	and Banneker as Surveyor	02/15/80	.35	.20	4.50	(12)	1.00	160
a	Horizontal pair, imperf. vertically		800.00					

1787

1788

1789

1790

1791  1792

1793  1794

1794a

1795  1796

1797  1798

1798b

1799

1800

1801

1802

1803

1804

1805

1807

1809

1813

1806

1808

1810

1818

Frances Perkins
USA **15c**

1821

1822

Emily Bissell
Crusader Against Tuberculosis
USA 15c

1823

HELEN KELLER
ANNE SULLIVAN

1824

Veterans
Administration

Fifty
Years of Service
USA 15c

1825

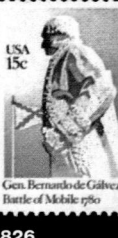
Gen. Bernardo de Gálvez
Battle of Mobile 1780
1826

1827   **1828**

Coral Reefs USA 15c   Coral Reefs USA 15c
Brain Coral: U.S. Virgin Islands *Elkhorn Coral: Florida*

Coral Reefs USA 15c   Coral Reefs USA 15c
Chalice Coral: American Samoa *Finger Coral: Hawaii*
 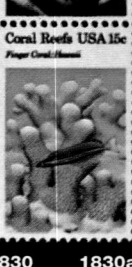

1829   **1830**   **1830a**

	Issues of 1980		Un	U	PB/LP	#	FDC	Q(M)
	Letter Writing Issue, Perf. 11							
1805	15¢ Letters Preserve Memories	02/25/80	.30	.20			1.00	39
1806	15¢ purple P.S. Write Soon	02/25/80	.30	.20			1.00	39
1807	15¢ Letters Lift Spirits	02/25/80	.30	.20			1.00	39
1808	15¢ green P.S. Write Soon	02/25/80	.30	.20			1.00	39
1809	15¢ Letters Shape Opinions	02/25/80	.30	.20			1.00	39
1810	15¢ red and blue P.S. Write Soon	02/25/80	.30	.20			1.00	39
a	Vertical Strip of 6, #1805-10		1.85	2.00	11.00	(36)	2.50	
	Issues of 1980-81, Americana Issue, Coil Stamps, Perf. 10 Vertically							
	(See also #1581-82, 1584-85, 1590-99, 1603-06, 1608, 1610-19, 1622-23, 1625)							
1811	1¢ dark blue, greenish Inkwell							
	and Quill (1581)	03/06/80	.20	.20	.40	(2)	1.00	
a	Imperf., pair		*175.00*		*275.00*	(2)		
1812	Not assigned							
1813	3.5¢ Weaver Violins	06/23/80	.20	.20	1.00	(2)	1.00	
a	Untagged (Bureau precanceled)			.20				
b	Imperf., pair		*225.00*		*450.00*	(2)		
1814-15	Not assigned							
1816	12¢ red brown, *beige* Torch from							
	Statue of Liberty (1594)	04/08/81	.25	.20	1.50	(2)	1.00	
a	Untagged (Bureau precanceled)			.25				
b	Imperf., pair		*200.00*		*400.00*	(2)		
1817	Not assigned							
	Issues of 1981, Perf. 11 x 10.5							
1818	(18¢) "B" Stamp	03/15/81	.35	.20	1.60	(4)	1.00	
	Booklet Stamp, Perf. 10							
1819	(18¢) "B" Stamp (1818),							
	single from booklet	03/15/81	.40	.20			1.00	
a	Booklet pane of 8	03/15/81	3.75	1.75			3.00	
	Coil Stamp, Perf. 10 Vertically							
1820	(18¢) "B" Stamp (1818)	03/15/81	.40	.20	1.60	(2)	1.00	
a	Imperf., pair		*100.00*		*250.00*	(2)		
	Issues of 1980 (continued), Perf. 10.5 x 11							
1821	15¢ Frances Perkins	04/10/80	.30	.20	1.30	(4)	1.00	164
	Perf. 11							
1822	15¢ Dolley Madison	05/20/80	.30	.20	1.40	(4)	1.00	257
1823	15¢ Emily Bissell	05/31/80	.35	.20	1.75	(4)	1.00	96
a	Vertical pair, imperf. horizontally		*400.00*					
1824	15¢ Helen Keller/Anne Sullivan	06/27/80	.30	.20	1.30	(4)	1.00	154
1825	15¢ Veterans Administration	07/21/80	.30	.20	1.30	(4)	1.50	160
a	Horizontal pair, imperf. vertically		*450.00*					
	American Bicentennial Issue							
1826	15¢ General Bernardo de Galvez,							
	Battle of Mobile	07/23/80	.30	.20	1.30	(4)	1.00	104
a	Red, brown and blue omitted		*800.00*					
b	Bl., brn., red and yel. omitted		*1,400.00*					
	Coral Reefs Issue							
1827	15¢ Brain Coral, Beaugregory							
	Fish	08/26/80	.30	.20			1.00	51
1828	15¢ Elkhorn Coral, Porkfish	08/26/80	.30	.20			1.00	51
1829	15¢ Chalice Coral, Moorish Idol	08/26/80	.30	.20			1.00	51
1830	15¢ Finger Coral, Sabertooth							
	Blenny	08/26/80	.30	.20			1.00	51
a	Block of 4, #1827-30		1.25	1.10	4.00	(12)	2.00	
b	As "a," imperf.		*1,000.00*					
c	As "a," imperf. between, vertically		—					
d	As "a," imperf. vertically		*3,000.00*					

	Issues of 1980		Un	U	PB	#	FDC	Q(M)
1831	15¢ Organized Labor	09/01/80	.30	.20	3.50	(12)	1.00	167
a	Imperf., pair		375.00					
	Literary Arts Issue, Edith Wharton, Perf. 10.5 x 11							
1832	15¢ Edith Wharton Reading							
	Letter	09/05/80	.30	.20	1.30	(4)	1.00	163
	Perf. 11							
1833	15¢ Education	09/12/80	.30	.20	1.90	(6)	1.00	160
a	Horizontal pair, imperf. vertically		240.00					
	American Folk Art Issue, Pacific Northwest Indian Masks							
1834	15¢ Heiltsuk, Bella Bella Tribe	09/25/80	.30	.20			1.00	39
1835	15¢ Chilkat Tlingit Tribe	09/25/80	.30	.20			1.00	39
1836	15¢ Tlingit Tribe	09/25/80	.30	.20			1.00	39
1837	15¢ Bella Coola Tribe	09/25/80	.30	.20			1.00	39
a	Block of 4, #1834-37		1.25	1.25	3.50	(10)	2.00	
	American Architecture Issue							
1838	15¢ Smithsonian Institution,							
	by James Renwick	10/09/80	.30	.20			1.00	39
1839	15¢ Trinity Church, by Henry							
	Hobson Richardson	10/09/80	.30	.20			1.00	39
1840	15¢ Pennsylvania Academy							
	of Fine Arts, by Frank Furness	10/09/80	.30	.20			1.00	39
1841	15¢ Lyndhurst, by Alexander							
	Jefferson Davis	10/09/80	.30	.20			1.00	39
a	Block of 4, #1838-41		1.25	1.25	1.50	(4)	2.00	
b	As "a", red omitted on #1838,1839		350.00					
	Christmas Issue							
1842	15¢ Madonna and Child							
	from Epiphany Window,							
	Washington Cathedral	10/31/80	.30	.20	4.00	(12)	1.00	693
a	Imperf., pair		70.00					
	Pair with full vertical gutter between		—					
1843	15¢ Wreath and Toys	10/31/80	.30	.20	6.50	(20)	1.00	719
a	Imperf., pair		70.00					
b	Buff omitted		25.00					
c	Vertical pair, imperf. horizontally		—					
d	Horizontal pair, imperf. between		4,000.00					

Roy Andersen

Roy Andersen is celebrated for his powerful, realist paintings of the American West. He has created outstanding illustrations for books, movie posters, and magazines including *Time*, *Sports Illustrated*, and *National Geographic.* An award-winning member of the Cowboy Artists of America, he credits his success as an artist with the discipline and love for research that he learned in the world of commercial art. The subject of a book titled *Dream Spinner: The Art of Roy Andersen*, he raises show dogs and horses that appear in his historical paintings and has created the artwork for 15 United States postage stamps. ■

1831

1832

1834

1835

1836

1837   **1837a**

1833

1838

1839

1840

1841   **1841a**

1842

1843

1980-1985

 Dorothea Dix USA 1c
1844

 Igor Stravinsky 2c
1845

 Henry Clay USA 3c
1846

 Carl Schurz 4c USA
1847

 Pearl Buck USA 5c
1848

 Walter Lippmann 6c USA
1849

 Abraham Baldwin USA 7
1850

 Henry Knox USA 8
1851

 Sylvanus Thayer USA 9
1852

 Richard Russell USA 10c
1853

 Alden Partridge USA 11
1854

 USA 13c Crazy Horse
1855

 Sinclair Lewis USA 14
1856

 Rachel Carson USA 17c
1857

 George Mason USA 18c
1858

 USA 19c Sequoyah
1859

 Ralph Bunche USA 20c

 Thomas H Gallaudet USA 20c

 Harry S Truman USA 20c

John J Audubon USA 22

Issues of 1980-85		Un	U	PB	#	FDC
Great Americans Issue, Perf. 11 (See also #2168-73, 2176-80, 2182-86, 2188, 2190-92, 2194-97)						
1844	1¢ Dorothea Dix	09/23/83	.20	.20	.35	(6)	1.00
a	Imperf., pair		300.00				
b	Vertical pair, imperf. between		3,000.00				
c	Perf. 10.9, small block tagging		.20	.20	.35	(6)	
d	Perf. 10.9, large block tagging		.20	.20	.35	(6)	
e	Vertical pair, imperf. horizontally		—				
	Perf. 11 x 10.5						
1845	2¢ Igor Stravinsky	11/18/82	.20	.20	.35	(4)	1.00
	Vertical pair, full gutter between		—				
1846	3¢ Henry Clay	07/13/83	.20	.20	.55	(4)	1.00
a	Tagging omitted		4.00				
1847	4¢ Carl Schurz	06/03/83	.20	.20	.65	(4)	1.00
a	Tagging omitted		4.00				
1848	5¢ Pearl Buck	06/25/83	.20	.20	.70	(4)	1.00
	Perf. 11						
1849	6¢ Walter Lippman	09/19/85	.20	.20	.85	(6)	1.00
a	Vertical pair, imperf. between		2,250.00				
1850	7¢ Abraham Baldwin	01/25/85	.20	.20	.95	(6)	1.00
1851	8¢ Henry Knox	07/25/85	.20	.20	.85	(4)	1.00
1852	9¢ Sylvanus Thayer	06/07/85	.20	.20	1.30	(6)	1.00
1853	10¢ Richard Russell	05/31/84	.25	.20	2.00	(6)	1.00
a	Large block tagging		.30	.20	2.25	(6)	
b	Vertical pair, imperf. between						
	and at bottom		900.00				
c	Horizontal pair, imperf. between		2,250.00				
1854	11¢ Alden Partridge	02/12/85	.25	.20	1.25	(4)	1.00
a	Tagging omitted		9.00				
	Perf. 11 x 10.5						
1855	13¢ Crazy Horse	01/15/82	.25	.20	2.00	(4)	1.50
a	Tagging omitted		7.50				
	Perf. 11						
1856	14¢ Sinclair Lewis	03/21/85	.30	.20	2.25	(6)	1.00
a	Large block tagging		.30	.20	2.25	(6)	
b	Vertical pair, imperf. horizontally		125.00				
c	Horizontal pair, imperf. between		9.00				
d	Vertical pair, imperf. between		1,500.00				
	Perf. 11 x 10.5						
1857	17¢ Rachel Carson	05/28/81	.35	.20	2.00	(4)	1.00
a	Tagging omitted		10.00				
1858	18¢ George Mason	05/07/81	.35	.20	3.00	(4)	1.00
a	Tagging omitted		6.00				
1859	19¢ Sequoyah	12/27/80	.40	.20	2.75	(4)	1.50
1860	20¢ Ralph Bunche	01/12/82	.40	.20	3.75	(4)	1.00
a	Tagging omitted		6.00				
1861	20¢ Thomas H. Gallaudet	06/10/83	.45	.20	4.00	(4)	1.25
	Perf. 11						
1862	20¢ Harry S. Truman	01/26/84	.40	.20	4.50	(6)	1.25
a	Perf. 11.2, large block tagging, dull gum		.40	.20	3.00	(4)	
b	Perf. 11.2, overall tagging, dull gum		.40	—	3.00	(4)	
c	Perf. 11.2, tagging omitted		10.00				
1863	22¢ John J. Audubon	04/23/85	.55	.20	6.00	(6)	1.00
a	Large block tagging		1.00	.20	8.00	(6)	
b	Perf. 11.2, large block tagging		.55	.20	8.00	(4)	
c	Tagging omitted		6.00				
d	Vertical pair, imperf. horizontally		2,500.00				
e	Vertical pair, imperf. between		—				
f	Horizontal pair, imperf. between		2,500.00				

1981-1985

	Issues of 1981-85		Un	U	PB/PNC	#	FDC	Q(M)
	Great Americans Issue (continued), Perf. 11							
1864	30¢ Frank C. Laubach	09/02/84	.55	.20	3.50	(6)	1.25	
a	Perf. 11.2, large block tagging		.55	.20	3.25	(4)		
b	Perf. 11, overall tagging		1.50	.20	22.50	(4)		
	Perf. 11 x 10.5							
1865	35¢ Charles R. Drew, MD	06/03/81	.70	.20	4.00	(4)	1.25	
1866	37¢ Robert Millikan	01/26/82	.75	.20	3.50	(4)	1.25	
a	Tagging omitted		10.00					
	Perf. 11							
1867	39¢ Grenville Clark	03/20/85	.80	.20	5.50	(6)	1.25	
a	Vertical pair, imperf. horizontally		600.00					
b	Vertical pair, imperf. between		2,000.00					
c	Perf. 10.9, large block tagging		.80	.20	5.50	(6)		
d	Perf. 11.2, large block tagging		.75	.20	5.50	(4)		
1868	40¢ Lillian M. Gilbreth	02/24/84	.80	.20	6.00	(6)	1.25	
a	Perf. 11.2, large block tagging		.80	.20	6.50	(4)		
1869	50¢ Chester W. Nimitz	02/22/85	.95	.20	7.50	(4)	2.00	
a	Perf. 11.2, large block tagging, dull gum		.95	.20	6.25	(4)		
b	Tagging omitted		10.00					
c	Perf. 11.2, tagging omitted, dull gum		7.50					
d	Perf. 11.2, overall tagging, dull gum		1.50	.20	8.50	(4)		
e	Perf. 11.2, prephosphored uncoated paper, shiny gum		.90	.20	5.00	(4)		
1870-73	Not assigned							
1874	15¢ Everett Dirksen	01/04/81	.30	.20	1.40	(4)	1.00	160
	Black Heritage Issue							
1875	15¢ Whitney Moore Young at Desk	01/30/81	.35	.20	1.75	(4)	1.00	160
	Flower Issue							
1876	18¢ Rose	04/23/81	.35	.20			1.00	53
1877	18¢ Camellia	04/23/81	.35	.20			1.00	53
1878	18¢ Dahlia	04/23/81	.35	.20			1.00	53
1879	18¢ Lily	04/23/81	.35	.20			1.00	53
a	Block of 4, #1876-79		1.40	1.25	1.75	(4)	2.50	
	Wildlife Booklet Issue							
1880	18¢ Bighorn Sheep	05/14/81	.55	.20			1.00	
1881	18¢ Puma	05/14/81	.55	.20			1.00	
1882	18¢ Harbor Seal	05/14/81	.55	.20			1.00	
1883	18¢ Bison	05/14/81	.55	.20			1.00	
1884	18¢ Brown Bear	05/14/81	.55	.20			1.00	
1885	18¢ Polar Bear	05/14/81	.55	.20			1.00	
1886	18¢ Elk (Wapiti)	05/14/81	.55	.20			1.00	
1887	18¢ Moose	05/14/81	.55	.20			1.00	
1888	18¢ White-Tailed Deer	05/14/81	.55	.20			1.00	
1889	18¢ Pronghorn Antelope	05/14/81	.55	.20			1.00	
a	Booklet pane of 10, #1880-89		8.50	7.00			5.00	
	#1880-89 issued only in booklets. All stamps are imperf. at one side or imperf. at one side and bottom.							
	Flag and Anthem Issue							
1890	18¢ "...for amber waves of grain"	04/24/81	.35	.20	2.25	(6)	1.00	
a	Imperf., pair		125.00					
b	Vertical pair, imperf. horizontally		850.00					
	Coil Stamp, Perf. 10 Vertically							
1891	18¢ "...from sea to shining sea"	04/24/81	.35	.20	4.25	(3)	1.00	
a	Imperf., pair		30.00					

Beginning with #1891, all coil stamps except 1947 feature a small plate number at the bottom of the design at varying intervals in a roll, depending on the press used. The basic "plate number coil" (PNC) collecting unit is a strip of three stamps, with the plate number appearing on the middle stamp. PNC values are for the most common plate number.

1864
1865
1866

1867
1868
1869

1876   1877

1874   1875

Rose USA 18c   Camellia USA 18c

Dahlia USA 18c   Lily USA 18c

1878   1879   1879a

1880   1881
1882   1883
1884   1885
1886   1887
1888   1889

1889a

1890   1891

1892

1893

1893a

1894

1897

1897A

1898

1898A

1899

1900

1901

1902

1903

1904

Issues of 1981-82		Un	U	PB/PNC/LP	#	FDC	Q(M)
Booklet Stamps, Perf. 11							
1892 6¢ USA Circle of Stars,							
single from booklet (1893a)	04/24/81	.50	.20			1.00	
1893 18¢ "...for purple mountain majesties,"							
single from booklet (1893a)	04/24/81	.30	.20			1.00	
a Booklet pane of 8 (2 #1892 & 6 #1893)		3.00	2.25			2.50	
b As "a," imperf. vertically between		75.00					
c Se-tenant pair, #1892 and #1893		.90	1.00				
#1892-93 issued only in booklets. All stamps are imperf. at one side or imperf. at one side and bottom.							
Flag Over Supreme Court Issue							
1894 20¢ Flag Over Supreme Court	12/17/81	.40	.20	2.75	(6)	1.00	
a Imperf., pair		35.00					
b Vertical pair, imperf. horizontally		550.00					
c Dark blue omitted		85.00					
d Black omitted		325.00					
e Perf. 11.2, shiny gum		.35	.20	2.50	(6)		
Coil Stamp, Perf. 10 Vertically							
1895 20¢ Flag Over Supreme							
Court (1894)	12/17/81	.40	.20	4.25	(3)	1.00	
a Narrow block tagging		.40	.20	4.25	(3)		
b Untagged (Bureau precanceled)		.50	.50	57.50	(3)		
c Tagging omitted		—					
d Imperf., pair		10.00					
e Pair, imperf. between		1,250.00					
f Black omitted		50.00					
g Blue omitted		1,500.00					
Booklet Stamp, Perf. 11 x 10.5							
1896 20¢ Flag over Supreme Court							
(1894), single from booklet	12/17/81	.40	.20			1.00	
a Booklet pane of 6	12/17/81	3.00	2.00			6.00	
b Booklet pane of 10	06/01/82	5.25	3.25			10.00	
Issues of 1981-84, Transportation Issue, Coil Stamps, Perf. 10 Vertically							
(See also #2123-36, 2225-26, 2228, 2231, 2252-66, 2452-53A, 2457, 2464, 2468)							
1897 1¢ Omnibus 1880s	08/19/83	.20	.20	.45	(3)	1.00	
b Imperf., pair		675.00		—	(2)		
1897A 2¢ Locomotive 1870s	05/20/82	.20	.20	.45	(3)	1.50	
e Imperf., pair		55.00		—	(2)		
1898 3¢ Handcar 1880s	03/25/83	.20	.20	.65	(3)	1.00	
1898A 4¢ Stagecoach 1890s	08/19/82	.20	.20	1.00	(3)	1.00	
b Untagged (Bureau precanceled)		.20	.20	6.00	(3)		
c As "b," imperf., pair		750.00					
d Imperf., pair		900.00		—			
1899 5¢ Motorcycle 1913	10/10/83	.20	.20	1.00	(3)	2.00	
a Imperf., pair		2,750.00					
1900 5.2¢ Sleigh 1880s	03/21/83	.20	.20	7.50	(3)	1.00	
a Untagged (Bureau precanceled)		.20	.20	11.00	(3)		
1901 5.9¢ Bicycle 1870s	02/17/82	.25	.20	8.00	(3)	1.50	
a Untagged (Bureau precanceled)		.20	.20	25.00	(3)		
b As "a," imperf., pair		200.00		—	(2)		
1902 7.4¢ Baby Buggy 1880s	04/07/84	.20	.20	8.50	(3)	1.00	
a Untagged (Bureau precanceled)		.20	.20	4.50	(3)		
1903 9.3¢ Mail Wagon 1880s	12/15/81	.30	.20	8.50	(3)	1.00	
a Untagged (Bureau precanceled)		.25	.25	3.00	(3)		
b As "a," imperf., pair		125.00		200.00	(2)		
1904 10.9¢ Hansom Cab 1890s	03/26/82	.30	.20	18.00	(3)	1.00	
a Untagged (Bureau precanceled)		.30	.25	25.00	(3)		
b As "a," imperf., pair		150.00			(2)		

	Issues of 1981-84		Un	U	PB	#	FDC	Q(M)
	Transportation Issue (continued)							
1905	11¢ RR Caboose 1890s	02/03/84	.30	.20	4.00	(3)	1.50	
a	Untagged (Bureau precanceled)		.25	.20	3.25	(3)		
1906	17¢ Electric Auto 1917	06/25/81	.35	.20	2.25	(3)	1.00	
a	Untagged (Bureau precanceled)		.35	.35	4.00	(3)		
b	Imperf., pair		165.00		—	(2)		
c	As "a," imperf., pair		650.00		—	(2)		
1907	18¢ Surrey 1890s	05/18/81	.35	.20	3.25	(3)	1.00	
a	Imperf., pair		150.00		—	(2)		
1908	20¢ Fire Pumper 1860s	12/10/81	.35	.20	3.00	(3)	3.00	
a	Imperf., pair		110.00		300.00	(2)		

Values for plate # coil strips of 3 stamps for #1897-1908 are for the most common plate numbers. Other plate #s and strips of 5 stamps may have higher values.

	Issue of 1983, Express Mail Booklet Issue, Perf. 10 Vertically							
1909	$9.35 Eagle and Moon,							
	single from booklet	08/12/83	21.00	15.00			45.00	
a	Booklet pane of 3		65.00	—			125.00	

#1909 issued only in booklets. All stamps are imperf. at top and bottom or imperf. at top, bottom and right side.

	Issues of 1981, Perf. 10.5 x 11							
1910	18¢ American Red Cross	05/01/81	.35	.20	1.50	(4)	1.00	165
	Perf. 11							
1911	18¢ Savings and Loans	05/08/81	.35	.20	1.50	(4)	1.00	107
	Space Achievement Issue, Perf. 11							
1912	18¢ Exploring the Moon —							
	Moon Walk	05/21/81	.40	.20			1.00	42
1913	18¢ Benefiting Mankind (upper							
	left) Columbia Space Shuttle	05/21/81	.40	.20			1.00	42
1914	18¢ Benefiting Mankind— Space							
	Shuttle Deploying Satellite	05/21/81	.40	.20			1.00	42
1915	18¢ Understanding the Sun—							
	Skylab	05/21/81	.40	.20			1.00	42
1916	18¢ Probing the Planets—							
	Pioneer 11	05/21/81	.40	.20			1.00	42
1917	18¢ Benefiting Mankind—							
	Columbia Space Shuttle							
	Lifting Off	05/21/81	.40	.20			1.00	42
1918	18¢ Benefiting Mankind—Space							
	Shuttle Preparing to Land	05/21/81	.40	.20			1.00	42
1919	18¢ Comprehending the							
	Universe — Telescope	05/21/81	.40	.20			1.00	42
a	Block of 8, #1912-19		3.25	3.00	3.75	(8)	3.00	
b	As "a," imperf.		9,000.00					
1920	18¢ Professional Management	06/18/81	.35	.20	1.50	(4)	1.00	99
	Preservation of Wildlife Habitats Issue							
1921	18¢ Save Wetland Habitats—							
	Great Blue Heron	06/26/81	.35	.20			1.00	45
1922	18¢ Save Grassland Habitats—							
	Badger	06/26/81	.35	.20			1.00	45
1923	18¢ Save Mountain Habitats—							
	Grizzly Bear	06/26/81	.35	.20			1.00	45
1924	18¢ Save Woodland Habitats—							
	Ruffled Grouse	06/26/81	.35	.20			1.00	45
a	Block of 4, #1921-24		1.50	1.25	2.00	(4)	2.50	

1905

1906

1907

1908

1909

1910

1911

1912 **1913** **1914** **1915**

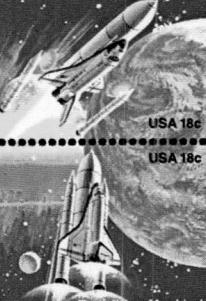

1916 **1917** **1918** **1919** **1919a**

1920

1921 **1922**

1923 **1924**

1924a

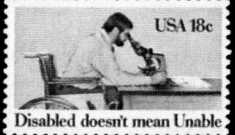

1925

1926

1927

1928

1929

1930

1931

1932

1931a

1933

1934

1935

1936

1937

1938

1938a

Issues of 1981		Un	U	PB	#	FDC	Q(M)
Preservation of Wildlife Habitats Issue, Perf. 11							
1925	18¢ International Year						
	of the Disabled 06/29/81	.35	.20	1.50	(4)	1.00	100
a	Vertical pair, imperf. horizontally	2,750.00					
1926	18¢ Edna St. Vincent Millay 07/10/81	.35	.20	1.50	(4)	1.00	100
a	Black omitted	350.00	—				
1927	18¢ Alcoholism 08/19/81	.40	.20	10.00	(6)	1.25	98
a	Imperf., pair	400.00					
b	Vertical pair, imperf. horizontally	2,500.00					
American Architecture Issue							
1928	18¢ NYU Library, by						
	Sanford White 08/28/81	.40	.20			1.00	42
1929	18¢ Biltmore House, by						
	Richard Morris Hunt 08/28/81	.40	.20			1.00	42
1930	18¢ Palace of the Arts,						
	by Bernard Maybeck 08/28/81	.40	.20			1.00	42
1931	18¢ National Farmer's Bank,						
	by Louis Sullivan 08/28/81	.40	.20			1.00	42
a	Block of 4, #1928-31	1.65	1.50	2.10	(4)	2.50	
American Sports Issue, Perf. 10.5 x 11							
1932	18¢ Babe Zaharias Holding						
	Trophy 09/22/81	.40	.20	3.00	(4)	7.00	102
1933	18¢ Bobby Jones Teeing off 09/22/81	.40	.20	3.00	(4)	8.00	99
Perf. 11							
1934	18¢ Frederic Remington 10/09/81	.35	.20	1.60	(4)	1.00	101
a	Vertical pair, imperf. between	275.00					
b	Brown omitted	475.00					
1935	18¢ James Hoban 10/13/81	.35	.20	1.60	(4)	1.00	101
1936	20¢ James Hoban 10/13/81	.35	.20	1.65	(4)	1.00	167
American Bicentennial Issue							
1937	18¢ Battle of Yorktown 1781 10/16/81	.35	.20			1.00	81
1938	18¢ Battle of the Virginia						
	Capes 1781 10/16/81	.35	.20			1.00	81
a	Attached pair, #1937-38	.90	.75	2.00	(4)	1.50	
b	As "a," black omitted	400.00					

Walter DuBois Richards

Walter DuBois Richards graduated from the Cleveland School of Art and moved to New York in 1936 where he created illustrations for Madison Avenue advertising accounts and national publications.
A gifted draftsman, watercolorist, and lithographer, he has traveled the world on assignment for *Life* magazine, the United States Air Force, and many American corporations. His paintings have been exhibited at the Metropolitan Museum of Art and are included in the permanent collections of the Whitney Museum of American Art, the New Britain Museum, and the Pentagon. His 37 United States postage stamp designs include a series honoring 16 national architectural treasures. ■

	Issues of 1981		Un	U	PB/LP	#	FDC	Q(M)
	Christmas Issue							
1939	20¢ Madonna and Child,							
	by Botticelli	10/28/81	.40	.20	1.75	(4)	1.00	598
a	Imperf., pair		125.00					
b	Vertical pair, imperf. horizontally		1,650.00					
1940	20¢ Felt Bear on Sleigh	10/28/81	.40	.20	1.75	(4)	1.00	793
a	Imperf., pair		275.00					
b	Vertical pair, imperf. horizontally		2,500.00					
1941	20¢ John Hanson	11/05/81	.40	.20	1.75	(4)	1.00	167
	Desert Plants Issue, Perf. 11							
1942	20¢ Barrel Cactus	12/11/81	.35	.20			1.00	48
1943	20¢ Agave	12/11/81	.35	.20			1.00	48
1944	20¢ Beavertail Cactus	12/11/81	.35	.20			1.00	48
1945	20¢ Saguaro	12/11/81	.35	.20			1.00	48
a	Block of 4, #1942-45		1.50	1.25	1.90	(4)	2.50	
b	As "a," deep brown omitted		7,500.00					
c	#1945 vertical pair, imperf.		5,250.00					
	Perf. 11 x 10.5							
1946	(20¢) "C" Stamp	10/11/81	.40	.20	2.00	(4)	1.00	
a	Tagging omitted		9.00					
	Coil Stamp, Perf. 10 Vertically							
1947	(20¢) "C" brown Eagle (1946)	10/11/81	.60	.20	1.50	(2)	1.00	
a	Imperf., pair		1,500.00		—	(2)		
	Booklet Stamp, Perf. 11 x 10.5							
1948	(20¢) "C" brown Eagle (1946),							
	single from booklet	10/11/81	.40	.20			1.00	
a	Booklet pane of 10	10/11/81	4.50	3.00			3.50	
	Issues of 1982, Perf. 11							
1949	20¢ Bighorn Sheep,							
	single from booklet	01/08/82	.55	.20			1.00	
a	Booklet pane of 10		5.50	2.50			6.00	
b	As "a," imperf. between		110.00					
c	Type II		.55	.20				
d	Type II, booklet pane of 10		11.00	—				
e	As #1949, tagging omitted		3.00	—				
f	As "e," booklet pane of 10		30.00					
	#1949 issued only in booklets. All stamps are imperf. at one side or imperf. at one side and bottom.							
1950	20¢ Franklin D. Roosevelt	01/30/82	.40	.20	1.75	(4)	1.00	164
	Perf. 11 x 10.5							
1951	20¢ Love	02/01/82	.40	.20	1.75	(4)	1.00	447
b	Imperf., pair		275.00					
c	Blue omitted		225.00					
d	Yellow omitted		900.00					
e	Purple omitted		—					
1951A	Perf. 11.25 x 10.5		.65	.20	3.00	(4)		
	Perf. 11							
1952	20¢ George Washington	02/22/82	.40	.20	1.75	(4)	1.00	181

1939

1940

1941

1942   **1943**   **1945**

1944   **1945a**

1946

1949

1950

1951

1952

State	Denom.	Bird & Flower	Year
 Alabama	USA 20c	Yellowhammer & Camellia	1953
 Alaska	USA 20c	Willow Ptarmigan & Forget-Me-Not	1954
 Arizona	USA 20c	Cactus Wren & Saguaro Cactus Blossom	1955
 Arkansas	USA 20c	Mockingbird & Apple Blossom	1956
 California	USA 20c	California Quail & California Poppy	1957
 Colorado	USA 20c	Lark Bunting & Rocky Mountain Columbine	1958
 Connecticut	USA 20c	Robin & Mountain Laurel	1959
 Delaware	USA 20c	Blue Hen Chicken & Peach Blossom	1960
 Florida	USA 20c	Mockingbird & Orange Blossom	1961
 Georgia	USA 20c	Brown Thrasher & Cherokee Rose	1962
 Hawaii	USA 20c	Hawaiian Goose & Hibiscus	1963
 Idaho	USA 20c	Mountain Bluebird & Syringa	1964
 Illinois	USA 20c	Cardinal & Violet	1965
 Indiana	USA 20c	Cardinal & Peony	1966
 Iowa	USA 20c	Eastern Goldfinch & Wild Rose	1967
Kansas	USA 20c	Western Meadowlark & Sunflower	1968
Kentucky	USA 20c	Cardinal & Goldenrod	1969
Louisiana	USA 20c	Brown Pelican & Magnolia	1970
Maine	USA 20c	Chickadee & White Pine Cone and Tassel	1971
Maryland	USA 20c	Baltimore Oriole & Black-Eyed Susan	1972
Massachusetts	USA 20c	Black-Capped Chickadee & Mayflower	1973
Michigan	USA 20c	Robin & Apple Blossom	1974
Minnesota	USA 20c	Common Loon & Showy Lady Slipper	1975
Mississippi	USA 20c	Mockingbird & Magnolia	1976
Missouri	USA 20c	Eastern Bluebird & Red Hawthorn	1977

Issues of 1982		Un	U	FDC	Q(M)
State Birds & Flowers Issue, Perf. 10.5 x 11					
1953	20¢ Alabama: Yellowhammer and Camellia	04/14/82	.50	.25	1.25	13
1954	20¢ Alaska: Willow Ptarmigan and Forget-Me-Not	04/14/82	.50	.25	1.25	13
1955	20¢ Arizona: Cactus Wren and Saguaro Cactus Blossom	04/14/82	.50	.25	1.25	13
1956	20¢ Arkansas: Mockingbird and Apple Blossom	04/14/82	.50	.25	1.25	13
1957	20¢ California: California Quail and California Poppy	04/14/82	.50	.25	1.25	13
1958	20¢ Colorado: Lark Bunting and Rocky Mountain Columbine	04/14/82	.50	.25	1.25	13
1959	20¢ Connecticut: Robin and Mountain Laurel	04/14/82	.50	.25	1.25	13
1960	20¢ Delaware: Blue Hen Chicken and Peach Blossom	04/14/82	.50	.25	1.25	13
1961	20¢ Florida: Mockingbird and Orange Blossom	04/14/82	.50	.25	1.25	13
1962	20¢ Georgia: Brown Thrasher and Cherokee Rose	04/14/82	.50	.25	1.25	13
1963	20¢ Hawaii: Hawaiian Goose and Hibiscus	04/14/82	.50	.25	1.25	13
1964	20¢ Idaho: Mountain Bluebird and Syringa	04/14/82	.50	.25	1.25	13
1965	20¢ Illinois: Cardinal and Violet	04/14/82	.50	.25	1.25	13
1966	20¢ Indiana: Cardinal and Peony	04/14/82	.50	.25	1.25	13
1967	20¢ Iowa: Eastern Goldfinch and Wild Rose	04/14/82	.50	.25	1.25	13
1968	20¢ Kansas: Western Meadowlark and Sunflower	04/14/82	.50	.25	1.25	13
1969	20¢ Kentucky: Cardinal and Goldenrod	04/14/82	.50	.25	1.25	13
1970	20¢ Louisiana: Brown Pelican and Magnolia	04/14/82	.50	.25	1.25	13
1971	20¢ Maine: Chickadee and White Pine Cone and Tassel	04/14/82	.50	.25	1.25	13
1972	20¢ Maryland: Baltimore Oriole and Black-Eyed Susan	04/14/82	.50	.25	1.25	13
1973	20¢ Massachusetts: Black-Capped Chickadee and Mayflower	04/14/82	.50	.25	1.25	13
1974	20¢ Michigan: Robin and Apple Blossom	04/14/82	.50	.25	1.25	13
1975	20¢ Minnesota: Common Loon and Showy Lady Slipper	04/14/82	.50	.25	1.25	13
1976	20¢ Mississippi: Mockingbird and Magnolia	04/14/82	.50	.25	1.25	13
1977	20¢ Missouri: Eastern Bluebird and Red Hawthorn	04/14/82	.50	.25	1.25	13

	Issues of 1982		Un	U	FDC	Q(M)
	State Birds & Flowers Issue (continued)					
1978	20¢ Montana: Western Meadowlark & Bitterroot	04/14/82	.50	.25	1.25	13
1979	20¢ Nebraska: Western Meadowlark & Goldenrod	04/14/82	.50	.25	1.25	13
1980	20¢ Nevada: Mountain Bluebird & Sagebrush	04/14/82	.50	.25	1.25	13
1981	20¢ New Hampshire: Purple Finch & Lilac	04/14/82	.50	.25	1.25	13
1982	20¢ New Jersey: American Goldfinch & Violet	04/14/82	.50	.25	1.25	13
1983	20¢ New Mexico: Roadrunner & Yucca Flower	04/14/82	.50	.25	1.25	13
1984	20¢ New York: Eastern Bluebird & Rose	04/14/82	.50	.25	1.25	13
1985	20¢ North Carolina: Cardinal & Flowering Dogwood	04/14/82	.50	.25	1.25	13
1986	20¢ North Dakota: Western Meadowlark & Wild Prairie Rose	04/14/82	.50	.25	1.25	13
1987	20¢ Ohio: Cardinal & Red Carnation	04/14/82	.50	.25	1.25	13
1988	20¢ Oklahoma: Scissor-tailed Flycatcher & Mistletoe	04/14/82	.50	.25	1.25	13
1989	20¢ Oregon: Western Meadowlark & Oregon Grape	04/14/82	.50	.25	1.25	13
1990	20¢ Pennsylvania: Ruffed Grouse & Mountain Laurel	04/14/82	.50	.25	1.25	13
1991	20¢ Rhode Island: Rhode Island Red & Violet	04/14/82	.50	.25	1.25	13
1992	20¢ South Carolina: Carolina Wren & Carolina Jessamine	04/14/82	.50	.25	1.25	13
1993	20¢ South Dakota: Ring-Necked Pheasant & Pasqueflower	04/14/82	.50	.25	1.25	13
1994	20¢ Tennessee: Mockingbird & Iris	04/14/82	.50	.25	1.25	13
1995	20¢ Texas: Mockingbird & Bluebonnet	04/14/82	.50	.25	1.25	13
1996	20¢ Utah: California Gull & Sego Lily	04/14/82	.50	.25	1.25	13
1997	20¢ Vermont: Hermit Thrush & Red Clover	04/14/82	.50	.25	1.25	13
1998	20¢ Virginia: Cardinal & Flowering Dogwood	04/14/82	.50	.25	1.25	13
1999	20¢ Washington: American Goldfinch & Rhododendron	04/14/82	.50	.25	1.25	13
2000	20¢ West Virginia: Cardinal & Rhododendron Maximum	04/14/82	.50	.25	1.25	13
2001	20¢ Wisconsin: Robin & Wood Violet	04/14/82	.50	.25	1.25	13
2002	20¢ Wyoming: Western Meadowlark & Indian Paintbrush	04/14/82	.50	.25	1.25	13
a	Any single, perf. 11.25 x 11		.55	.30		
b	Pane of 50 (with plate #)		25.00	—	30.00	
c	Pane of 50, perf. 11.25 x 11		27.50	—		
d	Pane of 50, imperf.		27,500.00			

© LEONARD EIGER

Arthur Singer (1917-1990)

One of America's finest wildlife painters, Arthur Singer was renowned for his illustrations of birds and animals in their natural habitats. After studying at the Cooper Union School of Art in New York, he worked with the Allies during World War II to conceive camouflage schemes for tanks, which required keen observations of terrain and moving objects when viewed from the air. His bold, fresh style emphasizing color, form and movement is evident in his many lavishly illustrated books, which are well known to bird watchers. His art also appears on fifty State Birds and Flowers stamps, illustrated for the United States Postal Service with his son, Alan D. Singer. ■

Montana USA 20c	Nebraska USA 20c	Nevada USA 20c	New Hampshire USA 20c	New Jersey USA 20c
Western Meadowlark & Bitterroot	*Western Meadowlark & Goldenrod*	*Mountain Bluebird & Sagebrush*	*Purple Finch & Lilac*	*American Goldfinch & Violet*
1978	1979	1980	1981	1982

New Mexico USA 20c	New York USA 20c	North Carolina USA 20c	North Dakota USA 20c	Ohio USA 20c
Roadrunner & Yucca Flower	*Eastern Bluebird & Rose*	*Cardinal & Flowering Dogwood*	*Western Meadowlark & Wild Prairie Rose*	*Cardinal & Red Carnation*
1983	1984	1985	1986	1987

Oklahoma USA 20c	Oregon USA 20c	Pennsylvania USA 20c	Rhode Island USA 20c	South Carolina USA 20c
Scissor-tailed Flycatcher & Mistletoe	*Western Meadowlark & Oregon Grape*	*Ruffed Grouse & Mountain Laurel*	*Rhode Island Red & Violet*	*Carolina Wren & Carolina Jessamine*
1988	1989	1990	1991	1992

South Dakota USA 20c	Tennessee USA 20c	Texas USA 20c	Utah USA 20c	Vermont USA 20c
Ring-Necked Pheasant & Pasqueflower	*Mockingbird & Iris*	*Mockingbird & Bluebonnet*	*California Gull & Sego Lily*	*Hermit Thrush & Red Clover*
1993	1994	1995	1996	1997

Virginia USA 20c	Washington USA 20c	West Virginia USA 20c	Wisconsin USA 20c	Wyoming USA 20c

Cardinal & Flowering Dogwood	*American Goldfinch & Rhododendron*	*Cardinal & Rhododendron Maximum*	*Robin & Wood Violet*	*Western Meadowlark & Indian Paintbrush*
1998	1999	2000	2001	2002

2003

2004

2005

2006

2007

2008

2009

2009a

2010

2012

2011

2013

2014

2015

2016

2019

2020

2017

2018

2021

2022

2022a

Issues of 1982		Un	U	PB/PNC/LP	#	FDC	Q(M)
Perf. 11							
2003 20¢ USA/The Netherlands	04/20/82	.40	.20	3.50	(6)	1.00	109
a Imperf., pair		325.00					
2004 20¢ Library of Congress	04/21/82	.40	.20	1.75	(4)	1.00	113
Coil Stamp, Perf. 10 Vertically							
2005 20¢ Consumer Education	04/27/82	.55	.20	30.00	(3)	1.00	
a Imperf., pair		100.00		400.00	(2)		
b Tagging omitted		7.50					

Value for plate no. coil strip of 3 stamps is for most common plate nos. Other plate nos. and strips of 5 stamps may have higher values.

		Un	U	PB/PNC/LP	#	FDC	Q(M)
Knoxville World's Fair Issue, Perf. 11							
2006 20¢ Solar Energy	04/29/82	.40	.20			1.00	31
2007 20¢ Synthetic Fuels	04/29/82	.40	.20			1.00	31
2008 20¢ Breeder Reactor	04/29/82	.40	.20			1.00	31
2009 20¢ Fossil Fuels	04/29/82	.40	.20			1.00	31
a Block of 4, #2006-09		1.65	1.50	2.00	(4)	2.50	
2010 20¢ Horatio Alger	04/30/82	.40	.20	1.75	(4)	1.00	108
2011 20¢ Aging Together	05/21/82	.40	.20	1.75	(4)	1.00	173
Performing Arts Issue							
2012 20¢ John, Ethel and Lionel Barrymore	06/08/82	.40	.20	1.75	(4)	1.25	107
2013 20¢ Dr. Mary Walker	06/10/82	.40	.20	1.75	(4)	1.00	109
2014 20¢ International Peace Garden	06/30/82	.40	.20	1.75	(4)	1.00	183
a Black and green omitted		260.00					
2015 20¢ America's Libraries	07/13/82	.40	.20	1.75	(4)	1.00	169
a Vertical pair, imperf. horizontally		300.00					
b Tagging omitted		7.50					
Black Heritage Issue, Perf. 10.5 x 11							
2016 20¢ Jackie Robinson and Robinson Stealing Home Plate	08/02/82	1.10	.20	5.50	(4)	6.00	164
Perf. 11							
2017 20¢ Touro Synagogue	08/22/82	.40	.20	11.00	(20)	1.00	110
a Imperf., pair		2,500.00					
2018 20¢ Wolf Trap Farm Park	09/01/82	.40	.20	1.75	(4)	1.00	111
American Architecture Issue							
2019 20¢ Fallingwater, by Frank Lloyd Wright	09/30/82	.45	.20			1.00	41
2020 20¢ Illinois Institute of Technology, by Ludwig Mies van der Rohe	09/30/82	.45	.20			1.00	41
2021 20¢ Gropius House, by Walter Gropius	09/30/82	.45	.20			1.00	41
2022 20¢ Dulles Airport by Eero Saarinen	09/30/82	.45	.20			1.00	41
a Block of 4, #2019-22		2.00	1.60	2.50	(4)	2.50	

1982-1983

	Issues of 1982		Un	U	PB	#	FDC	Q(M)
2023	20¢ St. Francis of Assisi	10/07/82	.40	.20	1.75	(4)	1.50	174
2024	20¢ Ponce de Leon	10/12/82	.40	.20	3.25	(6)	1.00	110
a	Imperf., pair		500.00					
	Christmas Issue							
2025	13¢ Puppy and Kitten	11/03/82	.25	.20	1.40	(4)	1.00	234
a	Imperf., pair		650.00					
2026	20¢ Madonna and Child,							
	by Tiepolo	10/28/82	.40	.20	11.00	(20)	1.00	703
a	Imperf., pair		150.00					
b	Horizontal pair, imperf. vertically		—					
c	Vertical pair, imperf. horizontally		—					
	Seasons Greetings Issue							
2027	20¢ Children Sledding	10/28/82	.50	.20			1.00	197
2028	20¢ Children Building							
	a Snowman	10/28/82	.50	.20			1.00	197
2029	20¢ Children Skating	10/28/82	.50	.20			1.00	197
2030	20¢ Children Trimming a Tree	10/28/82	.50	.20			1.00	197
a	Block of 4, #2027-30		2.25	1.50	2.75	(4)	2.50	
b	As "a," imperf.		2,750.00					
c	As "a," imperf. horizontally		3,250.00					
	Issues of 1983							
2031	20¢ Science & Industry	01/19/83	.40	.20	1.75	(4)	1.00	119
a	Black omitted		1,400.00					
	Balloons Issue							
2032	20¢ Intrepid, 1861	03/31/83	.40	.20			1.00	57
2033	20¢ Hot Air Ballooning							
	(wording lower right)	03/31/83	.40	.20			1.00	57
2034	20¢ Hot Air Ballooning							
	(wording upper left)	03/31/83	.40	.20			1.00	57
2035	20¢ Explorer II, 1935	03/31/83	.40	.20			1.00	57
a	Block of 4, #2032-35		1.65	1.50	1.75	(4)	2.50	
b	As "a," imperf.		4,250.00					
c	As "a," right stamp perf.,							
	otherwise imperf.		4,500.00					
2036	20¢ U.S./Sweden Treaty	03/24/83	.40	.20	1.75	(4)	1.00	118
2037	20¢ Civilian Conservation							
	Corps	04/05/83	.40	.20	1.75	(4)	1.00	114
a	Imperf., pair		2,750.00					
2038	20¢ Joseph Priestley	04/13/83	.40	.20	1.75	(4)	1.00	165
2039	20¢ Voluntarism	04/20/83	.40	.20	3.00	(6)	1.25	120
a	Imperf., pair		800.00					
2040	20¢ Concord-German							
	Immigration, Apr. 29	04/29/83	.40	.20	1.75	(4)	1.00	117

2023

2024

2025

2027 **2028**

2026

2029 **2030** **2030a**

2032 **2033**

2031

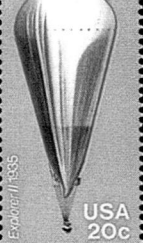

2034 **2035** **2035a**

2036

2037

2038

2039

2040

2041

2042

2043

2044

2045

2046

2047

2048   **2049**

2050   **2051**   **2051a**

2052

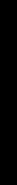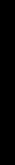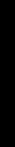

2053

2054

2055   **2056**

2057   **2058**   **2058a**

	Issues of 1983		Un	U	PB	#	FDC	Q(M)
2041	20¢ Brooklyn Bridge	05/17/83	.40	.20	1.75	(4)	1.00	182
2042	20¢ Tennessee Valley Authority	05/18/83	.40	.20	11.00	(20)	1.00	114
2043	20¢ Physical Fitness	05/14/83	.40	.20	3.00	(6)	1.00	112
	Black Heritage Issue							
2044	20¢ Scott Joplin Portrait							
	and Joplin Playing the Piano	06/09/83	.40	.20	1.75	(4)	1.00	115
a	Imperf., pair		475.00					
2045	20¢ Medal of Honor	06/07/83	.40	.20	1.75	(4)	4.00	109
a	Red omitted		250.00					
	American Sports Issue, Perf. 10.5 x 11							
2046	20¢ Babe Ruth Hitting							
	a Home Run	07/06/83	1.25	.20	7.00	(4)	5.00	185
	Literary Arts Issue, Perf. 11							
2047	20¢ Nathaniel Hawthorne,							
	by Cephus Giovanni Thompson	07/08/83	.45	.20	2.10	(4)	1.00	111
	Olympic Summer Games Issue (See also #2082-85, C101-12)							
2048	13¢ Discus Thrower	07/28/83	.35	.20			1.00	99
2049	13¢ High Jumper	07/28/83	.35	.20			1.00	99
2050	13¢ Archer	07/28/83	.35	.20			1.00	99
2051	13¢ Boxers	07/28/83	.35	.20			1.00	99
a	Block of 4, #2048-51		1.50	1.25	1.75	(4)	2.50	
	American Bicentennial Issue							
2052	20¢ Signing of Treaty of Paris							
	(John Adams, Benjamin Franklin							
	and John Jay observing David							
	Hartley), by Benjamin West	09/02/83	.40	.20	1.75	(4)	1.00	104
2053	20¢ Civil Service	09/09/83	.40	.20	3.00	(6)	1.00	115
2054	20¢ Metropolitan Opera	09/14/83	.40	.20	1.75	(4)	1.00	113
	American Inventors Issue							
2055	20¢ Charles Steinmetz							
	and Curve on Graph	09/21/83	.45	.20			1.00	48
2056	20¢ Edwin Armstrong and							
	Frequency Modulator	09/21/83	.45	.20			1.00	48
2057	20¢ Nikola Tesla and							
	Induction Motor	09/21/83	.45	.20			1.00	48
2058	20¢ Philo T. Farnsworth and							
	First Television Camera	09/21/83	.45	.20			1.00	48
a	Block of 4, #2055-58		1.80	1.25	2.50	(4)	2.50	
b	As "a," black omitted		350.00					

Charles Harper

A self-described minimal realist, Charles Harper reduces his subjects to the simplest terms while maintaining visual identity. His elegant images are tinged with humor and have appeared in magazines and on posters for such conservation-minded sites and organizations as the National Park Service, the Cincinnati Zoo, Everglades National Park, and Hawk Mountain Sanctuary. He has also created large-scale ceramic tile murals for federal buildings and universities, illustrated books about biology and the animal kingdom, and produced many limited-edition silkscreen prints. His artwork appears on four United States postage stamps. ■

Issues of 1983		Un	U	PB	#	FDC	Q(M)
Streetcars Issue, Perf. 11							
2059 20¢ First American Streetcar	10/08/83	.45	.20			1.00	52
2060 20¢ Early Electric Streetcar	10/08/83	.45	.20			1.00	52
2061 20¢ "Bobtail" Horsecar	10/08/83	.45	.20			1.00	52
2062 20¢ St. Charles Streetcar	10/08/83	.45	.20			1.00	52
a Block of 4, #2059-62		1.80	1.40	2.50	(4)	2.50	
b As "a," black omitted		425.00					
c As "a," black omitted on #2059, 2061		—					
Christmas Issue							
2063 20¢ Niccolini-Cowper							
Madonna, by Raphael	10/28/83	.40	.20	1.75	(4)	1.00	716
2064 20¢ Santa Claus	10/28/83	.40	.20	3.00	(6)	1.00	849
a Imperf., pair		175.00					
2065 20¢ Martin Luther	11/11/83	.40	.20	1.75	(4)	3.00	165
Issues of 1984							
2066 20¢ 25th Anniversary							
of Alaska Statehood	01/03/84	.40	.20	1.75	(4)	1.00	120
Winter Olympic Games Issue, Perf. 10.5 x 11							
2067 20¢ Ice Dancing	01/06/84	.50	.20			1.00	80
2068 20¢ Alpine Skiing	01/06/84	.50	.20			1.00	80
2069 20¢ Nordic Skiing	01/06/84	.50	.20			1.00	80
2070 20¢ Hockey	01/06/84	.50	.20			1.00	80
a Block of 4, #2067-70		2.10	1.50	3.00	(4)	2.50	
Perf. 11							
2071 20¢ Federal Deposit							
Insurance Corporation	01/12/84	.40	.20	1.75	(4)	1.00	103

Richard Leech (1932–1993)

Best known for his beautifully detailed drawings of automobiles, motorcycles, and locomotives, Richard Leech spent most of his life doing the exacting work of a technical illustrator, a profession that he deeply enjoyed. Born in England, he had an early fascination with locomotion and attended Southwest Essex College and Derby College of Art and Technology as a scholarship student. In 1964, he moved to California and began his own business, which served the advertising and illustration needs of such prominent companies as Yamaha, General Motors, Mazda, and Porsche. *National Geographic* and the United States Postal Service, for which he designed 14 commemorative stamps, have also commissioned his artwork. ■

2059　　2060

2061　　2062　　2062a

2063

2064

2065

2067　　2068

2066

2071

2069　　2070　　2070a

2072

2073

2074

2075

2076   **2077**

2080

2081

2078   **2079**   **2079a**

2082   **2083**

2086

2087

Issues of 1984		Un	U	PB	#	FDC	Q(M)
Perf. 11 x 10.5							
2072 20¢ Love	01/31/84	.40	.20	11.50	(20)	2.00	555
a	Horizontal pair, imperf. vertically	175.00					
b	Tagging omitted	5.00					
Black Heritage Issue, Carter G. Woodson, Perf. 11							
2073 20¢ Carter G. Woodson							
Holding History Book	02/01/84	.40	.20	1.75	(4)	1.00	120
a	Horizontal pair, imperf. vertically	1,600.00					
2074 20¢ Soil and Water							
Conservation	02/06/84	.40	.20	1.75	(4)	1.00	107
2075 20¢ 50th Anniversary							
of Credit Union Act	02/10/84	.40	.20	1.75	(4)	1.00	107
Orchids Issue							
2076 20¢ Wild Pink	03/05/84	.50	.20			1.00	77
2077 20¢ Yellow Lady's-Slipper	03/05/84	.50	.20			1.00	77
2078 20¢ Spreading Pogonia	03/05/84	.50	.20			1.00	77
2079 20¢ Pacific Calypso	03/05/84	.50	.20			1.00	77
a	Block of 4, #2076-79	2.00	1.50	2.50	(4)	2.50	
2080 20¢ 25th Anniversary							
of Hawaii Statehood	03/12/84	.40	.20	1.70	(4)	1.00	120
2081 20¢ National Archives	04/16/84	.40	.20	1.70	(4)	1.00	108
Olympic Summer Games Issue (See also #2048-52, C101-12)							
2082 20¢ Diving	05/04/84	.55	.20			1.00	78
2083 20¢ Long Jump	05/04/84	.55	.20			1.00	78
2084 20¢ Wrestling	05/04/84	.55	.20			1.00	78
2085 20¢ Kayak	05/04/84	.55	.20			1.00	78
a	Block of 4, #2082-85	2.40	1.90	3.50	(4)	2.50	
2086 20¢ Louisiana World							
Exposition	05/11/84	.40	.20	1.75	(4)	1.00	130
2087 20¢ Health Research	05/17/84	.40	.20	1.75	(4)	1.00	120

Jerry Pinkney

Jerry Pinkney began his career in the art department of a Boston greeting card company, but
soon became acquainted with the publishing
industry, which sought and nurtured his work.
Celebrated for his luminous narrative paintings
that provide historical accuracy, he has received
four Caldecott Honor Medals and many other
professional awards. The illustrator of more than
80 children's books, he has created images for
such diverse clients as *Time*, *National
Geographic*, NASA, the Franklin Mint, and
General Mills. His 12 United States postage
stamp designs include a series of Black Heritage
issues celebrating African-American achieve-

PHOTO BY MYLES C. PINKNEY

ment. A member of the Citizens' Stamp Advisory Committee from 1982 to
1992, he has also served on the United States Postal Service Quality
Assurance Committee. ∎

*"Stamps … have the power to reach many people in a way
that functions, educates and informs."*

— Jerry Pinkney

Issues of 1984		Un	U	PB	#	FDC	Q(M)
Performing Arts Issue, Perf. 11							
2088 20¢ Douglas Fairbanks Portrait							
and Fairbanks in Pirate Role	05/23/84	.40	.20	12.00	(20)	1.00	117
American Sports Issue							
2089 20¢ Jim Thorpe							
on Football Field	05/24/84	.40	.20	2.00	(4)	3.00	116
Performing Arts Issue							
2090 20¢ John McCormack Portrait							
and McCormack in Tenor Role	06/06/84	.40	.20	1.75	(4)	1.00	117
2091 20¢ 25th Anniversary							
of St. Lawrence Seaway	06/26/84	.40	.20	1.75	(4)	1.00	120
2092 20¢ Migratory Bird Hunting							
and Preservation Act	07/02/84	.50	.20	2.50	(4)	1.25	124
a Horizontal pair, imperf. vertically		400.00					
2093 20¢ Roanoke Voyages	07/13/84	.40	.20	1.75	(4)	1.00	120
Pair with full horizontal gutter between		—					
Literary Arts Issue							
2094 20¢ Herman Melville	08/01/84	.40	.20	1.75	(4)	2.00	117
2095 20¢ Horace Moses	08/06/84	.45	.20	3.50	(6)	1.00	117
2096 20¢ Smokey the Bear	08/13/84	.40	.20	2.00	(4)	5.00	96
a Horizontal pair, imperf. between		300.00					
b Vertical pair, imperf. between		250.00					
c Block of 4, imperf. between							
vertically and horizontally		5,500.00					
d Horizontal pair, imperf. vertically		1,750.00					
American Sports Issue							
2097 20¢ Roberto Clemente in Pirates Cap, Puerto							
Rican Flag in Background	08/17/84	1.60	.20	8.00	(4)	9.00	119
a Horizontal pair, imperf. vertically		2,000.00					
American Dogs Issue							
2098 20¢ Beagle and Boston Terrier	09/07/84	.45	.20			1.25	54
2099 20¢ Chesapeake Bay Retriever							
and Cocker Spaniel	09/07/84	.45	.20			1.25	54
2100 20¢ Alaskan Malamute							
and Collie	09/07/84	.45	.20			1.25	54
2101 20¢ Black and Tan Coonhound							
and American Foxhound	09/07/84	.45	.20			1.25	54
a Block of 4, #2098-2101		1.90	1.75	3.00	(4)	3.00	

Wendell Minor

Wendell Minor is well known for his paintings that illustrate children's books and appear on the jackets of best-selling books by authors such as David McCullough, Pat Conroy, Doris Kearns Goodwin, and Fannie Flagg. His work has been exhibited widely and is represented in the permanent collections of many prestigious institutions. The recipient of more than 250 awards from major graphics organizations, he has served as president of the Society of Illustrators and taught at the School of Visual Arts in New York City. A 25-year retrospective  of his book cover art, *Wendell Minor: Art For the Written Word*, was published in 1995. A graduate of the Ringling School of Art and Design in Sarasota, Florida, he writes and illustrates children's books and creates commissioned art from his studio in Connecticut. He has designed three stamped cards and one stamp for the U.S. Postal Service. ■

2088 **2089** **2090**

2091 **2092**

2093

2094 **2095** **2096** **2097**

2098 **2099**

2100 **2101** **2101a**

2102

2103

2104

2105

2106

2107

2108

2109

2110

2111

2114

2115b

2116

	Issues of 1984		Un	U	PB/PNC	#	FDC	Q(M)
2102	20¢ Crime Prevention	09/26/84	.40	.20	1.75	(4)	1.00	120
2103	20¢ Hispanic Americans	10/31/84	.40	.20	1.75	(4)	1.00	108
a	Vertical pair, imperf. horizontally		2,250.00					
2104	20¢ Family Unity	10/01/84	.40	.20	14.00	(20)	1.00	118
a	Horizontal pair, imperf. vertically		550.00					
b	Tagging omitted		6.00					
2105	20¢ Eleanor Roosevelt	10/11/84	.40	.20	1.75	(4)	1.00	113
2106	20¢ A Nation of Readers	10/16/84	.40	.20	1.75	(4)	1.00	117
	Christmas Issue							
2107	20¢ Madonna and Child,							
	by Fra Filippo Lippi	10/30/84	.40	.20	1.70	(4)	1.00	751
2108	20¢ Santa Claus	10/30/84	.40	.20	1.70	(4)	1.00	786
a	Horizontal pair, imperf. vertically		950.00					
2109	20¢ Vietnam Veterans'							
	Memorial	11/10/84	.40	.20	1.90	(4)	4.50	105
	Issues of 1985, Performing Arts Issue							
2110	22¢ Jerome Kern Portrait and							
	Kern Studying Sheet Music	01/23/85	.40	.20	1.75	(4)	1.00	125
a	Tagging omitted		7.50					
2111	(22¢)"D" Stamp	02/01/85	.55	.20	4.50	(6)	1.00	
a	Imperf., pair		50.00					
b	Vertical pair, imperf. horizontally		1,350.00					
	Coil Stamp, Perf. 10 Vertically							
2112	(22¢)"D" green Eagle (2111)	02/01/85	.60	.20	6.00	(3)	1.00	
a	Imperf., pair		47.50					
b	As "a," tagging omitted		140.00					
	Booklet Stamp, Perf. 11							
2113	(22¢)"D" green Eagle (2111),							
	single from booklet	02/01/85	.80	.20			1.00	
a	Booklet pane of 10	02/01/85	8.50	3.00			7.50	
b	As "a," imperf. between horizontally		—					
	Issues of 1985-87, Flag Over Capitol Issue							
2114	22¢ Flag Over Capitol	03/29/85	.40	.20	1.90	(4)	1.00	
	Pair with full horizontal gutter between		—					
	Coil Stamp, Perf. 10 Vertically							
2115	22¢ Flag Over Capitol (2114)	03/29/85	.40	.20	3.75	(3)	1.00	
a	Narrow block tagging		.40	.20	3.75	(3)	*1.00*	
b	Inscribed "T" at bottom	05/23/87	.50	.40	4.00	(3)		
c	Black field of stars		—	—				
	#2115b issued for test on prephosphored paper. Paper is whiter and colors are brighter							
	than on 2115.							
d	Tagging omitted		3.00					
e	Imperf., pair		15.00					
	Booklet Stamp, Perf. 10 Horizontally							
2116	22¢ Flag over Capitol,							
	single from booklet		.50	.20			1.00	
a	Booklet pane of 5	03/29/85	2.50	1.25			3.50	
	#2116 issued only in booklets. All stamps are imperf. at both sides or imperf. at both sides							
	and bottom.							

	Issues of 1985		Un	U	PNC	#	FDC
	Seashells Booklet Issue, Perf. 10						
2117	22¢ Frilled Dogwinkle	04/04/85	.40	.20			1.00
2118	22¢ Reticulated Helmet	04/04/85	.40	.20			1.00
2119	22¢ New England Neptune	04/04/85	.40	.20			1.00
2120	22¢ Calico Scallop	04/04/85	.40	.20			1.00
2121	22¢ Lightning Whelk	04/04/85	.40	.20			1.00
a	Booklet pane of 10		4.00	2.50			7.50
b	As "a," violet omitted		800.00				
c	As "a," imperf. between vertically		600.00				
e	Strip of 5, #2117-21		2.00	—			
	Express Mail Booklet Issue, Perf. 10 Vertically						
2122	$10.75 Eagle and Moon,						
	booklet single	04/29/85	19.00	7.50			40.00
a	Booklet pane of 3		60.00	—			95.00
b	Type II		21.00	10.00			
c	As "b," booklet pane of 3		65.00	—			
	#2122 issued only in booklets. All stamps are imperf. at top and bottom or at top, bottom and one side.						
	Issues of 1985-89, Coil Stamps, Transportation Issue (See also #1897-1908, 2225-31, 2252-66, 2451-68)						
2123	3.4¢ School Bus 1920s	06/08/85	.20	.20	1.10	(5)	1.00
a	Untagged (Bureau precanceled)		.20	.20	5.25	(5)	
2124	4.9¢ Buckboard 1880s	06/21/85	.20	.20	1.00	(5)	1.00
a	Untagged (Bureau precanceled)		.20	.20	1.75	(5)	
2125	5.5¢ Star Route Truck 1910s	11/01/86	.20	.20	1.90	(5)	1.00
a	Untagged (Bureau precanceled)		.20	.20	1.90	(5)	
2126	6¢ Tricycle 1880s	05/06/85	.20	.20	1.65	(5)	1.50
a	Untagged (Bureau precanceled)		.20	.20	1.90	(5)	
b	As "a," imperf., pair		200.00				
2127	7.1¢ Tractor 1920s	02/06/87	.20	.20	2.50	(5)	1.00
a	Untagged (Bureau precanceled "Nonprofit org.")		.20	.20	3.50	(5)	5.00
b	Untagged (Bureau precanceled "Nonprofit 5-Digit ZIP + 4")	05/26/89	.20	.20	2.00	(5)	
2128	8.3¢ Ambulance 1860s	06/21/85	.20	.20	1.90	(5)	1.00
a	Untagged (Bureau precanceled)		.20	.20	2.00	(5)	
2129	8.5¢ Tow Truck 1920s	01/24/87	.20	.20	3.25	(5)	1.00
a	Untagged (Bureau precanceled)		.20	.20	3.25	(5)	
2130	10.1¢ Oil Wagon 1890s	04/18/85	.25	.20	2.75	(5)	1.00
a	Untagged (Bureau precanceled, red)		.25	.25	2.50	(5)	1.00
	Untagged (Bureau precanceled, black)		.25	.25	3.00	(5)	
b	As "a," red precancel, imperf., pair		15.00		100.00	(6)	
	As "a," black precancel, imperf., pair		100.00				
2131	11¢ Stutz Bearcat 1933	06/11/85	.25	.20	2.00	(5)	1.25
2132	12¢ Stanley Steamer 1909	04/02/85	.25	.20	2.50	(5)	1.00
a	Untagged (Bureau precanceled)		.25	.25	2.75	(5)	
b	As "a," type II		.40	.30	21.00	(5)	
	Type II has "Stanley Steamer 1909" .5 mm shorter (17.5 mm) than #2132 (18mm).						
2133	12.5¢ Pushcart 1880s	04/18/85	.25	.20	3.25	(5)	1.25
a	Untagged (Bureau precanceled)		.25	.25	3.50	(5)	
b	As "a," imperf., pair		55.00				
2134	14¢ Iceboat 1880s	03/23/85	.30	.20	2.75	(5)	1.25
a	Imperf., pair		100.00				
b	Type II		.30	.20	4.25	(5)	
2135	17¢ Dog Sled 1920s	08/20/86	.30	.20	3.50	(5)	1.25
a	Imperf., pair		500.00				
2136	25¢ Bread Wagon 1880s	11/22/86	.45	.20	3.75	(5)	1.25
a	Imperf., pair		10.00				
b	Pair, imperf. between		750.00				
c	Tagging omitted		.20				

2117

2118

2119

2120

2121

2121a

2122

2123

School Bus 1920s
3.4 USA

Buckboard 1880s
USA 4.9

Star Route Truck
5.5 USA 1910s

2124

2125

Tricycle 1880s
6 USA

2126

Tractor 1920s
7.1 USA

2127

Ambulance 1860s
8.3 USA

2128

Tow Truck 1920s
8.5 USA

2129

Oil Wagon 1890s
10.1 USA

Stutz Bearcat 1933
11 USA

2130

2131

Stanley Steamer 1909
USA 12

2132

Pushcart 1880s
12.5 USA
USA

2133

Iceboat 1880s
USA 14

2134

Dog Sled 1920s
17 USA

2135

Bread Wagon 1880s
25 USA

2136

2137

2138   **2139**

2140   **2141**   **2141a**

2142

2143

2144

2145

2146

2147

2149

2150

2152   **2153**

Issues of 1985		Un	U	PB/PNC	#	FDC	Q(M)
Black Heritage Issue, Perf. 11							
2137	22¢ Mary McLeod Bethune 03/05/85	.40	.20	2.25	(4)	1.00	120
American Folk Art Issue							
2138	22¢ Broadbill Decoy 03/22/85	.65	.20			1.00	75
2139	22¢ Mallard Decoy 03/22/85	.65	.20			1.00	75
2140	22¢ Canvasback Decoy 03/22/85	.65	.20			1.00	75
2141	22¢ Redhead Decoy 03/22/85	.65	.20			1.00	75
a	Block of 4, #2138-41	4.00	2.25	6.50	(4)	2.75	
2142	22¢ Winter Special Olympics 03/25/85	.40	.20	1.75	(4)	1.00	121
a	Vertical pair, imperf. horizontally	600.00					
2143	22¢ Love 04/17/85	.40	.20	1.70	(4)	2.00	730
a	Imperf., pair	1,500.00					
2144	22¢ Rural Electrification Administration 05/11/85	.45	.20	20.00	(20)	1.00	125
2145	22¢ AMERIPEX '86 05/25/85	.40	.20	1.75	(4)	1.00	203
a	Red, black and blue omitted	200.00					
b	Red and black omitted	1,250.00					
2146	22¢ Abigail Adams 06/14/85	.40	.20	1.90	(4)	1.00	126
a	Imperf., pair	275.00					
2147	22¢ Frederic A. Bartholdi 07/18/85	.40	.20	1.90	(4)	1.00	130
2148	Not assigned						
Coil Stamps, Perf. 10 Vertically							
2149	18¢ George Washington, Washington Monument 11/06/85	.35	.20	4.00	(5)	1.25	
a	Untagged (Bureau precanceled)	.35	.35	4.00	(5)		
b	Imperf., pair	950.00					
c	As "a," imperf. pair	800.00					
d	Tagging omitted	—	—				
e	As "a," tagged (error), dull gum	2.00	1.75	—			
2150	21.1¢ Sealed Envelopes 10/22/85	.40	.20	4.00	(5)	1.25	
a	Untagged (Bureau precanceled)	.40	.40	4.25	(5)		
b	As "a," tagged (error)	.40	.40	5.50	(5)		
2151	Not assigned						
Perf. 11							
2152	22¢ Korean War Veterans 07/26/85	.40	.20	2.50	(4)	3.00	120
2153	22¢ Social Security Act, 50th Anniversary 08/14/85	.40	.20	1.90	(4)	1.00	120

Corita Kent (1918–1986)

A Roman Catholic nun from 1936 to 1968, Corita Kent gained recognition as an activist and an artist whose bright colors and slogans from the mass media convey strong social and religious messages. In her art and in her capacity as a beloved art department chair of Immaculate Heart College, she was in step with the widespread questioning of authority that epitomized America in the

1960s. Her most famous and controversial outdoor work—created during the Vietnam War—is her monumental rainbow painting on a huge gas storage tank on the Boston harbor front. Today, the Corita Art Center of the Immaculate Heart Community in California keeps the artist's love of life and humanity alive. Her artwork appears on the fourth Love stamp issued by the United States Postal Service. ∎

Issues of 1985, Perf. 11		Un	U	PB	#	FDC	Q(M)
2154 22¢ World War I Veterans	08/26/85	.40	.20	2.25	(4)	3.00	120
American Horses Issue							
2155 22¢ Quarter Horse	09/25/85	1.00	.20			1.50	37
2156 22¢ Morgan	09/25/85	1.00	.20			1.50	37
2157 22¢ Saddlebred	09/25/85	1.00	.20			1.50	37
2158 22¢ Appaloosa	09/25/85	1.00	.20			1.50	37
a Block of 4, #2155-58		6.00	4.50	8.50	(4)	3.00	
2159 22¢ Public Education	10/01/85	.45	.20	2.75	(4)	1.00	120
International Youth Year Issue							
2160 22¢ YMCA Youth Camping	10/07/85	.65	.20			1.00	33
2161 22¢ Boy Scouts	10/07/85	.65	.20			2.00	33
2162 22¢ Big Brothers/Big Sisters	10/07/85	.65	.20			1.00	33
2163 22¢ Camp Fire	10/07/85	.65	.20			1.00	33
a Block of 4, #2160-63		3.00	2.25	4.50	(4)	2.50	
2164 22¢ Help End Hunger	10/15/85	.45	.20	2.00	(4)	1.00	120
Christmas Issue							
2165 22¢ Genoa Madonna, by Luca Della Robbia	10/30/85	.40	.20	1.75	(4)	1.00	759
a Imperf., pair		100.00					
2166 22¢ Poinsettia Plants	10/30/85	.40	.20	1.70	(4)	1.00	758
a Imperf., pair		130.00					

Robert Alexander Anderson

Robert Alexander Anderson has been a fine painter of commissioned portraits for 30 years and has also created art for advertising, publishing, and the music industry. A spokesman and illustrator for the John H. Breck Company for 15 years, he created pastel portraits for shampoo print ads and television commercials for American and Canadian television. He has recently completed portraits of former Massachusetts governors Edward J. King and William F. Weld. His outstanding images are included in many public, private, and institutional collections and appear on 12 United States postage stamps. ■

2154

2155   **2156**

2157   **2158**   **2158a**

2160   **2161**

2159

2162   **2163**   **2163a**

2164

2165

2166

2167

2168

2169

2170

2171

2172

2173

2175

2176

2177

2178

2179

2180

2181

2182

2183

2184

2185

2186

2187

2188

2189

2190

2191

	Issues of 1986		Un	U	PB	#	FDC	Q(M)
2167	22¢ Arkansas Statehood	01/03/86	.40	.20	2.00	(4)	1.00	130
a	Vertical pair, imperf. horizontally		—					
Issues of 1986-91, Great Americans Issue (See also #1844-69)								
2168	1¢ Margaret Mitchell	06/30/86	.20	.20	.25	(4)	1.50	
a	Tagging omitted		5.00					
2169	2¢ Mary Lyon	02/28/87	.20	.20	.30	(4)	1.00	
a	Untagged		.20	.20	.35	(4)		
2170	3¢ Paul Dudley White, MD	09/15/86	.20	.20	.50	(4)	1.00	
a	Untagged, dull gum		.20	.20	.50	(4)		
2171	4¢ Father Flanagan	07/14/86	.20	.20	.60	(4)	1.00	
a	Grayish violet, untagged		.20	.20	.40	(4)		
b	Deep grayish blue, untagged		.20	.20	.50	(4)		
2172	5¢ Hugo L. Black	02/27/86	.20	.20	.65	(4)	1.00	
a	Tagging omitted		10.00					
2173	5¢ Luis Munoz Marin	02/18/90	.20	.20	.75	(4)	1.25	
a	Untagged		.20	.20	.60	(4)		
2174	Not assigned							
2175	10¢ Red Cloud	08/15/87	.20	.20	.85	(4)	1.50	
a	Overall tagging	1990	.30	.20	10.00	(4)		
b	Tagging omitted		15.00					
c	Prephosphored coated paper (solid tagging)		.30	.20	1.40	(4)		
d	Prephosphored uncoated paper (mottled tagging)		.20	.20	1.25	(4)		
e	Carmine, prephosphored uncoated paper (mottled tagging)		.25	.20	1.25	(4)		
2176	14¢ Julia Ward Howe	02/12/87	.25	.20	1.50	(4)	1.00	
2177	15¢ Buffalo Bill Cody	06/06/88	.30	.20	6.00	(4)	2.00	
a	Overall tagging	1990	.30	—	3.25	(4)		
b	Prephosphored coated paper (solid tagging)		.40	—	3.25	(4)		
c	Tagging omitted		15.00	—				
2178	17¢ Belva Ann Lockwood	06/18/86	.35	.20	2.00	(4)	1.00	
a	Tagging omitted		10.00					
	Perf. 11 x 11.1							
2179	20¢ Virginia Apgar	10/24/94	.40	.20	2.00	(4)	1.25	
a	Orange brown		.40	.20	2.25	(4)		
	Perf. 11							
2180	21¢ Chester Carlson	10/21/88	.40	.20	2.50	(4)	1.25	
2181	23¢ Mary Cassatt	11/04/88	.45	.20	2.50	(4)	1.25	
a	Overall tagging, dull gum		.45	—	5.00	(4)		
b	Prephosphored coated paper (solid tagging)		.60	—	3.25	(4)		
c	Prephosphored uncoated paper (mottled tagging)		.50	.20	3.25	(4)		
d	Tagging omitted		7.50					
2182	25¢ Jack London	01/11/86	.45	.20	2.75	(4)	1.25	
a	Booklet pane of 10	05/03/88	4.50	3.75			6.00	
b	Tagging omitted	1990	—					
2183	28¢ Sitting Bull	09/28/89	.50	.20	2.50	(4)	1.50	
2184	29¢ Earl Warren	03/09/92	.55	.20	2.50	(4)	1.25	
	Perf. 11.5 x 11							
2185	29¢ Thomas Jefferson	04/13/93	.50	.20	2.50	(4)	1.25	
2186	35¢ Dennis Chavez	04/03/91	.65	.20	3.25	(4)	1.25	
2187	40¢ Claire Lee Chennault	09/06/90	.70	.20	3.75	(4)	2.00	
a	Prephosphored coated paper (solid tagging)		.75	.35	4.25	(4)		
b	Prephosphored uncoated paper (mottled tagging)		.75	.20	7.50	(4)		
2188	45¢ Harvey Cushing, MD	06/17/88	.85	.20	3.75	(4)	1.25	
a	Overall tagging	1990	1.65	.20	11.00	(4)		
b	Tagging omitted		15.00					
2189	52¢ Hubert H. Humphrey	06/03/91	1.10	.20	7.50	(4)	1.40	
a	Prephosphored uncoated paper (mottled tagging)		1.10	—	5.50	(4)		
2190	56¢ John Harvard	09/03/86	1.10	.20	6.00	(4)	2.50	
2191	65¢ H.H. 'Hap' Arnold	11/05/88	1.20	.20	5.00	(4)	2.00	

	Issues of 1986-1990		Un	U	PB	#	FDC	Q(M)
	Perf. 11							
2192	75¢ Wendell Willkie	02/16/92	1.30	.20	5.50	(4)	1.50	
a	Prephosphored uncoated paper (mottled tagging)		1.30	—	5.50	(4)		
2193	$1 Bernard Revel	09/23/86	2.50	.50	14.00	(4)	3.00	
2194	$1 Johns Hopkins	06/07/89	1.75	.50	7.00	(4)	3.00	
b	Overall tagging	1990	1.75	.50	7.00	(4)		
c	Tagging omitted		10.00					
d	Dark blue, prephosphored coated paper (solid tagging)		1.75	.50	7.00	(4)		
e	Blue, prephosphored uncoated paper (mottled tagging)		2.00	.60	8.00	(4)		
f	Blue, prephosphored coated paper (grainy solid tagging)		1.75	.50	7.00	(4)		
2195	$2 William Jennings Bryan	03/19/86	3.50	.50	15.00	(4)	5.00	
a	Tagging omitted		45.00					
2196	$5 Bret Harte	08/25/87	8.00	1.00	32.50	(4)	20.00	
a	Tagging omitted		—					
b	Prephosphored paper (solid tagging)		8.00	—	32.50	(4)		
	Booklet Stamp, Perf. 10							
2197	25¢ Jack London (2182), single from booklet.		.45	.20			1.25	
a	Booklet pane of 6	05/03/88	3.00	2.25			4.00	
b	Tagging omitted		4.50					
c	As "b," booklet pane of 6		65.00					
	United States — Sweden Stamp Collecting Booklet Issue, Perf. 10 Vertically							
2198	22¢ Handstamped Cover	01/23/86	.45	.20			1.00	17
2199	22¢ Boy Examining Stamp Collection	01/23/86	.45	.20			1.00	17
2200	22¢ #836 Under Magnifying Glass	01/23/86	.45	.20			1.00	17
2201	22¢ 1986 Presidents Miniature Sheet	01/23/86	.45	.20			1.00	17
a	Booklet pane of 4, #2198-2201		2.00	1.75			4.00	17
b	As "a," black omitted on #2198, 2201		65.00					
c	As "a," blue omitted on #2198-2200		2,500.00					
d	As "a," buff omitted		—					
	#2198-2201 issued only in booklets. All stamps are imperf. at top and bottom or imperf. at top, bottom and right side.							
	Perf. 11							
2202	22¢ Love	01/30/86	.40	.20	1.75	(4)	1.75	949
	Black Heritage Issue							
2203	22¢ Sojourner Truth and Truth Lecturing	02/04/86	.40	.20	1.75	(4)	1.00	130
2204	22¢ Republic of Texas, 150th Anniversary	03/02/86	.40	.20	1.75	(4)	1.25	137
a	Horizontal pair, imperf. vertically		1,100.00					
b	Dark red omitted		2,750.00					
c	Dark blue omitted		8,500.00					
	Fish Booklet Issue, Perf. 10 Horizontally							
2205	22¢ Muskellunge	03/21/86	.50	.20			1.00	44
2206	22¢ Atlantic Cod	03/21/86	.50	.20			1.00	44
2207	22¢ Largemouth Bass	03/21/86	.50	.20			1.00	44
2208	22¢ Bluefin Tuna	03/21/86	.50	.20			1.00	44
2209	22¢ Catfish	03/21/86	.50	.20			1.00	44
a	Booklet pane of 5, #2205-09		4.50	2.75			2.50	44
	#2205-09 issued only in booklets. All stamps are imperf. at sides or imperf. at sides and bottom.							

92

2193

2194

2195

2196

98

2199

2200

2201

2201a

2202

2203

2205

2206

2207

2204

2208

2209

2209a

1986

2210

2211

2216a

2216b

2216c

2216d

2216e

2216f

2216g

2216h

2216i

2217a

2217b

2217c

2217d

2217e

2217f

2217g

2217h

2217i

Issues of 1986			Un	U	PB	#	FDC	Q(M)
Perf. 11								
2210	22¢ Public Hospitals	04/11/86	.40	.20	1.75	(4)	1.00	130
a	Vertical pair, imperf. horizontally		325.00					
b	Horizontal pair, imperf. vertically		1,350.00					
Performing Arts Issue								
2211	22¢ Duke Ellington							
	and Piano Keys	04/29/86	.40	.20	1.90	(4)	1.75	130
a	Vertical pair, imperf. horizontally		1,000.00					
2212-15	Not assigned							
AMERIPEX '86 Issue, Presidents Miniature Sheets								
2216	Sheet of 9	05/22/86	3.75	—			4.00	6
a	22¢ George Washington		.40	.25			1.50	
b	22¢ John Adams		.40	.25			1.50	
c	22¢ Thomas Jefferson		.40	.25			1.50	
d	22¢ James Madison		.40	.25			1.50	
e	22¢ James Monroe		.40	.25			1.50	
f	22¢ John Quincy Adams		.40	.25			1.50	
g	22¢ Andrew Jackson		.40	.25			1.50	
h	22¢ Martin Van Buren		.40	.25			1.50	
i	22¢ William H. Harrison		.40	.25			1.50	
j	Blue omitted		3,500.00					
k	Black inscription omitted		2,000.00					
l	Imperf.		10,500.00					
2217	Sheet of 9	05/22/86	3.75	—			4.00	6
a	22¢ John Tyler		.40	.25			1.50	
b	22¢ James Polk		.40	.25			1.50	
c	22¢ Zachary Taylor		.40	.25			1.50	
d	22¢ Millard Fillmore		.40	.25			1.50	
e	22¢ Franklin Pierce		.40	.25			1.50	
f	22¢ James Buchanan		.40	.25			1.50	
g	22¢ Abraham Lincoln		.40	.25			1.50	
h	22¢ Andrew Johnson		.40	.25			1.50	
i	22¢ Ulysses S. Grant		.40	.25			1.50	

#2216

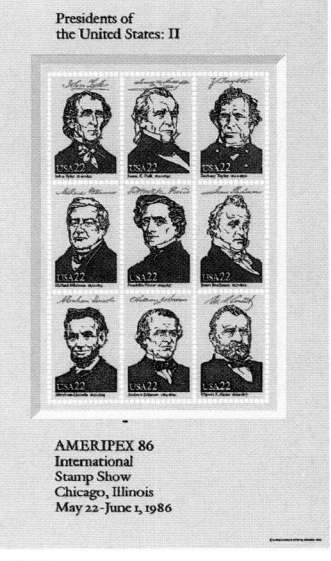

#2217

Issues of 1986			Un	U	FDC	Q(M)
AMERIPEX '86 Issue (continued), Presidents Miniature Sheets						
2218	Sheet of 9	05/22/86	3.75	—	4.00	6
a	22¢ Rutherford B. Hayes		.40	.25	1.50	
b	22¢ James A. Garfield		.40	.25	1.50	
c	22¢ Chester A. Arthur		.40	.25	1.50	
d	22¢ Grover Cleveland		.40	.25	1.50	
e	22¢ Benjamin Harrison		.40	.25	1.50	
f	22¢ William McKinley		.40	.25	1.50	
g	22¢ Theodore Roosevelt		.40	.25	1.50	
h	22¢ William H. Taft		.40	.25	1.50	
i	22¢ Woodrow Wilson		.40	.25	1.50	
j	Brown omitted		—			
k	Black inscription omitted		2,9000.00			
2219	Sheet of 9	05/22/86	3.75	—	4.00	6
a	22¢ Warren G. Harding		.40	.25	1.50	
b	22¢ Calvin Coolidge		.40	.25	1.50	
c	22¢ Herbert Hoover		.40	.25	1.50	
d	22¢ Franklin D. Roosevelt		.40	.25	1.50	
e	22¢ White House		.40	.25	1.50	
f	22¢ Harry S. Truman		.40	.25	1.50	
g	22¢ Dwight D. Eisenhower		.40	.25	1.50	
h	22¢ John F. Kennedy		.40	.25	2.50	
i	22¢ Lyndon B. Johnson		.40	.25	1.50	
j	Blackish blue inscription omitted		—			
k	Tagging omitted		15.00			

#2218

#2219

2218a

2218b

2218c

2218d

Benjamin Harrison 1889-1893
2218e

William McKinley 1897-1901
2218f

Theodore Roosevelt 1901-1909
2218g

William H. Taft 1909-1913
2218h

Woodrow Wilson 1913-1921
2218i

Warren G. Harding 1921-1923
2219a

Calvin Coolidge 1923-1929
2219b

Herbert C. Hoover 1929-1933
2219c

Franklin D. Roosevelt 1933-45
2219d

2219e

Harry S. Truman 1945-1953
2219f

Dwight D. Eisenhower 1953-1961
2219g

John F. Kennedy 1961-1963
2219h

Lyndon B. Johnson 1963-1969
2219i

2220 **2221**

USA22 Elisha Kent Kane

USA22 Adolphus W. Greely

USA22 Vilhjalmur Stefansson

USA22 Robert E. Peary, Matthew Henson

2222 **2223** **2223a**

Liberty 1886-1986
USA 22

2224

Omnibus 1880s
1 USA

2225

Locomotive 1870s
2 USA

2226

2235 **2236**

Navajo Art USA 22

Navajo Art USA 22

Navajo Art USA 22

Navajo Art USA 22

2237 **2238** **2238a**

T.S.Eliot
22 USA

2239

2240 **2241**

Wood Carving: Highlander Figure
Folk Art USA 22

Wood Carving: Ship Figurehead
Folk Art USA 22

Wood Carving: Nautical Figure
Folk Art USA 22

Wood Carving: Cigar-Store Figure
Folk Art USA 22

2242 **2243** **2243a**

CHRISTMAS 22 USA
Perugino, National Gallery

2244

USA 22
GREETINGS

2245

USA 22
1837-1987
Michigan Statehood

2246

22 USA
Pan American Games Indianapolis 1987

2247

LOVE
USA 22

2248

Jean Baptiste Pointe Du Sable 22
Black Heritage USA

	Issues of 1986		Un	U	PB/PNC	#	FDC	Q(M)
	Arctic Explorers Issue, Perf. 11							
2220	22¢ Elisha Kent Kane	05/28/86	.65	.20			1.00	33
2221	22¢ Adolphus W. Greely	05/28/86	.65	.20			1.00	33
2222	22¢ Vilhjalmur Stefansson	05/28/86	.65	.20			1.00	33
2223	22¢ Robt. Peary, Matt. Henson	05/28/86	.65	.20			1.00	33
a	Block of 4, #2220-23		2.75	2.25	4.50	(4)	2.50	
b	As "a," black omitted		9,500.00					
2224	22¢ Statue of Liberty	07/04/86	.40	.20	2.25	(4)	3.00	221
	Issues of 1986-87, Reengraved Transportation Issue, Coil Stamps, Perf. 10 Vertically							
	(See also #1897-1908, 2123-36, 2252-66, 2452-53A, 2457, 2464, 2468)							
2225	1¢ Omnibus	11/26/86	.20	.20	.90	(5)	1.00	
a	Prephosphored uncoated paper							
	(mottled tagging)		.20	.20	7.50	(5)		
b	Untagged, dull gum		.20	.20	.90	(5)		
c	Imperf., pair		2,250.00					
2226	2¢ Locomotive	03/06/87	.20	.20	1.00	(5)	1.50	
a	Untagged, dull gum		.20	.20	.75	(5)		
2227, 2229-30, 2232-34 Not assigned								
2228	4¢ Stagecoach (1898A)	08/86	.20	.20	1.50	(5)		
a	Overall tagging		.70	.20	15.00	(5)		
b	Imperf., pair		300.00					
2231	8.3¢ Ambulance (2128)							
	(Bureau precanceled)	08/29/86	.20	.20	4.50	(5)		
	On #2228, "Stagecoach 1890s" is 17mm long; on #1898A, it is 19.5mm long. On #2231, "Ambulance 1860s" is 18mm long; on #2128, it is 18.5mm long.							
	American Folk Art Issue, Perf. 11							
2235	22¢ Navajo Art, four "+" marks							
	horizontally through middle	09/04/86	.50	.20			1.00	60
2236	22¢ Navajo Art, vertical							
	diamond pattern	09/04/86	.50	.20			1.00	60
2237	22¢ Navajo Art, horizontal							
	diamond pattern	09/04/86	.50	.20			1.00	60
2238	22¢ Navajo Art, jagged line							
	horizontally through middle	09/04/86	.50	.20			1.00	60
a	Block of 4, #2235-38		2.50	2.00	4.00	(4)	2.50	
b	As "a," black omitted		350.00					
	Literary Arts Issue							
2239	22¢ T.S. Eliot	09/26/86	.40	.20	1.90	(4)	1.00	132
	American Folk Art Issue							
2240	22¢ Highlander Figure	10/01/86	.40	.20			1.00	60
2241	22¢ Ship Figurehead	10/01/86	.40	.20			1.00	60
2242	22¢ Nautical Figure	10/01/86	.40	.20			1.00	60
2243	22¢ Cigar Store Figure	10/01/86	.40	.20			1.00	60
a	Block of 4, #2240-43		1.75	1.75	3.00	(4)	2.50	
b	As "a," imperf. vertically		1,500.00					
	Christmas Issue							
2244	22¢ Madonna and Child	10/24/86	.40	.20	2.00	(4)	1.00	690
2245	22¢ Village Scene	10/24/86	.40	.20	1.90	(4)	1.00	882
	Issues of 1987							
2246	22¢ Michigan Statehood	01/26/87	.40	.20	1.90	(4)	1.00	167
	Pair with full vertical gutter between							
2247	22¢ Pan American Games	01/29/87	.40	.20	1.90	(4)	1.00	167
a	Silver omitted		1,500.00					
	Perf. 11.5 x 11							
2248	22¢ Love	01/30/87	.40	.20	1.90	(4)	1.75	842
	Black Heritage Issue, Perf. 11							
2249	22¢ Jean Baptiste Point Du Sable							
	and Chicago Settlement	02/20/87	.40	.20	1.90	(4)	1.00	143
a	Tagging omitted		10.00					

1987-1988

	Performing Arts Issue							
2250	22¢ Enrico Caruso as the Duke							
	of Mantua in Rigoletti	02/27/87	.40	.20	1.90	(4)	1.00	130
a	Black (engr.) omitted		5,000.00					
2251	22¢ Girl Scouts	03/12/87	.40	.20	1.90	(4)	2.50	150
a	All litho colors omitted		2,500.00					
	Coil Stamps, Transportation Issue, Perf. 10 Vertically (See also #1897-1908, 2123-36, 2225-31, 2451-68)							
2252	3¢ Conestoga Wagon 1800s	02/29/88	.20	.20	1.00	(5)	1.00	
a	Untagged, dull gum		.20	.20	1.25	(5)		
2253	5¢ Milk Wagon 1900s	09/25/87	.20	.20	1.10	(5)	1.00	
2254	5.3¢ Elevator 1900s,							
	Bureau precanceled	09/16/88	.20	.20	1.50	(5)	1.25	
2255	7.6¢ Carreta 1770s,							
	Bureau precanceled	08/30/88	.20	.20	2.40	(5)	1.25	
2256	8.4¢ Wheel Chair 1920s,							
	Bureau precanceled	08/12/88	.20	.20	2.10	(5)	1.25	
a	Imperf., pair		700.00					
2257	10¢ Canal Boat 1880s	04/11/87	.20	.20	1.75	(5)	1.00	
a	Overall tagging, dull gum		.20	.20	4.50	(5)		
b	Prephosphored uncoated paper		.20	.20	4.00	(5)		
d	Tagging omitted		25.00	—				
2258	13¢ Patrol Wagon 1880s,							
	Bureau precanceled	10/29/88	.25	.25	3.00	(5)	1.50	
2259	13.2¢ Coal Car 1870s,							
	Bureau precanceled	07/19/88	.25	.25	3.00	(5)	1.50	
a	Imperf., pair		100.00					
2260	15¢ Tugboat 1900s	07/12/88	.25	.20	2.75	(5)	1.25	
a	Overall tagging		.25	.20	3.75	(5)		
b	Tagging omitted		3.75					
c	Imperf., pair		800.00					
2261	16.7¢ Popcorn Wagon 1902,							
	Bureau precanceled	07/07/88	.30	.30	3.75	(5)	1.25	
a	Imperf., pair		225.00					
2262	17.5¢ Racing Car 1911	09/25/87	.30	.20	3.75	(5)	1.00	
a	Untagged (Bureau precanceled)		.35	.30	4.00	(5)		
b	Imperf., pair		2,250.00					
2263	20¢ Cable Car 1880s	10/28/88	.35	.20	3.75	(5)	1.25	
a	Imperf., pair		75.00					
b	Overall tagging		.35	.20	5.00	(5)		
2264	20.5¢ Fire Engine 1920s,							
	Bureau precanceled	09/28/88	.40	.40	4.00	(5)	2.00	
2265	21¢ Railroad Mail Car 1920s,							
	Bureau precanceled	08/16/88	.40	.40	4.00	(5)	1.50	
a	Imperf., pair		65.00					
2266	24.1¢ Tandem Bicycle 1890s,							
	Bureau precanceled	10/26/88	.45	.45	4.00	(5)	1.75	
	Issues of 1987 (continued), Special Occasions Booklet Issue, Perf. 10							
2267	22¢ Congratulations!	04/20/87	.60	.20			1.00	1,222
2268	22¢ Get Well!	04/20/87	.75	.20			1.00	611
2269	22¢ Thank you!	04/20/87	.75	.20			1.00	611
2270	22¢ Love You, Dad!	04/20/87	.75	.20			1.00	611
2271	22¢ Best Wishes!	04/20/87	.75	.20			1.00	611
2272	22¢ Happy Birthday!	04/20/87	.60	.20			1.00	1,222
2273	22¢ Love You, Mother!	04/20/87	.90	.20			1.00	611
2274	22¢ Keep In Touch!	04/20/87	.75	.20			1.00	611
a	Booklet pane of 10, #2268-71, 2273-74							
	and 2 each of #2267, 2272		8.00	5.00			5.00	611
	#2267-74 issued only in booklets. All stamps are imperf. at one or two sides or imperf. at sides and bottom.							

Enrico Caruso 22 USA

2250

GIRL SCOUTS USA 22

2251

Conestoga Wagon 1800s USA 3

2252

Milk Wagon 1900s 5 USA

2253

Elevator 1900s 5.3 USA Nonprofit Carrier Route Sort

2254

Carreta 1770s 7.6 USA Nonprofit

2255

Wheel Chair 1920s 8.4 USA Nonprofit

2256

Canal Boat 1880s 10 USA

2257

Patrol Wagon 1880s USA 13 Presorted First-Class

2258

Coal Car 1870s 13.2 Bulk Rate USA

2259

Tugboat 1900s USA 15

2260

Popcorn Wagon 16.7 USA 1902 Bulk Rate

2261

Racing Car 1911 USA 17.5

2262

USA 20 Cable Car 1880s

2263

Fire Engine 1900s 20.5 USA ZIP+4 Presort

2264

Railroad Mail Car 1920s Presorted First-Class 21 USA

2265

Tandem Bicycle 1890s 24.1 USA ZIP+4

2266

2268

Congratulations! 22 USA

2267

Get Well! USA 22 USA 22 Thank You!

2269

Love You, Dad! USA 22

2270

2271

Best Wishes! USA 22 Happy Birthday! USA 22

2272

2274

Love You, Mother! USA 22

2273

Keep In Touch! USA 22 Happy Birthday! USA 22

2272

2267

Congratulations! USA 22

2274a

2275

2276

2277

2278

2279

2280

2281

2283

2283c

2282a

2285b

2284   2285

	Issues of 1987		Un	U	PB/PNC	#	FDC	Q(M)
2275	22¢ United Way	04/28/87	.40	.20	1.90	(4)	1.00	157
2276	22¢ Flag with Fireworks	05/09/87	.40	.20	1.90	(4)	1.00	
a	Booklet pane of 20	11/30/87	8.50	—			8.00	
	Issues of 1988-89 (All issued in 1988 except #2280 on prephosphored paper)							
2277	(25¢) "E" Stamp	03/22/88	.45	.20	2.00	(4)	1.25	
2278	25¢ Flag with Clouds	05/06/88	.45	.20	1.90	(4)	1.25	
	Pair with full vertical gutter between		—					
	Coil Stamps, Perf. 10 Vertically							
2279	(25¢) "E" Earth	03/22/88	.45	.20	3.00	(5)	1.25	
a	Imperf., pair		90.00					
2280	25¢ Flag over Yosemite	05/20/88	.45	.20	4.00	(5)	1.25	
a	Prephosphored paper	02/14/89	.45	.20	4.00	(5)	1.25	
b	Imperf., pair, large block tagging		35.00					
c	Imperf., pair, prephosphored paper		15.00					
d	Tagging omitted		5.00	*				
e	Black trees		100.00	—				
f	Pair, imperf. between		800.00					
2281	25¢ Honeybee	09/02/88	.45	.20	3.25	(3)	1.25	
a	Imperf., pair		50.00					
b	Black (engr.) omitted		60.00					
c	Black (litho) omitted		450.00					
d	Pair, imperf. between		1,000.00					
e	Yellow (litho) omitted		1,250.00					
	Booklet Stamp, Perf. 10							
2282	(25¢) "E" Earth (#2277), single from booklet		.50	.20			1.25	
a	Booklet pane of 10	03/22/88	6.50	3.50			6.00	
	Pheasant Booklet Issue, Perf. 11							
2283	25¢ Pheasant, single from booklet		.50	.20			1.25	
a	Booklet pane of 10	04/29/88	6.00	3.50			6.00	
b	Single, red removed from sky		6.25	.20				
c	As "b," booklet pane of 10		67.50	—				
d	As "a," imperf. horizontally between		2,250.00					
	#2283 issued only in booklets. All stamps have one or two imperf. edges. Imperf. and part perf. pairs and panes exist from printer's waste.							
	Owl and Grosbeak Booklet Issue, Perf. 10							
2284	25¢ Grosbeak, single from booklet		.50	.20			1.25	
2285	25¢ Owl, single from booklet		.50	.20			1.25	
b	Booklet pane of 10,							
	5 each of #2284, 2285	05/28/88	5.00	3.50			6.00	
d	Pair, #2284, 2285		1.10	.25				
e	As "d," tagging omitted		12.50					
	#2284 and 2285 issued only in booklets. All stamps are imperf. at one side or imperf. at one side and bottom.							
2285A	25¢ Flag with Clouds							
	(#2278), single from booklet		.50	.20			1.25	
c	Booklet pane of 6	07/05/88	3.00	2.00			4.00	

Issues of 1987			Un	U	FDC	Q(M)
American Wildlife Issue, Perf. 11						
2286	22¢ Barn Swallow	06/13/87	.85	.20	1.50	13
2287	22¢ Monarch Butterfly	06/13/87	.85	.20	1.50	13
2288	22¢ Bighorn Sheep	06/13/87	.85	.20	1.50	13
2289	22¢ Broad-tailed Hummingbird	06/13/87	.85	.20	1.50	13
2290	22¢ Cottontail	06/13/87	.85	.20	1.50	13
2291	22¢ Osprey	06/13/87	.85	.20	1.50	13
2292	22¢ Mountain Lion	06/13/87	.85	.20	1.50	13
2293	22¢ Luna Moth	06/13/87	.85	.20	1.50	12
2294	22¢ Mule Deer	06/13/87	.85	.20	1.50	13
2295	22¢ Gray Squirrel	06/13/87	.85	.20	1.50	13
2296	22¢ Armadillo	06/13/87	.85	.20	1.50	13
2297	22¢ Eastern Chipmunk	06/13/87	.85	.20	1.50	13
2298	22¢ Moose	06/13/87	.85	.20	1.50	13
2299	22¢ Black Bear	06/13/87	.85	.20	1.50	13
2300	22¢ Tiger Swallowtail	06/13/87	.85	.20	1.50	13
2301	22¢ Bobwhite	06/13/87	.85	.20	1.50	13
2302	22¢ Ringtail	06/13/87	.85	.20	1.50	13
2303	22¢ Red-winged Blackbird	06/13/87	.85	.20	1.50	13
2304	22¢ American Lobster	06/13/87	.85	.20	1.50	13
2305	22¢ Black-tailed Jack Rabbit	06/13/87	.85	.20	1.50	13
2306	22¢ Scarlet Tanager	06/13/87	.85	.20	1.50	13
2307	22¢ Woodchuck	06/13/87	.85	.20	1.50	13
2308	22¢ Roseate Spoonbill	06/13/87	.85	.20	1.50	13
2309	22¢ Bald Eagle	06/13/87	.85	.20	1.50	13
2310	22¢ Alaskan Brown Bear	06/13/87	.85	.20	1.50	13

Chuck Ripper

One of America's premier wildlife artists, Chuck Ripper developed his interest in art and nature at an early age. A graduate of the Art Institute of Pittsburgh, he honed his technical skills as a staff artist at the Carnegie Museum. After serving in the Korean War, he worked as a commercial artist and illustrator of children's nature books before devoting himself fully to painting the natural world. Since then, his artwork has appeared in *National Geographic*, *Reader's Digest*, and on the covers of many outdoor magazines. The designer of 80 United States postage stamps, he has also created images for every National Wildlife Federation conservation stamp sheet issued since 1959. ■

"Stamps are something that everyone sees, though they don't think of them as paintings or know who created them."

— Chuck Ripper

22 USA — Barn Swallow — 2286
22 USA — Monarch — 2287
22 USA — Bighorn Sheep — 2288
22 USA — Broad-tailed Hummingbird — 2289
22 USA — Cottontail — 2290

22 USA — Osprey — 2291
22 USA — Mountain Lion — 2292
22 USA — Luna Moth — 2293
22 USA — Mule Deer — 2294
22 USA — Gray Squirrel — 2295

22 USA — Armadillo — 2296
22 USA — Eastern Chipmunk — 2297
22 USA — Moose — 2298
22 USA — Black Bear — 2299
22 USA — Tiger Swallowtail — 2300

22 USA — Bobwhite — 2301
22 USA — Ringtail — 2302
22 USA — Red-winged Blackbird — 2303
22 USA — American Lobster — 2304
22 USA — Black-tailed Jack Rabbit — 2305

22 USA — Scarlet Tanager — 2306
22 USA — Woodchuck — 2307
22 USA — Roseate Spoonbill — 2308
22 USA — Bald Eagle — 2309
22 USA — Alaskan Brown Bear — 2310

2311	2312	2313	2314	2315
2316	2317	2318	2319	2320
2321	2322	2323	2324	2325
2326	2327	2328	2329	2330
2331	2332	2333	2334	2335

	Issues of 1987		Un	U	FDC	Q(M)
	American Wildlife Issue (continued), Perf. 11					
2311	22¢ Iiwi	06/13/87	.85	.20	1.50	13
2312	22¢ Badger	06/13/87	.85	.20	1.50	13
2313	22¢ Pronghorn	06/13/87	.85	.20	1.50	13
2314	22¢ River Otter	06/13/87	.85	.20	1.50	13
2315	22¢ Ladybug	06/13/87	.85	.20	1.50	13
2316	22¢ Beaver	06/13/87	.85	.20	1.50	13
2317	22¢ White-tailed Deer	06/13/87	.85	.20	1.50	13
2318	22¢ Blue Jay	06/13/87	.85	.20	1.50	13
2319	22¢ Pika	06/13/87	.85	.20	1.50	13
2320	22¢ Bison	06/13/87	.85	.20	1.50	13
2321	22¢ Snowy Egret	06/13/87	.85	.20	1.50	13
2322	22¢ Gray Wolf	06/13/87	.85	.20	1.50	13
2323	22¢ Mountain Goat	06/13/87	.85	.20	1.50	13
2324	22¢ Deer Mouse	06/13/87	.85	.20	1.50	13
2325	22¢ Black-tailed Prairie Dog	06/13/87	.85	.20	1.50	13
2326	22¢ Box Turtle	06/13/87	.85	.20	1.50	13
2327	22¢ Wolverine	06/13/87	.85	.20	1.50	13
2328	22¢ American Elk	06/13/87	.85	.20	1.50	13
2329	22¢ California Sea Lion	06/13/87	.85	.20	1.50	13
2330	22¢ Mockingbird	06/13/87	.85	.20	1.50	13
2331	22¢ Raccoon	06/13/87	.85	.20	1.50	13
2332	22¢ Bobcat	06/13/87	.85	.20	1.50	13
2333	22¢ Black-footed Ferret	06/13/87	.85	.20	1.50	13
2334	22¢ Canada Goose	06/13/87	.85	.20	1.50	13
2335	22¢ Red Fox	06/13/87	.85	.20	1.50	13
a	Pane of 50, #2286-2335		47.50		50.00	

Example of 2335a

Issues of 1987-90		Un	U	PB	#	FDC	Q(M)
Ratification of the Constitution Issue, Perf. 11							
2336 22¢ Delaware	07/04/87	.60	.20	2.75	(4)	1.00	168
2337 22¢ Pennsylvania	08/26/87	.60	.20	2.75	(4)	1.00	187
2338 22¢ New Jersey	09/11/87	.60	.20	2.75	(4)	1.00	184
a Black omitted		6,000.00					
2339 22¢ Georgia	01/06/88	.60	.20	2.75	(4)	1.00	169
2340 22¢ Connecticut	01/09/88	.60	.20	2.75	(4)	1.25	155
2341 22¢ Massachusetts	02/06/88	.60	.20	2.75	(4)	1.00	102
2342 22¢ Maryland	02/15/88	.60	.20	2.75	(4)	1.00	103
2343 25¢ South Carolina	05/23/88	.60	.20	2.75	(4)	1.25	162
2344 25¢ New Hampshire	06/21/88	.60	.20	2.75	(4)	1.25	153
2345 25¢ Virginia	06/25/88	.60	.20	2.75	(4)	1.25	160
2346 25¢ New York	07/26/88	.60	.20	2.75	(4)	1.25	183
2347 25¢ North Carolina	08/22/89	.60	.20	2.75	(4)	1.25	
2348 25¢ Rhode Island	05/29/90	.60	.20	2.75	(4)	1.25	164
2349 22¢ Friendship with Morocco	07/18/87	.40	.20	1.75	(4)	1.00	157
a Black omitted		275.00					
Literary Arts Issue							
2350 22¢ William Faulkner	08/03/87	.40	.20	1.75	(4)	1.00	156
American Folk Art Issue							
2351 22¢ Squash Blossoms	08/14/87	.45	.20			1.00	41
2352 22¢ Floral Piece	08/14/87	.45	.20			1.00	41
2353 22¢ Floral Piece	08/14/87	.45	.20			1.00	41
2354 22¢ Dogwood Blossoms	08/14/87	.45	.20			1.00	41
a Block of 4, #2351-54		1.90	1.90	3.25	(4)	2.75	
b As "a," white omitted		950.00					

Libby Dorsett Thiel

Award-winning artist Libby Dorsett Thiel is the owner of Blueline Design, a silkscreen design studio in Maryland. A National Endowment for the Arts Design Arts Fellow, she has created brochures, posters, catalogues, and advertisements for such prestigious clients as US Sprint, the World Wildlife Fund, the World Bank, and the Kennedy Center. She has also designed and produced museum exhibitions for the Corcoran Gallery of Art, the Jewish Museum, and the Alexandria Black History Resource Center, among others. Her artwork has appeared on two United States postage stamps. ∎

"To put it mildly, it caused quite a stir in my household when I received the phone call asking me to propose some stamp designs."

— Libby Dorsett Thiel

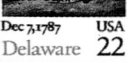
Dec 7,1787 USA
Delaware 22

2336

Dec 12,1787
Pennsylvania

2337

Dec 18,1787 USA
New Jersey 22

2338

22 USA
January 2, 1788
Georgia

2339

22 USA
January 9, 1788
Connecticut

2340

Feb 6, 1788
Massachusetts

2341

April 28, 1788 USA
Maryland 22

2342

25 USA
May 13, 1788
South Carolina

2343

25 USA
June 21, 1788
New Hampshire

2344

June 25, 1788 USA
Virginia 25

2345

July 26, 1788 USA
New York 25

2346

25 USA
November 21, 1789
North Carolina

2347

25 USA
May 29, 1790
Rhode Island

2348

2351   **2352**

Friendship
with Morocco
1787-1987
USA 22

2349

William Faulkner
USA 22

2350

Lacemaking USA 22   Lacemaking USA 22

Lacemaking USA 22   Lacemaking USA 22

2353   **2354**   **2354a**

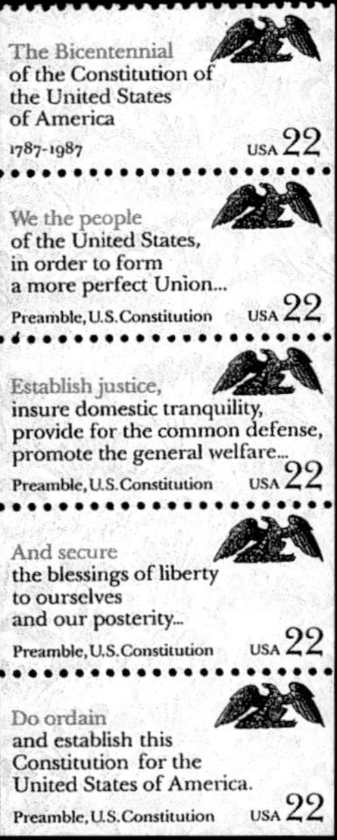
The Bicentennial of the Constitution of the United States of America
1787-1987
USA 22
We the people of the United States, in order to form a more perfect Union...
Preamble, U.S. Constitution
USA 22
Establish justice, insure domestic tranquility, provide for the common defense, promote the general welfare...
Preamble, U.S. Constitution
USA 22
And secure the blessings of liberty to ourselves and our posterity...
Preamble, U.S. Constitution
USA 22
Do ordain and establish this Constitution for the United States of America.
Preamble, U.S. Constitution
USA 22

2355

2356

2357

2358

2359

2359a

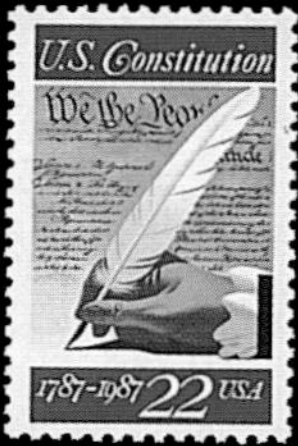
U.S. Constitution
1787-1987
22
USA

2360

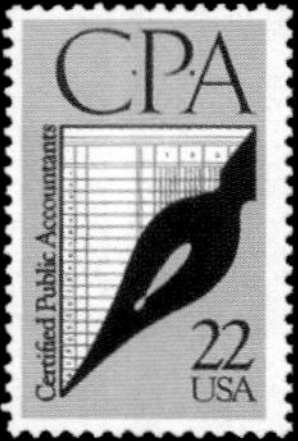
C·P·A
Certified Public Accountants
22
USA

2361

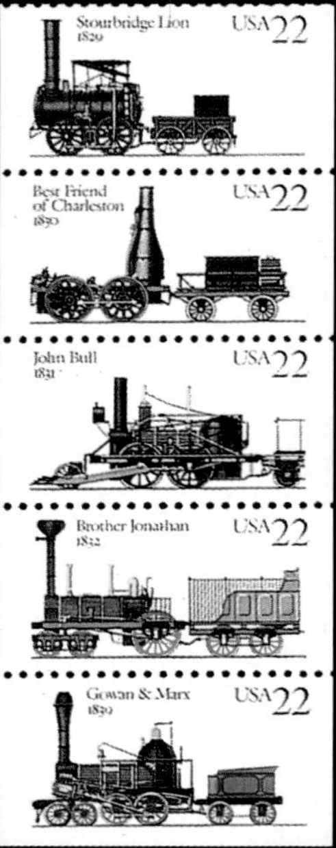
Stourbridge Lion
1829
USA 22
Best Friend of Charleston
1830
USA 22
John Bull
1831
USA 22
Brother Jonathan
1832
USA 22
Gowan & Marx
1839
USA 22

2362

2363

2364

2365

2366

2366a

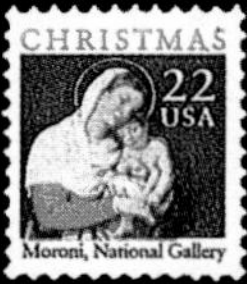
CHRISTMAS
22
USA
Moroni, National Gallery

2367

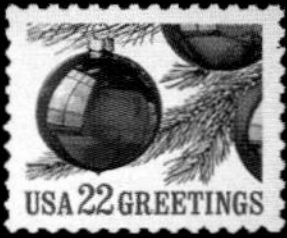
USA 22 GREETINGS

2368

Issues of 1987		Un	U	PB	#	FDC	Q(M)
Drafting of the Constitution Booklet Issue, Perf. 10 Horizontally							
2355	22¢ "The Bicentennial..." 08/28/87	.55	.20			1.00	122
2356	22¢ "We the people..." 08/28/87	.55	.20			1.00	122
2357	22¢ "Establish justice..." 08/28/87	.55	.20			1.00	122
2358	22¢ "And secure..." 08/28/87	.55	.20			1.00	122
2359	22¢ "Do ordain..." 08/28/87	.55	.20			1.00	122
a	Booklet pane of 5, #2355-59	2.75	2.25			3.00	122
#2355-59 issued only in booklets. All stamps are imperf. at sides or imperf. at sides and bottom.							
Signing of the Constitution Issue, Perf. 11							
2360	22¢ Constitution and Signer's Hand-Holding Quill Pen 09/17/87	.45	.20	2.25	(4)	1.00	169
2361	22¢ Certified Public Accountants 09/21/87	1.90	.20	8.50	(4)	3.50	163
a	Black omitted	900.00					
Locomotives Booklet Issue, Perf. 10 Horizontally							
2362	22¢ Stourbridge Lion, 1829 10/01/87	.55	.20			1.50	143
2363	22¢ Best Friend of Charleston, 1830 10/01/87	.55	.20			1.50	143
2364	22¢ John Bull, 1831 10/01/87	.55	.20			1.50	143
2365	22¢ Brother Jonathan, 1832 10/01/87	.55	.20			1.50	143
a	Red omitted	—					
2366	22¢ Gowan & Marx, 1839 10/01/87	.55	.20			1.50	143
a	Booklet pane of 5, #2362-66	2.75	2.50			4.50	143
#2362-66 issued only in booklets. All stamps are imperf. at sides or imperf. at sides and bottom.							
Christmas Issue, Perf. 11							
2367	22¢ Madonna and Child, by Moroni 10/23/87	.40	.20	2.00	(4)	1.00	529
2368	22¢ Christmas Ornaments 10/23/87	.40	.20	1.75	(4)	1.00	978
	Pair with full vertical gutter between	—					

Lou Nolan

A native of Washington, D.C., Lou Nolan studied fine art at the Corcoran School of Art and graduated from Parsons School of Design in 1952. After working as a book designer and illustrator in New York, he returned to his hometown and began a freelance career. Following a ten-year partnership at a graphic design firm, he returned to freelancing. Before retiring in 1995, he had created designs for NASA, the Smithsonian Institution, each branch of the U.S. Armed Forces, and many other federal agencies. His work has been honored by the Art Directors Club of New York and *Print* magazine. He won gold and silver medals from the Art Directors Club of Metropolitan Washington. The designer of more than a dozen United States postage stamps and many stamp products, this retiree enjoys reading, traveling, and competitively shooting antique Civil War muskets. ∎

1988

	Issues of 1988		Un	U	PB	#	FDC	Q(M)
	Winter Olympic Games Issue, Perf. 11							
2369	22¢ Skier and Olympic Rings	01/10/88	.40	.20	1.75	(4)	1.00	159
2370	22¢ Australia Bicentennial	01/10/88	.40	.20	1.75	(4)	1.00	146
	Black Heritage Issue							
2371	22¢ James Weldon Johnson and Music from "Lift Ev'ry Voice and Sing"	02/02/88	.40	.20	1.75	(4)	1.00	97
	American Cats Issue							
2372	22¢ Siamese and Exotic Shorthair	02/05/88	.45	.20			2.00	40
2373	22¢ Abyssinian and Himalayan	02/05/88	.45	.20			2.00	40
2374	22¢ Maine Coon and Burmese	02/05/88	.45	.20			2.00	40
2375	22¢ American Shorthair and Persian	02/05/88	.45	.20			2.00	40
a	Block of 4, #2372-75		1.90	1.90	3.75	(4)	4.50	
	American Sports Issue							
2376	22¢ Knute Rockne Holding Football on Field	03/09/88	.40	.20	2.25	(4)	4.00	97
2377	25¢ Francis Ouimet and Ouimet Hitting Fairway Shot	06/13/88	.45	.20	2.50	(4)	4.00	153
2378	25¢ Love	07/04/88	.45	.20	1.90	(4)	1.75	841
a	Imperf., pair		3,000.00					
2379	45¢ Love	08/08/88	.65	.20	3.25	(4)	1.75	180
	Summer Olympic Games Issue							
2380	25¢ Gymnast on Rings	08/19/88	.45	.20	1.90	(4)	1.25	157

Greg Rudd

As a child, Greg Rudd was captivated by the gallery of images that arrived at his family home each day on the corners of letters and packages. The art that appeared on postage inspired his interest in painting and fueled his dream to one day illustrate a stamp. A gifted portraitist and illustrator, he conveys the essence of his subjects by depicting them as simply and gracefully as possible with passion, color, and composition. He is known for capturing the history-makers of golf on canvas like no other, and first began painting the legends of the sport when commissioned to create a likeness of Francis Ouimet by the United States Postal Service. He considers his work on eight United States postage stamps to be a dream come true. ■

"I discerned what was essential to the subject and explained it as simply and gracefully as possible, using passion."

— Greg Rudd

2369

2370

2371

2372 **2373**

2374 **2375** **2375a**

2376

2377

2378

2379

2380

2381

1928 Locomobile

2382

1929 Pierce-Arrow

2383

1931 Cord

2384

1932 Packard

2385

1935 Duesenberg

2385a

2390   2391

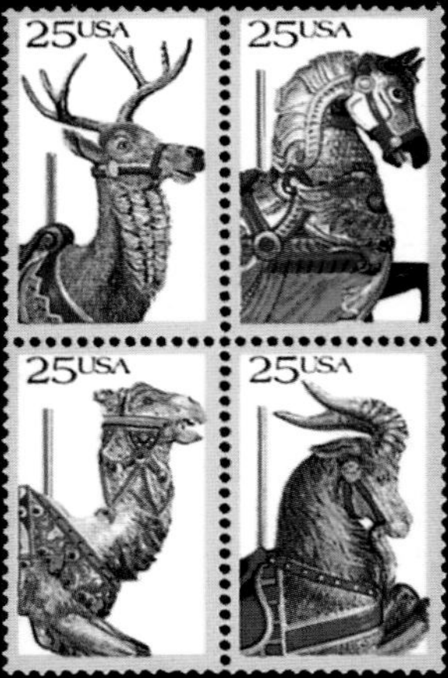

2392   2393   2393a

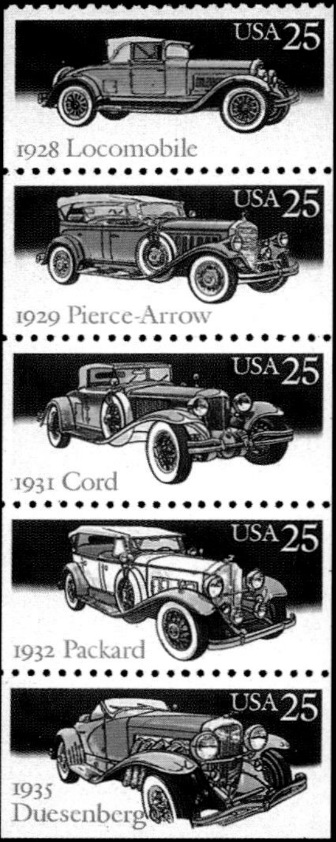

2386   2387

Nathaniel Palmer   Lt. Charles Wilkes

Richard E. Byrd   Lincoln Ellsworth

2388   2389   2389a

Issues of 1988		Un	U	PB	#	FDC	Q(M)
Classic Cars Booklet Issue, Perf. 10 Horizontally							
2381 25¢ 1928 Locomobile	08/25/88	.50	.20			1.25	127
2382 25¢ 1929 Pierce-Arrow	08/25/88	.50	.20			1.25	127
2383 25¢ 1931 Cord	08/25/88	.50	.20			1.25	127
2384 25¢ 1932 Packard	08/25/88	.50	.20			1.25	127
2385 25¢ 1935 Duesenberg	08/25/88	.50	.20			1.25	127
a Booklet pane of 5, #2381-85		5.00	*2.25*			3.00	127
#2381-85 issued only in booklets. All stamps are imperf. at sides or imperf. at sides and bottom.							
Antarctic Explorers Issue, Perf. 11							
2386 25¢ Nathaniel Palmer	09/14/88	.65	.20			1.25	41
2387 25¢ Lt. Charles Wilkes	09/14/88	.65	.20			1.25	41
2388 25¢ Richard E. Byrd	09/14/88	.65	.20			1.25	41
2389 25¢ Lincoln Ellsworth	09/14/88	.65	.20			1.25	41
a Block of 4, #2386-89		2.75	2.00	4.50	(4)	3.00	
b As "a," black omitted		*1,500.00*					
c As "a," imperf. horizontally		*3,000.00*					
American Folk Art Issue, Carousel Animals							
2390 25¢ Deer	10/01/88	.65	.20			2.50	76
2391 25¢ Horse	10/01/88	.65	.20			2.50	76
2392 25¢ Camel	10/01/88	.65	.20			2.50	76
2393 25¢ Goat	10/01/88	.65	.20			2.50	76
a Block of 4, #2390-93		3.00	2.00	4.00	(4)	5.00	

Gyo Fujikawa (1908-1998)
Born in Berkeley, California, to
Japanese parents, Gyo Fujikawa grew
up near Los Angeles and was educated
at the Chouinard Art Institute there.
Early in her career, she designed 25-
cent books for the Disney Studios.
In 1953, she illustrated a new edition of
Robert Louis Stevenson's *A Child's
Garden of Verses,* a project that led her
to write and illustrate more than 40
children's books. Her first two books,
Babies and *Baby Animals,* sold a
combined 1.3 million copies. She was
one of the first illustrators to feature
children of many races in her drawings.
When asked how she, an unmarried
woman with no children, wrote and
illustrated children's books so success-
fully, she remarked that she was herself
still like a child: "Part of me, I guess,
never grew up." She designed six U.S.
postage stamps. ■

	Issues of 1988		Un	U	PB	#	FDC	Q(M)
2394	$8.75 Express Mail	10/04/88	13.50	8.00	54.00	(4)	25.00	
	Special Occasions Booklet Issue							
2395	25¢ Happy Birthday	10/22/88	.50	.20			1.25	120
2396	25¢ Best Wishes	10/22/88	.50	.20			1.25	120
a	Booklet pane of 6, 3 #2395 and 3 #2396 with gutter between		3.50	3.25			4.00	
2397	25¢ Thinking of You	10/22/88	.50	.20			2.00	120
2398	25¢ Love You	10/22/88	.50	.20			2.00	120
a	Booklet pane of 6, 3 #2397 and 3 #2398 with gutter between		3.50	3.25			5.00	
b	As "a," imperf. horizontally		—					
	#2395-98a issued only in booklets. All stamps are imperf. on one side or on one side and top or bottom.							
	Christmas Issue							
2399	25¢ Madonna and Child, by Botticelli	10/20/88	.45	.20	1.90	(4)	1.25	844
a	Gold omitted		30.00					
2400	25¢ One-Horse Open Sleigh and Village Scene	10/20/88	.45	.20	1.90	(4)	1.25	1,038
	Pair with full vertical gutter between		—					

Ned Seidler

Born in New York and educated at the Art Students League and Pratt Institute, Ned Seidler was a freelance illustrator of books, magazines, and advertising for 21 years before becoming a staff artist for *National Geographic* in 1967. Since his retirement from the magazine in 1985, he has returned to freelance work and has created 26 United States postage stamp designs. A gifted painter of nature and historical subjects, his images have also been exhibited at such prominent venues as the National Gallery of Art in Washington, D.C., the Brandywine River Museum in Chadds Ford, Pennsylvania, and Grand Central Galleries in New York City. ■

2394

2395   2396   2396a

2397   2398   2398a

2399

2400

2401

2402

2404

2405

2406

2407

2408

2409

2409a

2410

2411

2403

2412

2413

2414

2415

2416

	Issues of 1989		Un	U	PB	#	FD	Q(M)
2401	25¢ Montana Statehood	01/15/89	.45	.20	2.00	(4)	1.25	165
	Black Heritage Issue							
2402	25¢ A. Philip Randolph, Pullman							
	Porters and Railroad Cars	02/03/89	.45	.20	2.00	(4)	1.25	152
2403	25¢ North Dakota Statehood	02/21/89	.45	.20	1.90	(4)	1.25	163
2404	25¢ Washington Statehood	02/22/89	.45	.20	2.00	(4)	1.25	265
	Steamboats Booklet Issue, Perf. 10 Horizontally							
2405	25¢ Experiment 1788-90	03/03/89	.45	.20			1.25	159
2406	25¢ Phoenix 1809	03/03/89	.45	.20			1.25	159
2407	25¢ New Orleans 1812	03/03/89	.45	.20			1.25	159
2408	25¢ Washington 1816	03/03/89	.45	.20			1.25	159
2409	25¢ Walk in the Water 1818	03/03/89	.45	.20			1.25	159
a	Booklet pane of 5, #2405-09		2.25	1.75			4.00	159
	#2405-09 issued only in booklets. All stamps are imperf. at sides or imperf. at sides and bottom.							
	Perf. 11							
2410	25¢ World Stamp Expo '89	03/16/89	.45	.20	1.90	(4)	1.25	164
	Performing Arts Issue							
2411	25¢ Arturo Toscanini							
	Conducting with Baton	03/25/89	.45	.20	2.00	(4)	1.25	152
	Issues of 1989-90, Constitution Bicentennial Issue							
2412	25¢ U.S. House of							
	Representatives	04/04/89	.50	.20	2.25	(4)	1.25	139
2413	25¢ U.S. Senate	04/06/89	.50	.20	2.25	(4)	1.25	138
2414	25¢ Executive Branch, George							
	Washington	04/16/89	.50	.20	2.25	(4)	1.25	139
2415	25¢ Supreme Court, Chief Justice							
	John Marshall	02/02/90	.50	.20	2.25	(4)	1.25	151
	Issues of 1989 (continued)							
2416	25¢ South Dakota							
	Statehood	05/03/89	.45	.20	1.90	(4)	1.25	165
	American Sports Issue							
2417	25¢ Lou Gehrig,							
	Gehrig Swinging Bat	06/10/89	.50	.20	3.00	(4)	4.00	263
	Literary Arts Issue							
2418	25¢ Ernest Hemingway, African							
	Landscape in Background	07/17/89	.45	.20	2.00	(4)	1.25	192

Barbara Higgins-Bond

A versatile artist whose work has attracted national attention, Barbara Higgins-Bond has been an illustrator and commercial artist for over 20 years. Her images have appeared in children's books and on magazine and book covers, posters, album covers, and collectors' plates created for such prominent clients as Anheuser-Busch, McGraw-Hill, *Essence* magazine, and The Franklin Mint. The first African-American female to illustrate a United States postage stamp, she has created outstanding designs for three Black Heritage issues. The Metropolitan Museum of Art and the DuSable Museum of African-American History have exhibited her work. ■

1989

	Issues of 1989		Un	U	PB	#	FDC	Q(M)
	Priority Mail Issue, Perf. 11 x 11.5							
2419	$2.40 Moon Landing	07/20/89	4.00	2.00	17.50	(4)	9.00	
a	Black (engr.) omitted		2,500.00					
b	Imperf., pair		750.00					
c	Black (litho.) omitted		4,500.00					
	Perf. 11							
2420	25¢ Letter Carriers	08/30/89	.45	.20	1.90	(4)	1.25	188
	Constitution Bicentennial Issue							
2421	25¢ Stylized U.S. Flag, Eagle							
	With Quill Pen in Mouth	09/25/89	.45	.20	3.00	(4)	1.25	192
a	Black omitted		325.00					
	Prehistoric Animals Issue							
2422	25¢ Tyrannosaurus	10/01/89	.65	.20			1.50	102
2423	25¢ Pteranodon	10/01/89	.65	.20			1.50	102
2424	25¢ Stegosaurus	10/01/89	.65	.20			1.50	102
2425	25¢ Brontosaurus	10/01/89	.65	.20			1.50	102
a	Block of 4, #2422-25		3.00	2.00	3.50	(4)	3.00	
b	As "a," black omitted		800.00					
	America/PUAS Issue (See also #C121)							
2426	25¢ Southwest Carved Figure							
	(A.D. 1150-1350), Emblem of the							
	Postal Union of the Americas	10/12/89	.45	.20	2.00	(4)	1.25	137
	Christmas Issue, Perf. 11.5							
2427	25¢ Madonna and							
	Child, by Caracci	10/19/89	.45	.20	2.00	(4)	1.25	913
a	Booklet pane of 10		4.75	3.50			6.00	
b	Red (litho.) omitted		850.00					
	Perf. 11							
2428	25¢ Sleigh Full of Presents	10/19/89	.45	.20	1.90	(4)	1.25	900
a	Vertical pair, imperf.							
	horizontally		2,000.00					
	Booklet Stamp Issue, Perf. 11.5 on 2 or 3 sides							
2429	25¢ Single from booklet							
	pane (#2428)	10/19/89	.45	.20			1.25	399
a	Booklet pane of 10		4.75	3.50			6.00	40
b	As "a," imperf. horiz. between		—					
c	Vertical pair, imperf. horizontally		—					
d	As "a," red omitted		—					
e	Imperf., pair		—					
	In #2429, runners on sleigh are twice as thick as in 2428; bow on package at rear of sleigh							
	is same color as package; board running underneath sleigh is pink.							
2430	Not assigned							
	Self-Adhesive, Die-Cut							
2431	25¢ Eagle and Shield	11/10/89	.50	.20			1.25	75
a	Booklet pane of 18		11.00					
b	Vertical pair, no							
	die-cutting between		850.00					
2432	Not assigned							

2419

2420

2421

2422 **2423**

2424 **2425**

2425a

2426

2427

2428

2431

2431 coil

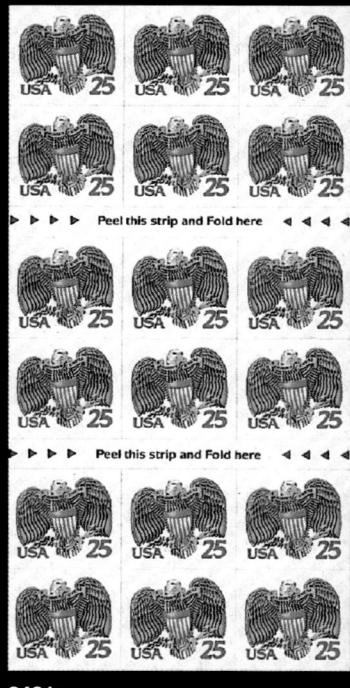

2431a

WORLD STAMP EXPO'89 ℠

The classic 1869 U.S. Abraham Lincoln stamp is reborn in these four larger versions commemorating World Stamp Expo'89, held in Washington, D.C. during the 20th Universal Postal Congress of the UPU. These stamps show the issued colors and three of the trial proof color combinations.

℠

2433

2434

2435

2436

2437

2437a

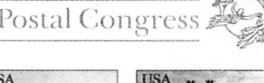

20ᵗʰ Universal Postal Congress

A review of historical methods of delivering the mail in the United States is the theme of these four stamps issued in commemoration of the convening of the 20th Universal Postal Congress in Washington, D.C. from November 13 through December 15, 1989. The United States, as host nation to the Congress for the first time in ninety-two years, welcomed more than 1,000 delegates from most of the member nations of the Universal Postal Union to the major international event.

2438

2439

2440

2442

2443

	Issues of 1989		Un	U	PB	#	FDC	Q(M)
	World Stamp Expo '89 Issue Souvenir Sheet, Imperf.							
2433	Reproduction of #122, 90¢ Lincoln,							
	and three essays of #122	11/17/89	14.00	9.00			7.00	2
a-d	Single stamp from sheet		2.00	1.75				
	20th UPU Congress Issues, Classic Mail Transportation, Perf. 11							
	(See also #C122-25)							
2434	25¢ Stagecoach	11/19/89	.45	.20			1.25	41
2435	25¢ Paddlewheel Steamer	11/19/89	.45	.20			1.25	41
2436	25¢ Biplane	11/19/89	.45	.20			1.25	41
2437	25¢ Depot-Hack Type							
	Automobile	11/19/89	.45	.20			1.25	41
a	Block of 4, #2434-37		2.00	1.00	3.75	(4)	3.00	
b	As "a," dark blue omitted		750.00					
	Souvenir Sheet, Imperf. (See also #C126)							
2438	Designs of #2434-37	11/28/89	4.00	1.75			2.00	2
a-d	Single stamp from sheet		.65	.25				
	Issues of 1990, Perf. 11							
2439	25¢ Idaho Statehood	01/06/90	.45	.20	2.00	(4)	1.25	173
	Perf. 12.5 x 13							
2440	25¢ Love	01/18/90	.45	.20	2.00	(4)	1.25	886
a	Imperf., pair		800.00					
	Booklet Stamp, Perf. 11.5							
2441	25¢ Love, single from booklet	01/18/90	.45	.20			1.25	995
a	Booklet pane of 10	01/18/90	4.75	3.50			6.00	
b	As "a," bright pink omitted		2,100.00					
c	As "b," single stamp		200.00					
	Black Heritage Issue, Perf. 11							
2442	25¢ Ida B. Wells,							
	Marchers in Background	02/01/90	.45	.20	2.00	(4)	1.25	153
	Beach Umbrella Booklet Issue, Perf. 11.5 x 11							
2443	15¢ Beach Umbrella,							
	single from booklet	02/03/90	.30	.20			1.25	
a	Booklet pane of 10	02/03/90	3.00	2.00			4.25	
b	As "a," blue omitted		1,900.00					
c	As #2443, blue omitted		170.00					

#2443 issued only in booklets. All stamps are imperf. at one side or imperf. at one side and bottom.

Thomas Blackshear II

Award-winning artist Thomas Blackshear began his career as an artist for the Hallmark Card Company. His beautifully crafted images have appeared in books, magazines, calendars, posters, and advertisements, commissioned by such clients as Coca-Cola, Coors, Jim Henson Studios, George Lucas, Universal Studios, and Milton Bradley. In addition to his many stamp designs for the United States Postal Service, he painted 28 portraits of celebrated African Americans that appear in *I Have a Dream*, a Black Heritage series commemorative book. ■

	Issues of 1990		Un	U	PB	#	FDC	Q(M)
	Perf 11							
2444	25¢ Wyoming Statehood	02/23/90	.45	.20	2.00	(4)	1.25	169
a	Black (engr.) omitted		2,500.00	—				
	Classic Films Issue							
2445	25¢ The Wizard of Oz	03/23/90	1.00	.20			2.50	44
2446	25¢ Gone With the Wind	03/23/90	1.00	.20			2.50	44
2447	25¢ Beau Geste	03/23/90	1.00	.20			2.50	44
2448	25¢ Stagecoach	03/23/90	1.00	.20			2.50	44
a	Block of 4, #2445-48		4.50	3.50	6.00	(4)	5.00	
	Literary Arts Issue							
2449	25¢ Marianne Moore	04/18/90	.45	.20	2.00	(4)	1.25	150
2450	Not assigned							
	Issues of 1990-95, Transportation Issue, Coil Stamps, Perf. 9.8 Vertically							
2451	4¢ Steam Carriage 1866	01/25/91	.20	.20	1.25	(5)	1.25	
a	Imperf., pair		700.00					
b	Untagged		.20	.20	1.40	(5)		
2452	5¢ Circus Wagon 1900s,							
	intaglio printing	08/31/91	.20	.20	1.40	(5)	1.50	
a	Untagged, dull gum		.20	.20	1.75	(5)		
c	Imperf., pair		900.00					
2452B	5¢ Circus Wagon							
	(2452), gravure printing	12/08/92	.20	.20	1.60	(5)	1.50	
f	Printed with luminescent ink		.20	.20	2.00	(5)		
2452D	5¢ Circus Wagon							
	(2452), gravure printing	03/20/95	.20	.20	1.60	(5)	1.50	
e	Imperf., pair		—					
g	Printed with luminescent ink		.20	.20	1.60	(5)		
2453	5¢ Canoe 1800s, precanceled,							
	intaglio printing	05/25/91	.20	.20	1.75	(5)	1.25	
a	Imperf., pair		350.00					
2454	5¢ Canoe 1800s,							
	precanceled, gravure printing	10/22/91	.20	.20	1.60	(5)	1.25	
2455-56	Not assigned							
2457	10¢ Tractor Trailer, Bureau							
	precanceled, intaglio printing	05/25/91	.20	.20	2.10	(5)	1.25	
a	Imperf., pair		350.00					
2458	10¢ Tractor Trailer, Bureau							
	precanceled, gravure printing	05/25/94	.20	.20	2.25	(5)	1.25	
2459-62	Not assigned							
2463	20¢ Cog Railway Car 1870s	06/09/95	.40	.20	4.00	(5)	1.25	
a	Imperf., pair		150.00					
2464	23¢ Lunch Wagon 1890s	04/12/91	.45	.20	4.00	(5)	1.25	
a	Prephosphored uncoated paper		.45	.20	5.00	(5)		
b	Imperf., pair		175.00					
2465	Not assigned							
2466	32¢ Ferryboat 1900s		.60	.20	6.50	(5)	1.25	
a	Imperf., pair		—					
b	Bright blue, prephosphored							
	uncoated paper		6.00	4.50	95.00	(5)		
2467	Not assigned							
2468	$1 Seaplane 1914	04/20/90	1.75	.50	11.00	(5)	2.50	
a	Imperf., pair		2,500.00	—				
b	Prephosphored uncoated paper		1.75	.50	10.00	(5)		
c	Prephosphored coated paper		1.75	.50	10.00	(5)		
2469	Not assigned							

2444

2445

2446

2447

2448

2448a

2449

2451

Circus Wagon 1900s

2452

Circus Wagon 1900s

2452D

2453

Canoe 1800s

2454

2457

Cog Railway 1870s

2463

2464

2466

2468

2474a

2470   2471   2472   2473   2474

2475

2476   2477   2478

2479   2480   2481   2482

2483   2484   2485

Issues of 1990-1995			Un	U	PB	#	FDC	Q(M)
Issues of 1990, Lighthouses Booklet Issue, Perf. 10 Vertically								
2470	25¢ Admiralty Head, WA	04/26/90	.45	.20			1.75	147
2471	25¢ Cape Hatteras, NC	04/26/90	.45	.20			1.75	147
2472	25¢ West Quoddy Head, ME	04/26/90	.45	.20			1.75	147
2473	25¢ American Shoals, FL	04/26/90	.45	.20			1.75	147
2474	25¢ Sandy Hook, NJ	04/26/90	.45	.20			1.75	147
a	Booklet pane of 5, #2470-74		2.50	2.00			4.50	147
b	As "a," white (USA 25) omitted		80.00					
	Self-Adhesive Issue, Die-Cut							
2475	25¢ Flag, single from pane	05/18/90	.50	.25			1.25	36
a	Pane of 12	05/18/90	6.00					
	Flora and Fauna Issues, Perf. 11							
2476	1¢ American Kestrel	06/22/91	.20	.20	.20	(4)	1.25	
2477	1¢ American Kestrel	05/10/95	.20	.20	.20	(4)	1.25	
2478	3¢ Eastern Bluebird	06/22/91	.20	.20	.30	(4)	1.25	
	Perf. 11.5 x 11							
2479	19¢ Fawn	03/11/91	.35	.20	1.75	(4)	1.25	
a	Tagging omitted		10.00					
b	Red omitted		850.00					
2480	30¢ Cardinal	06/22/91	.50	.20	2.25	(4)	1.25	
	Perf. 11							
2481	45¢ Pumpkinseed Sunfish	12/02/92	.80	.20	3.90	(4)	1.75	
a	Black omitted		525.00	—				
2482	$2 Bobcat	06/01/90	3.00	1.25	12.00	(4)	5.00	
a	Black omitted		300.00					
b	Tagging omitted		15.00					
	Perf. 10.9 x 9.8							
2483	20¢ Blue Jay	06/15/95	.40	.20			1.25	
a	Booklet pane of 10		4.00	2.25				
	Wood Duck Booklet Issue, Perf. 10							
2484	29¢ Black and multicolored	04/12/91	.50	.20			1.25	
a	Booklet pane of 10		5.50	3.75			5.00	
b	As "a," horizontal imperf. between		—					
c	Prephosphored coated paper		.40	.20				
d	As "c," booklet pane of 10		5.50	3.75				
	Perf. 11							
2485	29¢ Red and multicolored	04/12/91	.50	.20			1.25	
a	Booklet pane of 10		5.50	4.00			5.00	
b	Vertical pair, imperf. between		275.00					
c	As "b," booklet pane of 10		1,500.00					

#2484-85a issued only in bklts. All stamps are imperf. top or bottom, or top or bottom and right edge.

"I considered each image a graphic element, and approached the creation of a stamp as a 'mini' poster."

— Robert Guisti

	Issues of 1990-1995		Un	U	PB	#	FDC	Q(M)
	Perf. 10 x 11 on 2 or 3 sides							
2486	29¢ African Violet	10/08/93	.50	.20			1.25	
a	Booklet pane of 10		5.50	*4.00*			5.00	
2487	32¢ Peach	07/08/95	.60	.20			1.25	
2488	32¢ Pear	07/08/95	.60	.20			1.25	
a	Booklet pane, 5 each #2487-88		6.00	*4.25*			7.50	
b	Pair, #2487-88		1.25	.30				
	Issues of 1993, Self-Adhesive, Die-Cut							
2489	29¢ Red Squirrel	06/25/93	.50	.20			1.25	
a	Booklet pane of 18		10.00					
2490	29¢ Red Rose	08/19/93	.50	.20			1.25	
a	Booklet pane of 18		10.00					
2491	29¢ Pine Cone	11/05/93	.50	.20			1.25	
a	Booklet pane of 18		11.00					
b	Horizontal pair, no die cutting between		—					
c	Coil with plate #B1			4.25	6.00	(5)		
	Serpentine Die-Cut 11.3 x 11.7 on 2, 3 or 4 sides							
2492	32¢ Pink Rose	06/02/95	.60	.20			1.25	
a	Booklet pane of 20 plus label		12.00					
b	Booklet pane of 15 plus label		8.75					
c	Horizontal pair, no die cutting between		—					
d	As "a," 2 stamps and parts of 7 others printed on backing liner		—					
e	Booklet pane of 14		21.00					
f	Booklet pane of 16		21.00					
g	Coil with plate #S111		—	3.50	5.50	(5)		
h	Vertical pair, no die cutting between		—					
2493	32¢ Peach	07/08/95	.60	.20			1.25	
2494	32¢ Pear	07/08/95	.60	.20			1.25	
a	Booklet pane, 10 each #2493-2494		12.50					
b	Pair, #2493-2494		1.20					
	Coil Stamps, Serpentine Die Cut Vert.							
2495	32¢ Peach	07/08/95	.60	.20			1.25	
2495A	32¢ Pear	07/08/95	.60	.20			1.25	
b	Pair #2495-2495A		1.20		5.25	(5)		
	Issues of 1990, Olympians Issue, Perf. 11							
2496	25¢ Jesse Owens	07/06/90	.60	.20			1.25	36
2497	25¢ Ray Ewry	07/06/90	.60	.20			1.25	36
2498	25¢ Hazel Wightman	07/06/90	.60	.20			1.25	36
2499	25¢ Eddie Eagan	07/06/90	.60	.20			1.25	36
2500	25¢ Helene Madison	07/06/90	.60	.20			1.25	36
a	Strip of 5, #2496-2500		3.25	2.50	8.00	(10)	3.00	7
	Indian Headdresses Booklet Issue, Perf. 11 on 2 or 3 sides							
2501	25¢ Assiniboine Headdress	08/17/90	.55	.20			1.25	124
2502	25¢ Cheyenne Headdress	08/17/90	.55	.20			1.25	124
2503	25¢ Comanche Headdress	08/17/90	.55	.20			1.25	124
2504	25¢ Flathead Headdress	08/17/90	.55	.20			1.25	124
2505	25¢ Shoshone Headdress	08/17/90	.55	.20			1.25	124
a	Booklet pane of 10, 2 each of #2501-05		5.50	*3.50*			6.00	62
b	As "a," black omitted		*3,250.00*					
c	Strip of 5		2.75	1.00				
d	As "a," horizontal imperf. between		—					

#2501-05 issued only in booklets. All stamps imperf. top or bottom, or top or bottom and right edge.

2486

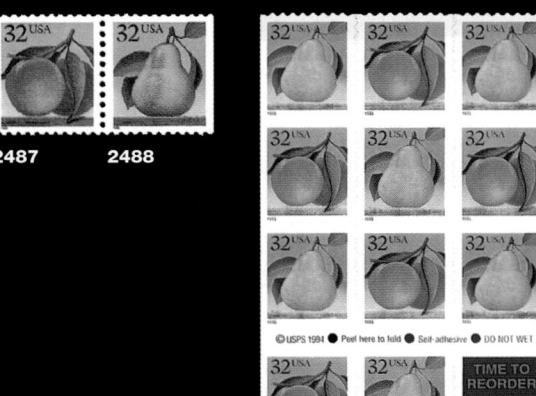

2487   **2488**

2487-2488a

2489

2490

2491

2492

2496   **2497**   **2498**   **2499**   **2500**   **2500a**

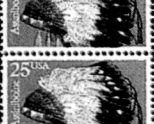

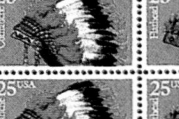

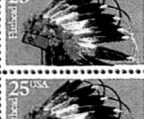

2501   **2502**   **2503**   **2504**   **2505**   **2505a**

2506   **2507**   **2507a**

2508   **2509**

2510   **2511**   **2511a**

2512

2513   **2514**   **2515**

2517   **2519**   **2520**   **2521**

2522   **2523**   **2523A**

	Issues of 1990		Un	U	PB	#	FDC	Q(M)
	Micronesia/Marshall Islands Issue, Perf. 11							
2506	25¢ Canoe and Flag of the							
	Federated States of Micronesia	09/28/90	.45	.20			1.25	76
2507	25¢ Stick Chart, Canoe and							
	Flag of the Marshall Islands	09/28/90	.45	.20			1.25	76
a	Pair, #2506-07		.90	.60	2.25	(4)	2.00	61
b	As "a," black omitted		3,750.00					
	Creatures of the Sea Issue							
2508	25¢ Killer Whales	10/03/90	.45	.20			1.25	70
2509	25¢ Northern Sea Lions	10/03/90	.45	.20			1.25	70
2510	25¢ Sea Otter	10/03/90	.45	.20			1.25	70
2511	25¢ Common Dolphin	10/03/90	.45	.20			1.25	70
a	Block of 4, #2508-11		1.90	1.75	2.50	(4)	3.00	70
b	As "a," black omitted		800.00					
	America/PUAS Issue, (See also #C127) 1990-1991							
2512	25¢ Grand Canyon	10/12/90	.45	.20	2.00	(4)	1.25	151
2513	25¢ Dwight D. Eisenhower	10/13/90	.60	.20	3.00	(4)	1.25	143
a	Imperf., pair		2,250.00					
	Christmas Issue, Perf. 11.5							
2514	25¢ Madonna and							
	Child, by Antonello	10/18/90	.45	.20	2.00	(4)	1.25	500
a	Booklet pane of 10		5.00	3.25			5.00	23
	Perf. 11							
2515	25¢ Christmas Tree	10/18/90	.45	.20	2.00	(4)	1.25	599
a	Vertical pair, imperf. horizontally		1,100.00					
	Booklet Stamp, Perf. 11.5 x 11 on 2 or 3 sides							
2516	Single (2515) from booklet pane	10/18/90	.45	.20			1.25	
a	Booklet pane of 10	10/18/90	5.00	3.25			6.00	32
	Issues of 1991, Perf. 13							
2517	(29¢) "F" Stamp	01/22/91	.50	.20	2.50	(4)	1.25	
a	Imperf., pair		750.00					
b	Horizontal pair, imperf. vertically		1,250.00					
	Coil Stamp, Perf. 10 Vertically							
2518	(29¢) "F" Tulip (2517)	01/22/91	.50	.20	4.25	(5)	1.25	
a	Imperf., pair		42.50					
	Booklet Stamps, Perf. 11 on 2 or 3 sides							
2519	(29¢) "F", single from booklet		.50	.20			1.25	
a	Booklet pane of 10	01/22/91	6.50	4.50			7.25	
2520	(29¢) "F", single from booklet		.50	.20			1.25	
a	Booklet pane of 10	01/22/91	18.00	4.50			7.25	
	#2519 has bull's-eye perforations that measure approximately 11.2. #2520 has less-pronounced							
	black lines in the leaf, which is a much brighter green than on #2519.							
	Perf. 11							
2521	(4¢) Makeup Rate	01/22/91	.20	.20	.40	(4)	1.25	
a	Vertical pair, imperf. horizontally		110.00					
	Self-Adhesive, Die-Cut, Imperf.							
2522	(29¢) F Flag, single from pane		.55	.25			1.25	
a	Pane of 12	01/22/91	7.00					
	Coil Stamps, Perf. 10 Vertically							
2523	29¢ Flag Over Mt. Rushmore,							
	intaglio printing	03/29/91	.50	.20	4.75	(5)	1.25	
b	Imperf., pair		25.00					
c	Blue, red and brown		5.00	—	150.00	(5)		
d	Prephosphored coated paper		5.00	—	550.00	(5)		
2523A	29¢ Flag Over Mt. Rushmore,							
	gravure printing	07/04/91	.50	.20	5.25	(5)	1.25	

	Issues of 1991		Un	U	PB	#	FDC	Q(M)
	Perf. 11							
2524	29¢ Tulip	04/05/91	.50	.20	2.25	(4)	1.25	
2524A	Perf. 13		.60	.20	2.90	(4)		
	Coil Stamps, Roulette 10 Vertically							
2525	29¢ Tulip	08/16/91	.50	.20	5.00	(5)	1.25	
	Issues of 1992, Perf. 10 Vertically							
2526	29¢ Tulip	03/03/92	.50	.20	5.00	(5)	1.25	
	Issues of 1991, Booklet Stamp, Perf. 11 on 2 or 3 sides							
2527	29¢ Tulip (2524), single from bklt.		.50	.20			1.25	
a	Booklet pane of 10	04/05/91	5.50	3.50			5.00	
b	As "a," vertically imperf. between		1,500.00					
c	Horizontal pair, imperf. vertically		300.00					
d	As "a," imperf. horizontally		2,750.00					
	Flag With Olympic Rings Booklet Issue, Perf. 11							
2528	29¢ U.S. Flag, Olympic Rings, single from booklet	04/21/91	.50	.20			1.25	
a	Booklet pane of 10	04/21/91	5.25	3.50			5.00	
	Issues of 1991-94, Perf. 10 Vertically							
2529	19¢ Fishing Boat	08/08/91	.35	.20	3.75	(5)	1.25	
a	New printing, Type II	1993	.35	.20	4.25	(5)		
b	As "a," untagged		1.00	.40	9.00	(5)		
	Perf. 9.8							
2529C	19¢ Fishing Boat	06/25/94	.50	.20	4.50	(5)	1.25	
	Type II stamps have finer dot pattern, smoother edges along type. #2529C has only one loop of rope tying up the boat.							
	Issue of 1991, Ballooning Booklet Issue, Perf. 10							
2530	19¢ Overhead View of Balloon, single from booklet	05/17/91	.35	.20			1.25	
a	Booklet pane of 10	05/17/91	3.50	2.75			5.00	
	#2530 was issued only in booklets. All stamps are imperf. on one side or on one side and bottom.							
	Perf. 11							
2531	29¢ Flags on Parade	05/30/91	.50	.20	2.25	(4)	1.25	
	Self-Adhesive, Die-Cut, Imperf.							
2531A	29¢ Liberty Torch, single stamp from pane	06/25/91	.55	.25			1.25	
b	Pane of 18	06/25/91	10.50					
	Perf. 11							
2532	50¢ Founding of Switzerland	02/22/91	1.00	.25	5.00	(4)	1.35	100
a	Vertical pair, imperf. horizontally		2,250.00					
2533	29¢ Vermont Statehood	03/01/91	.55	.20	2.75	(4)	1.50	0.1
2534	29¢ Savings Bonds	04/30/91	.50	.20	2.50	(4)	1.25	151
	Perf. 12.5 x 13							
2535	29¢ Love	05/09/91	.50	.20	2.50	(4)	1.25	631
2535A	Perf. 11		.60	.20	3.00	(4)		
	Booklet Stamp, Perf. 11 on 2 or 3 sides							
2536	29¢ (2535), single from booklet		.50	.20			1.25	
a	Booklet pane of 10	05/09/91	5.25	3.50			5.00	
	Perf. 11							
2537	52¢ Love	05/09/91	.90	.20	4.50	(4)	1.35	200

2524   2525   2526

2528   2529   2529C

2530   2531   2531A

2532   2533   2534

2535   2537

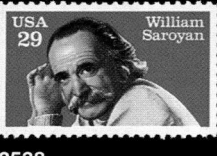

2538

2539

2540

2541

2542

2543

2544

2544A

2545 Royal Wulff

2546 Jock Scott

2547 Apte Tarpon Fly

2548 Lefty's Deceiver

2549 Muddler Minnow

2549a

Issues of 1991-95		Un	U	PB	#	FDC	Q(M)
Literary Arts Issue, Perf. 11							
2538	29¢ William Saroyan	05/22/91	.50	.20	2.50	(4)	1.25	161
Issues of 1991–93, Perf. 11							
2539	$1 USPS Logo/Olympic Rings	09/29/91	1.75	.50	8.00	(4)	2.25	
2540	$2.90 Priority Mail	07/07/91	5.00	2.50	20.00	(4)	4.50	
2541	$9.95 Domestic Express Mail	06/16/91	15.00	7.50	60.00	(4)	12.50	
2542	$14 International Express Mail	08/31/91	22.50	10.00	90.00	(4)	19.00	
a	Red omitted		1,500.00					
Perf 11 x 10.5							
2543	$2.90 Space Vehicle	06/03/93	5.00	2.25	22.50	(4)	6.00	
Perf. 11.2							
2544	$3 Space Shuttle *Challenger*	06/22/95	5.25	2.25	21.00	(4)	7.00	
Express Mail Rate, Perf. 11							
2544A	$10.75 Space Shuttle *Endeavour*	08/04/95	17.50	7.50	70.00	(4)	15.00	
Issues of 1991, Fishing Flies Booklet Issue, Perf. 11 Horizontally							
2545	29¢ Royal Wulff	05/31/91	.65	.20			1.25	149
2546	29¢ Jock Scott	05/31/91	.65	.20			1.25	149
2547	29¢ Apte Tarpon Fly	05/31/91	.65	.20			1.25	149
2548	29¢ Lefty's Deceiver	05/31/91	.65	.20			1.25	149
2549	29¢ Muddler Minnow	05/31/91	.65	.20			1.25	149
a	Booklet pane of 5, #2545-49		3.75	*2.50*			3.00	149

#2545-49 were issued only in booklets. All stamps are imperf. at sides or imperf. at sides and bottom.

Ron Miller

A renowned illustrator and author who specializes in astronomical, astronautical, and science fiction subjects, Ron Miller is an authority on early space flight and the writings of Jules Verne. He studied at the Columbus College of Art and served as an art director at the National Air and Space Museum's Albert Einstein Planetarium before becoming a freelance illustrator in 1977. Since then, his images have been featured in many magazines and books including *The Dream Machines*, his illustrated history of manned spacecraft. He has also been a production illustrator for such films as *Dune* and *Total Recall* and is a contributing editor for *Air & Space* and *Smithsonian* magazines. His art for ten United States postage stamps honors our advances in solar system exploration. ■

Issues of 1991		Un	U	PB	#	FDC	Q(M)
	Performing Arts Issue, Perf. 11						
2550	29¢ Cole Porter at Piano,						
	Sheet Music 06/08/91	.50	.20	2.50	(4)	1.25	150
a	Vertical pair, imperf. horizontally	650.00					
2551	29¢ Operations Desert Shield/						
	Desert Storm 07/02/91	.50	.20	2.50	(4)	2.50	200
a	Vertical pair, imperf. horizontally	2,000.00					
	Booklet Stamp, Perf. 11 on 1 or 2 sides						
2552	29¢ Operations Desert Shield/Desert						
	Storm (2551), single from booklet 07/02/91	.50	.20			2.50	200
a	Booklet pane of 5 07/02/91	2.75	2.25			4.50	40
	Summer Olympic Games Issue, Perf. 11						
2553	29¢ Pole Vaulter 07/12/91	.50	.20			1.25	34
2554	29¢ Discus Thrower 07/12/91	.50	.20			1.25	34
2555	29¢ Women Sprinters 07/12/91	.50	.20			1.25	34
2556	29¢ Javelin Thrower 07/12/91	.50	.20			1.25	34
2557	29¢ Women Hurdlers 07/12/91	.50	.20			1.25	34
a	Strip of 5, #2553-57	2.75	2.25	7.50	(10)	3.00	34
2558	29¢ Numismatics 08/13/91	.50	.20	2.50	(4)	1.25	150
	World War II Issue, 1941: A World at War, Miniature Sheet						
2559	Sheet of 10 and central label 09/03/91	5.25	4.50			7.00	15
a	29¢ Burma Road	.50	.30			1.50	15
b	29¢ America's First Peacetime Draft	.50	.30			1.50	15
c	29¢ Lend-Lease Act	.50	.30			1.50	15
d	29¢ Atlantic Charter	.50	.30			1.50	15
e	29¢ Arsenal of Democracy	.50	.30			1.50	15
f	29¢ Destroyer *Reuben James*	.50	.30			1.50	15
g	29¢ Civil Defense	.50	.30			1.50	15
h	29¢ Liberty Ship	.50	.30			1.50	15
i	29¢ Pearl Harbor	.50	.30			1.50	15
j	29¢ U.S. Declaration of War	.50	.30			1.50	15
k	29¢ Black omitted	10,000.00					

Jerry Dadds

An outstanding printmaker in the woodcut medium, Jerry Dadds is a founder of the Eucalyptus Tree Studio in Baltimore, Maryland. He has created illustrations and designs for corporations, government agencies, institutions, advertising agencies, book covers, magazines, and calendars throughout North America. The artist's presidential portraits appear on 36 United States postage stamps. A collector of presidential sculpture, portraits, and memorabilia, he is currently working on a bust of President Franklin D. Roosevelt for the Social Security Administration. ∎

"I gathered most of my research at old bookstores, antique shops and flea markets."

— Jerry Dadds

2550

2551

2553

2554

2555

2556

2557   2557a

2558

a   b   c   d   e

f   g   h   i   j   2559

2561

2560

2562

2563

2564

2565

2566　　**2566a**

2567

2568　　　**2569**　　　**2570**　　　**2571**　　　**2572**

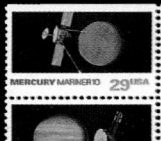

2573　　　**2574**　　　**2575**　　　**2576**　　　**2577**　　**2577a**

	Issues of 1991		Un	U	PB	#	FDC	Q(M)
2560	29¢ Basketball	08/28/91	.50	.20	2.50	(4)	2.00	150
2561	29¢ District of Columbia	09/07/91	.50	.20	2.50	(4)	1.25	149
a	Black omitted		125.00					
	Comedians Booklet Issue, Perf. 11 on 2 or 3 sides							
2562	29¢ Stan Laurel and Oliver Hardy	08/29/91	.50	.20			1.50	140
2563	29¢ Edgar Bergen and Dummy Charlie McCarthy	08/29/91	.50	.20			1.50	140
2564	29¢ Jack Benny	08/29/91	.50	.20			1.50	140
2565	29¢ Fanny Brice	08/29/91	.50	.20			1.50	140
2566	29¢ Bud Abbott and Lou Costello	08/29/91	.50	.20			1.50	140
a	Booklet pane of 10, 2 each of #2562-66		5.50	3.50			6.00	70
b	As "a," scarlet and bright violet omitted		750.00					
c	Strip of 5		2.50	—				
	#2562-66 issued only in booklets. All stamps are imperf. at top or bottom, or at top or bottom and right side.							
	Black Heritage Issue, Perf. 11							
2567	29¢ Jan Matzeliger and Shoe-Lasting Machine Diagram	09/15/91	.50	.20	2.50	(4)	1.25	149
a	Horizontal pair, imperf. vertically		1,750.00					
b	Vertical pair, imperf. horizontally		1,600.00					
c	Imperf., pair		2,750.00					
	Space Exploration Booklet Issue, Perf. 11 on 2 or 3 sides							
2568	29¢ Mercury, Mariner 10	10/01/91	.50	.20			1.25	33
2569	29¢ Venus, Mariner 2	10/01/91	.50	.20			1.25	33
2570	29¢ Earth, Landsat	10/01/91	.50	.20			1.25	33
2571	29¢ Moon, Lunar Orbiter	10/01/91	.50	.20			1.25	33
2572	29¢ Mars, Viking Orbiter	10/01/91	.50	.20			1.25	33
2573	29¢ Jupiter, Pioneer 11	10/01/91	.50	.20			1.25	33
2574	29¢ Saturn, Voyager 2	10/01/91	.50	.20			1.25	33
2575	29¢ Uranus, Voyager 2	10/01/91	.50	.20			1.25	33
2576	29¢ Neptune, Voyager 2	10/01/91	.50	.20			1.25	33
2577	29¢ Pluto	10/01/91	.50	.20			1.25	33
a	Booklet pane of 10, #2568-77		5.50	3.50			5.00	33
	#2568-77 issued only in booklets. All stamps are imperf. at top or bottom, or at top or bottom and right side.							

"My art had to stand on its own despite diminutive size restrictions and necessary type requirements. The greatest challenge was to simplify forms in order to enhance readability and viewer recognition."

— James Barkley

	Issues of 1991-1995		Un	U	PB	#	FDC	Q(M)
	Christmas Issue, Perf. 11							
2578	29¢ Madonna and Child,							
	by Romano	10/17/91	.50	.20	2.50	(4)	1.25	401
a	Booklet pane of 10		5.50	3.25				30
b	As "a," single, red and black omitted		3,500.00					
2579	29¢ Santa Claus Sliding							
	Down Chimney	10/17/91	.50	.20	2.50	(4)	1.25	900
a	Horizontal pair, imperf. vertically		325.00					
b	Vertical pair, imperf. horizontally		525.00					
	Booklet Stamps, Perf. 11 on 2 or 3 sides							
2580	29¢ Santa Claus (2579),							
	Type I, single from booklet	10/17/91	1.75	.20			1.25	
2581	29¢ Santa Claus (2579),							
	Type II, single from booklet	10/17/91	1.75	.20			1.25	
a	Pair, #2580, 2581	10/17/91	3.50	.25				28
b	Booklet pane, 2 each		7.50	1.25			2.50	
	The extreme left brick in top row of chimney is missing from Type II, #2581.							
2582	29¢ Santa Claus Checking							
	List, single from booklet	10/17/91	.50	.20			1.25	
a	Booklet pane of 4	10/17/91	2.00	1.25			2.50	28
2583	29¢ Santa Claus Leaving Present							
	Under Tree, single from booklet	10/17/91	.50	.20			1.25	
a	Booklet pane of 4	10/17/91	2.00	1.25			2.50	28
2584	29¢ Santa Claus Going Up							
	Chimney, single from booklet	10/17/91	.50	.20			1.25	
a	Booklet pane of 4	10/17/91	2.00	1.25			2.50	28
2585	29¢ Santa Claus Flying Away							
	in Sleigh, single from booklet	10/17/91	.50	.20			1.25	
a	Booklet pane of 4	10/17/91	2.00	1.25			2.50	28
	#2582-85 issued only in booklets. All stamps are imperf. at top or bottom, or at top or bottom and right side.							
	Perf. 11.2							
2587	32¢ James K. Polk	11/02/95	.60	.20	3.00	(4)	1.25	
	Issues of 1994, Perf. 11.5							
2590	$1 Victory at Saratoga	05/05/94	1.90	.50	7.60	(4)	2.00	
2592	$5 Washington and Jackson	08/19/94	8.00	2.50	40.00	(4)	9.00	

2578

2579

2580   **2581**   **2581a**

2582   **2583**

2584   **2585**

2587

2590   **2592**

2593

2594

2595

2596

2597

2598

2599

2602

2603

2604

2605

2606

2607

2608

2609

	Issues of 1991-1994		Un	U	PB	#	FDC	Q(M)
	Perf. 10							
2593	29¢ Pledge of Allegiance	09/08/92	.50	.20			1.25	
a	Booklet of 10		5.25	4.25			5.00	
	Perf. 11 x 10							
2593B	Pledge of Allegiance, shiny gum		.50	.20				
c	Booklet pane of 10, shiny gum		5.50	4.25				
	Issue of 1993, Perf. 11 x 10							
2594	29¢ Pledge of Allegiance	04/08/93	.50	.20				
a	Booklet of 10		5.25	4.25				
b	Imperf., pair		900.00					
	Issues of 1992, Self-Adhesive Booklet and Coil Stamps							
2595	29¢ Eagle and Shield							
	(brown lettering)	09/25/92	.50	.25			1.25	
a	Pane of 17 + label		13.00					
b	Pair, no die-cutting		225.00					
c	Brown omitted		475.00					
d	As "a," no die-cutting		1,800.00					
2596	29¢ Eagle and Shield							
	(green lettering)	09/25/92	.50	.25			1.25	
a	Pane of 17 + label		12.00					
2597	29¢ Eagle and Shield							
	(red lettering)	09/25/92	.50	.25			1.25	
a	Pane of 17 + label		10.00					
	Issues of 1994, Self-Adhesive, Die-Cut							
2598	29¢ Eagle	02/04/94	.50	.20			1.25	
a	Booklet pane of 18		10.00					
b	Coil		—	3.50	6.00	(5)		
2599	29¢ Statue of Liberty	06/24/94	.50	.20			1.25	
a	Booklet pane of 18		10.00					
b	Coil		—	3.50	6.00	(5)		
	Issues of 1991-93, Perf. 10 Vertically							
2602	10¢ Eagle and Shield							
	(inscribed "Bulk Rate USA")	12/13/91	.20	.20	3.50	(5)	1.25	
2603	10¢ Eagle and Shield							
	(inscribed "USA Bulk Rate")	05/29/93	.20	.20	4.00	(5)	1.25	
a	Imperf., pair		30.00					
b	Tagged (error), shiny gum		2.00	1.50	15.00	(5)		
2604	10¢ Eagle and Shield (metallic,							
	inscribed "USA Bulk Rate")	05/29/93	.20	.20	3.50	(5)	1.25	
2605	23¢ Flag, Presorted First-Class	09/27/91	.40	.40	4.25	(5)	1.25	
	Issues of 1992, Perf. 11							
2606	23¢ USA	07/21/92	.40	.40	4.75	(5)	1.25	
2607	23¢ USA (Bureau)							
	(In #2607, "23" is 7mm long)	10/09/92	.40	.40	4.75	(5)	1.25	
a	Tagged (error), shiny gum		5.00	4.50	85.00	(5)		
c	Imperf., pair		100.00					
2608	23¢ USA (violet)	05/14/93	.40	.40	4.75	(5)	1.25	
2609	29¢ Flag Over White House	04/23/92	.50	.20	4.75	(5)	1.25	
a	Imperf., pair		20.00					
b	Pair, imperf. between		100.00					

1992

	Issues of 1992		Un	U	PB	#	FDC	Q(M)
	Winter Olympic Games Issue							
2611	29¢ Hockey	01/11/92	.50	.20			1.25	32
2612	29¢ Figure Skating	01/11/92	.50	.20			1.25	32
2613	29¢ Speed Skating	01/11/92	.50	.20			1.25	32
2614	29¢ Skiing	01/11/92	.50	.20			1.25	32
2615	29¢ Bobsledding	01/11/92	.50	.20			1.25	32
a	Strip of 5, #2611-15		2.75	2.25	6.50	(10)	3.00	
2616	29¢ World Columbian							
	Stamp Expo	01/24/92	.50	.20	2.50	(4)	1.25	149
a	Tagging omitted		8.50					
	Black Heritage Issue							
2617	29¢ W.E.B. DuBois	01/31/92	.50	.20	2.50	(4)	1.25	150
2618	29¢ Love	02/06/92	.50	.20	2.50	(4)	1.25	835
a	Horizontal pair, imperf. vertically		800.00					
2619	29¢ Olympic Baseball	04/03/92	.50	.20	2.75	(4)	1.50	160
	First Voyage of Christopher Columbus Issue, Perf. 11 x 10.5							
2620	29¢ Seeking Queen Isabella's							
	Support	04/24/92	.50	.20			1.25	40
2621	29¢ Crossing The Atlantic	04/24/92	.50	.20			1.25	40
2622	29¢ Approaching Land	04/24/92	.50	.20			1.25	40
2623	29¢ Coming Ashore	04/24/92	.50	.20			1.25	40
a	Block of 4, #2620-23		2.00	1.90	2.50	(4)	2.75	

"It was a fascinating challenge to come up with an interesting concept and have the opportunity to collaborate on the execution of the designs."

— Naiad Einsel

2611 **2612** **2613** **2614** **2615** **2615a**

2616

2617 **2618** **2619**

2620 **2621**

2622 **2623** **2623a**

2624

2625

2626

2627

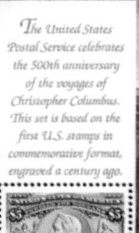

2628

2629

Issues of 1992		Un	U	PB	#	FDC	Q(M)
The Voyages of Columbus Souvenir Sheets, Perf. 10.5							
2624	First Sighting of Land,						
	sheet of 3	05/22/92	1.75	—			2.10	2
a	1¢ deep blue		.20	.20			1.25	
b	4¢ ultramarine		.20	.20			1.25	
c	$1 salmon		1.65	1.00			2.00	
2625	Claiming a New World,						
	sheet of 3	05/22/92	6.75	—			8.00	2
a	2¢ brown violet		.20	.20			1.25	
b	3¢ green		.20	.20			1.25	
c	$4 crimson lake		6.50	4.00			8.00	
2626	Seeking Royal Support,						
	sheet of 3	05/22/92	1.40	—			1.75	2
a	5¢ chocolate		.20	.20			1.25	
b	30¢ orange brown		.50	.30			1.25	
c	50¢ slate blue		.80	.50			1.50	
2627	Royal Favor Restored,						
	sheet of 3	05/22/92	5.25	—			6.25	2
a	6¢ purple		.20	.20			1.25	
b	8¢ magenta		.20	.20			1.25	
c	$3 yellow green		4.75	3.00			6.00	
2628	Reporting Discoveries,						
	sheet of 3	05/22/92	3.75	—			4.50	2
a	10¢ black brown		.20	.20			1.25	
b	15¢ dark green		.25	.20			1.25	
c	$2 brown red		3.25	2.00			4.00	
2629	$5 Christopher Columbus,						
	sheet of 1	05/22/92	8.50	—			10.00	2
a	$5 black		8.00	5.00				

John Falter (1910–1982)

Reared in Falls City, Nebraska, John Falter studied at the Kansas City Art Institute and at the Art Students League in New York City. Talented and prolific, he created illustrations for prominent agencies and publications, but was best known for his *Saturday Evening Post* covers depicting small towns and country settings. As a Navy lieutenant in World War II, he served on special art assignment and created more than 300 recruiting posters. He illustrated more than 40 books for *Reader's Digest* after the war, and completed portrait commissions for such dignitaries as Fleet Admiral William F. Halsey, Louis Armstrong, Olivia de Havilland, and James Cagney. In 1976, he was inducted into the Illustrators Hall of Fame for his artistic contributions. ■

	Issues of 1992		Un	U	PB	#	FDC	Q(M)
	Perf. 11							
2630	29¢ New York Stock Exchange							
	Bicentennial	05/17/92	.50	.20	2.50	(4)	1.75	148
	Space Adventures Issue							
2631	29¢ Cosmonaut, US Space							
	Shuttle	05/29/92	.50	.20			1.50	37
2632	29¢ Astronaut, Russian							
	Space Station	05/29/92	.50	.20			1.50	37
2633	29¢ Sputnik, Vostok, Apollo							
	Command and Lunar Modules	05/29/92	.50	.20			1.50	37
2634	29¢ Soyuz, Mercury and							
	Gemini Spacecraft	05/29/92	.50	.20			1.50	37
a	Block of 4, #2631-34		2.00	1.75	2.50	(4)	2.75	
2635	29¢ Alaska Highway, 50th							
	Anniversary	05/30/92	.50	.20	2.50	(4)	1.25	147
a	Black (engr.) omitted		*500.00*					
2636	29¢ Kentucky Statehood							
	Bicentennial	06/01/92	.50	.20	2.50	(4)	1.25	160
	Summer Olympic Games Issue							
2637	29¢ Soccer	06/11/92	.50	.20			1.25	32
2638	29¢ Gymnastics	06/11/92	.50	.20			1.25	32
2639	29¢ Volleyball	06/11/92	.50	.20			1.25	32
2640	29¢ Boxing	06/11/92	.50	.20			1.25	32
2641	29¢ Swimming	06/11/92	.50	.20			1.25	32
a	Strip of 5, #2637-41		2.50	2.25	5.50	(10)	3.00	
	Hummingbirds Issue							
2642	29¢ Ruby-Throated	06/15/92	.50	.20			1.25	88
2643	29¢ Broad-Billed	06/15/92	.50	.20			1.25	88
2644	29¢ Costa's	06/15/92	.50	.20			1.25	88
2645	29¢ Rufous	06/15/92	.50	.20			1.25	88
2646	29¢ Calliope	06/15/92	.50	.20			1.25	88
a	Booklet pane of 5, #2642-46		2.75	2.25			3.00	

Lonnie Busch

A native of St. Louis, Missouri, Lonnie Busch now creates his dynamic art from a studio located in Ocracoke, North Carolina. An alumnus of two St. Louis universities—Washington and Webster—he has also taught illustration at both institutions. For nearly 30 years, he has pursued a career as an illustrator and designer. His works—honored by distinguished design groups such as *Print* magazine, the Advertising Club of New York, and the Advertising Federation of St. Louis—include a *Newsweek* cover in 1984. They have been exhibited nationwide and in Japan. His first stamp design was issued in 1987 and has been followed by U.S. Postal Service commissions for another 13 commemorative stamps. ■

1992

2630

2631 **2632**

2633 **2634**

2634a

2635

2636

2637

2638

2639

2640

2641 **2641a**

2642

2643

2644

2645

2646 **2646a**

Indian Paintbrush **2647**
Fragrant Water Lily **2648**
Meadow Beauty **2649**
Jack-in-the-Pulpit **2650**
California Poppy **2651**

Large-flowered Trillium **2652**
Tickseed **2653**
Shooting Star **2654**
Stream Violet **2655**
Bluets **2656**

Herb Robert **2657**
Marsh Marigold **2658**
Sweet White Violet **2659**
Claret Cup Cactus **2660**
White Mountain Avens **2661**

Sessile Bellwort **2662**
Blue Flag **2663**
Harlequin Lupine **2664**
Twinflower **2665**
Common Sunflower **2666**

Sego Lily **2667**
Virginia Bluebells **2668**
Ohi'a Lehua **2669**
Rosebud Orchid **2670**
Showy Evening Primrose **2671**

Issues of 1992		Un	U	FDC	Q(M)
Wildflowers Issue, Perf. 11					
2647 29¢ Indian Paintbrush	07/24/92	.50	.20	1.25	11
2648 29¢ Fragrant Water Lily	07/24/92	.50	.20	1.25	11
2649 29¢ Meadow Beauty	07/24/92	.50	.20	1.25	11
2650 29¢ Jack-in-the-Pulpit	07/24/92	.50	.20	1.25	11
2651 29¢ California Poppy	07/24/92	.50	.20	1.25	11
2652 29¢ Large-Flowered Trillium	07/24/92	.50	.20	1.25	11
2653 29¢ Tickseed	07/24/92	.50	.20	1.25	11
2654 29¢ Shooting Star	07/24/92	.50	.20	1.25	11
2655 29¢ Stream Violet	07/24/92	.50	.20	1.25	11
2656 29¢ Bluets	07/24/92	.50	.20	1.25	11
2657 29¢ Herb Robert	07/24/92	.50	.20	1.25	11
2658 29¢ Marsh Marigold	07/24/92	.50	.20	1.25	11
2659 29¢ Sweet White Violet	07/24/92	.50	.20	1.25	11
2660 29¢ Claret Cup Cactus	07/24/92	.50	.20	1.25	11
2661 29¢ White Mountain Avens	07/24/92	.50	.20	1.25	11
2662 29¢ Sessile Bellwort	07/24/92	.50	.20	1.25	11
2663 29¢ Blue Flag	07/24/92	.50	.20	1.25	11
2664 29¢ Harlequin Lupine	07/24/92	.50	.20	1.25	11
2665 29¢ Twinflower	07/24/92	.50	.20	1.25	11
2666 29¢ Common Sunflower	07/24/92	.50	.20	1.25	11
2667 29¢ Sego Lily	07/24/92	.50	.20	1.25	11
2668 29¢ Virginia Bluebells	07/24/92	.50	.20	1.25	11
2669 29¢ Ohi'a Lehua	07/24/92	.50	.20	1.25	11
2670 29¢ Rosebud Orchid	07/24/92	.50	.20	1.25	11
2671 29¢ Showy Evening Primrose	07/24/92	.50	.20	1.25	11

April Greiman

A native of New York, April Greiman studied graphic design at the Kansas City Art Institute and the Allgemeine Kunst Gewerbeschule in Basel, Switzerland. In 1976 she opened her practice in Los Angeles where today she is a partner at Pentagram. An early and enthusiastic adapter of computer technology, she established her reputation as a new media pioneer with now-legendary projects for Esprit, the Walker Art Center, and the Southern California Institute of Architecture. One of the most honored designers in the world, she has received numerous medals and awards including both the Medal of the American Institute of Graphic Arts and the Chrysler Award for Innovation in 1998. A design teacher, she was honored as a finalist in the Inaugural National Design Awards in 2000. Her work has been represented in museum shows worldwide. Her first U.S. Postal Service commission honored the 19th Amendment. ■

	Issues of 1992		Un	U	FDC	Q(M)
	Wildflowers Issue (continued)					
2672	29¢ Fringed Gentian	07/24/92	.50	.20	1.25	11
2673	29¢ Yellow Lady's Slipper	07/24/92	.50	.20	1.25	11
2674	29¢ Passionflower	07/24/92	.50	.20	1.25	11
2675	29¢ Bunchberry	07/24/92	.50	.20	1.25	11
2676	29¢ Pasqueflower	07/24/92	.50	.20	1.25	11
2677	29¢ Round-Lobed Hepatica	07/24/92	.50	.20	1.25	11
2678	29¢ Wild Columbine	07/24/92	.50	.20	1.25	11
2679	29¢ Fireweed	07/24/92	.50	.20	1.25	11
2680	29¢ Indian Pond Lily	07/24/92	.50	.20	1.25	11
2681	29¢ Turk's Cap Lily	07/24/92	.50	.20	1.25	11
2682	29¢ Dutchman's Breeches	07/24/92	.50	.20	1.25	11
2683	29¢ Trumpet Honeysuckle	07/24/92	.50	.20	1.25	11
2684	29¢ Jacob's Ladder	07/24/92	.50	.20	1.25	11
2685	29¢ Plains Prickly Pear	07/24/92	.50	.20	1.25	11
2686	29¢ Moss Campion	07/24/92	.50	.20	1.25	11
2687	29¢ Bearberry	07/24/92	.50	.20	1.25	11
2688	29¢ Mexican Hat	07/24/92	.50	.20	1.25	11
2689	29¢ Harebell	07/24/92	.50	.20	1.25	11
2690	29¢ Desert Five Spot	07/24/92	.50	.20	1.25	11
2691	29¢ Smooth Solomon's Seal	07/24/92	.50	.20	1.25	11
2692	29¢ Red Maids	07/24/92	.50	.20	1.25	11
2693	29¢ Yellow Skunk Cabbage	07/24/92	.50	.20	1.25	11
2694	29¢ Rue Anemone	07/24/92	.50	.20	1.25	11
2695	29¢ Standing Cypress	07/24/92	.50	.20	1.25	11
2696	29¢ Wild Flax	07/24/92	.50	.20	1.25	11
a	Pane of 50, #2647-96		25.00		30.00	11

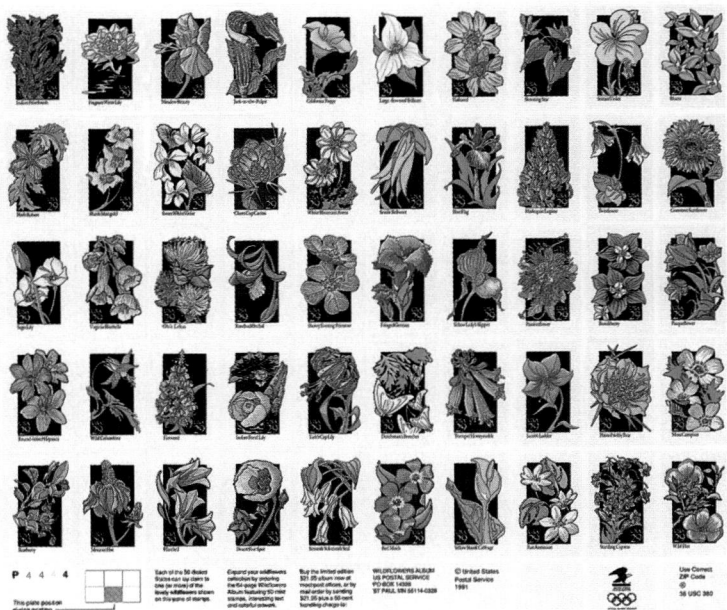

Example of #2696a

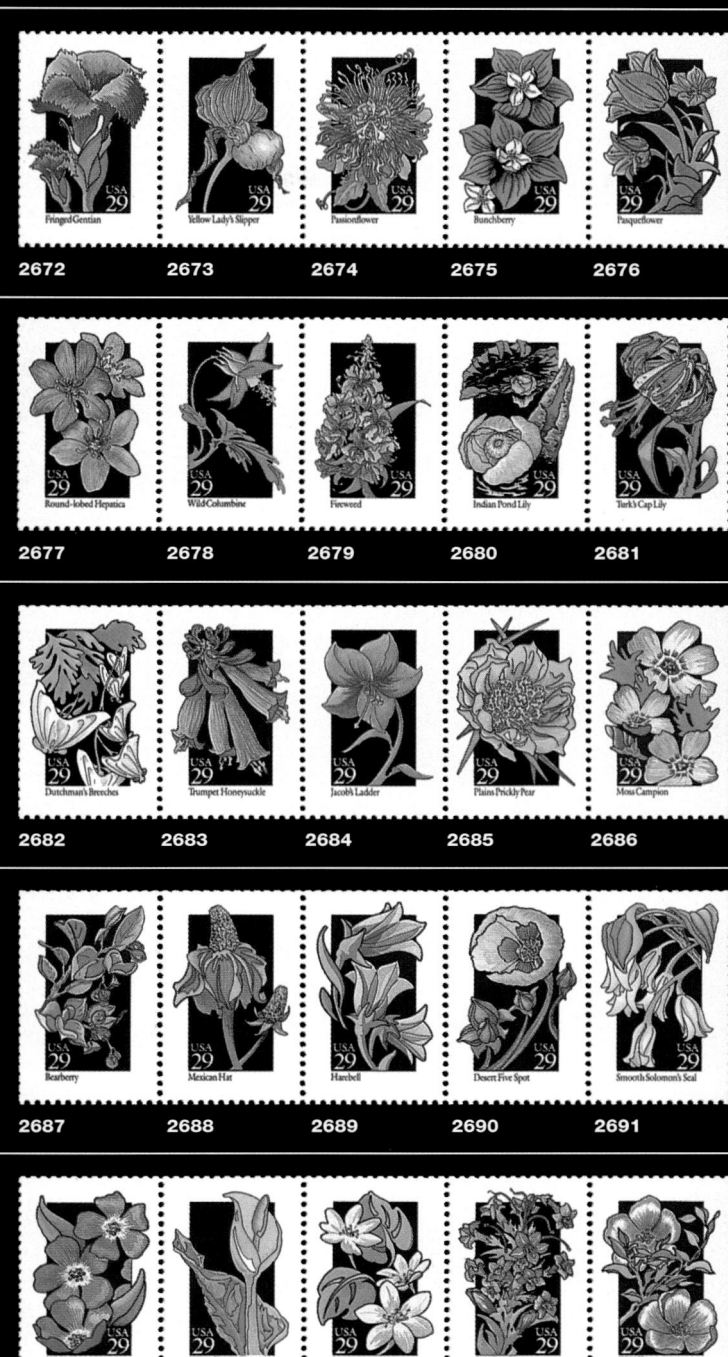

2672 Fringed Gentian
2673 Yellow Lady's Slipper
2674 Passionflower
2675 Bunchberry
2676 Pasqueflower

2677 Round-lobed Hepatica
2678 Wild Columbine
2679 Fireweed
2680 Indian Pond Lily
2681 Turk's Cap Lily

2682 Dutchman's Breeches
2683 Trumpet Honeysuckle
2684 Jacob's Ladder
2685 Plains Prickly Pear
2686 Moss Campion

2687 Bearberry
2688 Mexican Hat
2689 Harebell
2690 Desert Five Spot
2691 Smooth Solomon's Seal

2692 Red Maids
2693 Yellow Skunk Cabbage
2694 Rue Anemone
2695 Standing Cypress
2696 Wild Flax

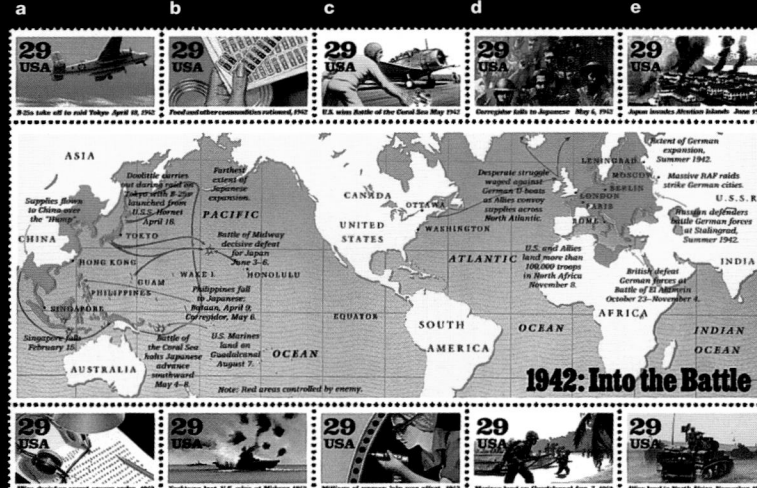

a   b   c   d   e

f   g   h   i   j   2697

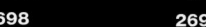

2698

2699

2700   2701

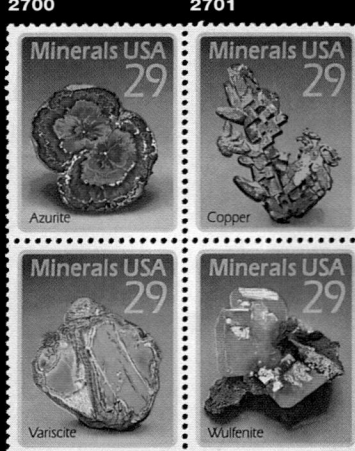

2702   2703   2703a

2704

340

Issues of 1992		Un	U	PB	#	FDC	Q(M)
World War II Issue, 1942: Into the Battle, Miniature Sheet, Perf. 11							
2697	Sheet of 10 and central label 08/17/92	5.25	4.50			7.00	12
a	29¢ B-25s Take Off to Raid Tokyo	.50	.30			1.50	12
b	29¢ Food and Other Commodities Rationed	.50	.30			1.50	12
c	29¢ U.S. Wins Battle of the Coral Sea	.50	.30			1.50	12
d	29¢ Corregidor Falls to Japanese	.50	.30			1.50	12
e	29¢ Japan Invades Aleutian Islands	.50	.30			1.50	12
f	29¢ Allies Decipher Secret Enemy Codes	.50	.30			1.50	12
g	29¢ *Yorktown* Lost	.50	.30			1.50	12
h	29¢ Millions of Women Join War Effort	.50	.30			1.50	12
i	29¢ Marines Land on Guadalcanal	.50	.30			1.50	12
j	29¢ Allies Land in North Africa	.50	.30			1.50	12
	Literary Arts Issue						
2698	29¢ Dorothy Parker 08/22/92	.50	.20	2.50	(4)	1.25	105
2699	29¢ Dr. Theodore von Karman 08/31/92	.50	.20	2.50	(4)	1.25	143
	Minerals Issue						
2700	29¢ Azurite 09/17/92	.50	.20			1.25	37
2701	29¢ Copper 09/17/92	.50	.20			1.25	37
2702	29¢ Variscite 09/17/92	.50	.20			1.25	37
2703	29¢ Wulfenite 09/17/92	.50	.20			1.25	37
a	Block of 4, #2700-03	2.00	1.75	2.50	(4)	2.75	
b	As "a," silver (litho.) omitted	8,500.00					
2704	29¢ Juan Rodriguez Cabrillo 09/28/92	.50	.20	2.50	(4)	1.25	85
a	Black (engr.) omitted	4,250.00					

Chris Calle

A graduate of the University of Michigan School of Art, where he studied illustration and design, Chris Calle has earned an international reputation as a stamp designer. He has created more than 200 stamps for the United Nations program and for countries as diverse as Sweden and the Republic of the Marshall Islands. His outstanding work also appears in many publications and is represented in corporate, private, and museum collections throughout the world. During his first year as a professional illustrator, he was commissioned to create the first of the 31 United States postage stamps designed by him. Chris is the son of artist Paul Calle. ■

"Coming up with a strong visual concept is of tremendous importance."

— Chris Calle

1992

	Issues of 1992		Un	U	PB	#	FDC	Q(M)
	Wild Animals Issue, Perf. 11 Horizontally							
2705	29¢ Giraffe	10/01/92	.50	.20			1.25	80
2706	29¢ Giant Panda	10/01/92	.50	.20			1.25	80
2707	29¢ Flamingo	10/01/92	.50	.20			1.25	80
2708	29¢ King Penguins	10/01/92	.50	.20			1.25	80
2709	29¢ White Bengal Tiger	10/01/92	.50	.20			1.25	80
a	Booklet pane of 5, #2705-09		2.50	2.00			3.25	
b	As "a," imperf.		3,000.00					
	Christmas Issue, Perf. 11.5 x 11							
2710	29¢ Madonna and Child by Giovanni Bellini	10/22/92	.50	.20	2.50	(4)	1.25	300
a	Booklet pane of 10		5.25	3.50			7.25	349
2711	29¢ Horse and Rider	10/22/92	.50	.20			1.25	125
2712	29¢ Toy Train	10/22/92	.50	.20			1.25	125
2713	29¢ Toy Steamer	10/22/92	.50	.20			1.25	125
2714	29¢ Toy Ship	10/22/92	.50	.20			1.25	125
a	Block of 4, #2711-14		2.00	1.10	2.50	(4)	2.75	
	Perf. 11							
2715	29¢ Horse and Rider	10/22/92	.50	.20			1.25	102
2716	29¢ Toy Train	10/22/92	.50	.20			1.25	102
2717	29¢ Toy Steamer	10/22/92	.50	.20			1.25	102
2718	29¢ Toy Ship	10/22/92	.50	.20			1.25	102
a	Booklet pane of 4, #2715-18		2.25	1.25			2.75	
2719	29¢ Toy Train (self-adhesive)	10/22/92	.60	.20			1.25	22
a	Booklet pane of 18		11.00					
	Lunar New Year Issue							
2720	29¢ Year of the Rooster	12/30/92	.50	.20	2.00	(4)	1.50	

Robert Giusti

Born in Switzerland and raised in New York City, Robert Giusti studied painting, sculpture, and graphics at the Tyler School of Fine Arts in Pennsylvania and the Cranbrook Academy in Michigan. He worked in advertising and publishing before setting out as a freelance illustrator and designer of book jackets, album covers, advertisements, packaging, logos, letterheads, and animated television commercials. The Cincinnati Zoo, the World Wildlife Fund, Columbia Records, Universal Pictures, *National Geographic*, and *The New York Times* are among his prestigious clients. His 13 United States postage stamps feature an array of colorful wildlife. ■

2705

2706

2707

2708

2709

2709a

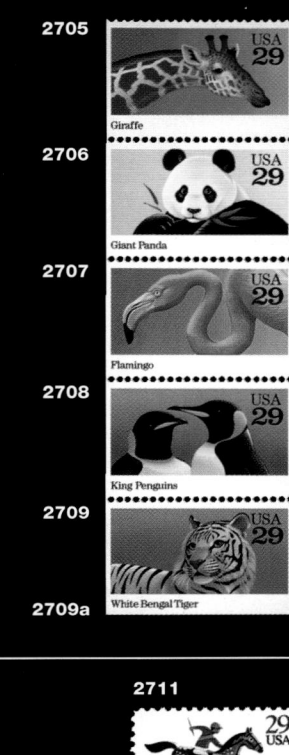

2710

2711   2712

2713   2714   2714a

2715   2716

2717   2718   2718a

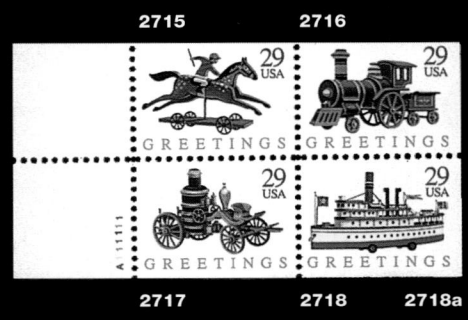

2719

2721

2722

2723

2724   **2725**   **2726**   **2727**   **2728**

2729   **2730**

2731
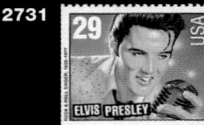

2732

2733

2734

2735

2736

2737

2731

2737b

2737a

	Issues of 1993		Un	U	PB	#	FDC	Q(M)
	Legends of American Music Series, Perf. 11							
2721	29¢ Elvis Presley	01/08/93	.50	.20	2.50	(4)	1.75	517
	Perf. 10							
2722	29¢ *Oklahoma!*	03/30/93	.50	.20	2.50	(4)	1.25	150
2723	29¢ Hank Williams	06/09/93	.50	.20	2.50	(4)	1.25	152
	Perf. 11.2 x 11.5							
2723A	29¢ Hank Williams		22.50	—	140.00	(4)	1.25	
	Legends of American Music Series, Rock & Roll/Rhythm & Blues Issue, Perf. 10							
2724	29¢ Elvis Presley	06/16/93	.60	.20			1.25	14
2725	29¢ Bill Haley	06/16/93	.60	.20			1.25	14
2726	29¢ Clyde McPhatter	06/16/93	.60	.20			1.25	14
2727	29¢ Ritchie Valens	06/16/93	.60	.20			1.25	14
2728	29¢ Otis Redding	06/16/93	.60	.20			1.25	14
2729	29¢ Buddy Holly	06/16/93	.60	.20			1.25	14
2730	29¢ Dinah Washington	06/16/93	.60	.20			1.25	14
a	Vertical strip of 7, #2724-30		4.25	—	6.50	(10)	5.00	
	Perf. 11 Horizontally							
2731	29¢ Elvis Presley	06/16/93	.50	.20			1.25	99
2732	29¢ Bill Haley (2725)	06/16/93	.50	.20			1.25	33
2733	29¢ Clyde McPhatter (2726)	06/16/93	.50	.20			1.25	33
2734	29¢ Ritchie Valens (2727)	06/16/93	.50	.20			1.25	33
2735	29¢ Otis Redding	06/16/93	.50	.20			1.25	66
2736	29¢ Buddy Holly	06/16/93	.50	.20			1.25	66
2737	29¢ Dinah Washington	06/16/93	.50	.20			1.25	66
a	Booklet pane, 2 #2731, 1 each #2732-37		4.25	2.25			5.25	
b	Booklet pane of 4, #2731, 2735-37		2.25	1.50			2.75	
2738-40	Not assigned							

Mark Stutzman

A graduate of the Art Institute of Pittsburgh, Mark Stutzman began his illustration career at a fast-paced television station where he worked on sets, created on-air graphics, painted weather maps, and created celebrity drawings that attracted industry attention. The co-founder of Eloqui, a studio devoted to the art of illustration, he works with clients from around the globe. His vibrant images portraying icons from popular culture appear on billboards, on posters, and in magazines, commissioned by such clients as McDonald's, D.C. Comics, and *Entertainment Weekly*. The artist's ground-breaking rendition of the young Elvis Presley for the United States Postal Service was one of four stamps that he created to honor the Legends of American Music. ■

"Stamps become such a permanent piece of art and history."

— Mark Stutzman

	Issues of 1993		Un	U	PB	#	FDC	Q(M)
	Space Fantasy Issue, Perf. 11 Vertically on 1 or 2 sides							
2741	29¢ multicolored	01/25/93	.50	.20			1.25	140
2742	29¢ multicolored	01/25/93	.50	.20			1.25	140
2743	29¢ multicolored	01/25/93	.50	.20			1.25	140
2744	29¢ multicolored	01/25/93	.50	.20			1.25	140
2745	29¢ multicolored	01/25/93	.50	.20			1.25	140
a	Booklet pane of 5, #2741-45		2.50	2.25			3.25	
2746	29¢ Percy Lavon Julian	01/29/93	.50	.20	2.50	(4)	1.25	105
2747	29¢ Oregon Trail	02/12/93	.50	.20	2.50	(4)	1.25	110
a	Tagging omitted		15.00					
2748	29¢ World University Games	02/25/93	.50	.20	2.50	(4)	1.25	110
2749	29¢ Grace Kelly	03/25/93	.50	.20	2.50	(4)	2.00	173
	Circus Issue, Perf. 11							
2750	29¢ Clown	04/06/93	.55	.20			1.50	66
2751	29¢ Ringmaster	04/06/93	.55	.20			1.50	66
2752	29¢ Trapeze Artist	04/06/93	.55	.20			1.50	66
2753	29¢ Elephant	04/06/93	.55	.20			1.50	66
a	Block of 4, #2750-53		2.25	1.75	4.50	(6)	3.00	
2754	29¢ Cherokee Strip	04/17/93	.50	.20	2.00	(4)	1.25	110
2755	29¢ Dean Acheson	04/21/93	.50	.20	2.50	(4)	1.25	116
	Sporting Horses Issue, Perf. 11 x 11.5							
2756	29¢ Steeplechase	05/01/93	.50	.20			1.75	40
2757	29¢ Thoroughbred Racing	05/01/93	.50	.20			1.75	40
2758	29¢ Harness Racing	05/01/93	.50	.20			1.75	40
2759	29¢ Polo	05/01/93	.50	.20			1.75	40
a	Block of 4, #2756-59		2.00	1.75	2.50	(4)	3.50	

C. Michael Dudash

Renowned for his dramatic realist paintings, Michael Dudash is an award-winning artist whose images appear to be bathed in light. He began his career in publishing, but has worked as a freelance illustrator since 1978, creating images for books, magazines, advertising agencies, film companies, and corporations. *The Reader's Digest*, *Sports Illustrated*, DC Comics, Eddie Bauer, and Paramount Pictures are among his impressive client roster. He has also worked collaboratively with Christian publishers toward the creation of fine art prints and is the illustrator of seven United States postage stamps. ■

"Printing and the quality of reproduction can vary dramatically from very good to very bad. Postal stamps are generally very good."

— C. Michael Dudash

2741   2742   2743   2744   2745   2745a

2746

2747

2748

2749

2750   2751

2752   2753

2753a

2754

2755

2756   2757

2758   2759

2759a

2760   2761   2762   2763   2764   2764a

a   b   c   d   e

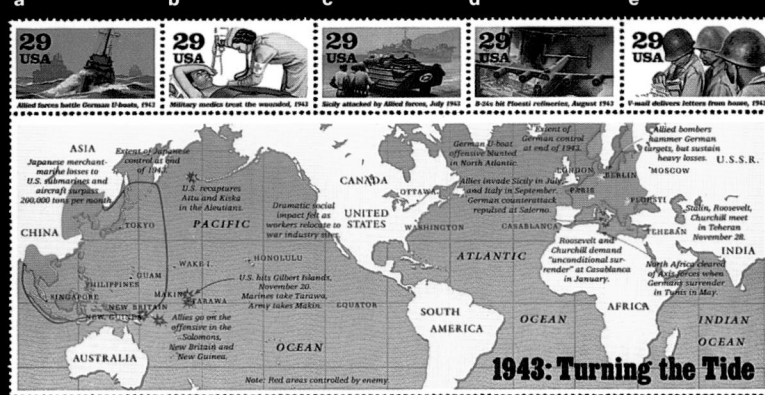

f   g   h   i   j   2765

2766

2767

2768

2769

2770

2770a

Issues of 1993		Un	U	PB	#	FDC	Q(M)
Garden Flowers Issue, Perf. 11 Vertically							
2760	29¢ Hyacinth 05/15/93	.50	.20			1.25	200
2761	29¢ Daffodil 05/15/93	.50	.20			1.25	200
2762	29¢ Tulip 05/15/93	.50	.20			1.25	200
2763	29¢ Iris 05/15/93	.50	.20			1.25	200
2764	29¢ Lilac 05/15/93	.50	.20			1.25	200
a	Booklet pane of 5, #2760-64	2.50	2.00			3.25	
b	As "a," black omitted	300.00					
c	As "a," imperf.	2,500.00					
World War II Issue, 1943: Turning The Tide, Miniature Sheet, Perf. 11							
2765	Sheet of 10 and central label 05/31/93	5.25	4.50			7.00	
a	29¢ Allied Forces Battle German U-boats	.50	.30			1.50	12
b	29¢ Military Medics Treat the Wounded.	.50	.30			1.50	12
c	29¢ Sicily Attacked by Allied Forces	.50	.30			1.50	12
d	29¢ B-24s Hit Ploesti Refineries	.50	.30			1.50	12
e	29¢ V-Mail Delivers Letters from Home.	50	.30			1.50	12
f	29¢ Italy Invaded by Allies	.50	.30			1.50	12
g	29¢ Bonds and Stamps Help War Effort	.50	.30			1.50	12
h	29¢ "Willie and Joe" Keep Spirits High.	50	.30			1.50	12
i	29¢ Gold Stars Mark World War II Losses	.50	.30			1.50	12
j	29¢ Marines Assault Tarawa	.50	.30			1.50	12
2766	29¢ Joe Louis 06/22/93	.50	.20	2.50	(4)	1.50	160
Legends of American Music Series, Broadway Musicals Issue, Perf. 11 Horizontally							
2767	29¢ *Show Boat* 07/14/93	.50	.20			1.25	129
2768	29¢ *Porgy & Bess* 07/14/93	.50	.20			1.25	129
2769	29¢ *Oklahoma!* 07/14/93	.50	.20			1.25	129
2770	29¢ *My Fair Lady* 07/14/93	.50	.20			1.25	129
a	Booklet pane of 4, #2767-70	2.50	2.00			3.25	

Wilson McLean

Born in Scotland, Wilson McLean began his career at the age of 15 in a London silk-screen shop. After attending art school at night he worked as a freelance artist in advertising and publishing and became familiar with the work of American illustrators. Inspired to move to New York in 1966, he has since received virtually every professional award and honor in the field of illustration, including a prestigious Clio for excellence in advertising. His artwork appears on four United States postage stamps and is included in the permanent collections of the Smithsonian Institution and the London Transport Museum. He has also taught aspiring artists at the School of Visual Arts and at Syracuse University. ■

	Issues of 1993		Un	U	PB	#	FDC	Q(M)
	Legends of American Music Series, Country & Western Issue, Perf. 10							
2771	29¢ Hank Williams (2775)	09/25/93	.55	.20			1.25	25
2772	29¢ Patsy Cline (2777)	09/25/93	.55	.20			1.25	25
2773	29¢ The Carter Family (2776)	09/25/93	.55	.20			1.25	25
2774	29¢ Bob Willis (2778)	09/25/93	.55	.20			1.25	25
a	Block or horiz. strip of 4, #2771-74		2.20	1.75	2.20	(4)	2.75	
	Booklet Stamps, Perf. 11 Horizontally							
2775	29¢ Hank Williams	09/25/93	.50	.20			1.25	170
2776	29¢ The Carter Family	09/25/93	.50	.20			1.25	170
2777	29¢ Patsy Cline	09/25/93	.50	.20			1.25	170
2778	29¢ Bob Willis	09/25/93	.50	.20			1.25	170
a	Booklet pane of 4, #2775-78		2.50	*2.00*			2.75	
	National Postal Museum Issue, Perf. 11							
2779	Independence Hall, Benjamin Franklin, Printing Press, Colonial Post Rider	07/30/93	.50	.20			1.25	38
2780	Pony Express Rider, Civil War Soldier, Concord Stagecoach	07/30/93	.50	.20			1.25	38
2781	Biplane, Charles Lindbergh, Railway Mail Car, 1931 Model A Ford Mail Truck	07/30/93	.50	.20			1.25	38
2782	California Gold Rush Miner's Letter, Barcode and Circular Date Stamp	07/30/93	.50	.20			1.25	38
a	Block or strip of 4, #2779-82		2.00	1.75	2.00	(4)	2.75	
c	As "a," imperf.		*3,500.00*					
	American Sign Language Issue, Perf. 11.5							
2783	29¢ Recognizing Deafness	09/20/93	.50	.20			1.25	42
2784	29¢ American Sign Language	09/20/93	.50	.20			1.25	42
a	Pair, #2783-84		1.00	.65	2.00	(4)	2.00	
	Classic Books Issues, Perf. 11							
2785	29¢ *Rebecca of Sunnybrook Farm*	10/23/93	.50	.20			1.25	38
2786	29¢ *Little House on the Prairie*	10/23/93	.50	.20			1.25	38
2787	29¢ *The Adventures of Huckleberry Finn*	10/23/93	.50	.20			1.25	38
2788	29¢ *Little Women*	10/23/93	.50	.20			1.25	38
a	Block or horiz. strip of 4, #2785-88		2.00	1.75	4.75	(4)	2.75	
b	As "a," imperf.		*3,000.00*					

James Lamb

James Lamb's love of plein-air painting is evident in the light-filled images that he creates for exhibition and a broad range of clients. A professional illustrator for 15 years, his diverse national accounts have included the Smithsonian Institution, the White House, NASA, the National Football League, and the United States Postal Service, for which he has designed six stamps. His images have also been commissioned by major motion picture studios and advertising agencies, and have been published as limited-edition prints and collectible plates. Exhibited widely, his paintings are included in many public and private collections. ■

2771 2772

2773 2774 2774a

2775

2776

2777

2778

2778a

2779 2780

2781 2782 2782a

2783 2784 2784a

2785 2786

2787 2788 2788a

2789

2790

2791   **2792**

2793   **2794**   **2794a**

2795   **2796**

2797   **2798**   **2798c**

2799   **2800**

2801   **2802**   **2802a**

2803

2804

2805

2806

2806a

Issues of 1993			Un	U	PB	#	FDC	Q(M)
Christmas Issue, Perf. 11								
2789	29¢ Madonna and Child	10/21/93	.50	.20	2.50	(4)	1.25	500
Booklet Stamps, Perf. 11.5 x 11 on 2 or 3 sides								
2790	29¢ Madonna and Child (2789)	10/21/93	.50	.20			1.25	500
a	Booklet pane of 4		2.25	1.75			2.00	
Perf. 11.5								
2791	29¢ Jack-in-the-Box	10/21/93	.50	.20			1.25	250
2792	29¢ Red-Nosed Reindeer	10/21/93	.50	.20			1.25	250
2793	29¢ Snowman	10/21/93	.50	.20			1.25	250
2794	29¢ Toy Soldier	10/21/93	.50	.20			1.25	250
a	Block or strip of 4, #2791-94		2.00	1.75	2.75	(4)	2.75	
Booklet Stamps, Perf. 11 x 10 on 2 or 3 sides								
2795	29¢ Toy Soldier (2794)	10/21/93	.50	.20			1.25	200
2796	29¢ Snowman (2793)	10/21/93	.50	.20			1.25	200
2797	29¢ Red-Nosed Reindeer (2792)	10/21/93	.50	.20			1.25	200
2798	29¢ Jack-in-the-Box (2791)	10/21/93	.50	.20			1.25	200
a	Booklet pane, 3 each #2795-96, 2 each #2797-98		5.00	4.00			6.50	
b	Booklet pane, 3 each #2797-98, 2 each #2795-96		5.00	4.00			6.50	
c	Block of 4		2.00	1.75				
Self-Adhesive, Die-Cut								
2799	29¢ Snowman	10/28/93	.50	.20			1.25	120
a	Coil with plate		—	3.50	5.50	(5)		
2800	29¢ Toy Soldier	10/28/93	.50	.20			1.25	120
2801	29¢ Jack-in-the-Box	10/28/93	.50	.20			1.25	120
2802	29¢ Red-Nosed Reindeer	10/28/93	.50	.20			1.25	120
a	Booklet pane, 3 each #2799-2802		7.00					
b	Block of 4		2.00					
2803	29¢ Snowman	10/28/93	.50	.20			1.25	18
a	Booklet pane of 18		10.00					
Perf. 11								
2804	29¢ Northern Mariana Islands	11/04/93	.50	.20	2.00	(4)	1.25	88
2805	29¢ Columbus Landing in Puerto Rico	11/19/93	.50	.20	2.50	(4)	1.25	105
2806	29¢ AIDS Awareness	12/01/93	.50	.20	2.50	(4)	1.25	100
a	Booklet version		.50	.20			1.25	250
b	Booklet pane of 5		2.50	2.00			3.25	

1994

	Issues of 1994		Un	U	PB	#	FDC	Q(M)
	Winter Olympic Games Issue, Perf. 11.2							
2807	29¢ Slalom	01/06/94	.50	.20			1.25	36
2808	29¢ Luge	01/06/94	.50	.20			1.25	36
2809	29¢ Ice Dancing	01/06/94	.50	.20			1.25	36
2810	29¢ Cross-Country Skiing	01/06/94	.50	.20			1.25	36
2811	29¢ Ice Hockey	01/06/94	.50	.20			1.25	36
a	Strip of 5, #2807-11		2.50	2.25	5.00	(10)	3.00	36
2812	29¢ Edward R. Murrow	01/21/94	.50	.20	2.50	(4)	1.25	151
2813	29¢ Love Sunrise	01/27/94	.50	.20	6.00	(5)	1.25	358
a	Booklet of 18 (self-adhesive)		11.00					
b	Coil with plate		—	3.50				
	Perf. 10.9 x 11.1							
2814	29¢ Love Stamp	02/14/94	.50	.20			1.25	830
a	Booklet pane of 10		5.50	*3.50*			6.50	
	Perf. 11.1							
2814C	29¢ Love Stamp	06/11/94	.50	.20	2.50	(4)	1.25	300
	Perf. 11.2							
2815	52¢ Love Birds	02/14/94	1.00	.20	5.00	(4)	1.40	175
2816	29¢ Dr. Allison Davis	02/01/94	.50	.20	2.00	(4)	1.25	156
	Lunar New Year Issue							
2817	29¢ Year of the Dog	02/05/94	.55	.20	2.20	(4)	1.75	105
	Perf. 11.5 x 11.2							
2818	29¢ Buffalo Soldiers	04/22/94	.50	.20	2.00	(4)	1.50	186
	Stars of the Silent Screen Issue, Perf. 11.2							
2819	29¢ Rudolph Valentino	04/27/94	.50	.20			1.50	19
2820	29¢ Clara Bow	04/27/94	.50	.20			1.50	19
2821	29¢ Charlie Chaplin	04/27/94	.50	.20			1.50	19
2822	29¢ Lon Chaney	04/27/94	.50	.20			1.50	19
2823	29¢ John Gilbert	04/27/94	.50	.20			1.50	19
2824	29¢ Zasu Pitts	04/27/94	.50	.20			1.50	19
2825	29¢ Harold Lloyd	04/27/94	.50	.20			1.50	19
2826	29¢ Keystone Cops	04/27/94	.50	.20			1.50	19
2827	29¢ Theda Bara	04/27/94	.50	.20			1.50	19
2828	29¢ Buster Keaton	04/27/94	.50	.20			1.50	19
a	Block of 10 #2819-2828		5.00	4.00	6.00	(10)	6.50	19
b	As "a," black (litho.) omitted		—					
c	As "a," black, red & bright violet (litho.) omitted		—					

Al Hirschfeld

Al Hirschfeld's signature style includes sweeping lines and intricate curves that capture the essence of likeness and personality. The most celebrated caricaturist of our time, he has documented the drama and humor of American film and theater for more than 75 years. Born in St. Louis in 1903, he studied at the Art Students League in New York and the Academie Julian in Paris before working for two major movie studios. His long relationship with *The New York Times* began in 1925 and continues today, and his drawings have appeared in *The Saturday Evening Post*, *Time*, *Rolling Stone,* and *TV Guide* among many others. The first artist to have his name published on a stamp booklet, he is also the first to include hidden writing in his designs. His 15 United States postage stamps honor noted comedians and silent film stars. ■

2807   2808   2809   2810   2811   2811a

               2813   2814   2814C

2812

2815   2817   2818

2816

2819   2820   2821   2822   2823

2824   2825   2826   2827   2828   2828a

| 29 USA *Lily* | 29 USA *Zinnia* | 29 USA *Gladiola* | 29 USA *Marigold* | 29 USA *Rose* |

2829   2830   2831   2832   2833 2833a

2834

2835

2836

a   b   c   d   e

| 29 USA Allied forces retake New Guinea, 1944 | 29 USA P-51s escort B-17s on bombing raids, 1944 | 29 USA Allies in Normandy, D-Day, June 6, 1944 | 29 USA Airborne units spearhead attacks, 1944 | 29 USA Submarines shorten war in Pacific, 1944 |

1944: Road to Victory

| 29 USA Allies free Rome, June 4; Paris, Aug. 25, 1944 | 29 USA U.S. troops clear Saipan bunkers, 1944 | 29 USA Red Ball Express speeds vital supplies, 1944 | 29 USA Battle for Leyte Gulf, October 23-26, 1944 | 29 USA Bastogne and Battle of the Bulge, Dec. 1944 |

f   g   h   i   j

2838

	Issues of 1994		Un	U	PB	#	FDC	Q(M)
	Garden Flowers Booklet Issue, Perf. 10.9 Vertically							
2829	29¢ Lily	04/28/94	.50	.20			1.25	166
2830	29¢ Zinnia	04/28/94	.50	.20			1.25	166
2831	29¢ Gladiola	04/28/94	.50	.20			1.25	166
2832	29¢ Marigold	04/28/94	.50	.20			1.25	166
2833	29¢ Rose	04/28/94	.50	.20			1.25	166
a	Booklet pane of 5, #2829-2833		2.50				3.25	
b	As "a," imperf.		2,500.00					
c	As "a," black (engr.) omitted		350.00					
	1994 World Cup Soccer Championships Issue, Perf. 11.1							
2834	29¢ Soccer Player	05/26/94	.50	.20	2.00	(4)	1.25	201
2835	40¢ Soccer Player	05/26/94	.80	.20	3.20	(4)	1.25	300
2836	50¢ Soccer Player	05/26/94	1.00	.20	4.00	(4)	1.35	269
2837	Souvenir Sheet of 3,							
	#2834-2836	05/26/94	2.50	2.00			2.50	60
a	29¢ Soccer Player							
b	40¢ Soccer Player							
c	50¢ Soccer Player							
	World War II Issue, 1944: Road to Victory Miniature, Sheet, Perf. 10.9							
2838	Sheet of 10 and central label	06/06/94	6.00	4.50			7.00	12
a	29¢ Allies Retake New Guinea		.60	.30			1.50	12
b	29¢ Bombing Raids		.60	.30			1.50	12
c	29¢ Allies in Normandy, D-Day		.60	.30			1.50	12
d	29¢ Airborne Units		.60	.30			1.50	12
e	29¢ Submarines Shorten War		.60	.30			1.50	12
f	29¢ Allies Free Rome, Paris		.60	.30			1.50	12
g	29¢ Troops Clear Siapan Bunkers		.60	.30			1.50	12
h	29¢ Red Ball Express		.60	.30			1.50	12
i	29¢ Battle for Leyte Gulf		.60	.30			1.50	12
j	29¢ Battle of the Bulge		.60	.30			1.50	12

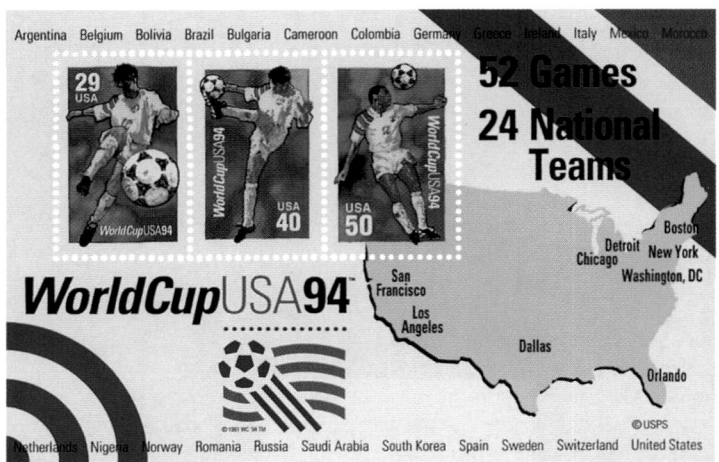

Example of #2837

	Issues of 1994		Un	U	PB	#	FDC	Q(M)
	Norman Rockwell Issue, Perf. 10.9 x 11.1							
2839	29¢ Rockwell Self-Portrait	07/01/94	.50	.20	2.50	(4)	1.25	209
2840	Four Freedoms souvenir sheet	07/01/94	4.00	2.75			3.50	20
a	50¢ Freedom from Want		1.00	.65			1.50	20
b	50¢ Freedom from Fear		1.00	.65			1.50	20
c	50¢ Freedom of Speech		1.00	.65			1.50	20
d	50¢ Freedom of Worship		1.00	.65			1.50	20
	First Moon Landing Issue, Perf. 11.2 x 11.1							
2841	29¢ sheet of 12	07/20/94	7.50	—			6.50	13
a	Single stamp		.60	.60			1.50	155
	Perf. 10.7 x 11.1							
2842	$9.95 Moon Landing	07/20/94	17.50	7.50	70.00	(4)	15.00	101
	Locomotives Issue, Perf. 11 Horizontally							
2843	29¢ Hudson's General	07/28/94	.50	.20			1.25	159
2844	29¢ McQueen's Jupiter	07/28/94	.50	.20			1.25	159
2845	29¢ Eddy's No. 242	07/28/94	.50	.20			1.25	159
2846	29¢ Ely's No. 10	07/28/94	.50	.20			1.25	159
2847	29¢ Buchanan's No. 999	07/28/94	.50	.20			1.25	159
a	Booklet pane of 5, #2843-2847		2.50	2.00			3.25	159
	Perf. 11.1 x 11							
2848	29¢ George Meany	08/16/94	.50	.20	2.50	(4)	1.25	151
	Legends of American Music Series, Popular Singers Issue, Perf. 10.1 x 10.2							
2849	29¢ Al Jolson	09/01/94	.60	.20			1.25	35
2850	29¢ Bing Crosby	09/01/94	.60	.20			1.25	35
2851	29¢ Ethel Waters	09/01/94	.60	.20			1.25	35
2852	29¢ Nat "King" Cole	09/01/94	.60	.20			1.25	35
2853	29¢ Ethel Merman	09/01/94	.60	.20			1.25	35
a	Vert. strip of 5, #2849-2853		3.00	2.00			3.25	

Norman Rockwell (1894–1978)

One of the most influential visual communicators of the 20th century, Norman Rockwell aspired to a career in illustration at an early age. He attended the Art Students League in New York and was 19 when he accepted the position of art editor at *Boys Life* magazine. At 22, his artwork was published on the cover of *The Saturday Evening Post*, which he called "the greatest show window in America for an illustrator." Best known for his 322 *Post* covers created between 1916 and 1963, his images have graced the covers and pages of more than 30 periodicals and were commissioned by many prominent corporations during his seven-decade career. In 1977 he received the Presidential Medal of Honor, the nation's highest civilian commendation, for his "vivid and affectionate portraits of our country." Although many of his works have been reproduced on United States postage stamps, only two issues were directly commissioned. ■

PHOTO BY LOUIE LAMONE, 1963

2839

a

b

c

d

2840

2841a

2842

2843

2844

2845

2846

2847

2847a

2848

2849

2850

2851

2852

2853

2853a

2854   2855   2856   2857   2858

2859   2860   2861

2862

2863   2864

2865   2866

2866a

	Issues of 1994		Un	U	PB	#	FDC	Q(M)
	Legends of American Music Series, Jazz and Blues Singers Issue, Perf. 11 x 10.8							
2854	29¢ Bessie Smith	09/17/94	.60	.20			1.25	25
2855	29¢ Muddy Waters	09/17/94	.60	.20			1.25	25
2856	29¢ Billie Holiday	09/17/94	.60	.20			1.25	25
2857	29¢ Robert Johnson	09/17/94	.60	.20			1.25	20
2858	29¢ Jimmy Rushing	09/17/94	.60	.20			1.25	20
2859	29¢ "Ma" Rainey	09/17/94	.60	.20			1.25	20
2860	29¢ Mildred Bailey	09/17/94	.60	.20			1.25	20
2861	29¢ Howlin' Wolf	09/17/94	.60	.20			1.25	20
a	Block of 9, #2854-2861							
	+ 1 additional stamp		4.50	3.50	8.00	(10)	6.00	
	Literary Arts Issue, Perf. 11							
2862	29¢ James Thurber	09/10/94	.50	.20	2.50	(4)	1.25	151
	Wonders of the Sea Issue, Perf. 11 x 10.9							
2863	29¢ Diver, Motorboat	10/03/94	.50	.20			1.25	56
2864	29¢ Diver, Ship	10/03/94	.50	.20			1.25	56
2865	29¢ Diver, Ship's Wheel	10/03/94	.50	.20			1.25	56
2866	29¢ Diver, Coral	10/03/94	.50	.20			1.25	56
a	Block of 4, #2963-2966		2.00	1.50	2.00	(4)	2.75	56
b	As "a" imperf.		2,000.00					
	Cranes Issue, Perf. 10.8 x 11							
2867	29¢ Black-Necked Crane	10/09/94	.50	.20			1.25	78
2868	29¢ Whooping Crane	10/09/94	.50	.20			1.25	78
a	Pair, #2867-2868		1.00	.65	2.00	(4)	2.00	78
b	Black and magenta (engr.) omitted		2,250.00					

"I got goosebumps when I saw some of my stamps being used on the envelopes of Christmas cards the month after they were issued."

— Kazuhiko Sano

1994

Issues of 1994		Un	U	PB	#	FDC	Q(M)
Legends of the West Issue, Perf. 10.1 x 10							
2869 Sheet of 20	10/18/94	12.00	—			14.00	20
a	29¢ Home on the Range	.60	.20			1.75	20
b	29¢ Buffalo Bill Cody	.60	.20			1.75	20
c	29¢ Jim Bridger	.60	.20			1.75	20
d	29¢ Annie Oakley	.60	.20			1.75	20
e	29¢ Native American Culture	.60	.20			1.75	20
f	29¢ Chief Joseph	.60	.20			1.75	20
g	29¢ Bill Pickett	.60	.20			1.75	20
h	29¢ Bat Masterson	.60	.20			1.75	20
i	29¢ John C. Fremont	.60	.20			1.75	20
j	29¢ Wyatt Earp	.60	.20			1.75	20
k	29¢ Nellie Cashman	.60	.20			1.75	20
l	29¢ Charles Goodnight	.60	.20			1.75	20
m	29¢ Geronimo	.60	.20			1.75	20
n	29¢ Kit Carson	.60	.20			1.75	20
o	29¢ Wild Bill Hickok	.60	.20			1.75	20
p	29¢ Western Wildlife	.60	.20			1.75	20
q	29¢ Jim Beckwourth	.60	.20			1.75	20
r	29¢ Bill Tilghman	.60	.20			1.75	20
s	29¢ Sacagawea	.60	.20			1.75	20
t	29¢ Overland Mail	.60	.20			1.75	20
2870 29¢ Sheet of 20 (recalled)	10/18/94	190.00	—				0.1

Clarence Lee

Born in Honolulu, Hawaii, Clarence Lee studied at the Yale University School of Art and Architecture and worked as a designer in New York City before returning to his home state. The founder of Clarence Lee Design & Associates, Inc., he has developed graphic symbols for such clients as Northwest Airlines, Capital Investments, and the Hawaii Convention Center. He has also designed interior displays for the Hawaii Pavilion at Osaka's World's Fair and packaging for Mauna Loa Macadamia Nuts and Royal Kona Coffee. Highly acclaimed for his work, he has created art for 14 United States postage stamps including a series celebrating the Chinese Lunar New Year. ■

"Stamp design has brought me more notoriety than any other project I have worked on."

— Clarence Lee

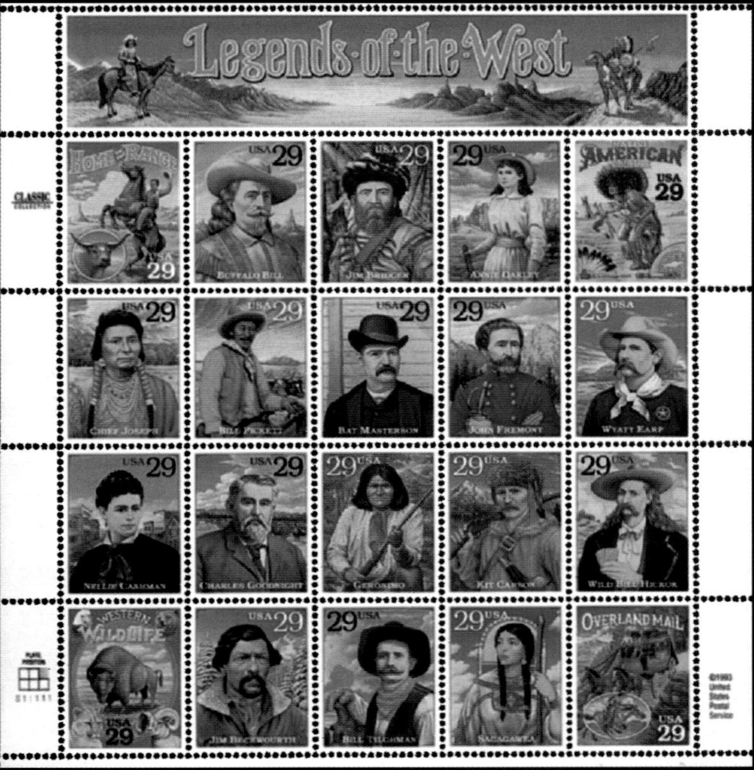

Legends of the West

CLASSIC COLLECTION

HOME ON THE RANGE 29 · BUFFALO BILL 29 · JIM BRIDGER 29 · ANNIE OAKLEY 29 · AMERICAN 29

CHIEF JOSEPH 29 · BILL PICKETT 29 · BAT MASTERSON 29 · JOHN FREMONT 29 · WYATT EARP 29

NELLIE CASHMAN 29 · CHARLES GOODNIGHT 29 · GERONIMO 29 · KIT CARSON 29 · WILD BILL HICKOK 29

WESTERN WILDLIFE 29 · JIM BECKWOURTH 29 · BILL TILGHMAN 29 · SACAGAWEA 29 · OVERLAND MAIL 29

©1993 United States Postal Service

2869	a	b	c	d	e
	f	g	h	i	j
	k	l	m	n	o
	p	q	r	s	t

2870g

2871

2872

2873

2874

2875

2876

Issues of 1994			Un	U	PB	#	FDC	Q(M)
	Christmas Issue, Perf. 11.1							
2871	29¢ Madonna and Child	10/20/94	.50	.20	2.50	(4)	1.25	
2871A	Perf. 9.8 x 10.8		.50	.20			1.25	
b	As "a," booklet pane of 10		5.25	3.50				50
c	As "a," Imperf.		—					
2872	29¢ Stocking	10/20/94	.50	.20	2.50	(4)	1.25	603
a	Booklet pane of 20		10.50	3.00				30
	Self-Adhesive							
2873	29¢ Santa Claus	10/20/94	.50	.20	6.00	(5)	1.25	240
a	Booklet pane of 12		6.25					20
2874	29¢ Cardinal in Snow	10/20/94	.50	.20			1.25	36
a	Booklet pane of 18		9.50					2
	Bureau of Engraving and Printing Issue, Perf.11							
2875	$2.00 Sheet of 4	11/03/94	15.00	—			12.00	5
a	Single stamp		3.00	1.25				20
	Lunar New Year Issue, Perf. 11.2 x 11.1							
2876	29¢ Year of the Boar	12/30/94	.55	.20	2.25	(4)	1.50	80
	Untagged, Perf. 11 x 10.8							
2877	(3¢) Dove Make-Up Rate	12/13/94	.20	.20	.30	(4)	1.25	
a	Imperf., pair		200.00					
	Perf. 10.8 x 10.9							
2878	(3¢) Dove Make-Up Rate	12/13/94	.20	.20	.30	(4)	1.25	

Peter Good

Graphic designer and illustrator Peter Good is well known for the powerful images he has created for corporations, museums, and arts organizations. With his wife, Janet Cummings, he is a principal in the seven-person graphic design studio, Cummings & Good. A graduate of the University of Connecticut, he has created a number of distinctive graphics for his alma mater, which in 1997 awarded him and his wife the University Medal for "outstanding professional achievement, leadership, and distinguished public service." His posters have been exhibited throughout the world and with other graphic designs are represented in the collections of such prestigious institutions as the Cooper-Hewitt Museum and the Library of Congress. The U.S. Postal Service has issued six commemorative stamps designed by this award-winning artist. ■

	Issues of 1994-1997		Un	U	PB	#	FDC	Q(M)
	Tagged, Perf. 11.2 x 11.1							
2879	(20¢) Old Glory Postcard Rate	12/13/94	.40	.20	5.00	(4)	1.25	
	Perf. 11 x 10.9							
2880	(20¢) Old Glory Postcard Rate	12/13/94	.50	.20	*9.00*	(4)	1.25	
	Perf. 11.2 x 11.1							
2881	(32¢) "G" Old Glory	12/13/94	.75	.20	*75.00*	(4)	1.25	
a	Booklet pane of 10		6.00	3.75			7.50	
	Perf. 11 x 10.9							
2882	(32¢) "G" Old Glory	12/13/94	.60	.20	3.00	(4)	1.25	
	Booklet Stamps, Perf. 10 x 9.9 on 2 or 3 sides							
2883	(32¢) "G" Old Glory	12/13/94	.60	.20			1.25	
a	Booklet pane of 10		6.25	3.75			7.50	
	Perf. 10.9							
2884	(32¢) "G" Old Glory	12/13/94	.60	.20			1.25	
a	Booklet pane of 10		6.00	3.75			7.50	
	Perf. 11 x 10.9							
2885	(32¢) "G" Old Glory	12/13/94	.65	.20			1.25	
a	Booklet pane of 10		6.50	3.75			7.50	
	Self-Adhesive, Die-Cut							
2886	(32¢) "G" Old Glory	12/13/94	.60	.20	5.75	(5)	1.25	
a	Booklet pane of 18		11.50					
b	Coil with plate		—	3.25				
2887	(32¢) "G" Old Glory	12/13/94	.60	.20			1.25	
a	Booklet pane of 18		11.50					
	Coil Stamps, Perf. 9.8 Vertically							
2888	(25¢) Old Glory First-Class Presort	12/13/94	.50	.50	5.00	(5)	1.25	
2889	(32¢) Black "G"	12/13/94	.60	.20	5.50	(5)	1.25	
a	Imperf., pair		*300.00*					
2890	(32¢) Blue "G"	12/13/94	.60	.20	5.75	(5)	1.25	
2891	(32¢) Red "G"	12/13/94	.60	.20	5.75	(5)	1.25	
	Rouletted							
2892	(32¢) Red "G"	12/13/94	.60	.20	5.75	(5)	1.25	
	Issue of 1995, Perf. 9.8 Vertically							
2893	(5¢) Green	01/12/95	.20	.20	1.90	(5)		
	Perf. 10.4							
2897	32¢ Flag Over Porch	05/19/95	.60	.20	3.00	(4)	1.25	
	Coil Stamps, Perf. 9.8 Vertically							
2902	(5¢) Butte	03/10/95	.20	.20	1.60	(5)	1.25	
a	Imperf., pair		750.00					
	Self-Adhesive, Serpentine Die-Cut 11.5 Vertically							
2902B	(5¢) Butte	06/15/96	.20	.20	1.60	(5)	1.25	550
	Perf. 9.8 Vertically							
2903	(5¢) Mountain, purple and multi	03/16/96	.20	.20	1.60	(5)	1.25	150
a	Tagged (error)		*4.00*	3.50	85.00	(5)		
2904	(5¢) Mountain, blue and multi	03/16/96	.20	.20	1.60	(5)	1.25	150
c	Imperf., pair		500.00					
	Self-Adhesive, Serpentine Die-Cut 11.2							
2904A	(5¢) Mountain, purple and multi	06/15/96	.20	.20	1.60	(5)	1.25	
	Self-Adhesive, Serpentine Die-Cut 9.8 Vertically							
2904B	(5¢) Mountain, purple and multi	01/24/97	.20	.20	1.60	(5)	1.25	148
c	Tagged (error)		*4.00*	3.50	85.00	(5)		
	Perf. 9.8 Vertically							
2905	(10¢) Automobile	03/10/95	.20	.20	2.75	(5)	1.25	
	Self-Adhesive, Serpentine Die-Cut 11.5 Vertically							
2906	(10¢) Automobile	06/15/96	.20	.20	2.75	(5)	1.25	450
2907	(10¢) Eagle and Shield	05/21/96	.20	.20	2.75	(5)	1.25	450

2879

2880

2881

2882

2883

2884

2885

2886

2887

2888

2889

2890

2891

2892

2893

2897

2902

2903

2904

2905

2906

2907

For details and illustrations of the new 2001 issues, see pages 22-53.

2908

2909

2910

2911

2912

2913

2914

2915

2916

2919

2920

2921

2933

2934

2935

2936

2938

2940

2941

	Issues of 1995-99		Un	U	PB	#	FDC	Q(M)
	Perf. 9.8 Vertically							
2908	(15¢) Auto Tail Fin, bureau printing	03/17/95	.30	.30	3.25	(5)	1.25	
2909	(15¢) Auto Tail Fin, private printing	03/17/95	.30	.30	3.25	(5)	1.25	
	Self-Adhesive, Serpentine Die-Cut 11.5 Vertically							
2910	(15¢) Auto Tail Fin	06/15/96						
	Perf. 9.8 Vertically							
2911	(25¢) Juke Box, bureau printing	03/17/95	.50	.50	4.50	(5)	1.25	
2912	(25¢) Juke Box, private printing	03/17/95	.50	.50	4.50	(5)	1.25	
	Self-Adhesive, Serpentine Die-Cut 11.5 Vertically							
2912A	(25¢) Juke Box	06/15/96	.50	.50	4.50	(5)	1.25	550
	Self-Adhesive, Serpentine Die-Cut 9.8 Vertically							
2912B	(25¢) Juke Box	01/24/97	.50	.50	4.00	(5)	1.25	20
	Perf. 9.8 Vertically							
2913	32¢ Flag Over Porch	05/19/95	.60	.20	5.75	(5)	1.25	
a	Imperf., pair		60.00					
2914	32¢ Flag Over Porch	05/19/95	.60	.20	5.25	(3)	1.25	
	Self-Adhesive, Serpentine Die-Cut 8.7 Vertically							
2915	32¢ Flag Over Porch	04/18/95	.60	.30	5.25	(5)	1.25	
	Self-Adhesive, Serpentine Die-Cut Perf. 9.8 Vertically							
2915A	32¢ Flag Over Porch	05/21/96	.60	.20	5.25	(5)	1.25	
	Self-Adhesive, Serpentine Die-Cut 11.5 Vertically							
2915B	32¢ Flag Over Porch	06/15/96	.60	.20	5.25	(5)	1.25	
	Self-Adhesive, Serpentine Die-Cut 10.9 Vertically							
2915C	32¢ Flag Over Porch	06/21/96	.60	.20	11.00	(5)	1.25	
	Self-Adhesive, Serpentine Die-Cut 9.8 Vertically							
2915D	32¢ Flag Over Porch	01/24/97	.60	.20	4.75	(5)	1.25	300
	Booklet Stamps, Perf. 10.8 x 9.8 on 2 or 3 adjacent sides							
2916	32¢ Flag Over Porch	05/19/95	.60	.20			1.25	
a	Booklet pane of 10		6.00	3.25			7.50	
b	As "a," imperf.		—					
	Self-Adhesive, Die-Cut							
2919	32¢ Flag Over Field	03/17/95	.60	.20			1.25	
a	Booklet pane of 18		11.00					
	Self-Adhesive, Serpentine Die-Cut 8.7 on 2, 3 or 4 adjacent sides							
2920	32¢ Flag Over Porch	04/18/95	.60	.20			1.25	
a	Booklet pane of 20 + label		12.00					
b	Small date		4.00	.20				
c	As "b," booklet pane of 20 + label		110.00					
f	As #2920, pane of 15 + label		9.00					
h	As #2920, booklet pane of 15		9.00					
	Self-Adhesive, Serpentine Die-Cut 11.3 on 3 sides							
2920D	32¢ Flag Over Porch	01/20/96	.60	.20				789
e	Booklet pane of 10		6.00					
	Self-Adhesive, Serpentine Die-Cut Perf. 9.8 on 2 or 3 sides							
2921	32¢ Flag Over Porch	05/21/96	.60	.20			1.25	7,344
a	Booklet pane of 10		6.00					
b	As #2921, dated red "1997"		.60	.20				
c	As "a," dated red "1997"		6.00					
d	Booklet pane of 5 + label		3.25					
	Great Americans Issue, Perf. 11.2							
2933	32¢ Milton S. Hershey	09/13/95	.60	.20	3.00	(4)	1.25	
2934	32¢ Cal Farley	04/26/96	.60	.20	3.00	(4)	1.25	150
2935	32¢ Henry R. Luce	04/03/98	.60	.20	2.40	(4)	1.25	
2936	32¢ Lila and DeWitt Wallace	07/16/98	.60	.20	2.40	(4)	1.25	
2938	46¢ Ruth Benedict	10/20/95	.90	.20	4.50	(4)	1.40	
2940	55¢ Alice Hamilton, MD	07/11/95	1.10	.20	5.50	(4)	1.40	
	Self-Adhesive, Serpentine Die-Cut 11.7 x 11.5							
2941	55¢ Justin S. Morrill	07/17/99	1.10	.20	4.40	(4)		

	Issues of 1995-1998		Un	U	PB	#	FDC
	Self-Adhesive, Serpentine Die-Cut 11.7 x 11.5						
2942	77¢ Mary Breckenridge	11/09/98	1.50	.20	6.00	(4)	1.75
	Perf. 11.2						
2943	78¢ Alice Paul	08/18/95	1.60	.20	7.50	(4)	1.50
a	78¢ dull violet		1.60	.20	7.50	(4)	
b	78¢ pale violet		1.75	.30	12.00	(4)	
	Love Issue, Perf. 11.2						
2948	(32¢) Love, Cherub from						
	Sistine Madonna, by Raphael	02/01/95	.60	.20	3.00	(4)	1.25
	Self-Adhesive, Die-Cut						
2949	(32¢) Love, Cherub from						
	Sistine Madonna, by Raphael	02/01/95	.60	.20			1.25
a	Booklet pane of 20 + label		12.00				
b	As "a," red (engr.) omitted		—				
	Perf. 11.1						
2950	32¢ Florida Statehood,						
	150th Anniversary	03/03/95	.60	.20	2.40	(4)	1.25
	Kids Care Earth Day Issue, Perf. 11.1 x 11						
2951	32¢ Earth Clean-Up	04/20/95	.60	.20			1.25
2952	32¢ Solar Energy	04/20/95	.60	.20			1.25
2953	32¢ Tree Planting	04/20/95	.60	.20			1.25
2954	32¢ Beach Clean-Up	04/20/95	.60	.20			1.25
a	Block of 4, #2951-54		2.40	1.75	2.40	(4)	2.75
	Perf. 11.2						
2955	32¢ Richard Nixon	04/26/95	.60	.20	3.00	(4)	1.25
a	Red (engr.) omitted		1,400.00				
	Black Heritage Issue						
2956	32¢ Bessie Coleman	04/27/95	.60	.20	3.00	(4)	1.25
	Love Issue						
2957	32¢ Love, Cherub from						
	Sistine Madonna, by Raphael	05/12/95	.60	.20	3.00	(4)	1.25
2958	55¢ Love, Cherub from						
	Sistine Madonna, by Raphael	05/12/95	1.10	.20	5.50	(4)	1.40
	Booklet Stamps, Perf. 9.8 x 10.8						
2959	32¢ Love, Cherub from						
	Sistine Madonna, by Raphael	05/12/95	.60	.20			1.25
a	Booklet pane of 10		6.00	3.25			7.50
	Self-Adhesive, Die-Cut						
2960	55¢ Love, Cherub from						
	Sistine Madonna, by Raphael	05/12/95	1.10	.20			1.40
a	Booklet pane of 20 + label		22.50				
	Recreational Sports Issue, Perf. 11.2						
2961	32¢ Volleyball	05/20/95	.60	.20			1.50
2962	32¢ Softball	05/20/95	.60	.20			1.50
2963	32¢ Bowling	05/20/95	.60	.20			1.50
2964	32¢ Tennis	05/20/95	.60	.20			1.50
2965	32¢ Golf	05/20/95	.60	.20			1.50
a	Vertical strip of 5, #2961-65		3.00	2.00	6.00	(10)	3.25
b	As "a," imperf.						
c	As "a," yellow omitted		2,500.00				
d	As "a," yellow, blue and						
	magenta omitted		2,500.00				
2966	32¢ Prisoners of War						
	and Missing in Action	05/29/95	.60	.20	2.40	(4)	2.00
	Pane of 20		12.00	—			

2942

2943

2948

2950

2951

2953

2952

2954

2955

2954a

2956

2958

2961

2962

2963

2965

2964

2966

2965a

Few other actresses personified the phrase "Hollywood movie star" as did Marilyn Monroe (1926-1962). Classically beautiful, Marilyn set the motion picture standard for glamour and sensuality in film favorites such as *Some Like It Hot, Gentlemen Prefer Blondes, Bus Stop,* and *The Seven Year Itch.*

2967

2968

2969

2970

2971

2972

2973   **2973a**

	Issues of 1995		Un	U	PB	#	FDC
	Legends of Hollywood Issue, Perf. 11.1						
2967	32¢ Marilyn Monroe	06/01/95	.60	.20	4.00	(4)	2.00
a	Imperf., pair		*600.00*				
	Perf. 11.2						
2968	32¢ Texas Statehood	06/16/95	.60	.20	2.40	(4)	1.25
	Great Lakes Lighthouses Issue, Perf. 11.2 Vertically						
2969	32¢ Split Rock, Lake Superior	06/17/95	.60	.20			1.75
2970	32¢ St. Joseph, Lake Michigan	6/17/95	.60	.20			1.75
2971	32¢ Spectacle Reef,						
	Lake Huron	06/17/95	.60	.20			1.75
2972	32¢ Marblehead, Lake Erie	06/17/95	.60	.20			1.75
2973	32¢ Thirty Mile Point,						
	Lake Ontario	06/17/95	.60	.20			1.75
a	Booklet pane of 5, #2969-73		3.00	2.75			5.00

Laura Smith

After graduating from Pasadena's Art
Center College of Design with a major in
illustration, Laura Smith moved to New
York City to jump-start her career.
Thirteen years later, she returned to her
native California and set up shop in
Hollywood. Over the years, she has
gained global recognition for the powerful graphic images she has created for
clients such as HBO, Ted Turner, Capitol
Records, *Time*, *Newsweek*, the New York
Knicks, Levi's, and Major League
Baseball. Her work—inspired by posters
and advertising of the 1930s, 40s, and
50s—has been recognized and honored
by many major award shows. Designer
of the 1996 commemorative stamps
honoring the statehood anniversaries of
Florida and Texas, she shares her
Hollywood studio with graphic
designer/lettering artist Michael Doret. ■

Issues of 1995		Un	U	PB	#	FDC
2974	32¢ United Nations,					
	50th Anniversary	06/26/95	.60	.20	2.40	(4)	1.25
	Civil War Issue, Perf. 10.1						
2975	Sheet of 20	06/29/95	12.00	—			13.00
a	32¢ *Monitor and Virginia*		.60	.20			1.50
b	32¢ Robert E. Lee		.60	.20			1.50
c	32¢ Clara Barton		.60	.20			1.50
d	32¢ Ulysses S. Grant		.60	.20			1.50
e	32¢ Battle of Shiloh		.60	.20			1.50
f	32¢ Jefferson Davis		.60	.20			1.50
g	32¢ David Farragut		.60	.20			1.50
h	32¢ Frederick Douglass		.60	.20			1.50
i	32¢ Raphael Semmes		.60	.20			1.50
j	32¢ Abraham Lincoln		.60	.20			1.50
k	32¢ Harriet Tubman		.60	.20			1.50
l	32¢ Stand Watie		.60	.20			1.50
m	32¢ Joseph E. Johnston		.60	.20			1.50
n	32¢ Winfield Hancock		.60	.20			1.50
o	32¢ Mary Chesnut		.60	.20			1.50
p	32¢ Battle of Chancellorsville		.60	.20			1.50
q	32¢ William T. Sherman		.60	.20			1.50
r	32¢ Phoebe Pember		.60	.20			1.50
s	32¢ "Stonewall" Jackson		.60	.20			1.50
t	32¢ Battle of Gettysburg		.60	.20			1.50

Mark Hess

Raised in Michigan, Mark Hess became a professional bull rider at the age of ten, but science and art captivated him. After studying painting at the University of Colorado, he honed his skills as an apprentice to his father, the acclaimed designer Richard Hess. His strong visual concepts and representational blend of surrealism, irony, and humor attracted industry attention quickly. The recipient of many professional awards and honors, he has created images for such diverse clients as *The New York Times*, *Rolling Stone*, *Newsweek*, Walt Disney Studios, IBM, American Express, and the United States Postal Service, for which he has illustrated 46 stamps. ■

CIVILWAR
1861   THE WAR BETWEEN THE STATES   1865

CLASSIC COLLECTION

MONITOR·VIRGINIA
USA 32

Robert E. Lee
32 USA

Clara Barton
32 USA

Ulysses S. Grant
32 USA

SHILOH
32 USA

Jefferson Davis
32 USA

David Farragut
32 USA

Frederick Douglass
32 USA

Raphael Semmes
32 USA

Abraham Lincoln
32 USA

Harriet Tubman
32 USA

Stand Watie
32 USA

Joseph E. Johnston
32 USA

Winfield Hancock
USA 32

Mary Chesnut
32 USA

PLATE POSITION
S 111

CHANCELLORSVILLE
USA 32

William T. Sherman
32 USA

Phoebe Pember
32 USA

"Stonewall" Jackson
32 USA

GETTYSBURG
32 USA

©1994
United
States
Postal
Service

2975   a   b   c   d   e

f   g   h   i   j

k   l   m   n   o

2976 **2977**

2980

2978 **2979** **2979a**

a **b** **c** **d** **e**

Issues of 1995		Un	U	PB	#	FDC
Carousel Horse Issue, Perf. 11						
2976 32¢ Golden Horse with Roses	07/21/95	.60	.20			1.25
2977 32¢ Black Horse with Gold Bridle	07/21/95	.60	.20			1.25
2978 32¢ Horse with Armor	07/21/95	.60	.20			1.25
2979 32¢ Brown Horse with						
Green Bridle	07/21/95	.60	.20			1.25
a Block of 4, #2976-79		2.40	1.75	2.40	(4)	3.25
Perf. 11.1 x 11						
2980 32¢ Women's Suffrage	08/26/95	.60	.20	3.00	(4)	1.25
a Black (engr.) omitted		425.00				
World War II Issue, 1945: Victory at Last, Miniature Sheet, Perf. 11.1						
2981 Block of 10 and central label	09/02/95	6.00	4.50			7.00
a 32¢ Marines Raise						
Flag on Iwo Jima		.60	.30			1.50
b 32¢ Fierce Fighting Frees Manila						
by March 3, 1945		.60	.30			1.50
c 32¢ Soldiers Advancing: Okinawa,						
the Last Big Battle		.60	.30			1.50
d 32¢ Destroyed Bridge: U.S. and						
Soviets Link Up at Elbe River		.60	.30			1.50
e 32¢ Allies Liberate Holocaust						
Survivors		.60	.30			1.50
f 32¢ Germany Surrenders at Reims		.60	.30			1.50
g 32¢ Refugees: By 1945, World 1.25						
War II Has Uprooted Millions		.60	.30			1.50
h 32¢ Truman Announces Japan's						
Surrender		.60	.30			1.50
i 32¢ Sailor Kissing Nurse: News of						
Victory Hits Home		.60	.30			1.50
j 32¢ Hometowns Honor Their						
Returning Veterans		.60	.30			1.50

William H. Bond

After serving in the British Royal Navy during World War II, William H. Bond studied art at Twickenham Art College and worked with some of England's leading illustrators during the post-war reconstruction of the city of London. Many of his paintings were created for the National Geographic Society during his 36 years as a staff artist there, and appear in the Society's magazines, books, and publications. His art is featured on 58 United States postage stamps, including an extraordinary series of 50 World War II commemorative issues. ■

	Issues of 1995		Un	U	PB	#	FDC	Q(M)
	Legends of American Music Series, Jazz Musicians Issue, Perf. 11.1 x 11							
2982	32¢ Louis Armstrong,							
	white denomination	09/01/95	.80	.20	2.40	(4)	1.25	
2983	32¢ Coleman Hawkins	09/16/95	.80	.20			1.25	
2984	32¢ Louis Armstrong,							
	black denomination	09/16/95	.80	.20			1.25	
2985	32¢ James W. Johnson	09/16/95	.80	.20			1.25	
2986	32¢ Jelly Roll Morton	09/16/95	.80	.20			1.25	
2987	32¢ Charlie Parker	09/16/95	.80	.20			1.25	
2988	32¢ Eubie Blake	09/16/95	.80	.20			1.25	
2989	32¢ Charles Mingus	09/16/95	.80	.20			1.25	
2990	32¢ Thelonious Monk	09/16/95	.80	.20			1.25	
2991	32¢ John Coltrane	09/16/95	.80	.20			1.25	
2992	32¢ Erroll Garner	09/16/95	.80	.20			1.25	
a	Vertical block of 10, #2983-92		8.00	—	8.00	(10)	6.50	
	Pane of 20		16.00	—				
	Garden Flowers Issue, Perf. 10.9 Vertically							
2993	32¢ Aster	09/19/95	.60	.20			1.25	800
2994	32¢ Chrysanthemum	09/19/95	.60	.20			1.25	800
2995	32¢ Dahlia	09/19/95	.60	.20			1.25	800
2996	32¢ Hydrangea	09/19/95	.60	.20			1.25	800
2997	32¢ Rudbeckia	09/19/95	.60	.20			1.25	800
a	Booklet pane of 5, #2993-97		3.00	2.25			4.00	
	Perf. 11.1							
2998	60¢ Eddie Rickenbacker,							
	Aviator	09/25/95	1.25	.25	6.25	(4)	1.50	
a	Large date, 2000		1.25	.25	6.25	(4)		
2999	32¢ Republic of Palau	09/29/95	.60	.20	3.00	(4)	1.25	

Dean Mitchell

Gifted realist painter Dean Mitchell began his experiments with paint when his grandmother gave him a paint-by-number set and encouraged him to explore his talent. After graduating from the Columbus College of Art, he worked as an illustrator for Hallmark and painted to satisfy the need for a more personal form of expression. He exhibited his works widely, and as his success mounted, he embarked on a career as a full-time painter. Since then, his masterful portraits, landscapes, and still-life paintings have received many professional honors and are included in the permanent collections of the

© 1996 JULIE F. ROBERTSON

Nelson-Atkins Museum of Art, the Xerox Corporation, and the Greenwich Workshop among others. His six United States postage stamp designs honor the Jazz Musicians. ■

"The Postal Service art director stressed good, simple, clean design because of the scale of the work when reduced to stamp size."

— Dean Mitchell

2982

2983 2984
2985 2986
2987 2988
2989 2990
2991 2992
2992a

2993 2994 2995 2996 2997 2997a

2998

2999

COMIC STRIP CLASSICS

  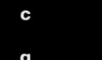

3000	a	b	c	d
	e	f	g	h
	i	j	k	l
	m	n	o	p
	q	r	s	t

Issues of 1995		Un	U	PB	#	FDC
Comic Strip Classics Issue, Perf. 10						
3000 Pane of 20	10/01/95	12.00	—			13.00
a	32¢ The Yellow Kid	.60	.20			1.75
b	32¢ Katzenjammer Kids	.60	.20			1.75
c	32¢ Little Nemo in Slumberland	.60	.20			1.75
d	32¢ Bringing Up Father	.60	.20			1.75
e	32¢ Krazy Kat	.60	.20			1.75
f	32¢ Rube Goldberg's Inventions	.60	.20			1.75
g	32¢ Toonerville Folks	.60	.20			1.75
h	32¢ Gasoline Alley	.60	.20			1.75
i	32¢ Barney Google	.60	.20			1.75
j	32¢ Little Orphan Annie	.60	.20			1.75
k	32¢ Popeye	.60	.20			1.75
l	32¢ Blondie	.60	.20			1.75
m	32¢ Dick Tracy	.60	.20			1.75
n	32¢ Alley Oop	.60	.20			1.75
o	32¢ Nancy	.60	.20			1.75
p	32¢ Flash Gordon	.60	.20			1.75
q	32¢ Li'l Abner	.60	.20			1.75
r	32¢ Terry and the Pirates	.60	.20			1.75
s	32¢ Prince Valiant	.60	.20			1.75
t	32¢ Brenda Starr, Reporter	.60	.20			1.75
Perf 10.9						
3001 32¢ U.S. Naval Academy, 150th Anniversary	10/10/95	.60	.20	2.40	(4)	1.25
Literary Arts Issue, Perf 11.1						
3002 32¢ Tennessee Williams	10/13/95	.60	.20	2.40	(4)	1.25

Bob Timberlake

Bob Timberlake is celebrated for his paintings that depict a fading rural lifestyle in the fast-growing South. Born in Salisbury, North Carolina, he has remained in his home state where he not only creates his popular paintings but also designs homes, furniture, home furnishings, and clothing. In 1995, he received the distinguished alumni award from the University of North Carolina in Chapel Hill—the same year the North Carolina Museum of History held a 25th anniversary retrospective celebrating his career. An avid collector, he surrounds himself with decoys, enamelware, quilts, and other reminders of the simple life he portrays in his paintings. The U.S. Postal Service has issued his designs for three U.S. postage stamps and for a stamped card marking the bicentennial of his alma mater. ■

	Issues of 1995		Un	U	PB	#	FDC
	Christmas Issue, Perf. 11.2						
3003	32¢ Madonna and Child,						
	by Giotto di Bondone	10/19/95	.60	.20	3.00	(4)	1.25
c	Black (engr., denom.) omitted		*250.00*				
	Booklet Stamp, Perf. 9.8 x 10.9						
3003A	32¢ Madonna and Child	10/19/95	.60	.20			1.25
b	Booklet pane of 10		6.00	*4.00*			7.25
3004	32¢ Santa Claus Entering Chimney	09/30/95	.60	.20			1.25
3005	32¢ Child Holding Jumping Jack	09/30/95	.60	.20			1.25
3006	32¢ Child Holding Tree	09/30/95	.60	.20			1.25
3007	32¢ Santa Claus Working on Sled	09/30/95	.60	.20			1.25
a	Block of 4, #3004-07		2.40	1.25	3.00	(4)	3.25
b	Booklet pane of 10, 3 each #3004-05,						
	2 each 3006-07		6.00	*4.00*			7.25
c	Booklet pane of 10, 2 each #3004-05,						
	3 each 3006-07		6.00	*4.00*			7.25
d	As "a," imperf.		*750.00*				
	Self-Adhesive, Serpentine Die-Cut						
3008	32¢ Santa Claus Working on Sled	09/30/95	.60	.20			1.25
3009	32¢ Child Holding Jumping Jack	09/30/95	.60	.20			1.25
3010	32¢ Santa Claus Entering Chimney	09/30/95	.60	.20			1.25
3011	32¢ Child Holding Tree	09/30/95	.60	.20			1.25
a	Booklet pane of 20, 5 each						
	#3008-11 + label		12.00				
3012	32¢ Midnight Angel	10/19/95	.60	.20			1.25
a	Booklet pane of 20 + label		12.00				
	Self-Adhesive, Die-Cut						
3013	32¢ Children Sledding	10/19/95	.60	.20			1.25
a	Booklet pane of 18		11.00				
	Self-Adhesive Coil Stamps, Serpentine Die-Cut Vertically						
3014	32¢ Santa Claus Working on Sled	09/30/95	.60	.30			1.25
3015	32¢ Child Holding Jumping Jack	09/30/95	.60	.30			1.25
3016	32¢ Santa Claus Entering Chimney	09/30/95	.60	.30			1.25
3017	32¢ Child Holding Tree	09/30/95	.60	.30			1.25
a	Strip of 4, #3014-17		2.40		6.50	(8)	3.25
3018	32¢ Midnight Angel	10/19/95	.60	.30	5.00	(5)	1.25

Chris Van Allsburg

Chris Van Allsburg was born in Grand Rapids, Michigan. He studied sculpture in college and exhibited his work in New England and New York City after receiving his graduate degree from the Rhode Island School of Design.

In 1979, he wrote and illustrated *The Garden of Abdul Gasazi*, which became a Caldecott Honor Book. Since then, he has written and illustrated eleven other books, including the Caldecott Medal books *Jumanji* and *The Polar Express*. Foreign language editions of his books have received honors in Europe and Japan. He currently resides in Providence, Rhode Island, with his wife Lisa and daughters, Sophia and Anna. His stamp design for Helping Children Learn was issued by the U.S. Postal Service in 1997. ■

3003

3004 | **3005**

3006 | **3007**

3007a

3008 **3009** **3010** **3011** **3011a**

3012

3013

3019

3020

3021

3022

3023

3023a

3024

3025   3026   3027   3028   3029   3029a

3030   3032   3033   3036   3044

3048   3049   3050   3052

Issues of 1995-1999		Un	U	PB	#	FDC	Q(M)
Antique Automobiles Issue							
3019	32¢ 1893 Duryea	11/03/95	.60	.20			1.25	
3020	32¢ 1894 Haynes	11/03/95	.60	.20			1.25	
3021	32¢ 1898 Columbia	11/03/95	.60	.20			1.25	
3022	32¢ 1899 Winton	11/03/95	.60	.20			1.25	
3023	32¢ 1901 White	11/03/95	.60	.20			1.25	
a	Vertical or horizontal strip of 5, #3019-23		3.00	2.00			3.25	
3024	32¢ Utah Statehood	01/04/96	.60	.20	3.00	(4)	1.25	
Issues of 1996, Garden Flowers Issue, Perf 10.9 Vertically							
3025	32¢ Crocus	01/19/96	.60	.20			1.25	
3026	32¢ Winter Asconite	01/19/96	.60	.20			1.25	
3027	32¢ Pansy	01/19/96	.60	.20			1.25	
3028	32¢ Snowdrop	01/19/96	.60	.20			1.25	
3029	32¢ Anemone	01/19/96	.60	.20			1.25	
a	Booklet pane of 5, #3025-3029		3.00	2.25			4.00	
Love Issue, Serpentine Die-Cut Perf. 11.3							
3030	32¢ Love Cherub from Sistine Madonna, by Raphael	01/20/96	.60	.20			1.25	
a	Booklet pane of 20 + label		12.00					
b	Booklet pane of 15 + label		9.00					
Flora and Fauna Issue, Self-Adhesive, Serpentine Die-Cut 10.5							
3031	1¢ American Kestrel	11/19/99	.20	.20	.25		1.25	120
Perf. 11							
3032	2¢ Red-Headed Woodpecker	02/02/96	.20	.20	.25	(4)	1.25	311
3033	3¢ Eastern Bluebird	04/03/96	.20	.20	.25	(4)	1.25	317
Self-Adhesive, Serpentine Die-Cut 11.5 x 11.25							
3036	$1 Red Fox	08/14/98	2.00	.50	8.00	(4)		
Coil Stamps, Perf. 9.75 Vertically							
3044	1¢ American Kestrel	01/20/96	.20	.20	.65	(5)	1.25	
a	Large date		.20	.20	.90	(5)		
3045	2¢ Red-Headed Woodpecker	6/22/99	.20	.20	.75	(5)	1.25	100
Booklet Stamps, Self-Adhesive, Serpentine Die-Cut 10.5 x 10.75 on 3 sides							
3048	20¢ Blue Jay	08/02/96	.40	.20			1.25	491
a	Booklet pane of 10		4.00					
b	Booklet pane of 4		1.60					
c	Booklet pane of 6		2.40					
Serpentine Die-Cut 11.25 x 11.75 on 2, 3 or 4 sides							
3049	32¢ Yellow Rose	10/24/96	.60	.20			1.25	2,900
a	Booklet pane of 20 and label		12.00					
b	Booklet pane of 4	12/96	2.75					
c	Booklet pane of 5	12/96	3.20					
d	Booklet pane of 6	12/96	3.60					
Serpentine Die-Cut 11.25 on 2 or 3 sides							
3050	20¢ Ring-neck Pheasant	07/31/98	.40	.20			1.25	
a	Booklet pane of 10		4.00					
Serpentine Die-Cut 10.5 x 11 on 3 sides							
3051	20¢ Ring-neck Pheasant	07/99	.40	.20				634
a	Serpentine Die-Cut 10.5 on 3 Sides		.40	.20				
b	Booklet pane of 5, 4 #3051, 1 #3051a turned sideways at top		2.00					
c	Booklet pane of 5, 4 #3051, 1 #3051a turned sideways at bottom		2.00					
Serpentine Die-Cut 11.5 x 11.25 on 2, 3 or 4 sides							
3052	33¢ Coral Pink Rose	8/13/99	.65	.20			1.25	1,000
a	Booklet pane of 4		2.60					
b	Booklet pane of 5 + label		3.25					
c	Booklet pane of 6		3.90					
d	Booklet pane of 20		13.00					

	Issues of 1996-2000		Un	U	PB	#	FDC	Q(M)
	Serpentine Die Cut 10.75 x 10.5 on 2 or 3 Sides							
3052E	33¢ Coral Pink Rose	4/7/00	.65	.20	1.25			
f	Booklet pane of 20		13.00					
	Coil Stamps, Serpentine Die-Cut 11.5 Vertically							
3053	20¢ Blue Jay	08/02/96	.40	.20	3.25	(5)	1.25	330
	Coil Stamps, Self-Adhesive, Serpentine Die-Cut 9.75 Vertically							
3054	32¢ Yellow Rose	08/01/97	.60	.20	5.00	(5)		
a	Imperf., pair		90.00					
3055	20¢ Ring-necked Pheasant	07/31/98	.40	.20	4.00	(5)		
	Black Heritage Issue, Perf. 11.1							
3058	32¢ Ernest E. Just	02/01/96	.60	.20	2.40	(4)	1.25	92
3059	32¢ Smithsonian Institution	02/07/96	.60	.20	2.40	(4)	1.25	115
	Lunar New Year Issue							
3060	32¢ Year of the Rat	02/08/96	.60	.20	2.40	(4)	1.50	93
	Pioneers of Communication Issue, Perf. 11.1 x 11							
3061	32¢ Eadweard Muybridge	02/22/96	.60	.20			1.25	96
3062	32¢ Ottmar Mergenthaler	02/22/96	.60	.20			1.25	96
3063	32¢ Frederic E. Ives	02/22/96	.60	.20			1.25	96
3064	32¢ William Dickson	02/22/96	.60	.20			1.25	96
a	Block or strip of 4, #3061-3064		2.40	1.75	2.40	(4)	3.25	
	Perf. 11.1							
3065	32¢ Fulbright Scholarships	02/28/96	.60	.20	3.00	(4)	1.25	130
	Pioneers of Aviation Issue							
3066	50¢ Jacqueline Cochran	03/09/96	1.00	.20	5.00	(4)	1.35	314
a	Black omitted		70.00					
3067	32¢ Marathon	04/11/96	.60	.20	2.40	(4)	1.25	209

Fred Otnes

Born in Junction City, Kansas, Fred Otnes studied at the Art Institute and the American Academy in Chicago. After graduation he moved to Connecticut where he lives and works today. Renowned for his masterful collages, he has won more than 200 awards for his art, including gold and silver medals from the Society of Illustrators. His work—the subject of numerous articles in design publications— has been widely exhibited and is represented in the collections of many prestigious corporations and institutions such as the National Geographic Society, the National Academy of Science, General Electric, NASA, and IBM. His commissioned illustrations have appeared in *The Atlantic Monthly* and *National Geographic* and on record covers for Atlantic Records. He has created designs for six commemorative stamps, including four collages honoring the Pioneers of Communication, issued by the U.S. Postal Service. ■

3058

3059

3060

3063

3064

3061

FREDERIC E. IVES (1856-1937) Halftone process

WILLIAM DICKSON (1860-1935) Motion pictures

3062

EADWEARD MUYBRIDGE (1830-1904) Photography

OTTMAR MERGENTHALER (1854-1899) Linotype

3064a

3065

3066

3067

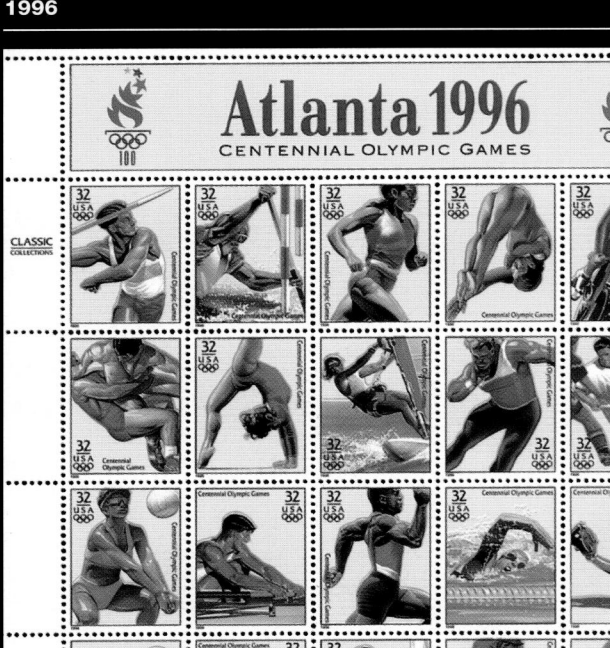

3068   a   b   c   d   e
         f   g   h   i   j
         k   l   m   n   o
         p   q   r   s   t

3069

3070

3072   3073   3074   3075   3076   3076a

	Issues of 1996		Un	U	PB	#	FDC	Q(M)
	Summer Olympic Games Issue, Perf. 11.1							
3068	Pane of 20	05/02/96	12.00	—			13.00	324
a	32¢ Decathlon		.60	.20			1.25	
b	32¢ Canoeing		.60	.20			1.25	
c	32¢ Women's running		.60	.20			1.25	
d	32¢ Women's diving		.60	.20			1.25	
e	32¢ Cycling		.60	.20			1.25	
f	32¢ Freestyle wrestling		.60	.20			1.25	
g	32¢ Women's gymnastic		.60	.20			1.25	
h	32¢ Women's sailboarding		.60	.20			1.25	
i	32¢ Shot put		.60	.20			1.25	
j	32¢ Women's soccer		.60	.20			1.25	
k	32¢ Beach volleyball		.60	.20			1.25	
l	32¢ Rowing		.60	.20			1.25	
m	32¢ Sprinting		.60	.20			1.25	
n	32¢ Women's swimming		.60	.20			1.25	
o	32¢ Women's softball		.60	.20			1.25	
p	32¢ Hurdles		.60	.20			1.25	
q	32¢ Swimming		.60	.20			1.25	
r	32¢ Gymnastics		.60	.20			1.25	
s	32¢ Equestrian		.60	.20			1.25	
t	32¢ Basketball		.60	.20			1.25	
	Perf. 11.6 x 11.4							
3069	32¢ Georgia O'Keeffe	05/23/96	.60	.20	2.75	(4)	1.25	156
a	Imperf., pair		200.00					
	Perf. 11.1							
3070	32¢ Tennessee Statehood	05/31/96	.60	.20	3.00	(4)	1.25	100
	Self-Adhesive, Serpentine Die-Cut 9.9 x 10.8							
3071	32¢ Tennessee Statehood	05/31/96	.60	.30			1.25	60
a	Booklet pane of 20		12.00					
	American Indian Dances Issue, Perf. 11.1							
3072	32¢ Fancy Dance	06/07/96	.60	.20			1.25	139
3073	32¢ Butterfly Dance	06/07/96	.60	.20			1.25	139
3074	32¢ Traditional Dance	06/07/96	.60	.20			1.25	139
3075	32¢ Raven Dance	06/07/96	.60	.20			1.25	139
3076	32¢ Hoop Dance	06/07/96	.60	.20			1.25	139
a	Strip of 5, #3072-3076		3.00	1.75	6.00	(10)	3.50	139

McRay Magleby

A distinguished professor of graphic design at the University of Utah and the recipient of its Distinguished Teaching Award, alumnus McRay Magleby also pursues a freelance design career from his studio in Provo. A highly regarded designer, illustrator, and design competition judge, he was named Designer of the Decade by the Council for Advancement and Support of Education (CASE) in 1986, the same year his *Wave of Peace* poster was voted Most Memorable Poster in the World by design professionals from 40 countries. Cited by *How* magazine as one of today's 12 most influential designers, his designs range from U.S. postage stamps to a stained glass window for the Provo public library, and from fine art paintings and drawings to sculptural designs for the facade of the Utah Governor's Mansion. ■

	Issues of 1996		Un	U	PB	#	FDC	Q(M)
	Prehistoric Animals Issue, Perf. 11.1 x 11							
3077	32¢ Eohippus	06/08/96	.60	.20			1.25	150
3078	32¢ Woolly Mammoth	06/08/96	.60	.20			1.25	150
3079	32¢ Mastodon	06/08/96	.60	.20			1.25	150
3080	32¢ Saber-tooth cat	06/08/96	.60	.20			1.25	150
a	Block or strip of 4, #3077-3080		2.40	1.50	2.40	(4)	3.25	150
	Pane of 20		12.00	—				
	Perf. 11.1							
3081	32¢ Breast Cancer Awareness	06/15/96	.60	.20	2.40	(4)	1.25	96
	Legends of Hollywood Issue, Perf. 11.1							
3082	32¢ James Dean	06/24/96	.60	.20	2.40	(4)	1.75	300
	Pane of 20		12.50	—				
a	Imperf., pair		425.00					
	Folks Heroes Issue, Perf. 11.1 x 11							
3083	32¢ Mighty Casey	07/11/96	.60	.20			1.25	113
3084	32¢ Paul Bunyan	07/11/96	.60	.20			1.25	113
3085	32¢ John Henry	07/11/96	.60	.20			1.25	113
3086	32¢ Pecos Bill	07/11/96	.60	.20			1.25	113
a	Block or strip of 4, #3083-3086		2.40	1.50	2.40	(4)	3.25	
	Centennial Olympic Games Issue, Perf. 11.1							
3087	32¢ Centennial Olympic Games	07/11/96	.65	.20	3.75	(4)	1.25	134
	Pane of 20		17.50	—				
3088	32¢ Iowa Statehood	08/01/96	.60	.20	3.00	(4)	1.25	103
	Booklet Stamp, Self-Adhesive, Serpentine Die-Cut 11.6 x 11.4							
3089	32¢ Iowa Statehood	08/01/96	.60	.30			1.25	60
a	Booklet pane of 20		12.00					
	Perf. 11.2 x 11							
3090	32¢ Rural Free Delivery	08/07/96	.60	.20	2.40	(4)	1.25	134

David LaFleur

A painter, illustrator, and designer, David LaFleur creates strong, whimsical images for clients throughout the nation from his Kansas studio. His designs for posters, billboards, packaging, menus, annual reports, calendars, apparel, CD covers, shopping bags, murals, and greeting cards have been commissioned by an impressive client roster that includes Milton Bradley, Federal Express, Starbucks, Heinz, and General Motors. Among the artist's seven United States postage stamps was the popular self-adhesive issue, Flag Over Porch. His artwork has been exhibited in galleries and museums throughout the United States. ■

3077 Eohippus
3078 Woolly mammoth
3079 Mastodon
3080 Saber-tooth cat
3080a

3081

3082

3083
3086
3085
3084

MIGHTY CASEY
PECOS BILL
JOHN HENRY
PAUL BUNYAN

3086a

3087

3088

3090

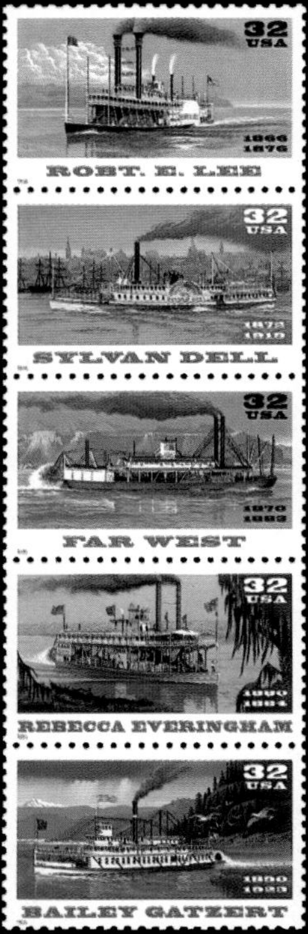

3091
ROBT. E. LEE

3092
SYLVAN DELL

3093
FAR WEST

3094
REBECCA EVERINGHAM

3095
BAILEY GATZERT

3095a

3096
32 USA
COUNT BASIE

3097
32 USA
TOMMY & JIMMY DORSEY

32 USA
GLENN MILLER

32 USA
BENNY GOODMAN

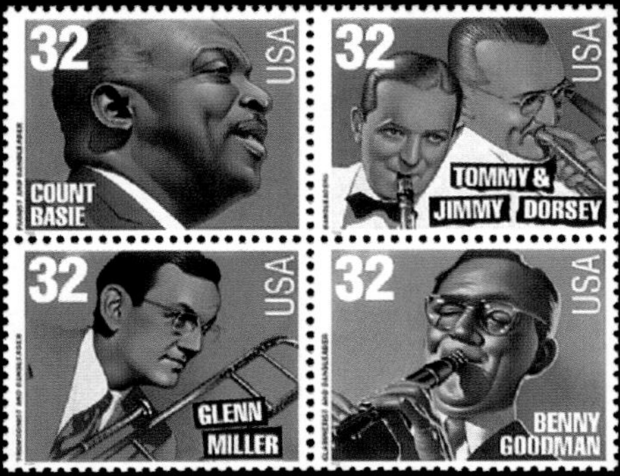

3098   3099   3099a

3100
32 USA
HAROLD ARLEN

3101
32 USA
JOHNNY MERCER

3102
32 USA
DOROTHY FIELDS

32 USA
HOAGY CARMICHAEL

3103

3103a

F. SCOTT FITZGERALD
23 USA

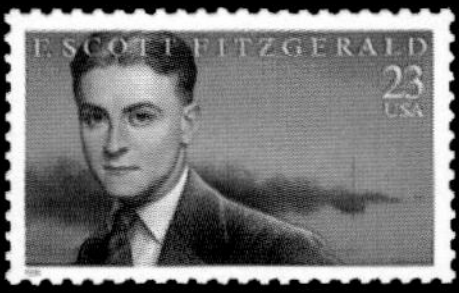

3104

Issues of 1996		Un	U	PB	#	FDC	Q(M)
Riverboats Issue, Serpentine Die-Cut 11 x 11.1							
3091 32¢ Robert E. Lee	08/22/96	.60	.20			1.25	160
3092 32¢ Sylvan Dell	08/22/96	.60	.20			1.25	160
3093 32¢ Far West	08/22/96	.60	.20			1.25	160
3094 32¢ Rebecca Everingham	08/22/96	.60	.20			1.25	160
3095 32¢ Bailey Gatzert	08/22/96	.60	.20			1.25	160
a Vertical strip of 5, #3091-3095		3.00		6.00	(10)	3.50	
b Strip of 5, #3091-3095 with							
special die-cutting		75.00	50.00	140.00	(10)		
Legends of American Music Series, Big Band Leaders Issue, Perf. 11.1 x 11							
3096 32¢ Count Basie	09/11/96	.60	.20			1.25	92
3097 32¢ Tommy and Jimmy Dorsey	09/11/96	.60	.20			1.25	92
3098 32¢ Glenn Miller	09/11/96	.60	.20			1.25	92
3099 32¢ Benny Goodman	09/11/96	.60	.20			1.25	92
a Block or strip of 4, #3096-3099		2.40	1.50	2.40	(4)	3.25	
Legends of American Music Series, Songwriters Issue							
3100 32¢ Harold Arlen	09/11/96	.60	.20			1.25	92
3101 32¢ Johnny Mercer	09/11/96	.60	.20			1.25	92
3102 32¢ Dorothy Fields	09/11/96	.60	.20			1.25	92
3103 32¢ Hoagy Carmichael	09/11/96	.60	.20			1.25	92
a Block or strip of 4, #3100-3103		2.40	1.50	2.40	(4)	3.25	
Literary Arts Issue, Perf. 11.1							
3104 23¢ F. Scott Fitzgerald	09/11/96	.45	.20	2.25	(4)	1.25	300

Bill Nelson

Bill Nelson is an internationally known illustrator and sculptor whose award-winning images have appeared on the covers and pages of *The New York Times Book Review*, *Newsweek*, *Time*, *TV Guide,* and *Atlantic Monthly*. He has also been commissioned to create artwork for such leading companies and agencies as Estée Lauder, Columbia Pictures, Sony, Reebok, The Kennedy Center, Bolla Wine, and the United States Postal Service, for which he has designed 11 stamps. The whimsical elves, gnomes, and fairies that appear in his fantasy sculptures have been exhibited in galleries throughout the world and are featured in the private collections of many celebrities. ■

"The scale that I had to work in seemed impossibly small until I saw the finished, printed stamp."

— Bill Nelson

Issues of 1996		Un	U	PB	#	FDC	Q(M)
	Endangered Species Issue, Perf. 11.1 x 11						
3105	Pane of 15 · · · · · · · · 10/02/96	9.00	—			7.50	224
a	32¢ Black-footed ferret	.60	.20			1.25	
b	32¢ Thick-billed parrot	.60	.20			1.25	
c	32¢ Hawaiian monk seal	.60	.20			1.25	
d	32¢ American crocodile	.60	.20			1.25	
e	32¢ Ocelot	.60	.20			1.25	
f	32¢ Schaus swallowtail butterfly	.60	.20			1.25	
g	32¢ Wyoming toad	.60	.20			1.25	
h	32¢ Brown pelican	.60	.20			1.25	
i	32¢ California condor	.60	.20			1.25	
j	32¢ Gilatrout	.60	.20			1.25	
k	32¢ San Francisco garter snake	.60	.20			1.25	
l	32¢ Woodland caribou	.60	.20			1.25	
m	32¢ Florida panther	.60	.20			1.25	
n	32¢ Piping plover	.60	.20			1.25	
o	32¢ Florida manatee	.60	.20			1.25	
	Perf. 10.9 x 11.1						
3106	32¢ Computer Technology · · · 10/08/96	.60	.20	3.00	(4)	1.25	94
	Christmas Issue, Perf. 11.1 x 11.2						
3107	32¢ Madonna and Child						
	by Paolo de Matteis · · · · 10/08/96	.60	.20	3.00	(4)	1.25	848
	Perf. 11.3						
3108	32¢ Family at Fireplace · · · 10/08/96	.60	.20			1.25	226
3109	32¢ Decorating Tree · · · · 10/08/96	.60	.20			1.25	226
3110	32¢ Dreaming of Santa Claus · 10/08/96	.60	.20			1.25	226
3111	32¢ Holiday Shopping · · · · 10/08/96	.60	.20			1.25	226
a	Block or strip of 4, #3108-3111	2.40	1.50	3.00	(4)	3.25	
	Self-Adhesive Booklet Stamps, Serpentine Die-Cut 10 on 2, 3 or 4 sides						
3112	32¢ Madonna and Child						
	by Paolo de Matteis · · · · 10/08/96	.60	.20			1.25	244
a	Booklet pane of 20 + label	12.00					
b	No die-cutting, pair	*75.00*					
3113	32¢ Family at Fireplace · · · 10/08/96	.60	.20			1.25	1,805
3114	32¢ Decorating Tree · · · · 10/08/96	.60	.20			1.25	1,805
3115	32¢ Dreaming of Santa Claus · 10/08/96	.60	.20			1.25	1,805
3116	32¢ Holiday Shopping · · · · 10/08/96	.60	.20			1.25	1,805
a	Booklet pane, 5 ea #3113-3116	12.00				3.25	
	Die-Cut						
3117	32¢ Skaters · · · · · · · · 10/08/96	.60	.20			1.25	495
a	Booklet pane of 18	11.00					
	Self-Adhesive, Serpentine Die-Cut 11.1						
3118	32¢ Hanukkah · · · · · · · 10/22/96	.60	.20	2.40	(4)	1.25	104
	Cycling Issue, Perf. 11 x 11.1						
3119	32¢ Souvenier sheet of 2 · · 11/01/96	2.00	2.00			2.50	
a	50¢ orange	1.00	1.00			1.50	
b	50¢ blue and green	1.00	1.00			1.50	

Endangered Species

National Stamp Collecting Month 1996 highlights these 18 species to promote awareness of endangered wildlife. Each generation must work to protect the delicate balance of nature, so that future generations may share a sound and healthy planet.

3105

a b c

d e f

g h i

j k l

m n o

3106

3107

3111a

3108   3111

3109   3110

3117   3118

3119a   3119b

3120

3121

3122

3123

3124

3125

3126

3127

3130

3131

3132

3133

3134

3135

	Issues of 1997		Un	U	PB	#	FDC	Q(M)
	Lunar New Year Issue, Perf. 11.2							
3120	32¢ Year of the Ox	01/05/97	.60	.20	2.40	(4)	1.50	106
	Black Heritage Issue, Serpentine Die-Cut 11.4							
3121	32¢ Brig. Gen. Benjamin							
	O. Davis Sr.	01/28/97	.60	.20	2.40	(4)	1.25	112
	Self-Adhesive Booklet Stamps, Serpentine Die-Cut 11 on 2, 3 or 4 sides							
3122	32¢ Statue of Liberty,							
	Type of 1994	02/01/97	.60	.20			1.25	2,855
a	Booklet panel of 20 + label		12.00					
b	Booklet pane of 4		2.50					
c	Booklet pane of 5 + label		3.20					
d	Booklet pane of 6		3.60					
	Self-Adhesive, Serpentine Die-Cut 11.5 x 11.8 on 2, 3 or 4 sides							
3122E	32¢ Statue of Liberty		.90	.20				
f	Booklet pane of 20 + label		35.00					
g	Booklet pane of 6		5.50					
	Self-Adhesive, Serpentine Die-Cut 11.8 x 11.6 on 2, 3 or 4 sides							
3123	32¢ Love Swans	02/04/97	.60	.20			1.25	1,660
a	Booklet pane of 20 + label		12.00					
b	No die-cutting, pair		250.00					
	Serpentine Die-Cut 11.6 x 11.8 on 2, 3 or 4 sides							
3124	55¢ Love Swans	02/04/97	1.00	.20			1.50	814
a	Booklet pane of 20 + label		21.00					
	Self-Adhesive, Serpentine Die-Cut 11.6 x 11.7							
3125	32¢ Helping Children Learn	02/18/97	.60	.20	2.40	(4)	1.25	122
	Merian Botanical Print Issues, Self-Adhesive,							
	Serpentine Die-Cut 10.9 x 10.2 on 2, 3 or 4 sides							
3126	32¢ Citron, Roth, Larvae,							
	Pupa, Beetle	03/03/97	.60	.20			1.25	2,048
3127	32¢ Flowering Pineapple,							
	Cockroaches	03/03/97	.60	.20			1.25	2,048
a	Booklet pane, 10 each #3126-3127 + label		12.00					
b	Pair, #3126-3127		1.20					
	Serpentine Die-Cut 11.2 x 10.8 on 2 or 3 sides							
3128	32¢ Citron, Roth, Larvae,							
	Pupa, Beetle	03/03/97	.60	.20			1.25	30
b	Booklet pane, 2 each #3128-3129		3.00					
3129	32¢ Flowering Pineapple,							
	Cockroaches	03/03/97	.60	.20			1.25	30
b	Booklet pane of 5,							
	2 each #3128-29, 1 #3129a		3.00					
c	Pair, #3128-3129		1.20					
	Pacific 97 Issues, Perf. 11.2							
3130	32¢ Sailing Ship	03/13/97	.60	.20			1.25	130
3131	32¢ Stagecoach	03/13/97	.60	.20			1.25	130
a	Pair #3130-31		1.25	.30	2.50	(4)	1.75	
	Coil Stamps, Self-Adhesive, Imperf.							
3132	25¢ Juke Box	03/14/97	.50	.50	4.50	(5)	1.25	24
	Coil Stamps, Serpentine Die-Cut 9.9 Vertically							
3133	32¢ Flag Over Porch	03/14/97	.60	.20	4.75	(5)	1.25	1
	Literary Arts Issue, Perf. 11.1							
3134	32¢ Thornton Wilder	04/17/97	.60	.20	2.40	(4)	1.25	98
3135	32¢ Raoul Wallenberg	04/24/97	.60	.20	2.40	(4)	1.50	96

	Issues of 1997		Un	U	FDC	Q(M)
	The World of Dinosaurs Issue, Perf. 11 x 11.1					
3136	Sheet of 15	05/01/97	9.00	—	7.50	219
a	32¢ Ceratosaurus		.60	.20	1.25	
b	32¢ Camptosaurus		.60	.20	1.25	
c	32¢ Camarasaurus		.60	.20	1.25	
d	32¢ Brachiosaurus		.60	.20	1.25	
e	32¢ Goniopholis		.60	.20	1.25	
f	32¢ Stegosaurus		.60	.20	1.25	
g	32¢ Allosaurus		.60	.20	1.25	
h	32¢ Opisthias		.60	.20	1.25	
i	32¢ Edmontonia		.60	.20	1.25	
j	32¢ Einiosaurus		.60	.20	1.25	
k	32¢ Daspletosaurus		.60	.20	1.25	
l	32¢ Palaeosaniwa		.60	.20	1.25	
m	32¢ Corythosaurus		.60	.20	1.25	
n	32¢ Ornithominus		.60	.20	1.25	
o	32¢ Parasaurolophus		.60	.20	1.25	
	Looney Tunes Issue, Self-Adhesive, Serpentine Die-Cut 11					
3137	Bugs Bunny Pane of 10	05/22/97	6.00			265
a	32¢ single		.60	.20	1.75	
b	Booklet pane of 9		5.40			
c	Booklet pane of 1		.60			
	Die-cutting on #3137b does not extend through the backing paper.					
3138	Pane of 10	05/22/97	*125.00*			
a	32¢ single		*2.00*			
b	Booklet pane of 9		—			
c	Booklet pane of 1, imperf.		—			
	Die-cutting on #3138b extends through the backing paper.					

James Gurney

Introduced to dinosaurs during a childhood museum visit, James Gurney studied anthropology at the University of California, Berkeley, and art at the Art Center College of Design in Los Angeles. His lavishly painted images bring realism to his work in fantasy and reveal his appreciation of both art and science.

Though he is best known for his highly acclaimed *Dinotopia* books, he has illustrated more than 70 science fiction and fantasy book covers, created historical and archeological illustrations for *National Geographic*, and worked as a background painter for an animated film. His World of Dinosaurs commemorative pane features 15 United States postage stamps. ■

"I wanted to recreate the full texture of the environment in order to make the postage stamps useful as an educational tool."

— James Gurney

3136   a   b   c   d   f   g

e   h

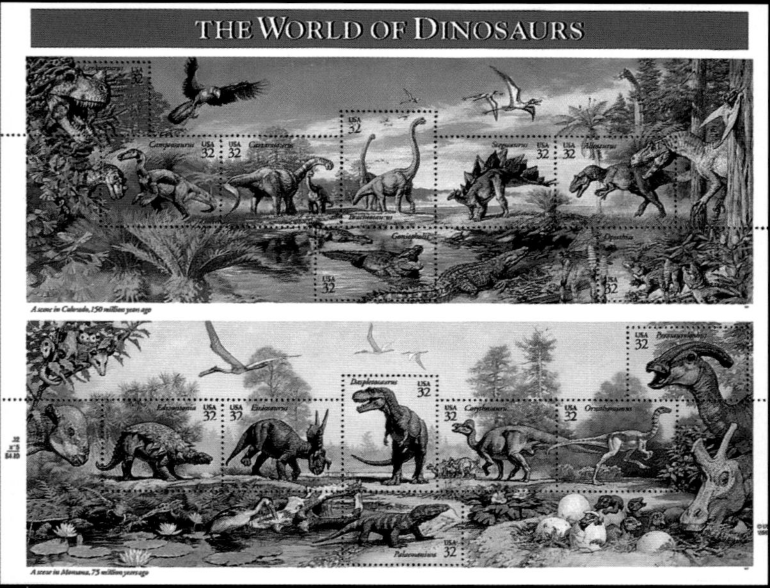

THE WORLD OF DINOSAURS

A scene in Colorado, 150 million years ago

A scene in Montana, 75 million years ago

i   j   k   m   n   o

l

3139

3140

Issues of 1997		Un	U	PB	#	FDC	Q(M)
Pacific 97 Issue, Perf. 10.5 x 10.4							
Benjamin Franklin							
3139 Pane of 12	05/29/97	12.00	—			12.00	56
a 50¢ single		1.00	.50			2.00	
George Washington							
3140 Pane of 12	05/30/97	14.50	—			14.50	56
a 60¢ single		1.20	.60			2.50	
The Marshall Plan, 50th Anniversary Issue, Perf. 11.1							
3141 32¢ The Marshall Plan	06/04/97	.60	.20	2.40	(4)	1.25	45

Marvin Mattelson

A renowned portrait painter and illustrator, Marvin Mattelson studied at the Philadelphia College of Art and refined his skills in classical painting techniques before setting out on a career as a freelance artist. During his 30-year career, his award-winning images for magazines, movie posters, and packaging have been commissioned by such prominent clients as *Time*, *Newsweek*, *National Geographic*, Dream Works, CBS, and Angel Records. His portraits are included in the permanent collection of the Smithsonian Institution and in many corporate and private collections. A respected teacher at the School of Visual Arts in New York, his artwork appears on two U.S. Postal Service Love stamps. ■

	Issues of 1997		Un	U	PB	#	FDC	Q(M)
	Classic American Aircraft Issue, Perf. 10.1							
3142	Pane of 20	07/19/97	12.00	—			15.00	161
a	32¢ Mustang		.60	.20			1.50	
b	32¢ Model B		.60	.20			1.50	
c	32¢ Cub		.60	.20			1.50	
d	32¢ Vega		.60	.20			1.50	
e	32¢ Alpha		.60	.20			1.50	
f	32¢ B-10		.60	.20			1.50	
g	32¢ Corsair		.60	.20			1.50	
h	32¢ Stratojet		.60	.20			1.50	
i	32¢ Gee Bee		.60	.20			1.50	
j	32¢ Staggerwing		.60	.20			1.50	
k	32¢ Flying Fortress		.60	.20			1.50	
l	32¢ Stearman		.60	.20			1.50	
m	32¢ Constellation		.60	.20			1.50	
n	32¢ Lightning		.60	.20			1.50	
o	32¢ Peashooter		.60	.20			1.50	
p	32¢ Tri-Motor		.60	.20			1.50	
q	32¢ DC-3		.60	.20			1.50	
r	32¢ 314 Clipper		.60	.20			1.50	
s	32¢ Jenny		.60	.20			1.50	
t	32¢ Wildcat		.60	.20			1.50	
	Legendary Football Coaches Issue, Perf. 11.2							
3143	32¢ Bear Bryant	07/25/97	.60	.20			1.50	90
3144	32¢ Pop Warner	07/25/97	.60	.20			1.50	90
3145	32¢ Vince Lombardi	07/25/97	.60	.20			1.50	90
3146	32¢ George Halas	07/25/97	.60	.20			1.50	90
a	Block or strip of 4, #3143-3146		2.40	—	2.40	(4)	4.00	

William S. Phillips

Renowned aviation artist William S. Phillips has had a love affair with flight for as long as he can remember. While in the Air Force during the Vietnam War, he took time to sketch military aircraft and spectacular cloud formations and began to sell his work. His research has taken him throughout the world, bringing him to the center of such combat missions and natural disasters as the Gulf War and the eruption of Mount St. Helens. A recipient of the Navy's Meritorious Public Service Award, he has been honored with a retrospective exhibition of his work at the National Air and Space Museum. His work appears in books, on limited-edition prints, and on 20 Classic American Aircraft stamps for the United States Postal Service. ■

"I had dreamed of having my work on a stamp from the time I was a small boy, when I saw my first Air Mail stamp."

— William S. Phillips

CLASSIC AMERICAN AIRCRAFT

Mustang 32 USA	Model B 32 USA	Cub 32 USA	Vega 32 USA
Alpha 32 USA	B-10 32 USA	Corsair 32 USA	Stratojet 32 USA
Gee Bee 32 USA	Staggerwing 32 USA	Flying Fortress 32 USA	Stearman 32 USA
Constellation 32 USA	Lightning 32 USA	Peashooter 32 USA	Tri-Motor 32 USA
DC-3 32 USA	314 Clipper 32 USA	Jenny 32 USA	Wildcat 32 USA

CLASSIC COLLECTION

.32 x20 $6.40

© 1996 United States Postal Service

3142

a	b	c	d
e	f	g	h
i	j	k	l
m	n	o	p
q	r	s	t

LEGENDARY Football Coaches

3145 **3146** **3143** **3144** **3146a**

3147

3148

3149

3150

CLASSIC
American Dolls

32
×15
$4.80

PLATE
POSITION
F11111

"Alabama Baby" and Martha Chase
"Baby Coos"
Ludwig Greiner

"The Columbian Doll"
Plains Indian
"Babs McCall"

Johnny Gruelle's "Raggedy Ann"
Izannah Walker
Percy Crosby's "Skippy"

Martha Chase
"Babyland Rag"
"Maggie Mix-up"

"American Child"
"Scootles"
Albert Schoenhut

The above names include doll makers, designers, trade names and common names.

3151   a   b   c   d   e

Issues of 1997		Un	U	PB	#	FDC	Q(M)
Legendary Football Coaches Issue with Red Bar above Coach's Name, Perf. 11							
3147	32¢ Vince Lombardi	08/05/97	.60	.30	2.40	(4)	1.50	20
3148	32¢ Bear Bryant	08/07/97	.60	.30	2.40	(4)	1.50	20
3149	32¢ Pop Warner	08/08/97	.60	.30	2.40	(4)	1.50	10
3150	32¢ George Halas	08/16/97	.60	.30	2.40	(4)	1.50	10
Classic American Dolls Issue, Perf. 10.9 x 11.1							
3151	Pane of 15	07/28/97	9.00	—			8.00	105
a	32¢ "Alabama Baby," and doll by Martha Chase		.60	.20			1.50
b	32¢ "Columbian Doll"		.60	.20			1.50
c	32¢ Johnny Gruelle's "Raggedy Ann"		.60	.20			1.50
d	32¢ Doll by Martha Chase		.60	.20			1.50
e	32¢ "American Child"		.60	.20			1.50
f	32¢ "Baby Coos"		.60	.20			1.50
g	32¢ Plains Indian		.60	.20			1.50
h	32¢ Doll by Izannah Walker		.60	.20			1.50
i	32¢ "Babyland Rag"		.60	.20			1.50
j	32¢ "Scootles"		.60	.20			1.50
k	32¢ Doll by Ludwig Greiner		.60	.20			1.50
l	32¢ "Betsy McCall"		.60	.20			1.50
m	32¢ Percy Crosby's "Skippy"		.60	.20			1.50
n	32¢ "Maggie Mix-up"		.60	.20			1.50
o	32¢ Dolls by Albert Schoenhut		.60	.20			1.50

Daniel A. Moore

An artist and an athlete, Daniel A. Moore studied commercial art and painting at the University of Alabama. Nationally acclaimed for his skillful realist paintings capturing great moments in sports history, he is the founder of New Life Art, a publishing company that issues fine limited-edition prints. He has also created images for such pro-fessional sports organizations as the National Football League, Major League Baseball, and the Professional Golf Association of America, and has illustrated four United States postage stamp honoring the achievements of Legendary Football Coaches. ∎

"I found it particularly rewarding to actually use the stamps created from my artwork."

— Daniel Moore

	Issues of 1997		Un	U	PB	#	FDC	Q(M)
	Legends of Hollywood Issue, Perf. 11.1							
3152	32¢ Humphrey Bogart	07/31/97	.60	.20	2.50	(4)	1.25	195
3153	32¢ "The Stars and Stripes							
	Forever"	08/21/97	.60	.20	3.00	(4)	1.25	323
	Legends of American Music Series, Opera Singers Issue, Perf. 11							
3154	32¢ Lily Pons	09/10/97	.65	.20			1.25	86
3155	32¢ Richard Tucker	09/10/97	.65	.20			1.25	86
3156	32¢ Lawrence Tibbett	09/10/97	.65	.20			1.25	86
3157	32¢ Rosa Ponselle	09/10/97	.65	.20			1.25	86
a	Block or strip of 4, #3154-3157		2.60	—	2.60	(4)	3.25	

Michael J. Deas

A classicist whose images seem to radiate light from within, Michael Deas is among the most accomplished realist painters of our day. Inclined to faithfully record the visual world, he attended art school in New York and turned to the art of the Old Masters for inspiration and information about traditional oil painting techniques. In addition to book cover illustration, he has painted for advertising, redesigned the logos for Columbia and Tri Star Pictures, and turned his brush to eight United States postage stamps. He is the recipient of many professional honors and awards. ∎

"Stamps are like tiny icons. Only one person can look at them at a time. That's what I like about them."

— Michael Deas

3152

3153

3154

3155

3156

3157

3157a

3158   3159   3160   3161

3162   3163   3164   3165   3165a

3167

3166

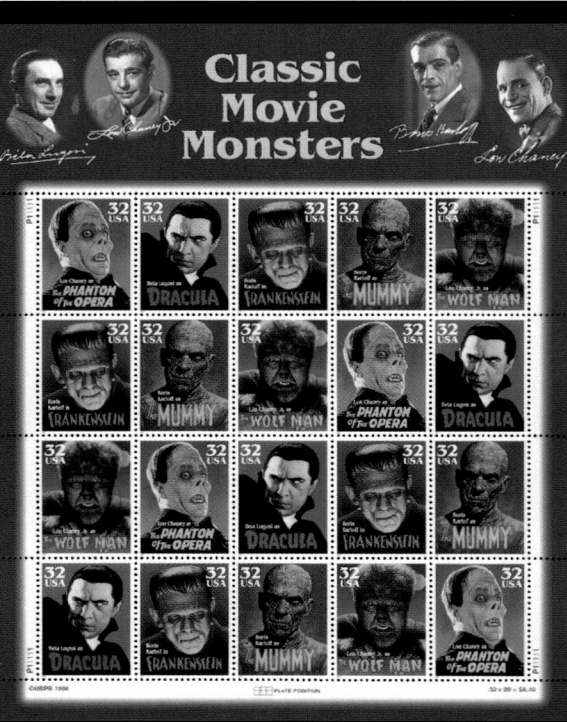

3169   3170   3171   3172   3168

	Issues of 1997		Un	U	PB	#	FDC	Q(M)
	Legends of American Music Series, Classical Composers & Conductors Issue, Perf. 11							
3158	32¢ Leopold Stokowski	09/12/97	.65	.20			1.25	86
3159	32¢ Arthur Fiedler	09/12/97	.65	.20			1.25	86
3160	32¢ George Szell	09/12/97	.65	.20			1.25	86
3161	32¢ Eugene Ormandy	09/12/97	.65	.20			1.25	86
3162	32¢ Samuel Barber	09/12/97	.65	.20			1.25	86
3163	32¢ Ferde Grofé	09/12/97	.65	.20			1.25	86
3164	32¢ Charles Ives	09/12/97	.65	.20			1.25	86
3165	32¢ Louis Moreau Gottschalk	09/12/97	.65	.20			1.25	86
a	Block of 8, #3158-3165		5.25	—	5.25	(8)	5.25	
	Perf. 11.2							
3166	32¢ Padre Félix Varela	09/15/97	.60	.20	2.40	(4)	1.25	2,855
	Department of the Air Force, 50th Anniversary Issue, Perf. 11.2 x 11.1							
3167	32¢ Thunderbirds Aerial Demonstration Squadron	09/18/97	.60	.20	2.40	(4)	1.25	45
	Classic Movie Monsters Issue, Perf. 10.2							
3168	32¢ Lon Chaney as the Phantom of the Opera	09/30/97	.60	.20			1.25	145
3169	32¢ Bela Lugosi as Dracula	09/30/97	.60	.20			1.25	145
3170	32¢ Boris Karloff as Frankenstein's Monster	09/30/97	.60	.20			1.25	145
3171	32¢ Boris Karloff as the Mummy	09/30/97	.60	.20			1.25	145
3172	32¢ Lon Chaney Jr. as the Wolf Man	09/30/97	.60	.20			1.25	145
a	Strip of 5, #3168-3172		3.00	—	6.00	(10)	3.75	

Beginning with No. 3167, a hidden 3-D design can be seen on some stamps when they are viewed with a special viewer sold by the post office.

Burton Silverman

Burton Silverman's art grows out of his responses to the world around him in his native New York City. His illustration career began with a commission to create a series of instructional drawings for *Sports Illustrated* in 1961. Since then, his masterful images have appeared in children's books, advertisements, and magazines for such prominent clients as *Time, Life, The New Yorker*, Exxon, CBS, Heinz, and IBM. As a distinguished easel painter, he has received many professional honors for his work, which has been exhibited at museums and galleries throughout the world. The artist's portraits focus on the interior worlds of his subjects and are featured on 12 United States postage stamps. ■

"The stamp program has really been a sort of national portrait gallery, and this appealed to me very much."

— Burton Silverman

Issues of 1997-98		Un	U	PB	#	FDC	Q(M)
Self-Adhesive, Serpentine Die-Cut 11.4							
3173 32¢ First Supersonic Flight,							
50th Anniversary	10/14/97	.60	.20	2.40	(4)	1.25	173
Perf. 11.1							
3174 32¢ Women in Military Service	10/18/97	.60	.20	2.40	(4)	1.25	
Self-Adhesive, Serpentine Die-Cut 11							
3175 32¢ Kwanzaa	10/22/97	.60	.20	3.00	(4)	1.25	133
Holiday Traditional Issue, Self-Adhesive Booklet Stamps, Serpentine Die-Cut 9.9							
on 2, 3 or 4 sides							
3176 32¢ Madonna and Child by							
Sano di Pietro	10/09/97	.60	.20			1.25	883
a Booklet pane of 20 + label		12.00					
Holiday Contemporary Issue, Self-Adhesive Booklet Stamps, Serpentine							
Die-Cut 11.2 x 11.8 on 2, 3 or 4 sides							
3177 32¢ American Holly	10/30/97	.60	.20			1.25	180
a Booklet pane of 20 + label		12.00					
b Booklet pane of 4		2.50					
c Booklet pane of 5 + label		3.00					
d Booklet pane of 6		3.75					
Mars Pathfinder, Perf. 11 x 11.1							
3178 $3 Mars Rover Sojourner	12/10/97	6.00	3.00			6.00	15
a $3, single stamp		5.50	2.75				
Lunar New Year Issue, Perf. 11.2							
3179 32¢ Year of the Tiger	01/05/98	.60	.20	2.40	(4)	1.25	

Synthia Saint James

Self-taught artist Synthia Saint James, a native of Los Angeles, California, began her career as an artist in New York City where, at age 19, she sold her first commissioned paintings. Today this inter-nationally recognized artist is also an award-winning author, illustrator, and

songwriter. Among her many awards are the Coretta Scott King Honor Award for Illustration, Oppenheim Gold Award, and National Parenting Publications Gold Award. Well known for her book covers, including *Waiting to Exhale* by Terry McMillan and *Acts of Faith* by Iyanla Vanzant, she designed the award-winning Kwanzaa stamp issued by the U.S. Postal Service in 1997. She has created commissioned art for more than 30 commissions for major organiza-tions, corporations, and individual collectors including Coca-Cola, *Essence* magazine, Maybelline, the Natural History Museum of Los Angeles, and attor-ney Johnnie L. Cochran, Jr. The designer of a 150-foot-long ceramic tile art mural in California's Ontario airport, she has also written and illustrated chil-dren's books and a cookbook. ■

73

3174

3176

3177

3178

3179

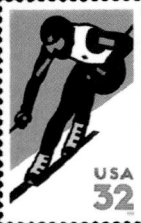

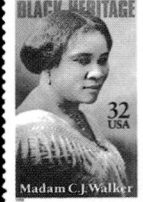

USA
32

BLACK HERITAGE
32
USA
Madam C.J. Walker

3180 3181

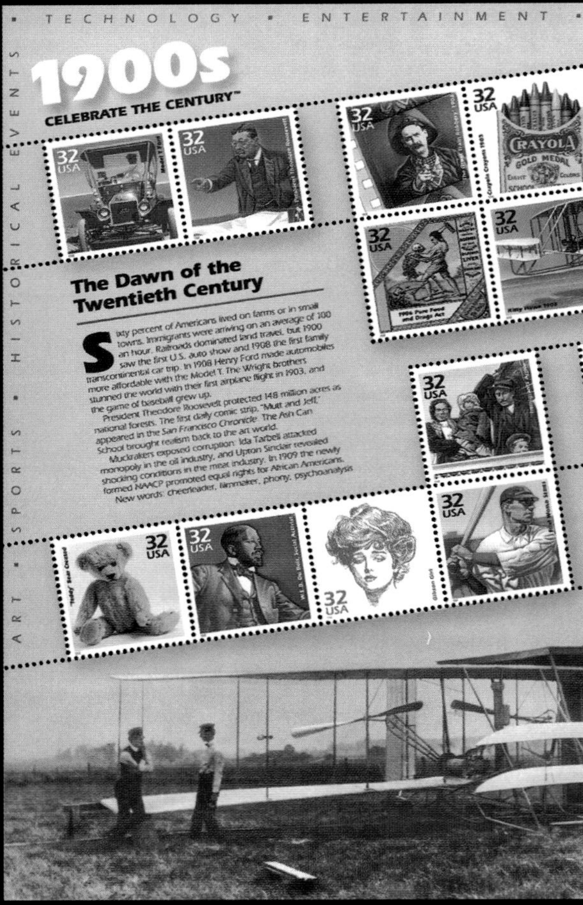
TECHNOLOGY • ENTERTAINMENT •
HISTORICAL EVENTS • SPORTS • ART •
1900s
CELEBRATE THE CENTURY™
32 USA
CRAYOLA
GOLD MEDAL
The Dawn of the Twentieth Century
Sixty percent of Americans lived on farms or in small towns. Immigrants were arriving on an average of 100 an hour. Railroads dominated land travel, but 1900 saw the first U.S. auto show and 1908 the first family transcontinental car trip. In 1908 Henry Ford made automobiles more affordable with the Model T. The Wright brothers stunned the world with their first airplane flight in 1903, and the game of baseball grew up.
President Theodore Roosevelt protected 148 million acres as national forests. The first daily comic strip, "Mutt and Jeff," appeared in the San Francisco Chronicle. The Ash Can School brought realism back to the art world.
Muckrakers exposed corruption: Ida Tarbell attacked monopoly in the oil industry, and Upton Sinclair revealed shocking conditions in the meat industry. In 1909 the newly formed NAACP promoted equal rights for African Americans.
New words: cheerleader, filmmaker, phony, psychoanalysis

3182 a b c d

f g

i

k l m n

Issues of 1998			Un	U	PB	#	FDC	Q(M)
Winter Sports Issue, Perf. 11.2								
3180	32¢ Winter Sports-Skiing	1/2/98	.60	.20	2.40	(4)	1.25	80
Black Heritage Issue, Self-Adhesive, Serpentine Die-Cut 11.6 x 11.3								
3181	32¢ Madam C. J. Walker	1/28/98	.60	.20	2.40	(4)	1.25	45
Celebrate The Century® Issue, Perf. 11.5								
3182	Pane of 15, 1900-1909	2/3/98	9.00	—			7.50	188
a	32¢ Model T Ford		.60	.30			1.25	
b	32¢ Theodore Roosevelt		.60	.30			1.25	
c	32¢ Motion picture, "The Great Train Robbery"		.60	.30			1.25	
d	32¢ Crayola Crayons introduced, 1903		.60	.30			1.25	
e	32¢ St. Louis World's Fair, 1904		.60	.30			1.25	
f	32¢ Design used on Hunt's Remedy stamp (#RS56), Pure Food & Drug Act, 1906		.60	.30			1.25	
g	32¢ Wright Brothers first flight, Kitty Hawk, 1903		.60	.30			1.25	
h	32¢ Boxing match shown in painting "Stag at Sharkey's," by George Bellows of the Ash Can School		.60	.30			1.25	
i	32¢ Immigrants arrive		.60	.30			1.25	
j	32¢ John Muir, preservationist		.60	.30			1.25	
k	32¢ "Teddy" Bear created		.60	.30			1.25	
l	32¢ W.E.B. Du Bois, social activist		.60	.30			1.25	
m	32¢ Gibson Girl		.60	.30			1.25	
n	32¢ First baseball World Series, 1903		.60	.30			1.25	
o	32¢ Robie House, Chicago, designed by Frank Lloyd Wright		.60	.30			1.25	

Richard Waldrep

Highly acclaimed for his artistic versatility, Richard Waldrep studied art at the University of Georgia and was a 15-year partner at Baltimore's Eucalyptus Tree Studio before setting out as a freelance artist. During his 28-year career, he has created award-winning illustrations for such editorial, publishing, advertising, and corporate clients as *Men's Health*, *U.S. News and World Report*, *The Washington Post*, Berkley Press, McDonald's, Parker Brothers, and others. His paintings honoring subjects as varied as the Olympic Games and American music and history have appeared on 39 United States postage stamps. ■

Issues of 1998		Un	U	FDC	Q(M)
Celebrate The Century® Issue, Perf. 11.5					
3183 Pane of 15, 1910-1919	02/03/98	9.00	—	7.50	188
a 32¢ Charlie Chaplin as the Little Tramp		.60	.30	1.25	
b 32¢ Federal Reserve System created, 1913		.60	.30	1.25	
c 32¢ George Washington Carver		.60	.30	1.25	
d 32¢ Avant-garde art introduced at Armory Show, 1913		.60	.30	1.25	
e 32¢ First transcontinental telephone line, 1914		.60	.30	1.25	
f 32¢ Panama Canal opens, 1914		.60	.30	1.25	
g 32¢ Jim Thorpe wins decathlon at Stockholm Olympics, 1912		.60	.30	1.25	
h 32¢ Grand Canyon National Park, 1919		.60	.30	1.25	
i 32¢ U.S. enters World War I		.60	.30	1.25	
j 32¢ Boy Scouts started in 1910, Girl Scouts formed in 1912		.60	.30	1.25	
k 32¢ Woodrow Wilson		.60	.30	1.25	
l 32¢ First crossword puzzle published, 1913		.60	.30	1.25	
m 32¢ Jack Dempsey wins heavyweight title, 1919		.60	.30	1.25	
n 32¢ Construction toys		.60	.30	1.25	
o 32¢ Child labor reform		.60	.30	1.25	

Dennis Lyall

An Iowa native and graduate of the University of Kansas, Dennis Lyall was still an art student when his art was awarded a prestigious gold medal by the Society of Illustrators in New York. During his 30-year career as an illustrator, he has created images for America's leading advertising agencies, corporations, and publishers. He is also an accomplished portraitist whose work is included in many public and private collections including those of the United States Air Force and the United States Coast Guard. His diverse client roster includes *Reader's Digest*, *National Geographic*, Random House, General Electric, and the United States Postal Service, for which he has illustrated 34 stamps. ■

"Stamps are very much like other projects, at least in the concept stage. I decide what is most important and build on the theme."

— Dennis Lyall

1998

· TECHNOLOGY · ENTERTAINMENT · SCIENCE ·

1910s
CELEBRATE THE CENTURY™

America Looks Beyond its Borders

Halley's comet lit up the sky to begin the decade. American workers began moving from farms to factories. The Ford Motor Co. refined the automobile assembly line. Traffic lights and white line dividers became part of the American landscape. Scientific and technological achievements changed society. In 1911, in New York, fingerprint evidence was used for the first time in the United States to arrest a burglar. Jim Thorpe was an international sports star, but Tarzan was an even more popular hero.

The accidental sinking of the luxury liner Titanic shocked the nation, but it was the sinking of another ship, the Lusitania, that upset society, leading to U.S. involvement in World War I. Two million American soldiers fought in Europe and more than 116,500 lost their lives. Americans saw the light as the decade ended: Daylight saving time was instituted in 1918.

New words: camouflage, electronics, troublemaker

I WANT YOU

TOYS

3183   a   b   c

1998

• TECHNOLOGY • ENTERTAINMENT • SCIENCE •

1920s
CELEBRATE THE CENTURY™

The Roaring Twenties

Two Constitutional amendments went into effect in 1920, turning the nation upside down. The 18th Amendment prohibited the manufacture and sale of alcoholic beverages, and the 19th gave women the right to vote. Prohibition backfired, leading to widespread disrespect for the law. A federal highway system was organized and the number of automobiles nearly tripled. Spreading electrification spurred the golden age of radio.

The Roaring Twenties, as the decade came to be known, was an age of thrill seekers and heroes. In 1926, Gertrude Ederle swam the English Channel faster than any man had. The following year Charles Lindbergh flew nonstop across the Atlantic alone and Babe Ruth hit 60 home runs.

The first feature-length film with talking parts, *The Jazz Singer*, appeared in 1927 and the first Academy Awards were presented in 1929. The prosperous times ended with the stock market crash of Thursday, October 24, 1929.

New words: motel, robot, fan mail, teenage.

3184   a   b   c   d   e

Issues of 1998		Un	U	FDC	Q(M)
Celebrate The Century® Issue, Perf. 11.5					
3184	Pane of 15, 1920-1929 5/28/98	9.00	—	7.50	188
a	32¢ Babe Ruth	.60	.30	1.25	
b	32¢ The Gatsby style	.60	.30	1.25	
c	32¢ Prohibition enforced	.60	.30	1.25	
d	32¢ Electric toy trains	.60	.30	1.25	
e	32¢ Nineteenth Amendment (woman voting)	.60	.30	1.25	
f	32¢ Emily Post's Etiquette	.60	.30	1.25	
g	32¢ Margaret Mead, anthropologist	.60	.30	1.25	
h	32¢ Flappers do the Charleston	.60	.30	1.25	
i	32¢ Radio entertains America	.60	.30	1.25	
j	32¢ Art Deco style (Chrysler Building)	.60	.30	1.25	
k	32¢ Jazz flourishes	.60	.30	1.25	
l	32¢ Four Horsemen of Notre Dame	.60	.30	1.25	
m	32¢ Lindbergh flies the Atlantic	.60	.30	1.25	
n	32¢ American realism (The Automat, by Edward Hopper)	.60	.30	1.25	
o	32¢ Stock Market crash, 1929	.60	.30	1.25	

Davis Meltzer

After studying at the Philadelphia Museum School of Art, Davis Meltzer spent four years in the Air Force during the Korean conflict before embarking on a career as a professional artist. Since 1958, he has created images for advertising and publishing and has acquired an extensive collection of research materials on almost every subject. The National Geographic Society, NASA, *Reader's Digest*, *Newsweek,* and Time-Life Books are among the many clients that have published his richly detailed illustrations. His illustrations appear on 25 United States postage stamps. ∎

"Most every stamp subject offered me was well-suited to my field of knowledge."

— Davis Meltzer

Issues of 1998			Un	U	FDC	Q(M)
Celebrate The Century Issue®, Perf. 11.5						
3185	Pane of 15, 1930-1939	9/10/98	9.00	—	7.50	188
a	32¢ Franklin D. Roosevelt		.60	.30	1.25	
b	32¢ The Empire State Building		.60	.30	1.25	
c	32¢ First Issue of Life Magazine, 1936		.60	.30	1.25	
d	32¢ Eleanor Roosevelt		.60	.30	1.25	
e	32¢ FDR's New Deal		.60	.30	1.25	
f	32¢ Superman arrives, 1938		.60	.30	1.25	
g	32¢ Household conveniences		.60	.30	1.25	
h	32¢ "Snow White and the Seven Dwarfs," 1937		.60	.30	1.25	
i	32¢ "Gone with the Wind," 1936		.60	.30	1.25	
j	32¢ Jesse Owens		.60	.30	1.25	
k	32¢ Streamline design		.60	.30	1.25	
l	32¢ Golden Gate Bridge		.60	.30	1.25	
m	32¢ America survives the Depression		.60	.30	1.25	
n	32¢ Bobby Jones wins Grand Slam, 1938		.60	.30	1.25	
o	32¢ The Monopoly Game		.60	.30	1.25	

Paul Calle

Paul Calle is a celebrated visual historian whose award-winning illustrations have chronicled America's heritage. A master painter and draftsman, he has documented our nation's space explorations in NASA's fine art program, and was commissioned by the United States Postal Service to create a stamp honoring the First Man on the Moon in 1969. Two paintings commemorating the 25th anniversary of this event are among his 37 memorable stamp designs. His work has been exhibited nationally and abroad at the National Gallery of Art, the National Air and Space Museum, the U.S. Department of the Interior, and in museums in Russia and Poland. ■

"I always investigate and try a number of approaches to each stamp design. I try to envision all possible solutions to the subject being portrayed."

— Paul Calle

TECHNOLOGY • ENTERTAINMENT • SCIENCE

1930s
CELEBRATE THE CENTURY™

Depression, Dust Bowl, and a New Deal

By 1933 the average wage was 60 percent less than in 1929 and unemployment had skyrocketed to 25 percent. Dust storms forced many farmers to give up their land.

Americans escaped harsh realities by playing Monopoly, reading the adventures of "Buck Rogers" and "Flash Gordon," and listening to Hoagy Carmichael's "Stardust." Popular films included King Kong and It Happened One Night. For the first time, African-American athletes became national idols. Joe Louis in boxing and Jesse Owens in track and field.

Prohibition was repealed in 1933. President Franklin Roosevelt fought the Great Depression with his New Deal programs. The "Star-Spangled Banner" was chosen as the national anthem. The Empire State Building rose above the Manhattan skyline and the Golden Gate Bridge spanned the San Francisco Bay. Back on the ground, the parking meter made its first appearance in 1935.

As the decade closed, many Americans were anxious about the growing war in Europe.

New words: all-star, oops, pizza, racism

3185   a   b   c   d   e

3186   a   b   c

Issues of 1999		Un	U	FDC	Q(M)
Celebrate The Century®, Perf. 11.5					
3186 Pane of 15, 1940-1949	02/18/99	9.75		7.50	12.5
a	33¢ World War II	.65	.30	1.25	
b	33¢ Antibiotics save lives	.65	.30	1.25	
c	33¢ Jackie Robinson	.65	.30	1.25	
d	33¢ Harry S. Truman	.65	.30	1.25	
e	33¢ Women support war effort	.65	.30	1.25	
f	33¢ TV entertains America	.65	.30	1.25	
g	33¢ Jitterbug sweeps nation	.65	.30	1.25	
h	33¢ Jackson Pollock, Abstract Expressionist	.65	.30	1.25	
i	33¢ GI Bill, 1944	.65	.30	1.25	
j	33¢ The Big Band Sound	.65	.30	1.25	
k	33¢ International style of architecture	.65	.30	1.25	
l	33¢ Postwar baby boom	.65	.30	1.25	
m	33¢ Slinky craze begins, 1945	.65	.30	1.25	
n	33¢ Broadway Hit, 1947	.65	.30	1.25	
o	33¢ Orson Welles' "Citizen Kane"	.65	.30	1.25	

Howard Koslow

Howard Koslow began his art training as a scholarship student at Pratt Institute in New York and served as an apprentice to the renowned French poster artist Jean Carlu. As a participant in the United States Air Force Historical Art Program, he has traveled on assignment exten-  sively. Beautifully realized, his paintings of military, historical, and travel subjects reflect his intensive research and painstaking attention to accuracy and detail. His work has been commissioned by NASA, the National Park Service, the United States Coast Guard, The Franklin Mint, Jacques Cousteau, and Random House among others. He has designed 40 United States postage stamps. ■

"Stamp design has allowed me, in a small way, to participate in the pictorial documentation of our American history."

— Howard Koslow

	Issues of 1999		Un	U	FDC	Q(M)
	Celebrate The Century®, Perf. 11.5					
3187	Pane of 15, 1950-1959	5/26/99	9.75	—	7.50	12.5
a	33¢ Polio vaccine developed		.65	.30	1.25	
b	33¢ Teen fashions		.65	.30	1.25	
c	33¢ The "Shot Heard 'Round the World"		.65	.30	1.25	
d	33¢ U.S. launches satellites		.65	.30	1.25	
e	33¢ Korean War		.65	.30	1.25	
f	33¢ Desegregating public schools		.65	.30	1.25	
g	33¢ Tail fins, chrome		.65	.30	1.25	
h	33¢ Dr. Seuss' "The Cat in the Hat"		.65	.30	1.25	
i	33¢ Drive-in movies		.65	.30	1.25	
j	33¢ World Series rivals		.65	.30	1.25	
k	33¢ Rocky Marciano, undefeated		.65	.30	1.25	
l	33¢ "I Love Lucy"		.65	.30	1.25	
m	33¢ Rock 'n Roll		.65	.30	1.25	
n	33¢ Stock car racing		.65	.30	1.25	
o	33¢ Movies go 3-D		.65	.30	1.25	

Dean Ellis

Dean Ellis studied art at the Cleveland Institute of Art and the Boston Museum School of Fine Arts, refining his skills as a painter and illustrator after serving as an infantryman in the Pacific during World War II. Named one of America's most prominent painters by *Life* magazine in 1950, he has enjoyed a successful five-decade career as an artist and illustrator. His striking images have appeared on book covers for science fiction, mystery, and best-selling novels, and his exquisite portraits hang in prominent institutions throughout the country. The first of his many United States postage stamp designs was created when postage was just six cents. ■

"The diminutive size of stamps is always a prime consideration. I try to use the famous design principle: less is more."

— Dean Ellis

TECHNOLOGY ▪ ENTERTAINMENT ▪ SCIENCE

1950s
CELEBRATE THE CENTURY™

POLITICAL FIGURES ▪ LIFESTYLE

HISTORICAL EVENTS ▪ SPORTS ▪ ART

Family Fun, Suburbia, and Nuclear Threats

The 1950s were, for the most part, years of peace and prosperity. Millions of families moved to the suburbs. Americans liked Dwight D. Eisenhower, their kindly war-hero President.

Television became popular; *I Love Lucy* and *Gunsmoke* were hits. Teenagers chose their own fashions and music. Elvis Presley thrilled young people and shocked their elders.

The decade also had a serious side. The Korean War took more than 50,000 American lives. The first hydrogen bomb was detonated. In 1954 the U.S. Supreme Court declared racial segregation in public schools unconstitutional, and in 1955, in Montgomery, Alabama, Rosa Parks refused to give up her bus seat to a white man. But in 1957 President Eisenhower had to use the Arkansas National Guard and paratroopers to enforce integration at a Little Rock high school.

In January 1959 Alaska was admitted as the 49th state, and in August Hawaii became the 50th state.

New words: brainwashing, ballpoint, high-rise, centerfold

3187   a   b   c   d   e

                   f   g   h

                   i   j

        k   l   m   n   o

3188   a   b   c   d   e

Issues of 1999		Un	U	FDC	Q(M)
Celebrate The Century®, Perf. 11.5					
3188 Pane of 15, 1960-1969	9/17/99	9.75	—	7.50	8
a	33¢ "I have a dream"	.65	.30	1.25	
b	33¢ Woodstock	.65	.30	1.25	
c	33¢ Man walks on the moon	.65	.30	1.25	
d	33¢ Green Bay Packers	.65	.30	1.25	
e	33¢ Star Trek	.65	.30	1.25	
f	33¢ The Peace Corps	.65	.30	1.25	
g	33¢ The Vietnam War	.65	.30	1.25	
h	33¢ Ford Mustang	.65	.30	1.25	
i	33¢ Barbie Doll	.65	.30	1.25	
j	33¢ The integrated circuit	.65	.30	1.25	
k	33¢ Lasers	.65	.30	1.25	
l	33¢ Super Bowl I	.65	.30	1.25	
m	33¢ Peace Symbol	.65	.30	1.25	
n	33¢ Roger Maris, 61 in '61	.65	.30	1.25	
o	33¢ The Beatles	.65	.30	1.25	

Keith Birdsong

A former journalist and self-taught artist, Keith Birdsong has been painting for 15 years. His powerful images have appeared in films, on book covers, and on collectors' plates for the Hamilton Collection and the Bradford Exchange. One of the major artistic contributors to George Lucas' *Star Wars*, he has also created designs for 13 United States postage stamps. These include an issuance honoring Native American Indian dance and six stamps that look back at the 1960s on a Celebrate The Century® pane. ■

"My stamp images emerged through terrific team work. Ideas did not come just from me, but from a task force of creative minds."

— Keith Birdsong

	Issues of 1999	Un	U	FDC	Q(M)
	Celebrate The Century®, Perf. 11.5				
3189	Pane of 15, 1970-1979 11/18/99	9.75	—	7.50	6
a	33¢ Earth Day celebrated	.65	.30	1.25	
b	33¢ TV series "All in the Family"	.65	.30	1.25	
c	33¢ "Sesame Street"	.65	.30	1.25	
d	33¢ Disco music	.65	.30	1.25	
e	33¢ Steelers win four Super Bowls	.65	.30	1.25	
f	33¢ U.S. celebrates 200th birthday	.65	.30	1.25	
g	33¢ Secretariat wins the Triple Crown	.65	.30	1.25	
h	33¢ VCRs transform entertainment	.65	.30	1.25	
i	33¢ Pioneer 10	.65	.30	1.25	
j	33¢ Women's Rights Movement	.65	.30	1.25	
k	33¢ 1970s fashions	.65	.30	1.25	
l	33¢ "Monday Night Football"	.65	.30	1.25	
m	33¢ America smiles	.65	.30	1.25	
n	33¢ Jumbo jet	.65	.30	1.25	
o	33¢ Medical imaging	.65	.30	1.25	

Kazuhiko Sano

A native of Japan, Kazuhiko Sano studied painting in Tokyo before moving to San Francisco in 1974 to study at the Academy of Art College, where he was awarded a merit scholarship and baccalaureate and masters degrees. During his 20-year career as a freelance illustrator and painter, he has created  advertising art and movie promotions for such prestigious clients as Lucasfilm, Coca-Cola, and American Express. His beautifully conceived images featuring subjects from the 1970s appear on 12 United States postage stamps in the Celebrate The Century® series. The artist's original works have been exhibited at the Central Museum in Tokyo and the Museum of American Illustration in New York. ■

"I enjoyed every moment of my work on stamps, and for all the scrutiny, it was still a lot easier than working on a movie promotion or an advertising illustration."

— Kazuhiko Sano

3189   a   b   c

3190   a   b   c   d   e

            f   g   h   i   j

            k   l   m

            n   o

CTC Issues of 2000		Un	U	FDC	Q(M)
Celebrate The Century®, Perf. 11.6					
3190 Pane of 15, 1980-1989	1/12/00	9.75	—	7.50	6
a	33¢ Space Shuttle Program	.65	.30	1.25	
b	33¢ "Cats", Broadway show	.65	.30	1.25	
c	33¢ San Fransico 49ers	.65	.30	1.25	
d	33¢ Hostages Come Home	.65	.30	1.25	
e	33¢ Figure Skating	.65	.30	1.25	
f	33¢ Cable TV	.65	.30	1.25	
g	33¢ Vietnam Veterans Memorial	.65	.30	1.25	
h	33¢ Compact Discs	.65	.30	1.25	
i	33¢ Cabbage Patch Kids	.65	.30	1.25	
j	33¢ "The Cosby Show"	.65	.30	1.25	
k	33¢ Fall of the Berlin Wall	.65	.30	1.25	
l	33¢ Video Games	.65	.30	1.25	
m	33¢ "E.T. The Extra-Terrestrial"	.65	.30	1.25	
n	33¢ Personal Computers	.65	.30	1.25	
o	33¢ Hip-Hop Culture	.65	.30	1.25	

Robert Rodriguez

New Orleans native Robert Rodriguez studied at the Chouinard Art Institute and has created powerful realist images for advertising, books, magazines, album covers, and movie posters since 1969. His art celebrating World Cup Soccer for AirTouch Cellular Phone Service was unveiled as a large-scale mural that hangs high above Broadway in downtown Los Angeles. The National Federation of Labor, Super Bowl XXVI, and the Royal Caribbean Classic PGA Tour are among his clients. The illustrator of 13 United States postage stamps, he received international attention when Cinco de Mayo was issued jointly by the United States Postal Service and the Mexican Postal Service in 1998. ■

"I had been trying to find out who to contact about doing a stamp when a Postal Service art director called me . . . Stamps touch people in a very personal way."

— Robert Rodriguez

CTC Issues of 2000			Un	U	FDC	Q(M)
Celebrate The Century®, Perf. 11.6						
3191	Pane of 15, 1990-1999	5/2/00	9.75	—	7.50	5.5
a	33¢ New Baseball Records		.65	.30	1.25	
b	33¢ Gulf War		.65	.30	1.25	
c	33¢ "Seinfeld", television series		.65	.30	1.25	
d	33¢ Extreme Sports		.65	.30	1.25	
e	33¢ Improving Education		.65	.30	1.25	
f	33¢ Computer Art and Graphics		.65	.30	1.25	
g	33¢ Recovering Species		.65	.30	1.25	
h	33¢ Return to Space		.65	.30	1.25	
i	33¢ Special Olympics		.65	.30	1.25	
j	33¢ Virtual Reality		.65	.30	1.25	
k	33¢ "Jurassic Park"		.65	.30	1.25	
l	33¢ "Titanic"		.65	.30	1.25	
m	33¢ Sports Utility Vehicle		.65	.30	1.25	
n	33¢ World Wide Web		.65	.30	1.25	
o	33¢ Cellular Phones		.65	.30	1.25	

Drew Struzan

A child who could draw almost before he could talk, Drew Struzan's future seemed indelibly charted at an early age. After graduating from the Art Center College of Design, he remained in Los Angeles, the heart of the entertainment business. His early professional assignments came from record industry clients for which he created dozens of album covers. Widely seen, they showcased his abilities and attracted movie industry attention. A master of the hand-painted poster, he has created images for more than 150 films including *E.T. the Extra-Terrestrial* and the *Star Wars*, *Indiana Jones,* and *Back to the Future* trilogies. His artwork appears on 29 United States postage stamps. ■

"Historic accuracy is the most important element, in my mind, to the Postal Service. Millions of citizens see stamps, every one with an opinion."

— Drew Struzan

1998

3192

3193   3194   3195   3196   3197   3197a

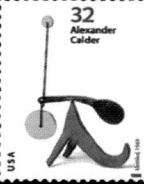   

3198   3199   3200   3201   3202   3202a

3203

 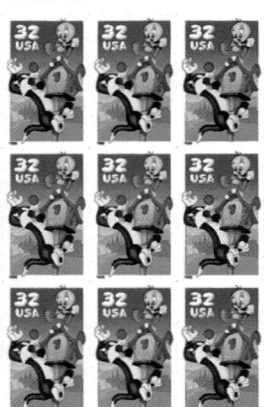 

3204b

Issues of 1998		Un	U	PB	#	FDC	Q(M)
Perf. 11.2 x 11							
3192 "Remember the Maine"							
Spanish-American War	2/15/98	.60	.20	2.40	(4)	1.25	30
Flowering Trees Issue, Die-Cut, Perf. 11.3							
3193 32¢ Southern Magnolia	3/19/98	.60	.20			1.25	
3194 32¢ Blue Paloverde	3/19/98	.60	.20			1.25	
3195 32¢ Yellow Poplar	3/19/98	.60	.20			1.25	
3196 32¢ Prairie Crab Apple	3/19/98	.60	.20			1.25	
3197 32¢ Pacific Dogwood	3/19/98	.60	.20			1.25	
a Strip of 5, #3193-3197	3/19/98	3.00		6.00	(10)	3.75	250
Alexander Calder Issue, Perf. 10.2							
3198 32¢ Black Cascade	3/25/98	.60	.20			1.25	
3199 32¢ Untitled	3/25/98	.60	.20			1.25	
3200 32¢ Rearing Stallion	3/25/98	.60	.20			1.25	
3201 32¢ Portrait of a Young Man	3/25/98	.60	.20			1.25	
3202 32¢ Un Effet du Japonais	3/25/98	.60	.20			1.25	
a Strip of 5, #3198-3202	3/25/98	3.00		6.00	(10)	3.75	80
Holiday Celebrations Issue, Self-Adhesive, Serpentine Die-Cut 11.7 x 10.9							
3203 32¢ Cinco de Mayo	4/16/98	.60	.20	2.40	(4)	1.25	85
Looney Tunes Issue, Self-Adhesive, Serpentine Die-Cut 11.1							
3204 Sylvester & Tweety Pane of 10	4/27/98	6.00					300
a 32¢ single		.60	.20			1.50	
b Booklet pane of 9, #3204a		5.40					
c Booklet pane of 1, #3204a		.60					

Gary Kelley

Renowned illustrator Gary Kelley has created award-winning images for many of America's major publications and corporations including *Time*, *The Atlantic Monthly*, *Rolling Stone*, the National Football League, and the Santa Fe Opera. Educated in his native Iowa at the University of Northern Iowa, he received an honorary doctor of humane letters from his alma mater in 1995. His work—honored by the Society of Illustrators as Best in Show as well as with gold and silver medals—has been exhibited throughout the U.S. as well as in Tokyo and Paris. He has lectured and taught at the Smithsonian Institution, the Corcoran School of Art, and the Art Center College of Art, among others. In 1998 the U.S. Postal Service issued his designs for four commemorative stamps. ∎

	Issues of 1998		Un	U	PB	#	FDC	Q(M)
	Self-Adhesive, Serpentine Die-Cut 10.8 x 10.9							
3206	32¢ Wisconsin Statehood	05/29/98	.60	.30	2.40	(4)	1.25	16
	American Scenes Issue, Coil Stamps, Perf. 10 Vertically							
3207	5¢ Wetlands (Nonprofit)	06/05/98	.20	.20	1.65	(5)	1.25	
	Coil Stamps, Self-Adhesive, Serpentine Die-Cut 9.7 Vertically							
3207A	5¢ Wetlands (Nonprofit)	12/04/98	.20	.20	1.65	(5)	1.25	650
	American Culture Issue, Coil Stamps, Perf. 10 Vertically							
3208	25¢ Diner	06/05/98	.50	.50	4.00	(5)	1.25	400
	Coil Stamps, Self-Adhesive, Serpentine Die-Cut 9.7 Vertically							
3208A	25¢ Diner	09/30/98	.50	.50	4.00	(5)	1.25	
	1898 Trans-Mississippi Reissue, Perf. 12 x 12.4							
3209	Pane of 9	06/18/98	7.75	5.00			6.50	19.8
a	1¢ Marquette on the Mississippi		.20	.20			1.25	
b	2¢ Mississippi River Bridge		.20	.20			1.25	
c	4¢ Indian Hunting Buffalo		.20	.20			1.25	
d	5¢ Fremont on the Rocky Mountains		.20	.20			1.25	
e	8¢ Troops Guarding Train		.20	.20			1.25	
f	10¢ Hardships of Emigration		.20	.20			1.25	
g	50¢ Western Mining Prospector		1.00	.60			1.50	
h	$1 Western Cattle in Storm		2.00	1.25			2.00	
i	$2 Farm in the West		4.00	2.50			4.00	
3210	Pane of 9 #3209h	06/18/98	18.00	—			15.00	
	Perf. 11.2							
3211	32¢ Berlin Airlift	06/26/98	.60	.20	2.40	(4)	1.25	30

Tom Engeman

Nationally acclaimed artist Tom Engeman, a resident of Kensington, Maryland, is well known for his poster and stamp designs. The winner of numerous design awards, he lists among his career accomplishments being the first art director for *Washingtonian* magazine, designing *Historic Preservation* magazine, and creating posters for the Washington subway system which were stolen as soon as they went up. His favorite stamp tale goes back to an early morning in July 1994, at the local post office in a small town in Idaho. Just ending a month-long drawing and painting trip, he was waiting in line to see which of his designs appeared on the newly issued Liberty stamp. From behind him someone called out to the postmaster, "Hey Bonnie, has that new Liberty stamp come in yet?" She replied, "Yes, and it's BEAUTIFUL!" In Tom's words, "You can imagine what that felt like to me, the designer of the stamp. I stayed and autographed stamps, glowing in my personal 15 minutes of fame." ■

3206

3207A

3208A

1998 Bi-Color Re-Issue of the 1898 Trans-Mississippi Stamp Designs

3209

a	b	c
d	e	f
g	h	i

3210

3211

1998

3212   **3213**

3214   **3215**   **3215a**

3219   **3218**

3216   **3217**   **3219a**

3220   **3221**

3222   **3223**

3225a

Issues of 1998		Un	U	PB	#	FDC	Q(M)
American Music Series, Folk Musicians, Perf. 10.1 x 10.2							
3212	32¢ Huddle "Leadbelly"						
	Ledbetter 6/26/98	.60	.20			1.25	
3213	32¢ Woody Guthrie 6/26/98	.60	.20			1.25	
3214	32¢ Sonny Terry 6/26/98	.60	.20			1.25	
3215	32¢ Josh White 6/26/98	.60	.20			1.25	
a	Block or strip of 4, #3212-3215 6/26/98	2.40	—	2.40	(4)	3.25	45
Legends of American Music Series, Gospel Singers Issue, Perf. 10.1 x 10.3							
3216	32¢ Mahalia Jackson 7/15/98	.60	.20			1.25	
3217	32¢ Roberta Martin 7/15/98	.60	.20			1.25	
3218	32¢ Clara Ward 7/15/98	.60	.20			1.25	
3219	32¢ Sister Rosetta Tharpe 7/15/98	.60	.20			1.25	
a	Block or strip of 4, #3216-3219 7/15/98	2.40	—	2.40	(4)	3.25	45
	Perf. 11.2						
3220	32¢ Spanish Settlement of						
	the Southwest 7/11/98	.60	.20	2.40	(4)	1.25	46
	Literary Arts Series						
3221	32¢ Stephen Vincent Benét 7/22/98	.60	.20	2.40	(4)	1.25	
	Tropical Birds Issue						
3222	32¢ Antillean Euphonia 7/29/98	.60	.20			1.25	
3223	32¢ Green-throated Carib 7/29/98	.60	.20			1.25	
3224	32¢ Crested Honeycreeper 7/29/98	.60	.20			1.25	
3225	32¢ Cardinal Honeyeater 7/29/98	.60	.20			1.25	
a	Block of 4, #3222-3225	2.40	—	2.40	(4)	3.25	70

Bernard Fuchs

Known for his fluid, evocative images, Bernard Fuchs began his career in Detroit where his automotive illustrations for advertising were an immediate success. His award-winning artwork has appeared in most national publications including *Fortune, Sports Illustrated*, *Esquire*, *Look,* and *Lithopinion*, a magazine that has encouraged him to travel and paint such varied events as the races at Longchamp in Paris, France, and the running of the bulls in Pamplona, Spain. A celebrated innovator in the field of illustration, he was inducted into the Society of Illustrators Hall of Fame in 1975. His artwork appears on five United States postage stamps. ■

1998

Issues of 1998		Un	U	PB	#	FDC	Q(M)
Legends of Hollywood Issue, Perf. 11.1							
3226	32¢ Alfred Hitchcock 8/3/98	.60	.20	2.40	(4)	1.25	65
Self-Adhesive, Serpentine Die-Cut 11.7							
3227	32¢ Organ & Tissue Donation 8/5/98	.60	.20	2.40	(4)	1.25	25
Coil Stamp, Self-Adhesive, Serpentine Die-Cut 9.8 Vertically							
3228	(10¢) Green Bicycle 8/14/98	.20	.20	2.50	(5)	1.25	
Coil Stamp, Perf. 9.9 Vertically							
3229	(10¢) Green Bicycle 8/14/98	.20	.20	2.50	(5)	1.25	
Bright Eyes Issue, Self-Adhesive, Serpentine Die-Cut 9.9							
3230	32¢ Dog 8/20/98	.60	.20			1.25	
3231	32¢ Goldfish 8/20/98	.60	.20			1.25	
3232	32¢ Cat 8/20/98	.60	.20			1.25	
3233	32¢ Parakeet 8/20/98	.60	.20			1.25	
3234	32¢ Hamster 8/20/98	.60	.20			1.25	
a	Strip of 5, #3230-3234 8/20/98	3.00		6.00	(8)	3.25	180
Perf. 11.1							
3235	32¢ Klondike Gold Rush 8/21/98	.60	.20	2.40	(4)	1.25	28

John C. Berkey

A staff artist at Brown & Bigelow for eight years, John Berkey produced more than 500 calendar images featuring everything from pastoral scenes to historic tableaus. He turned to freelance illustration in 1963 and has never looked back. Renowned for his robust, impressionist style, he has created paintings for book covers, movie posters, advertisements, and such periodicals as *National Geographic*, *Life*, *Time,* and *TV Guide*. Among those attracted to his masterful science fiction illustrations was the young George Lucas, who commissioned him to work on the pre-production designs for *Star Wars*. His images appear on 16 United States postage stamps. ■

3226

3227

3228

3230

3231

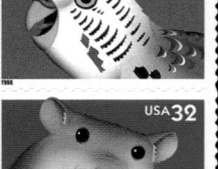

3232

3233

3234

3234a

3235

FOUR CENTURIES OF
American Art

John Foster (1648-1681) 32 USA	The Freake Limner (fl.c.1670) 32 USA	James Phillips (1788-1866) 32 USA	Rembrandt Peale (1778-1860) 32 USA	John James Audubon (1785-1851) 32 USA
George Caleb Bingham (1811-1879) 32 USA	Asher B. Durand (1796-1886) 32 USA	Joshua Johnson (active 1796-1824) 32 USA	William M. Harnett (1848-1892) 32 USA	Winslow Homer (1836-1910) 32 USA
George Catlin (1796-1872) 32 USA	Thomas Moran (1837-1926) 32 USA	Albert Bierstadt (1830-1902) 32 USA	Frederic Edwin Church (1826-1900) 32 USA	Mary Cassatt (1845-1926) 32 USA
Edward Hopper (1882-1967) 32 USA	Grant Wood (1891-1942) 32 USA	Charles Sheeler (1883-1965) 32 USA	Franz Kline (1910-1962) 32 USA	Mark Rothko (1903-1970) 32 USA

3236	a	b	c	d	e
	f	g	h	i	j
	k	l	m	n	o
	p	q	r	s	t

3237

Issues of 1998		Un	U	PB	#	FDC	Q(M)
Four Centuries of American Art Issue, Perf. 10.2							
3236 Pane of 20	08/27/98	12.00	—			9.50	80
a 32¢ "Portrait of Richard Mather," by John Foster		.60	.20			1.25	
b 32¢ "Mrs. Elizabeth Freake and Baby Mary," by The Freake Limner		.60	.20			1.25	
c 32¢ "Girl in Red Dress with Cat and Dog," by Ammi Phillips		.60	.20			1.25	
d 32¢ "Rubens Peale with a Geranium," by Rembrandt Peale		.60	.20			1.25	
e 32¢ "Long-billed Curlew, Numenius Longrostris," by John James Audubon		.60	.20			1.25	
f 32¢ "Boatmen on the Missouri," by George Caleb Bingham		.60	.20			1.25	
g 32¢ "Kindred Spirits," by Asher B. Durand		.60	.20			1.25	
h 32¢ "The Westwood Children," by Joshua Johnson		.60	.20			1.25	
i 32¢ "Music and Literature," by William Harnett		.60	.20			1.25	
j 32¢ "The Fog Warning," by Winslow Homer		.60	.20			1.25	
k 32¢ "The White Cloud, Head Chief of the Iowas," by George Catlin		.60	.20			1.25	
l 32¢ "Cliffs of Green River," by Thomas Moran		.60	.20			1.25	
m 32¢ "The Last of the Buffalo," by Alfred Bierstadt		.60	.20			1.25	
n 32¢ "Niagara," by Frederic Edwin Church		.60	.20			1.25	
o 32¢ "Breakfast in Bed," by Mary Cassatt		.60	.20			1.25	
p 32¢ "Nighthawks," by Edward Hopper		.60	.20			1.25	
q 32¢ "American Gothic," by Grant Wood		.60	.20			1.25	
r 32¢ "Two Against the White," by Charles Sheeler		.60	.20			1.25	
s 32¢ "Mahoning," by Franz Kline		.60	.20			1.25	
t 32¢ "No. 12" by Mark Rothko		.60	.20			1.25	
Perf. 10.9 x 11.1							
3237 32¢ Ballet	09/16/98	.60	.20	2.40	(4)	1.25	130

1998

Issues of 1998		Un	U	PB	#	FDC	Q(M)
Space Discovery Issue, Perf. 11.1							
3238	32¢ Multicolored	10/1/98	.60	.20			1.25	
3239	32¢ Multicolored	10/1/98	.60	.20			1.25	
3240	32¢ Multicolored	10/1/98	.60	.20			1.25	
3241	32¢ Multicolored	10/1/98	.60	.20			1.25	
3242	32¢ Multicolored	10/1/98	.60	.20			1.25	
a	Strip of 5, #3238-3242		3.00	—			3.75	
Self-Adhesive, Serpentine Die-Cut 11.1							
3243	32¢ Philanthropy,							
	Giving and Sharing	10/7/98	.60	.20			1.25	50
Holiday Traditional, Booklet Stamps, Self-Adhesive, Serpentine Die-Cut 10.1 x 9.9							
on 2, 3 or 4 sides							
3244	32¢ The Madonna and Child							
	by Hans Memling	10/15/98	.60	.20			1.25	925.2
a	Booklet pane of 20 + label		12.00					
Holiday Contemporary, Booklet Stamps, Self-Adhesive, Serpentine Die-Cut 11.3 x 11.6							
on 2 or 3 sides							
3245	32¢ Evergreen Wreath	10/15/98	.60	.20			1.25	
3246	32¢ Victorian Wreath	10/15/98	.60	.20			1.25	
3247	32¢ Chili Pepper Wreath	10/15/98	.60	.20			1.25	
3248	32¢ Tropical Wreath	10/15/98	.60	.20			1.25	
a	Booklet pane of 4, #3245-3248		2.50				3.25	
b	Booklet pane of 5, #3245, #3246,							
	3248, 2 #3247 and label		3.00					
c	Booklet pane of 6, #3247-3248,							
	2 each #3245-3246		3.60					
Serpentine Die-Cut 11.4 x 11.6 on 2, 3 or 4 sides							
3249	32¢ Evergreen Wreath	10/15/98	.60	.20			1.25	
3250	32¢ Victorian Wreath	10/15/98	.60	.20			1.25	
3251	32¢ Chili Pepper Wreath	10/15/98	.60	.20			1.25	
3252	32¢ Tropical Wreath	10/15/98	.60	.20			1.25	
a	Block of 4, #3249-3252		2.40				3.25	
b	Booklet pane, 5 each #3249-3252		12.00		2.40	(4)		
Perf. 11.2							
3257	(1¢) Make-Up Rate Weathervane	11/9/98	.20	.20	.25	(4)	1.25	
3258	(1¢) Make-Up Rate Weathervane	11/9/98	.20	.20	.25	(4)	1.25	
#3257 is 18mm high, has thin letters, white USA, and black 1998.							
#3258 is 17mm high, has thick letters, pale blue USA, and blue 1998.							
Self-Adhesive, Serpentine Die-Cut 10.8							
3259	22¢ Uncle Sam	11/9/98	.45	.20	1.80	(4)	1.25	
Perf. 11.2							
3260	(33¢) H-Series		.65	.20			1.25	

3238 **3239** **3240** **3241** **3242 3242a**

3243

3245 **3246**

3244

3247 **3248**

3248a

3258 **3259** **3260**

3261

3262

	Issues of 1998		Un	U	PB	#	FDC	Q(M)
	Self-Adhesive, Serpentine Die-Cut 11.5							
3261	$3.20 Space Shuttle Landing	11/9/98	6.00	3.00	24.00	(4)	6.00	245
	Self-Adhesive, Serpentine Die-Cut 11.5							
3262	$11.75 Express Mail	11/19/98	22.50	11.50	90.00	(4)	12.00	21
	Coil Stamps, Self-Adhesive, Serpentine Die-Cut 9.9 Vertically							
3263	22¢ Uncle Sam	11/9/98	.45	.20	3.50	(5)	1.25	
	Perf. 9.8 Vertically							
3264	33¢ Unce Sam's Hat	11/9/98	.65	.20	4.75	(5)	1.25	
	Self-Adhesive, Serpentine Die-Cut 9.9 Vertically							
3265	33¢ H-Series	11/9/98	.65	.20	4.75	(5)	1.25	
	Serpentine Die-Cut 9.9 Vertically							
3266	33¢ Uncle Sam's Hat	11/9/98	.65	.20	4.75	(5)	1.25	
	Booklet Stamps, Self-Adhesive, Serpentine Die-Cut 9.9 on 2 or 3 sides							
3267	33¢ H-Series	11/9/98	.65	.20			1.25	
a	Booklet pane of 10		6.50					
	Serpentine Die-Cut 11.2 x 11.1 on 2, 3 or 4 sides							
3268	33¢ Uncle Sam's Hat	11/9/98	.65	.20			1.25	
a	Booklet pane of 10		6.50					
b	Booklet pane of 20 + label		13.00					
	Die-Cut 8 on 2, 3 or 4 sides							
3269	33¢ Uncle Sam's Hat	11/9/98	.65	.20			1.25	
a	Booklet pane of 18		12.00					
	Coil Stamps, Perf. 9.8 Vertically							
3270	10¢ Eagle with Shield	12/14/98	.20	.20	2.25	(5)	1.25	
	Self-Adhesive, Serpentine Die-Cut 9.9 Vertically							
3271	10¢ Eagle with Shield	12/14/98	.20	.20	2.25	(5)	1.25	
a	Tagged (error)		1.25	1.10	10.00	(5)		
	Self-Adhesive, Serpentine Die-Cut 11							
B1	32¢ + 8¢ Breast Cancer Research	7/29/98	.80	.60	3.25	(4)		200

© 2001 WHITNEY SHERMAN

Whitney Sherman

Illustrator, designer, and educator Whitney Sherman creates commissioned art for a national clientele from her Baltimore, Maryland, studio. She holds a bachelor of fine arts degree in photography from the Maryland Institute, College of Art, where today she serves as chair of the illustration department. Self-taught in illustration and design, her work has been recognized by *American Illustration,* the Society of Illustrators, and *Communication Arts*. Her book and jacket illustrations have been commissioned by Henry Holt & Co., Clarkson N. Potter/Random House, and Scholastic Books, among others. Recent exhibits include "The Art of Transportation" at the San Francisco Metropolitan Transportation Commission Gallery and "Twenty Years of *Cricket* Covers" at the Art Institute of Chicago. Her illustration for the 1998 Breast Cancer semipostal was her first project for the U.S. Postal Service. ∎

1999

Issues of 1999		Un	U	PB	#	FDC	Q(M)
	Lunar New Year Issue, Perf. 11.2						
3272	33¢ Year of the Rabbit	01/5/99	.65	.20	2.60	(4)	1.25	51
	Black Heritage Issue, Self-Adhesive, Serpentine Die-Cut 11.4						
3273	33¢ Malcolm X	01/20/99	.65	.20	2.60	(4)	1.25	100
	Booklet Stamp, Self-Adhesive, Die-Cut						
3274	33¢ Love	01/28/99	.65	.20			1.25	1,500
a	Booklet pane of 20		13.00					
3275	55¢ Love	01/20/99	1.10	.20	4.40	(4)	2.00	300
	Serpentine Die-Cut 11.4						
3276	33¢ Hospice Care	02/9/99	.65	.20	2.60	(4)	1.25	100
	Perf. 11.2						
3277	33¢ City Flag	02/25/99	.65	.20	2.60	(4)	1.25	200
	Self-Adhesive, Serpentine Die-Cut 11.1 on 2, 3 or 4 sides						
3278	33¢ City Flag	02/25/99	.65	.20	2.60	(4)	1.25	
a	Booklet pane of 4		2.60					
b	Booklet pane of 5 + label		3.25					
c	Booklet pane of 6		3.90					
d	Booklet pane of 10		6.50					
e	Booklet pane of 20 + label		13.00					
	Booklet Stamps, Serpentine Die-Cut 11.5 x 11.75 on 2, 3 or 4 sides						
3278F	33¢ City Flag		.65	.20				
g	Booklet pane of 20 + label		13.00					
	Self-Adhesive, Serpentine Die-Cut 9.8 on 2 or 3 sides						
3279	33¢ City Flag	02/25/99	.65	.20			1.25	
a	Booklet pane of 10		6.50					
	Coil Stamps, Perf. 9.9 Vertically						
3280	33¢ City Flag	02/25/99	.65	.20	4.75	(5)	1.25	
	Self-Adhesive, Serpentine Die-Cut 9.8 Vertically						
3281	33¢ City Flag	02/25/99	.65	.20	4.75	(5)	1.25	
3282	33¢ City Flag	02/25/99	.65	.20	4.75	(5)	1.25	
	Rounded corners.						
	Booklet Stamp, Self-Adhesive, Serpentine Die-Cut 7.9 on 2, 3 or 4 sides						
3283	33¢ Flag and Chalkboard	03/13/99	.65	.20			1.25	306
a	Booklet pane of 18		12.00					
	Perf. 11.2						
3286	33¢ Irish Immigration	02/26/99	.65	.20	2.60	(4)	1.25	40.4
3287	33¢ Lunt & Fontanne	03/2/99	.65	.20	2.60	(4)	1.25	42.5

3272

3273

3274

3275

3276

3277

3278

3279

3280

3286

3287

3288   3289   3290   3291   3292   3292a

	Issues of 1999		Un	U	PB	#	FDC	Q(M)
	Arctic Animals Issue, Perf. 11							
3288	33¢ Arctic Hare	3/12/99	.65	.20			1.25	15.3
3289	33¢ Arctic Fox	3/12/99	.65	.20			1.25	15.3
3290	33¢ Snowy Owl	3/12/99	.65	.20			1.25	15.3
3291	33¢ Polar Bear	3/12/99	.65	.20			1.25	15.3
3292	33¢ Gray Wolf	3/12/99	.65	.20			1.25	15.3
a	Strip of 5, #3288-3292		3.25				3.75	

Alan D. Singer

A gifted artist, designer, and writer, Alan D. Singer is known for his accurate and exquisite botanical and wildlife images. During his 25-year career, his illustrations have been commissioned by leading publishers and magazines including Random House, Houghton Mifflin, *National Geographic,* and *Horticulture*. An associate professor at Rochester Institute of Technology, he has exhibited his originals at such museums and galleries as the Smithsonian Institution and the National Academy of Design. He worked in tandem with his father, Arthur Singer, to create the flowers that appear on 50 State Birds and Flowers stamps for the United States Postal Service. ■

© LEONARD EIGER

"I was an avid stamp collector, so for me this assignment was the fulfillment of a dream."

— Alan Singer

	Issues of 1999-2000		Un	U	PB	#	FDC	Q(M
	Sonoran Desert Issue, Self-Adhesive, Serpentine Die-Cut Perf. 11.2							
3293	Pane of 10	04/6/99	6.50				6.75	10.3
a	33¢ Cactus Wren, brittlebush,							
	teddy bear cholla		.65	.20			1.25	
b	33¢ Desert tortoise		.65	.20			1.25	
c	33¢ White-winged dove		.65	.20			1.25	
d	33¢ Gambel quail		.65	.20			1.25	
e	33¢ Saguaro cactus		.65	.20			1.25	
f	33¢ Desert mule deer		.65	.20			1.25	
g	33¢ Desert cottontail, hedgehog cactus		.65	.20			1.25	
h	33¢ Gila monster		.65	.20			1.25	
i	33¢ Western diamondback rattlesnake,							
	cactus mouse		.65	.20			1.25	
j	33¢ Gila woodpecker		.65	.20			1.25	
	Fruit Berries Issue, Self-Adhesive, Serpentine Die-Cut 11.25 x 11.75 on 2,3 or 4 sides,							
	Serpentine Die-Cut 11.5 x 11.75 on 2 or 3 sides (3294-3297a)							
3294	33¢ Blueberries	04/10/99	.65	.20			1.25	
a	Dated "2000"	03/15/00	.65	.20			1.25	
3295	33¢ Raspberries	04/10/99	.65	.20			1.25	
a	Dated "2000"	03/15/00	.65	.20			1.25	
3296	33¢ Strawberries	04/10/99	.65	.20			1.25	
a	Dated "2000"	03/15/00	.65	.20			1.25	
3297	33¢ Blackberries	04/10/99	.65	.20			1.25	
a	Dated "2000"	03/15/00	.65	.20			1.25	
b	Booklet pane, 5 each #3294-3297 + label		13.00	—			3.25	
c	Block of 4, #3294-3297		2.60					
d	Booklet pane, 5 #3297e		13.00					
e	Block of 4, #3294a-3297a		2.60					
	Serpentine Die-Cut 9.5 x 10 on 2 or 3 sides							
3298	33¢ Blueberries	04/10/99	.65	.20			1.25	
3299	33¢ Raspberries	04/10/99	.65	.20			1.25	
3300	33¢ Strawberries	04/10/99	.65	.20			1.25	
3301	33¢ Blackberries	04/10/99	.65	.20			1.25	
a	Booklet pane of 4							
	#3298-#3301		2.60				3.25	
b	Booklet pane of 5							
	#3298, #3299, #3301							
	2 #3300 + label		3.25					
c	Booklet pane of 6							
	#3300, #3301,							
	2 #3298, #3299		4.00					
d	Block of 4, #3298-#3301		2.60					
	Coil Stamps, Serpentine Die-Cut 8.5 Vertically							
3302	33¢ Blueberries	04/10/99	.65	.20			1.25	
3303	33¢ Raspberries	04/10/99	.65	.20			1.25	
3304	33¢ Strawberries	04/10/99	.65	.20			1.25	
3305	33¢ Blackberries	04/10/99	.65	.20			1.25	
a	Strip of 4		2.60				3.25	

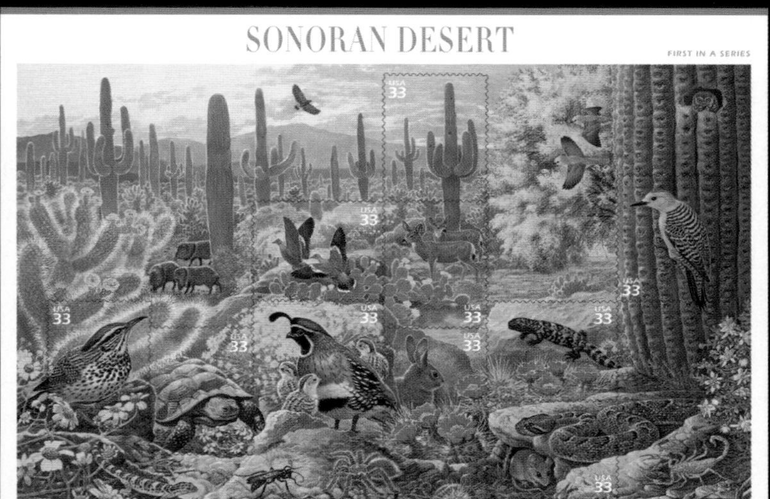
SONORAN DESERT
FIRST IN A SERIES
USA 33
N A T U R E O F A M E R I C A

3293

e

c f j

a b d g h

i

3294 3296

33USA
33USA
33USA
33USA

3295 3297

3297c

33USA
33USA
33USA
33USA

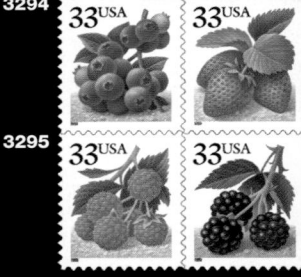

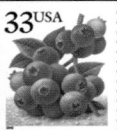

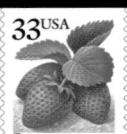

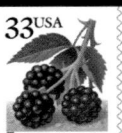

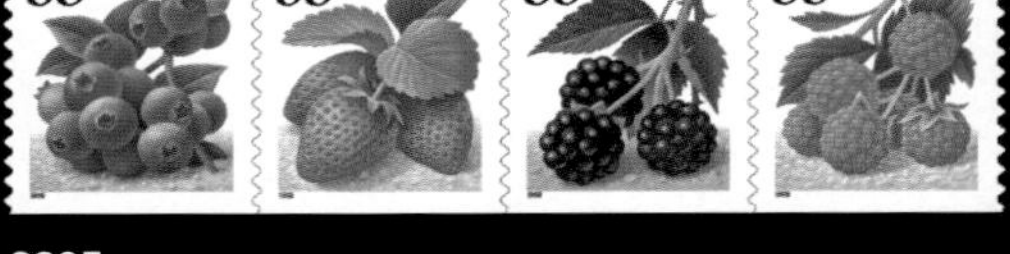

3305a

3306a

3308

3309

3310   3311

3312   3313   3313a

3314

3315

3316

3317   3318   3319   3320   3320a

	Issues of 1999		Un	U	PB	#	FDC	Q(M)
	Looney Tunes Issue, Self-Adhesive, Serpentine Die-Cut 11.1							
3306	Pane of 10	04/16/99	6.50					
a	33¢ Daffy Duck		.65	.20			1.25	427
b	Booklet pane of 9 #3306a		5.85					
c	Booklet pane of 1 #3306a		.65					
3307	Pane of 10		*6.50*					
a	33¢ Single		*.65*					
	Literary Arts Issue, Perf. 11.2							
3308	33¢ Ayn Rand	04/22/99	.65	.20	2.60	(4)	2.00	42.5
	Self-Adhesive, Serpentine Die-Cut 11.6 x 11.3							
3309	33¢ Cinco De Mayo	04/27/99	.65	.20	2.60	(4)	1.25	113
	Tropical Flowers Issue, Self-Adhesive, Serpentine Die-Cut 10.9 on 2 or 3 sides							
3310	33¢ Bird of Paradise	05/01/99	.65	.20			1.25	
3311	33¢ Royal Poinciana	05/01/99	.65	.20			1.25	
3312	33¢ Gloriosa Lily	05/01/99	.65	.20			1.25	
3313	33¢ Chinese Hibiscus	05/01/99	.65	.20			1.25	
a	Block of 4 #3310-3313		2.60				3.25	
b	Booklet pane of 5 #3313a		13.00					
	Self-Adhesive, Perf. 11.5							
3314	33¢ John & William Bartram	05/18/99	.65	.20	2.60	(4)	1.25	145
	Self-Adhesive, Perf. 11							
3315	33¢ Prostate Cancer Awareness	05/28/99	.65	.20	2.60	(4)	1.25	78
	Perf. 11.25							
3316	33¢ California Gold Rush 1849	06/18/99	.65	.20	2.60	(4)	1.25	89
	Aquarium Fish Issue, Self-Adhesive, Serpentine Die-Cut 11.5							
3317	33¢ Yellow fish, red fish, cleaner shrimp	06/24/99	.65	.20			1.25	39
3318	33¢ Fish, thermometer	06/24/99	.65	.20			1.25	39
3319	33¢ Red fish, blue & yellow fish	06/24/99	.65	.20			1.25	39
3320	33¢ Fish, heater/aerator	06/24/99	.65	.20			1.25	39
a	Strip of 4, #3317-3320		2.60		5.20	(8)	3.50	

Nicholas Gaetano

Nicholas Gaetano studied at the Art Center College of Design in Los Angeles and worked in advertising agencies on the East and West Coasts before embarking on a career as a freelance illustrator and designer. He has created award-winning television commercials and illustrations for books, magazines, posters, and records for such prestigious clients as Sony, Jell-O, Clairol, Maxwell House coffee and Norwegian Cruise Line. His artwork is included in the collections of the Library of Congress, the Smithsonian Institution, and many corporations and is featured on a striking Ayn Rand commemorative stamp. ∎

"The stamp design guidelines were very open. Constraints of size were the only real issue."

— Nicholas Gaetano

	Issues of 1999		Un	U	PB	#	FDC	Q(M)
	Extreme Sports Issue, Self-Adhesive, Serpentine Die-Cut 11							
3321	33¢ Skateboarding	6/25/99	.65	.20			1.25	38
3322	33¢ BMX Biking	6/25/99	.65	.20			1.25	38
3323	33¢ Snowboarding	6/25/99	.65	.20			1.25	38
3324	33¢ Inline Skating	6/15/99	.65	.20			1.25	38
a	Block of 4, #3321-3324		2.60		2.60	(4)	3.50	
	American Glass Issue, Perf. 11							
3325	33¢ Free-Blown Glass	6/29/99	.65	.20			1.25	29
3326	33¢ Mold-Blown Glass	6/29/99	.65	.20			1.25	29
3327	33¢ Pressed Glass	6/29/99	.65	.20			1.25	29
3328	33¢ Art Glass	6/29/99	.65	.20			1.25	29
a	Strip or block of 4, #3325-3328		2.60	—			3.50	
	Legends of Hollywood Issue, Perf. 11							
3329	33¢ James Cagney	7/22/99	.65	.20	2.60	(4)	1.25	75.5
	Pioneers of Aviation Issue, Self-Adhesive, Serpentine Die-Cut 9.75 x 10							
3330	55¢ Gen. William "Billy" L. Mitchell	7/30/99	1.10	.20	4.40	(4)	1.25	101
	Self-Adhesive, Serpentine Die Cut 11							
3331	33¢ Honoring Those Who Served	8/16/99	.65	.20	2.60	(4)	1.25	102
	Perf. 11							
3332	45¢ Universal Postal Union	8/25/99	.90	.20	3.60	(4)	1.40	43
	All Aboard!: Twentieth Century Trains Issue							
3333	33¢ Daylight	8/26/99	.65	.20			1.25	24
3334	33¢ Congressional	8/26/99	.65	.20			1.25	24
3335	33¢ 20th Century Limited	8/26/99	.65	.20			1.25	24
3336	33¢ Hiawatha	8/26/99	.65	.20			1.25	24
3337	33¢ Super Chief	8/26/99	.65	.20			1.25	24
a	Strip of 5, #3333-3337		3.25	—			3.75	

© JENNIFER ESPERANZA

Ted Rose

Ted Rose's dramatic watercolor paintings of the American landscape and 20th-century industrial culture reflect the lives of people and places in an ever-changing world.

A native of Milwaukee, Wisconsin, he studied painting, printmaking, and history at the University of Illinois. After serving in the Army during the Vietnam War, he settled in Santa Fe, New Mexico, where he lives and works today. The recipient of many professional honors and awards, he has been featured in such national publications as *The Artist's Magazine* and *Trains Illustrated*. His images also appear in calendars, on posters, and on the covers and pages of books. Five classic streamliners are represented in his first United States postage stamps. ■

3321 3322 3325 3326

SKATEBOARDING USA 33
BMX BIKING USA 33

Free-Blown Glass USA 33
Mold-Blown Glass USA 33

SNOWBOARDING USA 33
INLINE SKATING USA 33

Pressed Glass USA 33
Art Glass USA 33

3323 3324 3324a 3327 3328 3328a

3329

JAMES CAGNEY 33 USA

BILLY MITCHELL
USA 55

3330

DAYLIGHT 33 USA 3333

CONGRESSIONAL 33 USA 3334

Honoring Those Who Served
The United States of America 33

3331

20TH CENTURY LIMITED 33 USA 3335

HIAWATHA 33 USA 3336

UNIVERSAL POSTAL UNION
USA 45

3332

SUPER CHIEF 33 USA 3337

3337a

3338

3339

3340

3341

3342

3343

3344

3344a

3345

3346

3347

3348

3349

3350

3350a

Issues of 1999		Un	U	PB	#	FDC	Q(M)
Perf. 11							
3338 33¢ Frederck Law Olmstead	9/13/99	.65	.20	2.60	(4)	1.25	42.5
Legends of American Music Series, Hollywood Composers Issue							
3339 33¢ Max Steiner	9/16/99	.65	.20			1.25	
3340 33¢ Dimitri Tiomkin	9/16/99	.65	.20			1.25	
3341 33¢ Bernard Herrmann	9/16/99	.65	.20			1.25	
3342 33¢ Franz Waxman	9/16/99	.65	.20			1.25	
3343 33¢ Alfred Newman	9/16/99	.65	.20			1.25	
3344 33¢ Erich Wolfgang Korngold	9/16/99	.65	.20			1.25	
a Block of 6, #3339-3344		3.90		3.90	(6)	3.75	
Legends of American Music Series, Broadway Songwriters Issue							
3345 33¢ Ira & George Gershwin	9/21/99	.65	.65			1.25	
3346 33¢ Lerner & Lowe	9/21/99	.65	.65			1.25	
3347 33¢ Lorenz Hart	9/21/99	.65	.65			1.25	
3348 33¢ Rodgers & Hammerstein	9/21/99	.65	.65			1.25	
3349 33¢ Meredith Willson	9/21/99	.65	.65			1.25	
3350 33¢ Frank Loesser	9/21/99	.65	.65			1.25	
a Block of 6, #3345-3350		3.90		3.90	(6)	3.75	

Robert T. McCall

Highly acclaimed space artist Robert T. McCall is celebrated for his visionary masterpieces featuring the world beyond. His World War II service in the Army Air Corps inspired a lifelong interest in aerospace subjects. Among the first artists to be invited into NASA's fine art program, he has documented such history-making activities as the Mercury, Gemini, and Apollo missions. His multi-story murals in the National Air and Space Museum and his paintings for such films as *2001: A Space Odyssey* and *Star Trek: The Motion Picture* are regarded as icons of the genre. "United States in Space. . . A Decade of Achievement," two of the artist's 21 United States postage stamp designs, was cancelled on the moon before a worldwide television audience. ■

"I love the fact that millions of people collect and treasure stamps, and have received hundreds of letters from collectors over the years in response to my designs."

— Robert T. McCall

1999

	Issues of 1999		Un	U	PB	#	FDC	Q(M
	Insects & Spiders Issue, Perf. 11							
3351	Pane of 20	10/1/99	13.00	—			8.50	4.23
a	Black widow		.65	.20			1.25	
b	Elderberry longhorn		.65	.20			1.25	
c	Lady beetle		.65	.20			1.25	
d	Yellow garden spider		.65	.20			1.25	
e	Dogbane beetle		.65	.20			1.25	
f	Flower Fly		.65	.20			1.25	
g	Assassin bug		.65	.20			1.25	
h	Ebony jewelwing		.65	.20			1.25	
i	Velvet ant		.65	.20			1.25	
j	Monarch caterpillar		.65	.20			1.25	
k	Monarch butterfly		.65	.20			1.25	
l	Eastern Hercules beetle		.65	.20			1.25	
m	Bombardier beetle		.65	.20			1.25	
n	Dung beetle		.65	.20			1.25	
o	Spotted water beetle		.65	.20			1.25	
p	True katydid		.65	.20			1.25	
q	Spinybacked spider		.65	.20			1.25	
r	Periodical cicada		.65	.20			1.25	
s	Scorpionfly		.65	.20			1.25	
t	Jumping spider		.65	.20			1.25	

Steve Buchanan

Steve Buchanan was trained as a classical musician at the Oberlin College Conservatory of Music and earned his doctorate at the University of Texas. After 11 years as a college professor and concert pianist, he studied art and began an illustration career. Although he was trained in traditional art media and methods, he began to explore the art possibilities of desktop computers in the early 1990s. He now works exclusively in digital media focusing on horticulture, natural history, and wildlife subjects for an impressive client roster including *The New York Times*, *Scientific American*, *Country Living Gardener*, and Houghton Mifflin. His artwork appears on 24 United States postage stamps. ∎

INSECTS & SPIDERS

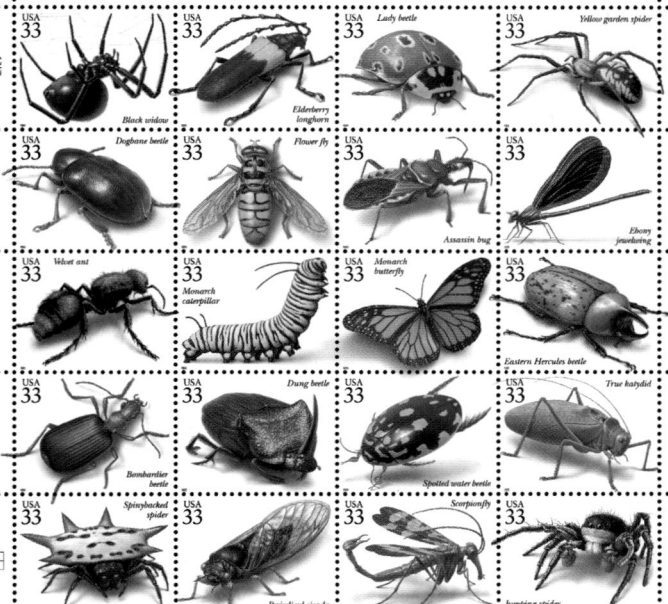

CLASSIC COLLECTION

33 x 20 $6.60

USA 33 — Black widow
USA 33 — Elderberry longhorn
USA 33 — Lady beetle
USA 33 — Yellow garden spider

USA 33 — Dogbane beetle
USA 33 — Flower fly
USA 33 — Assassin bug
USA 33 — Ebony jewelwing

USA 33 — Velvet ant
USA 33 — Monarch caterpillar
USA 33 — Monarch butterfly
USA 33 — Eastern Hercules beetle

USA 33 — Bombardier beetle
USA 33 — Dung beetle
USA 33 — Spotted water beetle
USA 33 — True katydid

USA 33 — Spinybacked spider
USA 33 — Periodical cicada
USA 33 — Scorpionfly
USA 33 — Jumping spider

PLATE POSITION
X1111

© USPS 1998

3351   a   b   c   d

3352

3353

3354

3355

3356      3357

3359   3358

3359a

3368

Issues of 1999		Un	U	PB	#	FDC	Q(M)
Self-Adhesive, Serpentine Die-Cut 11							
3352	33¢ Hanukkah 10/8/99	.65	.20	2.60	(4)	1.25	65
Coil Stamp, Perf. 9.75							
3353	22¢ Uncle Sam 10/8/99	.45	.20	3.50	(5)	1.25	150
Perf. 11.25							
3354	33¢ NATO 50th Anniversary 10/13/99	.65	.20	2.60	(4)	1.25	44.6
Holiday Traditional, Issue, Self-Adhesive Booklet Stamps, Serpentine Die-Cut 11.25 on 2 or 3 sides							
3355	33¢ Madonna and child by Bartolomeo Vivarini 10/20/99	.65	.20			1.25	1,556
a	Booklet pane of 20	13.00					
Holiday Contemporary Issue, Self-Adhesive, Serpentine Die-Cut 11.25							
3356	33¢ Red Deer 10/20/99	.65	.20			1.25	
3357	33¢ Blue Deer 10/20/99	.65	.20			1.25	
3358	33¢ Purple Deer 10/20/99	.65	.20			1.25	
3359	33¢ Green Deer 10/20/99	.65	.20			1.25	
a	Block or strip, #3356-3359	2.60		2.60	(4)	3.25	
Booklet Stamps, Serpentine Die-Cut 11.25 on 2, 3 or 4 sides							
3360	33¢ Red Deer 10/20/99	.65	.20			1.25	
3361	33¢ Blue Deer 10/20/99	.65	.20			1.25	
3362	33¢ Purple Deer 10/20/99	.65	.20			1.25	
3363	33¢ Green Deer 10/20/99	.65	.20			1.25	
a	Booklet pane of 20	13.00				3.25	
Booklet Stamps, Serpentine Die-Cut 11.5 x 11.25 on 2 or 3 sides							
3364	33¢ Red Deer 10/20/99	.65	.20			1.25	
3365	33¢ Blue Deer 10/20/99	.65	.20			1.25	
3366	33¢ Purple Deer 10/20/99	.65	.20			1.25	
3367	33¢ Green Deer 10/20/99	.65	.20			1.25	
a	Booklet pane of 4	2.60				3.25	
b	Block pane of 5, #3364, #3366, #3367 2 #3365 + label	3.25					
c	Block pane of 6, #3365, #3367, 2 #3364, #3366	4.00					
Self-Adhesive, Serpentine Die-Cut 11							
3368	33¢ Kwanzaa 10/29/99	.65	.20	2.60	(4)	1.25	95

Michael Cronan

Michael Cronan is creative director of the Cronan Group, a firm specializing in the creation of names and brands for new and growing technology companies such as TiVo, Ten Square, and Verio. He holds a degree in fine art from California State University in Sacramento. He also attended the California College of Arts and Crafts, where he later taught graphic design as an adjunct professor. In demand as a lecturer on a variety of design topics, he has also judged national and international design competitions. His work is

© 2001 TERRY LURANT

represented in collections at the Library of Congress, the Smithsonian Institution, the San Francisco Museum of Modern Art, and London's Victoria and Albert Museum. In 1999, his designs appeared on two commemorative stamps. ■

	Issues of 1999-2000		Un	U	PB	#	FDC	Q(M)
	Self-Adhesive, Serpentine Die-Cut 11.25							
3369	33¢ Year 2000	12/27/99	.65	.20	2.60	(4)	1.25	124
	Lunar New Year Issue, Perf. 11.25							
3370	33¢ Year of the Dragon	01/06/00	.65	.20	2.60	(4)	1.25	106
	Black Heritage Issue, Serpentine Die-Cut 11.5 x 11.25							
3371	33¢ Patricia Harris	01/27/00	.65	.20	2.60	(4)	1.25	150
	U.S. Navy Submarines Issue, Perf. 11							
3372	33¢ *Los Angeles* Class	03/27/00	.65	.20	2.60	(4)	1.25	65.15
3373	22¢ *S* Class	03/27/00	.45	.20			1.25	3
3374	33¢ *Los Angeles* Class	03/27/00	.65	.30			1.25	3
3375	55¢ *Ohio* Class	03/27/00	1.10	.50			1.50	3
3376	60¢ USS *Holland*	03/27/00	1.25	.55			1.50	3
3377	$3.20 *Gato* Class	03/27/00	6.50	3.00			6.00	3
a	Booklet Pane of 5, #3373-3377		10.00					

Jim Griffiths

An accomplished marine painter, Jim Griffiths is renowned for his realist depictions of ships at sea. His subjects of special interest include mid-to-late 19th-century clipper ships and United States Navy vessels constructed between 1898 and 1909 and from 1940 to the present. Impeccably researched, his images emphasize the depth and character of the ocean in its many moods. He has worked on several projects for the U. S. Navy including the official commemorative portrait of the aircraft carrier USS *Abraham Lincoln* (CVN-72) which is permanently assigned to hang aboard ship. The artist's five submarine stamps—his first U.S. Postal Service project—were issued on the centennial of the U.S. Navy Submarine Service. ■

3369

3370

3371

3372

3376

3377

3374

3373

3375

3377a

PACIFIC COAST RAIN FOREST

SECOND IN A SERIES

N A T U R E   O F   A M E R I C A

3378

           e

a   b   f   i

c   g   h   j

d

3379   3380   3381   3382   3383   3383a

	Issues of 2000		Un	U	PB	#	FDC	Q(M)
	Pacific Coast Rain Forest Issue, Self-Adhesive, Serpentine Die-Cut 11.25 x 11.5							
3378	Pane of 10	3/29/00	6.50					10
a	33¢ Harlequin duck		.65	.20			1.25	10
b	33¢ Dwarf oregongrape,							
	snail eating ground beetle		.65	.20			1.25	10
c	33¢ American dipper, horizontal		.65	.20			1.25	10
d	33¢ Cutthroat trout, horizontal		.65	.20			1.25	10
e	33¢ Roosevelt elk		.65	.20			1.25	10
f	33¢ Winter wren		.65	.20			1.25	10
g	33¢ Pacific giant salamander,							
	Rough-skinned newt		.65	.20			1.25	10
h	33¢ Western tiger swallowtail, horizontal		.65	.20			1.25	10
i	33¢ Douglass squirrel, foliose lichen		.65	.20			1.25	10
j	33¢ Foliose lichen, banana slug		.65	.20			1.25	10
	Louise Nevelson Issue, Perf. 11 x 11.25							
3379	33¢ Silent Music I	4/6/00	.65	.20	6.50	(10)	1.25	11
3380	33¢ Royal Tide I	4/6/00	.65	.20	6.50	(10)	1.25	11
3381	33¢ Black Chord	4/6/00	.65	.20	6.50	(10)	1.25	11
3382	33¢ Nightsphere-Light	4/6/00	.65	.20	6.50	(10)	1.25	11
3383	33¢ Dawn's Wedding Chapel I	4/6/00	.65	.20	6.50	(10)	1.25	11
a	Strip of 5, #3379-3383		3.25					

John D. Dawson

John D. Dawson is a gifted wildlife artist whose meticulous attention to detail and accuracy are inspired by countless hours of research, field observations, specimen studies, and consultations with scientists. The dramatic terrain of the West fueled many of his creative ideas, but in 1989, he traded the Rocky Mountains for the tropical rain forests of Hawaii where he lives and works today. His clients include *National Geographic*, the National Park Service, and the United States Postal Service, for which he has created 30 stamp designs. An exhibition of his original works has toured nationally. ■

"The collaboration between the artist and designer is an important, delicate balance. We go back and forth constantly with ideas, changes, more ideas and more changes until the art is completed. This takes a lot of energy on both sides, because we try to leave nothing compromised."

— John Dawson

	Issues of 2000		Un	U	PB	#	FDC	Q(M)
	Edwin Powell Hubble/Telescope, Perf. 11							
3384	33¢ Eagle Nebula	04/10/00	.65	.20	6.50	(10)	1.25	21.07
3385	33¢ Ring Nebula	04/10/00	.65	.20	6.50	(10)	1.25	21.07
3386	33¢ Lagoon Nebula	04/10/00	.65	.20	6.50	(10)	1.25	21.07
3387	33¢ Egg Nebula	04/10/00	.65	.20	6.50	(10)	1.25	21.07
3388	33¢ Galaxy NGC 1316	04/10/00	.65	.20	6.50	(10)	1.25	21.07
a	Strip of 5, #3384-3388		3.25					
3389	33¢ American Samoa	04/17/00	.65	.20	2.60	(4)	1.25	16
3390	33¢ Library of Congress	04/24/00	.65	.20	2.60	(4)	1.25	55
	Looney Tunes Issue, Self-Adhesive, Serpentine Die-Cut 11							
3391	Pane of 10	04/26/00	6.50					
a	33¢ Road Runner & Wile E. Coyote		.65	.20			1.25	300
	Distinguished Soldiers Issue, Perf. 11							
3393	33¢ Maj. Gen. John L. Hines	08/16/00	.65	.20	2.60	(4)	1.25	13.75
3394	33¢ Gen. Omar N. Bradley	08/16/00	.65	.20	2.60	(4)	1.25	13.75
3395	33¢ Sgt. Alvin C. York	08/16/00	.65	.20	2.60	(4)	1.25	13.75
3396	33¢ Second Lt. Audie L. Murphy	08/16/00	.65	.20	2.60	(4)	1.25	13.75
a	Block Strip of 4, #3393-3396		2.60					
	Perf. 11							
3397	33¢ Summer Sports	05/05/00	.65	.20	2.60	(4)	1.25	90.6

Herb Kawainui Kane

An artist, historian, and author with a special interest in Hawaii and the South Pacific, lives and works in rural south Kona on the island of Hawaii. Raised in Hawaii and Wisconsin, he holds a master's degree in art education from the School of the Art Institute of Chicago. Kane's clients include private collectors, the National Park Service, the National Geographic Society, and major publishers of books and periodicals who collect and commission his advertising art, publishing art, paintings, and architectural designs. Over the years, Kane's art has appeared on stamps honoring American Samoa, the Republic of the Marshall Islands, the Federated States of Micronesia, and the Republic of Palau. Elected a Living Treasure of Hawaii in 1984, Kane was the 1998 recipient of the Charles R. Bishop Medal, awarded by the Bishop Museum, Hawaii's state museum of natural and cultural history. ■

 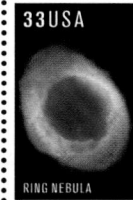   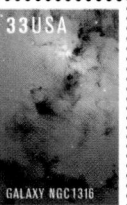

3384 **3385** **3386** **3387** **3388** **3388a**

3389

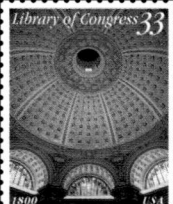 

3390 **3391a**

3393 **3394**

3395 **3396**

3396a

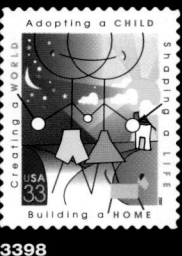

Adopting a CHILD
Creating a WORLD
Shaping a LIFE
Building a HOME
USA 33

3398

3399 3400

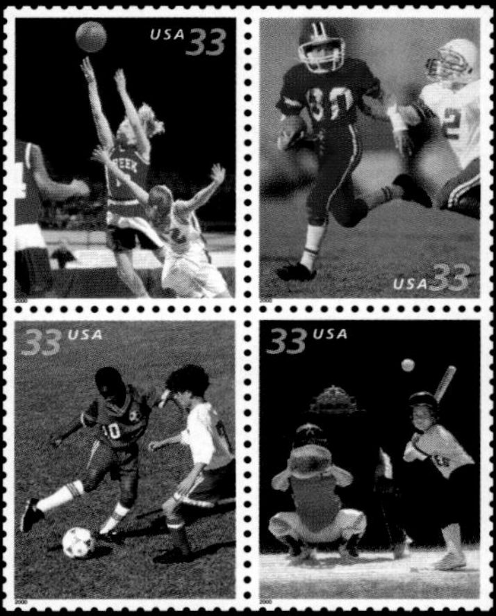
USA 33
USA 33
33 USA
33 USA

3401 3402

3402a

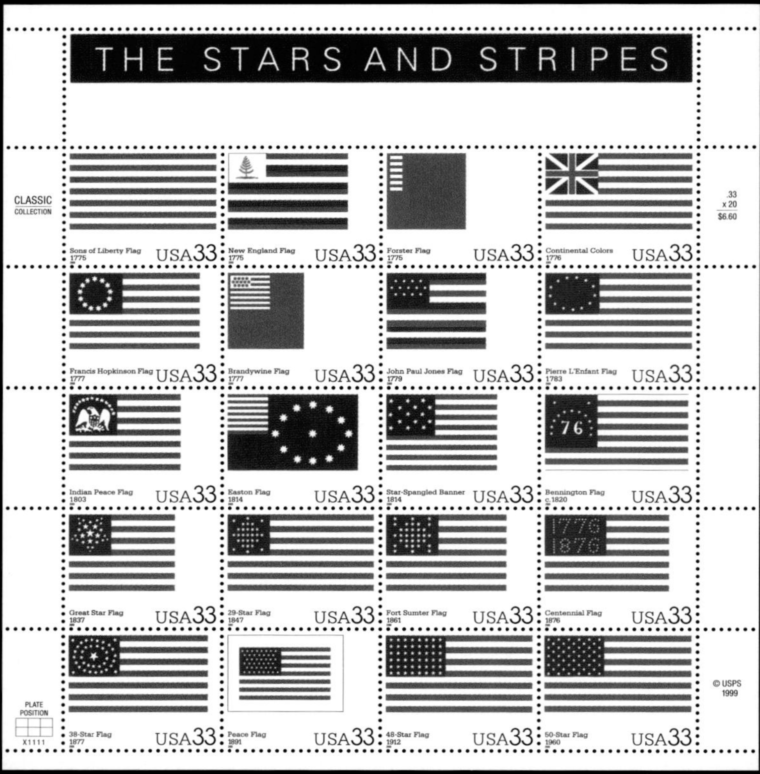
THE STARS AND STRIPES
CLASSIC COLLECTION
.33
x 20
$6.60
Sons of Liberty Flag 1775 USA33
New England Flag 1775 USA33
Forster Flag 1775 USA33
Continental Colors 1776 USA33
Francis Hopkinson Flag 1777 USA33
Brandywine Flag 1777 USA33
John Paul Jones Flag 1779 USA33
Pierre L'Enfant Flag 1783 USA33
Indian Peace Flag 1803 USA33
Easton Flag 1814 USA33
Star-Spangled Banner 1814 USA33
Bennington Flag c.1820 USA33
Great Star Flag 1837 USA33
29-Star Flag 1847 USA33
Fort Sumter Flag 1861 USA33
Centennial Flag 1876 USA33
38-Star Flag 1877 USA33
Peace Flag 1891 USA33
48-Star Flag 1912 USA33
50-Star Flag 1960 USA33
PLATE POSITION
X1111
© USPS 1999

3403

a	b	c	d
e	f	g	h
i	j	k	l
m	n	o	p
q	r	s	t

Issues of 2000		Un	U	PB	#	FDC	Q(M)
Self-Adhesive, Serpentine Die-Cut 11.5							
3398 33¢ Adoption	5/10/00	.65	.20	2.60	(4)	1.25	200
Youth Team Sports Issue, Self-Adhesive, Serpentine Die-Cut 11.5							
3399 33¢ Basketball	5/27/00	.65	.20	2.60	(4)	1.25	22
3400 33¢ Football	5/27/00	.65	.20	2.60	(4)	1.25	22
3401 33¢ Soccer	5/27/00	.65	.20	2.60	(4)	1.25	22
3402 33¢ Baseball	5/27/00	.65	.20	2.60	(4)	1.25	22
a Block strip of 4, #3399-3402		2.60					
The Stars and Stripes Issue, Perf. 10.5 x 11							
3403 Pane of 20	6/14/00	13.00					
a 33¢ Sons of Liberty Flag, 1775		.65	.30			1.25	80
b 33¢ New England Flag, 1775		.65	.30			1.25	80
c 33¢ Forster Flag, 1775		.65	.30			1.25	80
d 33¢ Continental Colors, 1776		.65	.30			1.25	80
e 33¢ Francis Hopkinson Flag, 1779		.65	.30			1.25	80
f 33¢ Brandywine Flag, 1777		.65	.30			1.25	80
g 33¢ John Paul Jones Flag, 1779		.65	.30			1.25	80
h 33¢ Pierre L'Enfant Flag, 1783		.65	.30			1.25	80
i 33¢ Indian Peace Flag, 1803		.65	.30			1.25	80
j 33¢ Easton Flag, 1814		.65	.30			1.25	80
k 33¢ Star-Spangled Banner, 1814		.65	.30			1.25	80
l 33¢ Bennington Fla, c. 1820		.65	.30			1.25	80
m 33¢ Great Star Flag, 1837		.65	.30			1.25	80
n 33¢ 29-Star Flag, 1847		.65	.30			1.25	80
o 33¢ Fort Sumter Flag, 1861		.65	.30			1.25	80
p 33¢ Centennial Flag, 1876		.65	.30			1.25	80
q 33¢ 38-Star Flag, 1912		.65	.30			1.25	80
r 33¢ Peace Flag, 1891		.65	.30			1.25	80
s 33¢ 48-Star Flag, 1912		.65	.30			1.25	80
t 33¢ 50-Star Flag, 1960		.65	.30			1.25	80

"I was delighted to be asked to create postage stamps, and honored to have my name included on 'Comedians by Hirschfeld,' my first set."

— Al Hirschfeld

	Issues of 2000		Un	U	PB	#	FDC	Q(M)
Fruit Berries Issue, Self-Adhesive, Serpentine Die-Cut 8.5 Horizontally								
3404	33¢ Blueberries	6/16/00	.65	.20			1.25	82.5
3405	33¢ Strawberries	6/16/00	.65	.20			1.25	82.5
3406	33¢ Blackberries	6/16/00	.65	.20			1.25	82.5
3407	33¢ Raspberries	6/16/00	.65	.20			1.25	82.5
a	Strip of 4, #3404-3407			2.60				
Legends of Baseball Issue, Self-Adhesive, Serpentine Die-Cut 11.25								
3408	Pane of 20	7/6/00	13.00					
a	33¢ Jackie Robinson		.65	.20			1.25	11.25
b	33¢ Eddie Collins		.65	.20			1.25	11.25
c	33¢ Christy Mathewson		.65	.20			1.25	11.25
d	33¢ Ty Cobb		.65	.20			1.25	11.25
e	33¢ George Sisler		.65	.20			1.25	11.25
f	33¢ Rogers Hornsby		.65	.20			1.25	11.25
g	33¢ Mickey Cochrane		.65	.20			1.25	11.25
h	33¢ Babe Ruth		.65	.20			1.25	11.25
i	33¢ Walter Johnson		.65	.20			1.25	11.25
j	33¢ Roberto Clemente		.65	.20			1.25	11.25
k	33¢ Lefty Grove		.65	.20			1.25	11.25
l	33¢ Tris Speaker		.65	.20			1.25	11.25
m	33¢ Cy Young		.65	.20			1.25	11.25
n	33¢ Jimmie Foxx		.65	.20			1.25	11.25
o	33¢ Pie Traynor		.65	.20			1.25	11.25
p	33¢ Satchel Paige		.65	.20			1.25	11.25
q	33¢ Honus Wagner		.65	.20			1.25	11.25
r	33¢ Josh Gibson		.65	.20			1.25	11.25
s	33¢ Dizzy Dean		.65	.20			1.25	11.25
t	33¢ Lou Gehrig		.65	.20			1.25	11.25

Joseph Saffold

A native of Savannah, Georgia, Joseph Saffold created fine realist images for a variety of clients from his Atlanta studio for 20 years. His award-winning posters, promotional materials, and advertisements have been commissioned by the Atlanta Braves, the National Football League, AT&T, Kodak, United Airlines, and others. Several years ago, he returned to his hometown to build a studio on the Savannah River. While he still accepts commercial assignments, his primary focus is on more personal imagery that is inspired by the world around him. His artwork appears on 20 United States postage stamps honoring the Legends of Baseball. ■

3404   3405   3406   3407 3407a

Legends of Baseball

ALL CENTURY TEAM

CLASSIC
COLLECTION

 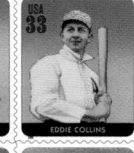 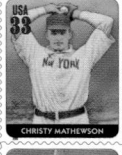 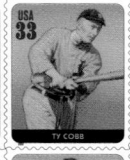 

.33
x 20
$6.60

JACKIE ROBINSON   EDDIE COLLINS   CHRISTY MATHEWSON   TY COBB   GEORGE SISLER

   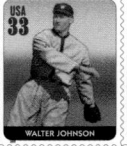 

ROGERS HORNSBY   MICKEY COCHRANE   BABE RUTH   WALTER JOHNSON   ROBERTO CLEMENTE

   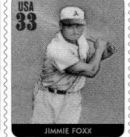 

LEFTY GROVE   TRIS SPEAKER   CY YOUNG   JIMMIE FOXX   PIE TRAYNOR

© USPS
2000

 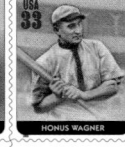   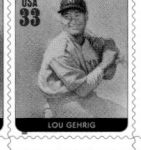

SATCHEL PAIGE   HONUS WAGNER   JOSH GIBSON   DIZZY DEAN   LOU GEHRIG

PLATE
POSITION
X1111

3408   a   b   c   d   e

f   g   h   i   j

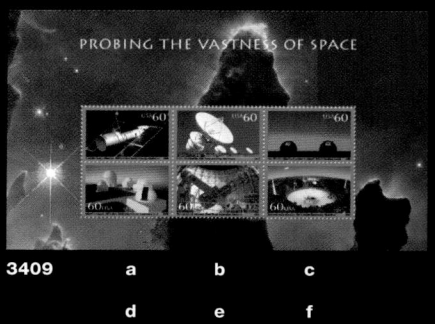

3409   a   b   c

                  d   e   f

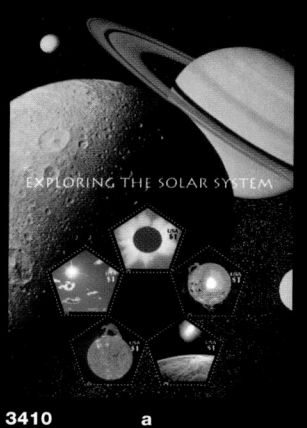

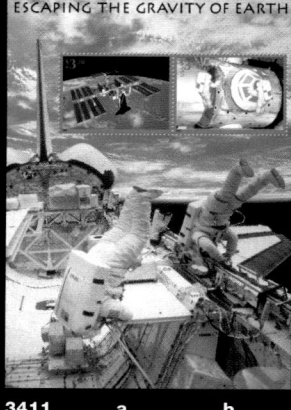

3410   a   **3411**   a   b

       e   b

      d   c

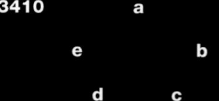

3412

3413

Issues of 2000		Un	U	PB	#	FDC	Q(M)
Space Issue, Perf. 10.5 x 11							
3409 Probing the Vastness of Space	7/10/00	7.50	—			6.00	1.695
a 60¢ Hubble Space Telescope		1.25	.60			1.50	
b 60¢ Radio interferometer very large array, New Mexico		1.25	.60			1.50	
c 60¢ Optical and infrared telescopes, Keck Observatory, Hawaii		1.25	.60			1.50	
d 60¢ Optical telescopes Cerro Tololo Observatory, Chile		1.25	.60			1.50	
e 60¢ Optical telescope, Mount Wilson Observatory, California		1.25	.60			1.50	
f 60¢ Radio telescope, Arecibo Observatory, Puerto Rico		1.25	.60			1.50	
Perf. 10.75							
3410 Exploring the Solar System	7/11/00	10.00	—			9.00	1.695
a $1 Sun and corona		2.00	1.00			2.00	
b $1 Cross-section of sun		2.00	1.00			2.00	
c $1 Sun and earth		2.00	1.00			2.00	
d $1 Sun and solar flare		2.00	1.00			2.00	
e $1 Sun and clouds		2.00	1.00			2.00	
Hologram, Perf. 10.5, 10.75 (#3412)							
3411 Escaping the Gravity of Earth	7/9/00	12.50	—			6.00	1.695
a $3.20 Space Shuttle and Space Station		6.25	3.00			3.75	
b $3.20 Astronauts working in space		6.25	3.00			3.75	
3412 $11.75 Space Achievement and Exploration	7/7/00	22.50	11.50			14.00	1.695
3413 $11.75 Landing on the Moon	7/8/00	22.50	11.50			14.00	1.695
Uncut sheet of 5 panes #3409-3412 (not shown)		75.00					

Teresa Fasolino

Teresa Fasolino lives and works adjacent to her alma mater, the School of Visual Arts, where she teaches aspiring illustrators about narrative image-making. A freelance artist for the past 15 years, she has created artwork for major magazines, publishers, and advertising agencies and has collaborated with architects and interior designers on a wide range of projects. The New York Zoological Society, *The New York Times*, the United Nations Environmental Program, The World Trade Center and several New York City restaurants are among her impressive client roster. Her lushly painted *Aquarium Fish* was the artist's first United States postage stamp commission. ■

"It was a thrill to see my work in stamp form, a democratic and accessible art that goes into the homes of millions of people."

— Teresa Fasolino

Issues of 2000		Un	U	PB	#	FDC	Q(M)
Stampin' The Future™ Issue, Self-Adhesive, Serpentine Die-Cut 11.25							
3414 33¢ By Zachary Canter	7/13/00	.65	.20	5.25	(8)	1.25	25
3415 33¢ By Sarah Lipsey	7/13/00	.65	.20	5.25	(8)	1.25	25
3416 33¢ By Morgan Hill	7/13/00	.65	.20	5.25	(8)	1.25	25
3417 33¢ By Ashley Young	7/13/00	.65	.20	5.25	(8)	1.25	25
a Horizontal Strip of 4, #3414-3417		2.60		5.25	(8)		
Perf. 11							
3420 10¢ Joseph W. Stillwell	8/24/00	.20	.20	.80	(4)	1.25	100
3426 33¢ Claude Pepper	9/7/00	.65	.20	2.00	(4)	1.25	56
Self-Adhesive, Serpentine Die-Cut 11							
3438 33¢ California Statehood	9/8/00	.65	.20	2.60	(4)	1.25	53
Deep Sea Creatures Issue, Perf. 10 x 10.25							
3439 33¢ Fanfin Angelfish	10/2/00	.65	.20			1.25	17
3440 33¢ Sea Cucumber	10/2/00	.65	.20			1.25	17
3441 33¢ Fangtooth	10/2/00	.65	.20			1.25	17
3442 33¢ Amphipod	10/2/00	.65	.20			1.25	17
3443 33¢ Medusa	10/2/00	.65	.20			1.25	17
a Vertical Strip 5, #3439-3443		3.25					

Mark Summers

Mark Summers, whose portraits of literary and historical figures are regular features in the *New York Times Book Review,* works from his studio in Ontario, Canada. His technique—known as scratchboard— is distinguished by a dense network of horizontal lines etched with exquisite precision. He was introduced to scratchboard by the respected Canadian political cartoonist, Duncan Macpherson, while attending the Ontario College of Art in 1976. His award-winning art includes book covers, as well as editorial, institutional, and advertising artwork. Some of his best known work has appeared on Barnes & Noble shopping bags, banners, and vans. Publishing clients include *Time, Rolling Stone, Sports Illustrated,* and *The Atlantic Monthly.* The winner of gold and silver medals from the Society of Illustrators, he has illustrated three commemorative stamps for the U.S. Postal Service including the first issued in the Distinguished Americans series. ∎

3414

3415

3416

3417

3417a

3420

3426

3438

3439

3440

3441

3442

3443

3443a

3444

3445

3446

3447

3448

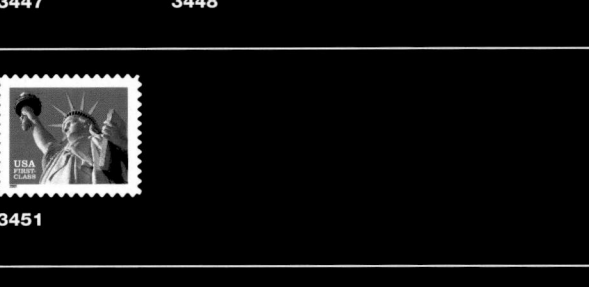

3451

3454

3455

3456

3457

	Issues of 2000		Un	U	PB	#	FDC	Q(M)
	Literary Arts Issue, Perf. 11							
3444	33¢ Thomas Wolfe	10/3/00	.65	.20	2.00	(4)	1.25	53
	Serpentine Die-Cut 11.25							
3445	33¢ White House	10/18/00	.65	.20	2.00	(4)	1.25	125
	Legends of Hollywood Issue, Perf. 11							
3446	33¢ Edward G. Robinson	10/24/00	.65	.20	2.00	(4)	1.25	52
	Serpentine Die-Cut 11.5 Vertically							
3447	10¢ The New York Public Library	11/9/00	.20	.20			1.25	100
	Perf. 11.25							
3448	34¢ Flag Over Farm	12/15/00	.65	.20	2.60	(4)		25
	Self-Adhesive, Serpentine Die-Cut 11.25							
3449	34¢ Flag Over Farm	12/15/00	.65	.20	2.60	(4)		200
	Booklet Stamps, Self-Adhesive, Serpentine Die-Cut 8 on 2, 3 or 4 sides							
3450	34¢ Flag Over Farm	12/15/00	.65	.20				
a	Booklet Pane of 18							300
	Booklet Stamps, Self-Adhesive, Serpentine Die-Cut 11 on 2, 3 or 4 sides							
3451	34¢ Statue of Liberty	12/15/00	.65	.20	2.60	(4)		1.5
	Coil Stamps, Perf. 9.75 Vertically							
3452	34¢ Statue of Liberty	12/15/00	.65	.20	4.75	(5)		200
	Serpentine Die-Cut 10 Vertically							
3453	34¢ Statue of Liberty	12/15/00	.65	.20	4.75	(5)		
	Booklet Stamps, Self-Adhesive, Serpentine Die-Cut 10.25 x 10.75 on 2 or 3 sides							
3454	34¢ Purple Flower	12/15/00	.65	.20				375
3455	34¢ Tan Flower	12/15/00	.65	.20				375
3456	34¢ Green Flower	12/15/00	.65	.20				375
3457	34¢ Red Flower	12/15/00	.65	.20				375
a	Block of 4		2.60					
b	Booklet pane of 20		18.00					
c	Booklet pane of 4		2.60					
d	Booklet pane of 6		3.50					
e	Booklet pane of 5		3.50					
	Coil Stamps, Serpentine Die-Cut 8.5 Vertically							
3462	34¢ Green Flower	12/15/00	.65	.20				125
3463	34¢ Red Flower	12/15/00	.65	.20				125
3464	34¢ Tan Flower	12/15/00	.65	.20				125
3465	34¢ Purple Flower	12/15/00	.65	.20				125
a	Strip of 4		2.60		4.75	(5)		

The Official Inaugural Keepsake

Limited Edition Folio

The 2001 Presidential Inauguration will be an exceptional one for future generations to remember.

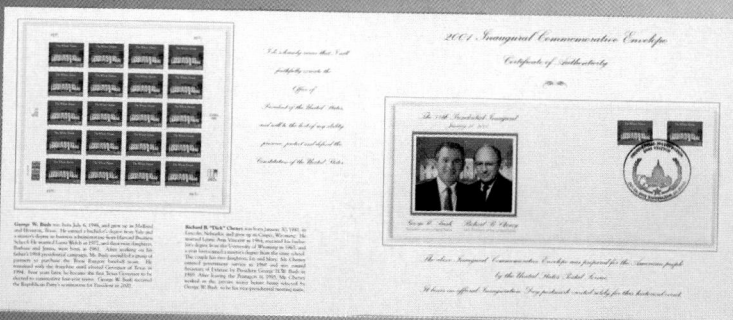

■ What better way to recall this event than with the *Official Inaugural Keepsake* issued by the United States Postal Service to commemorate the 2001 presidential inauguration celebration.

■ This limited edition folio, honoring **President George W. Bush** and **Vice President Richard B. Cheney** includes brief biographies and a silk cachet envelope featuring the President and Vice-President,

20 White House stamps and a specially designed inaugural pictorial cancellation dated January 20, 2001. Only 50,000 commemorative keepsake folios were produced. So order yours today.

■ To order or for more information call **1 800 STAMP-24**. Customers may order online by visiting the Postal Service's Web site at **www.usps.com** and clicking on the Postal Store. Source Code: #39004

479

Airmail and Special Delivery Stamps

1918-1938

C1

C2

C3

C3a

C4

C5

C6

C7

C10

C11

C12

C13

C14

C15

C18

C20

C21

C23

Issues of 1918		Un	U	PB	#	FDC	Q(M)
Perf. 11							
For prepayment of postage on all mailable matter sent by airmail. All unwatermarked.							
C1	6¢ Curtiss Jenny	12/10/18	75.00	30.00	800.00	(6)	32,500.00	3
	Double transfer		95.00	45.00				
C2	16¢ Curtiss Jenny	07/11/18	100.00	35.00	1,200.00	(6)	32,500.00	4
C3	24¢ Curtiss Jenny	05/13/18	100.00	35.00	475.00	(4)	27,500.00	2
a	Center Inverted		*170,000.00*		*1,200,000.00*	(4)		0.0001
	Issues of 1923							
C4	8¢ Airplane Radiator and							
	Wooden Propeller	08/15/23	27.50	14.00	260.00	(6)	450.00	6
C5	16¢ Air Service Emblem	08/17/23	100.00	30.00	1,900.00	(6)	650.00	5
C6	24¢ De Havilland Biplane	08/21/23	110.00	30.00	2,500.00	(6)	850.00	5
	Issues of 1926-27							
C7	10¢ Map of U.S. and							
	Two Mail Planes	02/13/26	2.90	.35	35.00	(6)	60.00	42
	Double transfer		5.75	1.10				
C8	15¢ olive brown (C7)	09/18/26	3.25	2.50	37.50	(6)	75.00	16
C9	20¢ yellow green (C7)	01/25/27	8.50	2.00	85.00	(6)	100.00	18
	Issue of 1927-28							
C10	10¢ Lindbergh's							
	"Spirit of St. Louis"	06/18/27	8.00	2.50	95.00	(6)	25.00	20
a	Booklet pane of 3	05/26/28	85.00	65.00			825.00	
	Issue of 1928							
C11	5¢ Beacon on Rocky							
	Mountains	07/25/28	5.25	.75	175.00	(8)	50.00	107
	Recut frame line at left		6.75	1.25				
a	Vertical pair, imperf. between		*5,500.00*					
	Issues of 1930							
C12	5¢ Winged Globe	02/10/30	11.00	.50	140.00	(6)	12.00	98
a	Horizontal pair, imperf. between		*4,500.00*					
	Graf Zeppelin Issue							
C13	65¢ Zeppelin over							
	Atlantic Ocean	04/19/30	250.00	160.00	2,300.00	(6)	1,250.00	0.09
C14	$1.30 Zeppelin							
	Between Continents	04/19/30	500.00	375.00	5,750.00	(6)	1,100.00	0.07
C15	$2.60 Zeppelin							
	Passing Globe	04/19/30	800.00	575.00	8,250.00	(6)	1,250.00	0.06
	Issues of 1931-32, Perf. 10.5 x 11							
C16	5¢ violet (C12)	08/19/31	5.50	.60	80.00	(4)	175.00	57
C17	8¢ olive bister (C12)	09/26/32	2.40	.40	27.50	(4)	15.00	77
	Issue of 1933, Century of Progress Issue, Perf. 11							
C18	50¢ Zeppelin, Federal Building							
	at Chicago Exposition and							
	Hangar at Friedrichshafen	10/02/33	75.00	70.00	575.00	(6)	200.00	0.3
	Beginning with #C19, unused values are for never-hinged stamps.							
	Issue of 1934, Perf. 10.5 x 11							
C19	6¢ dull orange (C12)	06/30/34	3.50	.25	22.50	(4)	*175.00*	302
	Issues of 1935-37, Trans-Pacific Issue, Perf. 11							
C20	25¢ "China Clipper"							
	over the Pacific	11/22/35	1.40	1.00	20.00	(6)	40.00	10
C21	20¢ "China Clipper"							
	over the Pacific	02/15/37	11.00	1.75	100.00	(6)	45.00	13
C22	50¢ carmine (C21)	02/15/37	10.00	5.00	100.00	(6)	50.00	9
	Issue of 1938							
C23	6¢ Eagle Holding Shield,							
	Olive Branch and Arrows	05/14/38	.50	.20	8.00	(4)	15.00	350
	6¢ ultramarine and carmine		150.00		1,500.00	(4)		
a	Vertical pair, imperf. horizontally		350.00					
b	Horizontal pair, imperf. vertically		12,500.00		37,500.00	(4)		

Issue of 1939		Un	U	PB/LP	#	FDC	Q(M)
	Transatlantic Issue, Perf. 11						
C24	30¢ Winged Globe 05/16/39	10.50	1.50	140.00	(6)	47.50	20
	Issues of 1941-44, Perf. 11 x 10.5						
C25	6¢ Twin-Motor Transport 06/25/41	.20	.20	.65	(4)	2.50	4,477
a	Booklet pane of 3 03/18/43	5.00	1.50			25.00	
	Singles of #C25a are imperf. at sides or imperf. at sides and bottom.						
b	Horizontal pair, imperf. between	2,250.00					
C26	8¢ olive green (C25) 03/21/44	.20	.20	1.10	(4)	3.75	1,745
C27	10¢ violet (C25) 08/15/41	1.25	.20	7.00	(4)	8.00	67
C28	15¢ brn. carmine (C25) 08/19/41	2.75	.35	13.50	(4)	10.00	78
C29	20¢ bright green (C25) 08/27/41	2.25	.30	11.00	(4)	12.50	42
C30	30¢ blue (C25) 09/25/41	2.50	.35	12.00	(4)	20.00	60
C31	50¢ orange (C25) 10/29/41	11.00	3.00	60.00	(4)	40.00	11
	Issue of 1946						
C32	5¢ DC-4 Skymaster 09/25/46	.20	.20	.45	(4)	2.00	865
	Issues of 1947, Perf. 10.5 x 11						
C33	5¢ DC-4 Skymaster 03/26/47	.20	.20	.50	(4)	2.00	972
	Perf. 11 x 10.5						
C34	10¢ Pan American Union Bldg., Washington, D.C. and Martin 2-0-2 08/30/47	.25	.20	1.10	(4)	2.00	208
a	Dry printing	.40	.20	1.75	(4)		
C35	15¢ Statue of Liberty, N.Y. Skyline and Lockheed Constellation 08/20/47	.35	.20	1.50	(4)	2.00	756
a	Horizontal pair, imperf. between	2,100.00					
b	Dry printing	.55	.20	2.50	(4)		
C36	25¢ San Francisco-Oakland Bay Bridge and Boeing Stratocruiser 07/30/47	.85	.20	3.50	(4)	2.50	133
a	Dry printing	1.00	.20	4.25	(4)		
	Issues of 1948, Coil Stamp, Perf. 10 Horizontally						
C37	5¢ carmine (C33) 01/15/48	1.00	.80	10.00	(2)	1.75	33
	Perf. 11 x 10.5						
C38	5¢ New York City 07/31/48	.20	.20	3.75	(4)	1.75	38
	Issues of 1949, Perf. 10.5 x 11						
C39	6¢ carmine (C33) 01/18/49	.20	.20	.50	(4)	1.50	5,070
a	Booklet pane of 6 11/18/49	10.00	5.00				
b	Dry printing	.50	.20	2.25	(4)		
c	As "a," dry printing	15.00	—				
	Perf. 11 x 10.5						
C40	6¢ Alexandria, Virginia 05/11/49	.20	.20	.50	(4)	1.50	75
	Coil Stamp, Perf. 10 Horizontally						
C41	6¢ carmine (C33) 08/25/49	3.25	.20	15.00	(2)	1.25	260
	Universal Postal Union Issue, Perf. 11 x 10.5						
C42	10¢ Post Office Dept. Bldg. 11/18/49	.20	.20	1.40	(4)	1.75	21
C43	15¢ Globe and Doves Carrying Messages 10/07/49	.30	.25	1.25	(4)	2.50	37
C44	25¢ Boeing Stratocruiser and Globe 11/30/49	.50	.40	5.75	(4)	3.50	16
C45	6¢ Wright Brothers 12/17/49	.20	.20	.65	(4)	3.00	80
	Issue of 1952						
C46	80¢ Diamond Head, Honolulu, Hawaii 03/26/52	5.00	1.25	22.50	(4)	17.50	19
	Issue of 1953						
C47	6¢ Powered Flight 05/29/53	.20	.20	.55	(4)	1.50	78
	Issue of 1954						
C48	4¢ Eagle in Flight 09/03/54	.20	.20	1.40	(4)	1.00	50

C24

C25

C32

C33

C34

C35

C36

C38

C40

C42

C43

C44

C45

C46

C47

C48

C49

C51

C53

C54

C55

C56

C57

C58

C59

C61

C62

C63

C64

C66

C67

C68

C69

C70

C71

Issue of 1957		Un	U	PB/LP	#	FDC	Q(M)
	Perf. 11 x 10.5						
C49	6¢ Air Force — 08/01/57	.20	.20	.75	(4)	1.75	63
	Issues of 1958						
C50	5¢ rose red (C48) — 07/31/58	.20	.20	1.40	(4)	1.00	72
	Perf. 10.5 x 11						
C51	7¢ Jet Airliner — 07/31/58	.20	.20	.60	(4)	1.00	1,327
a	Booklet pane of 6	14.00	*7.00*			9.00	221
	Coil Stamp, Perf. 10 Horizontally						
C52	7¢ blue (C51) — 07/31/58	2.25	.20	15.00	(2)	1.00	157
	Issues of 1959, Perf. 11 x 10.5						
C53	7¢ Alaska Statehood — 01/03/59	.20	.20	.60	(4)	1.00	90
	Perf. 11						
C54	7¢ Balloon Jupiter — 08/17/59	.20	.20	.60	(4)	1.10	79
	Perf. 11 x 10.5						
C55	7¢ Hawaii Statehood — 08/21/59	.20	.20	.60	(4)	1.00	85
	Perf. 11						
C56	10¢ Pan American Games — 08/27/59	.25	.25	1.25	(4)	1.00	39
	Issues of 1959-66						
C57	10¢ Liberty Bell — 06/10/60	1.25	.70	5.50	(4)	1.25	40
C58	15¢ Statue of Liberty — 11/20/59	.35	.20	1.50	(4)	1.25	98
C59	25¢ Abraham Lincoln — 04/22/60	.50	.20	2.00	(4)	1.75	
a	Tagged — 12/29/66	.60	.30	2.50	(4)	15.00	
	Issues of 1960, Perf. 10.5 x 11						
C60	7¢ carmine (C61) — 08/12/60	.20	.20	.60	(4)	1.00	1,289
	Pair with full horizontal gutter between						
a	Booklet pane of 6 — 08/19/60	17.50	*8.00*			9.50	
b	Vertical pair, imperf. between	*5,500.00*					
	Coil Stamp, Perf. 10 Horizontally						
C61	7¢ Jet Airliner — 10//22/60	4.25	.25	37.50	(2)	1.00	87
	Issues of 1961-67, Perf. 11						
C62	13¢ Liberty Bell — 06/28/61	.40	.20	1.65	(4)	1.00	
a	Tagged — 02/15/67	.75	.50	5.00	(4)	10.00	
C63	15¢ Statue of Liberty — 01/13/61	.30	.20	1.25	(4)	1.00	
a	Tagged — 01/11/67	.35	.20	1.50	(4)	15.00	
b	As "a," horiz. pair, imperf. vertically	*15,000.00*					
	#C63 has a gutter between the two parts of the design; C58 does not.						
	Issues of 1962-65, Perf. 10.5 x 11						
C64	8¢ Jetliner over Capitol — 12/05/62	.20	.20	.65	(4)	1.00	
a	Tagged — 08/01/63	.20	.20	.65	(4)	4.50	
b	Bklt. pane of 5 + label	7.00	*3.00*			3.50	
c	As "b," tagged — 1964	2.00	.75				
	Coil Stamp, Perf. 10 Horizontally						
C65	8¢ carmine (C64) — 12/05/62	.40	.20	3.75	(2)	1.00	
a	Tagged — 01/14/65	.35	.20	1.50	(2)		
	Issue of 1963, Perf. 11						
C66	15¢ Montgomery Blair — 05/03/63	.60	.55	2.75	(4)	1.10	42
	Issues of 1963-67, Perf. 11 x 10.5						
C67	6¢ Bald Eagle — 07/12/63	.20	.20	1.80	(4)	1.00	
a	Tagged — 02/15/67	4.00	3.00	55.00	(4)	15.00	
	Issue of 1963, Perf. 11						
C68	8¢ Amelia Earhart — 07/24/63	.20	.20	1.00	(4)	2.50	64
	Issue of 1964						
C69	8¢ Robert H. Goddard — 10/05/64	.40	.20	1.75	(4)	2.50	62
	Issues of 1967						
C70	8¢ Alaska Purchase — 03/30/67	.25	.20	1.40	(4)	1.00	56
C71	20¢ "Columbia Jays,"						
	by Audubon, (See also #1241) — 04/26/67	.80	.20	3.50	(4)	2.00	165
a	Tagging omitted	*10.00*					

	Issues of 1968		Un		PB/LP	#	FDC	Q(M)
	Unwmk., Perf. 11 x 10.5							
C72	10¢ 50-Star Runway	01/05/68	.20	.20	.90	(4)	1.00	
b	Booklet pane of 8		2.00	.75			3.50	
c	Booklet pane of 5 + label	01/06/68	3.75	.75			125.00	
	Coil Stamp, Perf. 10 Vertically							
C73	10¢ carmine (C72)	01/05/68	.30	.20	1.70	(2)	1.00	
a	Imperf., pair		600.00		900.00	(2)		
	Perf. 11							
C74	10¢ U.S. Air Mail Service	05/15/68	.25	.20	2.00	(4)	1.50	
a	Red (tail stripe) omitted			—				
b	Tagging omitted		7.50					
C75	20¢ USA and Jet	11/22/68	.35	.20	1.75	(4)	1.10	
a	Tagging omitted		7.50					
	Issue of 1969							
C76	10¢ Moon Landing	09/09/69	.25	.20	1.10	(4)	5.00	152
a	Rose red omitted		500.00	—				
	Issues of 1971-73, Perf. 10.5 x 11							
C77	9¢ Delta Wing Plane	05/15/71	.20	.20	.90	(4)	1.00	
	Perf. 11 x 10.5							
C78	11¢ Silhouette of Jet	05/07/71	.20	.20	.90	(4)	1.00	
a	Booklet pane of 4 + 2 labels		1.25	.75			1.75	
b	Untagged (Bureau precanceled)			.30				
c	Tagging omitted (not Bureau precanceled)		6.00					
C79	13¢ Winged Airmail Envelope	11/16/73	.25	.20	1.10	(4)	1.00	
a	Booklet pane of 5 + label	12/27/73	1.50	.75			1.75	
b	Untagged (Bureau precanceled)			.30				
	Perf. 11							
C80	17¢ Statue of Liberty	07/13/71	.35	.20	1.60	(4)	1.00	
a	Tagging omitted		10.00	—				
C81	21¢ USA and Jet	05/21/71	.40	.20	2.00	(4)	1.00	
a	Tagging omitted		7.50					
	Coil Stamps, Perf. 10 Vertically							
C82	11¢ carmine (C78)	05/07/71	.25	.20	.80	(2)	1.00	
a	Imperf., pair		300.00		450.00	(2)		
C83	13¢ carmine (C79)	12/27/73	.30	.20	1.10	(2)	1.00	
a	Imperf., pair		75.00		150.00	(2)		
	Issues of 1972, National Parks Centennial Issue, Perf. 11 (See also #1448-54)							
C84	11¢ Kii Statue and Temple at City of Refuge Historical National Park, Honaunau, Hawaii	05/03/72	.20	.20	.90	(4)	1.00	78
a	Blue and green omitted		900.00					
	Olympic Games Issue, Perf. 11 x 10.5 (See also #1460-62)							
C85	11¢ Skiers and Olympic Rings	08/17/72	.20	.20	2.50	(10)	1.00	96
	Issues of 1973, Progress in Electronics Issue, Perf. 11 (See also #1500-02)							
C86	11¢ DeForest Audions	07/10/73	.20	.20	.95	(4)	1.00	59
a	Vermilion and green omitted		1,400.00					
b	Tagging omitted		20.00					
	Issues of 1974							
C87	18¢ Statue of Liberty	01/11/74	.35	.25	1.50	(4)	1.00	
a	Tagging omitted		15.00					
C88	26¢ Mount Rushmore National Memorial	01/02/74	.50	.20	2.25	(4)	1.25	
a	Tagging omitted		10.00					
	Issues of 1976							
C89	25¢ Plane and Globes	01/02/76	.50	.20	2.25	(4)	1.25	
C90	31¢ Plane, Globes and Flag	01/02/76	.60	.20	2.75	(4)	1.25	
a	Tagging omitted		10.00					

C72   **C74**

C75

C76

C77

C78   **C79**   **C80**   **C81**

C85   **C86**

C84

C87   **C88**

C89   **C90**

C91 C93 C95

C92 C92a C94 C94a C96 C96a

C97

C98

C99

C100

C101 C102 C105 C106

C103 C104 C104a C107 C108 C108b

C109 C110

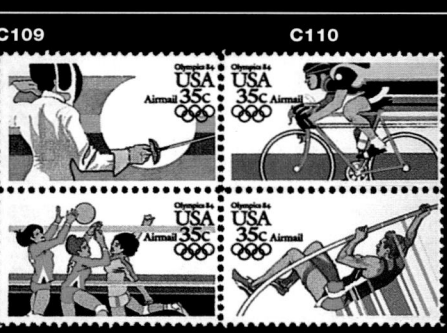

C111 C112 C112a

	Issues of 1978		Un	U	PB	#	FDC	Q(M)
	Aviation Pioneers Issue, Perf. 11 (See also #C93-96)							
C91	31¢ Wright Brothers, Flyer A	09/23/78	.65	.30			3.00	157
C92	31¢ Wright Brothers, Flyer A							
	and Shed	09/23/78	.65	.30			3.00	157
a	Vert. pair, #C91-92		1.30	1.10	3.00	(4)	4.00	
b	As "a," ultramarine and black omitted		800.00					
c	As "a," black omitted		—					
d	As "a," black, yellow, magenta,							
	blue and brown omitted		2,250.00					
	Issues of 1979, Aviation Pioneers Issue							
C93	21¢ Octave Chanute and Biplane							
	Hang-Glider	03/29/79	.70	.30			3.00	29
C94	21¢ Biplane Hang-Glider							
	and Chanute	03/29/79	.70	.30			3.00	29
a	Attached pair, #C93-94		1.40	1.10	3.25	(4)	4.00	
b	As "a," ultramarine and black omitted		4,500.00					
	Aviation Pioneers Issue (See also #C99-100)							
C95	25¢ Wiley Post and							
	"Winnie Mae"	11/20/79	1.10	.35			3.00	32
C96	25¢ NR-105-W, Post in							
	Pressurized Suit and Portrait	11/20/79	1.10	.35			3.00	32
a	Attached pair, #C95-96		2.25	1.25	8.00	(4)	4.00	
	Olympic Summer Games Issue (See also #1790-94)							
C97	31¢ High Jumper	11/01/79	.70	.30	9.50	(12)	1.25	47
	Issues of 1980-82							
C98	40¢ Philip Mazzei	10/13/80	.80	.20	10.00	(12)	1.40	81
b	Imperf., pair		3,250.00					
d	Tagging omitted		10.00					
	Perf. 10.5 x 11.25							
C98A	40¢ Philip Mazzei	1982	6.50	1.50	110.00	(12)		
	Issues of 1980, Aviation Pioneers Issue, Perf. 11							
C99	28¢ Blanche Stuart Scott							
	and Biplane	12/30/80	.60	.20	8.50	(12)	1.25	20
C100	35¢ Glen Curtiss							
	and "Pusher" Biplane	12/30/80	.65	.20	9.00	(12)	1.25	23
	Issues of 1983, Olympic Summer Games Issue (See also #2048-51 and 2082-85)							
C101	28¢ Gymnast	06/17/83	1.00	.30			1.25	43
C102	28¢ Hurdler	06/17/83	1.00	.30			1.25	43
C103	28¢ Basketball Player	06/17/83	1.00	.30			1.25	43
C104	28¢ Soccer Player	06/17/83	1.00	.30			1.25	43
a	Block of 4, #C101-04		4.50	2.00	6.75	(4)	3.75	
	Olympic Summer Games Issue, Perf. 11.2 Bullseye (See also #2048-51 and 2082-85)							
C105	40¢ Shotputter	04/08/83	.90	.40			1.40	67
a	Perf. 11 line		1.00	.45				
C106	40¢ Gymnast	04/08/83	.90	.40			1.40	67
a	Perf. 11 line		1.00	.45				
C107	40¢ Swimmer	04/08/83	.90	.40			1.40	67
a	Perf. 11 line		1.00	.45				
C108	40¢ Weightlifter	04/08/83	.90	.40			1.40	67
a	Perf. 11 line		1.00	.45				
b	Block of 4, #C105-#C108		4.25	2.50	5.00	(4)	5.00	
c	Block of 4, #C105a-#C108a		7.50	—	7.50	(4)		
d	Block of 4, imperf.		1,250.00					
	Olympic Summer Games Issue, Perf. 11 (See also #2048-51 and 2082-85)							
C109	35¢ Fencer	11/04/83	.90	.50			1.25	43
C110	35¢ Bicyclist	11/04/83	.90	.50			1.25	43
C111	35¢ Volleyball Players	11/04/83	.90	.50			1.25	43
C112	35¢ Pole Vaulter	11/04/83	.90	.50			1.25	43
a	Block of 4, #C109-12		4.00	3.00	7.00	(4)	4.50	

	Issues of 1985		Un	U	PB	#	FDC	Q(M)
	Aviation Pioneers Issues, Perf. 11							
C113	33¢ Alfred Verville							
	and Airplane Diagram	02/13/85	.65	.20	3.25	(4)	1.25	168
a	Imperf., pair		850.00					
C114	39¢ Lawrence and							
	Elmer Sperry	02/13/85	.80	.25	3.75	(4)	1.40	168
a	Imperf., pair		1,400.00					
C115	44¢ Transpacific Airmail	02/15/85	.85	.25	4.00	(4)	1.50	209
a	Imperf., pair		900.00					
C116	44¢ Junipero Serra	08/22/85	1.00	.30	8.50	(4)	1.50	164
a	Imperf., pair		1,500.00					
	Issues of 1988							
C117	44¢ New Sweden	03/29/88	1.00	.25	7.00	(4)	1.40	137
	Aviation Pioneers Issues (See also #C128-29)							
C118	45¢ Samuel P. Langley	05/14/88	.90	.20	4.25	(4)	1.40	406
a	Overall tagging		3.00	.50	30.00	(4)		
C119	36¢ Igor Sikorsky	06/23/88	.70	.20	3.25	(4)	3.00	179
	Issues of 1989, Perf. 11.5 x 11							
C120	45¢ French Revolution	07/14/89	.95	.20	4.75	(4)	1.40	38
	America/PUAS Issue, Perf. 11 (See also #2426)							
C121	45¢ Southeast Carved Wood Figure,							
	Key Marco Cat (A.D. 700-1450),							
	Emblem of the Postal Union of the							
	Americas and Spain	10/12/89	.90	.20	5.25	(4)	1.40	39
	20th UPU Congress Issue (See also #2434-38)							
C122	45¢ Hypersonic Airliner	11/27/89	1.00	.40			1.40	27
C123	45¢ Air-Cushion Vehicle	11/27/89	1.00	.40			1.40	27
C124	45¢ Surface Rover	11/27/89	1.00	.40			1.40	27
C125	45¢ Shuttle	11/27/89	1.00	.40			1.40	27
a	Block of 4, #C122-25		4.25	3.00	5.50	(4)	5.00	
b	As "a," light blue omitted		900.00					

Ken Dallison

Renowned automotive artist Ken Dallison studied art at Twickenham Art College and began his professional career in a London advertising agency. His interest in the artistry of automobiles inspired him to create a portfolio filled with studies of trains, buses and cars—particularly large 1950s American cars. During his 50-year career, he has created elegant images featuring automobiles and a wide range of subjects for such prominent clients as *Esquire*, *National Geographic*, *Sports Illustrated*, *Car and Driver*, Mercedes-Benz, General Motors, and IBM. A founder of the Automotive Fine Arts Society, his art appears on 28 United States postage stamps. ∎

C113

C114

C115

C116

C117

C118

C119

C120

C121

C122   **C123**

C124   **C125**

20th Universal Postal Congress

A glimpse at several potential mail delivery methods of the future is the theme of these four stamps issued by the U.S. in commemoration of the convening of the 20th Universal Postal Congress in Washington, D.C. from November 13 through December 14, 1989. The United States, as host nation to the Congress for the first time in ninety-two years, welcomed more than 1,000 delegates from most of the member nations of the Universal Postal Union to the major international event.

C126

C127

C128

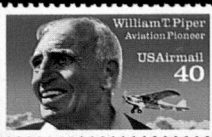

C129

C130

C131

C133

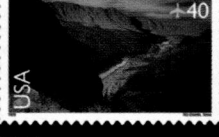

C134

C135

CE1

CE2

	Issues of 1989		Un	U	PB	#	FDC	Q(M)
	20th UPU Congress Issue Souvenir Sheet, Imperf.							
C126	Designs of #C122-25	11/24/89	4.75	3.75			3.00	2
a-d	Single stamp from sheet		1.00	.50				
	Issue of 1990, America/PUAS Issue, Perf. 11 (See also #2512)							
C127	45¢ Tropical Coast	10/12/90	.90	.20	6.25	(4)	1.40	39
	Issues of 1991, Aviation Pioneers Issues							
C128	50¢ Harriet Quimby							
	and Early Plane	04/27/91	1.00	.25	5.50	(4)	1.40	
a	Vertical pair, imperf. horizontally		2,000.00					
b	Perf. 11.2	04/27/91	1.10	.25	6.00	(4)		
C129	40¢ William T. Piper							
	and Piper Cub Airplane	05/17/91	.80	.20	4.00	(4)	1.25	
C130	50¢ Antarctic Treaty	06/21/91	1.00	.25	5.00	(4)	1.40	113
	Issues of 1991-93, America/PUAS Issue							
C131	50¢ Eskimo and Bering							
	Land Bridge	10/12/91	1.00	.25	5.25	(4)	1.40	15
	Perf. 11.2							
C132	40¢ William T. Piper	1993	1.20	.20	10.00	(4)		
	Issues of 1999, Self-Adhesive, Perf. 11							
C133	48¢ Niagra Falls	5/12/99	.95	.20	4.00	(4)	1.40	
	Self-Adhesive, Serpentine Die-Cut 11							
C134	40¢ RioGrande	7/30/99	.95	.20	3.20	(4)		
	Issue of 2000, Serpentine Die-Cut 11.25 x 11.5							
C135	60¢ Grand Canyon	1/20/2000	1.25	.25	5.00	(4)	1.50	100
	Airmail Special Delivery Stamps							
	Issues of 1934, Perf. 11							
CE1	16¢ Great Seal of the							
	United States	08/30/34	.60	.65	17.50	(6)	25.00	
	For imperforate variety see #77							
	Issue of 1936							
CE2	16¢ red and blue	02/10/36	.40	.25	6.50	(4)	17.50	
a	Horizontal pair, imperf. vertically		4,000.00					
	Special Delivery Stamps							
	Issue of 1885, Perf. 12, Unwmkd.							
E1	10¢ Messenger Running	10/01/85	325.00	45.00	14,000.00	(8)	8,500.00	
	Issue of 1888							
E2	10¢ blue Messenger Running (E3)	09/06/88	300.00	17.50	11,500.00	(8)		
	Issue of 1893							
E3	10¢ Messenger Running	01/24/93	200.00	22.50	7,250.00	(8)		
	Issue of 1894							
E4	10¢ Messenger Running	10/10/94	700.00	30.00	14,000.00	(6)		
	(Line under "Ten Cents")							

	Issue of 1895		Un	U	PB	#	FDC
	Wmkd. (191), Perf. 12						
E5	10¢ bl. Messenger Running (E4)	08/16/95	160.00	3.50	*4,000.00*	(6)	
	Double transfer		—	16.00			
	Line of color through "POSTAL DELIVERY"		210.00	12.50			
	Dots in curved frame above messenger		200.00	9.00			
	Issue of 1902						
E6	10¢ Messenger on Bicycle	12/09/02	110.00	3.25		(6)	
	Damaged transfer under "N" of "CENTS"		140.00	3.75			
	Issue of 1908						
E7	10¢ Mercury Helmet and						
	Olive Branch	12/12/08	60.00	40.00	*925.00*	(6)	
	Issue of 1911, Wmkd. (190), Perf. 12						
E8	10¢ ultramarine Messenger						
	on Bicycle (E6)	01/11	100.00	5.25	*2,000.00*	(6)	
	Top frame line missing		140.00	12.50			
	Issue of 1914, Perf. 10						
E9	10¢ ultramarine Messenger						
	on Bicycle (E6)	09/14	180.00	6.50	*3,250.00*	(6)	
	Issue of 1916, Unwmkd.						
E10	10¢ ultramarine Messenger						
	on Bicycle (E6)	10/19/16	275.00	27.50	*5,500.00*	(6)	
	Issue of 1917, Unwmkd., Perf. 11						
E11	10¢ ultramarine Messenger						
	on Bicycle (E6)	05/02/17	20.00	.50	225.00	(6)	
c	Blue		50.00	2.50	550.00	(6)	
	Issue of 1922, Unwmkd.						
E12	10¢ Postman and Motorcycle	07/12/22	35.00	.50	400.00	(6)	425.00
a	10¢ deep ultramarine		40.00	.60	425.00	(6)	
	Issues of 1925, Unwmkd.						
E13	15¢ Postman and Motorcycle	04/11/25	25.00	1.00	300.00	(6)	240.00
E14	20¢ Post Office Truck	04/25/25	2.00	1.00	32.50	(6)	95.00
	Issue of 1927, Unwmkd., Perf. 11 x 10.5						
E15	10¢ gray violet Postman						
	and Motorcycle (E12)	11/29/27	.60	.20	4.00	(4)	110.00
	Cracked plate		35.00				
c	Horizontal pair, imperf. between		300.00				
	Issue of 1931, Unwmkd.						
E16	15¢ orange Postman and						
	Motorcycle (E13)	08/13/31	.70	.20	3.75	(4)	125.00
	Beginning with #E17, unused values are for never-hinged stamps.						
	Issues of 1944, Unwmkd.						
E17	13¢ Postman and Motorcycle	10/30/44	.60	.20	3.00	(4)	12.00
E18	17¢ Postman and Motorcycle	10/30/44	2.75	1.75	20.00	(4)	12.00
	Issue of 1951, Unwmkd.						
E19	20¢ blk. Post Office Truck (E14)	11/30/51	1.25	.20	5.50	(4)	5.00
	Issues of 1954-57, Unwmkd.						
E20	20¢ Delivery of Letter	10/13/54	.40	.20	2.00	(4)	3.00
E21	30¢ Delivery of Letter	09/03/57	.50	.20	2.40	(4)	2.25
	Issues of 1969-71, Unwmkd., Perf. 11						
E22	45¢ Arrows	11/21/69	1.25	.25	5.50	(4)	3.50
E23	60¢ Arrows	05/10/71	1.25	.20	5.50	(4)	3.50

E6

E7

E12

E13

E14

E18

E20

E21

Registration, Certified Mail and Postage Due Stamps

1879-1955

F1

FA1

J2

J19

J25

J33

J69

J78

J88

J98

J101

	Issue of 1911		Un	U	PB	#	FDC	Q(M)
	Wmkd. (190), Perf. 12							
	Registration Stamp							
	Issued for the prepayment of registry; not usable for postage. Sale discontinued May 28, 1913.							
F1	10¢ Bald Eagle	12/01/11	75.00	7.50	*1,600.00*	(6)	*8,000.00*	
	Certified Mail Stamp							
	For use on First-Class mail for which no indemnity value was claimed, but for which proof of mailing and proof of delivery were available at less cost than registered mail.							
	Issue of 1955, Perf. 10.5 x 11							
FA1	15¢ Letter Carrier	06/06/55	.45	.30	4.00	(4)	3.25	54
	Postage Due Stamps							
	For affixing by a postal clerk to any mail to denote amount to be collected from addressee because of insufficient prepayment of postage.							
	Issues of 1879, Printed by American Bank Note Co., Design of #J2, Unwmkd., Perf. 12							
J1	1¢ brown		57.50	8.50	*1,100.00*	(10)		
J2	2¢ brown		375.00	7.50				
J3	3¢ brown		52.50	4.50	*1,050.00*	(10)		
J4	5¢ brown		575.00	45.00				
J5	10¢ brown	09/19/79	625.00	25.00				
a	Imperf., pair		*2,000.00*					
J6	30¢ brown	09/19/79	325.00	50.00	*4,250.00*	(10)		
J7	50¢ brown	09/19/79	475.00	60.00	*11,000.00*	(10)		
	Special Printing, Soft, Porous Paper							
J8	1¢ deep brown		*12,500.00*					
J9	2¢ deep brown		*7,500.00*					
J10	3¢ deep brown		*12,500.00*					
J11	5¢ deep brown		*7,500.00*					
J12	10¢ deep brown		*3,750.00*					
J13	30¢ deep brown		*3,750.00*					
J14	50¢ deep brown		*3,750.00*					
	Issues of 1884, Design of #J19, Unwmkd.							
J15	1¢ red brown		55.00	4.50	*1,250.00*	(10)		
J16	2¢ red brown		67.50	4.50	*1,400.00*	(10)		
J17	3¢ red brown		1,000.00	175.00				
J18	5¢ red brown		500.00	25.00				
J19	10¢ Figure of Value		475.00	17.50	*12,500.00*	(10)		
J20	30¢ red brown		165.00	50.00	*3,000.00*	(10)		
J21	50¢ red brown		1,650.00	175.00				
	Issues of 1891, Design of #J25, Unwmkd.							
J22	1¢ bright claret		26.00	1.00	*550.00*	(10)		
J23	2¢ bright claret		32.50	1.00	*675.00*	(10)		
J24	3¢ bright claret		62.50	8.00	*950.00*	(10)		
J25	5¢ Figure of Value		77.50	8.00	*1,150.00*	(10)		
J26	10¢ bright claret		125.00	17.50	*2,000.00*	(10)		
J27	30¢ bright claret		500.00	150.00	*7,500.00*	(10)		
J28	50¢ bright claret		525.00	150.00	*9,000.00*	(10)		
	Issues of 1894, Design of #J33, Unwmkd.							
J29	1¢ vermilion		1,750.00	400.00				
J30	2¢ vermilion		700.00	125.00	6,000.00	(6)		
	Issues of 1894-95, Design of #J33, Unwmkd.							
J31	1¢ deep claret	08/14/94	47.50	6.00	450.00	(6)		
J32	2¢ deep claret	07/20/94	40.00	4.00	400.00	(6)		
J33	3¢ Figure of Value	04/27/95	160.00	30.00	1,700.00	(6)		

	Issues of 1894-95		Un	U	PB	#
	Design of #J33, Unwmkd., Perf. 12					
J34	5¢ deep claret	04/27/95	240.00	35.00	2,000.00	(6)
J35	10¢ deep claret	09/24/94	240.00	25.00	2,000.00	(6)
J36	30¢ deep claret	04/27/95	400.00	90.00		
b	30¢ pale rose		325.00	85.00	2,850.00	(6)
J37	50¢ deep claret	04/27/95	1,250.00	250.00		
a	50¢ pale rose		1,200.00	250.00	9,500.00	(6)
	Issues of 1895-97, Design of #J33, Wmkd. (191)					
J38	1¢ deep claret	08/29/95	8.50	.75	225.00	(6)
J39	2¢ deep claret	09/14/95	8.50	.70	225.00	(6)
J40	3¢ deep claret	10/30/95	57.50	1.75	575.00	(6)
J41	5¢ deep claret	10/15/95	65.00	1.75	650.00	(6)
J42	10¢ deep claret	09/14/95	67.50	3.50	675.00	(6)
J43	30¢ deep claret	08/21/97	550.00	50.00	5,500.00	(6)
J44	50¢ deep claret	03/17/96	350.00	37.50	3,750.00	(6)
	Issues of 1910-12, Design of #J33, Wmkd. (190)					
J45	1¢ deep claret	08/30/10	32.50	3.00		
a	1¢ rose carmine		30.00	3.00	475.00	(6)
J46	2¢ deep claret	11/25/10	32.50	1.00		
a	2¢ rose carmine		30.00	1.00	450.00	(6)
J47	3¢ deep claret	08/31/10	600.00	30.00	5,500.00	(6)
J48	5¢ deep claret	08/31/10	95.00	6.50		
a	5¢ rose carmine		90.00	6.50	950.00	(6)
J49	10¢ deep claret	08/31/10	115.00	12.50	1,400.00	(6)
J50	50¢ deep claret	09/23/12	950.00	120.00	9,000.00	(6
	Issues of 1914, Design of #J33, Perf. 10					
J52	1¢ carmine lake		60.00	11.00	575.00	(6)
J53	2¢ carmine lake		47.50	.40	450.00	(6)
J54	3¢ carmine lake		875.00	37.50	7,500.00	(6)
J55	5¢ carmine lake		37.50	2.50	350.00	(6)
	5¢ deep claret		—	—		
J56	10¢ carmine lake		57.50	2.00	675.00	(6)
J57	30¢ carmine lake		240.00	17.50	2,750.00	(6)
J58	50¢ carmine lake		10,000.00	800.00	70,000.00	(6)
	Issues of 1916, Design of #J33, Unwmkd.					
J59	1¢ rose		2,500.00	325.00	17,500.00	(6)
	Experimental Bureau precancel, New Orleans			210.00		
J60	2¢ rose		160.00	20.00	1,450.00	(6)
	Issues of 1917-25, Design of #J33, Perf. 11					
J61	1¢ carmine rose		2.75	.25	45.00	(6)
J62	2¢ carmine rose		2.50	.25	40.00	(6)
J63	3¢ carmine rose		11.00	.25	100.00	(6)
J64	5¢ carmine		11.00	.25	100.00	(6)
J65	10¢ carmine rose		17.00	.30	160.00	(6)
	Double transfer		—	—		
J66	30¢ carmine rose		87.50	.75	725.00	(6)
J67	50¢ carmine rose		110.00	.30	900.00	(6)
J68	½¢ dull red	04/13/25	1.00	.25	12.50	(6)

	Issue of 1930-31		Un	U	PB	#
	Design of #J69, Perf. 11					
J69	½¢ Figure of Value		4.50	1.40	42.50	(6)
J70	1¢ carmine		3.00	.25	30.00	(6)
J71	2¢ carmine		4.00	.25	45.00	(6)
J72	3¢ carmine		21.00	1.75	275.00	(6)
J73	5¢ carmine		19.00	2.50	250.00	(6)
J74	10¢ carmine		40.00	1.00	450.00	(6)
J75	30¢ carmine		110.00	2.00	1,000.00	(6)
J76	50¢ carmine		150.00	.75	1,400.00	(6)
	Design of #J78					
J77	$1 carmine		30.00	.25	225.00	(6)
a	$1 scarlet		25.00	.25	275.00	(6)
J78	$5 "FIVE" on $		37.50	.25	300.00	(6)
a	$5 scarlet		32.50	.25	250.00	(6)
b	As "a," wet printing		35.00	.25	275.00	(6)
	Issues of 1931-56, Design of #J69, Perf. 11 x 10.5					
J79	½¢ dull carmine		.90	.20	22.50	(4)
J80	1¢ dull carmine		.20	.20	1.75	(4)
J81	2¢ dull carmine		.20	.20	1.75	(4)
J82	3¢ dull carmine		.25	.20		
a	3¢ scarlet		.25	.20	2.50	(4)
b	3¢ scarlet, wet printing		.50	.20		
J83	5¢ dull carmine		.40	.20	3.25	(4)
J84	10¢ dull carmine		1.10	.20	6.75	(4)
b	scarlet, wet printing		1.25	.20		
J85	30¢ dull carmine		7.50	.25	35.00	(4)
J86	50¢ dull carmine		10.00	.25		
a	50¢ scarlet		10.00	.25	52.50	(4)
	Design of J78, Perf. 10.5 x 11					
J87	$1 scarlet		32.50	.25	200.00	(4)
	Beginning with #J88, unused values are for never-hinged stamps.					
	Issues of 1959, Designs of #J88, J98 and J101, Perf. 11 x 10.5					
J88	½¢ Figure of Value	06/19/59	1.50	1.10	180.00	(4)
J89	1¢ carmine rose	06/19/59	.20	.20	.35	(4)
a	"1 CENT" omitted		300.00			
b	Pair, one without "1 CENT"		600.00			
J90	2¢ carmine rose	06/19/59	.20	.20	.45	(4)
J91	3¢ carmine rose	06/19/59	.20	.20	.50	(4)
J92	4¢ carmine rose	06/19/59	.20	.20	.60	(4)
J93	5¢ carmine rose	06/19/59	.20	.20	.65	(4)
J94	6¢ carmine rose	06/19/59	.20	.20	.70	(4)
a	Pair, one without "6 CENTS"		850.00			
J95	7¢ carmine rose	06/19/59	.20	.20	.80	(4)
J96	8¢ carmine rose	06/19/59	.20	.20	.90	(4)
J97	10¢ carmine rose	06/19/59	.20	.20	1.00	(4)
J98	30¢ Figure of Value	06/19/59	.75	.20	2.75	(4)
J99	50¢ carmine rose	06/19/59	1.10	.20	5.00	(4)
	Design of #J101					
J100	$1 carmine rose	06/19/59	2.00	.20	8.75	(4)
J101	$5 Outline Figure of Value	06/19/59	9.00	.20	45.00	(4)
	Issues of 1978-85, Designs of #J98					
J102	11¢ carmine rose	01/02/78	.25	.20	2.00	(4)
J103	13¢ carmine rose	01/02/78	.25	.20	2.00	(4)
J104	17¢ carmine rose	06/10/85	.40	.35	25.00	(4)

Official and Penalty Mail Stamps
1873-1999

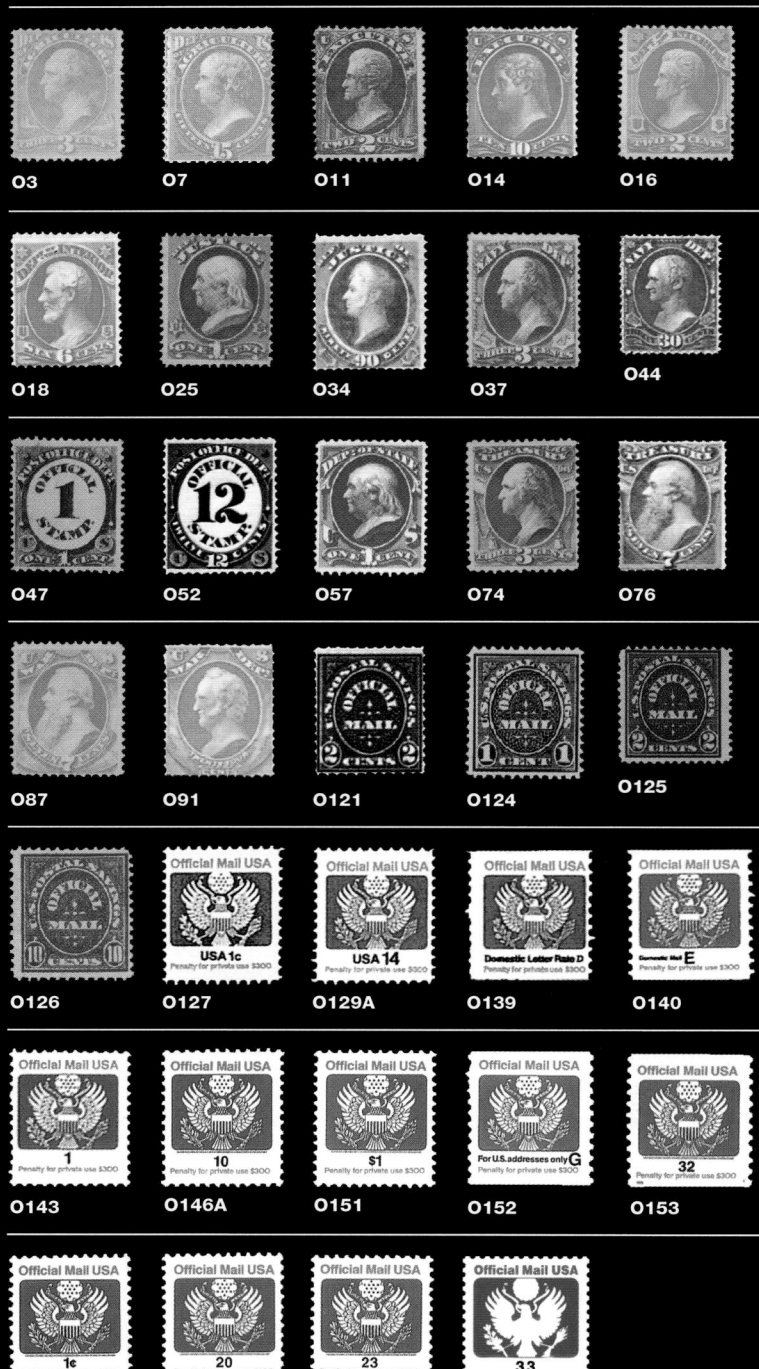

O3　　O7　　O11　　O14　　O16

O18　　O25　　O34　　O37　　O44

O47　　O52　　O57　　O74　　O76

O87　　O91　　O121　　O124　　O125

O126　　O127　　O129A　　O139　　O140

O143　　O146A　　O151　　O152　　O153

O154　　O155　　O156　　O157

Issues of 1873	Un	U

Thin, Hard Paper, Perf. 12, Unwmkd.

Official Stamps

The franking privilege having been abolished as of July 1, 1873, these stamps were provided for each of the departments of government for the prepayment on official matter. These stamps were supplanted on May 1, 1879, by penalty envelopes and on July 5, 1884, were declared obsolete.

Department of Agriculture Issue: Yellow

		Un	U
O1	1¢ Franklin	160.00	150.00
	Ribbed paper	170.00	150.00
O2	2¢ Jackson	130.00	60.00
O3	3¢ Washington	115.00	12.00
	Double transfer	—	—
O4	6¢ Lincoln	125.00	50.00
O5	10¢ Jefferson	260.00	175.00
	10¢ golden yellow	275.00	180.00
	10¢ olive yellow	290.00	185.00
O6	12¢ Clay	350.00	225.00
	12¢ golden yellow	375.00	230.00
O7	15¢ Webster	290.00	200.00
	15¢ olive yellow	325.00	220.00
O8	24¢ Scott	290.00	180.00
	24¢ golden yellow	325.00	190.00
O9	30¢ Hamilton	375.00	235.00
	30¢ olive yellow	425.00	250.00

Executive Dept. Issue: Carmine

		Un	U
O10	1¢ Franklin	650.00	400.00
O11	2¢ Jackson	425.00	200.00
O12	3¢ Washington	450.00	160.00
O13	6¢ Lincoln	725.00	475.00
O14	10¢ Jefferson	700.00	550.00

Dept. of the Interior Issue: Vermilion

		Un	U
O15	1¢ Franklin	35.00	8.00
	Ribbed paper	40.00	9.50
O16	2¢ Jackson	30.00	9.00
O17	3¢ Washington	47.50	5.00
O18	6¢ Lincoln	35.00	5.00
O19	10¢ Jefferson	35.00	15.00
O20	12¢ Clay	50.00	7.75
O21	15¢ Webster	85.00	17.00
	Double transfer of left side	140.00	25.00
O22	24¢ Scott	62.50	14.00
O23	30¢ Hamilton	85.00	14.00
O24	90¢ Perry	190.00	37.50

Dept. of Justice Issue: Purple

		Un	U
O25	1¢ Franklin	110.00	85.00
O26	2¢ Jackson	200.00	85.00
O27	3¢ Washington	200.00	20.00
O28	6¢ Lincoln	175.00	30.00

Issues of 1873	Un	U

Dept. of Justice Issue: Purple (continued)

		Un	U
O29	10¢ Jefferson	200.00	70.00
	Double transfer	—	—
O30	12¢ Clay	150.00	45.00
O31	15¢ Webster	300.00	150.00
O32	24¢ Scott	800.00	325.00
O33	30¢ Hamilton	675.00	250.00
	Double transfer at top	700.00	175.00
O34	90¢ Perry	1,000.00	500.00

Navy Dept. Issue: Ultramarine

		Un	U
O35	1¢ Franklin	75.00	37.50
a	1¢ dull blue	85.00	40.00
O36	2¢ Jackson	60.00	17.00
a	2¢ dull blue	70.00	15.00
	2¢ gray blue	65.00	15.00
O37	3¢ Washington	60.00	8.00
a	3¢ dull blue	70.00	11.00
O38	6¢ Lincoln	60.00	14.00
a	6¢ dull blue	70.00	14.50
	Vertical line through "N" of "NAVY"	125.00	25.00
O39	7¢ Stanton	425.00	175.00
a	7¢ dull blue	450.00	175.00
O40	10¢ Jefferson	80.00	30.00
a	10¢ dull blue	85.00	30.00
	Plate scratch	*170.00*	—
O41	12¢ Clay	95.00	30.00
	Double transfer of left side	250.00	175.00
O42	15¢ Webster	175.00	57.50
O43	24¢ Scott	175.00	65.00
a	24¢ dull blue	200.00	—
O44	30¢ Hamilton	140.00	35.00
O45	90¢ Perry	700.00	200.00
a	Double impression		*3,750.00*

Post Office Dept. Issue: Black

		Un	U
O47	1¢ Figure of Value	12.50	7.50
O48	2¢ Figure of Value	16.00	7.00
a	Double impression	325.00	300.00
O49	3¢ Figure of Value	5.25	1.00
	Cracked plate	—	—
O50	6¢ Figure of Value	16.00	6.00
	Vertical ribbed paper	—	11.00
O51	10¢ Figure of Value	70.00	40.00
O52	12¢ Figure of Value	35.00	8.25
O53	15¢ Figure of Value	47.50	14.00
	Double transfer	—	—
O54	24¢ Figure of Value	60.00	17.00
O55	30¢ Figure of Value	60.00	17.00
O56	90¢ Figure of Value	90.00	14.00

1873-1879

	Issues of 1873	Un	U
	Dept. of State Issue: Green, Perf. 12		
O57	1¢ Franklin	110.00	50.00
O58	2¢ Jackson	210.00	75.00
O59	3¢ Washington	85.00	17.00
	Double paper	—	—
O60	6¢ Lincoln	80.00	22.00
O61	7¢ Stanton	160.00	50.00
	Ribbed paper	180.00	55.00
O62	10¢ Jefferson	125.00	35.00
	Short transfer	160.00	47.50
O63	12¢ Clay	200.00	90.00
O64	15¢ Webster	210.00	65.00
O65	24¢ Scott	425.00	170.00
O66	30¢ Hamilton	400.00	130.00
O67	90¢ Perry	750.00	275.00
O68	$2 Seward	850.00	700.00
O69	$5 Seward	6,000.00	3,500.00
O70	$10 Seward	4,000.00	2,400.00
O71	$20 Seward	3,250.00	1,800.00
	Treasury Dept. Issue: Brown		
O72	1¢ Franklin	37.50	4.50
	Double transfer	45.00	6.25
O73	2¢ Jackson	47.50	4.50
	Double transfer	—	7.75
	Cracked plate	65.00	—
O74	3¢ Washington	32.50	1.25
	Shaded circle outside		
	right frame line	—	—
O75	6¢ Lincoln	42.50	2.25
	Worn plate	37.50	4.00
O76	7¢ Stanton	90.00	22.50
O77	10¢ Jefferson	90.00	7.75
O78	12¢ Clay	90.00	6.00
O79	15¢ Webster	85.00	7.75
O80	24¢ Scott	425.00	65.00
O81	30¢ Hamilton	145.00	9.00
	Short transfer top right	185.00	20.00
O82	90¢ Perry	150.00	10.00
	War Dept. Issue: Rose		
O83	1¢ Franklin	140.00	8.50
O84	2¢ Jackson	125.00	9.50
	Ribbed paper	135.00	11.50
O85	3¢ Washington	130.00	2.75
O86	6¢ Lincoln	425.00	6.00
O87	7¢ Stanton	125.00	72.50
O88	10¢ Jefferson	42.50	15.00

	Issues of 1873	Un	U
	War Dept. Issue (continued): Rose		
O89	12¢ Clay	160.00	10.00
	Ribbed paper	175.00	10.50
O90	15¢ Webster	37.50	11.00
	Ribbed paper	42.50	14.00
O91	24¢ Scott	37.50	6.75
O92	30¢ Hamilton	40.00	6.75
O93	90¢ Perry	90.00	40.00
	Issues of 1879, Soft, Porous Paper		
	Dept. of Agriculture: Yellow		
O94	1¢ Franklin, issued		
	without gum	3,250.00	
O95	3¢ Washington	290.00	65.00
	Dept. of the Interior Issue: Vermilion		
O96	1¢ Franklin	250.00	220.00
O97	2¢ Jackson	4.00	1.25
O98	3¢ Washington	3.50	1.00
O99	6¢ Lincoln	5.25	5.50
O100	10¢ Jefferson	65.00	60.00
O101	12¢ Clay	125.00	90.00
O102	15¢ Webster	300.00	225.00
	Double transfer	350.00	—
O103	24¢ Scott	*3,000.00*	
O104-05	Not assigned		
	Dept. of Justice Issue: Bluish Purple		
O106	3¢ Washington	100.00	65.00
O107	6¢ Lincoln	225.00	175.00
	Post Office Dept. Issue: Black		
O108	3¢ Figure of Value	15.00	5.00
	Treasury Dept. Issue: Brown		
O109	3¢ Washington	45.00	6.75
O110	6¢ Lincoln	85.00	35.00
O111	10¢ Jefferson	150.00	50.00
O112	30¢ Hamilton	1,250.00	275.00
O113	90¢ Perry	2,000.00	275.00
	War Dept. Issue: Rose Red		
O114	1¢ Franklin	3.50	2.75
O115	2¢ Jackson	5.00	3.25
O116	3¢ Washington	5.00	1.20
b	Double impression	*750.00*	
	Double transfer	8.50	4.75
O117	6¢ Lincoln	4.50	1.00
O118	10¢ Jefferson	37.50	37.50
O119	12¢ Clay	30.00	10.00
O120	30¢ Hamilton	80.00	67.50

Issues of 1910-1985	Un	U
Perf. 12		
Official Postal Savings Mail		

These stamps were used to prepay postage on official correspondence of the Postal Savings Division of the Post Office Department. Discontinued Sept. 23, 1914.

O121	2¢ Postal Savings	14.00	1.50
	Double transfer	19.00	2.50
O122	50¢ dark green	140.00	40.00
O123	$1 ultramarine	130.00	11.00
	Wmkd. (190)		
O124	1¢ dark violet	7.50	1.50
O125	2¢ Postal Savings (O121)	45.00	5.50
O126	10¢ carmine	17.00	1.60
Penalty Mail Stamps			

Stamps for use by government departments were reinstituted in 1983. Now known as Penalty Mail stamps, they help provide a better accounting of actual mail costs for official departments and agencies, etc.

Beginning with #O127, unused values are for never-hinged stamps.

Issues of 1983-85, Unwmkd.,			
Perf. 11 x 10.5, O129A is Perf. 11			
O127	1¢, Jan. 12, 1983	.20	.20
O128	4¢, Jan. 12, 1983	.20	.25
O129	13¢, Jan. 12, 1983	.45	.75
O129A	14¢, May 15, 1985	.45	.50
O130	17¢, Jan. 12, 1983	.60	.40

Issues of 1983-1999	Un	U
Perf. 11 x 10.5		
O131, O134, O137, O142 Not assigned		
O132 $1, Jan. 12, 1983	2.00	1.00
O133 $5, Jan. 12, 1983	9.00	9.00
Coil Stamps, Perf. 10 Vertically		
O135 20¢, Jan. 12, 1983	1.75	*2.00*
a Imperf. pair	*2,000.00*	
O136 22¢, May 15, 1985	.70	*2.00*
Perf. 11		
O138 "D" postcard rate		
(14¢) Feb. 4, 1985	5.25	*5.00*
Coil Stamps, Perf. 10 Vertically		
O138A 15¢, June 11, 1988	.45	.50
O138B 20¢, May 19, 1988	.45	.30
O139 "D" (22¢), Feb. 4, 1985	5.25	*3.00*
O140 "E" (25¢), Mar. 22, 1988	.75	*2.00*
O141 25¢, June 11, 1988	.65	.50
Perf. 11		
O143 1¢, July 5, 1989	.20	.20
Perf. 10		
O144 "F" (29¢), Jan. 22, 1991	.75	.50
O145 29¢, May 24, 1991	.65	.30
Perf. 11		
O146 4¢, Apr. 6, 1991	.20	*.30*
O146A 10¢, Oct. 19, 1993	.25	*.30*
O147 19¢, May 24, 1991	.40	*.50*
O148 23¢, May 24, 1991	.45	.30
O151 $1, Sept., 1993	2.00	.75
O152 (32¢), Dec. 13, 1994	.65	—
O153 32¢, May 9, 1995	.65	.30
O154 1¢, May 9, 1995	.20	.20
O155 20¢, May 9, 1995	.45	.30
O156 23¢, May 9, 1995	.50	.30
O157 33¢, Oct. 8, 1999	.65	—

Variable Rate Coil Stamps

These are coil postage stamps printed without denominations. The denomination is imprinted by the dispensing equipment called a Postage and Mailing Center (PMC). Denominations can be set between 1¢ and $99.99. In 1993, the minimum denomination was adjusted to 19¢ (the postcard rate at the time).

Date of Issue:
August 20, 1992
Printing: Intaglio

Date of Issue:
February 19, 1994
Printing: Gravure

Date of Issue:
January 26, 1996
Printing: Gravure

Parcel Post and
Special Handling Stamps

1913-1955

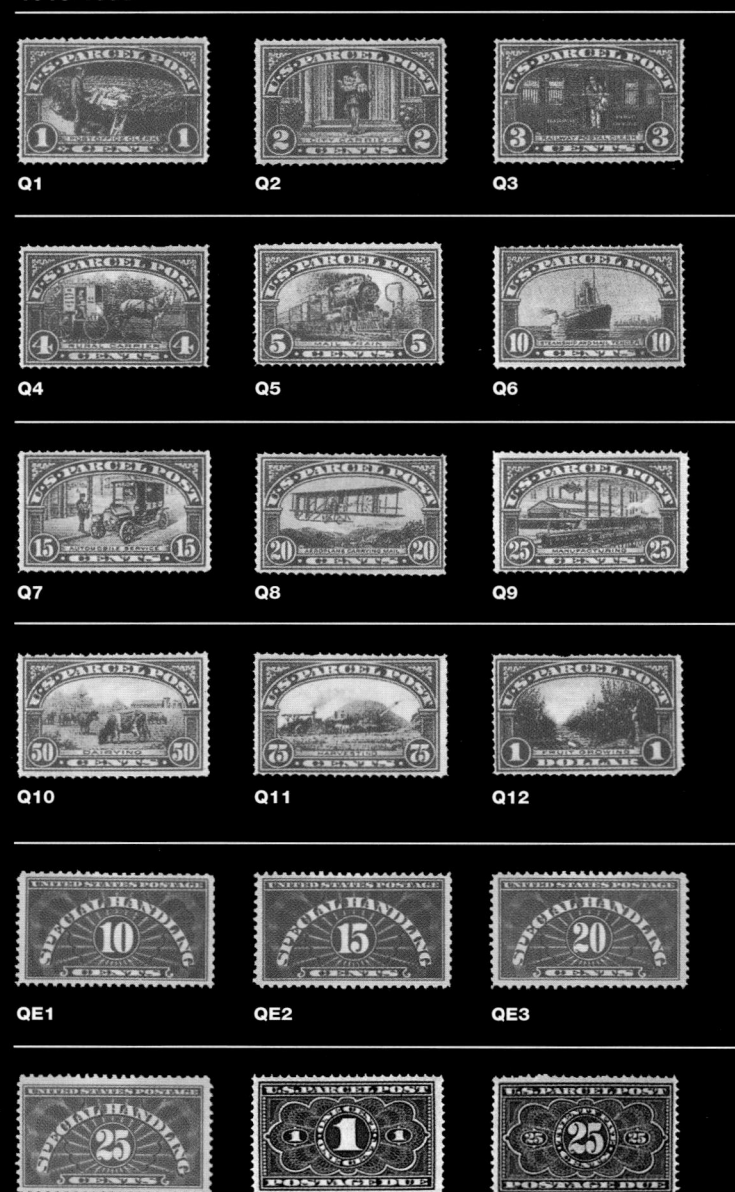

Q1	Q2	Q3
Q4	Q5	Q6
Q7	Q8	Q9
Q10	Q11	Q12
QE1	QE2	QE3
QE4	JQ1	JQ5

	Issues of 1913		Un	U	PB	#	FDC
	Parcel Post Stamps						
	Wmkd. (190), Perf. 12						
	Issued for the prepayment of postage on parcel post packages only. Beginning						
	July 1, 1913 these stamps were valid for all postal purposes.						
Q1	1¢ Post Office Clerk	07/01/13	5.25	1.50	42.50	(4)	*1,500.00*
	Double transfer		8.75	4.00			
Q2	2¢ City Carrier	07/01/13	6.75	1.25	47.50	(4)	*1,500.00*
	2¢ lake		—				
	Double transfer		—	—			
Q3	3¢ Railway Postal Clerk	04/05/13	13.50	5.75	100.00	(4)	*3,250.00*
	Retouched at lower						
	right corner		26.00	14.50			
	Double transfer		26.00	14.50			
Q4	4¢ Rural Carrier	07/01/13	37.50	3.00	360.00	(4)	*3,250.00*
	Double transfer		—	—			
Q5	5¢ Mail Train	07/01/13	32.50	2.25	350.00	(4)	*3,250.00*
	Double transfer		45.00	6.25			
Q6	10¢ Steamship and Mail Tender		52.50	3.00	440.00	(4)	
	Double transfer		—	—			
Q7	15¢ Automobile Service	07/01/13	67.50	12.00	700.00	(4)	
Q8	20¢ Aeroplane Carrying Mail		140.00	25.00	1,450.00	(4)	
Q9	25¢ Manufacturing		67.50	6.75	2,700.00	(6)	
Q10	50¢ Dairying	03/15/13	280.00	40.00	1,950.00	(4)	
Q11	75¢ Harvesting		95.00	35.00	4,000.00	(6)	
Q12	$1 Fruit Growing	01/03/13	350.00	35.00	*20,000.00*	(6)	
	Special Handling Stamps						
	Issued for use on parcel post packages to secure the same expeditious handling						
	accorded first class mail matter.						
	Issues of 1925, 1928-29, 1955, Unwmkd., Perf. 11						
QE1	10¢ Special Handling	1955	1.60	1.00	20.00	(6)	
a	Wet printing	06/25/28	3.25	1.00			45.00
QE2	15¢ Special Handling	1955	1.75	.90	30.00	(6)	
a	Wet printing	06/25/28	3.50	.90			45.00
QE3	20¢ Special Handling	1955	2.75	1.50	32.50	(6)	
a	Wet printing	06/25/28	4.25	1.50			45.00
QE4	25¢ Special Handling	1929	22.50	7.50	260.00	(6)	
a	25¢ deep grn.	04/11/25	32.50	5.50	330.00	(6)	225.00
	"A" and "T" of "STATES"						
	joined at top		50.00	22.50			
	"T" and "A" of "POSTAGE"						
	joined at top		50.00	45.00			
	Parcel Post Postage Due Stamps						
	Issued for affixing by a postal clerk to any parcel post package to denote the amount to be						
	collected from the addressee because of insufficient prepayment of postage. Beginning						
	July 1, 1913 these stamps were valid for use as regular postage due stamps.						
	Issues of 1913, Wmkd. (190), Perf. 12						
JQ1	1¢ Figure of Value	11/27/13	11.00	4.50	550.00	(6)	
JQ2	2¢ dark green	12/09/13	85.00	17.50	*3,750.00*	(6)	
JQ3	5¢ dark green	11/27/13	15.00	5.50	600.00	(6)	
JQ4	10¢ dark green	12/12/13	175.00	45.00	*9,750.00*	(6)	
JQ5	25¢ Figure of Value	12/16/13	105.00	5.00	*5,000.00*	(6)	

RW1

RW3

RW10

RW13

RW15

RW16

	Issues of 1934-1955		Un	U	PB	#	Q(M)
	Department of Agriculture Duck Stamps						
RW1	$1 Mallards Alighting	1934	750.00	125.00	11,500.00	(6)	0.6
a	Imperf. pair		—				
b	Vert. pair, imperf. horiz.		—				
RW2	$1 Canvasbacks	1935	675.00	140.00	8,750.00	(6)	0.4
RW3	$1 Canada Geese	1936	325.00	75.00	3,000.00	(6)	0.6
RW4	$1 Scaup Ducks	1937	275.00	57.50	2,250.00	(6)	0.8
RW5	$1 Pintail Drake						
	and Hen Alighting	1938	350.00	57.50	2,600.00	(6)	1
	Department of the Interior Duck Stamps						
RW6	$1 Green-winged Teal	1939	200.00	45.00	1,900.00	(6)	1
RW7	$1 Black Mallards	1940	200.00	45.00	1,800.00	(6)	1
RW8	$1 Ruddy Ducks	1941	200.00	45.00	1,800.00	(6)	1
RW9	$1 Baldpates	1942	200.00	45.00	1,800.00	(6)	1
RW10	$1 Wood Ducks	1943	75.00	40.00	625.00	(6)	1
RW11	$1 White-fronted Geese	1944	87.50	27.50	650.00	(6)	1
RW12	$1 Shoveller Ducks	1945	60.00	25.00	425.00	(6)	2
RW13	$1 Redhead Ducks	1946	45.00	16.00	300.00	(6)	2
RW14	$1 Snow Geese	1947	45.00	16.00	300.00	(6)	2
RW15	$1 Buffleheads in Flight	1948	50.00	16.00	350.00	(6)	2
RW16	$2 Goldeneye Ducks	1949	60.00	14.00	375.00	(6)	2
RW17	$2 Trumpeter Swans	1950	75.00	11.00	500.00	(6)	2
RW18	$2 Gadwall Ducks	1951	75.00	11.00	500.00	(6)	2
RW19	$2 Harlequin Ducks	1952	75.00	11.00	500.00	(6)	2
RW20	$2 Blue-winged Teal	1953	75.00	11.00	500.00	(6)	2
RW21	$2 Ring-necked Ducks	1954	75.00	10.50	500.00	(6)	2
RW22	$2 Blue Geese	1955	75.00	10.50	500.00	(6)	2

Migratory Bird hunting and Conservation Stamps (popularity known as "Duck Stamps") are sold as hunting permits. While they are sold through many post offices, they are not usable for postage.

1956-1987

	Issues of 1956-1987		Un	U	PB	#	Q(M)
	Department of the Interior Duck Stamps (continued)						
RW23	$2 American Merganser	1956	75.00	10.50	500.00	(6)	2
RW24	$2 American Eider	1957	75.00	10.50	500.00	(6)	2
RW25	$2 Canada Geese	1958	75.00	10.50	475.00	(6)	2
RW26	$3 Labrador Retriever						
	Carrying Mallard Drake	1959	95.00	11.00	450.00	(4)	2
RW27	$3 Redhead Ducks	1960	80.00	10.50	400.00	(4)	2
RW28	$3 Mallard Hen and Ducklings	1961	85.00	10.50	425.00	(4)	1
RW29	$3 Pintail Drakes	1962	95.00	10.50	450.00	(4)	1
RW30	$3 Pair of Brant Landing	1963	95.00	10.50	450.00	(4)	1
RW31	$3 Hawaiian Nene Geese	1964	95.00	10.50	2,100.00	(6)	2
RW32	$3 Three Canvasback Drakes	1965	95.00	10.50	475.00	(4)	2
RW33	$3 Whistling Swans	1966	95.00	10.50	475.00	(4)	2
RW34	$3 Old Squaw Ducks	1967	100.00	10.00	475.00	(4)	2
RW35	$3 Hooded Mergansers	1968	57.50	10.00	275.00	(4)	2
RW36	$3 White-winged Scoters	1969	57.50	7.00	260.00	(4)	2
RW37	$3 Ross's Geese	1970	62.50	7.00	290.00	(4)	2
RW38	$3 Three Cinnamon Teal	1971	40.00	8.00	190.00	(4)	2
RW39	$5 Emperor Geese	1972	25.00	7.00	110.00	(4)	2
RW40	$5 Steller's Eiders	1973	21.00	7.00	100.00	(4)	2
RW41	$5 Wood Ducks	1974	20.00	6.00	85.00	(4)	2
RW42	$5 Canvasbacks Decoy,						
	3 Flying Canvasbacks	1975	15.00	6.00	65.00	(4)	2
RW43	$5 Canada Geese	1976	15.00	6.00	60.00	(4)	2
RW44	$5 Pair of Ross's Geese	1977	15.00	6.00	60.00	(4)	2
RW45	$5 Hooded Merganser Drake	1978	12.50	6.00	55.00	(4)	2
RW46	$7.50 Green-winged Teal	1979	14.00	6.00	57.50	(4)	2
RW47	$7.50 Mallards	1980	14.00	6.00	57.50	(4)	2
RW48	$7.50 Ruddy Ducks	1981	14.00	6.00	57.50	(4)	2
RW49	$7.50 Canvasbacks	1982	15.00	6.00	60.00	(4)	2
RW50	$7.50 Pintails	1983	15.00	6.00	60.00	(4)	2
RW51	$7.50 Widgeons	1984	15.00	6.00	62.50	(4)	2
RW52	$7.50 Cinnamon Teal	1985	15.00	6.00	60.00	(4)	
RW53	$7.50 Fulvous Whistling Duck	1986	15.00	6.00	60.00	(4)	2
a	Black omitted		3,750.00				
RW54	$10 Redheads	1987	15.00	9.00	62.50	(4)	2

DUCK STAMP DOLLARS
BUY WETLANDS
FOR WATERFOWL.

IT IS UNLAWFUL TO HUNT
WATERFOWL UNLESS YOU
SIGN YOUR NAME IN INK
ON THE FACE OF THIS STAMP.

RW26-34

BUY DUCK STAMPS
SAVE WETLANDS

SEND IN ALL BIRD BANDS

SIGN YOUR DUCK STAMP
IT IS UNLAWFUL TO HUNT WATERFOWL UNLESS YOU
SIGN YOUR NAME IN INK ON THE FACE OF THIS STAMP

RW37-53

TAKE PRIDE IN AMERICA
BUY DUCK STAMPS
SAVE WETLANDS

SEND IN ALL BIRD BANDS

SIGN YOUR DUCK STAMPS
IT IS UNLAWFUL TO HUNT WATERFOWL OR USE THIS STAMP
AS A NATIONAL WILDLIFE ENTRANCE PASS UNLESS YOU
SIGN YOUR NAME IN INK ON THE FACE OF THIS STAMP

RW57

TAKE PRIDE IN AMERICA
BUY DUCK STAMPS
SAVE WETLANDS

SEND IN ALL BIRD BANDS

IT IS UNLAWFUL TO HUNT WATERFOWL OR USE THIS STAMP
AS A NATIONAL WILDLIFE REFUGE ENTRANCE PASS UNLESS
YOU SIGN YOUR NAME IN INK ON THE FACE OF THIS STAMP.

RW58-present

RW23

RW26

RW33

RW36

RW38

RW39

RW46

RW49

RW54

RW57

RW58

RW59

RW60

RW61

RW62

RW63

RW65

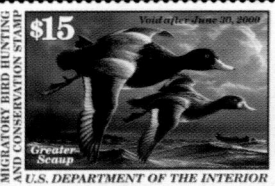

	Issues of 1988-2000		Un	U	PB	#	Q(M)
	Department of the Interior Duck Stamps (continued)						
RW55	$10 Snow Goose	1988	15.00	9.00	62.50	(4)	
RW56	$12.50 Lesser Scaup	1989	19.00	10.00	77.50	(4)	1
RW57	$12.50 Black Bellied						
	Whistling Duck	1990	19.00	10.00	77.50	(4)	1
RW58	$15 King Eiders	1991	22.50	11.00	92.50	(4)	1
RW59	$15 Spectacled Eider	1992	22.50	11.00	92.50	(4)	1
RW60	$15 Canvasbacks	1993	22.50	11.00	92.50	(4)	1
RW61	$15 Red-breasted Merganser	1994	22.50	11.00	92.50	(4)	1
RW62	$15 Mallards	'995	22.50	11.00	92.50	(4)	
RW63	$15 Surf Scoters	1996	22.50	11.00	92.50	(4)	
RW64	$15 Canada Goose	1997	22.50	11.00	92.50	(4)	
RW65	$15 Barrow's Goldeneye	1998	22.50	11.00	92.50	(4)	
RW66	$15 Greater Scaup	1999	22.50	11.00	100.00	(4)	
RW67	$15 Mottled Duck	2000	22.50	11.00	100.00	(4)	

Bob Hautman

Minnesota wildlife artist Bob Hautman is the designer of the 2001-2002 Duck Stamp. Hautman's acrylic painting of a northern pintail bested 316 other entries in the 2000 Federal Duck Stamp Contest, which is sponsored each year by the U.S. Fish and Wildlife Service. Hautman chose his winning design from among several sketches and spent two months working on the painting. He explained that he chose the northern pintail because of the species' striking beauty. This is the second time Hautman has won the Federal Duck Stamp Contest; in 1996 his painting of a Canada goose took top honors. ■

Stamped Envelopes

1853-1886

U9   U14   U19   U36

U45   U46   U62   U64

U84   U85   U97

U103   U113   U142

Issues of 1853-65	Un	U

Represented below is only a partial listing of stamped envelopes. At least one example is listed for most die types; most die types exist on several colors of envelope paper. Values are for cut squares; prices for entire envelopes are higher. Color in italic is the color of the envelope paper; when no color is specified, envelope paper is white. "W" with catalog number indicates wrapper instead of envelope.

		Un	U
U1	3¢ red Washington (top label 13mm wide), *buff*	290.00	26.00
U4	3¢ red Washington (top label 15mm wide) *buff*	290.00	22.50
U5	3¢ red (label has octagonal ends)	5,250.00	400.00
U7	3¢ red (label 20mm wide)	900.00	90.00
U9	3¢ red (label 14½mm)	32.50	3.50
U12	6¢ red Washington, *buff*	150.00	65.00
U14	6¢ green Washington, *buff*	175.00	85.00
U15	10¢ green Washington (label 15½mm wide)	425.00	85.00
U17	10¢ green (label 20mm)	275.00	125.00
a	10¢ pale green	275.00	100.00
U19	1¢ blue Franklin (period after "POSTAGE"), *buff*	32.50	15.00
U23	1¢ blue (bust touches inner frame line), *orange*	500.00	350.00
U24	1¢ blue (no period after "POSTAGE"), *buff*	250.00	125.00
U27	3¢ red, no label, *buff*	24.00	13.00
U28	3¢ + 1¢ (U12 and U9)	350.00	240.00
U30	6¢ red Wash., no label	2,500.00	1,250.00
U33	10¢ green, no label, *buff*	1,400.00	250.00
U34	3¢ pink Washington (outline lettering)	22.50	5.75
U36	3¢ pink, blue (letter sheet)	80.00	50.00
U39	6¢ pink Washington, *buff*	70.00	62.50
U40	10¢ yellow green Wash.	35.00	30.00
U42	12¢ red, brn. Wash., *buff*	190.00	160.00
U44	24¢ Washington, *buff*	200.00	175.00
U45	40¢ blk., red Wash., *buff*	325.00	300.00
U46	2¢ black Jackson ("U.S. POSTAGE" downstroke, tail of "2" unite near point)	37.50	20.00
U49	2¢ black ("POSTAGE" downstroke and tail of "2" touch but do not merge), *orange*	1,250.00	
U50	2¢ blk. Jack. ("U.S. POST." stamp 24-25mm wide), *buff*	13.50	9.00
W51	2¢ blk. Jack. ("U.S. POST." stamp 24-25mm wide), *buff*	300.00	160.00
U54	2¢ blk. Jack. ("U.S. POST." stp. 25½-26½mm), *buff*	13.00	9.00
W55	2¢ blk. Jack. ("U.S. POST." stp. 25½-26½mm), *buff*	80.00	57.50
U58	3¢ pink Washington (solid lettering)	8.00	1.60
U60	3¢ brown Washington	45.00	29.60
U62	6¢ pink Washington	72.50	29.00

Issues of 1863-86	Un	U
U64	6¢ purple Washington	50.00	26.00
U66	9¢ lemon Washington, *buff*	425.00	250.00
U67	9¢ orange Washington, *buff*	110.00	90.00
U68	12¢ brn. Wash., *buff*	325.00	250.00
U69	12¢ red brown Wash., *buff*	125.00	55.00
U70	18¢ red Washington, *buff*	95.00	95.00
U71	24¢ bl. Washington, *buff*	100.00	85.00
U72	30¢ green Washington, *buff*	125.00	75.00
U73	40¢ rose Washington, *buff*	60.00	250.00
U75	1¢ blue Franklin (bust points to end of "N" of "ONE"), *amber*	32.50	27.50
U78	2¢ brown Jackson (bust narrow at back; small, thick numerals)	37.50	16.00
U84	3¢ grn. Washington ("ponytail" projects below bust), *cream*	9.50	4.25
U85	6¢ dark red Lincoln (neck very long at back)	22.50	16.00
a	6¢ vermilion	22.50	16.00
U88	7¢ verm. Stanton (figures 7 normal), *amber*	47.50	*190.00*
U89	10¢ olive blk. Jefferson	650.00	750.00
U92	10¢ brown Jefferson, *amber*	72.50	50.00
U93	12¢ plum Clay (chin prominent)	90.00	82.50
U97	15¢ red orange Webster (has side whiskers), *amber*	200.00	225.00
U99	24¢ purple Scott (locks of hair project, top of head)	140.00	140.00
U103	30¢ black Hamilton (back of bust very narrow), *amber*	225.00	500.00
U105	90¢ carmine Perry (front of bust very narrow, pointed)	150.00	350.00
U113	1¢ lt. blue Frank. (lower part of bust points to end of "E" in "ONE")	1.75	1.00
a	1¢ dark blue	7.50	7.50
U114	1¢ lt. blue (lower part of bust points to end of "E" in "Postage"), *amber*	4.25	4.00
U122	2¢ brown Jackson (bust narrow at back; numerals thin)	100.00	40.00
U128	2¢ brown Jackson (numerals in long ovals)	42.50	32.50
U132	2¢ brown, die 3 (left numeral touches oval)	60.00	27.50
U134	2¢ brown Jackson (similar to U128-31 but "O" of "TWO" has center netted instead of plain)	1,000.00	140.00
U139	2¢ brown (bust broad; numerals short, thick)	45.00	35.00
U142	2¢ verm. Jackson (U139)	6.00	3.00

1874-1893

W155

U159

U172

U190

U204

U218

U250

U294

U314

U348

U351

U358

U368

U374

U377

U379   U386   U390

U393   U398   U400

U406   U416   U429

U447   U468   W485

U523   U524

Issues of 1899-1906	Un	U
U379 1¢ green Franklin, horizontal oval	.70	.20
U386 2¢ carm. Wash. (1 short, 2 long vertical lines at right of "CENTS"), *amber*	1.90	.20
U390 4¢ chocolate Grant	22.50	11.00
U393 5¢ blue Lincoln	20.00	12.50
U398 2¢ carm. Washington, recut die (lines at end of "TWO CENTS" all short), *blue*	3.50	.90
U400 1¢ grn. Frank., oval, die 1 (wide "D" in "UNITED")	.30	.20
U401a 1¢ grn. Frank., die 2 (narrow "D"), *amber*	.95	.70
U402b 1¢, grn. die 3 (wide "S" in "STATES"), *oriental buff*	6.50	1.50
U403c 1¢, die 4 (sharp angle at back of bust, "N," "E" of "ONE" are parallel), *blue*	4.25	1.25
U406 2¢ brn. red Wash., die 1 (oval "O" in "TWO" and "C" in "CENTS")	.80	.20
U407a 2¢, die 2 (like die 1, but hair recut in 2 distinct locks, top of head), *amb.*	100.00	45.00
U408b 2¢, die 3 (round "O" in "TWO" and "C" in "CENTS," coarse letters), *or. buff*	6.50	2.50
U411c 2¢ carmine, die 4 (like die 3 but lettering, hair lines fine, clear)	.40	.20
U412d 2¢ carmine Wash., die 5 (all S's wide), *amber*	.60	.35
U413e 2¢ carm., die 6 (like die 1 but front of bust narrow), *oriental buff*	.55	.35
U414f 2¢ carm., die 7 (like die 6 but upper corner of front of bust cut away), *blue*	30.00	19.00
g 2¢ carm., die 8 (like die 7 but lower stroke of "S" in "CENTS" straight line; hair as in die 2), *blue*	30.00	19.00
U416 4¢ blk. Wash., die 2 ("F" is 1¾mm from left "4")	4.00	2.25
a 4¢, die 1 ("F" is 1mm from left "4")	4.50	3.00
U420 1¢ grn. Frank., round, die 1 ("UNITED" nearer inner circle than outer circle)	.20	.20
U421a 1¢, die 2 (large "U"; "NT" closely spaced), *amber*	350.00	175.00
U423a 1¢ grn. die 3 (knob of hair at back of neck; large "NT" widely spaced), *blue*	.75	.45
b 1¢, die 4 ("UNITED" nearer outer circle than inner)	1.25	.65
c 1¢, die 5 (narrow, oval "C")	.80	.35

Issues of 1907-32	Un	U
U429 2¢ carmine Washington, die 1 (letters broad, numerals vertical, "E" closer than "N" to inner circle)	.20	.20
a 2¢, die 2 (like die 1 but "U" far from left circle), *amber*	9.00	6.00
b 2¢, die 3 (like die 2 but inner circles very thin)	30.00	25.00
U430b 2¢, die 4 (like die 1 but "C" very close to left circle), *amber*	40.00	20.00
c 2¢, die 5 (small head, 8¾mm from tip of nose to back of neck; "TS" of "CENTS" close at bottom)	1.10	.35
U431d 2¢, die 6 (like die 6 but "TS" of "CENTS" far apart at bottom; left numeral slopes right), *oriental buff*	3.00	2.00
e 2¢, die 7 (large head, both numerals slope right, T's have short top strokes)	2.75	1.75
U432h 2¢, die 8 (like die 7 but all T's have long top strokes), *blue*	.60	.25
i 2¢, die 9 (narrow, oval "C")	.90	.30
U436 3¢ dk. violet Washington, die 1 (as 2¢)	.55	.20
U440 4¢ black Washington	1.50	.60
U447 2¢ on 3¢ dark violet, rose surcharge	7.75	6.50
U458 Same as U447, black surcharge, bars 2mm apart	.50	.35
U468 Same as U458, bars 1½mm apart	.70	.45
U481 1½¢ brown Washington, die 1 (as U429)	.20	.20
W485 1½¢ brown, *manila*	.80	.20
U490 1½¢ on 1¢ grn. Franklin, black surcharge	4.00	3.50
U499 1½¢ on 1¢, *manila*	12.50	6.00
U510 1½¢ on 1¢ grn., outline numeral in surcharge	2.40	1.25
U522 2¢ carmine Liberty Bell	1.10	.50
a 2¢, center bar of "E" of "Postage" same length as top bar	7.00	3.75
U523 1¢ ol. grn. Mount Vernon	1.00	.80
U524 1½¢ choc. Mount Vernon	2.00	1.50

Issues of 1916-62		Un	U
U525	2¢ carmine Mount Vernon	.40	.20
a	2¢, die 2 "S" of		
	"POSTAGE" raised	70.00	16.00
U526	3¢ violet Mount Vernon	2.00	.35
U527	4¢ black Mount Vernon	18.00	16.00
U528	5¢ dark blue Mount Vernon	4.00	3.50
U529	6¢ orange Washington	5.50	4.00
U530	6¢ orange Wash., *amber*	11.00	8.00
U531	6¢ or. Washington, *blue*	11.00	10.00
U532	1¢ green Franklin	5.00	1.75
U533	2¢ carmine Wash. (oval)	.75	.25
U534	3¢ dk. violet Washington, die 4		
	(short N in UNITED,thin		
	crossbar in A of STATES)	.40	.20
U535	1½¢ brown Washington	5.00	3.50
U536	4¢ red violet Franklin	.80	.20
U537	2¢ + 2¢ Wash. (U429)	3.25	1.50
U538	2¢ + 2¢ Washington (U533)	.75	.20
U539	3¢ + 1¢ purple, die 1		
	(4½mm tall, thick "3")	15.00	11.00
U540	3¢ + 1¢ purple, die 3		
	(4mm tall, thin "3")	.50	.20
a	Die 2 (4½mm tall,		
	thin "3" in medium		
	circle), entire	—	—
U541	1¼¢ turquoise Franklin	.75	.50
a	Die 2 ("4" 3½mm		
	high), precanceled		1.50
U542	2½¢ dull blue Washington	.85	.50
U543	4¢ brn. Pony Express Rider	.60	.30
U544	5¢ dark blue Lincoln	.85	.20
c	With albino impression		
	of 4¢ U536)	50.00	—
U545	4¢ + 1¢, type 1 (U536)	1.40	.50
U546	5¢ New York World's Fair	.60	.40
U547	1¼¢ brown Liberty Bell		.20
U548	1⁴⁄10¢ brown Liberty Bell		.20
U548A	1⁶⁄10¢ orange Liberty Bell		.20
U549	4¢ blue Old Ironsides	.75	.20
U550	5¢ purple Eagle	.75	.20
a	Tagged	1.25	.20
U551	6¢ green Statue of Liberty	.70	.20
U552	4¢ + 2¢ brt. bl. (U549)	3.75	2.00
U553	5¢ + 1¢ brt. pur. (U550)	3.50	2.50
U554	6¢ lt. blue Herman Melville	.50	.20
U555	6¢ Youth Conference	.75	.20
U556	1⁷⁄10¢ lilac Liberty Bell		.20
U557	8¢ ultramarine Eagle	.40	.20
U561	6¢ + (2¢) lt. grn.	1.00	.30
U562	6¢ + (2¢) lt. blue	2.00	1.60
U563	8¢ rose red Bowling	.50	.20
U564	8¢ Aging Conference	.50	.20
U565	8¢ Transpo '72	.50	.20
U566	8¢ + 2¢ brt. ultra.	.40	.20
U567	10¢ emerald Liberty Bell	.40	.20
U568	1⁸⁄10¢ Volunteer Yourself		.20

Issues of 1962-78		Un	U
U569	10¢ Tennis Centenary	.30	.20
U571	10¢ Compass Rose	.30	.20
a	Brown "10¢/USA"		
	omitted, entire	*125.00*	
U572	13¢ Quilt Pattern	.35	.20
U573	13¢ Sheaf of Wheat	.35	.20
U574	13¢ Mortar and Pestle	.35	.20
U575	13¢ Tools	.35	.20
U576	13¢ Liberty Tree	.30	.20
U577	2¢ red Nonprofit		.20
U578	2.1¢ yel. green Nonprofit		.20
U579	2.7¢ green Nonprofit		.20
U580	15¢ orange Eagle, A	.40	.20
U581	15¢ red Uncle Sam	.40	.20
U582	13¢ emerald Centennial	.35	.20
U583	13¢ Golf	.45	.20
U584	13¢ Energy Conservation	.40	.20
d	Blk, red omitted, ent.	*425.00*	
U585	13¢ Energy Development	.40	.20
U586	15¢ on 16¢ blue USA	.35	.20
U587	15¢ Auto Racing	.35	.20
a	Black omitted, entire	*120.00*	
U588	15¢ on 13¢ (U576)	.35	.20
U589	3.1¢ ultramarine nonprofit		.20
U590	3.5¢ purple Violins		.20
U591	5.9¢ Auth Nonprofit Org		.20
U592	18¢ violet Eagle, B	.45	.20
U593	18¢ dark blue Star	.45	.20
U594	20¢ brown Eagle, C	.45	.20
U595	15¢ Veterinary Medicine	.35	.20
U596	15¢ Summer Oly. Games	.60	.20
a	Red, grn. omitted, ent.	*225.00*	
U597	15¢ Highwheeler Bicycle	.40	.20
a	Blue "15¢ USA"		
	omitted, entire	*100.00*	
U598	15¢ America's Cup	.40	.20
U599	Brown 15¢ Honeybee	.35	.20
a	Brown "15¢ USA"		
	omitted, entire	*125.00*	
U600	18¢ Blind Veterans	.45	.20
U601	20¢ Capitol Dome	.45	.20
U602	20¢ Great Seal of U.S.	.45	.20
U603	20¢ Purple Heart	.45	.20
U604	5.2¢ Auth Nonprofit Org		.20
U605	20¢ Paralyzed Veterans	.45	.20
U606	20¢ Small Business	.50	.20
U607	22¢ Eagle, D	.55	.20
U608	22¢ Bison	.55	.20
U609	6¢ *USS Constitution*		.20
U610	8.5¢ *Mayflower*		.20
U611	25¢ Stars	.60	.20
U612	8.4¢ *US Frigate Constellation*		.20
U613	25¢ Snowflake	.60	.25
U614	25¢ USA, Stars (Philatelic Mail)	.50	.25

U530

U531

U541

U542

U543

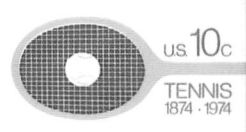

U569

U576

U581

U587

U601

U609

U610

U611

U614

U616

U617

U631

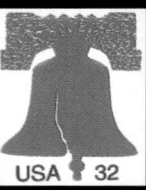

U632

U634

U635

U636

U637

Issues of 1989-92	Un	U
U615 25¢ Stars (lined paper)	.50	.25
U616 25¢ Love	.50	.25
U617 25¢ Space hologram	.60	.30
U618 25¢ Football hologram	.50	.25
U619 29¢ Star	.60	.30
U620 11.1¢ Birds		.20
U621 29¢ Love	.60	.30
U622 29¢ Magazine Industry	.60	.30
U623 29¢ Star and Bars	.60	.30
U624 29¢ Country Geese	.60	.60
U625 29¢ Space Shuttle	.60	.25
U626 29¢ Western Americana	.60	.30
U627 29¢ Protect the Environment	.60	.30
U628 19.8¢ Bulk Rate precanceled		.40

Issues of 1992-95	Un	U
U629 29¢ Disabled Americans	.60	.30
U630 29¢ Kitten	.60	.30
U631 29¢ Football	.60	.30
U632 32¢ Liberty Bell	.65	.30
U633 32¢ Old Glory	.65	.30
U634 32¢ Old Glory	.65	.30
U635 5¢ Nonprofit		.20
U636 10¢ Graphic Eagle		.20
U637 32¢ Spiral Heart	.65	.30

Ren Wicks (1911-1998)

In a career spanning 50 years, Ren Wicks influenced American perceptions through his work in media and advertising. Born in Syracuse and raised in Seattle, he was a freelance artist before helping to form Group West, Inc., a Los Angeles design and illustration studio where he served as chairman. Universal Pictures, CBS, *The Saturday Evening Post, Esquire,* and NASA were among his many accounts. A celebrated aviation artist, he worked directly with Howard Hughes on aviation and motion picture projects and accepted commissions from Lockheed and the United States Air Force. A founder of the American Society of Aviation Artists, he is the recipient of a prestigious Life Achievement Award from the Los Angeles Society of Illustrators. His art appears on six United States postage stamps. ∎

Issues of 1995-99		Un	U
U639	32¢ Space Shuttle	.65	.35
U640	32¢ Save Our Environment	.60	.30
U641	32¢ 1996 Paralympic Games	.60	.30
U642	33¢ Flag (yellow, red, blue)	.65	.30

Issues of 1999		Un	U
U643	33¢ Flag (blue & red)	.65	.30
U644	33¢ Victorian Love	.65	.30
U645	33¢ Lincoln	.65	.30

Julia Talcott

As a child, Julia Talcott wrote and illustrated her own stories. After graduating from Williams College in 1980 with a degree in studio art, she spent a year in Japan soaking up the culture and teaching English to Japanese businessmen and children. On returning to the States, she worked as a graphic designer at the Boston Children's Museum, and then attended graduate school at Cranbrook Academy of Art, receiving a degree in printmaking in 1984. Since then, she has pursued a freelance career as an illustrator, creating works for clients such as the Museum of Fine Arts in Boston, AT&T, *Newsweek*, Lotus Development Corporation, and *The Atlantic Monthly*. Married with three children, she lives in Newton, Massachusetts, and teaches illustration at the Art Institute of Boston. In 1996, the U.S Postal Service issued five of her stamp designs. ∎

U639

U640

U641

U642

U643

U644

U645

Buy the *Baseball's Legendary Playing Fields*
Commemoratives

A companion to the Legends of Baseball Classic Collection issued in 2000 — You won't want to miss this opportunity to buy stamps featuring ten of the most memorable playing fields in Major League Baseball®.

Collect the stamps and stamped cards — all with significant information on the back about each of the fields featured. And, for your convenience and collecting pleasure, we've created first day covers, uncut press sheets, and Collection II.

Collection II is A Great Deal! All of your baseball stamp collectibles are packaged together. You'll receive Legends of Baseball Classic Collection first day covers; and Baseball's Legendary Playing Fields stamps, first day covers, and stamped cards.

Ebbets Field, Brooklyn — USA 34

Tiger Stadium, Detroit — USA 34

FORBES FIELD, PITTSBURGH
With expansive foul territory and deep outfield dimensions, this park was a pitcher's friend. Ironically, in the 61 years that the Pittsburgh Pirates called Forbes Field home, no one ever pitched a no-hitter there.

Crosley Field, Cincinnati — USA 34

Polo Grounds, New York — USA 34

Fenway Park, Boston — USA 34

Shibe Park, Philadelphia — USA 34

Baseball's Legendary Playing Fields

Join the United States Postal Service and Major League Baseball in celebrating our national pastime.

To order or for more information call **1 800 STAMP-24.** Customers may order online by visiting the Postal Service's Web site at **www.usps.com** and clicking on the Postal Store.

Source Code: #39006

Item	Price	No.
Full Pane	$6.80	450840
Stamped Cards (Set of 10)	$6.95	450866
First Day Covers (Set of 10)	$7.40	450863
Uncut Press Sheet	$54.40	450884
Collection II	$28.95	450889

Airmail Envelopes and Aerogrammes

1929-1973

UC1

UC3

UC7

UC8

UC14

UC21

UC25

UC26

UC30

UC39

UC46

Issues of 1929-1945	Un	U
UC1 5¢ blue Airplane, die 1		
(vertical rudder is not		
semicircular)	3.50	2.00
1933 wmk., entire	*750.00*	*750.00*
1937 wmk., entire	—	*2,500.00*
Bicolored border		
omitted, entire	650.00	
UC2 5¢ blue, die 2 (vertical		
rudder is semicircular)	11.00	5.00
1929 wmk., entire	—	*1,500.00*
1933 wmk., entire	*650.00*	—
UC3 6¢ orange Airplane, die 2a		
("6" is 6½mm wide)	1.45	.40
a With #U436a added		
impression	*4,000.00*	
UC4 6¢ orange, die 2b		
("6" is 6mm wide)	2.75	2.00
UC5 6¢ orange, die 2c		
("6" is 5mm wide)	.75	.30
UC6 6¢ orange, die 3 (vertical		
rudder leans forward)	1.00	.35
a 6¢ orange, *blue*,		
entire	*3,500.00*	*2,400.00*
UC7 8¢ olive green Airplane	13.00	3.50
UC8 6¢ on 2¢ carm.		
Washington (U429)	1.25	.65
a 6¢ on 1¢ green		
(U420)	*1,750.00*	
c 6¢ on 3¢ purple		
(U437a)	*3,000.00*	
UC9 6¢ on 2¢ Wash. (U525)	75.00	40.00
Issues of 1946-56		
UC10 5¢ on 6¢ orange (UC3)	2.75	1.50
a Double surcharge	60.00	
UC11 5¢ on 6¢ orange (UC4)	9.00	5.50
UC13 5¢ on 6¢ orange (UC6)	.80	.60
a Double surcharge	60.00	
UC14 5¢ carm. DC-4, die 1		
(end of wing on right		
is smooth curve)	.75	.20
UC16 10¢ red, DC-4		
2-line back inscription,		
entire, *pale blue*	7.50	6.00
a "Air Letter" on face,		
4-line back inscription	16.00	14.00
Die-cutting reversed	275.00	
b 10¢ chocolate	400.00	
c "Air Letter" and		
"Aerogramme" on face	45.00	12.50
d 3-line back inscription	8.00	8.00

Issues of 1946-56	Un	U
UC17 5¢ Postage Centenary	.40	.25
UC18 6¢ carm. Airplane (UC14),		
type I (6's lean right)	.35	.20
a Type II (6's upright)	.75	.25
UC20 6¢ on 5¢ (UC15)	.80	.50
a 6¢ on 6¢ carmine,		
entire	*1,500.00*	
b Double surcharge	*250.00*	—
UC21 6¢ on 5¢ (UC14)	27.50	17.50
UC22 6¢ on 5¢ (UC14)	3.50	2.50
a Double surcharge	75.00	
UC23 6¢ on 5¢ (UC17)	1,250.00	
UC25 6¢ red Eagle	.75	.50
Issues of 1958-73		
UC26 7¢ blue (UC14)	.65	.50
UC27 6¢ + 1¢ orange (UC3)	250.00	225.00
UC28 6¢ + 1¢ orange (UC4)	65.00	75.00
UC29 6¢ + 1¢ orange (UC5)	37.50	50.00
UC30 6¢ + 1¢ (UC5)	1.00	.50
UC32 10¢ Jet Airliner, back		
inscription in 2 lines	6.00	5.00
a Type 1, entire	10.00	5.00
UC33 7¢ blue Jet Silhouette	.60	.25
UC34 7¢ carmine (UC33)	.60	.25
UC35 11¢ Jet, Globe, entire	2.75	2.25
a Red omitted	*875.00*	
Die-cutting reversed	35.00	
UC36 8¢ red Jet Airliner	.55	.20
UC37 8¢ red Jet in Triangle	.35	.20
a Tagged	1.25	.30
UC39 13¢ John Kennedy, entire	3.00	2.75
a Red omitted	*500.00*	
UC40 10¢ Jet in Triangle	.50	.20
UC41 8¢ + 2¢ (UC37)	.65	.20
UC42 13¢ Human Rights, entire	8.00	4.00
Die-cutting reversed	75.00	
UC43 11¢ Jet in Circle	.50	.20
UC44 15¢ gray, red, white		
and blue Birds in Flight	1.50	1.10
UC45 10¢ + (1¢) (UC40)	1.50	.20
UC46 15¢ red, white, bl.	.75	.40

	Issues of 1973-83	Un	U
UC47	13¢ red Bird in Flight	.30	.20
UC48	18¢ USA, entire	.90	.30
UC50	22¢ red and bl. USA, entire	.90	.40
UC51	22¢ blue USA, entire	.70	.25
	Die-cutting reversed	25.00	
UC52	22¢ Summer Olympic Games	1.50	.25
UC53	30¢ blue, red, brn. Tour the United States, entire	.65	.30
a	Red "30" omitted	*70.00*	
UC54	30¢ *yellow, magenta, blue and black* (UC53), entire	.65	.30
	Die-cutting reversed	20.00	
UC55	30¢ Made in USA, entire	.65	.30
UC56	30¢ World Communications Year, entire	.65	.30
	Die-cutting reversed	25.00	

	Issues of 1983-99	Un	U
UC57	30¢ Olympic Games, entire	.65	.30
UC58	36¢ Landsat, entire	.70	.35
UC59	36¢ Tourism Week, entire	.70	.35
UC60	36¢ Mark Twain/ Halley's Comet, entire	.70	.35
UC61	39¢ Envelope	.80	.40
UC62	39¢ Montgomery Blair	.80	.40
UC63	45¢ Eagle, entire, *blue*	.90	.45
a	White paper	.90	.45
UC64	50¢ Thaddeus Lowe, Balloonist	1.00	.50
UC65	60¢ Voyageurs Nat'l Park, Minnesota	1.25	.65

Hiro Kimura

Born in a Buddhist temple in Kyoto, Japan, Hiro Kimura studied art in Hawaii and California. From his home studio in Brooklyn, New York, he creates commissioned artwork for an impressive group of corporate clients such as Anheuser-Busch, Coca-Cola, Honda, IBM, McDonald's, Reebok, and Universal Studios. Publishing clients include *The Atlantic Monthly*, *BusinessWeek*, *Golf Digest*, the *New Yorker*, Avon Books, and Random House. He has been featured in graphic publications such as the Society of Illustrators' *Pro-Illustration Volume II* and *IDEA* magazine and received awards from the Society of Illustrators, *Communications Arts*, The Humor Show, Illustrators West, and the Art Directors Club of Metropolitan Washington, among others. His association with the Pushpin Group has led to exhibitions in Europe and Japan. His United States Postal Service commissions include designs for three United States postage stamps, each featuring the American flag. ■

UC48

UC52

UC53

UC56

UC57

UC59

UC63

UC64

UC65

UO1

UO16

UO20

UO73

UO84

UO88

Issues of 1873-1875		Un	U
Official Envelopes			
Post Office Department			
Numeral 9½mm high			
UO1	2¢ black, *lemon*	15.00	9.00
	Numeral 10½mm high		
UO5	2¢ black, *lemon*	6.00	4.00
UO9	3¢ black, *amber*	45.00	35.00
	Postal Service		
UO16	blue, *amber*	50.00	30.00
	War Department		
UO20	3¢ dk. red Washington	60.00	40.00
UO26	12¢ dark red Clay	110.00	50.00
UO39	10¢ vermilion Jefferson	250.00	
UO48	2¢ red Jackson, *amber*	25.00	14.00
UO55	3¢ red Washington, *fawn*	4.50	2.75

Issues of 1983-99		Un	U
Penalty Mail Envelopes			
UO73	20¢ blue Great Seal	1.25	*30.00*
UO74	22¢ (seal embossed)	.90	*5.00*
UO75	22¢ (seal typographed)	1.00	*20.00*
UO76	"E" (25¢) Great Seal	1.10	*20.00*
UO77	25¢ black, blue Great Seal (seal embossed)	.80	*15.00*
UO78	25¢ (seal typographed)	.90	*25.00*
UO79	45¢ (stars illegible)	1.25	—
UO80	65¢ (stars illegible)	1.75	—
UO81	45¢ (stars clear)	1.25	—
UO82	65¢ (stars clear)	1.60	—
UO83	"F" (29¢) Great Seal	1.10	*20.00*
UO84	29¢ black, blue, entire	.75	*10.00*
UO88	32¢ Official Mail	.80	*10.00*
UO89	33¢ Official Mail	.70	—

Robert Peak (1927-1992)

In a career spanning some 40 years, Robert Peak created award-winning art for a distinguished group of clients. Born in Denver, Colorado, he was educated at Wichita State University and the Art Center College of Design in Los Angeles. In his mid-30s he was named Artist of the Year by the Artists Guild of New York. He won more than 100 awards from the Society of Illustrators and was elected to its Hall of Fame in 1977. A teacher at the Art Center College of Design, the Art Students League in New York, and the Famous Artists School, he was featured in numerous articles and books. His art is found in the permanent collections of many major corporations and institutions. He designed 28 commemorative stamps for the U.S. Postal Service. ■

Postal Cards

1875-1968

UX5

UX6

UX11

UX14

UX16

UX18

UX25

UX27

UX28

UX37

UX43

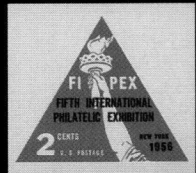
UX44

UX45

UX46

UX48

UX49

UX50

UX56

Issues of 1873-1917	Un	U

Represented below is only a partial listing of postal cards. Values are for entire cards. Color in italic is color of card. Cards preprinted with written address or message usually sell for much less.

		Un	U
UX1	1¢ brown Liberty, wmkd. (90 x 60mm)	325.00	17.50
UX3	1¢ brown Liberty, wmkd. (53 x 36mm)	70.00	2.25
UX4	1¢ blk. Liberty, wmkd., USPOD in monogram	2,000.00	300.00
UX5	1¢ blk. Liberty, unwmkd.	60.00	.40
UX6	2¢ blue Liberty, *buff*	25.00	17.50
a	2¢ dark blue, *buff*	30.00	19.00
UX7	1¢ (UX5), inscribed "Nothing But The Address"	60.00	.35
a	23 teeth below "One Cent"	500.00	30.00
b	Printed on both sides	*575.00*	*400.00*
UX8	1¢ brown Jefferson, large "one-cent" wreath	45.00	1.25
c	1¢ chocolate	85.00	6.00
UX9	1¢ blk. Jefferson, *buff*	17.50	.55
a	1¢ blk., *dark buff*	20.00	1.25
UX10	1¢ black Grant	32.50	1.40
UX11	1¢ blue Grant	12.50	2.50
UX12	1¢ black Jefferson, wreath smaller than UX14	35.00	.45
UX13	2¢ blue Liberty, *cream*	135.00	75.00
UX14	1¢ Jefferson	25.00	.40
UX15	1¢ black John Adams	40.00	15.00
UX16	2¢ black Liberty	10.00	9.00
UX17	1¢ black McKinley	*4,500.00*	
UX18	1¢ black McKinley, facing left	12.00	.30
UX19	1¢ black McKinley, triangles in top corners	37.50	.50
UX20	1¢ (UX19), correspondence space at left	50.00	4.00
UX21	1¢ blue McKinley, shaded background	90.00	6.50
a	1¢ bronze blue, *bluish*	165.00	12.50
UX22	1¢ blue McKinley, white background	13.00	.30
UX23	1¢ red Lincoln, solid background	8.00	5.50
UX24	1¢ red McKinley	9.00	.30
UX25	2¢ red Grant	1.25	8.50
UX26	1¢ green Lincoln, solid background	10.00	6.00
UX27	1¢ Jefferson, *buff*	.25	.25
a	1¢ green, *cream*	3.50	.60
UX27C	1¢ green Jefferson, *gray*, die I	*2,000.00*	150.00
UX28	1¢ green Lincoln, *cream*	.60	.30
a	1¢ green, *buff*	1.50	.60
UX29	2¢ red Jefferson, *buff*	40.00	2.00
a	2¢ lake, *cream*	47.50	2.50
c	2¢ vermilion, *buff*	275.00	60.00

Issues of 1918-68	Un	U

		Un	U
UX30	2¢ red Jefferson, *cream*	27.50	1.50
	Surcharged in one line by canceling machine.		
UX31	1¢ on 2¢ red Jefferson	*3,500.00*	*3,500.00*
	Surcharged in two lines by canceling machine.		
UX32	1¢ on 2¢ red Jeff., *buff*	50.00	12.50
a	1¢ on 2¢ vermilion	*95.00*	60.00
b	Double surcharge	—	82.50
UX33	1¢ on 2¢ red Jefferson, *cream*	12.00	1.90
a	Inverted surcharge	55.00	
b	Double surcharge	55.00	35.00
d	Triple surcharge	350.00	
	Surcharged in two lines by press printing.		
UX34	1¢ on 2¢ red (UX29)	500.00	47.50
UX35	1¢ on 2¢ red Jefferson, *cream*	200.00	32.50
UX36	1¢ on 2¢ red (UX25)		*50,000.00*
UX37	3¢ red McKinley, *buff*	4.00	10.00
UX38	2¢ carmine rose Franklin	.35	.25
a	Double impression	200.00	
	Surcharged by canceling machine in light green.		
UX39	2¢ on 1¢ green Jefferson, *buff*	.50	.35
b	Double surcharge	17.50	20.00
UX40	2¢ on 1¢ green (UX28)	.65	.45
	Surcharged typographically in dark green.		
UX41	2¢ on 1¢ green Jefferson, *buff*	4.50	1.75
a	Inverted surcharge lower left	75.00	125.00
UX42	2¢ on 1¢ green (UX29)	5.00	2.50
b	Surcharged on back	80.00	
UX43	2¢ carmine Lincoln	.30	*1.00*
UX44	2¢ FIPEX	.25	*1.00*
b	Dk. vio. blue omitted	450.00	225.00
UX45	4¢ Statue of Liberty	1.50	*40.00*
UX46	3¢ purple Statue of Liberty	.50	.20
a	"N GOD WE TRUST"	15.00	25.00
UX47	2¢ + 1¢ carmine rose Franklin	185.00	250.00
UX48	4¢ red violet Lincoln	.25	.20
UX49	7¢ World Vacationland	3.75	*35.00*
UX50	4¢ U.S. Customs	.50	*1.00*
a	Blue omitted	625.00	
UX51	4¢ Social Security	.40	*1.00*
b	Blue omitted	*750.00*	
UX52	4¢ blue & red Coast Guard	.30	*1.00*
UX53	4¢ Bureau of the Census	.30	*1.00*
UX54	8¢ blue & red (UX49)	3.75	*35.00*
UX55	5¢ emerald Lincoln	.30	*.50*
UX56	5¢ Women Marines	.35	*1.00*

1970-1990

Issues of 1970-83		Un	U
UX57	5¢ Weather Services	.30	*1.00*
a	Yellow, black omitted	*700.00*	*850.00*
b	Blue omitted	*650.00*	
c	Black omitted	*600.00*	
UX58	6¢ brown Paul Revere	.30	*1.00*
a	Double impression	*300.00*	
UX59	10¢ blue & red (UX49)	4.00	*35.00*
UX60	6¢ America's Hospitals	.30	*1.00*
a	Blue, yellow omitted	*700.00*	
UX61	6¢ USF *Constellation*	.85	*3.00*
a	Address side blank	*300.00*	
UX62	6¢ black Monument Valley	.40	*3.00*
UX63	6¢ Gloucester, MA	.40	*3.00*
UX64	6¢ blue John Hanson	.25	*1.00*
UX65	6¢ magenta Liberty	.25	*1.00*
UX66	8¢ orange Samuel Adams	.25	*1.00*
UX67	12¢ Visit USA/		
	Ship's Figurehead	.35	*30.00*
UX68	7¢ Charles Thomson	.30	*5.00*
UX69	9¢ John Witherspoon	.25	*1.00*
UX70	9¢ blue Caesar Rodney	.25	*1.00*
UX71	9¢ Federal Court House	.25	*1.00*
UX72	9¢ green Nathan Hale	.25	*1.00*
UX73	10¢ Cincinnati Music Hall	.30	*1.00*
UX74	10¢ John Hancock	.30	*1.00*
UX75	10¢ John Hancock	.30	*.20*
UX76	14¢ Coast Guard Eagle	.40	*15.00*
UX77	10¢ Molly Pitcher	.30	*1.00*
UX78	10¢ George Rogers Clark	.30	*1.00*
UX79	10¢ Casimir Pulaski	.30	*1.00*
UX80	10¢ Olympic Sprinter	.60	*1.00*
UX81	10¢ Iolani Palace	.30	*1.00*
UX82	14¢ Olympic Games	.60	*10.00*
UX83	10¢ Salt Lake Temple	.25	*1.00*
UX84	10¢ Landing of Rochambeau	.25	*1.00*
UX85	10¢ Battle of Kings Mtn.	.25	*1.00*
UX86	19¢ Drake's Golden Hinde	.65	*10.00*
UX87	10¢ Battle of Cowpens	.25	*2.50*
UX88	12¢ violet Eagle,		
	nondenominated	.30	*.50*
UX89	12¢ lt. bl. Isaiah Thomas	.30	*.50*
UX90	12¢ Nathanael Greene	.30	*1.00*
UX91	12¢ Lewis and Clark	.30	*3.00*
UX92	13¢ buff Robert Morris	.30	*.50*
UX93	13¢ buff Robert Morris	.30	*.50*
UX94	13¢ "Swamp Fox"		
	Francis Marion	.30	*.75*
UX95	13¢ LaSalle Claims		
	Louisiana	.30	*.75*
UX96	13¢ Academy of Music	.30	*.75*
UX97	13¢ Old Post Office,		
	St. Louis, Missouri	.30	*.75*
UX100	13¢ Olympic Yachting	.30	*.75*

Issues of 1984-90		Un	U
UX101	13¢ *Ark* and *Dove*, Maryland	.30	*.75*
UX102	13¢ Olympic Torch	.30	*.75*
UX103	13¢ Frederic Baraga	.30	*.75*
UX104	13¢ Dominguez Adobe	.30	*.75*
UX105	14¢ Charles Carroll	.30	*.50*
UX106	14¢ green Charles Carroll	.45	*.25*
UX107	25¢ Clipper *Flying Cloud*	.70	*5.00*
UX108	14¢ brt. grn. George Wythe	.30	*.50*
UX109	14¢ Settlement of		
	Connecticut	.30	*.75*
UX110	14¢ Stamp Collecting	.30	*.75*
UX111	14¢ Francis Vigo	.30	*.75*
UX112	14¢ Settling of Rhode Island	.30	*.75*
UX113	14¢ Wisconsin Territory	.30	*.75*
UX114	14¢ National Guard	.30	*.75*
UX115	14¢ Self-Scouring Plow	.30	*.50*
UX116	14¢ Constitutional		
	Convention	.30	*.50*
UX117	14¢ Stars and Stripes	.30	*.50*
UX118	14¢ Take Pride in		
	America	.30	*.50*
UX119	14¢ Timberline Lodge	.30	*.50*
UX120	15¢ Bison and Prairie	.30	*.50*
UX121	15¢ Blair House	.30	*.50*
UX122	28¢ *Yorkshire*	.60	*3.00*
UX123	15¢ Iowa Territory	.30	*.50*
UX124	15¢ Ohio, Northwest Terr.	.30	*.50*
UX125	15¢ Hearst Castle	.30	*.50*
UX126	15¢ The Federalist Papers	.30	*.50*
UX127	15¢ Hawk and Desert	.30	*.50*
UX128	15¢ Healy Hall	.30	*.50*
UX129	15¢ Blue Heron and Marsh	.30	*.50*
UX130	15¢ Settling of Oklahoma	.30	*.50*
UX131	21¢ Geese and Mountains	.40	*3.00*
UX132	15¢ Seagull and Seashore	.30	*.50*
UX133	15¢ Deer and Waterfall	.30	*.50*
UX134	15¢ Hull House, Chicago	.30	*.50*
UX135	15¢ Ind. Hall, Philadelphia	.30	*.50*
UX136	15¢ Inner Harbor, Baltimore	.30	*.50*
UX137	15¢ Bridge, New York	.30	*.50*
UX138	15¢ Capitol, Washington	.30	*.50*
	#UX139-42 issued in sheets of 4 plus 2		
	inscribed labels, rouletted 9½ on 2 or		
	3 sides.		
UX139	15¢ (UX135)	3.25	*.90*
UX140	15¢ The White House	3.25	*.90*
UX141	15¢ (UX137)	3.25	*.90*
UX142	15¢ (UX138)	3.25	*.90*
a	Sheet of 4,		
	#UX139-42	13.00	
UX143	15¢ The White House	1.00	1.00
UX144	15¢ Jefferson Memorial	1.00	1.00
UX145	15¢ Papermaking	.30	*.30*
UX146	15¢ World Literacy Year	.30	*.50*

UX70

UX79

UX81

UX83

UX94

UX109

UX112

UX113

UX115

UX116

UX118

UX119

UX131

UX143

UX144

UX143 (picture side)

UX144 (picture side)

1994-1998

UX174

UX175

UX176

UX177

UX198

UX199

UX219A

UX220

UX241

UX262

UX263

UX280

UX282

UX283

UX290

UX292

UX298

Issues of 1990-93		Un	U
UX147	15¢ George Caleb Bingham	1.00	1.00
UX148	15¢ Isaac Royall House	.30	.50
UX150	15¢ Stanford University	.30	.50
UX151	15¢ Constitution Hall	1.00	1.00
UX152	15¢ Chicago Orchestra Hall	.30	.50
UX153	19¢ Flag	.40	.50
UX154	19¢ Carnegie Hall	.40	.50
UX155	19¢ Old Red, UT-Galveston	.40	.50
UX156	19¢ Bill of Rights	.40	.50
UX157	19¢ Notre Dame	.40	.50
UX158	30¢ Niagara Falls	.75	1.40
UX159	19¢ The Old Mill	.40	.50
UX160	19¢ Wadsworth Atheneum	.40	.50
UX161	19¢ Cobb Hall	.40	.50
UX162	19¢ Waller Hall	.40	.50
UX163	19¢ America's Cup	1.00	1.75
UX164	19¢ Columbia River Gorge	.40	.50
UX165	19¢ Ellis Island	.40	.50
UX166	19¢ National Cathedral	.40	.50
UX167	19¢ Wren Building	.40	.50
UX168	19¢ Holocaust Memorial	1.00	1.75
UX169	19¢ Fort Recovery	.40	.50
UX170	19¢ Playmakers Theatre	.40	.50
UX171	19¢ O'Kane Hall	.40	.50

Issues of 1993-98		Un	U
UX172	19¢ Beecher Hall	.40	.50
UX173	19¢ Massachusetts Hall	.40	.50
UX174	19¢ Lincoln's Home	.40	.50
UX175	19¢ Wittenberg University	.40	.50
UX176	19¢ Canyon de Chelly	.40	.50
UX177	19¢ St. Louis Union Station	.40	.50
UX198	20¢ Red Barn	.40	.40
UX199	20¢ Old Glory	.60	.40
UX219A	50¢ Soaring Eagle	1.00	2.00
UX220	20¢ American Clipper Ships	.40	.40
UX241	20¢ Winter Scene	.40	.40
UX262	20¢ St. John's College	.40	.40
UX263	20¢ Princeton University	.40	.40
UX280	20¢ City College of New York	.40	.40
UX281	20¢ Bugs Bunny	1.20	1.75
UX282	20¢ Pacific 97 Golden Gate Bridge in Daylight	.40	.40
UX283	50¢ Pacific 97 Golden Gate Bridge at Sunset	1.00	1.00
UX284	20¢ Fort McHenry	.40	.40
UX290	20¢ University of Mississippi	.40	.40
UX291	20¢ Sylvester & Tweety	1.20	1.75
UX292	20¢ Girard College	.40	.40
UX298	20¢ Northeastern University	.40	.40

Bart Forbes

Internationally acclaimed artist Bart Forbes has been capturing the essence of sport for nearly 30 years. He attended the Art Center College in Los Angeles before embarking on a career as a freelance illustrator, which has taken him to all corners of the earth. Among the most sought-after artists of our time, his images have appeared in *Sports Illustrated* and *Time* as well as on posters for the Boston Marathon, The America's Cup, the Indianapolis 500, and the 1992 and 1996 Olympic Games. The designer of 24 United States postage stamps, he was selected by the Korean Olympic Committee as the official artist for the 1988 Seoul Olympics. ∎

"I was particularly excited about the opportunity to create the Lou Gehrig stamp, since baseball has always been a passion with me."

— Bart Forbes

1949-2000

Issues of 1998-2000	Un	U
UX299 20¢ Brandeis University	.40	.40
UX301 20¢ University of		
Wisconsin-Madison	.40	.40
UX302 20¢ Washington and		
Lee University	.40	.40
UX303 20¢ Redwood Library		
& Athenæum	.40	.40
UX305 20¢ Mount Vernon	.40	.40
UX306 20¢ Block Island Lighthouse	.40	.40
UX312 20¢ University of Utah	.40	.40
UX313 20¢ Ryman Auditorium	.40	.40
UX316 20¢ Middlebury College	.40	.40

Issues of 1949-1966	Un	U
Airmail Postal Cards		
UXC1 4¢ orange Eagle	.50	.75
UXC2 5¢ red Eagle (C48)	1.75	.75
UXC3 5¢ UXC2 redrawn "Air		
Mail-Postal Card" omitted	6.00	2.00
UXC4 6¢ red Eagle	.60	.75
UXC5 11¢ Visit The USA	.60	12.50

Richard Schlecht

Richard Schlecht grew up in Colorado and graduated from the University of Denver with a degree in journalism. He came to art as an illustrator of military subjects during his service in the Army, and worked at commercial graphics studios before embarking on a freelance career in 1967. A specialist on the subjects of underwater  archaeology, maritime history, and the visual reconstruction of historic and prehistoric archaeological sites, he has worked extensively with *National Geographic*, the National Park Service, Time-Life Books, and Colonial Williamsburg. He has created imagery for 21 United States postage stamps and spends several months each year painting in Italy for exhibition and pleasure. ■

UX299

UX301

UX302

UX303

UX305

UX306

UX312

UX313

UX316

UXC1

UXC2

UXC4

UXC5

UXC6

UXC7

UXC8

UXC9

UXC10

UXC11

UXC12

UXC13

UXC19

UXC20

UXC23

UXC25

UXC27

UY12

UY41

UZ6

Issues of 1967-1999	Un	U
UXC6 6¢ Virgin Islands	.40	*6.00*
a Red, yellow omitted	*1,700.00*	
UXC7 6¢ Boy Scout		
World Jamboree	.40	*6.00*
UXC8 13¢ blue & red (UXC5)	1.25	*8.00*
UXC9 8¢ Stylized Eagle	.60	*2.00*
UXC10 9¢ red & blue (UXC5)	.50	*1.00*
UXC11 15¢ Travel Service	1.75	*12.50*
UXC12 9¢ black Grand Canyon	.50	*8.00*
UXC13 15¢ black Niagara Falls	.65	*15.00*
UXC14 11¢ Stylized Eagle	.70	*2.00*
UXC15 18¢ Eagle Weather Vane	.85	*7.00*
UXC16 21¢ Angel Weather Vane	.80	*7.50*
UXC17 21¢ Curtiss Jenny	.75	*6.00*
UXC18 21¢ Olympic Gymnast	1.00	*10.00*
UXC19 28¢ First Transpacific Flight	.90	*4.00*
UXC20 28¢ Gliders	.90	*3.00*
UXC21 28¢ Olympic Speed Skater	.90	*2.00*
UXC22 33¢ China Clipper	.90	*2.00*
UXC23 33¢ AMERIPEX '86	.65	*2.00*
UXC24 36¢ DC-3	.70	*2.00*
UXC25 40¢ Yankee Clipper	.80	*1.00*
UXC27 Mt. Rainier	1.10	1.00

Issues of 1892-1995	Un	U
Paid Reply Postal Cards		
Prices are: Un=unsevered,		
U=severed card.		
UY1 1¢ + 1¢ black Grant	35.00	9.00
UY6 1¢ + 1¢ green G. and M.		
Washington, double		
frame line around		
instructions	150.00	25.00
UY7 1¢ + 1¢ green G. and M.		
Washington, single		
frame line	1.25	.50
UY12 3¢ + 3¢ red McKinley	9.00	25.00
UY18 4¢ + 4¢ Lincoln	3.00	*2.50*
UY23 6¢ + 6¢ John Adams	.90	*2.00*
UY31 "A" (12¢ + 12¢) Eagle	.75	*2.00*
UY39 15¢ + 15¢ Bison and Prairie	.75	*1.00*
UY40 19¢ + 19¢ Flag	.75	*1.00*
UY41 20¢ Red Barn	.80	*1.25*
Issues of 1913-95		
Official Mail Postal Cards		
UZ1 1¢ black Numeral	325.00	175.00
UZ2 13¢ blue Great Seal	.60	*35.00*
UZ3 14¢ blue Great Seal	.60	*35.00*
UZ4 15¢ blue Great Seal	.60	*35.00*
UZ5 19¢ blue Great Seal	.55	*30.00*
UZ6 20¢ Official Mail	.40	*30.00*

The **Souvenir Pages Subscription Program**

Collect Every **First Day Issue**

- Features stamps issued each year
- Complete with First Day cancellation and informative text
- A convenient, affordable way to collect

The U.S. Postal Service's Souvenir Pages Subscription Program is your ticket to the year's stamp issues. It's a great way to collect and learn about the stamps and stamp subjects honored during the year.

Fun and Attractive

A Souvenir Page is issued for most stamps—definitives and commemoratives, self-adhesive stamps, coil stamps and booklet panes. Each Souvenir Page includes the featured stamp(s), post-marked with a First Day of Issue cancellation, mounted on an 8" x 10 1/2" page. Information on relevant philatelic specifications and a lively narrative about the stamp's subject are included.

Affordable Collectibles

Souvenir Pages are printed in a limited quantity each year. The cost of a Souvenir Page is approximately $2.00 per page. (If the face value of the stamp[s] exceeds $2.00, the price will reflect the face value.)

Money-Back Guarantee

Just return your Souvenir Pages within 30 days for a full refund.

To order or for more information call **1 800 STAMP-24**. Customers may order online by visiting the Postal Service's Web site at **www.usps.com** and clicking on the Postal Store.
Source Code: #3907

Souvenir Pages

The Postal Service offers Souvenir Pages for new stamps. The series began with a page for the Yellowstone Park Centennial stamp issued March 1, 1972. The Pages feature one or more stamps tied by the first day cancel, along with technical data and information on the subject of the issue. More than just collectors' items, Souvenir Pages make wonderful show and conversation pieces. Souvenir Pages are issued in limited editions. Number in parentheses ( ) indicates the number of stamps on page if there are more than one.

The identifying numbers used below are based on the Postal Service's numbering system for Souvenir Pages; therefore, they do not follow the Scott numbering system.

	1972	
72-00	Family Planning	500.00
72-01	Yellowstone Park	90.00
72-01a	Yellowstone Park with DC cancel	—
72-02	2¢ Cape Hatteras	75.00
72-03	14¢ Fiorello LaGuardia	75.00
72-04	11¢ City of Refuge Park	80.00
72-05	6¢ Wolf Trap Farm Park	27.50
72-06	Colonial Craftsmen (4)	14.00
72-07	15¢ Mount McKinley	20.00
72-08	6¢-15¢ Olympic Games (4)	10.50
72-08E	Olympic Games with broken red circle on 6¢ stamp	—
72-09	PTA	5.50
72-10	Wildlife Conservation (4)	6.75
72-11	Mail Order	5.50
72-12	Osteopathic Medicine	5.50
72-13	Tom Sawyer	5.50
72-14	7¢ Benjamin Franklin	6.25
72-15	Christmas (2)	6.75
72-16	Pharmacy	10.00
72-17	Stamp Collecting	5.50
	1973	
73-01	$1 Eugene O'Neill	12.50
73-01E	$1 Eugene O'Neill picture perf. error	—
73-02	Love	6.50
73-03	Pamphleteer	4.25
73-04	George Gershwin	5.00
73-05	Broadside	5.75
73-06	Copernicus	4.75
73-07	Postal Employees	5.50
73-08	Harry S. Truman	4.25
73-09	Post Rider	5.50
73-10	21¢ Amadeo Giannini	4.50
73-11	Boston Tea Party (4)	5.50

73-12	6¢-15¢ Electronics (4)	6.25
73-13	Robinson Jeffers	4.00
73-14	Lyndon B. Johnson	3.50
73-15	Henry O. Tanner	5.00
73-16	Willa Cather	3.25
73-17	Colonial Drummer	4.00
73-18	Angus Cattle	3.50
73-19	Christmas (2)	5.75
73-20	13¢ Winged Envelope airmail	2.75
73-21	10¢ Crossed Flags	2.75
73-22	10¢ Jefferson Memorial	2.50
73-23	13¢ Winged Envelope airmail coil (2)	2.75
	1974	
74-01	26¢ Mount Rushmore airmail	4.75
74-02	ZIP Code	3.25
74-02E	ZIP Code with date error 4/4/74	—
74-03	18¢ Statue of Liberty airmail	5.50
74-04	18¢ Elizabeth Blackwell	2.00
74-05	VFW	2.50
74-06	Robert Frost	2.50
74-07	Expo '74	2.50
74-08	Horse Racing	3.75
74-09	Skylab	5.25
74-10	UPU (8)	4.75
74-11	Mineral Heritage (4)	5.00
74-12	Fort Harrod	2.50
74-13	Continental Congress (4)	4.00
74-14	Chautauqua	1.90
74-15	Kansas Wheat	1.90
74-16	Energy Conservation	1.90
74-17	6.3¢ Liberty Bell coil (2)	2.75
74-18	Sleepy Hollow	2.75
74-19	Retarded Children	2.00
74-20	Christmas (3)	5.00
	1975	
75-01	Benjamin West	2.25
75-02	Pioneer/Jupiter	5.00
75-03	Collective Bargaining	2.50
75-04	8¢ Sybil Ludington	2.50
75-05	Salem Poor	2.50
75-06	Haym Salomon	2.75

75-07	18¢ Peter Francisco	3.25
75-08	Mariner 10	4.25
75-09	Lexington & Concord	2.50
75-10	Paul Dunbar	3.25
75-11	D.W. Griffith	2.50
75-12	Bunker Hill	2.50
75-13	Military Uniforms (4)	5.00
75-14	Apollo Soyuz (2)	5.00
75-15	International Women's Year	2.00
75-16	Postal Service Bicentennial (4)	3.25
75-17	World Peace Through Law	2.00
75-18	Banking & Commerce (2)	2.00
75-19	Christmas (2)	3.00
75-20	3¢ Francis Parkman	2.50
75-21	11¢ Freedom of the Press	2.00
75-22	24¢ Old North Church	1.90
75-23	Flag over Independence Hall (2)	2.00
75-24	9¢ Freedom to Assemble	2.00
75-25	Liberty Bell coil (2)	2.00
75-26	Eagle & Shield	2.50
	1976	
76-01	Spirit of '76 (3)	3.25
76-01E	Spirit of '76 with cancellation error Jan. 2, 1976 (3)	—
76-02	25¢ and 31¢ Plane and Globes airmails (2)	2.75
76-03	Interphil '76	2.50
76-04	State Flags, DE to VA (10)	7.00
76-05	State Flags, NY to MS (10)	7.00
76-06	State Flags, IL to WI (10)	7.00
76-07	State Flags, CA to SD (10)	7.00
76-08	State Flags, MT to HI (10)	7.00
76-09	9¢ Freedom to Assemble coil (2)	1.75

No.	Description	Price
76-10	Telephone Centennial	1.75
76-11	Commercial Aviation	2.00
76-12	Chemistry	1.75
76-13	7.9¢ Drum coil (2)	1.90
76-14	Benjamin Franklin	1.75
76-15	Bicentennial souvenir sheet	8.00
76-15E	13¢ Bicentennial souvenir sheet with perforation and numerical errors	—
76-16	18¢ Bicentennial souvenir sheet	8.00
76-17	24¢ Bicentennial souvenir sheet	8.00
76-18	31¢ Bicentennial souvenir sheet	8.00
76-19	Declaration of Independence (4)	4.00
76-20	Olympics (4)	4.25
76-21	Clara Maass	1.75
76-22	Adolph S. Ochs	1.75
76-23	Christmas (3)	2.25
76-24	7.7¢ Saxhorns coil (2)	1.75
1977		
77-01	Washington at Princeton	1.90
77-02	Flag over Capitol booklet pane (9¢ and 13¢) Perf. 10 (8)	16.00
77-03	Sound Recording	1.75
77-04	Pueblo Pottery (4)	2.25
77-05	Lindbergh Flight	2.75
77-06	Colorado Centennial	1.90
77-07	Butterflies (4)	2.00
77-08	Lafayette	1.75
77-09	Skilled Hands (4)	2.25
77-10	Peace Bridge	1.60
77-11	Battle of Oriskany	1.60
77-12	Alta, CA, First Civil Settlement	1.60
77-13	Articles of Confederation	1.75
77-14	Talking Pictures	2.50
77-15	Surrender at Saratoga	2.50
77-16	Energy (2)	1.60
77-17	Christmas, Mailbox and Christmas, Valley Forge, Omaha cancel (2)	2.00
77-18	Same, Valley Forge cancel	—
77-19	10¢ Petition for Redress coil (2)	2.75
77-20	10¢ Petition for Redress sheet (2)	2.25
77-21	1¢-4¢ Americana (5)	2.00
1978		
78-01	Carl Sandburg	2.00
78-02	Indian Head Penny	2.00
78-03	Captain Cook, Anchorage cancel (2)	2.00
78-04	Captain Cook, Honolulu cancel (2)	2.00
78-05	Harriet Tubman	3.00
78-06	American Quilts (4)	2.50
78-07	16¢ Statue of Liberty sheet and coil (2)	1.90
78-08	29¢ Sandy Hook Lighthouse	1.90
78-09	American Dance (4)	2.50
78-10	French Alliance	1.90
78-11	Early Cancer Detection	2.50
78-12	"A" (15¢) sheet and coil (2)	4.50
78-13	Jimmie Rodgers	3.00
78-14	CAPEX '78 (8)	6.25
78-15	Oliver Wendell Holmes coil	1.90
78-16	Photography	1.90
78-17	Fort McHenry Flag sheet and coil (2)	2.00
78-18	George M. Cohan	1.60
78-19	Rose booklet single	2.50
78-20	8.4¢ Piano coil (2)	2.00
78-21	Viking Missions	3.75
78-22	28¢ Remote Outpost	2.00
78-23	American Owls (4)	2.50
78-24	31¢ Wright Brothers airmails (2)	2.75
78-25	American Trees (4)	2.75
78-26	Christmas, Madonna	2.00
78-27	Christmas, Hobby Horse	2.00
78-28	$2 Kerosene Lamp	5.25
1979		
79-01	Robert F. Kennedy	2.00
79-02	Martin Luther King, Jr.	3.50
79-03	International Year of the Child	1.90
79-04	John Steinbeck	1.90
79-05	Albert Einstein	2.25
79-06	21¢ Octave Chanute airmails (2)	2.75
79-07	Pennsylvania Toleware (4)	2.25
79-08	American Architecture (4)	2.25
79-09	Endangered Flora (4)	2.50
79-10	Seeing Eye Dogs	1.90
79-11	Candle & Holder	4.25
79-12	Special Olympics	1.90
79-13	$5 Lantern	10.50
79-14	30¢ Schoolhouse	3.00
79-15	10¢ Summer Olympics (2)	2.75
79-16	50¢ Whale Oil Lamp	3.25
79-17	John Paul Jones	2.00
79-18	Summer Olympics (4)	3.75
79-19	Christmas, Madonna	2.50
79-20	Christmas, Santa Claus	2.50
79-21	3.1¢ Guitar coil (2)	3.50
79-22	31¢ Summer Olympics airmail	4.00
79-23	Will Rogers	1.90
79-24	Vietnam Veterans	1.90
79-25	25¢ Wiley Post airmails (2)	3.25
1980		
80-01	W.C. Fields	2.00
80-02	Winter Olympics (4)	5.00
80-03	Windmills booklet pane (10)	4.00
80-04	Benjamin Banneker	3.50
80-05	Letter Writing (6)	2.25
80-06	1¢ Ability to Write (2)	1.60
80-07	Frances Perkins	1.50
80-08	Dolley Madison	3.00
80-09	Emily Bissell	1.90
80-10	3.5¢ Violins coil (2)	2.50
80-11	Helen Keller/ Anne Sullivan	1.90
80-12	Veterans Administration	1.50
80-13	General Bernardo de Galvez	1.50
80-14	Coral Reefs (4)	1.90
80-15	Organized Labor	3.25
80-16	Edith Wharton	3.00
80-17	Education	3.00
80-18	Indian Masks (4)	2.50
80-19	American Architecture (4)	1.90
80-20	40¢ Philip Mazzei airmail	2.75
80-21	Christmas, Madonna	2.50
80-22	Christmas, Antique Toys	2.50
80-23	Sequoyah	1.50
80-24	28¢ Blanche Scott airmail	1.60
80-25	35¢ Glenn Curtiss airmail	1.60
1981		
81-01	Everett Dirksen	1.50
81-02	Whitney M. Young	3.25
81-03	"B" (18¢) sheet and coil (3)	2.00
81-04	"B" (18¢) booklet pane (8)	2.25
81-05	12¢ Freedom of Conscience sheet and coil (3)	1.90
81-06	Flowers block (4)	2.00
81-07	Flag and Anthem sheet and coil (3)	2.50
81-08	Flag and Anthem booklet pane (8 - 6¢ and 18¢)	2.50
81-09	American Red Cross	1.50
81-10	George Mason	1.50
81-11	Savings & Loans	1.50
81-12	Wildlife booklet pane (10)	3.50
81-13	Surrey coil (2)	2.75
81-14	Space Achievement (8)	6.75
81-15	17¢ Rachel Carson (2)	1.40
81-16	35¢ Charles Drew, MD	2.50
81-17	Professional Management	1.40
81-18	17¢ Electric Auto coil (2)	3.25
81-19	Wildlife Habitat (4)	2.00
81-20	International Year of the Disabled	1.50
81-21	Edna St. Vincent Millay	2.50
81-22	Alcoholism	2.50
81-23	American Architecture (4)	2.50
81-24	Babe Zaharias	4.25
81-25	Bobby Jones	4.25
81-26	Frederic Remington	1.50
81-27	"C" (20¢) sheet and coil (3)	3.25
81-28	"C" (18¢) booklet pane (10)	3.25
81-29	18¢ and 20¢ Hoban (2)	1.60
81-30	Yorktown/ Virginia Capes (2)	2.00
81-31	Christmas, Madonna	2.75
81-32	Christmas, Bear on Sleigh	3.00
81-33	John Hanson	1.40
81-34	Fire Pumper coil (2)	5.00
81-35	Desert Plants (4)	2.50

81-36	9.3¢ Mail Wagon coil (3)	3.75
81-37	Flag over Supreme Court sheet and coil (3)	3.75
81-38	Flag over Supreme Court booklet pane (6)	3.25

1982

82-01	Sheep booklet pane (10)	3.00
82-02	Ralph Bunche	4.00
82-03	13¢ Crazy Horse (2)	1.60
82-04	37¢ Robert Millikan	1.40
82-05	Franklin D. Roosevelt	1.50
82-06	Love	1.50
82-07	5.9¢ Bicycle coil (4)	5.75
82-08	George Washington	3.25
82-09	10.9¢ Hansom Cab coil (2)	4.25
82-10	Birds & Flowers, AL-GE (10)	10.00
82-11	Birds & Flowers, HI-MD (10)	10.00
82-12	Birds & Flowers, MA-NJ (10)	10.00
82-13	Birds & Flowers, NM-SC (10)	10.00
82-14	Birds & Flowers, SD-WY (10)	10.00
82-15	USA/Netherlands	1.50
82-16	Library of Congress	1.40
82-17	Consumer Education coil (2)	3.25
82-18	Knoxville World's Fair (4)	1.75
82-19	Horatio Alger	1.50
82-20	2¢ Locomotive coil (2)	3.50
82-21	Aging Together	1.50
82-22	The Barrymores	2.50
82-23	Mary Walker	1.60
82-24	Peace Garden	1.60
82-25	America's Libraries	1.40
82-26	Jackie Robinson	14.00
82-27	4¢ Stagecoach coil (3)	4.00

82-28	Touro Synagogue	1.50
82-29	Wolf Trap Farm Park	1.40
82-30	American Architecture (4)	2.00
82-31	Francis of Assisi	1.40
82-32	Ponce de Leon	1.40
82-33	13¢ Kitten & Puppy (2)	2.75
82-34	Christmas, Madonna	2.50
82-35	Christmas, Seasons Greetings (4)	2.75
82-36	2¢ Igor Stravinsky (2)	2.00

1983

83-01	1¢, 4¢, 13¢ Penalty Mail (5)	2.50
83-02	17¢ Penalty Mail (4)	2.25
83-03	Penalty Mail coil (2)	3.25
83-04	$1 Penalty Mail	4.00
83-05	$5 Penalty Mail	9.50
83-06	Science & Industry	1.60
83-07	5.2¢ Antique Sleigh coil (4)	4.75
83-08	Sweden/USA Treaty	2.00
83-09	3¢ Handcar coil (3)	3.25
83-10	Balloons (4)	1.90
83-11	Civilian Conservation Corps	1.25
83-12	40¢ Olympics airmails (4)	2.75
83-13	Joseph Priestley	1.60
83-14	Volunteerism	1.50
83-15	Concord/German Immigration	1.50
83-16	Physical Fitness	1.60
83-17	Brooklyn Bridge	2.00
83-18	TVA	1.50
83-19	4¢ Carl Schurz (5)	1.50
83-20	Medal of Honor	2.50
83-21	Scott Joplin	3.25
83-22	Thomas H. Gallaudet	1.50
83-23	28¢ Olympics (4)	3.00
83-24	5¢ Pearl S. Buck (4)	1.60

83-25	Babe Ruth	10.00
83-26	Nathaniel Hawthorne	1.60
83-27	3¢ Henry Clay (7)	1.40
83-28	13¢ Olympics (4)	3.25
83-29	$9.35 Eagle booklet single	110.00
83-30	$9.35 Eagle booklet pane (3)	140.00
83-31	1¢ Omnibus coil (3)	3.50
83-32	Treaty of Paris	1.90
83-33	Civil Service	1.50
83-34	Metropolitan Opera	1.90
83-35	Inventors (4)	2.00
83-36	1¢ Dorothea Dix (3)	1.90
83-37	Streetcars (4)	2.25
83-38	5¢ Motorcycle coil (4)	4.75
83-39	Christmas, Madonna	2.00
83-40	Christmas, Santa Claus	1.90
83-41	35¢ Olympics airmails (4)	2.50
83-42	Martin Luther	2.50
83-43	Flag over Supreme Court booklet pane (10)	3.00

1984

84-01	Alaska Statehood	2.00
84-02	Winter Olympics (4)	2.25
84-03	FDIC	1.60
84-04	Harry S. Truman	1.50
84-05	Love	1.60
84-06	Carter G. Woodson	3.25
84-07	11¢ RR Caboose coil (2)	3.50
84-08	Soil & Water Conservation	1.60
84-09	Credit Union Act	1.60
84-10	40¢ Lillian M. Gilbreth	1.40
84-11	Orchids (4)	2.25
84-12	Hawaii Statehood	1.60
84-13	7.4¢ Baby Buggy coil (3)	3.50
84-14	National Archives	1.50

Claude Pepper

84-15	20¢ Summer Olympics (4)	3.50
84-16	New Orleans World's Fair	1.50
84-17	Health Research	1.50
84-18	Douglas Fairbanks	1.90
84-19	Jim Thorpe	7.75
84-20	10¢ Richard Russell (2)	1.25
84-21	John McCormack	2.00
84-22	St. Lawrence Seaway	1.60
84-23	Migratory Bird Hunting and Conservation Stamp Act	4.00
84-24	Roanoke Voyages	1.60
84-25	Herman Melville	1.75
84-26	Horace Moses	1.60
84-27	Smokey Bear	4.75
84-28	Roberto Clemente	11.00
84-29	30¢ Frank C. Laubach	1.40
84-30	Dogs (4)	3.25
84-31	Crime Prevention	2.00
84-32	Family Unity	2.50
84-33	Eleanor Roosevelt	2.50
84-34	Nation of Readers	2.25
84-35	Christmas, Madonna	2.25
84-36	Christmas, Santa Claus	2.25
84-37	Hispanic Americans	1.50
84-38	Vietnam Veterans Memorial	2.75

1985

85-01	Jerome Kern	2.50
85-02	7¢ Abraham Baldwin (3)	2.50
85-03	"D" (22¢) sheet and coil (3)	2.25
85-04	"D" (22¢) booklet pane (10)	3.75
85-05	"D" (22¢) Penalty Mail sheet and coil (3)	1.60
85-06	11¢ Alden Partridge (2)	1.50
85-07	33¢ Alfred Verville airmail	1.60
85-08	39¢ Lawrence & Elmer Sperry airmail	2.00
85-09	44¢ Transpacific airmail	2.00
85-10	50¢ Chester Nimitz	1.75
85-11	Mary McLeod Bethune	2.50
85-12	39¢ Grenville Clark	1.25
85-13	14¢ Sinclair Lewis (2)	1.50
85-14	Duck Decoys (4)	2.25
85-15	14¢ Iceboat coil (2)	3.50
85-16	Winter Special Olympics	2.00
85-17	Flag over Capitol sheet and coil (3)	2.25
85-18	Flag over Capitol booklet pane (5)	2.50
85-19	12¢ Stanley Steamer coil (2)	3.75
85-20	Seashells booklet pane (10)	3.75
85-21	Love	3.25
85-22	10.1¢ Oil Wagon coil (3)	2.75
85-23	12.5¢ Pushcart coil (2)	3.25
85-24	John J. Audubon	1.90
85-25	$10.75 Eagle booklet single	37.50
85-26	$10.75 Eagle booklet pane (3)	72.50
85-27	6¢ Tricycle coil (4)	3.25
85-28	Rural Electrification Administration	1.60

85-29	14¢ and 22¢ Penalty Mail sheet and coil (4)	3.25
85-30	AMERIPEX '86	1.60
85-31	9¢ Sylvanus Thayer (3)	2.00
85-32	3.4¢ School Bus coil (7)	4.25
85-33	11¢ Stutz Bearcat coil (2)	3.50
85-34	Abigail Adams	1.50
85-35	4.9¢ Buckboard coil (5)	4.25
85-36	8.3¢ Ambulance coil (3)	4.00
85-37	Frederic Bartholdi	3.25
85-38	8¢ Henry Knox (3)	1.50
85-39	Korean War Veterans	2.50
85-40	Social Security Act	2.00
85-41	44¢ Father Junipero Serra airmail	2.00
85-42	World War I Veterans	2.00
85-43	6¢ Walter Lippmann (4)	1.75
85-44	Horses (4)	3.50
85-45	Public Education	2.00
85-46	International Youth Year (4)	2.50
85-47	Help End Hunger	2.00
85-48	21.1¢ Letters coil (2)	2.50
85-49	Christmas, Madonna	2.00
85-50	Christmas, Poinsettias	2.50
85-51	18¢ Washington/ Washington Monument coil (2)	2.25

1986

86-01	Arkansas Statehood	1.50
86-02	25¢ Jack London	1.75
86-03	Stamp Collecting booklet pane (4)	4.00
86-04	Love	2.25
86-05	Sojourner Truth	2.75
86-06	5¢ Hugo L. Black (5)	2.50
86-07	Republic of Texas (2)	1.50
86-08	$2 William Jennings Bryan	3.75
86-09	Fish booklet pane (5)	3.50
86-10	Public Hospitals	1.25
86-11	Duke Ellington	3.25
86-12	Presidents, Washington- Harrison (9)	4.25
86-13	Presidents, Tyler-Grant (9)	4.25
86-14	Presidents, Hayes-Wilson (9)	4.25
86-15	Presidents, Harding-Johnson (9)	4.25
86-16	Polar Explorers (4)	3.25
86-17	17¢ Belva Ann Lockwood (2)	2.25
86-18	1¢ Margaret Mitchell (3)	1.90
86-19	Statue of Liberty	3.00
86-20	4¢ Father Flanagan (3)	1.60
86-21	17¢ Dog Sled coil (2)	3.00
86-22	56¢ John Harvard	1.75
86-23	Navajo Blankets (4)	2.75
86-24	3¢ Paul Dudley White, MD (8)	2.00
86-25	$1 Bernard Revel	2.00
86-26	T.S. Eliot	1.50
86-27	Wood-Carved Figurines (4)	2.00

86-28	Christmas, Madonna	2.25
86-29	Christmas, Village Scene	2.25
86-30	5.5¢ Star Route Truck coil (4)	3.25
86-31	25¢ Bread Wagon coil	3.25

1987

87-01	8.5¢ Tow Truck coil (5)	2.50
87-02	Michigan Statehood	2.50
87-03	Pan American Games	2.50
87-04	Love	3.00
87-05	7.1¢ Tractor coil (5)	2.50
87-06	14¢ Julia Ward Howe (2)	1.50
87-07	Jean Baptiste Pointe Du Sable	4.50
87-08	Enrico Caruso	2.00
87-09	2¢ Mary Lyon (3)	2.00
87-10	Reengraved 2¢ Locomotive coil (6)	2.75
87-11	Girl Scouts	3.25
87-12	10¢ Canal Boat coil (5)	3.00
87-13	Special Occasions booklet pane (10)	4.50
87-14	United Way	1.75
87-15	Flag with Fireworks	1.75
87-16	Flag over Capitol coil, prephosphored paper (2)	—
87-17	Wildlife, Swallow- Squirrel (10)	5.00
87-18	Wildlife, Armadillo- Rabbit (10)	5.00
87-19	Wildlife, Tanager- Ladybug (10)	5.00
87-20	Wildlife, Beaver- Prairie Dog (10)	5.00
87-21	Wildlife, Turtle-Fox (10)	5.00
87-22	Delaware Statehood	1.90
87-23	U.S./Morocco Friendship	1.75
87-24	William Faulkner	1.75
87-25	Lacemaking (4)	3.25
87-26	10¢ Red Cloud (3)	1.50
87-27	$5 Bret Harte	9.50
87-28	Pennsylvania Statehood	2.00
87-29	Drafting of the Constitution booklet pane (5)	3.25
87-30	New Jersey Statehood	2.50
87-31	Signing of Constitution	2.00
87-32	Certified Public Accountants	3.75
87-33	5¢ Milk Wagon and 17.5¢ Racing Car coils (4)	3.00
87-34	Locomotives booklet pane (5)	6.75
87-35	Christmas, Madonna	2.00
87-36	Christmas, Ornaments	1.75
87-37	Flag with Fireworks booklet-pair	2.75

1988

88-01	Georgia Statehood	2.00
88-02	Connecticut Statehood	2.00
88-03	Winter Olympics	1.75
88-04	Australia Bicentennial	1.90
88-05	James Weldon Johnson	3.00
88-06	Cats (4)	3.50
88-07	Massachusetts Statehood	2.25

88-08	Maryland Statehood	2.25	88-54	24.1¢ Tandem		90-08	Classic Films (4)	5.00
88-09	3¢ Conestoga			Bicycle coil (2)	3.00	90-09	Marianne Moore	2.00
	Wagon coil (8)	2.50	88-55	20¢ Cable Car		90-10	$1 Seaplane	
88-10	Knute Rockne	5.00		coil (2)	3.00		coil (2)	5.75
88-11	"E" (25¢) Earth sheet		88-56	13¢ Patrol Wagon		90-11	Lighthouses	
	and coil (3)	2.00		coil (2)	3.00		booklet pane (5)	5.00
88-12	"E" (25¢) Earth		88-57	23¢ Mary Cassatt	1.90	90-12	Plastic Flag stamp	3.25
	booklet pane (10)	4.75	88-58	65¢ H.H. "Hap" Arnold	2.25	90-13	Rhode Island	
88-13	"E" (25¢) Penalty			**1989**			Statehood	2.75
	Mail coil (2)	2.00	89-01	Montana Statehood	1.75	90-14	$2 Bobcat	5.00
88-14	44¢ New Sweden		89-02	A. Philip Randolph	3.25	90-15	Olympians (5)	5.75
	airmail	2.00	89-03	Flag over Yosemite		90-16	Indian Headdresses	
88-15	Pheasant			coil, prephosphored			booklet pane (10)	6.50
	booklet pane (10)	4.25		paper (2)	2.50	90-17	5¢ Circus Wagon	
88-16	Jack London		89-04	North Dakota			coil (5)	3.25
	booklet pane (6)	3.25		Statehood	1.90	90-18	40¢ Claire Lee	
88-17	Jack London		89-05	Washington			Chennault	3.25
	booklet pane (10)	4.25		Statehood	1.90	90-19	Federated	
88-18	Flag with Clouds	1.60	89-06	Steamboats			States of Micronesia/	
88-19	45¢ Samuel Langley			booklet pane (5)	3.50		Marshall Islands (2)	2.75
	airmail	2.00	89-07	World Stamp		90-20	Creatures of	
88-19A	20¢ Penalty Mail			Expo '89	2.00		the Sea (4)	4.75
	coil (2)	2.25	89-08	Arturo Toscanini	1.75	90-21	25¢ and 45¢	
88-20	Flag over Yosemite		89-09	U.S. House			PUAS/America (2)	3.00
	coil (2)	2.00		of Representatives	2.25	90-22	Dwight D.	
88-21	South Carolina		89-10	U.S. Senate	2.25		Eisenhower	2.25
	Statehood	2.00	89-11	Executive Branch	2.25	90-23	Christmas,	
88-22	Owl & Grosbeak		89-12	South Dakota			Madonna, sheet and	
	booklet pane (10)	4.00		Statehood	2.00		booklet pane (11)	5.75
88-23	15¢ Buffalo Bill		89-13	7.1¢ Tractor coil,		90-24	Christmas, Yule Tree,	
	Cody (2)	1.90		precancel (4)	2.50		sheet and	
88-24	15¢ and 25¢		89-14	$1 Johns Hopkins	2.50		booklet pane (11)	5.75
	Penalty Mail coils (4)	2.75	89-15	Lou Gehrig	9.25		**1991**	
88-25	Francis Ouimet	6.00	89-16	1¢ Penalty Mail	2.75	91-01	"F" (29¢) Flower	
88-26	45¢ Harvey		89-17	45¢ French Revolution			sheet and coil (3)	3.25
	Cushing, MD	1.60		airmail	3.00	91-02	"F" (29¢) Flower	
88-27	New Hampshire		89-18	Ernest Hemingway	1.60		booklet panes (20)	11.00
	Statehood	2.00	89-19	$2.40 Moon Landing	12.50	91-03	4¢ Makeup	2.25
88-28	36¢ Igor Sikorsky		89-20	North Carolina		91-04	"F" (29¢) ATM	
	airmail	2.75		Statehood	2.00		booklet single	2.75
88-29	Virginia Statehood	2.00	89-21	Letter Carriers	1.60	91-05	"F" (29¢) Penalty	
88-30	10.1¢ Oil Wagon		89-22	28¢ Sitting Bull	1.75		Mail coil (2)	3.25
	coil, precancel (3)	—	89-23	Drafting		91-06	4¢ Steam Carriage	
88-31	Love	2.00		of the Bill of Rights	2.00		coil (7)	3.25
88-32	Flag with Clouds		89-24	Prehistoric		91-07	50¢ Switzerland	2.75
	booklet pane (6)	4.00		Animals (4)	7.50	91-08	Vermont Statehood	2.75
88-33	16.7¢ Popcorn		89-25	25¢ and 45¢		91-09	19¢ Fawn (2)	2.75
	Wagon coil (2)	2.50		PUAS-America (2)	2.50	91-10	Flag over Mount	
88-34	15¢ Tugboat coil (2)	2.00	89-26	Christmas, Madonna	7.00		Rushmore coil (2)	2.75
88-35	13.2¢ Coal Car		89-27	Christmas,		91-11	35¢ Dennis	
	coil (2)	3.00		Antique Sleigh	6.75		Chavez	2.50
88-36	New York Statehood	2.50	89-28	Eagle and Shield,		91-12	Flower sheet and	
88-37	45¢ Love	2.00		self-adhesive	2.25		booklet pane (10)	6.25
88-38	8.4¢ Wheelchair		89-29	World Stamp		91-13	4¢ Penalty Mail (8)	2.50
	coil (3)	2.50		Expo '89		91-14	Wood Duck	
88-39	21¢ Railroad Mail Car			souvenir sheet	7.00		booklet panes (10)	11.00
	coil (2)	3.00	89-30	Classic Mail		91-15	23¢ Lunch	
88-40	Summer Olympics	2.00		Transportation (4)	2.75		Wagon coil (2)	2.75
88-41	Classic Cars		89-31	Future Mail		91-16	Flag with Olympic	
	booklet pane (5)	4.75		Transportation			Rings booklet	
88-42	7.6¢ Carreta coil (4)	3.00		souvenir sheet	5.25		pane (10)	6.25
88-43	Honeybee coil (2)	4.25	89-32	45¢ Future Mail		91-17	50¢ Harriet Quimby	2.75
88-44	Antarctic			Transportation		91-18	Savings Bond	2.25
	Explorers (4)	2.75		airmails (4)	5.25	91-19	Love sheet and	
88-45	5.3¢ Elevator coil (5)	3.00	89-33	Classic Mail			booklet pane,	
88-46	20.5¢ Fire Engine			Transportation			52¢ Love (12)	9.25
	coil (2)	3.50		souvenir sheet	5.75	91-20	19¢ Balloon booklet	
88-47	Carousel Animals (4)	3.25		**1990**			pane (10)	4.50
88-48	$8.75 Eagle	20.00	90-01	Idaho Statehood	2.00	91-21	40¢ William Piper	
88-49	Christmas, Madonna	2.00	90-02	Love sheet			airmail	2.75
88-50	Christmas,			and booklet		91-22	William Saroyan	2.75
	Snow Scene	2.00		pane (10)	4.75	91-23	Penalty Mail coil	
88-51	21¢ Chester Carlson	1.50	90-03	Ida B. Wells	3.75		and 19¢ and 23¢	
88-52	Special Occasions		90-04	U.S. Supreme Court	2.00		sheet (4)	3.50
	booklet pane (6),		90-05	15¢ Beach Umbrella		91-24	5¢ Canoe and	
	Love You,			booklet pane (10)	3.50		10¢ Tractor Trailer	
	Thinking of You	9.25	90-06	5¢ Luis Munoz			coils (4)	3.25
88-53	Special Occasions			Marin (5)	2.00	91-25	Flags on Parade	2.75
	booklet pane (6),		90-07	Wyoming Statehood	2.00	91-26	Fishing Flies booklet	
	Happy Birthday,						pane (5)	5.25
	Best Wishes	14.00						

91-27	52¢ Hubert H. Humphrey	2.75
91-28	Cole Porter	2.75
91-29	50¢ Antarctic Treaty airmail	3.25
91-30	1¢ Kestrel, 3¢ Bluebird and 30¢ Cardinal (3)	2.75
91-31	Torch ATM booklet single	2.75
91-32	Desert Shield/ Desert Storm sheet and booklet pane (11)	5.75
91-33	Flag over Mount Rushmore coil, gravure printing (darker, 3)	2.75
91-34	Summer Olympics (5)	5.75
91-35	Flower coil, slit perforations (3)	2.75
91-36	Numismatics	2.50
91-37	Basketball	5.75
91-38 through 91-47 are unassigned		
91-48	19¢ Fishing Boat coil (3)	3.00
91-49	Comedians booklet pane (10)	6.75
91-50	World War II miniature sheet (10)	7.25
91-51	District of Columbia	2.50
91-52	Jan Matzeliger	4.50
91-53	$1 USPS/ Olympic Logo	4.00
91-54	Space Exploration booklet pane (10)	6.75
91-55	50¢ PUASP/America airmail	2.75
91-56	Christmas, Madonna sheet and booklet pane (10)	8.50
91-57	Christmas, Santa Claus sheet and booklet pane (11)	12.50
91-58	5¢ Canoe coil, gravure printing (red, 6)	3.25
91-59	29¢ Eagle and Shield, self-adhesive (3)	6.00
91-60	23¢ Flag presort	3.25
91-61	$9.95 Express Mail	22.50
91-62	$2.90 Priority Mail	7.50
91-63	$14.00 Express Mail International	30.00
1992		
92-01	Winter Olympic Games (5)	4.75
92-02	World Columbian Stamp Expo '92	2.75
92-03	W.E.B. DuBois	5.75
92-04	Love	2.75
92-05	75¢ Wendell Willkie	3.25
92-06	29¢ Flower coil, round perforations (2)	2.75
92-07	Earl Warren	3.75
92-08	Olympic Baseball	12.50
92-09	Flag over White House, coil (2)	2.75
92-10	First Voyage of Christopher Columbus (4)	4.00
92-11	New York Stock Exchange	2.50
92-12	Columbian-Columbus	12.00
92-13	Columbian-Seeking Royal Support (3)	12.00
92-14	Columbian-First Sighting of Land (3)	12.00
92-15	Columbian-Claiming New World (3)	12.00

92-16	Columbian-Reporting Discoveries (3)	12.00
92-17	Columbian-Royal Favor Restored (3)	12.00
92-18	Space Adventures (4)	4.75
92-19	Alaska Highway	2.50
92-20	Kentucky Statehood	2.50
92-21	Summer Olympic Games (5)	4.75
92-22	Hummingbirds booklet pane (5)	5.50
92-22A	23¢ Presort (3)	3.25
92-23	Wildflowers (10)	6.50
92-24	Wildflowers (10)	6.50
92-25	Wildflowers (10)	6.50
92-26	Wildflowers (10)	6.50
92-27	Wildflowers (10)	6.50
92-28	World War II miniature sheet (10)	8.00
92-29	29¢ Variable Rate	2.75
92-30	Dorothy Parker	2.75
92-31	Theodore von Karman	4.25
92-32	Pledge of Allegiance (10)	10.00
92-33	Minerals (4)	4.75
92-34	Eagle and Shield (3)	3.50
92-35	Juan Rodriguez Cabrillo	2.50
92-36	Wild Animals booklet pane (5)	5.50
92-37	23¢ Presort (3)	4.00
92-38	Christmas Contemporary, sheet and booklet pane (8)	7.50
92-39	Christmas Traditional, sheet and booklet pane (11)	8.75
92-40	Pumpkinseed Sunfish	2.75
92-41	Circus Wagon	3.50
92-42	Year of the Rooster	6.00
1993		
93-01	Elvis	11.00
93-02	Space Fantasy (5)	7.00
93-03	Percy Lavon Julian	4.75
93-04	Oregon Trail	3.50
93-05	World University Games	3.75
93-06	Grace Kelly	5.50
93-07	Oklahoma!	3.75
93-08	Circus	5.50
93-09	Thomas Jefferson	3.50
93-10	Cherokee Strip	3.50
93-11	Dean Acheson	3.50
93-12	Sporting Horses	5.50
93-13	USA Coil	3.50
93-14	Garden Flowers, booklet pane (5)	5.50
93-15	Eagle and Shield, coil	3.25
93-16	World War II miniature sheet (10)	6.75
93-17	Futuristic Space Shuttle	10.00
93-18	Hank Williams, sheet	6.00
93-19	Rock & Roll/Rhythm & Blues, sheet single, booklet pane (8)	10.00
93-20	Joe Louis	7.50
93-21	Red Squirrel	4.00
93-22	Broadway Musicals, booklet pane (4)	6.75
93-23	National Postal Museum, strip (4)	4.75
93-24	Rose	4.00
93-25	American Sign Language, pair	3.50
93-26	Country & Western Music, sheet and booklet pane (4)	9.25
93-27	African Violets, booklet pane (10)	6.00

93-28	10¢ Official Mail	3.25
93-29	Contemporary Christmas, booklet pane (10), sheet and self-adhesive stamps	8.50
93-30	Traditional Christmas, sheet, booklet pane (4)	6.25
93-31	Classic Books, strip (4)	5.50
93-32	Mariana Islands	4.25
93-33	Pine Cone	4.00
93-34	Columbus' Landing in Puerto Rico	4.75
93-35	AIDS Awareness	7.50
1994		
94-01	Winter Olympics	5.50
94-02	Edward R. Murrow	3.50
94-03	Love, self-adhesive	3.50
94-04	Dr. Allison Davis	6.00
94-05	29¢ Eagle, self-adhesive	5.25
94-06	Year of the Dog	5.25
94-07	Love, booklet pane (10), single sheet stamp	8.00
94-08	Postage and Mailing Center	5.00
94-09	Buffalo Soldiers	8.00
94-10	Silent Screen Stars	7.25
94-11	Garden Flowers, booklet pane (5)	8.50
94-12	Victory at Saratoga	7.00
94-13	10¢ Tractor Trailer gravure printing	5.00
94-14	World Cup Soccer	8.75
94-15	World Cup Soccer souvenir sheet	9.25
94-16	World War II miniature sheet (10)	5.50
94-17	Love, sheet stamp	5.25
94-18	Statue of Liberty	5.25
94-19	Fishing Boat, reissue	5.25
94-20	Norman Rockwell	8.00
94-21	$9.95 and 29¢ Moon Landing	15.00
94-22	Locomotives (5)	7.00
94-23	George Meany	5.25
94-24	$5.00 Washington/ Jackson	11.00
94-25	Popular Singers (5)	10.00
94-26	James Thurber	5.25
94-27	Jazz Singers/Blues Singers (10)	14.00
94-28	Wonders of the Sea (4)	8.75
94-29	Chinese/Joint Issue (2)	8.00
94-30	Holiday Traditional (10)	14.00
94-31	Holiday Contemporary (4)	12.00
94-32	Holiday, self-adhesive	9.25
94-33	20¢ Virginia Apgar	7.25
94-34	BEP Centennial	17.50
94-35	Year of the Boar	9.00
94-G1	G1 (4) Rate Change	12.00
94-G2	G2 (6) Rate Change	12.00
94-G3	G3 (5) Rate Change	12.00
94-G4	G4 (2) Rate Change	12.00
94-36	Legends of West	12.00
1995		
95-01	Love (2)	12.00
95-02	Florida State	12.00
95-03	Butte (7)	12.00
95-04	Automobile (4)	12.00
95-05	Flag Over Field, self-adhesive	12.00
95-06	Juke Box (2+2)	12.00
95-07	Tail Fin (2+2)	12.00
95-08	Circus Wagon (7)	6.00

95-09	Kids Care (4)	12.00
95-10	Richard Nixon	12.00
95-11	Bessie Coleman	12.00
95-12	Official Mail	12.00
95-13	Kestrel with cent sign	8.00
95-14	Love 1 oz. and 2 oz.	12.00
95-15	Flag Over Porch	12.00
95-16	Recreational Sports (5)	12.00
95-17	POW & MIA	12.00
95-18	Marilyn Monroe	12.00
95-19	Pink Rose	8.00
95-20	Ferry Boat (3)	8.00
95-21	Cog Railway Car (3)	8.00
95-22	Blue Jay (10)	8.00
95-23	Texas Statehood	12.00
95-24	Great Lake Lighthouses (5)	12.00
95-25	Challenger Shuttle	12.00
95-26	United Nations	12.00
95-27	Civil War (front and back)	16.00
95-28	Two Fruits	8.00
95-29	Alice Hamilton	12.00
95-30	Carousel Horses	12.00
95-31	Endeavor Shuttle	24.00
95-32	Alice Paul	12.00
95-33	Women's Suffrage	12.00
95-34	Louis Armstrong	12.00
95-35	World War II	12.00
95-36	Milton Hershey	12.00
95-37	Jazz Musicians	14.00
95-38	Fall Garden Flowers (5)	12.00
95-39	Eddie Rickenbacker (airmail)	12.00
95-40	Republic of Palau	12.00
95-41	Holiday Contemporary/ Santa (4)	14.00
95-42	American Comic Strips	20.00
95-43	Naval Academy	12.00
95-44	Tennessee Williams	12.00
95-45	Holiday Children Sledding	12.00
95-46	Holiday Traditional sheet and booklet pane (10)	14.00
95-47	Holiday Midnight Angel	12.00
95-48	Ruth Bendict	12.00
95-49	James K. Polk	12.00
95-50	Antique Automobiles, strip (5)	14.00
1996		
96-01	Utah Statehood	12.00
96-02	Garden Flowers	14.00
96-03	Love/Kestrel	16.00
96-04	Postage and Mailing Center (3)	5.00
96-05	Ernest E. Just	12.00
96-06	Woodpecker	14.00
96-07	Smithsonian Institution	12.00
96-08	Year of the Rat	12.00
96-09	Pioneers of Communication	14.00
96-10	Fulbright Scholarships	12.00
96-11	Jacqueline Cochran	12.00
96-12	Mountain	12.00
96-13	Bluebird	6.00
96-14	Marathon	6.00
96-15	Flag over Porch/ Eagle & Shield	7.50
96-16	Cal Farley	6.00
96-17	Classic Olympic Collection	8.00
96-18	Georgia O'Keefe Art	6.00
96-19	Tennessee	6.00

96-20	American Indian Dances	9.00
96-21	Prehistoric Animals	9.00
96-22	Breast Cancer Awareness	6.00
96-23	Flag over Porch/ Juke Box/Butte/Tail Fin Automobile/Mountain	9.00
96-24	James Dean	6.00
96-25	Folk Heroes	9.00
96-26	Olympic/Discus	6.00
96-27	Iowa	6.00
96-28	Blue Jay	6.00
96-29	Rural Free Delivery	6.00
96-30	Riverboats	9.00
96-31	Big Band Leaders	9.00
96-32	Songwriters	9.00
96-33	F. Scott Fitzgerald	6.00
96-34	Endangered Species	10.00
96-35	Computer Technology	6.00
96-36	Family Scenes	7.50
96-37	Skaters	6.00
96-38	Hanukkah	6.00
96-39	Madonna and Child	7.50
96-40	Yellow Rose	6.00
96-41	Cycling	10.00
1997		
97-01	Year of the Ox	6.00
97-02	Flag Over Porch/ Juke Box/Mountain	9.00
97-03	Benjamin O. Davis Sr.	6.00
97-04	Statue of Liberty	6.00
97-05	Love Swans	6.00
97-06	Helping Children Learn	6.00
97-07	Merian Botanical Plants	7.50
97-08	Pacific 97 - Stagecoach and Ship	7.50
97-09	Linerless Flag Over Porch/Juke Box	9.00
97-10	Thornton Wilder	6.00
97-11	Raoul Wallenberg	6.00
97-12	Dinosaurs	10.00
97-13	Pacific '97 - Franklin	15.00
97-14	Pacific '97 - Washington	15.00
97-15	Bugs Bunny	6.00
97-16	The Marshall Plan	6.00
97-17	Humphrey Bogart	6.00
97-18	Classic Aircraft	15.00
97-19	Classic American Dolls	15.00
97-20	Football Coaches	7.50
97-20A	George Halas	6.00
97-20B	Vince Lombardi	6.00
97-20C	Pop Warner	6.00
97-20D	Bear Bryant	6.00
97-21	Yellow Rose	6.00
97-22	"Stars and Stripes Forever"	6.00
97-23	Padre Félix Varela	6.00
97-24	Composers and Conducters	7.50
97-25	Opera Singers	7.50
97-26	Air Force	6.00
97-27	Movie Monsters	7.50
97-28	Supersonic Flight	6.00
97-29	Women in Military	6.00
97-30	Kwanzaa	6.00
97-31	Holiday Traditional, Madonna and Child	6.00
97-32	Holly	6.00
97-33	Mars Pathfinder	12.00
1998		
98-01	Year of the Tiger	6.00
98-02	Winter Sports	6.00
98-03	Madam C. J. Walker	6.00
98-03A	Celebrate The Century® 1900s	10.00
98-03B	Celebrate The Century® 1910s	10.00

98-04	Spanish American War	6.00
98-05	Flowering Trees	6.00
98-06	Alexander Calder	6.00
98-07	Henry R. Luce	6.00
98-08	Cinco De Mayo	6.00
98-09	Sylvester & Tweety	6.00
98-09A	Celebrate The Century® 1920s	10.00
98-10	Wisconsin	6.00
98-11	Trans-Mississippi Reissue of 1898	10.00
98-12	Trans-Mississippi (single stamp)	6.00
98-13	Folk Singers	6.00
98-14	Berlin Airlift	6.00
98-15	Diner/Wetlands coil	6.00
98-16	Spanish Settlement of the Southwest	6.00
98-17	Gospel Singers	6.00
98-18	The Wallaces	6.00
98-19	Stephen Vincent Benet	6.00
98-20	Tropical Birds	6.00
98-21	Breast Cancer Research (semi-postal)	6.00
98-22	Ring-Neck Pheasant	6.00
98-23	Alfred Hitchcock	6.00
98-24	Organ Donations	6.00
98-24A	Red Fox	6.00
98-24B	Green Bicycle coil	6.00
98-25	Bright Eyes	7.50
98-26	Klondike Gold Rush	6.00
98-26A	Celebrate The Century® 1930s	10.00
98-27	American Art	10.00
98-28	Ballet	6.00
98-28A	Diner coil	6.00
98-29	Space Fantasy	7.50
98-30	Philanthropy	6.00
98-31	Holiday Traditional	6.00
98-32	Holiday Contemporary	7.50
98-33	Hat Rate Change "H" Series/Makeup Rate	10.00
98-34	Uncle Sam — Rate Change	6.00
98-35	Hat Rate Change "H" Series	10.00
98-36	Hat Rate Change "H" Series	10.00
98-37	Mary Breckinridge	6.00
98-38	Space Shuttle Landing	10.00
98-39	Shuttle Piggyback	20.00
98-40	Wetlands non-denominated nonprofit coil and Eagle & Shield non-denominated presort coil	10.00
1999		
99-01	Year of the Hare	6.00
99-02	Malcolm X	6.00
99-03	33¢ Victorian — Love	6.00
99-04	55¢ Victorian — Love	6.00
99-05	Hospice Care	6.00
99-06	Celebrate The Century® 1940s	10.00
99-07	City Flag	6.00
99-08	Irish Immigration	6.00
99-09	Alfred Lunt and Lynn Fontanne	6.00
99-10	Arctic Animals	6.00
99-10A	Classroom Flag	6.00
99-11	Nature of America Sonoran Desert	10.00
99-11A	Fruit Berries	7.50
99-12	Daffy Duck	6.00
99-13	Ayn Rand	6.00
99-14	Cinco de Mayo	6.00

Note: Numbers and prices may be changed without notice due to additional USPS stamp issues and/or different information that may become available on older issues.

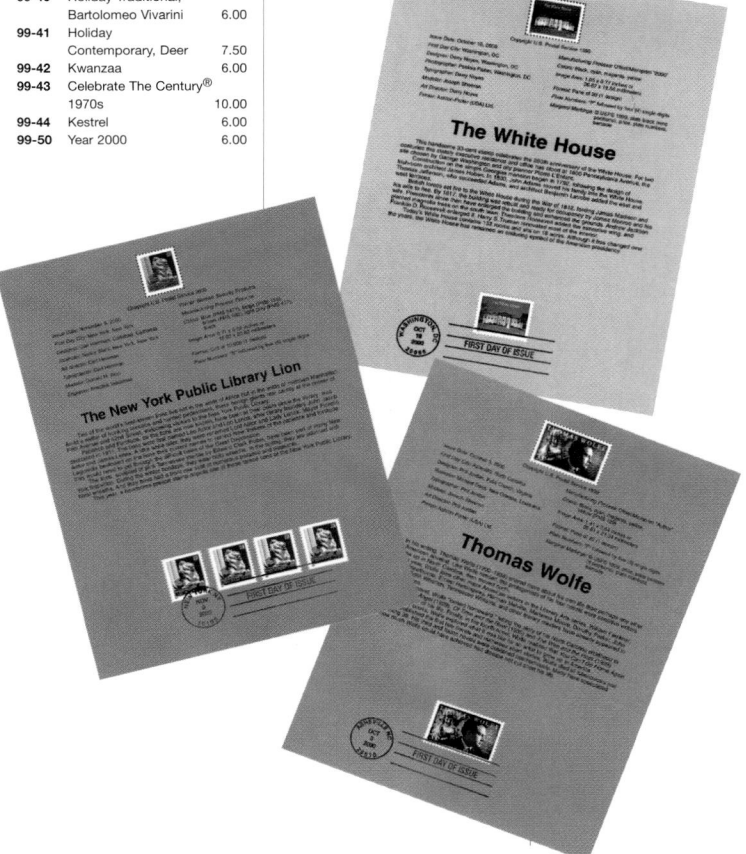

The White House

The New York Public Library Lion

Thomas Wolfe

American Commemorative Panels

The Postal Service offers American Commemorative Panels for each new commemorative stamp and special Holiday and Love stamp issued. The series began in 1972 with the Wildlife Commemorative Panel. The panels feature mint stamps complemented by fine reproductions of steel line engravings and the stories behind the commemorated subjects.

The identifying numbers used below are based on the Postal Service's numbering system for American Commemorative Panels; therefore, they do not follow the Scott numbering system.

1972
1	Wildlife	6.00
2	Mail Order	5.75
3	Osteopathic Medicine	5.75
4	Tom Sawyer	5.25
5	Pharmacy	9.00
6	Christmas, Angels	9.00
7	Christmas, Santa Claus	9.00
7E	Same with error date (1882)	—
8	Stamp Collecting	5.50

1973
9	Love	6.75
10	Pamphleteers	5.50
11	George Gershwin	6.00
12	Posting a Broadside	5.50
13	Copernicus	5.50
14	Postal People	5.25
15	Harry S. Truman	7.50
16	Post Rider	5.00
17	Boston Tea Party	15.00
18	Electronics	5.50
19	Robinson Jeffers	5.50
20	Lyndon B. Johnson	5.00
21	Henry O. Tanner	5.50
22	Willa Cather	5.50
23	Drummer	8.25
24	Angus Cattle	5.50
25	Christmas, Madonna	8.75
26	Christmas Tree, Needlepoint	8.75

1974
27	VFW	5.75
28	Robert Frost	5.75
29	Expo '74	6.50
30	Horse Racing	7.00
31	Skylab	8.50
32	Universal Postal Union	7.00
33	Mineral Heritage	5.00
34	First Kentucky Settlement	5.75

35	Continental Congress	7.00
35A	Same with corrected logo	—
36	Chautauqua	5.75
37	Kansas Wheat	5.75
38	Energy Conservation	5.75
39	Sleepy Hollow	5.75
40	Retarded Children	5.75
41	Christmas, Currier & Ives	8.50
42	Christmas, Angel Altarpiece	8.50

1975
43	Benjamin West	5.50
44	Pioneer	8.50
45	Collective Bargaining	5.75
46	Contributors to the Cause	5.50
47	Mariner 10	6.50
48	Lexington & Concord	6.25
49	Paul Laurence Dunbar	7.00
50	D.W. Griffith	5.75
51	Bunker Hill	6.25
52	Military Uniforms	5.00
53	Apollo Soyuz	8.25
54	World Peace Through Law	5.50
54A	Same with August 15, 1975 date	—
55	Women's Year	5.75
56	Postal Service Bicentennial	7.00
57	Banking and Commerce	7.00
58	Early Christmas, Card	7.75
59	Christmas, Madonna	7.75

1976
60	Spirit of '76	8.50
61	Interphil 76	7.50
62	State Flags	9.50

63	Telephone	6.75
64	Commercial Aviation	9.25
65	Chemistry	8.00
66	Benjamin Franklin	7.75
67	Declaration of Independence	7.50
68	12th Winter Olympics	7.50
69	Clara Maass	7.00
70	Adolph S. Ochs	8.25
70A	Same with charter logo	—
71	Christmas, Winter Pastime	8.75
71A	Same with charter logo	—
72	Christmas, Nativity	8.75
72A	Same with charter logo	—

1977
73	Washington at Princeton	10.00
73A	Same with charter logo	—
74	Sound Recording	17.50
74A	Same with charter logo	—
75	Pueblo Art	55.00
75A	Same with charter logo	—
76	Solo Transatlantic Lindbergh Flight	60.00
77	Colorado Statehood	14.00
78	Butterflies	14.00
79	Lafayette	14.00
80	Skilled Hands	14.00
81	Peace Bridge	14.00
82	Battle of Oriskany	14.00
83	Alta, CA, Civil Settlement	14.00
84	Articles of Confederation	15.00
85	Talking Pictures	20.00
86	Surrender at Saratoga	15.00
87	Energy	14.00

88	Christmas, Valley Forge	14.00
89	Christmas, Mailbox	25.00

1978

90	Carl Sandburg	8.00
91	Captain Cook	14.00
92	Harriet Tubman	8.50
93	Quilts	15.00
94	Dance	10.00
95	French Alliance	10.00
96	Early Cancer Detection	8.25
97	Jimmie Rodgers	11.00
98	Photography	8.00
99	George M. Cohan	14.00
100	Viking Missions	26.00
101	Owls	26.00
102	Trees	26.00
103	Christmas, Madonna	12.00
104	Christmas, Hobby Horse	12.00

1979

105	Robert F. Kennedy	7.25
106	Martin Luther King, Jr.	7.50
107	International Year of the Child	6.75
108	John Steinbeck	6.75
109	Albert Einstein	7.25
110	Pennsylvania Toleware	6.75
111	Architecture	6.50
112	Endangered Flora	8.00
113	Seeing Eye Dogs	8.00
114	Special Olympics	8.00
115	John Paul Jones	8.25
116	15¢ Olympics	9.50
117	Christmas, Madonna	9.50
118	Christmas, Santa Claus	9.50
119	Will Rogers	8.00
120	Vietnam Veterans	9.50
121	10¢, 31¢ Olympics	10.00

1980

122	W.C. Fields	7.50
123	Winter Olympics	7.50
124	Benjamin Banneker	10.00
125	Frances Perkins	6.00
126	Emily Bissell	6.00
127	Helen Keller/ Anne Sullivan	6.00
128	Veterans Administration	6.00
129	General Bernardo de Galvez	6.00
130	Coral Reefs	8.00
131	Organized Labor	6.00
132	Edith Wharton	6.00
133	Education	6.00
134	Indian Masks	6.00
135	Architecture	6.75
136	Christmas, Epiphany Window	9.00
137	Christmas, Toys	6.50

1981

138	Everett Dirksen	7.00
139	Whitney Moore Young	7.00
140	Flowers	8.00
141	Red Cross	7.50
142	Savings & Loans	6.75
143	Space Achievement	10.00
144	Professional Management	6.75
145	Wildlife Habitats	10.50
146	Int'l. Year of Disabled Persons	6.25
147	Edna St. Vincent Millay	6.25
148	Architecture	6.50
149	Babe Zaharias/ Bobby Jones	15.00
150	James Hoban	6.75
151	Frederic Remington	6.75
152	Battle of Yorktown/ Virginia Capes	6.75
153	Christmas, Madonna	9.25
154	Christmas, Bear and Sleigh	6.50
155	John Hanson	7.00
156	U.S. Desert Plants	8.00

1982

157	Roosevelt	8.25
158	Love	10.00
159	George Washington	9.50
160	State Birds & Flowers	17.00
161	U.S./ Netherlands	10.00
162	Library of Congress	10.50
163	Knoxville World's Fair	10.00
164	Horatio Alger	8.75
165	Aging Together	11.00
166	The Barrymores	12.00
167	Dr. Mary Walker	10.00
168	Peace Garden	11.00
169	America's Libraries	11.00
170	Jackie Robinson	24.00
171	Touro Synagogue	10.50
172	Architecture	12.00
173	Wolf Trap Farm Park	12.00
174	Francis of Assisi	12.00
175	Ponce de Leon	12.00
176	Christmas, Madonna	14.00
177	Christmas, Season's Greetings	14.00
178	Kitten & Puppy	14.00

1983

179	Science and Industry	5.25
180	Sweden/ USA Treaty	5.75
181	Balloons	6.00

182	Civilian Conservation Corps	5.25
183	40¢ Olympics	6.50
184	Joseph Priestley	5.25
185	Voluntarism	4.50
186	Concord/German Immigration	5.25
187	Physical Fitness	4.25
188	Brooklyn Bridge	6.00
189	TVA	5.25
190	Medal of Honor	6.50
191	Scott Joplin	9.00
192	28¢ Olympics	6.50
193	Babe Ruth	10.00
194	Nathaniel Hawthorne	5.75
195	13¢ Olympics	8.00
196	Treaty of Paris	6.50
197	Civil Service	6.50
198	Metropolitan Opera	6.50
199	Inventors	6.75
200	Streetcars	8.00
201	Christmas, Madonna	8.75
202	Christmas, Santa Claus	8.75
203	35¢ Olympics	8.00
204	Martin Luther	8.00

1984

205	Alaska Statehood	4.50
206	Winter Olympics	5.00
207	FDIC	4.75
208	Love	4.00
209	Carter G. Woodson	6.75
210	Soil and Water Conservation	4.75
211	Credit Union Act	4.75
212	Orchids	6.75
213	Hawaii Statehood	6.25
214	National Archives	4.50
215	20¢ Olympics	6.75
216	Louisiana World Exposition	6.00
217	Health Research	4.75
218	Douglas Fairbanks	5.25
219	Jim Thorpe	8.25
220	John McCormack	4.75
221	St. Lawrence Seaway	6.25
222	Preserving Wetlands	7.50
223	Roanoke Voyages	4.75
224	Herman Melville	4.75
225	Horace Moses	5.25
226	Smokey Bear	5.00
227	Roberto Clemente	20.00
228	Dogs	6.25
229	Crime Prevention	5.25
230	Family Unity	6.25
231	Christmas, Madonna	6.75
232	Christmas, Santa Claus	6.75
233	Eleanor Roosevelt	5.50
234	Nation of Readers	5.50
235	Hispanic Americans	5.25
236	Vietnam Veterans Memorial	8.25

1985

237	Jerome Kern	5.75
238	Mary McLeod Bethune	7.00
239	Duck Decoys	7.25
240	Winter Special Olympics	6.00
241	Love	5.00
242	Rural Electrification Administration	5.00
243	AMERIPEX '86	6.75
244	Abigail Adams	4.75
245	Frederic Auguste Bartholdi	6.50
246	Korean War Veterans	6.25
247	Social Security Act	5.00
248	World War I Veterans	5.75
249	Horses	9.00
250	Public Education	4.50
251	Youth	6.75
252	Help End Hunger	5.00
253	Christmas, Madonna	8.00
254	Christmas, Poinsettias	5.00

1986

255	Arkansas Statehood	5.25
256	Stamp Collecting Booklet	6.75
257	Love	5.00
258	Sojourner Truth	7.50
259	Republic of Texas	6.25
260	Fish Booklet	6.75
261	Public Hospitals	4.75
262	Duke Ellington	7.50
263	U.S. Presidents' Sheet #1	6.25
264	U.S. Presidents' Sheet #2	6.25
265	U.S. Presidents' Sheet #3	6.25
266	U.S. Presidents' Sheet #4	6.25
267	Polar Explorers	6.75
268	Statue of Liberty	7.50
269	Navajo Blankets	6.75
270	T.S. Eliot	6.25
271	Wood-Carved Figurines	6.00
272	Christmas, Madonna	5.75
273	Christmas, Village Scene	5.75

1987

274	Michigan Statehood	5.75
275	Pan American Games	3.50
276	Love	7.00
277	Jean Baptiste Pointe Du Sable	5.00
278	Enrico Caruso	3.50
279	Girl Scouts	4.00
280	Special Occasions Booklet	6.00

281	United Way	4.75
282	#1 American Wildlife	6.50
283	#2 American Wildlife	6.50
284	#3 American Wildlife	6.50
285	#4 American Wildlife	6.50
286	#5 American Wildlife	6.50
287	Delaware Statehood	5.75
288	Morocco/U.S. Diplomatic Relations	4.75
289	William Faulkner	4.75
290	Lacemaking	4.75
291	Pennsylvania Statehood	5.25
292	Constitution Booklet	4.75
293	New Jersey Statehood	5.75
294	Signing of the Constitution	4.75
295	Certified Public Accountants	5.75
296	Locomotives Booklet	5.75
297	Christmas, Madonna	6.25
298	Christmas, Ornaments	5.75

1988

299	Georgia Statehood	6.25
300	Connecticut Statehood	6.25
301	Winter Olympics	6.25
302	Australia	5.75
303	James Weldon Johnson	5.00
304	Cats	6.50
305	Massachusetts Statehood	6.25
306	Maryland Statehood	6.25
307	Knute Rockne	9.50
308	New Sweden	5.75
309	South Carolina Statehood	6.25
310	Francis Ouimet	12.00
311	New Hampshire Statehood	6.25
312	Virginia Statehood	6.25
313	Love	7.00
314	New York Statehood	6.25
315	Summer Olympics	6.25
316	Classic Cars Booklet	6.75
317	Antarctic Explorers	6.25
318	Carousel Animals	6.75
319	Christmas, Madonna, Sleigh	7.00
320	Special Occasions Booklet	6.75

1989

321	Montana Statehood	6.25
322	A. Philip Randolph	8.75
323	North Dakota Statehood	6.25
324	Washington Statehood	6.25
325	Steamboats Booklet	8.00
326	World Stamp Expo '89	6.25
327	Arturo Toscanini	6.25
328	U.S. House of Representatives	7.25
329	U.S. Senate	7.25
330	Executive Branch	7.25
331	South Dakota Statehood	6.25
332	Lou Gehrig	15.00
333	French Revolution	7.50
334	Ernest Hemingway	7.25
335	North Carolina Statehood	6.25
336	Letter Carriers	7.25
337	Drafting of the Bill of Rights	7.25
338	Prehistoric Animals	12.50
339	25¢ and 45¢ America/PUAS	7.25
340	Christmas, Traditional and Contemporary	8.50
341	Classic Mail Transportation	7.25
342	Future Mail Transportation	8.00

1990

343	Idaho Statehood	7.25
344	Love	7.25
345	Ida B. Wells	11.00
346	U.S. Supreme Court	7.25
347	Wyoming Statehood	6.25
348	Classic Films	9.25
349	Marianne Moore	6.25
350	Lighthouses Booklet	10.00
351	Rhode Island Statehood	6.75
352	Olympians	10.00
353	Indian Headdresses Booklet	10.00
354	Micronesia/ Marshall Islands	8.75
355	25¢ and 45¢ America/PUAS	7.50
356	Eisenhower	8.25
357	Creatures of the Sea	13.00
358	Christmas, Traditional and Contemporary	9.50

1991

359	Switzerland	8.75
360	Vermont Statehood	7.25
361	Savings Bonds	6.25
362	29¢ and 52¢ Love	8.00
363	Saroyan	7.50
364	Fishing Flies Booklet	12.50
365	Cole Porter	8.00
366	Antarctic Treaty	8.00
367	Desert Shield/ Desert Storm	20.00
368	Summer Olympics	8.75
369	Numismatics	7.50
370	Basketball	12.50
371	World War II Miniature Sheet	12.00
372	Comedians Booklet	9.50
373	District of Columbia	8.00
374	Jan Matzeliger	7.50
375	Space Exploration Booklet	12.50
376	America/PUAS	8.00
377	Christmas, Traditional and Contemporary	9.50

1992

378	Winter Olympics	10.00
379	World Columbian Stamp Expo '92	8.75
380	W.E.B. Du Bois	8.75
381	Love	8.75
382	Olympic Baseball	25.00
383	Columbus' First Voyage	10.00
384	Space Adventures	12.00
385	New York Stock Exchange	11.00
386	Alaska Highway	8.75
387	Kentucky Statehood	8.75
388	Summer Olympics	10.50
389	Hummingbirds Booklet	11.00
390	World War II Miniature Sheet	11.00
391	Dorothy Parker	8.75
392	Theodore von Karman	10.00
393	Minerals	9.50
394	Juan Rodriguez Cabrillo	10.00
395	Wild Animals Booklet	12.50
396	Christmas, Traditional and Contemporary	9.25
397	Columbus Souvenir Sheets	40.00
398	Columbus Souvenir Sheets	40.00
399	Columbus Souvenir Sheets	40.00
400	Wildflowers #1	20.00
401	Wildflowers #2	20.00
402	Wildflowers #3	20.00
403	Wildflowers #4	20.00

404	Wildflowers #5	20.00
405	Happy New Year	15.00

1993

406	Elvis	22.50
407	Space Fantasy	14.00
408	Percy Julian	12.50
409	Oregon Trail	10.50
410	World Univ.Games	11.00
411	Grace Kelly	13.00
412	Oklahoma!	12.00
413	Circus	12.00
414	Cherokee Strip	9.25
415	Dean Acheson	10.50
416	Sport Horses	13.00
417	Garden Flowers	13.00
418	World War II	13.00
419	Hank Williams	15.00
420	Rock & Roll/R&B	20.00
421	Joe Louis	20.00
422	Broadway Musicals	12.50
423	National Postal Museum	12.00
424	Deaf Communication	12.00
425	Country Western	15.00
426	Christmas, Traditional	13.00
427	Youth Classics	13.00
428	Mariana Islands	12.00
429	Columbus Landing In Puerto Rico	10.50
430	AIDS Awareness	12.00

1994

431	Winter Olympics	12.00
432	Edward R. Murrow	9.50
433	Dr. Allison Davis	10.00
434	Year of the Dog	14.00
435	Love	9.50
436	Buffalo Soldiers	16.00
437	Silent ScreenStars	14.00
438	Garden Flowers	12.00
439	World Cup Soccer	12.50
440	World War II	15.00
441	Norman Rockwell	13.00
442	Moon Landing	16.00
443	Locomotives	13.00
444	George Meany	10.00
445	Popular Singers	14.00
446	James Thurber	10.00
447	Jazz/Blues	15.00
448	Wonders of the Sea	13.00
449	Birds (Cranes)	13.00
450	Christmas, Madonna	10.00
451	Christmas, Stocking	10.00
452	Year of the Boar	13.00

1995

453	Florida Statehood	12.50
454	Bessie Coleman	15.00
455	Kids Care!	11.00
456	Richard Nixon	15.00
457	Love	15.00
458	Recreational Sports	15.00
459	POW & MIA	14.00
460	Marilyn Monroe	20.00

461	Texas Statehood	12.50
462	Great Lakes Lighthouses	14.00
463	United Nations	11.00
464	Carousel Horses	17.50
465	Jazz Musicians	17.50
466	Women's Suffrage	11.00
467	Louis Armstrong	15.00
468	World War II	15.00
469	Fall Garden Flowers	12.50
470	Republic of Palau	12.50
471	Christmas, Contemporary	15.00
472	Naval Academy	15.00
473	Tennessee Williams	14.00
474	Christmas, Traditional	15.00
475	James K. Polk	12.50
476	Antique Automobiles	17.50

1996

477	Utah Statehood	10.00
478	Winter Garden Flowers	10.00
479	Ernest E. Just	12.50
480	Smithsonian Institution	10.00
481	Year of the Rat	17.50
482	Pioneers of Communication	14.00
483	Fulbright Scholarships	10.00
484	Olympics	30.00
485	Marathon	15.00
486	Georgia O'Keefe	10.00
487	Tennessee Statehood	10.00
488	James Dean	17.50
489	Prehistoric Animals	17.50
490	Breast Cancer Awareness	11.00
491	American Indian Dances	17.50
492	Folk Heroes	17.50
493	Centennial Games (Discus)	12.50
494	Iowa Statehood	10.00
495	Rural Free Delivery	10.00
496	Riverboats	17.50
497	Big Band Leaders	17.50
498	Songwriters	17.50
499	Endangered Species	30.00
500	Family Scenes (4 designs)	15.00
501	Hanukkah	15.00
502	Madonna and Child	15.00
503	Cycling	20.00
503A	F. Scott Fitzgerald	17.50
503B	Computer Technology	17.50

1997

504	Year of the Ox	15.00
505	Benjamin O. Davis	15.00
506	Love	15.00
507	Helping Children Learn	12.50
508	Pacific 97 Triangle Stamps	17.50
509	Thornton Wilder	15.00
510	Raoul Wallenberg	15.00
511	Dinosaurs	20.00
512	Bugs Bunny	16.00
513	Pacific 97 Franklin	50.00
514	Pacific 97 Washington	50.00
515	The Marshall Plan	12.50
516	Classic Aircraft	30.00
517	Football Coaches	17.50
518	Dolls	22.50
519	Humphrey Bogart	17.50
520	Stars and Stripes	15.00
521	Opera Singers	15.00
522	Composers and Conductors	17.50
523	Padre Varela	14.00
524	Air Force	15.00
525	Movie Monsters	17.50
526	Supersonic Flight	15.00
527	Women in the Military	14.00
528	Holiday Kwanzaa	15.00
529	Holiday, Traditional	22.50
530	Holiday Holly	22.50

1998

531	Year of the Tiger	15.00
532	Winter Sports	14.00
533	Madam C.J. Walker	15.00
533A	Celebrate The Century® 1900s	25.00
533B	Celebrate The Century® 1910s	25.00
534	Spanish American War	15.00
535	Flowering Trees	16.00
536	Alexander Calder	16.00
537	Cinco de Mayo	14.00
538	Sylvester & Tweety	17.50
538A	Celebrate The Century® 1920s	25.00
539	Wisconsin Statehood	16.00
540	Trans-Mississippi	20.00
541	Folk Singers	16.00
542	Berlin Airlift	14.00
543	Spanish Settlement of the Southwest	16.00
544	Gospel Singers	14.00
545	Stephen Vincent Benet	15.00
546	Tropical Birds	16.00
546A	Breast Cancer Research	15.00
547	Alfred Hitchcock	16.00
548	Organ Donations	15.00
549	Bright Eyes	16.00

550	Klondike Gold Rush	15.00
551	American Art	25.00
551A	Celebrate The Century® 1930s	25.00
552	Ballet	15.00
553	Space Discovery	16.00
554	Philanthropy	15.00
555	Holiday, Traditional	20.00
556	Holiday, Contemporary	15.00

1999

557	Year of the Hare	15.00
558	Malcolm X	15.00
559	33¢ Victorian - Love	20.00
560	55¢ Victorian - Love	15.00
561	Hospice Care	15.00
562	Celebrate The Century® 1940s	25.00
563	Irish Immigration	15.00
564	Alfred Lunt and Lynn Fontanne	15.00
565	Arctic Animals	15.00
566	Nature of America Sonoran Desert	25.00
567	Daffy Duck	25.00
568	Ayn Rand	15.00
569	Cinco de Mayo	15.00
570	John and William Bartram	15.00
571	Celebrate The Century® 1950s	25.00
572	Prostate Cancer	16.00
573	California Gold Rush	16.00
574	Aquarium Fish	16.00
575	Xtreme Sports	16.00
576	American Glass	16.00
577	James Cagney	16.00
578	Honoring Those Who Served	16.00
579	All Aboard!	16.00
580	Frederick Law Olmsted	16.00
581	Hollywood Composers	16.00
582	Celebrate The Century® 1960s	25.00
583	Broadway Songwriters	16.00
584	Insects and Spiders	25.00
585	Hanukkah	16.00
586	Nato	16.00
587	Holiday Traditional, Bartolomeo Vivarini	16.00
588	Holiday Contemporary, Deer	16.00
589	Kwanzaa	16.00
590	Celebrate The Century® 1970s	25.00
591	Year 2000	16.00

2000

592	Year of the Dragon	16.00
593	Celebrate The Century® 1980s	25.00
594	Patricia Roberts Harris	16.00
595	U.S. Navy Submarines – *Los Angeles* Class	—
596	Pacific Coast Rain Forest	—
597	Louise Nevelson	—
598	Edwin Powell Hubble	—
599	American Samoa	—
600	Library of Congress	—
601	Wile E. Coyote/ Road Runner	—
602	Celebrate The Century® 1990s	—
603	Summer Sports	—
604	Adoption	—
605	Youth Team Sports	—
606	Distinguished Soldiers	—
607	The Stars and Stripes	—
608	Legends of Baseball	—
609	Stampin' The Future™	—
610	Edward G. Robinson	—
611	California Statehood	—
612	Deep Sea Creatures	—
613	Thomas Wolfe	—
614	The White House	—

Glossary

Accessories
The tools used by stamp collectors, such as tongs, hinges, etc.

Aerophilately
Stamp collecting that focuses on stamps or postage relating to airmail.

Airmail
Mail which has been transported by air, as distinct from "surface" mail. Most long-distance mail is now transported by air; in the U.S., the distinction (and premium) for domestic airmail ceased in the late 1970s, and for foreign mail in the mid-1990s (now generically called "international rate").

Album
A book designed to hold stamps and covers.

Approvals
Stamps sent by a dealer to a collector for examination. Approvals must either be bought or returned to the dealer within a specified time.

Auction
A sale at which philatelic material is sold to the highest bidder.

Block
An unseparated group of stamps, at least two stamps high and two stamps wide.

Bogus
A completely fictitious, worthless "stamp," created only for sale to collectors. Bogus stamps include labels for nonexistent values added to regularly issued sets, issues for nations without postal systems, etc.

Booklet Pane
A small sheet of stamps specially cut to be sold in booklets.

Bourse
A marketplace, such as a stamp exhibition, where stamps are bought, sold or exchanged.

Cachet (ka-shay')
A design on an envelope describing an event. Cachets appear on first day of issue, first flight and stamp exhibition covers, etc.

Cancellation
A mark placed on a stamp by a postal authority to show that it has been used.

Centering
The position of the design on a postage stamp. On perfectly centered stamps the design is exactly in the middle.

Cinderella
Any stamp-like label without an official postal value.

Classic
An early stamp issue. Most people consider these to be rare stamps, but classic stamps aren't necessarily rare.

Coils
Stamps issued in rolls (one stamp wide) for use in dispensers or vending machines.

Commemoratives
Stamps that honor anniversaries, important people, special events or aspects of national culture.

Compound Perforations
Different gauge perforations on different (normally adjacent) sides of a single stamp.

Condition
Condition is the most important characteristic in determining the value of a stamp. It refers to the state of a stamp regarding such details as centering, color and gum.

Cover
An envelope that has been sent through the mail.

Cracked Plate
A term used to describe stamps which show evidence that the plate from which they were printed was cracked.

Definitives
Regular issues of postage stamps, usually sold over long periods of time.

Denomination
The postage value appearing on a stamp, such as 5 cents.

Die Cut
Scoring of self-adhesive stamps that allows stamp separation from liner.

Directory Markings
Postal markings that indicate a failed delivery attempt, stating reasons such as "No Such Number" or "Address Unknown."

Double Transfer
The condition on a printing plate that shows evidence of a duplication of all or part of the design.

Duplicates
Extra copies of stamps that can be sold or traded. Duplicates should be examined carefully for color and perforation variations.

Entire
An intact piece of postal stationery, in contrast to a cut-out of the printed design.

Error
A stamp with some-thing incorrect in its design or manufacture.

Exploded (booklet)
A stamp booklet that has been separated into its various components for display.

Face Value
The monetary value or denomination of a stamp.

Fake
A genuine stamp that has been altered in some way to make it more attractive to collectors. It may be repaired, reperfed or regummed to resemble a more valuable variety.

First Day Cover (FDC)
An envelope with a new stamp and cancellation showing the date the stamp was issued.

Foreign Entry
When original transfers are erased incompletely from a plate, they can appear with new transfers of a different design which are subsequently entered on the plate.

Franks
Marking on the face of a cover, indicating it is to be carried free of postage. Franks may be written, hand-stamped, imprinted or represented by special adhesives. Such free franking is usually limited to official correspondence, such as the President's mail.

Freak
An abnormal variety of stamps occurring because of paper fold, over-inking, perforation shift, etc., as opposed to a continually appearing variety or a major error.

Grill
A pattern of small, square pyramids in parallel rows impressed or embossed on the stamp to break paper fibers, allowing cancellation ink to soak in and preventing washing and reuse.

Gum
The coating of glue on the back of an unused stamp.

Hinges
Small strips of gummed material used by collectors to affix stamps to album pages.

Imperforate
Indicates stamps without perforations or separating holes. They usually are separated by scissors and collected in pairs.

Label
Any stamp-like adhesive that is not a postage stamp.

Laid Paper
When held to the light, the paper shows alternate light and dark crossed lines.

Line Pairs (LP)
Most coil stamp rolls prior to 1981 freature a line of ink (known as a "joint line") printed between two stamps at various intervals, caused by the joining of two or more curved plates around the printing cylinder.

Liner
The backing paper for self-adhesive stamps.

Linerless Coil
Self-adhesive roll of coil stamps without a liner.

Miniature Sheet
A single stamp or block of stamps with a margin on all sides bearing some special wording or design.

On Paper
Stamps "on paper" are those that still have portions of the original envelope or wrapper stuck to them.

Overprint
Additional printing on a stamp that was not part of the original design.

Packet

A presorted unit of all different stamps. One of the most common and economical ways to begin a collection.

Pane

A full "sheet" of stamps as sold by a Post Office. Four panes typically make up the original sheet of stamps as printed.

Par Avion

French for mail transported "by air."

Perforations

Lines of small holes or cuts between rows of stamps that make them easy to separate.

Philately

The collection and study of postage stamps and other postal materials.

Pictorials

Stamps with a picture of some sort, other than portraits or static designs such as coats of arms.

Plate Block (PB) (or Plate Number Block)

A block of stamps with the margin attached that bears the plate number used in printing that sheet.

Plate Number Coils (PNC)

For most coil stamp rolls beginning with #1891, a small plate number appears at varying intervals in the roll in the design of the stamp.

Postage Due

A stamp issued to collect unpaid postage.

Postal Stationery

Envelopes, postal cards and aerogrammes with stamp designs printed or embossed on them.

Postal Cards

See "stamped cards."

Postcards

Commercially-produced mailable cards, but without imprinted postage (postage must be affixed).

Postmark

A mark put on envelopes or other mailing pieces showing the date and location of the post office where it was mailed.

Precancels

Cancellations applied to stamps before the stamps were affixed to mail.

Presort Stamp

A discounted stamp used by qualified mailers who presort mail.

Registered Mail

First-Class mail with a numbered receipt, including a valuation of the registered item. This guarantees customers will get their money back if an item is lost in the mail.

Reissue

An official reprinting of a stamp that was no longer being printed.

Replicas

Reproductions of stamps sold during the early days of collecting. Usually printed in one color on a sheet containing a number of different designs. Replicas were never intended to deceive either the post office or the collector.

Reprint

A stamp printed from the original plate after the issue is no longer valid for postage. Official reprints are sometimes made for presentation purposes, official collections, etc., and are often distinguished in some way from the "real" ones.

Revenue Stamps

Stamps not valid for postal use but issued for collecting taxes.

Ribbed Paper

Paper which shows fine parallel ridges on one or both sides of a stamp.

Rouletting

The piercing of the paper between stamps to facilitate their separation. No paper is actually removed from the sheet, as is the case in the punching method used in most perforating. Instead, rouletting often gives the appearance of a series of dashes.

Se-tenant

An attached pair, strip or block of stamps that differ in design, value or surcharge.

Secret Marks

Many stamps have included tiny reference points in their designs to foil attempts at counterfeiting and to differentiate issues.

Self-Adhesive Stamp

A stamp with a pressure sensitive adhesive.

Selvage

The unprinted paper around panes of stamps, sometimes called the margin.

Series

A number of individual stamps or sets of stamps having a common purpose or theme, issued over an extended period of time (generally a year or more), including all variations of design and/or denomination.

Set

A group of stamps with a common design or theme issued at one time for a common purpose or over a limited perid of time (generally less than a year).

Souvenir Sheet

A small sheet of stamps with a commemorative inscription of some sort.

Special Issues

Stamps which supplement definitives, while meeting specific needs and having a more commemorative appearance. These include Christmas, Love, Holiday Celebration, airmail, international rate, Express Mail and Priority Mail stamps.

Speculative

A stamp or issue released primarily for sale to collectors, rather than to meet any legitimate postal need.

Stamped Cards

The current term for postal cards, which are mailable cards with postage imprinted directly on them.

Stamped Envelopes

Mailable envelopes with postage embossed and/or imprinted on them.

Strip

Three or more unseparated stamps in a row.

Surcharge

An overprint that changes the denomination of a stamp from its original face value.

Sweatbox

A closed box with a grill over which stuck-together unused stamps are placed. A wet, sponge-like material under the grill creates humidity so the stamps can be separated without removing the gum.

Tagging

The marking of stamps with a phosphor or similar coating (which may be in lines, bars, letters, overall design area or entire stamp surface), done by many countries for use with automatic mail-handling equipment. When a stamp is issued both with and without this marking, catalogs will often note varieties as "tagged" or "untagged."

Thematic

A stamp collection that relates to a specific theme and is arranged to present a logical story and progression.

Tied On

Indicates a stamp whose postmark touches the envelope.

Tongs

A tool, used to handle stamps, that resembles a tweezers with rounded or flattened tips.

Topicals

Indicates a group of stamps with the same theme—space travel, for example.

Unhinged

A stamp without hinge marks, but not necessarily with original gum.

Unused

The condition of a stamp that has no cancellation or other sign of use.

Used

The condition of a stamp that has been canceled.

Variety

A stamp which varies in some way from its standard or original form. Varieties can include missing colors or perforations, constant plate flaws, changes in ink or paper, differences in printing method or in format, such as booklet and coil "varieties" of the same stamp.

Want List

A list of philatelic material needed by a collector.

Watermark

A design pressed into stamp paper during its manufacture.
Water Activated Gum Water soluable adhesives such as sugar based starches on back of unused stamps.

Water Activated Gum

Water soluable adhesives such as sugar based starches on back of unused stamps.

Wove Paper

A uniform paper which, when held to the light, shows no light or dark figures.

Organizations

Please enclose a stamped, self-addressed envelope when writing to these organizations.

American Air Mail Society
Rudy Roy
P.O. Box 5367
Virginia Beach, VA 23471-0367
(p) 757/499-5234
AAMSinformation@aol.com
http://ourworld.compuserve.com/homepages/aams/

Specializes in all phases of aerophilately. Membership services include Advance Bulletin Service, Auction Service, free want ads, Sales Department, monthly journal, discounts on Society publications, translation service.

American First Day Cover Society
Douglas Kelsey
Executive Director
P.O. Box 65960
Tucson, AZ 85728-5960
(p) 520/321-0880
520/321-0879
AFDCS@aol.com
http://www.afdcs.org

A full-service, not-for-profit, noncommercial society devoted exclusively to First Day Covers and First Day Cover collecting. Publishes 90-page magazine, First Day, *eight times a year. Offers information on 300 current cachet producers, expertizing, foreign covers, translation service, color slide programs and archives covering First Day Covers.*

American Ceremony Program Society
John E. Peterson
ACPS Secretary/Treasurer
6987 Coleshill Drive
San Diego, CA 92119-1953
jkpete@pacebell.net
www.webacps.org

The American Ceremony Program Society (ACPS) is a place to learn about First Day and Supplemental (Second Day or later) stamp Ceremonies and Ceremony Programs. The Society publishes a journal, The Ceremonial, *which is available online. The Society dues are $5 a year.*

American Philatelic Society
Robert E. Lamb
Executive Director
P.O. Box 8000
State College, PA 16803-8000
(p) 814/237-3803
(f) 814/237-6128
flsente@stamps.org
http://www.stamps.org

A full complement of services and resources for stamp collectors. Annual membership offers: library services, educational seminars and correspondence courses, expertizing service, estate advisory service, translation service, a stamp theft committee that functions as a clearinghouse for philatelic crime information, on-line intramember sales service and a monthly journal, The American Philatelist, *sent to all members. Membership 53,000 worldwide.*

American Society for Philatelic Pages and Panels
Gerald Blankenship
P.O. Box 475
Crosby, TX 77532-0475
(p) 281/324-2709
gblank1941@aol.com

Focuses on souvenir pages and commemorative panels. Free ads, member auction, publishes a quarterly journal sent to all members with reports on new issues, varieties, errors, oddities and discoveries.

American Stamp Dealers Association
Joseph B. Savarese
3 School St., Suite 205
Glen Cove, NY 11542-2548
(p) 516/759-7000
(f) 516/759-7014
asdashows@erols.com
http://www.asdaonline.com

Association of dealers engaged in every facet of philately, with 11 regional chapters nationwide. Sponsors national and local shows. Will send you a complete listing of dealers in your area or collecting specialty. A #10 SASE must accompany your request.

American Topical Association
Paul E. Tyler
Executive Director
P.O. Box 50820
Albuquerque, NM 87181-0820
(p) 505/323-8595
(f) 505/323-8795
ATAStamps@juno.com
http://home.prcn.org/~pauld/ata

A service organization concentrating on the specialty of topical stamp collecting. Offers handbooks and checklists on specific topics; exhibition awards; Topical Time, *a bimonthly publication dealing with topical interest areas; a slide loan service, and information, translation and sales services.*

Ebony Society of Philatelic Events and Reflections
Sanford L. Byrd
P.O. Box 8888
Corpus Christi, TX 78468-8888
(f) 361/980-8675
esper@attglobal.net
http://slsabyrd.com

Junior Philatelists of America
Jennifer Arnold
Executive Secretary
P.O. Box 2625
Albany, OR 97321-0643
Exec.sec@jpastamps.org
http://www.jpastamps.org/

Member services include: pen pals, philatelic library, stamp identification, contests, study groups, and other services to young collectors. Members receive a bimonthly newsletter, The Philatelic Observer. *Adult supporting membership and gift memberships are available. The JPA also publishes various brochures on stamp collecting.*

Mailer's Postmark Permit Club
Joseph LoPreiato
165 Old Farm Drive
Newington, CT 06111-1819
(p) 860/666-5244
(f) 860/666-7041
EnotriaLP@aol.com

Publishes bimonthly newsletter, Permit Patter, *which covers all aspects of mailer's precancel postmarks, as well as a catalog and two checklists. Also available, a 10-page step by step brochure "How to obtain a Mailer's Postmark Permit...a basic guide."*

Plate Number Coil Collectors Club
Don Eastman
Secretary PNC[3]
24 Bemis Street
Berlin, NH 03570-3304
www.pnc3.org

The Plate Number Coil Collectors Club (PNC[3]) is an organization that studies the plate numbers and plate varieties of United States coil stamps issued since 1981. The PNC[3] publishes a monthly newsletter, Coil Line. *The website discusses plate number coils and PNC[3] at length.*

Postal History Society
Kalman V. Illyefalvi
8207 Daren Court
Pikesville, MD 21208-2211
(p) 410/653-0665
kalphyl@juno.com

Devoted to the study of various aspects of the development of the mails and local, national and international postal systems; UPU treaties; and means of transporting mail.

The Souvenir Card Collectors Society, Inc.
Dana M. Marr
P.O. Box 4155
Tulsa, OK 74159-0155
(p) 918/664-6724
DMARR5569@aol.com

Provides member auctions, a quarterly journal and access to limited-edition souvenir cards.

United Postal Stationery Society
UPSS Central Office
Cora Collins
Executive Director
P.O. Box 1792
Norfolk, VA 23501-1792

Universal Ship Cancellation Society
David Kent
P.O. Box 127
New Britian, CT 06050-0127
(p) 860/667-1400
kentdave@aol.com
http://www.uscs.org

Specializes in naval ship postmarks.

United States Postal Service
Stamp Services
475 L'Enfant Plaza SW
Washington, D.C. 20260-2437

United States Stamp Society
Executive Secretary
P.O. Box 6634
Katy, TX 77491-6634
http://www.usstamps.org

Devoted to the study of all U.S. stamps, principally those produced by the Bureau of Engraving and Printing.

Expertisers

American Philatelic Expertizing Service (APEX)
Mercer Bristow
Director of Expertizing
P.O. Box 8000
State College, PA 16803-8000
Ambristo@stamps.org

Krystal Harter
Expertizing Coordinator
P.O. Box 8000
State College, PA 16803-8000
Krharter@stamps.org

(p) 814/237-3803
(f) 814/237-6128
http://www.stamps.org

A joint project of the American Philatelic Society and the American Stamp Dealers' Association, APEX utilizes the high-tech equipment and outstanding reference collection at APS headquarters in conjunction with the nation's best philatelic scholars to pass judgement on the identification,

authenticity and condition of stamps from all countries. APEX certificates are accepted by all legitimate auction firms, dealers and collectors.

Philatelic Foundation
Attention: Chairman
501 Fifth Ave. Rm. 1901
New York, NY 10017-6102
(p) 212/867-3699

A nonprofit organization known for its excellent expertization service. The Foundation's broad resources, including extensive reference collections, 5,000-volume library and Expert Committee, provide collectors with comprehensive consumer protection. Slide and cassette programs are available on such subjects as the Pony Express, classic U.S. stamps, Confederate Postal History and collecting basics for beginners. Book series include expertizing case histories in Opinions, *Foundation seminar subjects in "textbooks" and specialized U.S. subjects in monographs.*

Professional Stamp Experts, Inc.
P.O. Box 6170
Newport Beach, CA 92658
(p) 877/782-6788
http://www.collectors.com/pse

A for-profit organization comprised of more than 70 of the leading philatelic experts in the U.S. in the identification and authentication of all U.S. and British Commonwealth postage stamps, covers, revenues, etc. The PSE's expansive resources include a 2,500-volume reference library plus postage stamp reference collection for direct comparison, examination and authentication. PSE issues a Certificate of Authenticity on each submission it receives. These expert opinions are accepted by all legitimate auction firms, dealers and collectors. All submissions are fully insured once reviewed by PSE until items are returned to the original submitter.

Periodicals

The following publications will send you a free copy of their magazine or newspaper upon request.

Global Stamp News
P.O. Box 97
Sidney, OH 45365-0097
(p) 937/492-3183
global@bright.net

America's largest-circulation monthly stamp magazine featuring U.S. and foreign issues.

Linn's Stamp News
P.O. Box 29
Sidney, OH 45365-0097
(p) 937/498-0801
(f) 800/340-9501 (US only)
(f) 937/498-0814 (outside US)
linns@linns.com
www.linns.com

The largest weekly stamp newspaper.

Mekeel's & Stamps Magazine
John Dunn
P.O. Box 5050-fa
White Plains, NY 10602-5050
Stampnews@aol.com
http://www.stampnews.com

World's oldest stamp weekly, for intermediate and advanced collectors.

Stamp Collector
Wayne Youngblood
Publisher, Stamps Dept.
700 E. State St.
Iola, WI 54990-0001
(p) 715/445-2214
youngbloodw@krause.com

For beginning and advanced collectors of all ages.

Stamp Wholesaler
Wayne Youngblood
Publisher, Stamps Dept.
700 E. State St.
Iola, WI 54990-0001
(p) 715/445-2214
youngbloodw@krause.com

For dealers of all levels and those interested in the stamp business. (Published monthly as part of Stamp Collector.)

USA Philatelic
Information Fulfillment
Dept. 6270
U.S. Postal Service
P.O. Box 219014
Kansas City, MO 64121-9014
(p) 1 800 STAMP-24

U.S. Stamp News
John Dunn
P.O. Box 5050-fb
White Plains, NY 10602-5050
Stampnews@aol.com
http://www.stampnews.com

Monthly magazine for all collectors of U.S. stamps, covers and postal history.

Museums, Libraries and Displays

Please contact the institutions before visiting to confirm hours and any entry fees.

American Philatelic Research Library
Robert E. Lamb
P.O. Box 8000
State College, PA 16803-8000
(p) 814/237-3803
(f) 814/237-6128
gini@stamps.org
http://www.stamps.org

Founded in 1968; now the largest philatelic library in the U.S. Currently receives more than 400 worldwide periodical titles and houses extensive collections of bound journals, books, auction catalogs and dealer pricelists. Directly serves members of the APS and APRL (library members also receive the quarterly Philatelic Literature Review). *The public may purchase photocopies directly or borrow materials through the national interlibrary loan system.*

The Collectors Club
Irene Bromberg
Executive Secretary
22 E. 35th Street
New York, NY 10016-3806
(p) 212/683-0559
(f) 212/481-1269
collectorsclub@nac.net
http://www.collectorsclub.org

Bimonthly journal, publication of various reference works, one of the most extensive reference libraries in the world, reading and study rooms. Regular meetings on the first and third Wednesdays of each month at 6:30 p.m., except July and August.

Friends of the Western Philatelic Library
P.O. Box 2219
Sunnyvale, CA 94087-2219
(p) 408/733-0336
http://www.fwpl.org/

National Postal Museum
Smithsonian Institution
Washington, D.C. 20560-0570
(p) 202/633-9360
http://www.si.edu/postal/
Hours:
7 days 10:00 a.m.-5:30 p.m., except 12/25

Located in the Old City Post Office building at 2 Massachusetts Avenue, NE, near Union Station, the National Postal Museum houses more than 16 million items for exhibition and study purposes. Collections research may be conducted separately or jointly with library materials. Call the museum and its library separately to schedule an appointment.

The Postal History Foundation
Betsy Towle
P.O. Box 40725
Tucson, AZ 85717-0725
(p) 520/623-6652
(f) 520/623-6652
phf3@mindspring.com
Hours:
M-F 8:00 a.m.-3:00 p.m.

Regular services include a library, USPS contract post office, philatelic sales, archives, artifacts and collections and a Youth Department. Membership includes subscription to a quarterly journal, The Heliograph.

San Diego County Philatelic Library
Ralph H. Armington
7403C Princess View Drive
San Diego, CA 92120
(p) 619/229-8813-1345
Hours:
M & Th 6:00 p.m.-9:00 p.m. and Sat noon to 3 p.m.

Spellman Museum of Stamps and Postal History

Viki Sand
Executive Director
235 Wellesley Street
Weston, MA 02193-1538
(p) 781/768-8367
(f) 781/768-7332
info@spellman.org
www.spellman.org
Hours: Th-S 12 noon-5 p.m.
(closed holidays)
Adults: $5; students/seniors: $3; members, visitors to the Museum Store and Post office, and children 16 and under: free.

Located on the campus of Regis College. America's first fully accredited museum devoted to the display, collection and preservation of stamps and postal history. The three galleries' exhibitions feature international rarities, United States, and worldwide collections. Philatelic research library and family activity center open with admission. Museum Store and Post Office has collectibles, collecting supplies, and U.S. postage stamps.

Western Philatelic Library

P.O. Box 2219
Sunnyvale, CA 94087-2219
(p) 408/733-0336
stulev@ix.netcom.com
http://www.pbbooks.com/wpl.htm

Wineburgh Philatelic Research Library

Erik D. Carlson, Ph.D.
McDermott Library
University of Texas at Dallas
P.O. Box 830643
Mailstation: MC33
Richardson, TX 75083-0643
(p) 972/883-2570
http://www.utdallas.edu/library/special/wprl.html
Hours:
M-T 9:00 a.m.–6:00 p.m.;
F 9:00 a.m.-5:00 p.m.

Exchange Service

Stamp Master

Charles Bergeron
P.O. Box 17
Putnam Hall, FL 32185-0017
Cbergero@bellsouth.net

An "electronic connection" for philatelists via modem and computer to display/review members' stamp inventories for trading purposes, etc.

Literature

ArtCraft First Day Cover Price List

Washington Press
2 Vreeland Road
Florham Park, NJ 07932-1501
(p) 973/966-0001
info@washpress.com
http://www.washpress.com

Includes Presidential Inaugural covers.

Basic Philately

Wayne Youngblood
Publisher, Stamps Dept.
700 E. State St.
Iola, WI 54990-0001
(p) 715/445-2214
youngbloodw@krause.com

Brookman's 1st Edition Black Heritage First Day Cachet Cover Catalog

Arlene Dunn
Brookman/Barrett & Worthen
10 Chestnut Drive
Bedford, NH 03110-5566
(p) 603/472-5575
(f) 603/472-8795

Illustrated 176-page perfect bound book.

Brookman's 2nd Edition Price Guide for Disney Stamps

Arlene Dunn
Brookman/Barrett & Worthen
10 Chestnut Drive
Bedford, NH 03110-5566
(p) 603/472-5575
(f) 603/472-8795

Illustrated 256-page perfect bound book.

2001 Brookman Price Guide of U.S., U.N. and Canada Stamps and Postal Collectibles

Arlene Dunn
Brookman/Barrett & Worthen
10 Chestnut Drive
Bedford, NH 03110-5566
(p) 603/472-5575
(f) 603/472-8795

Illustrated 364-page catalog.

Commemorative Cancellation Catalog

Paul Brenner
General Image, Inc.
P.O. Box 335
Maplewood, NJ 07040-0335
Postmark1@earthlink.net
http://home.earthlink.net/~postmark1
(How-to-do-it is excellent for beginners)

Catalog covering all pictorial cancellations used in the U.S. during 1988-1989 is available. Please send self-addressed, stamped envelope for prices and description. Weekly newsletter is available which also provides descriptive information on U.S. pictorial postmarks. A sample newsletter is available at no charge if you send a SASE and specifically ask for a copy.

Compilation of U.S. Souvenir Cards

Dana M. Marr
P.O. Box 4155
Tulsa, OK 74159-4155
(p) 918/664-6724
DMARR5569@aol.com

Durland Plate Number Catalog

United States Stamp Society
Executive Secretary
P.O. Box 6334
Katy, TX 77491-6634
http://www.stamps.org

Fleetwood's Standard First Day Cover Catalog

Fleetwood
Unicover Corporation
1 Unicover Center
Cheyenne, WY 82008-0001
(p) 307/771-3000
(p) 800/443-4225
http://www.unicover.com

The Hammarskjold Invert

Washington Press
2 Vreeland Road
Florham Park, NJ 07932-1501
(p) 973/966-0001
info@washpress.com
http://www.washpress.com

Tells the story of the Dag Hammarskjold error/invert. FREE for #10 SASE.

Linn's U.S. Stamp Yearbook

P.O. Box 29
Sidney, OH 45365-0097
(p) 937/498-0801
(f) 800/340-9501 (US only)
(f) 937/498-0814 (outside US)
linns@linns.com
www.linns.com

A series of books providing facts and annual figures on every collectible variety of U.S. stamps, postal stationery and souvenir cards issued since 1983. A sample newsletter is available, at no charge, if you send a SASE and ask for one.

Linn's World Stamp Almanac
P.O. Box 29
Sidney, OH 45365-0097
(p) 937/498-0801
(f) 800/340-9501 (US only)
(f) 937/498-0814 (outside US)
linns@linns.com
www.linns.com

The most useful single reference source for stamp collectors. Contains detailed information on U.S. stamps.

19th Century Envelopes Catalog
UPSS Central Office
Cora Collins
Executive Director
P.O. Box 1792
Norfolk, VA 23501-1792

Precancel Stamp Society Catalogs
Dick Laetsch
108 Ashwamp Road
Scarborough, ME 04070
(p) 207/883-2505
precancel@aol.com
http://members.aol.com/precancel

Scott Specialized Catalogue of U.S. Stamps and Covers
P.O. Box 828
Sidney, OH 45365-0828
(p) 937/498-0802
(p) 800/572-6885
(f) 937/498-0807
ssm@scottonline.com
http://www.scottonline.com

Scott Stamp Monthly
P.O. Box 828
Sidney, OH 45365-0828
(p) 937/498-0802
(p) 800/572-6885
(f) 937/498-0807
ssm@scottonline.com
http://www.scottonline.com

Scott Standard Postage Stamp Catalogue
P.O. Box 828
Sidney, OH 45365-0828
(p) 937/498-0802
(p) 800/572-6885
(f) 800/488-5349
ssm@scottonline.com
http://www.scottonline.com

Stamp Collecting Made Easy
P.O. Box 29
Sidney, OH 45365-0029

An illustrated, easy-to-read, 96-page booklet for beginning collectors.

The 24¢ 1918 Air Mail Invert
Washington Press
2 Vreeland Road
Florham Park, NJ 07932-1501
(p) 973/966-0001
info@washpress.com
http://www.washpress.com

Tells all there is to know about this famous stamp. FREE for #10 SASE.

20th Century Envelops Catalog
UPSS Central Office
Cora Collins
Executive Director
P.O. Box 1792
Norfolk, VA 23501-1792

U.S. Postal Card Catalog
UPSS Central Office
Cora Collins
Executive Director
P.O. Box 1792
Norfolk, VA 23501-1792

The U.S. Transportation Coils
Washington Press
2 Vreeland Road
Florham Park, NJ 07932-1501
(p) 973/966-0001
info@washpress.com
http://www.washpress.com

FREE for #10 SASE.

International Agents

Japan Philatelic Agency
PO Box 96 Toshima
Tokyo 170-8668
JAPAN

Max Stern
234 Flinders Street
Box 997 H
GPO Melbourne 3001
AUSTRALIA

Harry Allen
PO Box 5
Watford Herts WD2 5SW
UNITED KINGDOM

Nordfrim
DK 5450 Otterup
DENMARK

DeRosa S.P.A.
Via Privata Maria Teresa 11
I-20123 Milan
ITALY

Hermann Sieger GMBH
Venusberg 32-34
D73545 Lorch Wurttemberg
GERMANY

Alberto Bolaffi
Via Cavour 17
10123 Torino
ITALY

International House of Stamps
98/2 Soi Tonson
Langsuan Rd
Lumpinee, Pathumwan
Bangkok 10330
THAILAND

Philatelic Centers

In addition to the more than 20,000 postal facilities authorized to sell philatelic products, the Postal Service also maintains Philatelic Centers located in major population centers. These Philatelic Centers have been established to serve stamp collectors and make it convenient for them to acquire an extensive range of current postage stamps, postal stationery and philatelic products issued by the Postal Service.

Centers are located at Main Post Offices with a ZIP + 4 of 9998 unless otherwise indicated. For questions about a Philatelic Center near you, call 800-275-8777.

Please note that Philatelic Centers in this listing include offices that may have only one philatelic window or limited hours dedicated to philatelic services.

Alabama
351 24th St. N
Birmingham, AL
35203-9816

379 N. Oates St.
Dothan, AL
36302-

Downtown Station
615 Clinton Ave. W
Huntsville, AL
35801-

250 St. Joseph St.
Mobile, AL
36601-

6701 Winton Blount
Blvd.
Montgomery, AL
36124-

Alaska
315 Barnette St.
Fairbanks, AK
99701-4532

Downtown Station
344 W. Third Ave.
Anchorage, AK
99510-2337

Arizona
2400 N. Postal Blvd.
Flagstaff, AZ
86004-4300

Osborne Station
3905 N. Seventh Ave.
Phoenix, AZ
85013-3349

General Mail Facility
4949 E. Van Buren St.
Phoenix, AZ
85026-9800

1501 S. Cherrybell St.
Tucson, AZ
85726-9713

Arkansas
600 E. Capitol Ave.
Little Rock, AR
72202-

California
1180 W. Ball Rd.
Anaheim, CA
92812-2730

2730 W. Tregallas Rd.
Antioch, CA
94509-4912

3400 Pegasus Dr.
Bakersfield, CA
93380-

2000 Allston Way
Berkeley, CA
94704-1418

2140 N. Hollywood Way
Burbank, CA
91505-

18122 Carmenita Rd.
Cerritos, CA
90703-6330

6330 Fountain Square Dr.
Citrus Heights, CA
95621-5500

2121 Meridian Park
Blvd.
Concord, CA
94520-5708

2020 Fifth St.
Davis, CA
95616-

8111 Firestone Blvd.
Downey, CA
90241-

401 W. Lexington Ave.
El Cajon, CA
92020-4415

Cutten Station
3901 Walnut Dr.
Eureka, CA
95501-9991

600 Kentucky St.
Fairfield, CA
94533-5531

1900 E St.
Fresno, CA
93706-

313 E. Broadway
Glendale, CA
91205-1010

Hillcrest Station
300 E. Hillcrest Blvd.
Inglewood, CA
50301-

300 N. Long Beach Blvd.
Long Beach, CA
90802-2427

900 N. Alameda St.
Los Angeles, CA
90012-2904

Village Station
11100 W. Wilshire Blvd.
Los Angeles, CA
90024-

Worldway Philatelic
Center
5800 Century Blvd.
Ste. 12
Los Angeles, CA
90009-

407 C St.
Marysville, CA
95901-

2334 M St.
Merced, CA
95340-

715 Kearney Ave.
Modesto, CA
95350-

Napa Station
1625 Trancas St.
Napa, CA
94558-

Civic Center Annex
201 13th St.
Oakland, CA
94612-3921

211 Brooks St.
Oceanside, CA
92054-3404

281 E. Colorado Blvd.
Pasadena, CA
91101-1903

4300 Black Ave.
Pleasanton, CA
94566-6103

2323 Churn Creek Rd.
Redding, CA
96049-

1201 N. Catalina
Redondo Beach, CA
90277-

2000 Royal Oaks Dr.
Sacramento, CA
95813-0100

390 W. Fifth St.
San Bernardino, CA
92401-

2535 Midway Dr.
San Diego, CA
92111-3223

180 Steuart St.
San Francisco, CA
94105-1239

1750 Maridian Ave.
San Jose, CA
95125-

40 Bellum Blvd.
San Rafael, CA
94901-

12935 Alcosta Blvd.
San Ramon, CA
94583-

Spurgeon Station
615 Bush St.
Santa Ana, CA
92701-4103

836 Anacapa St.
Santa Barbara, CA
93102-

201 E. Battles Rd.
Santa Maria, CA
93454-7203

730 Second St.
Santa Rosa, CA
95402-

200 Prairie Ct.
Vacaville, CA
95687-

15701 Sherman Way
Van Nuys, CA
91409-

396 S. California Ave.
West Covina, CA
91793-9000

Colorado

16890 E. Alameda Pkwy.
Aurora, CO
80017-

1905 15th St.
Boulder, CO
80302-

201 E. Pikes Peak Ave.
Rm. 205
Colorado Springs, CO
80903-1933

1823 Stout St.
Denver, CO
80202-2500

7500 E. 53rd Place
Denver, CO
80217-

222 W. Eighth St.
Durango, CO
81301-

301 E. Broadwalk Dr.
Fort Collins, CO
80528-

241 N. Fourth St.
Grand Junction, CO
81501-

5753 S. Prince St.
Littleton, CO
80120-1927

1905 15th St.
Longmont, CO
80501-

Connecticut

70 Water St.
Danielson, CT
06239-

141 Weston St.
Hartford, CT
06101-9000

11 Silver St.
Middletown, CT
06457-

50 Brewery St.
New Haven, CT
06511-

469 Main St.
Ridgefield, CT
06877-4513

135 Grand St.
Waterbury, CT
06701-9991

Delaware

55 The Plaza
Dover, DE
19901-

Wilmington P&DC
147 Quigley Blvd.
New Castle, DE
19720-9696

Rodney Square Station
1101 N. King St.
Wilmington, DE
19801-

District of Columbia

Pavillion Postique
1100 Penn. Ave. NW
Washington, DC
20004-2501

Postal Square
2 Mass. Ave. NE
Washington, DC
20002-9997

Florida

321 Montgomery Rd.
Altamonte Springs, FL
32714-

Bradenton MOWU
824 Manatee Ave.
W. Bradenton, FL
34205-

Brooksville MOWU
19101 Cortez Blvd.
Brooksville, FL
34601-

Clearwater MOWU
100 S. Belcher Rd.
Clearwater, FL
33765-

336 E. New York Ave.
Deland, FL
32724-

1900 W. Oakland Pk.
Blvd.
Fort Lauderdale, FL
33310-0116

Renaissance Contract
Postal Unit
8695 College Pkwy
Ste. 131
Fort Myers, FL
33919-4892

5000 W. Midway Rd.
Fort Pierce, FL 34981-

1801 Polk St.
Hollywood, FL
33022-0079

210 N. Missouri Ave.
Lakeland, FL
33815-

Leesburg Station
1201 S. 14th St.
Leesburg, FL
34748-9996

Longwood Wekiva
Station
920 Wekiva Springs Rd.
Longwood, FL
32779-9996

2200 NW 72nd Ave.
Miami, FL
33152-9000

1200 Goodlette Rd. N
Naples, FL
34102-5254

New Port Richey
MOWU
6550 Nebraska Ave.
New Port Richey, FL
34653-

1335 Kingsley Ave.
Orange Park, FL
32073-4507

46 E. Robinson St.
Orlando, FL
32801-

518 N. Ridgewood Dr.
Sebring, FL
33870-

St. Petersburg MOWU
3135 First Ave. N
St. Petersburg, FL
33730-

Tampa Airport MOWU
Postal Store
5201 W. Spruce St.
Tampa, FL
33630-

1538 Harrison Ave.
Titusville, FL
32780-

3200 Summit Blvd.
W. Palm Beach, FL
33406-

Georgia

1072 W. Peachtree St.
NW
Atlanta, GA
30309-

Perimeter Branch
4707 Ashford
Dunwoody Rd.

Atlanta, GA
31146-

3470 McClure Bridge Rd.
Duluth, GA
30136-

364 Green St. NE
Gainesville, GA
30501-

451 College St.
Macon, GA
31213-9812

257 Lawrence St. NE
Marietta, GA
30060-

2 N. Farm St., Rm 14
Savannah, GA
31402-

Hawaii

335 Merchant St.
Honolulu, HI
96813-

Idaho

770 S. 13th St.
Boise, ID
83708-

220 E. Fifth St.
Moscow, ID
83843-

730 E. Clark St.
Pocatello, ID
83201-

Illinois

909 W. Euclid Ave.
Arlington Heights, IL
60004-

525 N. Broadway
Aurora, IL
60507-

Moraine Valley Station
7401 W. 100th Place
Bridgeview, IL
60455-

1301 E. Main St.
Carbondale, IL
62901-

Loop Station
11 S. Clark St.
Chicago, IL
60604-

433 W. Harrison St.
2nd Fl.
Chicago, IL
60607-9208

1000 E. Oakton St.
Des Plaines, IL
60018-

1101 Davis St.
Evanston, IL
60201-

2359 Madison Ave.
Granite City, IL
62040-

2000 McDonough St.
Joliet, IL
60436-

1750 W. Ogden Ave.
Naperville, IL
60540-

123 Indianwood Blvd.
Park Forest, IL
60466-

N. University Station
6310 N. University St.
Peoria, IL
61614-3454

401 William
River Forest, IL
60305-1900

5225 Harrison Ave.
Rockford, IL
61125-

1956 Second Ave.
Rock Island, IL
61201-9700

450 W. Schaumburg Rd.
Schaumburg, IL
60194-

2105 E. Cook St.
Springfield, IL
62703-

326 N. Genesee St.
Waukegan, IL
60085-

Indiana

North Park Branch
4490 First Ave.
Evansville, IN
47710-

1501 S. Clinton St.
Fort Wayne, IN
46802-

5530 Sohl St.
Hammond, IN
46320-

3450 State Rd. 26 E
Lafayette, IN
47901-

424 S. Michigan St.
South Bend, IN
46624-

Iowa

615 Sixth Ave. SE
Cedar Rapids, IA
52401-9830

1165 Second Ave.
Des Moines, IA
50318-9755

214 Jackson St.
Sioux City, IA
51101-

Kansas

6029 Broadmoor St.
Shawnee Mission, KS
66202-

424 S. Kansas Ave.
Topeka, KS
66603-

330 W. Second St. N
Wichita, KS
67202-

Kentucky

1088 Nandino Blvd.
Lexington, KY
40511-

St. Mathews Station
4600 Shelbyville Rd.
Louisville, KY
40207-

Louisiana

3401 Government St.
Alexandria, LA
71302-9996

8101 Bluebonnet St.
Baton Rouge, LA
70826-2830

1105 Moss St.
Lafayette, LA
70501-

921 Moss St.
Lake Charles, LA
70601-

3301 17th St.
Metairie, LA
70009-

501 Sterlington Rd.
Monroe, LA
71201-

Carrollton Station
3400 S. Carrollton Ave.
New Orleans, LA
70118-4581

701 Loyola Ave.
New Orleans, LA
70113-

Vieux Carre Station
1022 Iberville St.
New Orleans, LA
70112-3145

2400 Texas Ave.
Shreveport, LA
71102-9711

Maine

40 Western Ave.
Augusta, ME
04330-

125 Forest Ave.
Portland, ME
04101-

Maryland

1 Church Cir.
Annapolis, MD
21401-

900 E. Fayette St.
Baltimore, MD
21233-9713

215 Park St.
Cumberland, MD
21502-

6411 Baltimore Ave.
Riverdale, MD
20737-

100 E. Carroll St.
Salisbury, MD
21801-

Massachusetts

McCormack Office
90 Devonshire St.
Boston, MA
02109-

120 Commercial St.
Brockton, MA
02402-9997

5 Bedford St.
Burlington, MA
01803-9996

2 Government Center
Fall River, MA
02722-

881 Main St.
Fitchburg, MA
01420-

431 Common St.
Lawrence, MA
01842-

155 Father Morissette
Blvd.
Lowell, MA
01854-

695 Pleasant St.
New Bedford, MA
02740-

212 Fenn St.
Pittsfield, MA
01201-

2 Margin St.
Salem, MA
01270-

1883 Main St.
Springfield, MA
01101-

178 Ave. A
Turner Falls, MA
01376-

4 E. Central St.
Worcester, MA
01613-

Michigan

2075 W. Stadium Blvd.
Ann Arbor, MI
48106-

90 S. McCamly St.
Battle Creek, MI
49016-

26200 Ford Rd.
Dearborn Hgts., MI
48127-

1401 W. Fort St.
Detroit, MI
48233-

250 E. Boulevard Dr.
Flint, MI
48502-

225 Michigan NW
Grand Rapids, MI
49599-

113 W. Michigan Ave.
Jackson, MI
49201-

1121 Miller Rd.
Kalamazoo, MI
49001-

General Mail Facility
4800 Collins Rd.
Lansing, MI
48924-

2900 Rodd St.
Midland, MI
48640-

735 W. Huron St.
Pontiac, MI
48343-9997

1300 Military St.
Port Huron, MI
48060-

30550 Gratiot St.
Roseville, MI
48066-

200 W. Second St.
Royal Oak, MI
48068-6800

1233 S. Washington St.
Saginaw, MI
48605-2510

6300 Wayne Rd.
Westland, MI
48185-3169

Minnesota

2800 W. Michigan
Duluth, MN
55806-1742

100 S. First St.
Minneapolis, MN
55401-2037

Mississippi

401 E. South St.
Jackson, MS
39205-5200

Missouri

401 S. Washington St.
Chillicothe, MO
64601-

2300 Bernadette Dr.
Columbia, MO
65203-4607

315 W. Pershing Rd.
Kansas City, MO
64108-

Northwest Plaza Station
500 Northwest Plaza
St. Ann, MO
63074-2209

201 S. Eighth St.
St. Joseph, MO
64501-

Clayton Branch
7750 Maryland Ave.
St. Louis, MO
63105-

500 W. Chestnut
Expwy.
Springfield, MO
65801-

Montana

841 S. 26th St.
Billings, MT
59101-

215 First Ave. N.
Stop 1
Great Falls, MT
59401-9911

Nebraska

W. South Front St.
Grand Island, NE
68801-

700 R St.
Lincoln, NE
68501-9804

300 E. Third St.
North Platte, NE
69101-4000

1124 Pacific St.
Omaha, NE
68108-9630

Nevada

1001 E. Sunset Rd.
Rm 1053
Las Vegas, NV
89199-

2000 Vassar St.
Reno, NV
89510-

New Hampshire

955 Goffs Falls Rd.
Manchester, NH
03103-9713

New Jersey

1701 Atlantic Ave.
Atlantic City, NJ
08401-

421 Beningo Blvd.
Bellmawr, NJ
08031-2520

25 Veterans Plaza
Bergenfield, NJ
07621-

3 Miln St.
Cranford, NJ
07016-

21 Kilmore Rd.
Edison, NJ
08899-9706

229 Main St.
Fort Lee, NJ
07024-

65 Hazlet Ave.
Hazlet, NJ
07730-

5 Wannamaker
Municipal Complex
Island Heights, NJ
08732-0001

69 Montgomery St.
Jersey City, NJ
07303-

160 Maplewood Ave.
Maplewood, NJ
07040-2532

Morristown/Convent
Station
1 Convent Rd.
Morristown, NJ
07961-9999

Nutley Branch
372 Franklin Ave.
Nutley, NJ
07110-1663

171 Broad St.
Red Bank, NJ
07701-

680 US Highway Rt. 130
Trenton, NJ
08650-9611

150 Pompton Plains
Cross Rd.
Wayne, NJ
07470-9994

155 Clinton Rd.
W. Caldwell, NJ
07006-

35 N. Broad St.
Woodbury, NJ
08096-

411 Greenwood Ave.
Wyckoff, NJ
07481-

New Mexico

1135 Broadway SE
Albuquerque, NM
87101-

200 E. Las Cruces Ave.
Las Cruces, NM
88001-9994

415 N. Pennsylvania Ave.
Roswell, NM
88201-4752

New York

50001 Colonie Ctr. Mall
Albany, NY
12205-

Empire State Plaza
Albany, NY
12220-

1620 Grand Ave. N
Baldwin, NY
11510-1807

345 Hicksville Rd.
Bethpage, NY
11714-3401

115 Henry St.
Binghamton, NY
13902-

Bronx General PO
558 Grand Concourse
Bronx, NY
10451-

1200 William St.
Buffalo, NY
14240-8500

124 Grove Ave.
Cedarhurst, NY
11516-2315

297 Larkfield Rd.
East Northport, NY
11731-2417

Downtown Station
55 Clemens Center Pkwy.
Elmira, NY
14902-3091

41-65 Main St.
Flushing, NY
11351-0001

Roosevelt Field Mall
630 Old Country Rd.
Unit 507
Garden City, NY
11530-3500

16 Hudson Ave.
Glen Falls, NY
12801-4356

77 Old Glenham Rd.
Glenham, NY
12527-

185 W. John St.
Hicksville, NY
11801-9671

445 Furrows Rd.
Holbrook, NY
11741-2720

55 Gerard St.
Huntington, NY
11743-6978

888 E. Hericho Turnpike
Huntingon Station, NY
11746-7505

8840 164th St.
Jamaica, NY
11431-4049

300 E. Third St.
Jamestown, NY
14701-5552

65 E. Hoffman Ave.
Lindenhurst, NY
11747-5005

324 Broadway
Monticello, NY
12701-1183

Church St. Station
90 Church St.
New York, NY
10007-

441 Eighth Ave.
New York, NY
10001-9291

Rockefeller Center
610 Fifth Ave.
New York, NY
10020-9991

909 Third Ave.
New York, NY
10022-

352 Main St.
Oneonta, NY
13820-

33 S. Main St.
Pearl River, NY
10965-2456

10 Miller St.
Plattsburgh, NY
12901-1820

55 Mansion St.
Poughkeepsie, NY
12601-

1335 Jefferson Rd.
Rochester, NY
14692-9205

29 Jay St.
Schenectady, NY
12305-1912

25 Route 111
Smithtown, NY
11787-3712

550 Manor Rd.
Staten Island, NY
10314-9648

40 Queens St.
Syosset, NY
11791-3006

5640 E. Taft Rd.
Syracuse, NY
13220-9800

108 Main St.
Warwick, NY
10990-1370

100 Fisher Ave.
White Plains, NY
10602-1907

79-81 Main St.
Yonkers, NY
10701-2740

North Carolina

West Asheville Station
1302 Patton Ave.
Asheville, NC
28806-2604

Starmount Finance Unit
6241 S. Blvd.
Charlotte, NC
28224-9798

Four Seasons Station
301 Four Seasons Town
Ctr.
Greensboro, NC
27427-

311 New Bern Ave.
Raleigh, NC
27601-1442

North Dakota

220 E. Rosser Ave.
Bismarck, ND
58502-

675 Second Ave. N
Fargo, ND
58102-4701

Ohio

675 Wolf Ledges Pky.
Akron, OH
44309-9902

4420 Dressier Rd. NW
Canton, OH
44718-

525 Vine St. (Skywalk)
Cincinnati, OH
45202-3905

2400 Orange Ave.
Cleveland, OH
44101-9997

6316 Nicholas Dr.
Columbus, OH
43235-

1111 E. Fifth St.
Rm. 212A
Dayton, OH
45401-9712

345 E. Bridge St.
Elyria, OH
44035-5222

200 N. Diamond St.
Mansfield, OH
44901-9996

150 N. Third St.
Steubenville, OH
43952-

435 S. St. Clair St.
Toledo, OH
43601-0101

201 High St. NE
Warren OH
44481-

99 S. Walnut St.
Youngstown, OH
44501-9713

Oklahoma

115 W. Broadway
Enid, OK
73701-

525 E. Okmulgee St.
Muskogee, OK
74401-

129 W. Gray
Norman, OK
73069-

Postique
320 SW Fifth Ave.
Oklahoma City, OK
73125-9100

333 W. Fourth St.
Tulsa, OK
74103-9612

Oregon

520 Willamette St.
Eugene, OR
97401-2627

751 NW Hoyt St.
Portland, OR
97208-

Pennsylvania

442 W. Hamilton St.
Allentown, PA
18101-1611

535 Wood St.
Bethlehem, PA
18616-

115 Boylston St.
Bradford, PA
16701-

229 Beaver Dr.
Du Bois, PA
15801-2517

1314 Griswold Plaza
Erie, PA
16501-1730

1025 Valley Forge Rd.
Fairview Village, PA
19409-

238 S. Pennsylvania
Greensburg, PA
15601-

1425 Crooked Hill Rd.
Harrisburg, PA
17107-9714

111 Franklin St.
Johnstown, PA
15901-

Downtown Station
4 W. Chestnut St.
Lancaster, PA
17603-3581

980 Wheeler Way
Langhorne, PA
19047-

17 S. Commerce Way
Lehigh Valley, PA
18002-9999

435 S. Cascade St.
New Castle, PA
16108-

501 11th St.
New Kensington, PA
15068-

Grant Street Station
700 Grant St., Ste. B
Pittsburgh, PA
15219-1906

William Penn Annex
Station
900 Market St.
Philadelphia, PA
19107-

Gus Yatron Facility
2100 N. 13th St.
Reading PA
19612-

Southeastern Window
Unit
1000 W. Valley Rd.
Southeastern, PA
19399-

237 S. Fraser St.
State College, PA
16801-4827

701 Ann St.
Stroudsburg, PA
18360-2016

300 S. Main St.
Wilkes Barre, PA
18701-

Center City Finance
Station
621 Hepburn St.
Williamsport, PA
17703-

200 S. George St.
York, PA
17405-5554

Puerto Rico

585 Ave. Fed.
Roosevelt, Ste. 180
San Juan, PR
00936-9711

Rhode Island

320 Thames St.
Newport, RI
02840-

40 Montgomery St.
Pawtucket, RI
02860-

24 Corliss St.
Providence, RI
02904-9713

South Carolina

7075 Cross County Rd.
Charleston, SC
29423-

1601 Assembly St.
Columbia, SC
29201-9713

600 W. Washington St.
Greenville, SC
29602-9918

South Dakota

320 S. Second Ave.
Sioux Falls, SD
57104-

Tennessee

General Mail Facility
6050 Shallowford Rd.
Chattanooga, TN
37421-5500

200 Martin Luther
King Dr.
Jackson, TN
38301-6921

530 E. Main St.
Johnson City, TN
37601-

General Mail Facility
1237 E. Weisgarber Rd.
Knoxville, TN
37950-8502

Colonial Station
4695 Southern Ave.
Memphis, TN
38124-4809

Crosstown Station
1520 Union Ave.
Memphis, TN
38124-3700

Broadway Station
901 Broadway
Nashville, TN
37203-3806

Texas

3401 Pine St.
Abilene, TX
79604-9996

2301 S. Ross
Amarillo, TX
79120-9604

300 E. South St.
Arlington, TX
76004-

510 Guadolupe St.
Austin, TX
78701-

1535 Los Ebanos Blvd.
Brownsville, TX
78520-8634

2121 E. Wm. J. Bryan Pky.
Bryan, TX
77801-

809 Nueces Bay Blvd.
Corpus Christi, TX
78469-

400 N. Ervay St.
Dallas, TX
75201-

Olla Podrida Post Office
12215 Coit Rd.
Dallas, TX
75251-

101 E. McKinney St.
Denton, TX
76206-

8401 Boeing Dr.
El Paso, TX
79910-

251 W. Lancaster Ave.
Fort Worth, TX
76102-

401 Franklin Ave.
Houston, TX
77201-9901

Copper Mountain
Station
3100 S. W.S. Young Dr.
Killeen, TX
76542-

601 E. Pecan
McAllen, TX
78501-9995

100 E. Wall St.
Midland, TX
79701-

433 Belle Grove Dr.
Richardson, TX
75080-

1 S. Bryant Blvd.
San Angelo, TX
76902-

Downtown Station
615 E. Houston
San Antonio, TX
78205-

10410 Perrin Beitel Rd.
San Antonio, TX
78284-

430 W. State Hwy. 6
Waco, TX
76702-

202 E. Erwin St.
Tyler, TX
75702-

1000 Lamar St.
Wichita Falls, TX
76301-

Utah

3680 Pacific Ave.
Ogden, UT 8
4401-

1760 W. 2100 S.
Salt Lake City, UT
84199-

Vermont

204 Main St.
Brattleboro, VT
05301-2837

11 Elmwood Ave.
Burlington, VT
05401-5700

10 Sykes Mountain Ave.
White River Junction, VT
05001-

Virginia

111 Sixth St.
Bristol, VA
24201-9996

1155 Seminole Tr.
Charlottesville, VA
22906-9996

1425 Battlefield Blvd.
N. Chesapeake, VA
23327-

700 Main St.
Danville, VA
24542-

809 Aberdeen Rd.
Hampton, VA
23670-

300 Odd Fellows Rd.
Lynchburg, VA
24506-9996

Denigh Station
14104 Warwick Blvd.
Newport News, VA
23608-

600 Church St.
Norfolk, VA
23501-

29 Franklin St.
Petersburg, VA
23804-

933 Broad St.
Portsmouth, VA
23707-

901 First St.
Radford, VA
24141

1801 Brook Rd.
Richmond, VA
23232-

419 Rutherford Ave. NE.
Roanoke, VA
24022-9993

501 Viking Dr.
Virginia Beach, VA
23451-

1430 N. Augusta
Staunton, VA
24401-2401

425 N. Boundary St.
Williamsburg, VA
23187-

Washington

11 Third St. NW
Auburn, WA
98002-4033

15800 NE Eighth St.
Bellevue, WA
98008-3906

315 Prospect St.
Bellingham, WA
98225-4001

3102 Hoyt Ave.
Everett, WA
98225-

3500 W. Court
Pasco, WA
99301-

424 E. First St.
Port Angeles, WA
98362-

301 Union St.
Seattle, WA 9
8101-2205

904 N. Riverdale Ave.
Spokane, WA
99201-

1102 A St.
Tacoma, WA
98402-

205 W. Washington Ave.
Yakima, WA
98903-

West Virginia

3010 E. Cumberland Rd.
Bluefield, WV
24701-9995

1057 Charleston Town
Center
Charleston, WV
25357-

500 W. Pike St.
Clarksburg, WV
26301-9995

1000 Virginia Ave. W
Huntington, WV
25704-1726

1355 Old Courthouse Sq.
Martinsburg, WV
25401-9995

Wisconsin

126 N. Barstow St.
Eau Claire, WI
54703-3572

425 State St.
La Crosse, WI
54601-3346

3902 Milwaukee St.
Madison, WI
53714-

345 W. St. Paul Ave.
Milwaukee, WI
53203-3096

1025 W. 20th Ave.
Oshkosh, WI
54901-6617

235 Forrest St.
Wausau, WI
54403-

Wyoming

2120 Capitol Ave.
Cheyenne, WY
82001-9996

Index

The Numbers listed next to the stamp description are the Scott numbers, and the numbers in the parentheses are the numbers of the pages on which the stamps are listed.

E

G

H

I

N

Naismith-Basketball, 1189 (164)
Narrows Bridge, Verrazano-, 1258 (171)
Nassau Hall (Princeton University), 1083 (155), 1704 (220)
Nation of Readers, A, 2106 (269)
National
  Apprenticeship Program, 1201 (167)
  Archives, 227 (71), 2081 (265)
  Capitol, 990–992 (144)
  Defense, 899–901 (133)
  Education Association, 1093 (156)
  Farmer's Bank, 1931 (249)
  Grange, 1323 (176)
  Guard, 1017 (147)
  Park Service, 1314 (175)
  Parks (39), (43), 740–751 (118), 756–765 (121), 769–770 (121), 952 (140), 1448–1451 (191), 1453–1454 (191), 2018 (257), C84 (486), C135 (493), UC65 (528), UXC28 (31)
  Postal Museum, 2779–2782 (350)
  Recovery Act, 732 (117)
  Stamp Exhibition, 735 (118), 768 (121)
Native American Culture, 2869e (362)
Nativity, by John Singleton Copley, 1701 (220)
NATO, 1008 (147), 1127 (159)
  50th Anniversary, 3354 (461)
Natural History, 1387–1390 (183)
Nature of America (39), 3293a-j (450), 3378 (465), 3378a-j (465)
Nautical Figure, 2242 (285)
Nautilus, 1128 (159)
Navajo Blanket, 2238 (285)
Naval
  Academy, US, 794 (125)
  Aviation, 1185 (164)
  Review, International, 1091 (156)
Navy, 790–794 (125)
  Continental, 1556 (203)
Navy, US, 935 (137), 1013 (147)
  Submarines, 3373–3377 (462)
  Submarines, *Gato* Class, 3377 (462)
  Submarines, *Los Angeles* Class, 3372 (462), 3374 (462)
  Submarines, *Ohio* Class, 3375 (462)
  Submarines, USS *Holland*, 3376 (462)

Nebraska, 1669 (215), 1979 (254)
  Statehood, 1328 (176)
  Territory, 1060 (152)
Nebula
  Eagle, 3384 (466)
  Egg, 3387 (466)
  Lagoon, 3386 (466)
  Ring, 3385 (466)
Nelson, Thomas, Jr., 1686d (216), 1687c (216)
Neptune, 1112 (159), 2576 (325)
New England, 2119 (270)
Netherlands, 913 (134), 2003 (257)
Nevada, 1668 (215), 1980 (254)
  Settlement, 999 (144)
  Statehood, 1248 (168)
Nevelson, Louise, 3379–3383 (465)
  Black Chord, 3381 (465)
  Dawn's Wedding Chapel I, 3383 (465)
  Nightsphere-Light, 3382 (465)
  Royal Tide, 3380 (465)
  Silent Music I, 3379 (465)
Nevin, Ethelbert, 883 (130)
New
  Amsterdam Harbor, NY, 1027 (147)
  Baseball Records, 3191a (430)
  Deal, FDR's, 3185e (418)
  England Flag, 1775, 3403b (469)
  England Neptune, 2119 (270)
  Hampshire, 1068 (152), 1641 (211), 1981 (254)
  Hampshire Statehood, 2344 (294)
  Jersey, 1635 (211), 1982 (254)
  Jersey Settlement, 1247 (168)
  Jersey Statehood, 2338 (294)
  Mexico, 1679 (215), 1983 (254)
  Mexico, Radio interferometer very large array, 3409b (473)
  Mexico (Chavez, Dennis), 2186 (277)
  Mexico Statehood, 1191 (164)
  Orleans, 2407 (305)
  Sweden, C117 (490)
  Year, Chinese, 2720 (342), 2817 (354), 2876 (365), 3060 (386), 3120 (397), 3179 (410), 3272 (446), 3370 (462), 3500 (23)
  York, 1643 (211), 1984 (254), C38 (482)
  York City, 1027 (147)
  York City Coliseum, 1076 (155)
  York Public Library, 3447 (477)
  York Skyline, C35 (482)

York Statehood, 2346 (294)
York Stock Exchange, 2630 (334)
York World's Fair '39, 853 (129)
York World's Fair '64, 1244 (168)
York, Newburgh, 727 (117), 731 (117), 767 (121)
Newburgh, New York, 752 (121)
Newman, Alfred, 3343 (457)
Newspaper Boys, 1015 (147)
Newt, Rough-skinned, 3378g (465)
Niagara, 3236n (441)
Niagara Falls, 297 (83), 568 (105), 699 (114), C133 (493)
  Railway Suspension Bridge, 961 (140)
Nicolet, Jean, 739 (118)
Nie Nederland, 614 (106)
Nighthawks, 3236p (441)
Nightsphere-Light, 3382 (465)
Nimitz, Chester W., 1869 (242)
Nine-Mile Prairie, C136 (35)
1970s Fashions, 3189k (426)
Nineteenth Amendment, 1406 (184), 3184e (417)
  Suffrage, 784 (122), 1051 (151), 1406 (184)
Nisqually, Fort, 1604 (207)
Nixon, Richard, 2955 (370)
Nobel Prize, The, 3504 (36)
Nonprofit, 2902 (366)
Norris
  Dam, 1184 (164)
  Sen. George W., 1184 (164)
Norse-American, 620–621 (109)
North
  Carolina, 1644 (211), 1985 (254)
  Carolina (Great Smoky Mountains National Park), 749 (118), 765 (121)
  Carolina Statehood, 2347 (294)
  Dakota, 1671 (215), 1986 (254)
  Dakota Statehood, 858 (129), 2403 (305)
  Pole, 1128 (159)
Northeastern University, UX298 (537)
Northern
  Mariana Islands, 2804 (353)
  Sea Lion, 2509 (317)
Northwest Territory
  Ordinance, 795 (125)
  Sesquicentennial, 837 (129)
Northwestern University (40)
Norway, 911 (134)
Number 12, 1949, 3236t (441)
Numismatics, 2558 (322)
Nurse, 702 (114), 1699 (220), 1910 (246)
Nursing, 1190 (164)
NYU Library, 1928 (249)

Q

X

Y

Postmasters General of the United States

Appointed by the Continental Congress

1775	Benjamin Franklin, PA
1776	Richard Bache, PA
1782	Ebenezer Hazard, NY

Appointed by the President with the advice and consent of the Senate

1789	Samuel Osgood, MA
1791	Timothy Pickering, PA
1795	Joseph Habersham, GA
1801	Gideon Granger, CT
1814	Return J. Meigs, Jr., OH
1823	John McLean, OH
1829	William T. Barry, KY
1835	Amos Kendall, KY
1840	John M. Niles, CT
1841	Francis Granger, NY
1841	Charles A. Wickliffe, KY
1845	Cave Johnson, TN
1849	Jacob Collamer, VT
1850	Nathan K. Hall, NY
1852	Samuel D. Hubbard, CT
1853	James Campbell, PA
1857	Aaron V. Brown, TN
1859	Joseph Holt, KY
1861	Horatio King, ME
1861	Montgomery Blair, DC
1864	William Dennison, OH
1866	Alexander W. Randall, WI
1869	John A.J. Creswell, MD
1874	James W. Marshall, NJ
1874	Marshall Jewell, CT
1876	James N. Tyner, IN
1877	David McK. Key, TN
1880	Horace Maynard, TN
1881	Thomas L. James, NY
1882	Timothy O. Howe, WI
1883	Walter Q. Gresham, IN
1884	Frank Hatton, IA
1885	William F. Vilas, WI
1888	Don M. Dickinson, MI
1889	John Wanamaker, PA
1893	Wilson S. Bissell, NY
1895	William L. Wilson, WV
1897	James A. Gary, MD
1898	Charles Emory Smith, PA
1902	Henry C. Payne, WI
1904	Robert J. Wynne, PA
1905	George B. Cortelyou, NY
1907	George von L. Meyer, MA
1909	Frank H. Hitchcock, MA
1913	Albert S. Burleson, TX
1921	Will H. Hays, IN
1922	Hubert Work, CO
1923	Harry S. New, IN
1929	Walter F. Brown, OH
1933	James A. Farley, NY
1940	Frank C. Walker, PA
1945	Robert E. Hannegan, MO
1947	Jesse M. Donaldson, IL
1953	Arthur E. Summerfield, MI
1961	J. Edward Day, CA
1963	John A. Gronouski, WI
1965	Lawrence F. OíBrien, MA
1968	W. Marvin Watson, TX
1969	Winton M. Blount, AL

Selected by the Presidentially appointed U.S. Postal Service Board of Governors

1971	Elmer T. Klassen, MA
1975	Benjamin Franklin Bailar, MD
1978	William F. Bolger, CT
1985	Paul N. Carlin, WY
1986	Albert V. Casey, MA
1986	Preston R. Tisch, NY
1988	Anthony M. Frank, CA
1992	Marvin Runyon, TN
1998	William J. Henderson, NC
2001	John E. Potter, NY

Acknowledgments

This stamp collecting catalog was produced by Public Affairs and Communications, Stamp Services, United States Postal Service.

UNITED STATES POSTAL SERVICE

John E. Potter
Postmaster General and Chief Executive Officer

Deborah K. Willhite
Senior Vice President, Government Relations and Public Policy

Azeezaly S. Jaffer
Vice President, Public Affairs and Communications

Catherine Caggiano
Executive Director, Stamp Services

Terrence McCaffrey
Manager, Stamp Development

Kelly Spinks
Project Manager and Editor

Tammy Blackburn
Project Assistant

HARPERCOLLINS PUBLISHERS

Megan Newman
Editorial Director, HarperResource

Greg Chaput
Associate Editor, HarperResource

Lucy Albanese
Design Director, General Books Group

Chin-Yee Lai
Art Director, HarperResource

DESIGN AND PRODUCTION SERVICES

Roberta Wojtkowski Design & Associates
10992 Thrush Ridge Road
Reston, VA 20191

Night & Day Design
41 River Terrace #2104
New York, NY 10282

RESEARCH AND WRITING SERVICES

PhotoAssist, Inc.
4400 Jenifer Street NW
Washington, DC 20015

COLOR SEPARATION AND DIGITAL PREPRESS SERVICES

Dodge Color
4827 Rugby Avenue
Bethesda, MD 20814

PRINTING AND BINDING

R. R. Donnelly & Sons Company
Crawfordsville, IN 47933

The United States Postal Service wishes to thank The Norman Rockwell
Museum at Stockbridge and Stephanie H. Plunkett, Curator of
Illustration Art, for their support of *The Postal Service Guide to U.S.
Stamps*. Many of the artist biographies that appear here have been
drawn from *Pushing the Envelope: The Art of the Postage Stamp*.
This special exhibition highlighting the art and evolution of U.S. postage
stamp design has been organized by The Norman Rockwell Museum in
collaboration with the U.S. Postal Service. Please check the museum's
Web site at www.nrm.org for exhibition travel information.

Notes

Notes

Notes

Notes

Notes

Notes

Notes

Notes